EAST–WEST RELATIONS

East–West Relations

Volume 2: Methodology and Data

Daniel Frei
Dieter Ruloff
University of Zurich

with the collaboration of
Urs Luterbacher
Pierre Allan

Oelgeschlager, Gunn & Hain, Publishers, Inc.
Cambridge, Massachusetts

International Standard Book Number: 0-89946-137-9

Library of Congress Catalog Card Number: 81-22356

Printed in the U.S.A.

Library of Congress Cataloging in Publication Data

Frei, Daniel.
East-West relations.

Bibliography: p.
Contents: v. 1. A systematic survey—v. 2. Methodology and data.
1. World politics—1965-1975. 2. World politics—1975-1985. 3. Détente. I. Ruloff, Dieter. II. Title.
D849.F688   327'.0904   81-22356
ISBN 0-89946-136-0 (v. 1)   AACR2
ISBN 0-89946-137-9 (v. 2)

Contents

List of Graphs vii

List of Tables ix

List of Abbreviations xiii

Note to the Reader xv

Appendix A1 Measuring Tensions and "Détente" in East–West Relations: Current Approaches 1
Measures Based on Events Data 1
Measures Based on Perceptual Data 6
Measures Based on Transaction-Flow Data 8
Nonrelational Tension Scales 8
A Critical Assessment and Conclusions 13

Appendix A2 A Content Analysis of CSCE Statements, 1973–1980 19
A2.1 Content Analysis: An Evaluation of Techniques and Coding Instructions 19
A2.2 Category Scores 41
A2.3 The Major Issues of East–West Relations: Highest-Scoring Categories in Rank–Order for Individual Countries 102
A2.4 The Factor Analysis of the Content-Analytical Data 173
A2.5 The Cluster Analysis of the Content-Analytical Data 200

Appendix A3 **The Structure and Dynamics of East–West Relations: Additional Tables** 223
A3.2 Disarmament and Security 223
A3.3 Cooperative and Conflictive Interactions 232
A3.4 Economic Cooperation: Additional Tables 254
A3.5 Human Rights and Human Contacts: Additional Data 270
A3.6 Sovereignty and Independence: Intra- and Intersystemic Interactions 275

Appendix A4 **Index Values Computed for the Master Dimensions of East–West Relations** 283

Appendix A5 **The Future of East–West Relations: A Computer Simulation of Five Scenarios,** *by Pierre Allan and Urs Luterbacher* 285
Introduction 285
Simulation of Political, Economic, and Strategic Interactions (SIMPEST Model) 286
Simulations and Scenarios 288
Synthesis of the Results 317

Bibliography 319

About the Authors 333

List of Graphs

A5.1 Strategic, Army, and Naval Forces Index for the US 290

A5.2 Soviet Strategic, Army, and Naval Forces Index 291

A5.3 Satisfaction of the Military Elite, the Civilian Elites, and the Population in the Soviet Union 293

A5.4 Soviet Agricultural and Nonagricultural Production 294

A5.5 Eastern and Western Security Index Values 296

A5.6 Strategic Indices for the Détente Scenario 298

A5.7 Army Indices for the Détente Scenario 299

A5.8 Navy Indices for the Détente Scenario 300

A5.9 Navy Indices for the Cold War Scenario 302

A5.10 Strategic Indices for the US Unilateral Disarmament Scenario 304

A5.11 Army Indices for the US Unilateral Disarmament Scenario 305

A5.12 US GNP Figures for the Scenario of a Unilateral American Disarmament 306

A5.13 US Military Expenditure for the Scenario of a Unilateral American Disarmament 307

A5.14 US Private Consumption for the Scenario of a Unilateral American Disarmament 308

A5.15 Approval of the US President's Policies (Popularity), in Percentages 310

A5.16 Strategic Indices for the Scenario of Unilateral Soviet Disarmament 311

A5.17 Army Indices for the Scenario of Soviet Unilateral Disarmament 312

A5.18 US Military Expenditure for the Scenario of Negotiating from a Position of Strength 314

A5.19 Strategic Indices for the Scenario of Negotiations from a Position of Strength 315

A5.20 Army Indices for the Scenario of Negotiations from a Position of Strength 316

List of Tables

A1.1	A Synopsis of International Tension Scales	9
A2.1	Summary of Approaches to Content Analysis	33
A2.2	Category Labels and Associated Numeric Category Codes for the Content Analysis of CSCE Statements	36
A2.3	Category Scores and Percentages: The 1973 Helsinki Statements	42
A2.4	Category Scores and Percentages: The 1975 Helsinki Statements	54
A2.5	Category Scores and Percentages: The Belgrade Opening Statements	66
A2.6	Category Scores and Percentages: The Belgrade Closing Statements	78
A2.7	Category Scores and Percentages: The Madrid Opening Statements	90
A2.8	Rank-Order of Categories: The 1973 Helsinki Statements	102
A2.9	Rank-Order of Categories: The 1975 Helsinki Statements	117
A2.10	Rank-Order of Categories: The Belgrade Opening Statements	131
A2.11	Rank-Order of Categories: The Belgrade Closing Statements	145
A2.12	Rank-Order of Categories: The Madrid Opening Statements	159
A2.13	Varimax Rotated-Factor Matrix: The 1973 Helsinki Statements	177
A2.14	Varimax Rotated-Factor Matrix: The 1975 Helsinki Statements	178
A2.15	Varimax Rotated-Factor Matrix: The Belgrade Opening Statements	179
A2.16	Varimax Rotated-Factor Matrix: The Belgrade Closing Statements	180
A2.17	Varimax Rotated-Factor Matrix: The Madrid Opening Statements	181

A2.18 Varimax Rotated-Factor Matrix for All Five Sets of Statements 182
A2.19 Factor Scores: The 1973 Helsinki Statements 183
A2.20 Factor Scores: The 1975 Helsinki Statements 184
A2.21 Factor Scores: The Belgrade Opening Statements 185
A2.22 Factor Scores: The Belgrade Closing Statements 186
A2.23 Factor Scores: The Madrid Opening Statments 187
A2.24 Factor Scores for All Fives Sets of Statements 188
A2.25 The 1973 Helsinki Statements: Percentage Distribution of Attention on Dimensions of East-West Relations 190
A2.26 The 1975 Helsinki Statements: Percentage Distribution of Attention on Dimensions of East-West Relations 192
A2.27 The Belgrade Opening Statements: Percentage Distribution of Attention on Dimensions of East-West Relations 194
A2.28 The Belgrade Closing Statements: Percentage Distribution of Attention on Dimensions of East-West Relations 196
A2.29 The Madrid Opening Statements: Percentage Distribution of Attention on Dimensions of East-West Relations 198
A2.30 The 1973 Helsinki CSCE Statements: Correlations Between Countries 202
A2.31 The 1975 Helsinki Statements: Correlations Between Countries 206
A2.32 The Belgrade Opening Statements: Correlations Between Countries 210
A2.33 The Belgrade Closing Statements: Correlations Between Countries 214
A2.34 The Madrid Opening Statements: Correlations Between Countries 218
A3.1 Military Expenditure of NATO Countries 224
A3.2 Military Expenditure of WTO Countries 225
A3.3 Military Expenditure of Neutral and Nonaligned Countries 226
A3.4 Rates of Change of Military Expenditure of NATO Countries 227
A3.5 Rates of Change of Military Expenditure of WTO Countries 228
A3.6 Rates of Change of Military Expenditure of Neutral and Nonaligned Countries 229
A3.7 US and USSR Strategic Nuclear Forces 230
A3.8 Eurostrategic Weapons of NATO and WTO 231
A3.9 Cooperative Interactions in Europe: Time Series for Selected Dyads 232
A3.10 Conflictive Interactions in Europe: Time Series for Selected Dyads 237

A3.11 Proximity Between Nations: Cooperation, 1960-1964 242
A3.12 Proximity Between Nations: Cooperation, 1965-1969 243
A3.13 Proximity Between Nations: Cooperation, 1970-1974 244
A3.14 Proximities Between Nations: Cooperation, 1975-1978 245
A3.15 Proximity Between Nations: Conflict, 1960-1964 246
A3.16 Proximity Between Nations: Conflict, 1965-1969 247
A3.17 Proximity Between Nations: Conflict, 1970-1974 248
A3.18 Proximities Between Nations: Conflict, 1975-1978 249
A3.19 Interblock Affinities in UN Voting Behavior 250
A3.20 Intrablock Affinities in UN Voting Behavior 251
A3.21 UN Voting Affinities among Neutral and Nonaligned Nations 252
A3.22 UN Voting Affinities of Neutral and Nonaligned Nations with the USA and the USSR 253
A3.23 Commercial Exchange Between Selected East-West Pairs of Countries 254
A3.24 Exports as Percentage of Total Exports for Selected East-West Pairs 255
A3.25 Imports as Percentage of Total Imports for Selected East-West Pairs 256
A3.26 SITC-7 Commercial Exchange Between Selected East-West Pairs of Countries 257
A3.27 SITC-3 Commerical Exchange Between Selected East-West Pairs of Countries 258
A3.28 SITC-7 Exports as Percentage of Total Exports to Respective Countries for Selected East-West Pairs 259
A3.29 SITC-3 Exports as Percentage of Total Exports to Respective Countries for Selected East-West Pairs 260
A3.30 Trade Between CSCE Countries, 1965 261
A3.31 Trade Between CSCE Countries, 1970 263
A3.32 Trade Between CSCE Countries, 1975 265
A3.33 Measures of Proximity Between CSCE Nations: Trade, 1965 267
A3.34 Measures of Proximity Between CSCE Nations: Trade, 1970 268
A3.35 Measures of Proximity Between CSCE Nations: Trade, 1975 269
A3.36 Number of Political Sanctions in WTO Countries 270
A3.37 Unemployment in Europe as Percent of Total Labor Force 271
A3.38 Tourism Between East and West for Selected Pairs of Countries 272
A3.39 The Exchange of Visitors Between the GDR and the FRG 273
A3.40 Migration from East to West in Europe and Associated Indicators 274
A3.41 Cooperative Interactions Between "Camps" as Percentage of Total Cooperative Interactions 275

A3.42 Cooperative Interactions with NATO Countries, in Percent of Total Cooperative Interactions with CSCE Countries 276
A3.43 Cooperative Interactions with WTO Countries, in Percent of Total Cooperative Interactions with CSCE Countries 278
A3.44 Cooperative Interactions with Neutral and Non-aligned Countries, in Percent of Total Cooperative Interactions with CSCE Countries 280
A4.1 Standardized Index Values for the Master Dimensions of East-West Relations 283

List of Abbreviations

ABM	Anti-Ballistic Missile
ACDA	Arms Control and Disarmament Agency
AI	Amnesty International
AUST	Austria
BIB	Bundesministerium für Innerdeutsche Bezichungen, Bonn
BJC	Bibilotheque Juive Contemporaire, Paris
BLGM	Belgium
BLGR	Bulgaria
CMEA	Council for Mutual Economic Assistance
CNDA	Canada
COCOM	Coordinating Committee for East–West Trade Policy
COPDAB	Azar's Conflict and Peace Data Bank
CSCE	Conference on Security and Cooperation in Europe
CYPR	Cyprus
CPRI	Canadian Peace Research Institute, Dundas, Ontario (see Newcombe and Wert 1979)
CPSU	Communist Party of the Soviet Union
CZCH	Czechoslovakia
DNMK	Denmark
EC	European Communities
EDC	European Defense Community
EEC	European Economic Community
FOBS	Forward Based Systems
FNLD	Finland
FRNC	France
FRG	Federal Republic of Germany
GDR	German Democratic Republic
GLCM	Ground-Launched Cruise Missile
GRCE	Greece
HNGR	Hungary
ICBM	Intercontinental Ballistic Missile
ICLD	Iceland
IRBM	Intermediate-Range Ballistic Missile

IRLD	Ireland
IISS	International Institute for Strategic Studies
INF	Intermediate-Range Nuclear Forces
ITLY	Italy
LICH	Liechtenstein
LRTNF	Long-Range TNF
LXBG	Luxembourg
MBFR	Mutual Balanced Force Reductions (Conference on MBFR in Vienna)
MFN	Most-Favored Nation
MIRV	Multiple Independently Targetable Re-entry Vehicle
MLTA	Malta
MNCO	Monaco
MRBM	Medium-Range Ballistic Missile
MRTNF	Medium-Range TNF
NATO	North Atlantic Treaty Organization
N + N	Neutral and Nonaligned Countries
NTHL	Netherlands
NRWY	Norway
OECD	Organization for Economic Cooperation and Development, Paris
PLND	Poland
PRTG	Portugal
RMNA	Romania
SALT	Strategic Arms Limitation Talks
SANM	San Marino
SITC	Standard International Trade Classification
SITC-3	Section 3 of the SITC: Hydrocarbons and Fuels
SICT-7	Section 7 of the SITC: Machinery and Transport Equipment
SIPRI	Stockholm International Peace Research Institute
SLBM	Submarine-Launched Ballistic Missile
SPAN	Spain
START	Strategic Arms Reduction Talks
SWDN	Sweden
SWTZ	Switzerland
TNF	Theatre Nuclear Forces
TRKY	Turkey
UK	United Kingdom of Great Britain and Northern Ireland
UN	United Nations
USA	United States of America
USSR	Union of the Socialist Soviet Republic
VATC	Vatican (Holy See)
WB	World Bank
WHB3	World Handbook of Political and Social Indicators (3rd edition); see Taylor (1981)
WTO	Warsaw Treaty Organization
WTOG	World Tourism Organization, Madrid
YGSL	Yugoslavia

Note to the Reader

For convenience, this study on East-West relations is divided into two volumes. The first volume offers a comprehensive survey of the findings, written in a form accessible to any interested reader irrespective of his or her acquaintance with modern social science approaches. This volume is structured as an appendix. It offers additional information not included in Volume 1. In particular, it presents exhaustive descriptions of the methodology applied for collecting and analyzing the data. Furthermore, the full sets of data are presented as well as additional transformations and analyses of the data.

The sections in Volume 2 are numbered according to the system used in Volume 1, putting an A for "Appendix" before each section number. For instance, *A3.2*, comprising data on armaments and defense expenditure, corresponds to Section 3.2 ("Disarmament and Security") in Volume 1.

Section A5 presents in addition to Chapter 5 of Volume 1 the results of a computer simulation by Professor Urs Luterbacher and Dr. Pierre Allan.

Appendix A1

Measuring Tensions and "Détente" in East–West Relations: Current Approaches

Although research on East–West relations is rapidly increasing, few contributions have been made that make use of modern social-science methodology for observing and monitoring the degree of tension or "détente" existing in Europe. It seems that many social scientists–and diplomatic practitioners as well–are satisfied with merely listing events or consulting tables presenting the number of weapons acquired by each country (Hermann 1981).

Yet there is a very substantial body of literature pertaining to the conceptualization and operationalization of less specific constructs such as "tension," "conflictivity," "relaxation of tension," and "cooperation." Therefore, before taking any new steps in the direction of monitoring East–West relations, it is worth while to examine those more general measures and the corresponding research findings.

According to the source of the data, we may distinguish three types of measures: (1) measures based on events data, (2) measures based on perceptual data, and (3) measures based on transaction flow data. Most of the scales developed so far refer to dyadic relationships and a few measures are nonrelational.

MEASURES BASED ON EVENTS DATA

The great majority of attempts to measure international conflict and cooperation, in a more systematic and less impressionistic manner, use events data, that is, the scaling of international interactions according to the position of each event on a conflict-cooperation continuum. Usually events data are coded per actor and dyad indicating the source, the target, and the type of action.

The first scheme of this kind was the Moses-Brody scale, consisting of four sets of thirty marker cards with each set ranked in order of increasing conflict from 1 to 30 (Moses et al. 1967).

A more comprehensive attempt toward scaling cooperation and conflict was made by Charles McClelland in his World Events Interaction Survey (WEIS) (McClelland and Hoggard 1969). It is based on interaction events coded on the basis of daily issues of the *New York Times* as the sole source. According to McClelland and Hoggard, interactions are "single action items of a non-routine, extraordinary, or newsworthy character that in some clear sense are directed across a national boundary and have, in most instances, a specific foreign target." The data refer to verbal as well as nonverbal events and are listed in a category system of sixty-three types of actions according to a cooperation-through-conflict ordering that can be condensed into twenty-two more general classes of behavior. This listing has been done on what the authors call "*a priori* and 'logical' grounds." Although the authors claim that the interaction categories have not been assumed to be locations on a single continuum of conflict or of conflict and cooperation, the twenty-two-point index is subsequently used as if it were on a continuum.

A statistical transformation of the twenty-two-point index has been suggested by Andriole and Young (1977) by combining volume and level of cooperative vs. conflictual behavior events, respectively. This derived indicator is called "tension level" and reflects the percentage of the total number of events that are cooperative and conflictual.

A more sophisticated measure has been designed by McClelland (1972), who proposed to look at the "deviation" of the distribution of different kinds of acts, that is, a variety measure. The unequal distribution of acts can be compared with the "standard" distribution by taking the ratio of the sum of logarithmic numbers for the unequal distribution and the similar sum of the logarithmic numbers for a corresponding equal distribution. This ratio is called "relative uncertainty," or *Hrel.* As Hrel approaches 1.0, it suggests that behaviors show increasing signs of disorderliness: as Hrel decreases toward 0.0, the suggestion is that a large amount of highly patterned and repetitive behavior may be present. According to the findings presented by McClelland, noncrisis (which might also be interpreted as nontension) periods have Hrel figures below .700. Apart from Hrel, there are several additional proposals by other scholars who use related approaches to identify dramatic changes in behavioral patterns. They are summed up and evaluated in Hermann (1973).

A more refined version of this approach has been offered by

ninety-five categories and ranked on a ratio scale. The intensity values assigned to the individual ninety-five types of interactive events are the result of an expert panel study, composed of scholars and practitioners of diplomacy. However, the Corson data apply primarily to US–USSR relations plus a few additional selected dyads. (For a more detailed description of the Corson scale, see Leng 1975 and Ruloff 1975, pp. 152–163.)

Starting in the early seventies, Edward Azar and associates at the University of North Carolina at Chapel Hill built up a Conflict and Peace Data Bank (COPDAB) (Azar and Sloan 1975; Sloan 1975). The daily events are scaled on what the authors call the Cooperation and Conflict Interaction Scale (CCIS), which consists of fifteen points, with point 1 being the value given to the most cooperative event between two nations (for example, Nation A and B unite to form one nation-state), and scale value 15 representing the most conflictive event between two or more nations (for example, total war). The individual events are ranked by graduate-student coders who assign them to specific dimensions of interactions and intensity on the fifteen-point scale.

Since the original Azar-Sloan scale is only ordinal and does not indicate how to weight the coded events in terms of exact intensity—that is, how much more serious, intense, or conflictive one event is in relation to another—the authors developed what they called the Dimension of Interaction (DI) scale, which is the measure of frequency and intensity of the interactions monitored by the fifteen-point Azar-Sloan scale (Azar and Sloan 1975). It was computed by eighteen expert scholars and practitioners, who assessed in numerical terms the amount of conflictiveness or cooperativeness represented by each of the points of the scale in relation to the neutral point 1. In contrast to the original scale, conflict and cooperation are no longer placed on the same continuum.

Based on the Inter-Nation Events scale, Azar (1974) and Sloan (1975; 1978) also developed a scale, which they called the Normal Relations Range. This is a specific interaction range on the scale, extending from very friendly to very hostile, which tends to incorporate most of the events exchanged between two nations, bound by upper and lower critical thresholds. The continuing occurrence of interactions above the upper critical threshold for more than a very short time implies that hostile situations of a crisis magnitude have begun. The "normal" interaction range is calculated by placing a confidence interval of one standard deviation around the mean level of a dyad's international interactions.

Another scale developed by the same research team and based again on Inter-Nation Events scale (Azar et al. 1977) is the Inter-Nation Relations Trend (INRT), which indicates the liklihood of a crisis occurring within one year by monitoring changes in the Dimension of Interactions Index. The INRT measure equals the sum of the logged and smoothed changes in cooperation and conflict directed by one nation at another. The crucial variable therefore is the change in interaction rates from year to year regardless of the volume of previous exchange.

In addition, an index called the Affinity Index is being prepared. Computed on a monthly basis, it will allow identification of affinity based on the share of attention mutually given by the units of a dyad.

The third among the large-scale and comprehensive events-data projects is CREON (Comparative Research on the Events of Nations), directed by Charles F. Hermann and Margaret G. Hermann (Hermann and Hermann 1976). The CREON dataset offers twelve ways of conceptualizing foreign-policy behavior, with events coded for a set of thirty-eight countries. Among the twelve dimensions used by CREON, two have a definite bearing on the measurement of cooperative versus conflictive behavior.

The first is the Affect Index, which refers to the affective feelings ranging from friendliness to hostility that policymakers express toward the policies, actions, or government of another nation. The index is composed of two partial dimensions: (1) direction (indicating whether the feeling expressed is positive or negative), and (2) intensity (indicating the degree of the feeling that is expressed). Values on a seven-point scale are assigned by coders who look at both the meaning of an event and at its desirability by the target or recipient state (Hutchins 1979).

The second is the Acceptance/Rejection Ratio. This measure provides information about the feedback for a nation's foreign policy. Again coding is done on the basis of judging individual acts as to their "rejective" or "acceptive" nature, partly using WEIS categories (Hermann 1979).

The variety of events datasets is quite bewildering. In an empirical study, Havener and Peterson (1975) tried to compare some of them in a systematic way. They started from the assumption that since scales were designed to measure conflict/cooperation in international relations, an alteration of the collection of events to be coded should not affect the reliability of a scaling instrument. Therefore, the measures should provide highly correlated indices when applied to the same set of data. They coded a particular event (the 1967 Middle East Crisis) using the Moses-Brody, Azar, and Corson schemes and found surprisingly low correlations between the indices of conflict/cooperation determined on one scale with those of the other scales. Interpreting this finding, Havener and Peterson conclude:

> The four instruments might be measuring qualitatively different properties of events.... Events categories are semantic variables. They many not measure syntactic changes such as the effect of armaments changes between 1914 and 1968 on categories....

Similar, though less pessimistic, findings are reported by Leng (1975).

Another comparison of data sets collected by different methods of measuring international tension resulted in similar low rank-order agreements (Thompson and Modelski 1977). The poor match reveals that critical attention with respect to serious validity problems is necessary. Other, less ambitious attempts to code events, such as the one made by Gamson and Modigliani (1971), suffer from the same weaknesses.

Due to the popularity of peace and conflict research in the past two decades, a high degree of attention has been devoted by scholars to the development of conflict-behavior measures. However, they are only of indirect relevance to the present study since they focus solely on the conflictive aspects of international relations and usually do not take into consideration the cooperation aspect. Furthermore, they are more suitable to measure intense conflict as expressed, for instance, by violent acts, protests, and threats, while neglecting "milder" intensities of hostile behavior. Yet some of them reflect a very high degree of sophistication and may be suggestive in view of developing new measures for "détente."

In the Dimensionality of Nations (DON) Project, concepts were developed to measure the behavior of nations dyads for a selected sample of fourteen nations (Rummel 1972; Rummel 1976). The set of variable includes variables for certain categories of events (like protests, accusations, aid to subversive groups or enemy, boycott or embargo, and military action) measured at five-year intervals (1950, 1955, 1960, 1963, 1965). A factor analysis based on thirteen variables yields a dimension called "Foreign Conflict." The statistical characteristics of this dimension lead to the conclusion "that international conflict behavior can be considered to be a continuum in international relations" (Rummel 1972, p. 337).

Some authors felt that data collections serving a general or "multitheoretical" purpose may not be appropriate for developing indicators suitable for measuring the specific nature of East–West relations in Europe. Thus they decided to develop more refined indicators. An example is Nygren's 1979; 1981) "peaceful interaction" measure, which is based on the aggregate amount of (1) official interaction between each of a pair of countries, comprising meetings/visits/, agreements/treaties/negotiations and diplomatic notes and; (2) societal interaction comprising the value of trade in constant prices, business communications, tourism, and students exchange.

A very productive field of application is the attempt to set up an early-warning system suitable for forecasting international crises. Although the problem of predicting acute international crises and crisis-like short-term increase in international tension is somewhat different from the task of measuring the state of East–West relations, it may be worthwhile considering them too. Based on WEIS data, Hopple (1980) developed an automated crisis-warning and monitoring system, using WEIS events categories and various statistical transformations of these data as predictor valuables for either crisis or noncrisis situations.

In the meantime a variety of crisis-management projects have been launched, most of them aiming at some kind of early-warning indicators (Daly and Andriole 1980). The most comprehensive system of indicators so far available has been suggested by Wilkenfeld et al. (1979). It is based on the assumption that a variety of societal, interstate, and global factors interact to generate conflict behavior in the international arena. Variable clusters include psychological, political, societal, interstate, and global components using causal modeling and econometric techniques. The authors successfully try to explain the foreign-policy behavior of states thus presenting indicators that can detect significant charges in those determinants of foreign behavior (described in terms of WEIS data) whose variation can be measured on a more long-term basis, in particular, those that affect the preconditions of conflict at the interstate level (see also Rossa et al. 1980).

All these efforts serve a particular and explicit purpose: to predict international crises. Related to these indicators are indicators referring to war or to "peak interactions," providing a metricized and subjectively scaled measure of violence in action, coded on a thirty-point scale (Choucri and North 1976, p. 13). The most precise operationalization of violent conflict available so far is the one suggested by Singer and Small (1974) and their definition of "war" based on the dimensions of magnitude (measured by nation months of war) and severity (measured by battle deaths). The same authors have also proposed early-warning indicators based on system properties and indicating the probability of an outbreak of violence (Wallace 1979). However, as crises (or the probability of nonoccurrence of crises) or war (or the probable absence of war) are rather special, although highly important phenomena of international politics, the indicators and measurement efforts aiming at these phenomena do not necessarily contribute to the measurement of East–West relations. Or, more precisely, they refer to a small fraction only of the large variety of types and intensities of East–West interactions. Therefore, it would not be meaningful to simply take them over and/or adapting them to the purpose of this study.

MEASURES BASED ON PERCEPTUAL DATA

In his pioneering study on crises, escalation, and war, Ole R. Holsti (1972) has suggested conceptualizing crisis tension as a state of mind of the actors concerned, which can most conveniently be interpreted as stress. He also suggests measuring stress in terms of perception of hostility (p. 38). Consequently, this approach of measuring tension had to rely on the method of content analysis of documents written by the relevant actors. Using a very simple but highly reliable set of categories, Holsti proposed and applied a content-analytical technique for an analysis of the international process of escalation of tension, which finally led to the outbreak of World War I. In another study, he applied the same tools to the 1962 Cuban missle crisis, again analyzing documents referring to the activity of the decision-making elite.

In order to validate this measure, Holsti compared the content data with a series of financial indices, assuming that the financial community would also be sensitive to international developments since all forms of investment are affected by them. Among the financial indicators used are prices of stocks and bonds, the flow of gold, wheat futures, exchange rates, and interest rates. These indicators reveal patterns of responses to developments in Europe strikingly similar to the measure of stress derived by content analysis of the diplomatic documents.

Assuming that the economic elite and the markets perceive and react to foreign events in a matter similar to the political decision makers, a whole range of economic indicators would become of interest to the measurement of "détente," as, for example stock prices and exchange rates. In a simulation study of the Vietnam war, Milstein and Mitchell (1968) used the black-market dollar value of the piastre as an indicator of the popular confidence in the government. However, such types of indicators can be expected to reflect external events only if, first, all economic reasons such as a poor balance of payment or high inflation rate are not dominating, and second, if those external events are of a somewhat spectacular character. The type of documents that were used in Holsti's historical study are of course not available for the measurement of "détente" simply because they tend to remain classified for a considerable period of time.

An alternative means might be the direct interviewing of the elites. This approach was chosen by Schössler (1977) who collected data on perceptions of "détente" by interviewing West German elites in a Delphi-type study. Yet this method as well, even though it may have certain merits, must be said to be of little use when it comes to monitoring contemporary developments in the tension "détente" dimension.

Regular content analysis of leading articles in the prestige press, which can be expected to reflect public opinion to some extent, should be discussed as a substitute. Pool's study of editorials (1962) is an excellent example of this type of research.

The most satisfactory solution in this respect was suggested by Goldmann (1974; 1979). Regarding tension as essentially synonymous with mutual-threat perception, he defines "tension" as the extent to which two opponents expect conflict behavior to occur between themselves. By adapting the Janis-Fadner coefficient-of-imbalance technique, he content analyzes public governmental statements from 1945 through 1975. The coefficient proposed by Goldmann varies from +1, if all units of content are favorable, and −1, if all units of content are unfavorable. Although

Goldmann used this technique with reference to general statements on "détente" and thus limited himself to a nonrelational inquiry, the method he proposed is also easily applicable to dyadic relationships.

MEASURES BASED ON TRANSACTION-FLOW DATA

The use of events data and perceptual data implies a certain risk of overemphasizing the conflict aspect of international relations. This bias can be avoided by using data on transaction flows, that is, on routine, aggregate, nonpolitical flows such as mail, trade, or travel patterns. They in turn may tend to overemphasize the cooperative aspects. As a matter of fact, they were originally developed in the context of integration theory. They offer various possibilities to measure the "distance" between political communities in terms of interrelatedness. The data used refer to trade, movement of people, and the flow of ideas (Deutsch and Eckstein 1961; Finsterbsuch 1975; Galtung 1975; Katzenstein 1975, Jodice and Taylor 1979 and 1981). The meaning of such indicators can be ameliorated by calculating percentage shares for dyads or, in a more sophisticated statistical transformation, indices of Relative Acceptance (RA Indices) (Deutsch and Isard 1966; Russett 1970; Alker and Puchala 1968). Furthermore, dynamic trends can be assessed by collecting data of this type in view of time series. In the context of East-West relations, they are also useful with regard to identifying the degree of cohesion of groups of states or blocks, as well as the tendency toward concentration or dissolution of such blocks within a certain time span.

There has been an ample and thorough discussion about these measures during the past two decades. There is therefore no need to come back again to the merits and limitations of this approach, and this brief promemoria note will suffice.

NONRELATIONAL TENSION SCALES

There are some highly valid and reliable tension scales that, however, refer to individual countries only. In other words, they are nonrelational, indicating the state of tension around individual countries without specifying the dyads experiencing conflict and tension, without identifying their respective opponents. Tension scales of this type allow general conclusions only, such as: "A rise in tension results from a rise of the country's perception of the hostile intent of one of its neighbors."

The majority of nonrelational tension scales are based in one way or another on the observation of military-expenditure development as suggested, for the first time, by Richardson (1960). However, when

Table A1.1. A Synopsis of International Tension Scales

Author	*Name of Scale*	*Dimension(s)*	*Level of Measurement*	*Method of Data Collection*	*Validation*	*Data Source*
Azar and Sloan (1975) Sloan (1975)	CCIS Cooperation and Conflict Interaction Scale	Events in terms of conflict/cooperation (15 points)	Ordinal/ interval	Coding events, Q-sort by judges	Construct	Various periodicals
Azar and Sloan (1975)	DI (Dimensions of Interaction)	Frequency and intensity of conflict/ cooperation as measured by Azar-Sloan scale	Interval	Same + assessment by experts	"Empirical" by expert judgment (18 scholars and practitioners)	Same
Azar (1974) Sloan (1975) (1978)	NRR (Normal Relations Range)	Same	Interval	Statistical transformation	Construct	Same
Azar et al. (1977)	INRT (Inter-Nation Relations Trend)	Degree of change in interaction rates	Interval	Statistical transformation	Construct	Same
Azar (unpublished)	Affinity Index	Share of attention given each other by the units of a dyad	?	Statistical transformation	?	Same
Köhler (1975)	Tensiometer	Similar to Azar's DI	Ordinal	Coding events	Construct	Same
Hutchinson (1979) Hermann and Hermann (1976)	Affect (CREON)	Direction and intensity of hostility/ friendliness	Ordinal	Coding events	Construct	Deadline Data on World Affairs

Table A.1.1 *(cont.)*

Hermann (1979)	Acceptance/ Rejection Ratio (CREON)	Negative/positive feedback of actions within dyads	Interval	Statistical transformation	Construct	Same
McClelland and Hoggard (1969)	Cooperative/ Conflict Behavior Types of WEIS (World Event Interaction Survey)	cooperation/conflict plus neutral category (= "participation") (22 categories)	Ordinal	Coding events (a priori)	Construct *Times*	*New York*
Andriole and Young (1977)	Tension Level	Relative share of conflicting behavior	Ratio	Statistical transformation of above data	Construct	Same
McClelland (1972)	Hrel	Degree of dis- orderliness and decrease of patterns in dyadic relations	Ratio	Same	Construct	Same
Moses et al. (1967)	Cooperation/ conflict scale	Cooperation/ conflict	Ordinal	Coding events	Construct	?
Corson (1970)	Conflict and cooperation intensity ratio scale	Intensity of conflict and cooperation	Ratio	Coding events	Face validity expert judgment	?
Gamson and Modigliani (1971)	R/C and b/a scales	Events according to their refractory/ conciliatory and belligerent/ accommodation nature	Ordinal	Coding events	Construct	*New York Times*

Rummel (1972, 1976)	Foreign conflict behavior	Conflict	Interval	Factor analysis of 13 events variables	Construct, partly face	Various periodicals
Choucri and North (1976)	Peak interactions index	Violent action (30 point scale)	Matrix	Coding events	Construct "subjectively coded"	Various periodicals
Singer and Small (1974)	Magnitude of war	Nation months of war	Interval	Coding cases	Construct/face	Historical material
	Severity of war	Battle deaths	Interval			
Holsti (1972)	Crisis stress	Perception of hostility	Nominal	Content analysis of diplomatic documents	Empirical	Original documents
Schössler (1977)	Various attitude dimensions regarding détente			Elite interviews		
Goldmann (1974, 1979)	Tension	Mutual threat perception according coefficient of imbalance	Ratio	Content analysis of public statements	Construct + empirical	Keesing's Archive
Newcombe, Newcombe, and Landrus (1974)	T.R. (Tension Ratio)	Military expenditure, adjusted for GNP	Interval	Aggregate data	Construct and predictive correlations with deadly quarrels	(Standard)
			Interval	Aggregate data		
Rossa, Hopple, and Wilkenfeld (1980)	Crisis early-warning indicators	Various	Interval	Aggregate data/ events data	Empirical	Various

looking at several countries at the same time, conclusions based on military expenditures may become misleading since military expenditures depend to a large degree on the GNP of countries concerned. This is why Newcombe, Newcombe, and Landrus (1974) suggested a tension scale based on military expenditures adjusted to GNP. They describe a method of calculating military expenditures as if these expenditures depended solely on the GNP; the value of the military expenditures thus obtained is called the "theoretical military expenditure"(M.E.Th.). Dividing the actual military expenditure by M.E.Th. (and multiplying by 100) yields a pure number, the Tension Ratio (T.R.). The T.R. identifies "overspenders" experiencing a high degree of international tension and "underspenders" perceiving few or no particular threats (See also Newcombe/Andrighetti 1977).

There are, however, certain reasons that cast some doubts on the Newcombes' assumption that overspending or underspending is somehow related to military ambitions or at least might be regarded as an indicator of perceived threat and insecurity. First of all, military expenditures depend on a number of factors, such as the local strategic situation, geographical differences, the structure of the army (militia systems, universal conscription, professional armies and so on), traditional reasons, which are hardly related to the phenomenon the Newcombes are supposed to measure. Second, the defense budget usually has some impact on the economic system. An increase or decrease in military expenditures could simply reflect certain fiscal measures of the government. Third, the costs of research and development (usually hidden in the budgets of other departments) have to be taken into account, as well as the level of foreign military assistance which is, in some cases, of considerable importance, but is nevertheless extremely difficult to measure in hard figures. Without a correction for these factors, defense budgets remain a rather unreliable measure.

Other authors prefer to look at the dynamic aspects of military-spending behavior. Consequently, an indicator of a nation's conflict intensity (or perceived conflict intensity) is the rate of change of its military expenditures. However, as Thompson and Modelski (1977) have quite correctly argued, it cannot be denied that military expenditures are necessarily related to international conflict or perceived hostility. There may be 'noise' affecting the validity of indicators based on military expenditures such as domestic economic and political processes or gestation periods required for development of new weaponry.

All indicators of this type are relatively simple. They usually rest on more or less elaborate and more or less explicit theoretical assumptions about cause-effect relationships: *If* there is a growth in military expenditure (or something similar), *then* there will be tension. The degree of theoretical sophistication of such assumptions is obviously quite low, and the same must be said about their empirical substance; in other words, most indicators of this type are not properly validated.

There is one exception, however, to be mentioned in this context. Crisis research has produced some indicators that, as "early-warning indicators," serve a useful purpose and often are solidly validated. Yet they deal with a rather specific case of international tension and focus on predicting escalation processes within the range of crisis and war only, paying by definition no attention to other types of interstate relation. Therefore, they are of only minor importance when it comes to measuring the more general state of relations within a system of states such as the European system. Nevertheless, they deserve interest because of their methodological properties. For instance, Rossa, Hopple, and Wilkenfield (1980) use a complex set of structural variables (economic dimensions such as energy consumption per capita, capability dimensions like defense expenditure, and political dimensions like legislative effectiveness) on the one hand and events data on the other hand, looking at the interrelationship between the two sets of variables by applying causal modeling and econometric methods. Similar methods might also be applied to monitor nonmilitary conflict behavior.

A CRITICAL ASSESSMENT AND CONCLUSIONS

The widespread and excellent work done with regard to measuring the increase of relaxation of international tension has also produced an equally impressive amount of critical discussions about the manifold merits and limitations of the various approaches. In some cases, different measures have also been compared by careful intercorrelation analysis (for example, Havener and Peterson 1975; Leng, 1975; Thompson and Modelski 1977), which leads to firmly grounded conclusions about the quality of those measures. However, indicators should not be confused with the phenomenon they are supposed to measure. Apparently, in the case of events analysis, this tendency is all too evident. Andriole and Young 1977 combine both volume and level of cooperative and conflictive behavior in a index that is referred to as "tension level." The use of both concepts, tension and "détente," on the one side and conflict and cooperation on the other is justified only if they represent different things. Cooperation is perhaps an indicator for "détente," but it is not exactly the same.

A few aspects of "détente" should be made clear even if a substantial definition of "détente" has to be avoided on the grounds previously discussed. In the common-sense meaning of the word, "détente" is understood as a process or as a property of bilateral and multilateral relationships. The connection between "détente" and the actual behavior of the actors appears, on the one hand, to be a process raising the expectation of future cooperative or at least nonconflictive relations, whereas cooperation and peaceful relationships are regarded as advantageous to further progress in détente. "Détente" and the actual behavior of actors are connected by a complex feedback relationship. Data on the behavior of the actors alone cannot be considered seriously to measure "détente."

It may be useful to express a few additional critical remarks from the perspective of this specific study. Such a critical assessment and the conclusions to be drawn from it may be summed up in the following four points.

Avoiding Theoretical Preemption

Monitoring political processes necessarily presupposes a choice among a host of dimensions that might be selected for operationalization and for which data might be collected—this is, of course, a basic truism that does not need any further comment. However, it must not be forgotten that this truism has serious consequences: The very choice of which dimension to use means that, implicitly or explicitly, one has a theory guiding this selection.

As far as the attempts to measure "détente" are concerned, the majority of the contributions available are based on theories that are only implicit by nature, that is, most authors do not pay much (any) attention to reflections about the reasons for the choice of the dimensions finally selected. They tend to consider only those aspects of "détente" that, for one reason or another, mostly unconsciously, are regarded as the most relevant ones. Economic cooperation, for example, is often considered synonymous with "détente"; consequently, the growth rates in East-West trade serve as an indicator. Or one might think that the respect for human rights is crucial for "détente"; hence statistics about political prisoners, free movement of people across borders, and the like are compiled.

From the methodological point of view, such an approach is disadvantageous for two reasons: First, it only considers those dimensions that seem relevant right in the beginning. Thus there is a danger of merely confirming one's own prejudices or of making nothing but random considerations. Second, the theoretical evaluation underlying the choice of those dimensions regarded as the most relevant ones may be politically acceptable to one side or to one school of thought but unacceptable to others.

Since this project is aimed at providing a base of monitoring "détente" acceptable to all member states of the CSCE group, such an approach toward unreflective "ad-hoc operationalization" based on a more or less explicit but preemptive choice of a theory of "détente" must be avoided.

The same argument applies equally to all those attempts to provide criteria for the selection of relevant dimensions by referring explicitly to elaborate theories of cooperation and conflict. The theoretical framework suggested by Goldmann (1974; 1979), for instance, may easily satisfy the needs of a sophisticated Western theorist. However, when proposing to look at the extent of mutual-threat perception, a theorist not sharing the Western bias may argue that perceptions are quite superficial and that it is far better to look directly at the objective premises promoting or impeding the progress of "détente." A similar argument may also be raised against the theories underlying the various events-data approaches. Those who do not share the metatheoretical assumptions held by the authors of those instruments may again claim that behavior too is superficial and that it is indispensible to grasp the underlying forces directly. This does not mean that the great number of theoretical designs to conceptualize "détente" (Haftendorn 1975; Willms 1976; Feger 1976; Rotfeld 1977; Klein 1977; Jahn 1977; Mitrovic 1977; and many other contributions) have no bearing on the development of a generally acceptable instrument to monitor "détente"—quite the contrary holds true. But we do maintain that choosing any *single* theory from this large number of theoretical designs may be harmful to the purpose of such a project in that it amounts to a kind of "theoretical preemption."

Avoiding Normative Preemption

A closer glance at the problem suggests the conclusion that the issue of "theoretical preemption" can be traced back to the issue of "normative preemption." Assessing political developments such as "détente" means matching them against certain normative standards, which provide a measure for evaluating whether the actual process can be said to be progress, stagnation, or retrogression. Yet it is precisely this choice of normative standards which either makes discussions about "détente" more difficult or even impedes them.

Sometimes social scientists are tempted to set such standards by themselves or they simply assume universal standards recognized by all groups and individuals concerned. This approach has been suggested, for example, by Snyder, Hermann, and Lasswell (1976) who proposed the creation of a global monitoring system using standardized indicators to monitor government actions and their impact on the attainment and distribution of basic human values, which can be summarized as "human dignity." Human dignity is conceptualized as a set of eight Lasswellian categories (power, enlightenment, wealth, well-being, skills, affection, rectitude, respect). It is quite obvious that neither the rank order of these (partly conflicting) values nor their interpretation will easily be agreed upon in today's multicultural and multi-ideological world.

And the same turns out to be true, and even more so, in the case of East-West relations, where the existence of different social and political systems makes any attempt at normative preemption a very futile endeavor. If a monitoring system for "détente" is to serve as a basis for serious businesslike discussions among all members of the East-West system, then it has to carefully avoid any preemption of norms going beyond the small margin of commonly shared values such as the recognition of the fact that one has "to agree to disagree."

The development of a proper definition of "détente," which would meet scientific standards, is not only not required in this study, it is also not even desirable. Although the thirty-five nations participating in the CSCE talks agreed on a final act in Helsinki, a number of differences have apparently remained. Thus adopting one definition or another would place us right in the middle of the ongoing political dispute, which is, in turn, more a disadvantage than a help to the project of monitoring the "détente" process. The social sciences should not evade moral problems. However, in the long run, a multitheoretical approach that refrains from moral preemption can be expected to be more valuable to "détente" (whatever it means in detail) than insisting on certain abstract principles.

Avoiding Construct Validation

The main problem of indicator development and index construction is the problem of validity. As Singer and Small (1974) note with regard to foreign-policy indicators, "validity always remains partially a matter of judgment." The most widely used procedure to support the validity of indicators in the field of research concerning international tensions and "détente" is construct validity, that is, the author of an indicator proposal usually offers a series of theoretical reasons why he believes that his indicator really does reflect the phenomenon ("tension," "détente," "cooperation," and so on) he claims to be grasping and measuring. For instance, Hermann (1981), when suggesting the construction of the Acceptance/Rejection Ratio as an instrument to measure the degree of favorable-unfavorable reactions that a government's foreign behavior receives from governments and international actors, provides an excellent theoretical framework based on a feedback concept. Yet someone not sharing this concept may easily question the validity of the Acceptance/Rejection Ratio measure and propose an alternative measure based on another theoretical reasoning.

The conclusion, therefore, is that indicators validated solely by construct-validity procedures are to be avoided if possible. Preference should be given to indicators that have some kind of face validity. If necessary, procedures of empirical validation may be applied. However, there again the danger exists that theoretical considerations have to be made that may not be universally acceptable. Validation by expert judgment may be another way out—although it is to be expected that experts coming from different "camps" would reflect different biases. To the author's knowledge, until now this has only been the case with the Corson (1970) scale of conflict and cooperation. Corson used experts (scholars and practitioners) from both East and West. Most other scales relying on expert judgment were developed with the assistance of experts from only one particular political culture, such as American graduate students. There is no need to emphasize that scales supported by such a limited validation procedure will hardly meet the quality of standards required for a substantial discussion among representatives of different social and political systems about current problems of East–West relations.

Avoiding a Biased Data Base

It goes without saying that the selection and the use of data sources pose serious problems as well. As far as measures based on events data are concerned, this problem has been abundantly discussed in the past years. Azar (1975) and Hoggard (1975) have shown that the data collection widely used—that is, relying on the *New York Times*—has serious deficiencies that can be partly overcome by using multiple sources or even getting access to government papers (see also Gamson and Modigliani 1971, Appendix B). Yet the problem of bias cannot be solved since no source is capable of really providing "all the news that's fit for print." Therefore, events-data measures not only have an indicator construct-validity problem but also a source-validity problem. Perceptual measures and measures referring to international transactions may, in this respect, be easier to handle than events data.

Appendix A2

A Content Analysis of CSCE Statements, 1973–1980

A2.1 CONTENT ANALYSIS: AN EVALUATION OF TECHNIQUES AND CODING INSTRUCTIONS

Introduction

Stone and Mochmann (1976) suggested that content analysis be used as a tool to guide the selection of social and political indicators. Since indicator research in social science is to a large extent concerned with the selection of appropriate measures and indicators, the question of which kinds of criteria to use becomes of utmost importance, as opposed to mere intuitive insights into the relevance of certain indicators and measures and their validity. The study of monitoring the process of East–West relations is concerned with exactly the same problem. According to Holsti (1969), *content analysis* is any technique for making references by objectively and systematically identifying specific characteristics of messages. A *message* is any symbolic output, written or oral, that conveys information. Content analysis is usually referred to only as the systematic analysis of texts of all kinds.

As the choice of dimensions used in this study was to be based on a content analysis of statements presented by the official spokesmen of the thirty-five states participating in the CSCE, it was important to make a careful selection among the various content analytical techniques developed so far.

The following section presents, first, a discussion of some of the most important approaches to content analysis and, second, an evaluation of these approaches with respect to the needs of this study.

Word-Frequency Approaches to Content Analysis: Contingency Analysis, the WORDS System, Assertion Analysis, and the General Inquirer

A simple form of content analysis is counting words or the occurence of certain specified concepts or categories in a text in order to compute frequencies. Since a complete account of the frequency of virtually all words in a text is practically impossible with manual counting techniques (a text of average length such as one of the CSCE statements may contain up to 5,000 words with a vocabulary of several hundreds of different words), two possible methods are usually considered: automatic word counting or predetermined categories.

The automatic counting of words by a computer requires two conditions, however. The text has to be transposed into machine-readable form. Then a computer program must be developed if one is not available already. The results are usually printed either by listing all the words alphabetically and their respective frequencies or by ranking words according to their frequency in a text.

A second possible solution to the problem is, of course, the use of predetermined categories. In contrast to mere word counting, this approach regards the occurrence or cooccurrence of words in a text as indicators of specific categories or concepts. These categories or concepts have to be determined on the basis of theoretical considerations. Again there are two different approaches.

The first uses manual coding of texts. A list of categories is set up, and the text is scanned by coders for the occurrence of words that would represent this category in the text. The occurrence of words such as *factory, industry, production,* or *machine* could represent one single category ("labor"). Previously, decisions have to be made as to what is the context unit (a sentence, a paragraph, or an entire document) and the recording unit (the word or clusters of words). In order to ensure a fast and efficient coding of texts, coding rules cannot be too specific. Often the compilation of lists including all synonyms for the categories under study are discussed in the literature. This, however, would not be of much help because looking up synonyms in these lists would slow down coding considerably without increasing reliability. The bulk of the decision-making work has to be left to the coders. Extensive reliability tests and careful selection of coders are, of course, prerequisites to the interpretation or further analysis of the data.

The second approach places the decision as to which words should be regarded as idicators of specific categories or concepts at the beginning of the process, in order to avoid the difficulties when attaching words with concepts or categories during the coding procedure by mere intuitive judgment because of the reliability problems mentioned previously. The result of this work is a dictionary that attaches so-called entries, that is, words that are taken as indicators for the presence of a certain concept in the text, to all categories or concepts selected previously on theoretical grounds. The compilation of a dictionary is of course a time-consuming task because several thousand words have to be attached to the appropriate concepts. Furthermore, the dictionary would be of no help in manual coding because looking up each word in the dictionary in order to determine the exact category it represents is much too slow for efficient coding. Thus dictionaries should be used only in computerized content analysis. This poses in principle no technical problems because the only requirement is a comparison of those subsequent strings of characters in a text with those listed in the dictionary. Since the computer works at high speed, the identification of words that would keep a coder busy for hours takes only fractions of seconds. Other technical problems are likely to turn up, however. One is, for example, that a dictionary contains words in the root form whereas the same words in a text appear in all different forms. Without a special routine for cutting off endings, the computer would not regard "root" and "roots" as the same words. We now turn to the detailed discussion of some of the more important approaches to content analysis that are based on word frequencies.

Contingency Analysis. Simple word frequencies are of course valuable indicators for testing specific hypotheses, as demonstrated, for example, by Merritt (1966). There is, however, a growing interest in word frequencies or frequencies of categories as a data base for further analysis. One early and still widely practiced example is Osgood's contingency analysis (Osgood and Anderson 1957; Osgood 1959).

Osgood's basic assumption (1959, pp. 44–45) is that it is "reasonalbe to assume that greater-than-chance contingencies of items in messages would be indicative of associations in the thinking of a source. If, in the past experience of a source, events A and B have often occurred together, the subsequent occurrence of one of them should be a condition facilitating the occurrence of the other." Osgood's contingency analysis requires, first, a set of categories that are of importance in the text under study. In contrast to mere word counting, this requires of course an intimate knowledge about the kinds of subjects treated in the text. Otherwise, relevant items might be missed without even knowing it. Extensive pretests and perhaps word counting on a subsample are usually necessary.

The context units in Osgood's studies are paragraphs with a length of 120 up to 210 words that are found to represent one associational sequence, that is, a space big enough to include on the average all words associated with a special theme and small enough not to include unrelated items to a greater extent (Osgood 1959, pp. 61 ff.). Then a raw-data matrix containing the absolute or relative frequencies is compiled and transformed into what is called a contingency matrix, passing through the following stages:

1. The average frequency of all categories is computed, for example, category *A* might occur in 50 percent of all context units and category *B* in 30 percent, on the average.
2. The expected frequency of the cooccurrence of all pairs of categories is computed simply by taking the product of the average single frequencies ($A - B = 0.5 \times 0.3 = 0.15$). Thus, in 15 percent of all context units, one would expect the cooccurrence of categories *A* and *B*.
3. Expected values of cooccurrences are then compared with the actual values of coocurrences. If the coocurrence of two categories is considerably higher or lower than the expected value, that is, associational or dissociational relationships appear to be significantly different from what would be expected by chance (taking the distribution of word occurrences for granted), these combinations of categories are selected.

As a method for computing significances, Osgood proposes the standard error of percentages. Contingency analysis allows for the detection of associational or dissociational structures that would have remained probably hidden in the source text otherwise.

The WORDS System. A further approach to content analysis on the basis of word frequencies and word coocurrences is Iker's WORDS system (Iker and Klein 1974). In contrast to Osgood's contingency analysis (Osgood 1959), which is based on the presence or absence of a given word or attribute within a specified content area, that is, a "contingent" upon that area, Iker's approach relies on contiguity relationships that merely demand the proximity of words within a given sampling mesh (the sentence, the paragraph, the page, and so on). Thus Iker's approach does not demand the advance imposition of a category system, which is, in fact a great advantage. Therefore, the precoding of the text or the construction of a dictionary is not necessary.

The WORDS system has now developed into an integrated set of computer programs that allows for a fully automatic processing of texts of all kinds. Since even the difficult task of selecting a subset of associationally rich words from the raw-data matrix of all word frequencies for further analysis appears to be solved, content analysis with the WORDS system might well be said to proceed untouched by human hands from the beginning right to the end. In detail, the analysis of a given text passes through the following series of different stages:

1. The text is divided into segments of equally long context units.
2. All function words, such as, articles and conjunctions, are removed.

3. From the rest of the words, endings are removed and words brought into root form.
4. The frequency of every remaining word in each of the segments is counted.
5. A subset of these words is selected automatically.
6. An intercorrelation matrix is computed on this subset of words.
7. The correlation matrix is factor analyzed according to the principal-component algorithm.
8. The resulting structure is rotated orthogonally to simple structure against a varimax criterion (that is, simplifying the columns of a factor matrix).

The resulting factors are supposed to represent the major content schemes of a given document or text (Iker and Harway 1969). The critical stage in this procedure is of course the selection of the appropriate subset of words (step 5) because this is where theoretical reasoning usually comes in. Iker developed a computer program (1974/75) that solves the problem on the basis of the assumption that associationally rich words are usually those that are highly correlated with a maximum number of other words. The program proceeds in the following way: After lemmatizing, all words with a frequency of less than or equal to ten are removed. The remaining set of words is correlated, and again all correlations not passing a test of significance are set to zero. The rest of the remaining correlations is raised to the fifth power, and, for each remaining pair of words, its correlations (transformed as previously described) are summed up.

Raising the correlation to the fifth power prior to summing up is essential because with simple correlations, a bias in favor of low correlations is likely to develop. In this case, ten common correlations of .1 would outnumber one high correlation of .9 with the possible effect that the respective pair of words is not selected, although highly associative. One possible shortcoming of the WORDS system is perhaps the use of correlation coefficients as a measure of proximity of words that requires, above all, a nearly normal distribution of words in the text. This assumption however, holds only for certain (in general the most common) words and for certain texts. A text that is already structured by the speaker according to the subjects treated, is likely to contain outliers that would affect the results in some way. A further shortcoming of correlation coefficients is that not only the combined presence of two words in a context counts but also the combined absence of two words. The assumption that two words not coocurring in a context are related holds only for the most common words. So far both problems appear to be neglected in content analysis. In this study much attention was devoted to the solution of this problem.

Assertion Analysis. A different and perhaps more valid measure of proximity of words in a text was presented by Weymann in a content analysis of articles on adult training in Germany

(Weymann 1973). The theoretical basis of this approach was adopted from studies on verbal behavior revealing that people, if confronted with a series of random stimuli (words), tend to respond on request by not reproducing these inputs in the original sequence but by rearranging words according to their semantic proximity. Thus not only the occurrence of a word in a given context appears to be of interest but also the sequence of their appearance in a context. Various measures were discussed (Shuell 1969) in the literature, one of which also seems to be useful in the general context of content analysis.

In his pilot study, Weymann first defined a set of categories that were developed during discussions on the subject, thus taking into account only a limited aspect of his texts. Recording units were words; context units were paragraphs with 120 up to 210 words. For each of the paragraphs, not only the frequency of every category but also the sequence of its occurrence in the text was reported.Results were compiled in a matrix. The matrix of proximity coefficients is then factor analyzed. Other methods of multivariate reduction such as cluster analysis or multidimensional scaling may also be applied.

The General Inquirer. The General Inquirer is a set of integrated computer programs that performs automatic content analysis on the basis of word frequencies (Stone et al. 1966). In contrast to other approaches, the General Inquirer uses predefined categories that are related to the relevant words in a text (the entries) by means of a machine-readable dictionary. The basic unit of information is the word (an entry in the text); as context unit, the sentence is usually selected. According to the entries detected in a sentence, respective labels (tags) are distributed that identify a sentence as containing a certain category or a combination of categories. The General Inquirer performs the following tasks (assuming that the text is in machine-readable form and a dictionary in the appropriate format is available):

1. Instances of words and phrases that belong to categories specified by the investigator are systematically identified.
2. Occurrences and specified coocurrences of categories in the text are counted.
3. Results are presented in various forms (prints and graphs).
4. Univariate and multivariate statistical tests on the results of frequency counts are performed.
5. Sentences are sorted and regrouped in accordance with user-provided specifications (occurrence of one or more entries or categories).

Since the programs are available and transforming a text into machine-readable format is only a matter of cost and time, the major obstacle appears to be the construction of a dictionary if none of the existing dictionaries can be used such as the *Stanford Political Dictionary*.

Studies with the *Stanford Political Dictionary* include the Cuban missile crisis of 1962 (Holsti et al. 1965), Sino–Soviet relations (Holsti 1966), the integration of the Socialist countries (Hopmann 1967), and other applications.

Syntax Structure Approaches to Content Analysis: Evaluative Assertion Analysis and Cognitive Mapping

The General Inquirer offers the option to take into account the syntactical position of words. This, however, requires manual preediting of the text with the effect that some of the advantages of automatic content analysis vanish since coding texts is usually a time-consuming task. Also reliability problems surface again. Computer programs for syntactical analysis of texts are available in linguistics, but they have not yet been applied to content analysis.

A further approach in content analysis is focused on syntactical relationships in sentences as its principal measure. Two of these techniques are discussed below.

Evaluative Assertion Analysis. Originally designed for the study of evaluative attitudes on a "good–bad" continuum, evaluative assertion analysis, as a technique for preparing, coding, and finally evaluating texts, has become an important approach in content analysis.

As a first step, evaluative assertion analysis of texts requires the isolation of *attitude objects* that are those concepts or symbols in a text about which people can be expected to disagree with respect to their evaluative meanings. These concepts or symbols should be related somehow to the variables or dimensions of a theory that is to be tested. As a next step, these attitude objects are masked in the text, which means they are substituted for by a series of symbols in order to avoid the coders' affectual identification with these attitude objects. Afterward, the text with masked attitude objects is translated into one of the two following standardized or generic assertion forms:

Type A: attitude object 1 / verbal connector / common meaning term
(AO_1) (c) (cm)

Type B: attitude object 1 / verbal connector / attitude object 2
(AO_1) (c) (AO_2)

Two sample sentences from the context of the CSCE meetings should suffice for demonstrating the logic of evaluative assertion analysis:

Type A: Mutual confidence / is / necessary.

Type B: Mutual confidence / is a prerequisite / for détente.

Sentences of these types are then transformed into a seven-column chart that contains the information on the sentence in the following sequence:

1. The source of the sentence.
2. Attitude object 1.
3. The verbal connector.
4. Scale value for the verbal connector.
5. Common-meaning term or attitude object 2.
6. Scale value for common 5.
7. Value product (columns 4 and 6 multiplied).

Holsti suggested that in the case of more than one dimension with which words (attitude objects, verbal connectors, and common-meaning terms) are scaled, either further columns should be entered into the chart or separate data charts prepared. Next the (associative or dissociative) direction of attitudes has to be determined (as plus or minus) as well as their intensity (as one, two, or three) for both verbal connectors and common-meaning terms. Verbs receive a value of 3. Only hypothetical relationships are ranked as 1. The determination of values for attitude objects is a more difficult task. However, a relative safe way is to rely on the assertions of type *A* in order to scale attitude objects. All assertions describing one specific attitude are listed in a table. The results are summed up and are finally attached to the attitude object, the value of which needs to be determined.

The scaling of common-meaning terms and verbal connectors is usually handed over to the coders, which is justified on the assumption that a rank-order scale of this type with a range of three values is a safe, although crude, measure. More sophisticated scaling techniques may be applied if coders are merely requested to translate a text into generic assertion forms without ranking verbal connectors and common-meaning terms. In a further step, all verbal connectors and common-meaning terms are compiled in lists and scaled, for example, by q-sorting or expert judgment.

Evaluative assertion analysis was first developed and applied by Osgood and his associates (Osgood et al. 1956). Various applications in political science include, for instance, a thorough examination of Secretary of State John Foster Dulles' attitude toward the Soviet Union that revealed that although he admitted positive changes in the relations, his negative attitude remained unchanged (Holsti 1969a). One major shortcoming of evaluative assertion analysis tends to remain, even though coders can be trained rapidly and no serious reliability problems are to be expected: The technique is too laborious to use with large volumes of texts. It should be reserved for those cases in which exact data on a limited number of attitude objects has to be collected.

Cognitive Mapping. Events analysis and cognitive mapping should be regarded as special applications of evaluative assertion analysis on a limited aspect of text contents. In this context, only cognitive mapping is relevant because the speeches at the CSCE meetings of Helsinki and Belgrade are not to be inspected for events but rather for the level of attention that is dedicated to certain aspects of détente.

A cognitive map is a representation of a part of a person's belief system in form of a list of assertions connecting pairs of concepts. Only assertions of type B are relevant in cognitive mapping.The information is derived either from documentary material (Axelrod 1976) or openended interviews (Bonham and Shapiro 1973, 1976, 1977). Texts are translated into simple assertions of the following type.

Cause concept / verbal connector or linkage / effect concept

Cause concepts and effect concepts are classified on the basis of the following scheme:

1. *Cognitive concepts* are abstract events of all types that the person or the authors of a document believe to be of relevance in a certain context.
2. *Affect concepts* are references made to immediate policy objectives by the decision-makers.
3. *Policy concepts* are alternatives or policy options; they usually function as cause concepts.
4. *Value concepts* are references to preferred final states or utilities. Value concepts are normally effect concepts.

According to the coding rules for cognitive mapping (Wrightson 1976), seven types of linkages between cause-and-effect concepts should be distinguished:

1. Positive linkages (+) for verbal connections as "enhances," "maintains," "increases," "promotes," and so on.
2. Negative linkages (−) for verbal connections as "retards," "inhibits," "removes," and "decreases."
3. Zero linkages (0) for assertions of the form "*A* has no effect on *B*."
4. Plus or zero linkages (+/0) for assertions of the form "will not hurt" or "does not prevent."
5. Minus or zero linkages (−/0) for assertions of the form "will not help" or "does not promote."
6. Plus, minus, zero linkages (coded as "u") for assertions such as "may or may not affect."
7. Plus or minus linkages (coded as "m") for assertions as "effects in one way or another," "definitely matters."

Bonham and Shapiro restrict themselves to the first three types of linkages. A high level of coder reliability is reported from all studies that might be due to the fact that coding rules are precise and simple and scaling not required. The identification of concepts and linkages appears to be a safe procedure because in most cases the solution is self-evident.

The analysis of data in cognitive mapping proceeds in various ways. Bonham, Shapiro, and Nozicka (1976) developed a computer program that traces so-called antecedence paths and consequence paths, beginning with one "highlighted" concept and then tracing the consequences and consequences of consequences, or, respectively, the causes, and the causes of causes, thereby virtually "simulating" chains of events.

One of the most interesting features of cognitive mapping is of course the possibility of comparing different cognitive maps. An index of concept similarity (ICS) was developed that measures the extent to which different people perceive a given problem in terms of similar sets of concepts. This is simply the fraction of concepts shared by both cognitive maps. A further index is concerned with relationship similarity (IRS), which measures the similarity of the signed relationships among the subset of common concepts. The following formula was applied:

$$\text{IRS} = \frac{S}{S + D}$$

Where S is the number of shared relationships perceived to be similar, and D is the number of shared relationships perceived dissimilar. The index ranges from zero to one with 0 indicating perfect disagreement and 1 indicating perfect agreement.

For the requirements of this study, additional measures indicating the attention dedicated to each of the concepts are easy to develop. One solution would be to measure the centrality of a concept by listing all possible antecedence and consequence paths and summing up for all occurrences of each of the concepts. As in the case of evaluative assertion analysis, one problem seems to remain, however. Cognitive mapping is an extremely laborious task that can be justified only if single texts or documents are to be studied. It is of course not applicable to the more voluminous kind of written material.

Scaling and Classification Approaches in Content Analysis: Pair-Comparison Scaling, Q-Sorting, Classification of Attention Levels, and Symbols Analysis

One of the basic assumptions of all previously discussed approaches to content analysis was that all content units (words, concepts, categories, assertions, and so on) can be treated with *equal weight.* Evaluative assertion analysis, however, is still only an "atomic" approach to coding for intensity (Holsti 1969, p. 124); the same is true for cognitive mapping since all assertions are treated as equal. The only way out is of course scaling concepts or assertions according to their intensity or designing classification schemes in order to score words or concepts with respect to their intensity.

Among the many scaling techniques, there appear to be of special relevance for content analysis: pair comparison, Q-sorting, and rank-ordering. Finally, we discuss a simple classification scheme for attention measurement in texts.

Pair-Comparison Scaling. The basic idea behind pair comparison is that it is still easy and safe to judge two different items with respect to certain properties as, for example intensity. With three or even more items, severe problems develop. Strictly speaking, pair comparison is a misnomer since this technique of scaling does not require pair comparisons on the entire set of statements or concepts in a study but rather on a small sample (North et al. 1963, p. 79). In principle, pair comparison proceeds as follows.

From a larger set of assertions or concepts one or more samples are selected, each containing up to ten or a few more items. Then all possible pairs between items are generated. Since a number of N items results in $F = N(N-1)/2$ pairs, the number of items should not exceed certain limits. Then for each pair a judge is requested to decide which is the more intense one in each of the pairs. The "winning" items in each pair receive a "vote". Finally all votes for each item are summed up, and items are ranked according to the number of votes they received. Coder reliability can be computed by rank-order correlation between the results different judges yield on the same set of items.

If various subsamples of items have been scaled in this manner, the results provide sufficient material for the generation of a "yardstick" against which the rest of items can be judged (Zinnes 1968, p. 97). In a pair comparison of eleven samples (with ten to sixteen items) from a total number of 2,000 hostility statements taken from the World War I context, a standard scale of twelve levels of hostility was developed by Zinnes (1968). The highest-ranking types of statements refer to "destruction, annihilation, disposal" and "declaration of war, attacks, bombing." For the identification of specific hostility statements with those general statements of the standard measure, judgment has to come in again. Coder reliability can be checked either by employing two or more judges on the same subset of items, or by coding a sub-sample of the material twice.

Q-Sorting. Pair comparison, even if only applied to a small sample of the items, is of course a laborious task. A further method for scaling concepts or assertions with respect to intensity is Q-sorting. As in the case of pair comparison, Q-sorting assumes a rank-order in the given universe of items. This rank-order is "forced" into a nine-category scale that (North et. al. 1963, p. 59) yields a rank-order of classes of items rather than a rank-order of items. The distribution is supposed to simulate normality in order to force judges to make the necessary fine distinctions.

One major advantage of Q-sorting is of course its easy application, which allows for a scaling of masses of items in a short period. Various measures for computing interjudge reliability are available, as, for example, correlations among results of different judges or the same judge repeating a certain subset of items after a specified period of time. In some instances, however, the assumption of forced quasi-normal distribution does not hold. In this case, either pair comparison should be considered or a "free" ranking of items by judges.

Free Rank-ordering. This procedure requires some personnel. The items to be rank-ordered are typed on cards and handed over to judges who are asked to arrange the cards according to a specified criterion, for example "intensity of expressed concern" or "hostility." Then the level of agreement between the results of each pair of judges is computed. Again Spearman's rank-order correlation is an appropriate measure. In a study on the Cuban missile crisis, Holsti and his associates (Holsti et al. 1969) had Soviet and American actions rank-ordered by three judges according to the degree of violence. A more sophisticated procedure was applied by Corson in his study of East–West interaction. Corson's Conflict Intensity Ratio Scale (Corson 1970) was constructed in two phases. First, fifty-four conflictive actions from his events data (over 10,000 events) were printed on cards and presented to judges in irregular order who were then asked to arrange these actions in a rank-order with respect to their intensity. On the basis of the returns, a fifty-four item rank-order conflict-intensity scale was constructed. Second, fourteen out of the original fifty-four actions were selected. The subsample covered the full range of intensity. These fourteen actions were again printed on cards and presented to judges in irregular sequence. The respondents were asked to assign numbers to each action proportional to its intensity, as perceived by them. From this data, Corson constructed his fourteen-item intensity scale. The remaining forty items from the original sample were merged into this scale by interpolation. The same procedure was applied to cooperative actions. In a similar procedure Azar transformed events originally rank-ordered on a fifteen-point scale onto his more precise Dimension of Interaction (DI) scale (see previous section, Appendix A1).

Classification of Attention Levels in Texts. The previous discussed scaling techniques have to be applied to a sample of items (concepts or assertions) before coding texts. The objective is to develop a "yardstick" scale which then is used to scale the rest of the items, either during the coding procedure or afterward. The criterion for scaling is semantical similarity between words or expressions. Since the precise meaning of words or expressions can be expected to differ among coders to a certain degree, basic reliability problems remain. One way out of these difficulties is classification on the basis of "hard" criteria or manifest attributes of the text.

The following simple classification scheme allows for a classification of categories within texts with regard to the amount of attention received by the authors. It is much less sensitive than the scales discussed previously, but it is much more reliable and much more efficient for coding.

1. Simple occurrence of a category in a broader context.
2. Simple occurrence of a category in a broader context, however qualified as important in one or another way.
3. Main category of the context (up to five lines of text).
4. Main category of the context (up to ten lines of text).
5. Main category of the context (over ten lines of text).

Reliability tests can be performed by computing rank-order correlations between the returns from two or more coders scanning the same sample texts. This type of rank-ordering categories should not be regarded, however, as a substitute for frequency counts but rather as an additional measure that is in fact also the case with all other scales in content analysis. A similar method was finally applied in the content analysis of this study.

Symbols Analysis. An interesting approach to content analysis, combining both intensity measurement based on word frequencies and scaling as a basis for direction measurement, was presented by Pool, Lasswell, and Lerner (Lerner et al. 1951; Lasswell et al. 1952; Pool 1951, 1952, 1962). The frequency and distribution of key categories in a text were computed. Futhermore, each category had to be classified as positive, negative, or neutral with respect to its evaluation in the text. In his study of the editorials of leading European newspapers for the period from 1890 to 1950, Pool (1962) detected a number of changes in the evaluation and distribution of key categories but also certain stereotypes and rather resistant beliefs that continued to prevail despite all changes in the social, economic, and political settings. The London *Times* especially proved to be considerably stable in its evaluations. More recent applications of similar techniques include studies in the field of events analysis, especially Goldmann's coefficient of imbalance (Goldmann 1974) and, of course, the Hermanns' affect index (Hermann and Hermann 1976).

Evaluation of the Approaches

The following criteria were used as guiding principles in this attempt to evaluate the previously discussed approaches to content analysis:

1. *Reliability* is concerned with the question of whether the methods applied can be expected to reproduce the same results if applied again on the same data, irrespective of the person who is coding, scaling, or operating a system.
2. *Validity* concerns the question of whether the indicators or categories selected do in fact measure those phenomena one is aiming at. The various aspects of validity (see, for example,

Holsti 1969, pp. 142 ff.) will not be discussed here.
3. *Efficiency* depends on the ability of a technique to allow for the rapid coding, scaling, or processing of larger amounts of texts. The time necessary for the implementation of computer programs is not taken into account. The expense of preparing the text (preediting or transposing the text onto cards or disk) is taken into consideration, however.
4. *Rigidity of the approach* concerns the question of whether a certain technique is generally applicable to a wide range of problems or whether it is restricted to a special kind of theoretical approach.
5. *Technical level* refers to the degree of sophistication of the method. High scores indicate fully computerized approaches, medium scores are given to semicomputerized approaches that require a certain amount of manual coding or scaling.

No systematic test for comparing various approaches to content analysis was performed. Reports in relevant publications, however, provide some insights into the advantages and disadvantages of these approaches. Table 2.1 gives a summary.

Contingency analysis, assertion analysis, evaluative assertion analysis, and cognitive mapping all require *manual coding*. WORDS and the General Inquirer require a text in machine-readable form that is still costly to prepare. Furthermore, the General Inquirer works on costly user-provided dictionaries. If none of the presently existing dictionaries can be used, the construction of a dictionary will cause considerable expense. All methods using manual coding usually face reliability problems that do not occur in automatic text processing. Those methods that require predefined category systems have to face validity problems to some extent. Evaluative assertion analysis and also cognitive mapping are extremely laborious as far as coding is concerned. Larger volumes of text are likely to cause considerable expenses. All methods of scaling and scoring involve both reliability problems *and* validity problems. A great number of tests are required. Symbols analysis measures the intensity of items only on a frequency basis. Direction is classified by scoring items on a three-category scheme that is a safe, though rather rigid and simple measure. One difficulty with the WORDS system is that a comparison of results from different texts is hardly possible since every single analysis is likely to produce a rather individual factor structure. The same is true to a certain extent for all approaches using multivariate-reduction methods. A final decision as to what methods should be employed has to take into account at least the following criteria:

1. The specific objectives of the study;
2. The kind of data required;
3. The amount of text to be coded; and
4. The time and resources available.

Table A2.1. Summary of Approaches to Content Analysis

	Reliability Problems	*Validity Problems*	*Efficiency*	*Rigidity*	*Technical Level*	*Sources Authors*
1. Contingency analysis	Some	Some	Medium	Medium	Medium	Osgood 1959
2. WORDS	None	None	High*	Low	High	Iker 1974
3. Assertion analysis	Some	Some	Medium	Low	Medium	Weymann 1973
4. General Inquirer	None	Some	Medium**	Low	High	Stone et al. 1966
5. Evaluative assertion	Some	Some	Low	Medium	Medium	Osgood et al. 1956
6. Cognitive mapping	Some	Some	Low	High	Medium	Axelrod 1976
7. Pair comparison***	Many	Many	Medium	Low	Medium	Various
8. Q-sorting***	Many	Many	High	Medium	Low	Various
9. Rank-ordering***	Many	Many	Medium	Low	Low	Corson 1970
10. Classification***	Some	Many	High	Low	Low	Various
11. Symbols analysis	Some	Some	High	Low	Low	Pool 1962

*With short texts; medium with more data.

**With short text; construction of dictionary taken into account (if dictionary available: high).

***These techniques are usually applied in combination with other approaches.

Conclusions for This Study

The objectives of this study are well defined. With the list of categories of the Final Act of Helsinki as a frame of reference, the importance attributed to each of these categories by each of the thirty-five participating governments has to be determined. In a content analysis of the statements presented at CSCE meetings at Helsinki, Belgrade, and Madrid by the representatives of the thirty-five governments, the necessary information will be collected. In a further stage of the study, the results are to be employed for the selection of appropriate indicators for monitoring the "détente" process.

The development of a category system based only on theoretical considerations is fortunately not required since the participants in the CSCE meetings have already compiled a list of relevant categories in the text of the Final Act. This list of categories can be assumed to be valid because it emerged out of discussions during the conference. Thus the CSCE is one of the extremely rare instances in which the authors of texts provide a list of categories that can be used for a content analysis of these texts *on their own*.

Frequency counts of all words in the texts are not required, as a first consequence, because we know which kinds of concepts are relevant in this study. The application of Iker's WORDS system and the General Inquirer, however, are also not justified because the WORDS system proceeds without predefined category systems, and the development of a proper dictionary would generate expenses that cannot be justified by the limited objectives of this study. Evaluative assertion analysis and cognitive mapping are inappropriate for the quantity of texts and the objectives of this study. In addition, we are not interested in the belief system of the actors but merely their preference for different issues within East-West relations and détente in particular.

Thus, as a feasible approach, assertion analysis was selected, with scaling or classification of categories as an additional measure. Also the sequence of categories was coded.

Coding Instructions and Examples of Coding

In content analysis, the context unit is the equivalent of a "case" in ordinary empirical research. The data file in this study consists of 175 statements of the CSCE meetings at Helsinki, Belgrade, and Madrid (5 x 35 statements). Each single statement represents a subfile containing, on the average, 10 to 20 associational sequences, the equivalent of a "case." The subdivision of each of the speeches into associational sequences is a prerequisite for computing intercorrelations between categories, the "variables" in this study. Only those categories mentioned in connection with the same broader theme or issue should be correlated since it can be argued that only these categories represent the same *dimension* of content. With the sentence as context unit, we would not detect these relationships because the sentence is a too narrow basis for an analysis of the cooccurrence of categories. The statement as context unit, on the other hand, is of course much too broad a basis because all dimensions would overlap, that is, virtually all categories would cooccur.

The identification of associational sequences poses fewer problems than one would expect. The following rules are to be applied in dividing the text into associational sequences:

1. Divisions in the text are made clear where clear and evident changes in the subject are detected.
2. Associational sequences have a length of 120 to 210 words, on the average.
3. Due to the fact that the CSCE statements are formal addresses, exceptions with respect to the length of associational sequences are to be expected. Thus no formal upper or lower threshold is specified.

Tests suggest that these provisions suffice for a reliable subdivision of statements into context units. For the computation of *overall frequencies* of categories (for each single speech or groups of speeches), the division of statements into associational sequencs is of course of no relevance since the sum of category frequencies of all associational sequences of a statement is equivalent to the frequency of categories observed on the level of the statement as the context unit. Finally, the associational sequence is of course less arbitrary a basis as context unit than the sentence because the length of a sentence is in no way connected with the content of a statement. Most sentences can be divided up or combined with following sentences without changing the meaning at all.

The following examples are taken from the statement by Ambassador Albert Weitnauer, head of the Swiss delegation to the Belgrade CSCE meeting held on 4 October 1977. The change of the associational sequence is indicated by a slash (/).

1. ...which in their turn will give us the framework in which human rights may favorably develop. / Mr. Chairman, ladies and gentlemen, I now speak of the implementation of the Final Act....
2. The prior notice of military maneuvers...is a modest measure, but nevertheless, we should note the results obtained. / These few examples show that all this is possible when there is a will to achieve it...(but) certain provisions of the Final Act have remained a dead letter so far. Thus, in a sphere to which we attach great importance, that of information, we note little progress. Another sector which deserves development is that of science.
3. ...the difficulties inherent to the international situation of ideological divergences, should not be an obstacle to our efforts.

Table A2.2. Category Labels and Associated Numeric Category Codes for the Content Analysis of CSCE Statements

001 BASKET ONE: QUESTIONS RELATING TO SECURITY IN EUROPE
002 GENERAL REMARKS CONCERNING THE DECLARATION ON PRINCIPLES GUIDING RELATIONS
003 SOVEREIGN EQUALITY, RESPECT FOR THE RIGHTS INHERENT IN SOVEREIGNTY
004 REFRAINING FROM THE THREAT OR USE OF FORCE
005 INVIOLABILITY OF FRONTIERS
006 TERRITORIAL INTEGRITY OF STATES
007 PEACEFUL SETTLEMENT OF DISPUTES
008 NON-INTERVENTION IN INTERNAL AFFAIRS
009 RESPECT FOR HUMAN RIGHTS AND FUNDAMENTAL FREEDOMS
010 EQUAL RIGHTS AND SELF-DETERMINATION OF PEOPLES
011 COOPERATION AMONG STATES AS A PRINCIPLE OF INTERNATIONAL RELATIONS
012 FULFILLMENT IN GOOD FAITH OF OBLIGATIONS UNDER INTERNATIONAL LAW
013 OTHER ASPECTS CONCERNING THE DECLARATION ON PRINCIPLES GUIDING RELATIONS
014 DOCUMENT ON CONFIDENCE-BUILDING MEASURES AND CERTAIN ASPECTS OF SECURITY AND DISARMAMENT
015 PRIOR NOTIFICATION OF MILITARY MANOEUVRES
016 QUESTIONS RELATING TO DISARMAMENT
017 QUESTIONS RELATING TO SECURITY
018 OTHER ASPECTS CONCERNING CONFIDENCE-BUILDING MEASURES, SECURITY, DISARMAMENT
019 BASKET TWO: COOPERATION IN THE FIELD OF ECONOMICS, SCIENCE, TECHNOLOGY, AND THE ENVIRONMENT
020 GENERAL REMARKS CONCERNING COMMERCIAL EXCHANGES
021 GENERAL PROVISIONS CONCERNING THE EXPANSION OF MUTUAL TRADE
022 BUSINESS CONTACTS AND FACILITIES
023 ECONOMIC AND COMMERCIAL INFORMATION
024 MARKETING AND TRADE PROMOTION
025 OTHER ASPECTS OF COMMERCIAL EXCHANGE
026 INDUSTRIAL COOPERATION AND PROJECTS OF COMMON INTEREST
027 SPECIFIC ISSUES OF INDUSTRIAL COOPERATION
028 PROJECTS OF COMMON INTEREST
029 OTHER ASPECTS CONCERNING INDUSTRIAL COOPERATION AND PROJECTS OF COMMON INTEREST
030 PROVISIONS CONCERNING TRADE AND INDUSTRIAL COOPERATION
031 HARMONIZATION OF STANDARDS
032 ARBITRATION IN INDUSTRIAL DISPUTES
033 SPECIFIC BILATERAL ARRANGEMENTS CONCERNING TRADE AND INDUSTRIAL COOPERATION
034 OTHER ASPECTS OF TRADE AND INDUSTRIAL COOPERATION
035 COOPERATION IN SCIENCE AND TECHNOLOGY
036 POSSIBILITIES FOR IMPROVING COOPERATION IN SCIENCE AND TECHNOLOGY
037 FIELDS OF COOPERATION IN SCIENCE AND TECHNOLOGY
038 FORMS AND METHODS OF COOPERATION IN SCIENCE AND TECHNOLOGY
039 OTHER ASPECTS CONCERNING SCIENCE AND TECHNOLOGY
040 COOPERATION IN THE FIELD OF ENVIRONMENT
041 AIMS OF COOPERATION IN THE FIELD OF ENVIRONMENT
042 FIELDS OF COOPERATION IN THE FIELD OF ENVIRONMENT
043 FORMS AND METHODS OF COOPERATION IN THE FIELD OF ENVIRONMENT
044 OTHER ASPECTS OF COOPERATION IN THE FIELD OF ENVIRONMENT
045 COOPERATION IN OTHER SPECIFIC AREAS
046 DEVELOPMENT OF TRANSPORT
047 PROMOTION OF TOURISM
048 ECONOMIC AND SOCIAL ASPECTS OF MIGRANT LABOUR
049 TRAINING OF PERSONNEL
050 OTHER ASPECTS OF COOPERATION IN VARIOUS FIELDS
051 SECTION ON THE MEDITERRANEAN: GENERAL REMARKS
052 DEVELOPMENT OF GOOD NEIGHBOURLY RELATIONS IN THE MEDITERRANEAN
053 INCREASING MUTUAL CONFIDENCE, SECURITY, STABILITY IN THE MEDITERRANEAN
054 COOPERATION WITH NON-PARTICIPATING MEDITERRANEAN COUNTRIES
055 ECONOMIC DEVELOPMENT IN THE MEDITERRANEAN AREA
056 ENVIRONMENTAL QUESTIONS CONCERNING THE MEDITERRANEAN

Table A2.2. *(cont.)*

057 OTHER ASPECTS OF COOPERATION IN THE MEDITERRANEAN
058 BASKET THREE: COOPERATION IN HUMANITARIAN AND OTHER FIELDS
059 GENERAL REMARKS CONCERNING HUMAN CONTACTS
060 CONTACTS AND REGULAR MEETINGS ON THE BASIS OF FAMILY TIES
061 REUNIFICATION OF FAMILIES
062 MARRIAGE BETWEEN CITIZENS OF DIFFERENT STATES
063 TRAVEL FOR PERSONAL OR PROFESSIONAL REASONS
064 IMPROVEMENT OF THE CONDITIONS FOR TOURISM ON AN INDIVIDUAL OR COLLECTIVE BASIS
065 MEETINGS AMONG YOUNG PEOPLE
066 COOPERATION IN THE FIELD OF SPORTS
067 EXPANSION OF CONTACTS AMONG GOVERNMENTAL AND NON-GOVERNMENTAL INSTITUTIONS
068 OTHER ASPECTS OF HUMAN CONTACTS
069 COOPERATION IN THE FIELD OF INFORMATION EXCHANGE
070 IMPROVEMENT OF THE CIRCULATION, ACCESS TO, AND EXCHANGE OF INFORMATION
071 AGREEMENTS AND ARRANGEMENTS IN THE FIELD OF INFORMATION EXCHANGE
072 IMPROVEMENT OF WORKING CONDITIONS FOR JOURNALISTS
073 OTHER ASPECTS IN THE FIELD OF INFORMATION EXCHANGE
074 COOPERATION AND EXCHANGES IN THE FIELD OF CULTURE
075 PROMOTION OF MUTUAL KNOWLEDGE
076 CULTURAL EXCHANGE
077 ACCESS TO THE CULTURE OF OTHER PARTICIPATING STATES
078 DEVELOPMENT OF CONTACTS AND COOPERATION IN THE FIELD OF CULTURE
079 FIELDS AND FORMS OF CULTURAL COOPERATION
080 CULTURAL CONTRIBUTIONS OF NATIONAL MINORITIES
081 OTHER ASPECTS OF EXCHANGES IN THE FIELD OF CULTURE
082 COOPERATION AND EXCHANGES IN THE FIELD OF EDUCATION
083 EXPANSION AND IMPROVEMENT OF COOPERATION AND LINKS IN THE FIELD OF EDUCATION
084 ACCESS TO EDUCATION SYSTEMS AND EXCHANGES OF STUDENTS
085 COOPERATION IN THE FIELD OF SCIENTIFIC RESEARCH
086 ENCOURAGING THE STUDY OF FOREIGN LANGUAGES
087 EXCHANGE OF INFORMATION ON TEACHING METHODS
088 THE ROLE OF NATIONAL MINORITIES IN THE FIELD OF EDUCATION
089 OTHER ASPECTS CONCERNING COOPERATION IN THE FIELD OF EDUCATION
090 GOOD-NEIGHBOURLY RELATIONS
091 PEACEFUL CORRECTION OF FRONTIERS
092 SOLIDARITY AMONG COUNTRIES
093 VIGILANCE
094 DANGERS OF NUCLEAR PROLIFERATION
095 ENERGY PROBLEMS
096 EFFECTIVE EXERCISE OF THE FREEDOM OF RELIGION
097 INTERNATIONAL CONFERENCES
098 INTERNATIONAL ORGANISATIONS OTHER THAN UN
099 UN AND UN SPECIAL ORGANISATIONS
100 FEDERALISM
101 NON-ALIGNMENT
102 NEUTRALITY
103 PEACE
104 CONFLICT AND CONFRONTATION
105 DEFENCE
106 DEMOCRACY AND DEMOCRATIC INSTITUTIONS
107 JUDICIAL SYSTEMS AND LEGAL INSTITUTIONS
108 IDEOLOGY AND IDEAS
109 FREEDOM
110 JUSTICE
111 WELFARE AND PROSPERITY
112 RESPONSIBILITY
113 PUBLIC OPINION

Table A2.2. *(cont.)*

```
114 POLITICAL COOPERATION AND POLITICAL DISCUSSIONS
115 FREEDOM OF RELIGION OR BELIEF
116 PEACEFUL COEXISTENCE
117 REMARKS CONCERNING DEVELOPING COUNTRIES
118 REMARKS CONCERNING THE NEW ECONOMIC ORDER
119 SPECIFIC INTERNATIONAL AGREEMENTS
120 STABILITY, STRATEGIC AND POLITICAL BALANCE
```

> On the contrary, an additional incentive to show the great spirit of comprehension and cooperation in pursuing the noble aids of the Act of Helsinki. / The Swiss are deeply attached to the ideas of protection of human dignity, of liberty and of democracy....

In all these examples there is a considerable change in the theme at the place indicated. A closer look at the respective context above and below the sentences cited (which cannot be presented here, of course) would suffice to justify the distinctions made. In the first example, some general remarks on the importance of human rights are followed by a closer look at some aspects of the third "basket." In the second example, remarks on confidence-building measures being those aspects of the Final Act in which modest improvements have been made, are confronted in the following paragraph with aspects showing little progress, from the point of view of the Swiss delegation. In the third example, a paragraph on ideological divergences is followed by one on human rights.

The Recording Unit

Text entries with assigned category codes are the recording units in this study. The recording unit is equivalent to a variable in empirical research. One specific category, the "variable," is associated with a number of entries, the "indicators." Entries, however, are not specified in advance. It is up to the coder to make decisions on whether a certain element of the text is to be treated as an entry, that is, as a relevant "indicator," or not. The following rules are to be applied in coding:

1. Recording units are concepts consisting of single words or groups of words *within one sentence.*
2. Entries are those concepts that either represent aspects of the Final Act or aspects of "détente" and East-West relations which are not treated in the Final Act.
3. Furthermore, other concepts are treated as entries if they are important in the context of a speech, even if they are not connected with "détente" or East-West relations.
4. Entries that cannot be associated with any of the categories from the Final Act receive a three-digit "free" code. Codes from separate coders are cleared later in a computer program.
5. Entries in the text that appear to be associated with more than

one category may receive up to three different codes. These codes are either attached in the sequence of aptness (the best interpretation first, the second best following, and so on) or, if this does not apply, in the sequence of numerically increasing codes.
6. Pronouns or other expressions that are clear references to entries in previous sentences are coded as if these concepts occurred again.
7. The interpretation of concepts in the frame of the category system should not be carried too far. It is recommended rather to omit an entry or to assign a "free" code than to exaggerate.
8. The interpretation of concepts should not distort the common meaning of terms.

In the following examples we draw again upon the statement by the head of the Swiss delegation to the CSCE meeting at Belgrade, Ambassador Weitnauer. First, we present a list of normal concepts that pose no problems for coding. The assigned code is given in brackets: independence (3); deepening of relations (11); reaching a better understanding (11); armed forces (16); lethal weapons (16); human rights (9); family reunions (61); and marriages with nationals of other countries (62). These concepts are easily identified as representing certain aspects of the Final Act.

The following concepts were treated as entries even though they clearly do not represent specific elements of the Final Act. They are included in the analysis because they appear to be important concepts in Ambassador Weitnauer's speech: nonalignment; neutrality; federalism; struggle of ideas; ideological confrontation; freedom. These entries would receive three-digit "free" codes (100 ff.). A double code was assigned to the following entries: cooperation (11/19); security (1/17); economic cooperation (20/26). "Cooperation" is interpreted as a reference to one of the ten principles in the first "basket" and as a general reference to the second "basket" of the Final Act. "Economic cooperation" refers to cooperation in the fields of both trade and industrial projects. "Security" is treated as a reference to the first "basket" in general and, additionally, to the section on security and confidence-building measures.

The following sentences from Ambassador Weitnauer's statement are examples for the preediting of texts, as required in coding of pronouns and equivalent expressions. The entries are italic; the additional information for coding references is added in brackets.

1. The *struggle of ideas* is one of the most marked characteristics of European civilization. *This struggle* [the struggle of ideas] explains the flowering of thought....
2. ...the Helsinki Act proclaimed the *respect of human rights*.... *This proclamation* [of human rights] which was willed by all the participating states, established a safeguard of *human rights*....
3. The *prior notice of military maneuvers*, in spite of a number of

omissions, is gradually becoming a habit, and that, in the vast *sphere of disarmament*, is a modest measure, but nevertheless, we should note the results obtained. *These few examples* [prior notice of military maneuvers, sphere of disarmament] show that all this is possible....

4. The *exchanges* and *economic cooperation, trade* among countries with different systems have become fortunately heavily increased for some years now. We esteem that *they* [exchange, economic cooperation, trade] could yet be further developed.

It should be noted that only references to previous *sentences* are coded. References to parts of the current sentence are omitted in order to assure fast and efficient coding. In the following example, no preediting is necessary since all references remain within the current sentence:

5. ...for we see in the application of *human rights* a means to strengthen *confidence* among the states and thus to increase security and deepen *security* and détente, which in their turn will give us the framework in which *human rights* may favorably develop.

Verbal Qualifications

So far the analysis of the content of the Helsinki, Belgrade, and Madrid statements is based merely on the *frequency* of categories, which is a valid, although simple indicator of the attention devoted to certain aspects of "détente" and other issues of the statements. As an additional measure, the speakers' qualifications of the concepts used in the statement is taken into account. These qualifications are classified on the following five-point scale:

0 = no verbal qualification
1 = light positive qualification [might be important, requires our attention, etc.]
2 = positive comparison or modest positive qualifications [is more important than..., is important, is useful]
3 = expression of high emphasis and stressed positive qualifications [deep concern, high importance]
4 = maximum emphasis or superlatives [the most important of all, all our attention, measures that count most]

The following sentences from Ambassador Weitnauer's statement should suffice as examples. Verbal qualifications and entries are italic. The codes for both are provided in brackets.

1. The Swiss are *deeply attached* to the ideas of protection of *human dignity* [code: 9; qualification: 3], of *liberty* [code: 109; qualification: 3], and of *democracy* [code: 106; qualification: 3].
2. Switzerland *appreciates* the initiative...in the field of *business contracts* [code: 22; qualification: 2]...

3. European *public opinion* [code: 113; qualification: 4], whose support is of the *first importance* for détente, will be following our work...
4. Favorably too, we *appreciate* the efforts... as regards the *environment* [code: 40; qualification: 2].

Only those expressions are coded that qualify as an entry on the dimension of *importance* or *attention* (important—unimportant; much attention—no attention). Importance and attention should not be confused with the dimension of evaluation (good—bad) or other dimensions of verbal qualification. As demonstrated in the first example, one verbal qualification may apply to more than one entry in the text. Since style and rhetoric is likely to vary among speeches, differences in the "density" of verbal qualifications are to be expected: Some speakers will use more verbal qualifications than others. Coders should make no attempts to "normalize" the distribution of verbal qualifications by manipulating the scale. The necessary computations are performed later.

Length of Association Sequences

In order to control for the potential effects of differences in the size of association sequences, coders are requested to count the lines of each of the association sequences.

Coding and Computations

For coding a coding sheet was prepared providing one record for each associational sequence. Category codes with associated values for verbal qualification are entered into the coding sheet in the sequence of their occurrence. These raw data were read on a disk space and manipulated with a set of computer programs. Attention scores for categories as presented in the subsequent tables were computed by counting the occurrence of categories in the respective statement of a delegate and adding the values for the verbal qualification. In order to compensate for varying length of statements, also relative frequencies were computed. Measures of distance between categories were computed using a program operating on the individual associational sequence as the context unit (or "case"), as in assertion analysis (Weymann 1973).

A2.2 CATEGORY SCORES

The first line of each table heading refers to the category codes. For each of the thirty-five countries of the CSCE there are subsequently two lines, the first line presenting raw category scores, the second line row percentages.

Table A2.3. Category Scores and Percentages: The 1973 Helsinki Statements

COUNTRIES	1	2	3	4	5	6	7	8	9	10	11	12	13	14	15	16	17	18	19	20
1 AUST	9	7	0	0	0	0	2	0	8	0	9	1	0	4	2	3	5	0	3	0
	7.7	6.0	0.0	0.0	0.0	0.0	1.7	0.0	6.8	0.0	7.7	0.9	0.0	3.4	1.7	2.6	4.3	0.0	2.6	0.0
2 BLGM	5	5	0	4	1	0	1	0	4	0	7	1	0	6	0	10	1	0	14	1
	3.4	3.4	0.0	2.8	0.7	0.0	0.7	0.0	2.8	0.0	4.8	0.7	0.0	4.1	0.0	6.9	0.7	0.0	9.7	0.7
3 BLGR	15	0	0	0	6	5	1	0	0	0	10	0	0	4	0	0	1	0	6	1
	14.4	0.0	0.0	0.0	5.8	4.8	1.0	0.0	0.0	0.0	9.6	0.0	0.0	3.8	0.0	0.0	1.0	0.0	5.8	1.0
4 CNDA	5	5	0	1	0	0	1	0	0	0	7	0	0	5	0	1	4	0	3	0
	6.5	6.5	0.0	1.3	0.0	0.0	1.3	0.0	0.0	0.0	9.1	0.0	0.0	6.5	0.0	1.3	5.2	0.0	3.9	0.0
5 CYPR	13	6	2	6	0	1	7	6	0	1	11	1	0	5	0	5	1	0	6	0
	10.3	4.8	1.6	4.8	0.0	0.8	5.6	4.8	0.0	0.8	8.7	0.8	0.0	4.0	0.0	4.0	0.8	0.0	4.8	0.0
6 CZCH	8	1	0	0	3	0	0	1	0	0	16	0	0	2	0	0	2	0	8	1
	6.7	0.8	0.0	0.0	2.5	0.0	0.0	0.8	0.0	0.0	13.4	0.0	0.0	1.7	0.0	0.0	1.7	0.0	6.7	0.8
7 DNMK	1	4	1	1	3	0	2	0	3	0	8	1	0	7	0	4	4	0	3	2
	1.2	4.7	1.2	1.2	3.5	0.0	2.4	0.0	3.5	0.0	9.4	1.2	0.0	8.2	0.0	4.7	4.7	0.0	3.5	2.4
8 FNLD	18	2	7	0	0	0	1	0	0	2	16	0	0	3	2	7	0	0	5	0
	14.0	1.6	5.4	0.0	0.0	0.0	0.8	0.0	0.0	1.6	12.4	0.0	0.0	2.3	1.6	5.4	0.0	0.0	3.9	0.0
9 FRNC	11	0	2	2	2	0	0	1	0	1	4	1	0	5	0	2	2	0	3	2
	13.4	0.0	2.4	2.4	2.4	0.0	0.0	1.2	0.0	1.2	4.9	1.2	0.0	6.1	0.0	2.4	2.4	0.0	3.7	2.4
10 FRG	1	4	2	6	1	0	1	0	1	2	23	0	0	7	0	0	6	0	6	0
	0.6	2.4	1.2	3.6	0.6	0.0	0.6	0.0	0.6	1.2	13.9	0.0	0.0	4.2	0.0	0.0	3.6	0.0	3.6	0.0
11 GDR	11	1	2	1	12	10	3	0	0	0	17	2	0	4	1	0	4	0	3	0
	7.3	0.7	1.3	0.7	7.9	6.6	2.0	0.0	0.0	0.0	11.3	1.3	0.0	2.6	0.7	0.0	2.6	0.0	2.0	0.0
12 GRCE	12	5	1	4	0	0	0	0	0	0	15	0	0	9	0	0	0	0	3	0
	10.7	4.5	0.9	3.6	0.0	0.0	0.0	0.0	0.0	0.0	13.4	0.0	0.0	8.0	0.0	0.0	0.0	0.0	2.7	0.0
13 HNGR	9	1	0	0	0	0	0	0	0	0	14	0	0	3	0	5	0	0	8	8
	9.1	1.0	0.0	0.0	0.0	0.0	0.0	0.0	0.0	0.0	14.1	0.0	0.0	3.0	0.0	5.1	0.0	0.0	8.1	8.1
14 ICLD	4	1	0	0	0	1	0	0	0	0	4	0	0	6	0	7	2	0	3	0
	7.3	1.8	0.0	0.0	0.0	1.8	0.0	0.0	0.0	0.0	7.3	0.0	0.0	10.9	0.0	12.7	3.6	0.0	5.5	0.0
15 IRLD	15	9	1	0	2	0	5	0	0	1	15	0	0	9	0	7	3	0	5	0
	6.9	4.2	0.5	0.0	0.9	0.0	2.3	0.0	0.0	0.5	6.9	0.0	0.0	4.2	0.0	3.2	1.4	0.0	2.3	0.0
16 ITLY	9	1	2	2	2	0	0	0	1	2	11	0	0	6	1	1	4	0	0	0
	9.3	1.0	2.1	2.1	2.1	0.0	0.0	0.0	1.0	2.1	11.3	0.0	0.0	6.2	1.0	1.0	4.1	0.0	0.0	0.0
17 LICH	3	0	2	2	0	0	1	0	0	0	4	1	0	2	0	0	0	0	2	0
	11.5	0.0	7.7	7.7	0.0	0.0	3.8	0.0	0.0	0.0	15.4	3.8	0.0	7.7	0.0	0.0	0.0	0.0	7.7	0.0
18 LXBG	7	1	3	3	3	2	3	0	2	2	6	0	0	8	0	1	7	0	5	0
	6.1	0.9	2.6	2.6	2.6	1.8	2.6	0.0	1.8	1.8	5.3	0.0	0.0	7.0	0.0	0.9	6.1	0.0	4.4	0.0

19	MLTA	13	0	1	1	0	0	3	0	0	0	9	0	0	2	0	4	1	0	5	0
		18.6	0.0	1.4	1.4	0.0	0.0	4.3	0.0	0.0	0.0	12.9	0.0	0.0	2.9	0.0	5.7	1.4	0.0	7.1	0.0
20	MNCO	3	0	0	0	0	0	0	0	0	0	1	0	0	0	0	0	1	0	0	0
		14.3	0.0	0.0	0.0	0.0	0.0	0.0	0.0	0.0	0.0	4.8	0.0	0.0	0.0	0.0	0.0	4.8	0.0	0.0	0.0
21	NTHL	12	8	1	0	2	0	0	2	2	5	3	5	0	10	0	1	0	0	2	1
		9.8	6.5	0.8	0.0	1.6	0.0	0.0	1.6	1.6	4.1	2.4	4.1	0.0	8.1	0.0	0.8	0.0	0.0	1.6	0.8
22	NRWY	11	2	2	0	0	0	3	0	1	0	14	0	0	10	2	0	1	2	2	0
		7.3	1.3	1.3	0.0	0.0	0.0	2.0	0.0	0.7	0.0	9.3	0.0	0.0	6.7	1.3	0.0	0.7	1.3	1.3	0.0
23	PLND	17	1	3	0	8	7	0	0	0	0	18	0	0	4	0	4	10	0	10	0
		9.4	0.6	1.7	0.0	4.4	3.9	0.0	0.0	0.0	0.0	9.9	0.0	0.0	2.2	0.0	2.2	5.5	0.0	5.5	0.0
24	PRTG	12	6	2	2	1	0	2	0	0	0	13	2	0	3	0	3	5	0	3	0
		10.9	5.5	1.8	1.8	0.9	0.0	1.8	0.0	0.0	0.0	11.8	1.8	0.0	2.7	0.0	2.7	4.5	0.0	2.7	0.0
25	RMNA	17	6	6	4	1	1	1	2	0	3	21	2	0	15	1	10	2	0	4	0
		8.6	3.0	3.0	2.0	0.5	0.5	0.5	1.0	0.0	1.5	10.7	1.0	0.0	7.6	0.5	5.1	1.0	0.0	2.0	0.0
26	SANM	1	8	4	4	0	1	2	2	4	2	10	0	0	1	0	3	3	0	0	0
		0.9	6.9	3.4	3.4	0.0	0.9	1.7	1.7	3.4	1.7	8.6	0.0	0.0	0.9	0.0	2.6	2.6	0.0	0.0	0.0
27	SPAN	14	3	1	0	0	0	0	0	0	0	16	1	0	6	0	2	7	0	6	0
		9.8	2.1	0.7	0.0	0.0	0.0	0.0	0.0	0.0	0.0	11.2	0.7	0.0	4.2	0.0	1.4	4.9	0.0	4.2	0.0
28	SWDN	5	5	3	0	0	0	4	0	0	1	19	2	0	7	0	11	6	0	6	0
		2.9	2.9	1.8	0.0	0.0	0.0	2.4	0.0	0.0	0.6	11.2	1.2	0.0	4.1	0.0	6.5	3.5	0.0	3.5	0.0
29	SWTZ	7	2	1	3	0	0	5	0	0	0	4	2	0	2	0	0	0	0	0	0
		11.5	3.3	1.6	4.9	0.0	0.0	8.2	0.0	0.0	0.0	6.6	3.3	0.0	3.3	0.0	0.0	0.0	0.0	0.0	0.0
30	TRKY	13	13	3	2	1	1	0	1	0	0	10	1	0	6	0	3	1	0	9	0
		8.8	8.8	2.0	1.4	0.7	0.7	0.0	0.7	0.0	0.0	6.8	0.7	0.0	4.1	0.0	2.0	0.7	0.0	6.1	0.0
31	USSR	19	11	5	2	2	5	2	3	1	1	21	1	0	13	1	2	6	0	4	1
		8.4	4.9	2.2	0.9	0.9	2.2	0.9	1.3	0.4	0.4	9.3	0.4	0.0	5.8	0.4	0.9	2.7	0.0	1.8	0.4
32	UK	9	1	0	0	0	0	0	0	0	0	3	0	0	13	0	1	2	0	1	3
		12.0	1.3	0.0	0.0	0.0	0.0	0.0	0.0	0.0	0.0	4.0	0.0	0.0	17.3	0.0	1.3	2.7	0.0	1.3	4.0
33	USA	8	4	2	7	1	0	2	1	5	1	3	0	0	9	1	4	0	0	0	0
		6.6	3.3	1.7	5.8	0.8	0.0	1.7	0.8	4.1	0.8	2.5	0.0	0.0	7.4	0.8	3.3	0.0	0.0	0.0	0.0
34	VATC	18	5	2	3	0	1	2	2	2	1	9	1	0	4	0	1	1	0	1	0
		17.3	4.8	1.9	2.9	0.0	1.0	1.9	1.9	1.9	1.0	8.7	1.0	0.0	3.8	0.0	1.0	1.0	0.0	1.0	0.0
35	YGSL	25	7	6	1	0	0	1	0	1	0	12	0	0	2	0	1	4	0	6	0
		17.4	4.9	4.2	0.7	0.0	0.0	0.7	0.0	0.7	0.0	8.3	0.0	0.0	1.4	0.0	0.7	2.8	0.0	4.2	0.0

Table A2.3. *(cont.)*

COUNTRIES	21	22	23	24	25	26	27	28	29	30	31	32	33	34	35	36	37	38	39	40
1 AUST	0	0	0	0	0	0	0	0	0	1	0	0	0	0	0	0	0	0	0	0
	0.0	0.0	0.0	0.0	0.0	0.0	0.0	0.0	0.0	0.9	0.0	0.0	0.0	0.0	0.0	0.0	0.0	0.0	0.0	0.0
2 BLGM	0	1	0	0	0	0	1	0	0	0	0	0	0	0	0	0	0	0	0	0
	0.0	0.7	0.0	0.0	0.0	0.0	0.7	0.0	0.0	0.0	0.0	0.0	0.0	0.0	0.0	0.0	0.0	0.0	0.0	0.0
3 BLGR	2	0	1	0	0	1	2	0	0	0	1	0	0	0	2	0	0	0	0	1
	1.9	0.0	1.0	0.0	0.0	1.0	1.9	0.0	0.0	0.0	1.0	0.0	0.0	0.0	1.9	0.0	0.0	0.0	0.0	1.0
4 CNDA	4	0	0	0	0	0	0	0	0	1	0	0	0	0	0	0	0	0	0	0
	5.3	0.0	0.0	0.0	0.0	0.0	0.0	0.0	0.0	1.3	0.0	0.0	0.0	0.0	0.0	0.0	0.0	0.0	0.0	0.0
5 CYPR	0	0	0	0	0	0	0	0	0	0	0	0	0	0	0	0	0	0	0	2
	0.0	0.0	0.0	0.0	0.0	0.0	0.0	0.0	0.0	0.0	0.0	0.0	0.0	0.0	0.0	0.0	0.0	0.0	0.0	1.6
6 CZCH	0	0	0	0	0	0	2	1	0	0	0	0	0	0	7	1	0	0	0	2
	0.0	0.0	0.0	0.0	0.0	0.0	1.7	0.8	0.0	0.0	0.0	0.0	0.0	0.0	5.9	0.8	0.0	0.0	0.0	1.7
7 DNMK	0	0	0	0	0	0	0	0	0	0	0	0	0	0	0	0	0	0	0	1
	0.0	0.0	0.0	0.0	0.0	0.0	0.0	0.0	0.0	0.0	0.0	0.0	0.0	0.0	0.0	0.0	0.0	0.0	0.0	1.2
8 FNLD	7	1	0	0	0	0	1	1	0	0	0	0	0	0	0	0	0	0	0	1
	5.5	0.8	0.0	0.0	0.0	0.0	0.8	0.8	0.0	0.0	0.0	0.0	0.0	0.0	0.0	0.0	0.0	0.0	0.0	0.8
9 FRNC	0	0	0	0	0	0	0	0	0	2	0	0	2	0	0	0	0	0	0	0
	0.0	0.0	0.0	0.0	0.0	0.0	0.0	0.0	0.0	2.4	0.0	0.0	2.4	0.0	0.0	0.0	0.0	0.0	0.0	0.0
10 FRG	2	2	1	0	0	0	0	0	0	2	0	0	0	0	3	0	0	0	0	1
	1.2	1.2	0.6	0.0	0.0	0.0	0.0	0.0	0.0	1.2	0.0	0.0	0.0	0.0	1.8	0.0	0.0	0.0	0.0	0.6
11 GDR	0	0	0	0	0	0	0	0	0	0	0	0	0	0	0	0	0	0	0	2
	0.0	0.0	0.0	0.0	0.0	0.0	0.0	0.0	0.0	0.0	0.0	0.0	0.0	0.0	0.0	0.0	0.0	0.0	0.0	1.3
12 GRCE	1	0	0	0	0	0	1	0	0	0	0	0	0	0	2	0	0	0	0	2
	0.9	0.0	0.0	0.0	0.0	0.0	0.9	0.0	0.0	0.0	0.0	0.0	0.0	0.0	1.8	0.0	0.0	0.0	0.0	1.8
13 HNGR	1	0	0	0	0	0	0	0	0	1	0	0	0	0	0	0	0	0	0	4
	1.0	0.0	0.0	0.0	0.0	0.0	0.0	0.0	0.0	1.0	0.0	0.0	0.0	0.0	0.0	0.0	0.0	0.0	0.0	4.1
14 ICLD	0	0	0	0	0	0	0	0	0	0	0	0	0	0	2	0	0	0	0	4
	0.0	0.0	0.0	0.0	0.0	0.0	0.0	0.0	0.0	0.0	0.0	0.0	0.0	0.0	3.7	0.0	0.0	0.0	0.0	7.4
15 IRLD	0	1	1	0	0	0	1	0	0	0	0	0	0	0	1	0	0	0	0	1
	0.0	0.5	0.5	0.0	0.0	0.0	0.5	0.0	0.0	0.0	0.0	0.0	0.0	0.0	0.5	0.0	0.0	0.0	0.0	0.5
16 ITLY	1	0	0	0	0	0	0	0	0	2	0	0	0	0	1	0	0	0	0	4
	1.0	0.0	0.0	0.0	0.0	0.0	0.0	0.0	0.0	2.1	0.0	0.0	0.0	0.0	1.0	0.0	0.0	0.0	0.0	4.1
17 LICH	0	0	0	0	0	0	0	0	0	0	0	0	0	0	0	0	0	0	0	0
	0.0	0.0	0.0	0.0	0.0	0.0	0.0	0.0	0.0	0.0	0.0	0.0	0.0	0.0	0.0	0.0	0.0	0.0	0.0	0.0

18	LXBG	1	0	0	0	0	0	0	0	0	0	0	0	0	0	0	0	0	0	0	0
		0.9	0.0	0.0	0.0	0.0	0.0	0.0	0.0	0.0	0.0	0.0	0.0	0.0	0.0	0.0	0.0	0.0	0.0	0.0	0.0
19	MLTA	0	0	0	0	0	0	0	0	0	0	0	0	0	0	0	0	0	0	0	0
		0.0	0.0	0.0	0.0	0.0	0.0	0.0	0.0	0.0	0.0	0.0	0.0	0.0	0.0	0.0	0.0	0.0	0.0	0.0	0.0
20	MNCO	0	0	0	0	0	0	0	0	0	0	0	0	0	0	2	0	0	0	0	3
		0.0	0.0	0.0	0.0	0.0	0.0	0.0	0.0	0.0	0.0	0.0	0.0	0.0	0.0	9.5	0.0	0.0	0.0	0.0	14.3
21	NTHL	1	1	1	0	0	0	1	0	0	0	0	0	0	0	2	0	0	0	0	1
		0.8	0.8	0.8	0.0	0.0	0.0	0.8	0.0	0.0	0.0	0.0	0.0	0.0	0.0	1.6	0.0	0.0	0.0	0.0	0.8
22	NRWY	5	0	0	0	0	4	0	1	0	0	0	0	0	0	4	0	0	0	0	20
		3.4	0.0	0.0	0.0	0.0	2.7	0.0	0.7	0.0	0.0	0.0	0.0	0.0	0.0	2.7	0.0	0.0	0.0	0.0	13.5
23	PLND	1	0	0	0	0	0	1	1	0	0	0	0	0	0	0	0	0	0	0	1
		0.6	0.0	0.0	0.0	0.0	0.0	0.6	0.6	0.0	0.0	0.0	0.0	0.0	0.0	0.0	0.0	0.0	0.0	0.0	0.6
24	PRTG	0	0	0	0	0	0	0	0	0	0	0	0	0	0	1	0	0	0	0	0
		0.0	0.0	0.0	0.0	0.0	0.0	0.0	0.0	0.0	0.0	0.0	0.0	0.0	0.0	0.9	0.0	0.0	0.0	0.0	0.0
25	RMNA	1	0	0	0	0	0	0	0	0	5	0	0	0	0	2	0	0	0	0	1
		0.5	0.0	0.0	0.0	0.0	0.0	0.0	0.0	0.0	2.6	0.0	0.0	0.0	0.0	1.0	0.0	0.0	0.0	0.0	0.5
26	SANM	0	0	0	0	0	0	0	0	0	0	0	0	0	0	1	0	0	0	0	6
		0.0	0.0	0.0	0.0	0.0	0.0	0.0	0.0	0.0	0.0	0.0	0.0	0.0	0.0	0.9	0.0	0.0	0.0	0.0	5.3
27	SPAN	1	0	1	0	0	3	0	0	0	1	0	0	0	0	0	0	0	0	0	4
		0.7	0.0	0.7	0.0	0.0	2.1	0.0	0.0	0.0	0.7	0.0	0.0	0.0	0.0	0.0	0.0	0.0	0.0	0.0	2.8
28	SWDN	2	1	1	0	0	0	0	0	0	0	0	0	0	0	0	0	0	0	0	3
		1.2	0.6	0.6	0.0	0.0	0.0	0.0	0.0	0.0	0.0	0.0	0.0	0.0	0.0	0.0	0.0	0.0	0.0	0.0	1.8
29	SWTZ	1	0	0	0	0	0	0	0	0	1	0	0	0	0	0	0	0	0	0	0
		1.6	0.0	0.0	0.0	0.0	0.0	0.0	0.0	0.0	1.6	0.0	0.0	0.0	0.0	0.0	0.0	0.0	0.0	0.0	0.0
30	TRKY	0	0	0	0	0	0	0	0	0	0	0	0	0	0	0	0	0	0	0	8
		0.0	0.0	0.0	0.0	0.0	0.0	0.0	0.0	0.0	0.0	0.0	0.0	0.0	0.0	0.0	0.0	0.0	0.0	0.0	5.4
31	USSR	0	0	0	0	0	0	0	0	0	0	0	0	0	0	0	0	0	0	0	0
		0.0	0.0	0.0	0.0	0.0	0.0	0.0	0.0	0.0	0.0	0.0	0.0	0.0	0.0	0.0	0.0	0.0	0.0	0.0	0.0
32	UK	0	1	1	0	0	0	0	0	0	0	0	0	0	0	0	0	0	0	0	1
		0.0	1.3	1.3	0.0	0.0	0.0	0.0	0.0	0.0	0.0	0.0	0.0	0.0	0.0	0.0	0.0	0.0	0.0	0.0	1.3
33	USA	3	1	1	0	0	0	1	0	0	0	0	0	0	0	1	0	0	0	0	0
		2.6	0.9	0.9	0.0	0.0	0.0	0.9	0.0	0.0	0.0	0.0	0.0	0.0	0.0	0.9	0.0	0.0	0.0	0.0	0.0
34	VATC	0	0	0	0	0	0	0	0	0	0	0	0	0	0	0	0	0	0	0	0
		0.0	0.0	0.0	0.0	0.0	0.0	0.0	0.0	0.0	0.0	0.0	0.0	0.0	0.0	0.0	0.0	0.0	0.0	0.0	0.0
35	YGSL	0	0	0	0	0	0	0	0	0	0	0	0	0	0	0	0	0	0	0	0
		0.0	0.0	0.0	0.0	0.0	0.0	0.0	0.0	0.0	0.0	0.0	0.0	0.0	0.0	0.0	0.0	0.0	0.0	0.0	0.0

Table A2.3. *(cont.)*

COUNTRIES	41	42	43	44	45	46	47	48	49	50	51	52	53	54	55	56	57	58	59	60
1 AUST	0	0	0	0	0	1	0	0	0	0	0	0	0	0	0	0	0	2	2	0
	0.0	0.0	0.0	0.0	0.0	0.9	0.0	0.0	0.0	0.0	0.0	0.0	0.0	0.0	0.0	0.0	0.0	1.7	1.7	0.0
2 BLGM	0	0	0	0	0	0	0	0	0	0	0	0	0	0	0	0	0	7	1	0
	0.0	0.0	0.0	0.0	0.0	0.0	0.0	0.0	0.0	0.0	0.0	0.0	0.0	0.0	0.0	0.0	0.0	4.8	0.7	0.0
3 BLGR	0	0	0	0	0	0	0	0	0	2	0	0	0	0	0	0	0	1	3	0
	0.0	0.0	0.0	0.0	0.0	0.0	0.0	0.0	0.0	1.9	0.0	0.0	0.0	0.0	0.0	0.0	0.0	1.0	2.9	0.0
4 CNDA	0	0	0	0	0	0	0	0	0	0	0	0	0	0	0	0	0	1	7	0
	0.0	0.0	0.0	0.0	0.0	0.0	0.0	0.0	0.0	0.0	0.0	0.0	0.0	0.0	0.0	0.0	0.0	1.3	9.3	0.0
5 CYPR	0	0	0	0	0	0	0	0	0	0	7	0	1	0	0	0	0	1	0	0
	0.0	0.0	0.0	0.0	0.0	0.0	0.0	0.0	0.0	0.0	5.6	0.0	0.8	0.0	0.0	0.0	0.0	0.8	0.0	0.0
6 CZCH	0	0	0	0	0	1	0	0	0	0	0	0	0	0	0	0	0	0	1	0
	0.0	0.0	0.0	0.0	0.0	0.8	0.0	0.0	0.0	0.0	0.0	0.0	0.0	0.0	0.0	0.0	0.0	0.0	0.8	0.0
7 DNMK	0	0	0	0	0	0	0	0	0	0	0	0	0	0	0	0	0	7	6	1
	0.0	0.0	0.0	0.0	0.0	0.0	0.0	0.0	0.0	0.0	0.0	0.0	0.0	0.0	0.0	0.0	0.0	8.2	7.1	1.2
8 FNLD	0	0	0	0	0	0	0	0	0	0	0	0	0	0	0	0	0	2	1	0
	0.0	0.0	0.0	0.0	0.0	0.0	0.0	0.0	0.0	0.0	0.0	0.0	0.0	0.0	0.0	0.0	0.0	1.6	0.8	0.0
9 FRNC	0	0	0	0	0	0	0	0	0	0	0	0	0	0	0	0	0	0	1	0
	0.0	0.0	0.0	0.0	0.0	0.0	0.0	0.0	0.0	0.0	0.0	0.0	0.0	0.0	0.0	0.0	0.0	0.0	1.2	0.0
10 FRG	0	0	0	0	0	0	0	0	0	0	0	0	0	0	0	0	0	3	5	0
	0.0	0.0	0.0	0.0	0.0	0.0	0.0	0.0	0.0	0.0	0.0	0.0	0.0	0.0	0.0	0.0	0.0	1.8	3.0	0.0
11 GDR	0	0	0	0	0	1	0	0	0	0	0	0	0	0	0	0	0	1	0	0
	0.0	0.0	0.0	0.0	0.0	0.7	0.0	0.0	0.0	0.0	0.0	0.0	0.0	0.0	0.0	0.0	0.0	0.7	0.0	0.0
12 GRCE	0	0	0	0	0	1	0	0	0	0	2	0	2	0	0	0	0	1	0	0
	0.0	0.0	0.0	0.0	0.0	0.9	0.0	0.0	0.0	0.0	1.8	0.0	1.8	0.0	0.0	0.0	0.0	0.9	0.0	0.0
13 HNGR	0	0	0	0	0	0	0	0	0	0	1	0	0	0	0	0	0	0	2	0
	0.0	0.0	0.0	0.0	0.0	0.0	0.0	0.0	0.0	0.0	1.0	0.0	0.0	0.0	0.0	0.0	0.0	0.0	2.0	0.0
14 ICLD	0	0	0	0	0	0	0	0	0	0	0	0	0	0	0	0	0	0	5	0
	0.0	0.0	0.0	0.0	0.0	0.0	0.0	0.0	0.0	0.0	0.0	0.0	0.0	0.0	0.0	0.0	0.0	0.0	9.3	0.0
15 IRLD	0	0	0	0	0	0	0	0	0	0	0	0	0	0	0	0	0	0	1	0
	0.0	0.0	0.0	0.0	0.0	0.0	0.0	0.0	0.0	0.0	0.0	0.0	0.0	0.0	0.0	0.0	0.0	0.0	0.5	0.0
16 ITLY	0	0	0	0	0	0	0	0	0	0	2	0	0	1	0	0	0	2	2	0
	0.0	0.0	0.0	0.0	0.0	0.0	0.0	0.0	0.0	0.0	2.1	0.0	0.0	1.0	0.0	0.0	0.0	2.1	2.1	0.0
17 LICH	0	0	0	0	0	0	0	0	0	0	0	0	0	0	0	0	0	1	0	0
	0.0	0.0	0.0	0.0	0.0	0.0	0.0	0.0	0.0	0.0	0.0	0.0	0.0	0.0	0.0	0.0	0.0	3.8	0.0	0.0

18	LXBG	0	0	0	0	0	0	0	0	0	0	0	0	0	0	0	0	0	0	4	0
		0.0	0.0	0.0	0.0	0.0	0.0	0.0	0.0	0.0	0.0	0.0	0.0	0.0	0.0	0.0	0.0	0.0	0.0	3.5	0.0
19	MLTA	0	0	0	0	0	0	0	0	0	0	8	0	1	1	0	0	0	0	1	0
		0.0	0.0	0.0	0.0	0.0	0.0	0.0	0.0	0.0	0.0	11.6	0.0	1.4	1.4	0.0	0.0	0.0	0.0	1.4	0.0
20	MNCO	0	0	0	0	0	0	1	0	0	0	3	0	0	0	0	0	0	0	0	0
		0.0	0.0	0.0	0.0	0.0	0.0	4.8	0.0	0.0	0.0	14.3	0.0	0.0	0.0	0.0	0.0	0.0	0.0	0.0	0.0
21	NTHL	0	0	0	0	0	1	0	0	0	0	0	0	0	0	0	0	0	0	2	0
		0.0	0.0	0.0	0.0	0.0	0.8	0.0	0.0	0.0	0.0	0.0	0.0	0.0	0.0	0.0	0.0	0.0	0.0	1.6	0.0
22	NRWY	2	0	0	0	0	0	0	0	0	0	0	0	0	0	0	0	0	0	4	0
		1.4	0.0	0.0	0.0	0.0	0.0	0.0	0.0	0.0	0.0	0.0	0.0	0.0	0.0	0.0	0.0	0.0	0.0	2.7	0.0
23	PLND	0	0	0	0	0	1	0	0	0	3	0	0	0	0	0	0	0	1	3	0
		0.0	0.0	0.0	0.0	0.0	0.6	0.0	0.0	0.0	1.7	0.0	0.0	0.0	0.0	0.0	0.0	0.0	0.6	1.7	0.0
24	PRTG	0	0	0	0	0	0	0	0	0	0	1	0	0	0	0	0	0	6	1	0
		0.0	0.0	0.0	0.0	0.0	0.0	0.0	0.0	0.0	0.0	0.9	0.0	0.0	0.0	0.0	0.0	0.0	5.6	0.9	0.0
25	RMNA	0	1	0	0	0	1	1	0	0	0	0	0	0	0	0	0	0	0	2	0
		0.0	0.5	0.0	0.0	0.0	0.5	0.5	0.0	0.0	0.0	0.0	0.0	0.0	0.0	0.0	0.0	0.0	0.0	1.0	0.0
26	SANM	0	0	0	0	0	0	0	0	0	0	0	0	0	0	0	0	0	1	0	0
		0.0	0.0	0.0	0.0	0.0	0.0	0.0	0.0	0.0	0.0	0.0	0.0	0.0	0.0	0.0	0.0	0.0	0.9	0.0	0.0
27	SPAN	0	0	0	0	0	1	5	2	1	0	10	0	3	0	1	0	0	0	1	0
		0.0	0.0	0.0	0.0	0.0	0.7	3.5	1.4	0.7	0.0	7.0	0.0	2.1	0.0	0.7	0.0	0.0	0.0	0.7	0.0
28	SWDN	0	0	0	0	0	4	0	0	0	0	0	0	0	0	0	0	0	2	3	0
		0.0	0.0	0.0	0.0	0.0	2.4	0.0	0.0	0.0	0.0	0.0	0.0	0.0	0.0	0.0	0.0	0.0	1.2	1.8	0.0
29	SWTZ	0	0	0	0	0	0	0	0	0	0	0	0	0	0	0	0	0	1	2	0
		0.0	0.0	0.0	0.0	0.0	0.0	0.0	0.0	0.0	0.0	0.0	0.0	0.0	0.0	0.0	0.0	0.0	1.6	3.3	0.0
30	TRKY	0	0	0	0	0	3	0	9	0	0	6	0	9	1	0	0	0	0	1	1
		0.0	0.0	0.0	0.0	0.0	2.0	0.0	6.1	0.0	0.0	4.1	0.0	6.1	0.7	0.0	0.0	0.0	0.0	0.7	0.7
31	USSR	0	0	0	0	0	0	0	0	0	0	0	0	0	0	0	0	0	0	3	0
		0.0	0.0	0.0	0.0	0.0	0.0	0.0	0.0	0.0	0.0	0.0	0.0	0.0	0.0	0.0	0.0	0.0	0.0	1.3	0.0
32	UK	0	0	0	0	0	0	0	0	0	0	0	0	0	0	0	0	0	0	6	0
		0.0	0.0	0.0	0.0	0.0	0.0	0.0	0.0	0.0	0.0	0.0	0.0	0.0	0.0	0.0	0.0	0.0	0.0	8.0	0.0
33	USA	0	0	0	0	0	0	0	0	0	0	0	0	0	0	0	0	0	2	9	0
		0.0	0.0	0.0	0.0	0.0	0.0	0.0	0.0	0.0	0.0	0.0	0.0	0.0	0.0	0.0	0.0	0.0	1.7	7.8	0.0
34	VATC	0	0	0	0	0	0	0	0	0	0	0	0	0	0	0	0	0	2	0	0
		0.0	0.0	0.0	0.0	0.0	0.0	0.0	0.0	0.0	0.0	0.0	0.0	0.0	0.0	0.0	0.0	0.0	2.0	0.0	0.0
35	YGSL	0	0	0	0	0	0	0	1	0	0	2	0	0	0	0	0	0	0	2	0
		0.0	0.0	0.0	0.0	0.0	0.0	0.0	0.7	0.0	0.0	1.4	0.0	0.0	0.0	0.0	0.0	0.0	0.0	1.4	0.0

Table A2.3. *(cont.)*

COUNTRIES	61	62	63	64	65	66	67	68	69	70	71	72	73	74	75	76	77	78	79	80
1 AUST	1	1	1	1	1	0	0	0	0	0	0	0	0	1	0	1	0	0	0	0
	0.9	0.9	0.9	0.9	0.9	0.0	0.0	0.0	0.0	0.0	0.0	0.0	0.0	0.9	0.0	0.9	0.0	0.0	0.0	0.0
2 BLGM	0	0	0	0	4	0	0	0	1	2	0	0	0	3	1	5	1	0	1	0
	0.0	0.0	0.0	0.0	2.8	0.0	0.0	0.0	0.7	1.4	0.0	0.0	0.0	2.1	0.7	3.4	0.7	0.0	0.7	0.0
3 BLGR	0	0	0	0	0	0	0	0	1	3	0	0	0	3	0	2	0	1	0	0
	0.0	0.0	0.0	0.0	0.0	0.0	0.0	0.0	1.0	2.9	0.0	0.0	0.0	2.9	0.0	1.9	0.0	1.0	0.0	0.0
4 CNDA	2	1	0	0	0	0	0	0	0	1	0	0	0	0	0	0	0	0	0	0
	2.7	1.3	0.0	0.0	0.0	0.0	0.0	0.0	0.0	1.3	0.0	0.0	0.0	0.0	0.0	0.0	0.0	0.0	0.0	0.0
5 CYPR	0	0	0	0	0	0	1	0	0	0	0	0	0	0	0	1	0	0	0	0
	0.0	0.0	0.0	0.0	0.0	0.0	0.8	0.0	0.0	0.0	0.0	0.0	0.0	0.0	0.0	0.8	0.0	0.0	0.0	0.0
6 CZCH	0	0	0	0	0	0	0	0	1	2	0	0	0	1	1	2	0	1	0	0
	0.0	0.0	0.0	0.0	0.0	0.0	0.0	0.0	0.8	1.7	0.0	0.0	0.0	0.8	0.8	1.7	0.0	0.8	0.0	0.0
7 DNMK	1	0	0	0	0	0	0	0	1	1	0	0	0	1	0	0	0	0	0	0
	1.2	0.0	0.0	0.0	0.0	0.0	0.0	0.0	1.2	1.2	0.0	0.0	0.0	1.2	0.0	0.0	0.0	0.0	0.0	0.0
8 FNLD	0	0	0	0	0	0	0	0	2	0	0	0	0	1	0	0	0	0	0	0
	0.0	0.0	0.0	0.0	0.0	0.0	0.0	0.0	1.6	0.0	0.0	0.0	0.0	0.8	0.0	0.0	0.0	0.0	0.0	0.0
9 FRNC	0	0	0	0	0	0	0	0	0	0	0	0	0	1	0	0	0	0	0	0
	0.0	0.0	0.0	0.0	0.0	0.0	0.0	0.0	0.0	0.0	0.0	0.0	0.0	1.2	0.0	0.0	0.0	0.0	0.0	0.0
10 FRG	2	0	0	1	0	0	1	0	6	1	0	1	0	0	0	1	0	0	0	0
	1.2	0.0	0.0	0.6	0.0	0.0	0.6	0.0	3.7	0.6	0.0	0.6	0.0	0.0	0.0	0.6	0.0	0.0	0.0	0.0
11 GDR	0	0	0	0	0	0	0	0	0	0	0	0	0	2	0	0	0	0	0	0
	0.0	0.0	0.0	0.0	0.0	0.0	0.0	0.0	0.0	0.0	0.0	0.0	0.0	1.3	0.0	0.0	0.0	0.0	0.0	0.0
12 GRCE	0	0	0	0	0	0	0	0	2	1	0	0	0	2	0	0	0	0	0	0
	0.0	0.0	0.0	0.0	0.0	0.0	0.0	0.0	1.8	0.9	0.0	0.0	0.0	1.8	0.0	0.0	0.0	0.0	0.0	0.0
13 HNGR	0	0	0	0	0	0	0	0	0	1	0	0	0	1	0	1	0	0	0	0
	0.0	0.0	0.0	0.0	0.0	0.0	0.0	0.0	0.0	1.0	0.0	0.0	0.0	1.0	0.0	1.0	0.0	0.0	0.0	0.0
14 ICLD	0	0	0	0	0	0	0	0	0	0	0	0	0	0	1	0	0	0	0	0
	0.0	0.0	0.0	0.0	0.0	0.0	0.0	0.0	0.0	0.0	0.0	0.0	0.0	0.0	1.9	0.0	0.0	0.0	0.0	0.0
15 IRLD	2	0	5	0	0	0	1	0	1	6	0	0	0	1	1	0	0	2	0	0
	0.9	0.0	2.3	0.0	0.0	0.0	0.5	0.0	0.5	2.8	0.0	0.0	0.0	0.5	0.5	0.0	0.0	0.9	0.0	0.0
16 ITLY	0	1	0	1	0	0	0	0	0	3	0	0	0	0	0	1	0	0	0	0
	0.0	1.0	0.0	1.0	0.0	0.0	0.0	0.0	0.0	3.1	0.0	0.0	0.0	0.0	0.0	1.0	0.0	0.0	0.0	0.0
17 LICH	0	0	0	0	0	0	0	0	0	1	0	0	0	0	0	0	0	0	0	0
	0.0	0.0	0.0	0.0	0.0	0.0	0.0	0.0	0.0	3.8	0.0	0.0	0.0	0.0	0.0	0.0	0.0	0.0	0.0	0.0

18	LXBG	1	0	0	0	0	0	0	0	0	5	0	1	0	0	0	0	0	0	0	0
		0.9	0.0	0.0	0.0	0.0	0.0	0.0	0.0	0.0	4.4	0.0	0.9	0.0	0.0	0.0	0.0	0.0	0.0	0.0	0.0
19	MLTA	0	0	0	0	0	0	0	0	0	1	0	0	0	0	0	2	0	0	0	0
		0.0	0.0	0.0	0.0	0.0	0.0	0.0	0.0	0.0	1.4	0.0	0.0	0.0	0.0	0.0	2.9	0.0	0.0	0.0	0.0
20	MNCO	0	0	0	0	0	0	0	0	0	0	0	0	0	0	0	1	0	0	0	0
		0.0	0.0	0.0	0.0	0.0	0.0	0.0	0.0	0.0	0.0	0.0	0.0	0.0	0.0	0.0	4.8	0.0	0.0	0.0	0.0
21	NTHL	4	0	3	0	0	0	0	0	2	1	0	2	0	0	5	0	0	0	0	0
		3.3	0.0	2.4	0.0	0.0	0.0	0.0	0.0	1.6	0.8	0.0	1.6	0.0	0.0	4.1	0.0	0.0	0.0	0.0	0.0
22	NRWY	4	3	3	0	8	0	9	0	0	3	0	0	0	0	0	0	0	0	0	0
		2.7	2.0	2.0	0.0	5.4	0.0	6.1	0.0	0.0	2.0	0.0	0.0	0.0	0.0	0.0	0.0	0.0	0.0	0.0	0.0
23	PLND	0	0	0	0	0	0	0	0	0	3	0	0	0	5	0	0	0	0	0	0
		0.0	0.0	0.0	0.0	0.0	0.0	0.0	0.0	0.0	1.7	0.0	0.0	0.0	2.9	0.0	0.0	0.0	0.0	0.0	0.0
24	PRTG	0	0	0	0	0	0	0	0	0	0	0	0	0	2	0	0	0	0	0	0
		0.0	0.0	0.0	0.0	0.0	0.0	0.0	0.0	0.0	0.0	0.0	0.0	0.0	1.9	0.0	0.0	0.0	0.0	0.0	0.0
25	RMNA	0	0	0	0	0	0	1	0	1	0	0	0	0	3	0	0	0	0	0	0
		0.0	0.0	0.0	0.0	0.0	0.0	0.5	0.0	0.5	0.0	0.0	0.0	0.0	1.5	0.0	0.0	0.0	0.0	0.0	0.0
26	SANM	0	0	0	0	0	0	0	0	0	0	0	0	0	0	0	0	0	0	0	0
		0.0	0.0	0.0	0.0	0.0	0.0	0.0	0.0	0.0	0.0	0.0	0.0	0.0	0.0	0.0	0.0	0.0	0.0	0.0	0.0
27	SPAN	1	0	0	0	0	0	1	0	0	4	0	0	0	5	1	0	1	1	0	0
		0.7	0.0	0.0	0.0	0.0	0.0	0.7	0.0	0.0	2.8	0.0	0.0	0.0	3.5	0.7	0.0	0.7	0.7	0.0	0.0
28	SWDN	0	0	0	1	0	0	0	0	0	6	0	0	0	0	1	1	0	0	0	0
		0.0	0.0	0.0	0.6	0.0	0.0	0.0	0.0	0.0	3.6	0.0	0.0	0.0	0.0	0.6	0.6	0.0	0.0	0.0	0.0
29	SWTZ	0	0	1	0	0	0	0	0	0	0	0	0	0	0	1	0	0	0	0	0
		0.0	0.0	1.6	0.0	0.0	0.0	0.0	0.0	0.0	0.0	0.0	0.0	0.0	0.0	1.6	0.0	0.0	0.0	0.0	0.0
30	TRKY	1	0	1	0	0	0	0	0	0	0	0	0	0	0	0	1	0	0	0	0
		0.7	0.0	0.7	0.0	0.0	0.0	0.0	0.0	0.0	0.0	0.0	0.0	0.0	0.0	0.0	0.7	0.0	0.0	0.0	0.0
31	USSR	0	0	0	1	1	0	0	0	0	2	0	0	0	3	0	0	0	0	0	0
		0.0	0.0	0.0	0.4	0.4	0.0	0.0	0.0	0.0	0.9	0.0	0.0	0.0	1.3	0.0	0.0	0.0	0.0	0.0	0.0
32	UK	0	0	0	0	0	0	0	0	0	1	0	0	0	0	0	0	0	0	0	0
		0.0	0.0	0.0	0.0	0.0	0.0	0.0	0.0	0.0	1.3	0.0	0.0	0.0	0.0	0.0	0.0	0.0	0.0	0.0	0.0
33	USA	1	0	1	0	1	0	0	0	0	7	0	1	0	0	1	0	0	0	0	0
		0.9	0.0	0.9	0.0	0.9	0.0	0.0	0.0	0.0	6.1	0.0	0.9	0.0	0.0	0.9	0.0	0.0	0.0	0.0	0.0
34	VATC	0	0	0	0	0	0	0	0	0	0	0	0	0	0	0	0	0	1	0	0
		0.0	0.0	0.0	0.0	0.0	0.0	0.0	0.0	0.0	0.0	0.0	0.0	0.0	0.0	0.0	0.0	0.0	1.0	0.0	0.0
35	YGSL	0	0	0	0	0	0	0	0	1	0	0	0	0	1	0	1	0	0	0	1
		0.0	0.0	0.0	0.0	0.0	0.0	0.0	0.0	0.7	0.0	0.0	0.0	0.0	0.7	0.0	0.7	0.0	0.0	0.0	0.7

Table A2.3. *(cont.)*

COUNTRIES	81	82	83	84	85	86	87	88	89	90	91	92	93	94	95	96	97	98	99	100
1 AUST	0	1	0	1	1	0	0	0	0	0	0	0	0	0	0	0	1	3	2	0
	0.0	0.9	0.0	0.9	0.9	0.0	0.0	0.0	0.0	0.0	0.0	0.0	0.0	0.0	0.0	0.0	0.9	2.6	1.7	0.0
2 BLGM	0	0	0	0	0	0	0	0	0	0	0	3	0	0	0	0	0	1	1	0
	0.0	0.0	0.0	0.0	0.0	0.0	0.0	0.0	0.0	0.0	0.0	2.1	0.0	0.0	0.0	0.0	0.0	0.7	0.7	0.0
3 BLGR	0	0	0	0	0	0	0	0	0	1	0	0	0	0	0	0	1	0	1	0
	0.0	0.0	0.0	0.0	0.0	0.0	0.0	0.0	0.0	1.0	0.0	0.0	0.0	0.0	0.0	0.0	1.0	0.0	1.0	0.0
4 CNDA	0	0	0	0	0	0	0	0	0	0	0	0	0	0	0	0	1	0	0	0
	0.0	0.0	0.0	0.0	0.0	0.0	0.0	0.0	0.0	0.0	0.0	0.0	0.0	0.0	0.0	0.0	1.3	0.0	0.0	0.0
5 CYPR	0	0	1	0	0	0	0	0	0	0	0	0	0	0	0	0	0	1	5	0
	0.0	0.0	0.8	0.0	0.0	0.0	0.0	0.0	0.0	0.0	0.0	0.0	0.0	0.0	0.0	0.0	0.0	0.8	4.0	0.0
6 CZCH	0	1	0	1	4	0	0	0	0	0	0	0	0	0	3	0	3	0	0	0
	0.0	0.8	0.0	0.8	3.4	0.0	0.0	0.0	0.0	0.0	0.0	0.0	0.0	0.0	2.5	0.0	2.5	0.0	0.0	0.0
7 DNMK	0	1	0	0	0	0	0	0	0	0	0	0	0	0	0	0	0	1	0	0
	0.0	1.2	0.0	0.0	0.0	0.0	0.0	0.0	0.0	0.0	0.0	0.0	0.0	0.0	0.0	0.0	0.0	1.2	0.0	0.0
8 FNLD	0	1	0	0	0	0	0	0	0	0	0	0	0	0	1	0	0	0	2	0
	0.0	0.8	0.0	0.0	0.0	0.0	0.0	0.0	0.0	0.0	0.0	0.0	0.0	0.0	0.8	0.0	0.0	0.0	1.6	0.0
9 FRNC	0	1	0	0	1	0	0	0	0	0	0	0	0	0	0	0	0	1	1	0
	0.0	1.2	0.0	0.0	1.2	0.0	0.0	0.0	0.0	0.0	0.0	0.0	0.0	0.0	0.0	0.0	0.0	1.2	1.2	0.0
10 FRG	0	0	0	1	9	0	0	0	0	0	0	0	0	0	1	0	0	2	1	0
	0.0	0.0	0.0	0.6	5.5	0.0	0.0	0.0	0.0	0.0	0.0	0.0	0.0	0.0	0.6	0.0	0.0	1.2	0.6	0.0
11 GDR	0	0	0	0	0	0	0	0	0	2	0	0	0	0	0	0	1	0	7	0
	0.0	0.0	0.0	0.0	0.0	0.0	0.0	0.0	0.0	1.3	0.0	0.0	0.0	0.0	0.0	0.0	0.7	0.0	4.7	0.0
12 GRCE	0	0	0	0	0	0	0	0	0	0	0	0	0	0	2	0	0	0	1	0
	0.0	0.0	0.0	0.0	0.0	0.0	0.0	0.0	0.0	0.0	0.0	0.0	0.0	0.0	1.8	0.0	0.0	0.0	0.9	0.0
13 HNGR	0	0	0	0	0	0	0	0	0	0	0	0	0	0	0	0	0	0	0	0
	0.0	0.0	0.0	0.0	0.0	0.0	0.0	0.0	0.0	0.0	0.0	0.0	0.0	0.0	0.0	0.0	0.0	0.0	0.0	0.0
14 ICLD	0	0	0	0	0	0	0	0	0	0	0	0	0	0	0	0	0	0	1	0
	0.0	0.0	0.0	0.0	0.0	0.0	0.0	0.0	0.0	0.0	0.0	0.0	0.0	0.0	0.0	0.0	0.0	0.0	1.9	0.0
15 IRLD	0	0	1	0	0	0	0	0	0	0	0	1	0	0	0	1	2	6	9	0
	0.0	0.0	0.5	0.0	0.0	0.0	0.0	0.0	0.0	0.0	0.0	0.5	0.0	0.0	0.0	0.5	0.9	2.8	4.2	0.0
16 ITLY	0	0	0	1	0	0	1	0	0	0	0	0	0	0	0	0	0	1	1	0
	0.0	0.0	0.0	1.0	0.0	0.0	1.0	0.0	0.0	0.0	0.0	0.0	0.0	0.0	0.0	0.0	0.0	1.0	1.0	0.0
17 LICH	0	0	0	0	0	0	0	0	0	0	0	0	0	0	0	0	0	0	0	0
	0.0	0.0	0.0	0.0	0.0	0.0	0.0	0.0	0.0	0.0	0.0	0.0	0.0	0.0	0.0	0.0	0.0	0.0	0.0	0.0

18	LXBG	0	0	0	0	0	0	0	0	0	0	0	0	0	0	0	0	0	2	2	0
		0.0	0.0	0.0	0.0	0.0	0.0	0.0	0.0	0.0	0.0	0.0	0.0	0.0	0.0	0.0	0.0	0.0	1.8	1.8	0.0
19	MLTA	0	0	0	0	0	0	0	0	0	0	0	0	0	0	0	0	0	1	0	0
		0.0	0.0	0.0	0.0	0.0	0.0	0.0	0.0	0.0	0.0	0.0	0.0	0.0	0.0	0.0	0.0	0.0	1.4	0.0	0.0
20	MNCO	0	0	0	0	0	0	0	0	0	0	0	0	0	0	0	0	0	0	1	0
		0.0	0.0	0.0	0.0	0.0	0.0	0.0	0.0	0.0	0.0	0.0	0.0	0.0	0.0	0.0	0.0	0.0	0.0	4.8	0.0
21	NTHL	0	0	0	0	0	0	0	0	0	0	0	0	0	0	0	0	6	1	5	0
		0.0	0.0	0.0	0.0	0.0	0.0	0.0	0.0	0.0	0.0	0.0	0.0	0.0	0.0	0.0	0.0	4.9	0.8	4.1	0.0
22	NRWY	0	0	0	0	0	0	0	0	0	0	0	0	0	0	0	0	2	0	0	0
		0.0	0.0	0.0	0.0	0.0	0.0	0.0	0.0	0.0	0.0	0.0	0.0	0.0	0.0	0.0	0.0	1.4	0.0	0.0	0.0
23	PLND	0	2	0	0	1	0	0	0	0	1	0	0	0	1	0	0	3	3	1	0
		0.0	1.2	0.0	0.0	0.6	0.0	0.0	0.0	0.0	0.6	0.0	0.0	0.0	0.6	0.0	0.0	1.7	1.7	0.6	0.0
24	PRTG	0	0	0	0	0	0	0	0	0	0	0	0	0	0	0	0	1	1	0	0
		0.0	0.0	0.0	0.0	0.0	0.0	0.0	0.0	0.0	0.0	0.0	0.0	0.0	0.0	0.0	0.0	0.9	0.9	0.0	0.0
25	RMNA	0	1	0	0	0	0	0	0	0	5	0	0	0	2	1	0	1	0	3	0
		0.0	0.5	0.0	0.0	0.0	0.0	0.0	0.0	0.0	2.6	0.0	0.0	0.0	1.0	0.5	0.0	0.5	0.0	1.5	0.0
26	SANM	0	0	0	0	0	0	0	0	0	0	0	0	0	0	0	0	0	0	0	0
		0.0	0.0	0.0	0.0	0.0	0.0	0.0	0.0	0.0	0.0	0.0	0.0	0.0	0.0	0.0	0.0	0.0	0.0	0.0	0.0
27	SPAN	0	2	0	0	1	0	0	0	0	0	0	1	0	0	0	0	1	0	3	0
		0.0	1.4	0.0	0.0	0.7	0.0	0.0	0.0	0.0	0.0	0.0	0.7	0.0	0.0	0.0	0.0	0.7	0.0	2.1	0.0
28	SWDN	0	0	0	0	0	0	0	0	0	0	0	0	1	0	2	0	6	0	7	0
		0.0	0.0	0.0	0.0	0.0	0.0	0.0	0.0	0.0	0.0	0.0	0.0	0.6	0.0	1.2	0.0	3.6	0.0	4.2	0.0
29	SWTZ	0	0	0	0	0	0	0	0	0	0	0	1	0	0	0	0	0	0	0	0
		0.0	0.0	0.0	0.0	0.0	0.0	0.0	0.0	0.0	0.0	0.0	1.6	0.0	0.0	0.0	0.0	0.0	0.0	0.0	0.0
30	TRKY	0	0	0	0	0	0	0	0	0	0	0	0	1	0	0	0	1	0	5	0
		0.0	0.0	0.0	0.0	0.0	0.0	0.0	0.0	0.0	0.0	0.0	0.0	0.7	0.0	0.0	0.0	0.7	0.0	3.4	0.0
31	USSR	0	0	0	0	0	0	0	0	0	2	0	0	0	1	0	0	2	0	2	0
		0.0	0.0	0.0	0.0	0.0	0.0	0.0	0.0	0.0	0.9	0.0	0.0	0.0	0.4	0.0	0.0	0.9	0.0	0.9	0.0
32	UK	0	0	0	0	0	0	0	0	0	0	0	0	0	0	0	0	3	1	1	0
		0.0	0.0	0.0	0.0	0.0	0.0	0.0	0.0	0.0	0.0	0.0	0.0	0.0	0.0	0.0	0.0	4.0	1.3	1.3	0.0
33	USA	0	0	5	0	0	0	0	0	0	0	0	0	0	0	0	0	0	2	0	0
		0.0	0.0	4.3	0.0	0.0	0.0	0.0	0.0	0.0	0.0	0.0	0.0	0.0	0.0	0.0	0.0	0.0	1.7	0.0	0.0
34	VATC	0	0	0	0	0	0	0	0	0	0	0	0	0	0	0	0	0	0	0	0
		0.0	0.0	0.0	0.0	0.0	0.0	0.0	0.0	0.0	0.0	0.0	0.0	0.0	0.0	0.0	0.0	0.0	0.0	0.0	0.0
35	YGSL	0	1	0	0	0	0	0	0	0	1	0	0	0	0	0	0	2	0	5	0
		0.0	0.7	0.0	0.0	0.0	0.0	0.0	0.0	0.0	0.7	0.0	0.0	0.0	0.0	0.0	0.0	1.4	0.0	3.5	0.0

Table A2.3. *(cont.)*

COUNTRIES		101	102	103	104	105	106	107	108	109	110	111	112	113	114	115	116	117	118	119	120
1	AUST	0	4	9	9	0	0	2	4	0	0	0	1	1	2	0	0	0	0	0	0
		0.0	3.4	7.8	7.8	0.0	0.0	1.7	3.4	0.0	0.0	0.0	0.9	0.9	1.7	0.0	0.0	0.0	0.0	0.0	0.0
2	BLGM	6	6	1	3	0	1	3	5	1	0	1	1	5	2	0	1	5	0	3	4
		4.1	4.1	0.7	2.1	0.0	0.7	2.1	3.4	0.7	0.0	0.7	0.7	3.4	1.4	0.0	0.7	3.4	0.0	2.1	2.8
3	BLGR	0	0	10	2	0	0	1	2	0	0	0	2	0	4	0	0	0	0	1	0
		0.0	0.0	9.6	1.9	0.0	0.0	1.0	1.9	0.0	0.0	0.0	1.9	0.0	3.8	0.0	0.0	0.0	0.0	1.0	0.0
4	CNDA	1	0	0	1	0	0	4	3	0	0	2	2	0	5	0	2	1	0	1	1
		1.3	0.0	0.0	1.3	0.0	0.0	5.3	4.0	0.0	0.0	2.7	2.7	0.0	6.7	0.0	2.7	1.3	0.0	1.3	1.3
5	CYPR	0	0	10	3	0	0	4	1	0	0	1	0	0	2	0	0	2	0	4	1
		0.0	0.0	8.0	2.4	0.0	0.0	3.2	0.8	0.0	0.0	0.8	0.0	0.0	1.6	0.0	0.0	1.6	0.0	3.2	0.8
6	CZCH	0	1	16	1	0	2	0	7	0	0	0	1	0	1	0	2	0	0	2	1
		0.0	0.8	13.6	0.8	0.0	1.7	0.0	5.9	0.0	0.0	0.0	0.8	0.0	0.8	0.0	1.7	0.0	0.0	1.7	0.8
7	DNMK	0	0	1	4	0	0	1	1	0	0	0	0	0	2	0	0	0	0	5	1
		0.0	0.0	1.2	4.7	0.0	0.0	1.2	1.2	0.0	0.0	0.0	0.0	0.0	2.4	0.0	0.0	0.0	0.0	5.9	1.2
8	FNLD	0	8	7	4	0	0	0	7	0	0	0	8	0	0	0	1	1	1	2	0
		0.0	6.3	5.5	3.1	0.0	0.0	0.0	5.5	0.0	0.0	0.0	6.3	0.0	0.0	0.0	0.8	0.8	0.8	1.6	0.0
9	FRNC	0	0	6	7	0	0	0	2	3	0	3	0	5	1	0	0	0	0	4	1
		0.0	0.0	7.3	8.5	0.0	0.0	0.0	2.4	3.7	0.0	3.7	0.0	6.1	1.2	0.0	0.0	0.0	0.0	4.9	1.2
10	FRG	3	2	4	5	0	0	1	10	1	0	0	2	3	7	0	0	0	0	8	4
		1.8	1.2	2.4	3.0	0.0	0.0	0.6	6.1	0.6	0.0	0.0	1.2	1.8	4.3	0.0	0.0	0.0	0.0	4.9	2.4
11	GDR	0	0	15	2	0	0	0	6	0	0	1	0	0	4	0	4	0	0	17	3
		0.0	0.0	10.1	1.3	0.0	0.0	0.0	4.0	0.0	0.0	0.7	0.0	0.0	2.7	0.0	2.7	0.0	0.0	11.4	2.0
12	GRCE	0	0	9	9	0	1	3	4	0	0	2	1	1	1	0	1	1	0	1	3
		0.0	0.0	8.2	8.2	0.0	0.9	2.7	3.6	0.0	0.0	1.8	0.9	0.9	0.9	0.0	0.9	0.9	0.0	0.9	2.7
13	HNGR	2	0	3	11	0	0	3	5	0	0	0	2	0	6	0	2	0	0	5	0
		2.0	0.0	3.1	11.2	0.0	0.0	3.1	5.1	0.0	0.0	0.0	2.0	0.0	6.1	0.0	2.0	0.0	0.0	5.1	0.0
14	ICLD	0	0	3	2	0	1	0	0	1	0	2	0	0	0	0	0	0	0	2	1
		0.0	0.0	5.6	3.7	0.0	1.9	0.0	0.0	1.9	0.0	3.7	0.0	0.0	0.0	0.0	0.0	0.0	0.0	3.7	1.9
15	IRLD	2	2	6	8	0	2	5	9	1	3	0	9	3	3	1	0	7	0	7	8
		0.9	0.9	2.8	3.7	0.0	0.9	2.3	4.2	0.5	1.4	0.0	4.2	1.4	1.4	0.5	0.0	3.3	0.0	3.3	3.7
16	ITLY	2	1	8	0	0	2	1	1	2	0	1	1	0	4	0	0	0	0	4	0
		2.1	1.0	8.2	0.0	0.0	2.1	1.0	1.0	2.1	0.0	1.0	1.0	0.0	4.1	0.0	0.0	0.0	0.0	4.1	0.0
17	LICH	0	0	2	2	0	1	0	1	1	0	0	0	0	0	0	0	0	0	0	0
		0.0	0.0	7.7	7.7	0.0	3.8	0.0	3.8	3.8	0.0	0.0	0.0	0.0	0.0	0.0	0.0	0.0	0.0	0.0	0.0

18	LXBG	0	0	5	8	0	1	0	4	0	0	1	0	1	8	1	0	0	0	4	0
		0.0	0.0	4.4	7.0	0.0	0.9	0.0	3.5	0.0	0.0	0.9	0.0	0.9	7.0	0.9	0.0	0.0	0.0	3.5	0.0
19	MLTA	0	0	3	4	0	0	0	1	0	0	1	0	0	1	0	0	0	0	1	0
		0.0	0.0	4.3	5.8	0.0	0.0	0.0	1.4	0.0	0.0	1.4	0.0	0.0	1.4	0.0	0.0	0.0	0.0	1.4	0.0
20	MNCO	0	0	2	0	0	0	0	0	0	0	0	0	0	0	0	0	0	0	2	0
		0.0	0.0	9.5	0.0	0.0	0.0	0.0	0.0	0.0	0.0	0.0	0.0	0.0	0.0	0.0	0.0	0.0	0.0	9.5	0.0
21	NTHL	0	0	5	2	0	1	0	0	1	0	2	1	0	1	0	0	2	1	0	2
		0.0	0.0	4.1	1.6	0.0	0.8	0.0	0.0	0.8	0.0	1.6	0.8	0.0	0.8	0.0	0.0	1.6	0.8	0.0	1.6
22	NRWY	0	0	4	4	0	0	1	0	0	0	1	1	0	6	1	0	3	0	2	1
		0.0	0.0	2.7	2.7	0.0	0.0	0.7	0.0	0.0	0.0	0.7	0.7	0.0	4.1	0.7	0.0	2.0	0.0	1.4	0.7
23	PLND	0	0	9	6	0	0	6	5	1	0	1	1	0	11	0	3	1	0	3	1
		0.0	0.0	5.2	3.5	0.0	0.0	3.5	2.9	0.6	0.0	0.6	0.6	0.0	6.4	0.0	1.7	0.6	0.0	1.7	0.6
24	PRTG	0	0	10	5	0	0	0	7	0	0	0	0	1	2	0	0	0	0	6	3
		0.0	0.0	9.3	4.6	0.0	0.0	0.0	6.5	0.0	0.0	0.0	0.0	0.9	1.9	0.0	0.0	0.0	0.0	5.6	2.8
25	RMNA	0	0	16	7	0	1	2	4	0	2	12	3	2	4	0	0	3	0	2	1
		0.0	0.0	8.2	3.6	0.0	0.5	1.0	2.1	0.0	1.0	6.2	1.5	1.0	2.1	0.0	0.0	1.5	0.0	1.0	0.5
26	SANM	1	8	28	3	0	1	1	3	5	3	3	0	0	0	2	0	0	0	1	1
		0.9	7.1	24.8	2.7	0.0	0.9	0.9	2.7	4.4	2.7	2.7	0.0	0.0	0.0	1.8	0.0	0.0	0.0	0.9	0.9
27	SPAN	0	0	8	6	0	0	3	0	0	1	2	3	0	1	0	0	0	0	0	1
		0.0	0.0	5.6	4.2	0.0	0.0	2.1	0.0	0.0	0.7	1.4	2.1	0.0	0.7	0.0	0.0	0.0	0.0	0.0	0.7
28	SWDN	2	3	7	11	0	0	2	2	0	0	1	0	3	4	0	0	3	0	2	2
		1.2	1.8	4.2	6.5	0.0	0.0	1.2	1.2	0.0	0.0	0.6	0.0	1.8	2.4	0.0	0.0	1.8	0.0	1.2	1.2
29	SWTZ	1	5	2	5	0	0	6	1	0	0	0	1	0	0	0	0	0	0	3	2
		1.6	8.2	3.3	8.2	0.0	0.0	9.8	1.6	0.0	0.0	0.0	1.6	0.0	0.0	0.0	0.0	0.0	0.0	4.9	3.3
30	TRKY	0	0	10	4	0	0	0	3	0	0	1	2	1	2	0	0	2	0	2	2
		0.0	0.0	6.8	2.7	0.0	0.0	0.0	2.0	0.0	0.0	0.7	1.4	0.7	1.4	0.0	0.0	1.4	0.0	1.4	1.4
31	USSR	0	1	46	14	0	0	1	8	0	0	0	1	0	8	1	5	0	0	13	2
		0.0	0.4	20.5	6.3	0.0	0.0	0.4	3.6	0.0	0.0	0.0	0.4	0.0	3.6	0.4	2.2	0.0	0.0	5.8	0.9
32	UK	1	1	4	5	0	0	0	0	0	1	1	0	1	0	0	0	0	0	2	3
		1.3	1.3	5.3	6.7	0.0	0.0	0.0	0.0	0.0	1.3	1.3	0.0	1.3	0.0	0.0	0.0	0.0	0.0	2.7	4.0
33	USA	0	0	10	8	0	0	0	0	0	0	0	0	0	2	0	0	0	0	5	3
		0.0	0.0	8.7	7.0	0.0	0.0	0.0	0.0	0.0	0.0	0.0	0.0	0.0	1.7	0.0	0.0	0.0	0.0	4.3	2.6
34	VATC	0	0	19	3	0	0	0	1	0	6	1	3	0	0	1	0	1	0	4	7
		0.0	0.0	18.6	2.9	0.0	0.0	0.0	1.0	0.0	5.9	1.0	2.9	0.0	0.0	1.0	0.0	1.0	0.0	3.9	6.9
35	YGSL	6	0	10	6	0	5	2	0	4	0	2	2	0	2	0	1	3	0	3	2
		4.3	0.0	7.1	4.3	0.0	3.5	1.4	0.0	2.8	0.0	1.4	1.4	0.0	1.4	0.0	0.7	2.1	0.0	2.1	1.4

Table A2.4. Category Scores and Percentages: The 1975 Helsinki Statements

COUNTRIES		1	2	3	4	5	6	7	8	9	10	11	12	13	14	15	16	17	18	19	20
1	AUST	0	2	0	0	0	0	1	0	0	1	8	0	0	0	0	0	0	0	8	1
		0.0	4.1	0.0	0.0	0.0	0.0	2.0	0.0	0.0	2.0	16.3	0.0	0.0	0.0	0.0	0.0	0.0	0.0	16.3	2.0
2	BLGM	14	5	2	4	0	0	4	5	4	0	10	0	1	0	2	12	16	0	8	1
		9.3	3.3	1.3	2.6	0.0	0.0	2.6	3.3	2.6	0.0	6.6	0.0	0.7	0.0	1.3	7.9	10.6	0.0	5.3	0.7
3	BLGR	6	1	0	1	1	1	0	0	0	1	8	0	0	0	0	5	7	0	9	2
		8.5	1.4	0.0	1.4	1.4	1.4	0.0	0.0	0.0	1.4	11.3	0.0	0.0	0.0	0.0	7.0	9.9	0.0	12.7	2.8
4	CNDA	7	0	0	1	1	0	1	0	0	0	3	0	0	0	0	5	6	0	4	7
		9.3	0.0	0.0	1.3	1.3	0.0	1.3	0.0	0.0	0.0	4.0	0.0	0.0	0.0	0.0	6.7	8.0	0.0	5.3	9.3
5	CYPR	12	19	5	8	1	6	0	1	3	0	3	0	0	0	0	0	12	0	3	3
		9.0	14.2	3.7	6.0	0.7	4.5	0.0	0.7	2.2	0.0	2.2	0.0	0.0	0.0	0.0	0.0	9.0	0.0	2.2	2.2
6	CZCH	7	7	1	3	0	0	0	0	0	0	8	0	0	0	0	3	8	1	8	5
		6.9	6.9	1.0	3.0	0.0	0.0	0.0	0.0	0.0	0.0	7.9	0.0	0.0	0.0	0.0	3.0	7.9	1.0	7.9	5.0
7	DNMK	4	1	0	0	0	0	0	0	0	0	4	0	0	4	0	0	10	0	5	3
		5.9	1.5	0.0	0.0	0.0	0.0	0.0	0.0	0.0	0.0	5.9	0.0	0.0	5.9	0.0	0.0	14.7	0.0	7.4	4.4
8	FNLD	17	10	11	0	0	0	0	0	0	0	16	0	0	0	0	3	18	0	14	1
		12.1	7.1	7.9	0.0	0.0	0.0	0.0	0.0	0.0	0.0	11.4	0.0	0.0	0.0	0.0	2.1	12.9	0.0	10.0	0.7
9	FRNC	5	0	1	0	0	0	0	0	0	0	2	0	0	0	0	1	6	0	1	0
		11.9	0.0	2.4	0.0	0.0	0.0	0.0	0.0	0.0	0.0	4.8	0.0	0.0	0.0	0.0	2.4	14.3	0.0	2.4	0.0
10	FRG	1	4	4	1	1	0	0	0	0	0	4	5	0	2	2	6	2	0	3	8
		1.0	4.2	4.2	1.0	1.0	0.0	0.0	0.0	0.0	0.0	4.2	5.2	0.0	2.1	2.1	6.3	2.1	0.0	3.1	8.3
11	GDR	10	3	3	1	4	1	0	0	0	0	2	1	0	0	0	3	10	0	2	2
		14.1	4.2	4.2	1.4	5.6	1.4	0.0	0.0	0.0	0.0	2.8	1.4	0.0	0.0	0.0	4.2	14.1	0.0	2.8	2.8
12	GRCE	2	24	3	3	4	0	2	1	0	0	3	2	0	2	1	2	3	0	3	2
		2.8	33.3	4.2	4.2	5.6	0.0	2.8	1.4	0.0	0.0	4.2	2.8	0.0	2.8	1.4	2.8	4.2	0.0	4.2	2.8
13	HNGR	5	6	4	1	1	0	2	0	0	0	4	0	0	0	0	7	5	0	3	7
		5.1	6.1	4.0	1.0	1.0	0.0	2.0	0.0	0.0	0.0	4.0	0.0	0.0	0.0	0.0	7.1	5.1	0.0	3.0	7.1
14	ICLD	4	2	1	1	0	0	1	0	0	0	3	0	2	1	0	4	4	0	4	6
		4.8	2.4	1.2	1.2	0.0	0.0	1.2	0.0	0.0	0.0	3.6	0.0	2.4	1.2	0.0	4.8	4.8	0.0	4.8	7.2
15	IRLD	2	6	0	1	0	0	0	0	5	0	8	0	1	0	0	0	1	0	12	0
		2.1	6.3	0.0	1.0	0.0	0.0	0.0	0.0	5.2	0.0	8.3	0.0	1.0	0.0	0.0	0.0	1.0	0.0	12.5	0.0
16	ITLY	4	5	1	1	1	0	1	0	8	0	5	0	0	0	0	0	4	0	5	3
		3.6	4.5	0.9	0.9	0.9	0.0	0.9	0.0	7.2	0.0	4.5	0.0	0.0	0.0	0.0	0.0	3.6	0.0	4.5	2.7
17	LICH	1	1	2	0	0	0	0	0	0	0	1	0	0	0	0	0	0	0	3	0
		4.3	4.3	8.7	0.0	0.0	0.0	0.0	0.0	0.0	0.0	4.3	0.0	0.0	0.0	0.0	0.0	0.0	0.0	13.0	0.0

18	LXBG	10	10	2	2	0	0	4	0	5	1	5	1	1	4	2	2	9	0	6	0
		8.8	8.8	1.8	1.8	0.0	0.0	3.5	0.0	4.4	0.9	4.4	0.9	0.9	3.5	1.8	1.8	7.9	0.0	5.3	0.0
19	MLTA	5	0	0	0	1	0	0	0	0	0	3	0	0	5	0	2	5	0	2	5
		6.3	0.0	0.0	0.0	1.3	0.0	0.0	0.0	0.0	0.0	3.8	0.0	0.0	6.3	0.0	2.5	6.3	0.0	2.5	6.3
20	MNCO	2	0	0	0	0	0	0	0	0	0	0	0	0	0	0	0	2	0	0	0
		5.3	0.0	0.0	0.0	0.0	0.0	0.0	0.0	0.0	0.0	0.0	0.0	0.0	0.0	0.0	0.0	5.3	0.0	0.0	0.0
21	NTHL	3	8	0	0	0	0	0	0	4	4	12	0	0	0	3	6	5	0	9	4
		2.5	6.7	0.0	0.0	0.0	0.0	0.0	0.0	3.3	3.3	10.0	0.0	0.0	0.0	2.5	5.0	4.2	0.0	7.5	3.3
22	NRWY	14	5	1	0	0	0	0	0	18	0	19	0	0	4	1	12	17	4	19	0
		8.0	2.9	0.6	0.0	0.0	0.0	0.0	0.0	10.3	0.0	10.9	0.0	0.0	2.3	0.6	6.9	9.8	2.3	10.9	0.0
23	PLND	3	5	5	2	1	2	0	1	0	0	11	0	0	0	0	1	4	1	12	1
		3.0	5.1	5.1	2.0	1.0	2.0	0.0	1.0	0.0	0.0	11.1	0.0	0.0	0.0	0.0	1.0	4.0	1.0	12.1	1.0
24	PRTG	4	4	2	1	0	0	1	2	1	2	8	1	0	1	2	0	6	0	6	1
		6.2	6.2	3.1	1.5	0.0	0.0	1.5	3.1	1.5	3.1	12.3	1.5	0.0	1.5	3.1	0.0	9.2	0.0	9.2	1.5
25	RMNA	21	12	14	6	0	0	0	5	2	5	23	0	0	2	3	22	25	0	26	1
		7.3	4.2	4.9	2.1	0.0	0.0	0.0	1.7	0.7	1.7	8.0	0.0	0.0	0.7	1.0	7.7	8.7	0.0	9.1	0.3
26	SANM	1	5	1	0	0	0	0	0	9	0	11	0	0	0	0	2	1	0	9	0
		0.9	4.6	0.9	0.0	0.0	0.0	0.0	0.0	8.3	0.0	10.1	0.0	0.0	0.0	0.0	1.8	0.9	0.0	8.3	0.0
27	SPAN	12	10	9	4	4	4	0	5	0	0	9	2	1	3	5	9	15	2	7	2
		7.2	6.0	5.4	2.4	2.4	2.4	0.0	3.0	0.0	0.0	5.4	1.2	0.6	1.8	3.0	5.4	9.0	1.2	4.2	1.2
28	SWDN	12	5	0	2	1	0	0	1	2	0	9	0	0	0	2	9	12	0	10	4
		8.5	3.5	0.0	1.4	0.7	0.0	0.0	0.7	1.4	0.0	6.4	0.0	0.0	0.0	1.4	6.4	8.5	0.0	7.1	2.8
29	SWTZ	6	8	9	1	1	0	8	1	6	0	3	1	0	0	0	2	6	0	3	5
		5.7	7.5	8.5	0.9	0.9	0.0	7.5	0.9	5.7	0.0	2.8	0.9	0.0	0.0	0.0	1.9	5.7	0.0	2.8	4.7
30	TRKY	9	29	4	5	2	2	0	2	17	0	15	1	0	2	0	1	17	0	4	7
		5.4	17.4	2.4	3.0	1.2	1.2	0.0	1.2	10.2	0.0	9.0	0.6	0.0	1.2	0.0	0.6	10.2	0.0	2.4	4.2
31	USSR	4	4	3	0	0	0	0	2	0	0	6	0	0	0	1	5	6	0	5	2
		6.0	6.0	4.5	0.0	0.0	0.0	0.0	3.0	0.0	0.0	9.0	0.0	0.0	0.0	1.5	7.5	9.0	0.0	7.5	3.0
32	UK	2	1	8	2	2	2	0	1	0	0	4	0	0	1	6	15	6	1	1	6
		1.0	0.5	4.1	1.0	1.0	1.0	0.0	0.5	0.0	0.0	2.1	0.0	0.0	0.5	3.1	7.8	3.1	0.5	0.5	3.1
33	USA	3	9	4	0	1	1	1	1	8	1	3	0	0	0	0	12	5	1	3	2
		1.8	5.4	2.4	0.0	0.6	0.6	0.6	0.6	4.8	0.6	1.8	0.0	0.0	0.0	0.0	7.2	3.0	0.6	1.8	1.2
34	VATC	7	4	1	1	0	0	1	0	8	2	8	1	0	0	0	2	7	0	9	0
		6.2	3.5	0.9	0.9	0.0	0.0	0.9	0.0	7.1	1.8	7.1	0.9	0.0	0.0	0.0	1.8	6.2	0.0	8.0	0.0
35	YGSL	14	5	18	1	7	2	0	7	0	0	14	0	2	2	2	12	18	0	13	5
		7.5	2.7	9.7	0.5	3.8	1.1	0.0	3.8	0.0	0.0	7.5	0.0	1.1	1.1	1.1	6.5	9.7	0.0	7.0	2.7

Table A2.4. *(cont.)*

COUNTRIES	21	22	23	24	25	26	27	28	29	30	31	32	33	34	35	36	37	38	39	40
1 AUST	0	0	0	0	0	0	0	0	0	0	0	0	0	0	0	0	0	0	0	0
	0.0	0.0	0.0	0.0	0.0	0.0	0.0	0.0	0.0	0.0	0.0	0.0	0.0	0.0	0.0	0.0	0.0	0.0	0.0	0.0
2 BLGM	0	0	0	0	0	0	0	0	0	0	0	0	0	0	0	0	0	0	0	0
	0.0	0.0	0.0	0.0	0.0	0.0	0.0	0.0	0.0	0.0	0.0	0.0	0.0	0.0	0.0	0.0	0.0	0.0	0.0	0.0
3 BLGR	0	0	0	0	2	0	0	0	0	0	0	0	3	0	0	0	0	1	0	1
	0.0	0.0	0.0	0.0	2.8	0.0	0.0	0.0	0.0	0.0	0.0	0.0	4.2	0.0	0.0	0.0	0.0	1.4	0.0	1.4
4 CNDA	0	0	0	0	0	0	0	0	0	0	0	0	0	0	0	0	0	0	0	0
	0.0	0.0	0.0	0.0	0.0	0.0	0.0	0.0	0.0	0.0	0.0	0.0	0.0	0.0	0.0	0.0	0.0	0.0	0.0	0.0
5 CYPR	0	1	0	0	0	0	0	0	0	0	0	0	0	0	1	0	0	0	0	0
	0.0	0.7	0.0	0.0	0.0	0.0	0.0	0.0	0.0	0.0	0.0	0.0	0.0	0.0	0.7	0.0	0.0	0.0	0.0	0.0
6 CZCH	1	0	0	0	0	1	0	0	0	0	0	0	0	0	1	0	0	1	0	0
	1.0	0.0	0.0	0.0	0.0	1.0	0.0	0.0	0.0	0.0	0.0	0.0	0.0	0.0	1.0	0.0	0.0	1.0	0.0	0.0
7 DNMK	0	0	0	0	0	0	0	0	0	0	0	0	0	0	0	0	0	0	0	0
	0.0	0.0	0.0	0.0	0.0	0.0	0.0	0.0	0.0	0.0	0.0	0.0	0.0	0.0	0.0	0.0	0.0	0.0	0.0	0.0
8 FNLD	0	0	0	0	0	0	0	0	0	0	0	0	0	0	0	0	0	0	0	0
	0.0	0.0	0.0	0.0	0.0	0.0	0.0	0.0	0.0	0.0	0.0	0.0	0.0	0.0	0.0	0.0	0.0	0.0	0.0	0.0
9 FRNC	0	0	0	0	0	0	0	0	0	0	0	0	0	0	0	0	0	0	0	0
	0.0	0.0	0.0	0.0	0.0	0.0	0.0	0.0	0.0	0.0	0.0	0.0	0.0	0.0	0.0	0.0	0.0	0.0	0.0	0.0
10 FRG	0	0	0	0	0	0	0	0	0	0	0	0	0	0	0	0	0	0	0	0
	0.0	0.0	0.0	0.0	0.0	0.0	0.0	0.0	0.0	0.0	0.0	0.0	0.0	0.0	0.0	0.0	0.0	0.0	0.0	0.0
11 GDR	0	0	0	0	0	0	0	0	0	0	0	0	0	0	1	0	0	0	0	0
	0.0	0.0	0.0	0.0	0.0	0.0	0.0	0.0	0.0	0.0	0.0	0.0	0.0	0.0	1.4	0.0	0.0	0.0	0.0	0.0
12 GRCE	0	0	0	0	0	0	0	0	0	0	0	0	0	0	0	0	0	0	0	0
	0.0	0.0	0.0	0.0	0.0	0.0	0.0	0.0	0.0	0.0	0.0	0.0	0.0	0.0	0.0	0.0	0.0	0.0	0.0	0.0
13 HNGR	0	0	0	0	0	0	0	0	0	0	0	0	0	0	2	0	0	0	0	0
	0.0	0.0	0.0	0.0	0.0	0.0	0.0	0.0	0.0	0.0	0.0	0.0	0.0	0.0	2.0	0.0	0.0	0.0	0.0	0.0
14 ICLD	0	0	0	2	1	0	0	0	0	0	0	0	0	0	0	0	0	0	0	0
	0.0	0.0	0.0	2.4	1.2	0.0	0.0	0.0	0.0	0.0	0.0	0.0	0.0	0.0	0.0	0.0	0.0	0.0	0.0	0.0
15 IRLD	0	0	0	0	0	0	0	0	0	0	0	0	0	0	0	0	0	0	0	0
	0.0	0.0	0.0	0.0	0.0	0.0	0.0	0.0	0.0	0.0	0.0	0.0	0.0	0.0	0.0	0.0	0.0	0.0	0.0	0.0
16 ITLY	0	0	0	0	0	0	0	0	0	0	0	0	0	0	0	0	0	0	0	0
	0.0	0.0	0.0	0.0	0.0	0.0	0.0	0.0	0.0	0.0	0.0	0.0	0.0	0.0	0.0	0.0	0.0	0.0	0.0	0.0
17 LICH	0	0	0	0	0	0	0	0	0	0	0	0	0	0	0	0	0	0	0	0
	0.0	0.0	0.0	0.0	0.0	0.0	0.0	0.0	0.0	0.0	0.0	0.0	0.0	0.0	0.0	0.0	0.0	0.0	0.0	0.0

18	LXBG	0	0	0	0	0	0	0	0	0	0	0	0	0	0	0	0	0	0	0	0
		0.0	0.0	0.0	0.0	0.0	0.0	0.0	0.0	0.0	0.0	0.0	0.0	0.0	0.0	0.0	0.0	0.0	0.0	0.0	0.0
19	MLTA	0	0	0	0	0	0	0	0	0	0	0	0	0	0	1	0	0	0	0	0
		0.0	0.0	0.0	0.0	0.0	0.0	0.0	0.0	0.0	0.0	0.0	0.0	0.0	0.0	1.3	0.0	0.0	0.0	0.0	0.0
20	MNCO	0	0	0	0	0	0	0	0	0	0	0	0	0	0	0	0	0	0	0	5
		0.0	0.0	0.0	0.0	0.0	0.0	0.0	0.0	0.0	0.0	0.0	0.0	0.0	0.0	0.0	0.0	0.0	0.0	0.0	13.2
21	NTHL	0	0	0	0	0	0	0	0	0	0	0	0	0	0	0	0	0	0	0	0
		0.0	0.0	0.0	0.0	0.0	0.0	0.0	0.0	0.0	0.0	0.0	0.0	0.0	0.0	0.0	0.0	0.0	0.0	0.0	0.0
22	NRWY	0	0	0	0	0	0	0	0	0	0	0	0	0	0	0	0	0	0	0	1
		0.0	0.0	0.0	0.0	0.0	0.0	0.0	0.0	0.0	0.0	0.0	0.0	0.0	0.0	0.0	0.0	0.0	0.0	0.0	0.6
23	PLND	0	0	0	0	0	0	1	0	0	0	0	0	0	0	1	0	0	0	0	1
		0.0	0.0	0.0	0.0	0.0	0.0	1.0	0.0	0.0	0.0	0.0	0.0	0.0	0.0	1.0	0.0	0.0	0.0	0.0	1.0
24	PRTG	0	0	0	0	0	0	0	0	0	0	0	0	0	0	0	0	0	0	0	0
		0.0	0.0	0.0	0.0	0.0	0.0	0.0	0.0	0.0	0.0	0.0	0.0	0.0	0.0	0.0	0.0	0.0	0.0	0.0	0.0
25	RMNA	0	0	0	0	1	0	0	0	0	0	0	0	0	0	0	0	0	0	0	0
		0.0	0.0	0.0	0.0	0.3	0.0	0.0	0.0	0.0	0.0	0.0	0.0	0.0	0.0	0.0	0.0	0.0	0.0	0.0	0.0
26	SANM	0	0	0	0	0	0	0	0	0	0	0	0	0	0	0	0	0	0	0	2
		0.0	0.0	0.0	0.0	0.0	0.0	0.0	0.0	0.0	0.0	0.0	0.0	0.0	0.0	0.0	0.0	0.0	0.0	0.0	1.8
27	SPAN	0	0	0	0	0	0	0	0	0	0	0	0	0	0	1	0	0	0	0	0
		0.0	0.0	0.0	0.0	0.0	0.0	0.0	0.0	0.0	0.0	0.0	0.0	0.0	0.0	0.6	0.0	0.0	0.0	0.0	0.0
28	SWDN	0	0	0	0	0	0	1	0	0	0	0	0	0	0	0	0	0	0	0	0
		0.0	0.0	0.0	0.0	0.0	0.0	0.7	0.0	0.0	0.0	0.0	0.0	0.0	0.0	0.0	0.0	0.0	0.0	0.0	0.0
29	SWTZ	0	0	0	0	0	1	0	0	0	0	0	0	0	0	2	0	0	0	0	0
		0.0	0.0	0.0	0.0	0.0	0.9	0.0	0.0	0.0	0.0	0.0	0.0	0.0	0.0	1.9	0.0	0.0	0.0	0.0	0.0
30	TRKY	0	0	0	0	0	0	2	0	0	0	0	0	0	0	0	0	0	0	0	0
		0.0	0.0	0.0	0.0	0.0	0.0	1.2	0.0	0.0	0.0	0.0	0.0	0.0	0.0	0.0	0.0	0.0	0.0	0.0	0.0
31	USSR	0	0	0	0	0	0	0	0	0	0	0	0	0	0	1	0	0	0	0	1
		0.0	0.0	0.0	0.0	0.0	0.0	0.0	0.0	0.0	0.0	0.0	0.0	0.0	0.0	1.5	0.0	0.0	0.0	0.0	1.5
32	UK	0	0	0	0	0	0	0	0	0	0	0	0	0	0	0	0	0	0	0	0
		0.0	0.0	0.0	0.0	0.0	0.0	0.0	0.0	0.0	0.0	0.0	0.0	0.0	0.0	0.0	0.0	0.0	0.0	0.0	0.0
33	USA	0	0	0	0	0	1	0	0	0	0	0	0	0	0	1	0	0	0	0	1
		0.0	0.0	0.0	0.0	0.0	0.6	0.0	0.0	0.0	0.0	0.0	0.0	0.0	0.0	0.6	0.0	0.0	0.0	0.0	0.6
34	VATC	0	0	0	0	0	0	0	0	0	0	0	0	0	0	0	0	0	0	0	0
		0.0	0.0	0.0	0.0	0.0	0.0	0.0	0.0	0.0	0.0	0.0	0.0	0.0	0.0	0.0	0.0	0.0	0.0	0.0	0.0
35	YGSL	0	0	0	0	0	0	0	0	0	0	0	0	0	0	0	0	0	0	0	0
		0.0	0.0	0.0	0.0	0.0	0.0	0.0	0.0	0.0	0.0	0.0	0.0	0.0	0.0	0.0	0.0	0.0	0.0	0.0	0.0

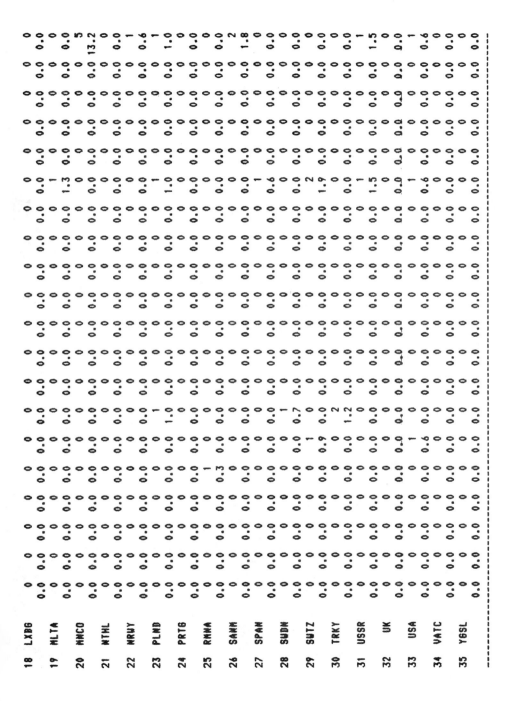

Table A2.4. *(cont.)*

COUNTRIES	41	42	43	44	45	46	47	48	49	50	51	52	53	54	55	56	57	58	59	60
1 AUST	0	0	0	0	0	0	0	0	0	0	0	0	0	0	0	0	0	1	0	0
	0.0	0.0	0.0	0.0	0.0	0.0	0.0	0.0	0.0	0.0	0.0	0.0	0.0	0.0	0.0	0.0	0.0	2.0	0.0	0.0
2 BLGM	0	0	0	0	0	0	0	0	0	0	1	0	1	0	0	0	0	1	3	0
	0.0	0.0	0.0	0.0	0.0	0.0	0.0	0.0	0.0	0.0	0.7	0.0	0.7	0.0	0.0	0.0	0.0	0.7	2.0	0.0
3 BLGR	0	0	0	0	0	0	0	0	0	0	0	0	0	0	0	0	0	0	1	0
	0.0	0.0	0.0	0.0	0.0	0.0	0.0	0.0	0.0	0.0	0.0	0.0	0.0	0.0	0.0	0.0	0.0	0.0	1.4	0.0
4 CNDA	0	0	0	0	0	0	0	0	0	0	0	0	0	0	0	0	0	0	1	0
	0.0	0.0	0.0	0.0	0.0	0.0	0.0	0.0	0.0	0.0	0.0	0.0	0.0	0.0	0.0	0.0	0.0	0.0	1.3	0.0
5 CYPR	0	0	0	0	0	0	0	0	0	0	2	0	0	1	0	0	2	0	2	0
	0.0	0.0	0.0	0.0	0.0	0.0	0.0	0.0	0.0	0.0	1.5	0.0	0.0	0.7	0.0	0.0	1.5	0.0	1.5	0.0
6 CZCH	0	0	0	0	0	0	0	0	0	0	0	0	0	0	0	0	0	0	1	0
	0.0	0.0	0.0	0.0	0.0	0.0	0.0	0.0	0.0	0.0	0.0	0.0	0.0	0.0	0.0	0.0	0.0	0.0	1.0	0.0
7 DNMK	0	0	0	0	0	0	0	0	0	0	0	0	0	0	0	0	0	12	2	0
	0.0	0.0	0.0	0.0	0.0	0.0	0.0	0.0	0.0	0.0	0.0	0.0	0.0	0.0	0.0	0.0	0.0	17.6	2.9	0.0
8 FNLD	0	0	0	0	0	0	0	0	0	0	0	0	0	0	0	0	0	3	1	0
	0.0	0.0	0.0	0.0	0.0	0.0	0.0	0.0	0.0	0.0	0.0	0.0	0.0	0.0	0.0	0.0	0.0	2.1	0.7	0.0
9 FRNC	0	0	0	0	0	0	0	0	0	0	0	0	0	0	0	0	0	0	1	0
	0.0	0.0	0.0	0.0	0.0	0.0	0.0	0.0	0.0	0.0	0.0	0.0	0.0	0.0	0.0	0.0	0.0	0.0	2.4	0.0
10 FRG	0	0	0	0	0	0	0	0	0	0	0	0	0	0	0	0	0	1	1	0
	0.0	0.0	0.0	0.0	0.0	0.0	0.0	0.0	0.0	0.0	0.0	0.0	0.0	0.0	0.0	0.0	0.0	1.0	1.0	0.0
11 GDR	0	0	0	0	0	0	0	0	0	0	0	0	0	0	0	0	0	0	0	0
	0.0	0.0	0.0	0.0	0.0	0.0	0.0	0.0	0.0	0.0	0.0	0.0	0.0	0.0	0.0	0.0	0.0	0.0	0.0	0.0
12 GRCE	0	0	0	0	0	0	0	0	0	0	1	0	1	0	0	0	0	0	0	0
	0.0	0.0	0.0	0.0	0.0	0.0	0.0	0.0	0.0	0.0	1.4	0.0	1.4	0.0	0.0	0.0	0.0	0.0	0.0	0.0
13 HNGR	0	0	0	0	0	0	0	0	0	0	0	0	0	0	0	0	0	2	2	0
	0.0	0.0	0.0	0.0	0.0	0.0	0.0	0.0	0.0	0.0	0.0	0.0	0.0	0.0	0.0	0.0	0.0	2.0	2.0	0.0
14 ICLD	4	3	0	0	0	0	0	0	0	0	0	0	0	0	0	0	0	5	3	0
	4.8	3.6	0.0	0.0	0.0	0.0	0.0	0.0	0.0	0.0	0.0	0.0	0.0	0.0	0.0	0.0	0.0	6.0	3.6	0.0
15 IRLD	0	0	0	0	0	0	0	0	0	0	1	0	0	0	0	0	0	4	5	0
	0.0	0.0	0.0	0.0	0.0	0.0	0.0	0.0	0.0	0.0	1.0	0.0	0.0	0.0	0.0	0.0	0.0	4.2	5.2	0.0
16 ITLY	0	0	0	0	0	0	0	0	0	0	2	1	0	2	0	0	0	0	4	0
	0.0	0.0	0.0	0.0	0.0	0.0	0.0	0.0	0.0	0.0	1.8	0.9	0.0	1.8	0.0	0.0	0.0	0.0	3.6	0.0
17 LICH	0	0	0	0	0	0	0	0	0	0	0	0	0	0	0	0	0	0	1	0
	0.0	0.0	0.0	0.0	0.0	0.0	0.0	0.0	0.0	0.0	0.0	0.0	0.0	0.0	0.0	0.0	0.0	0.0	4.3	0.0

18	LXBG	0	0	0	0	0	0	0	0	0	0	0	0	0	0	0	0	0	2	1	0
		0.0	0.0	0.0	0.0	0.0	0.0	0.0	0.0	0.0	0.0	0.0	0.0	0.0	0.0	0.0	0.0	0.0	1.8	0.9	0.0
19	MLTA	0	0	0	0	0	0	0	0	0	0	4	2	2	6	1	2	4	0	1	0
		0.0	0.0	0.0	0.0	0.0	0.0	0.0	0.0	0.0	0.0	5.1	2.5	2.5	7.6	1.3	2.5	5.1	0.0	1.3	0.0
20	MNCO	2	9	0	0	0	0	0	0	0	0	0	0	0	0	0	1	0	0	1	0
		5.3	23.7	0.0	0.0	0.0	0.0	0.0	0.0	0.0	0.0	0.0	0.0	0.0	0.0	0.0	2.6	0.0	0.0	2.6	0.0
21	NTHL	0	0	0	0	0	0	0	0	0	0	0	0	0	0	0	0	0	0	5	0
		0.0	0.0	0.0	0.0	0.0	0.0	0.0	0.0	0.0	0.0	0.0	0.0	0.0	0.0	0.0	0.0	0.0	0.0	4.2	0.0
22	NRWY	0	1	0	0	0	0	0	0	0	0	0	0	0	0	0	0	0	1	1	0
		0.0	0.6	0.0	0.0	0.0	0.0	0.0	0.0	0.0	0.0	0.0	0.0	0.0	0.0	0.0	0.0	0.0	0.6	0.6	0.0
23	PLND	0	0	0	0	0	0	0	0	0	0	0	0	0	0	0	0	0	0	1	0
		0.0	0.0	0.0	0.0	0.0	0.0	0.0	0.0	0.0	0.0	0.0	0.0	0.0	0.0	0.0	0.0	0.0	0.0	1.0	0.0
24	PRTG	0	0	0	0	0	0	0	0	0	0	3	0	1	1	0	0	0	1	0	1
		0.0	0.0	0.0	0.0	0.0	0.0	0.0	0.0	0.0	0.0	4.6	0.0	1.5	1.5	0.0	0.0	0.0	1.5	0.0	1.5
25	RMNA	0	0	0	0	0	0	0	1	0	0	2	0	0	4	0	0	0	4	1	0
		0.0	0.0	0.0	0.0	0.0	0.0	0.0	0.3	0.0	0.0	0.7	0.0	0.0	1.4	0.0	0.0	0.0	1.4	0.3	0.0
26	SANM	0	0	0	0	0	0	1	2	0	0	2	0	2	1	0	0	0	1	0	0
		0.0	0.0	0.0	0.0	0.0	0.0	0.9	1.8	0.0	0.0	1.8	0.0	1.8	0.9	0.0	0.0	0.0	0.9	0.0	0.0
27	SPAN	0	0	0	0	0	0	1	0	0	0	6	0	1	1	0	0	0	0	2	0
		0.0	0.0	0.0	0.0	0.0	0.0	0.6	0.0	0.0	0.0	3.6	0.0	0.6	0.6	0.0	0.0	0.0	0.0	1.2	0.0
28	SWDN	0	0	0	0	0	0	0	0	0	0	0	0	0	0	0	0	0	1	2	0
		0.0	0.0	0.0	0.0	0.0	0.0	0.0	0.0	0.0	0.0	0.0	0.0	0.0	0.0	0.0	0.0	0.0	0.7	1.4	0.0
29	SWTZ	0	0	0	0	0	0	0	0	0	0	0	0	0	0	0	0	0	0	4	0
		0.0	0.0	0.0	0.0	0.0	0.0	0.0	0.0	0.0	0.0	0.0	0.0	0.0	0.0	0.0	0.0	0.0	0.0	3.8	0.0
30	TRKY	0	0	0	0	0	0	0	0	0	0	5	3	4	0	0	0	4	0	0	0
		0.0	0.0	0.0	0.0	0.0	0.0	0.0	0.0	0.0	0.0	3.0	1.8	2.4	0.0	0.0	0.0	2.4	0.0	0.0	0.0
31	USSR	0	0	0	0	0	0	0	0	0	0	0	0	0	0	0	0	0	0	1	0
		0.0	0.0	0.0	0.0	0.0	0.0	0.0	0.0	0.0	0.0	0.0	0.0	0.0	0.0	0.0	0.0	0.0	0.0	1.5	0.0
32	UK	0	0	0	0	0	0	0	0	0	0	0	0	0	0	0	0	0	0	2	0
		0.0	0.0	0.0	0.0	0.0	0.0	0.0	0.0	0.0	0.0	0.0	0.0	0.0	0.0	0.0	0.0	0.0	0.0	1.0	0.0
33	USA	0	0	0	0	0	1	0	0	0	3	0	0	0	0	0	0	0	0	1	0
		0.0	0.0	0.0	0.0	0.0	0.6	0.0	0.0	0.0	1.8	0.0	0.0	0.0	0.0	0.0	0.0	0.0	0.0	0.6	0.0
34	VATC	0	0	0	0	0	0	0	0	0	0	3	0	0	0	0	0	1	1	0	0
		0.0	0.0	0.0	0.0	0.0	0.0	0.0	0.0	0.0	0.0	2.7	0.0	0.0	0.0	0.0	0.0	0.9	0.9	0.0	0.0
35	YGSL	0	0	0	0	0	0	0	0	0	0	0	0	0	0	0	0	0	0	0	0
		0.0	0.0	0.0	0.0	0.0	0.0	0.0	0.0	0.0	0.0	0.0	0.0	0.0	0.0	0.0	0.0	0.0	0.0	0.0	0.0

Table A2.4. *(cont.)*

COUNTRIES	61	62	63	64	65	66	67	68	69	70	71	72	73	74	75	76	77	78	79	80
1 AUST	0	0	0	0	0	0	0	0	0	0	0	0	0	0	0	0	0	0	0	0
	0.0	0.0	0.0	0.0	0.0	0.0	0.0	0.0	0.0	0.0	0.0	0.0	0.0	0.0	0.0	0.0	0.0	0.0	0.0	0.0
2 BLGM	0	0	4	0	0	0	0	0	0	4	0	0	0	0	0	0	0	0	0	0
	0.0	0.0	2.6	0.0	0.0	0.0	0.0	0.0	0.0	2.6	0.0	0.0	0.0	0.0	0.0	0.0	0.0	0.0	0.0	0.0
3 BLGR	0	0	0	0	0	0	0	0	0	0	1	0	0	1	0	0	0	0	0	0
	0.0	0.0	0.0	0.0	0.0	0.0	0.0	0.0	0.0	0.0	1.4	0.0	0.0	1.4	0.0	0.0	0.0	0.0	0.0	0.0
4 CNDA	1	0	0	0	0	0	0	0	0	0	0	0	0	0	0	1	0	0	0	0
	1.3	0.0	0.0	0.0	0.0	0.0	0.0	0.0	0.0	0.0	0.0	0.0	0.0	0.0	0.0	1.3	0.0	0.0	0.0	0.0
5 CYPR	0	0	0	0	0	0	0	3	0	0	0	0	0	1	0	1	0	0	0	0
	0.0	0.0	0.0	0.0	0.0	0.0	0.0	2.2	0.0	0.0	0.0	0.0	0.0	0.7	0.0	0.7	0.0	0.0	0.0	0.0
6 CZCH	0	0	0	1	1	1	0	2	0	1	0	0	0	1	0	1	0	0	1	0
	0.0	0.0	0.0	1.0	1.0	1.0	0.0	2.0	0.0	1.0	0.0	0.0	0.0	1.0	0.0	1.0	0.0	0.0	1.0	0.0
7 DNMK	0	0	1	0	0	0	0	1	0	2	0	0	1	1	0	0	0	0	0	0
	0.0	0.0	1.5	0.0	0.0	0.0	0.0	1.5	0.0	2.9	0.0	0.0	1.5	1.5	0.0	0.0	0.0	0.0	0.0	0.0
8 FNLD	0	0	0	0	0	0	0	0	0	0	0	0	0	0	0	0	0	0	0	0
	0.0	0.0	0.0	0.0	0.0	0.0	0.0	0.0	0.0	0.0	0.0	0.0	0.0	0.0	0.0	0.0	0.0	0.0	0.0	0.0
9 FRNC	0	0	1	0	0	0	0	0	0	2	0	0	0	1	0	1	0	0	0	0
	0.0	0.0	2.4	0.0	0.0	0.0	0.0	0.0	0.0	4.8	0.0	0.0	0.0	2.4	0.0	2.4	0.0	0.0	0.0	0.0
10 FRG	0	0	1	1	1	1	0	1	0	1	0	1	0	1	0	1	0	0	0	0
	0.0	0.0	1.0	1.0	1.0	1.0	0.0	1.0	0.0	1.0	0.0	1.0	0.0	1.0	0.0	1.0	0.0	0.0	0.0	0.0
11 GDR	0	0	0	0	0	1	0	0	0	0	0	0	0	1	0	0	0	0	0	0
	0.0	0.0	0.0	0.0	0.0	1.4	0.0	0.0	0.0	0.0	0.0	0.0	0.0	1.4	0.0	0.0	0.0	0.0	0.0	0.0
12 GRCE	0	0	0	0	0	0	0	0	0	0	0	0	0	0	0	0	0	0	0	0
	0.0	0.0	0.0	0.0	0.0	0.0	0.0	0.0	0.0	0.0	0.0	0.0	0.0	0.0	0.0	0.0	0.0	0.0	0.0	0.0
13 HNGR	0	0	1	1	0	0	0	2	3	1	0	0	0	4	2	0	0	0	0	0
	0.0	0.0	1.0	1.0	0.0	0.0	0.0	2.0	3.0	1.0	0.0	0.0	0.0	4.0	2.0	0.0	0.0	0.0	0.0	0.0
14 ICLD	0	0	6	0	0	0	0	0	5	3	0	0	0	5	0	0	5	0	0	0
	0.0	0.0	7.2	0.0	0.0	0.0	0.0	0.0	6.0	3.6	0.0	0.0	0.0	6.0	0.0	0.0	6.0	0.0	0.0	0.0
15 IRLD	0	0	0	0	0	0	0	0	1	0	0	0	0	1	0	0	0	0	0	0
	0.0	0.0	0.0	0.0	0.0	0.0	0.0	0.0	1.0	0.0	0.0	0.0	0.0	1.0	0.0	0.0	0.0	0.0	0.0	0.0
16 ITLY	0	0	0	0	0	0	0	0	3	1	0	0	0	3	0	1	0	0	0	0
	0.0	0.0	0.0	0.0	0.0	0.0	0.0	0.0	2.7	0.9	0.0	0.0	0.0	2.7	0.0	0.9	0.0	0.0	0.0	0.0
17 LICH	0	0	0	0	0	0	0	0	0	1	0	0	0	0	0	1	0	0	0	0
	0.0	0.0	0.0	0.0	0.0	0.0	0.0	0.0	0.0	4.3	0.0	0.0	0.0	0.0	0.0	4.3	0.0	0.0	0.0	0.0

18	LXBG	0	0	1	0	0	0	0	0	1	1	0	1	0	2	0	0	0	0	0	0
		0.0	0.0	0.9	0.0	0.0	0.0	0.0	0.0	0.9	0.9	0.0	0.9	0.0	1.8	0.0	0.0	0.0	0.0	0.0	0.0
19	MLTA	0	0	0	1	0	0	0	0	0	0	0	0	0	2	0	0	0	0	0	0
		0.0	0.0	0.0	1.3	0.0	0.0	0.0	0.0	0.0	0.0	0.0	0.0	0.0	2.5	0.0	0.0	0.0	0.0	0.0	0.0
20	MNCO	0	0	0	0	0	0	0	0	0	0	0	0	0	0	1	0	0	0	0	0
		0.0	0.0	0.0	0.0	0.0	0.0	0.0	0.0	0.0	0.0	0.0	0.0	0.0	0.0	2.6	0.0	0.0	0.0	0.0	0.0
21	NTHL	0	0	0	0	0	0	0	0	0	4	0	0	0	0	4	5	2	0	0	0
		0.0	0.0	0.0	0.0	0.0	0.0	0.0	0.0	0.0	3.3	0.0	0.0	0.0	0.0	3.3	4.2	1.7	0.0	0.0	0.0
22	NRWY	0	0	0	0	1	0	0	0	0	3	0	0	0	0	2	1	0	0	0	0
		0.0	0.0	0.0	0.0	0.6	0.0	0.0	0.0	0.0	1.7	0.0	0.0	0.0	0.0	1.1	0.6	0.0	0.0	0.0	0.0
23	PLND	0	0	0	0	0	0	0	0	0	0	0	0	0	2	0	0	0	0	0	0
		0.0	0.0	0.0	0.0	0.0	0.0	0.0	0.0	0.0	0.0	0.0	0.0	0.0	2.0	0.0	0.0	0.0	0.0	0.0	0.0
24	PRTG	1	0	0	1	0	0	0	0	0	1	0	1	0	0	0	0	0	0	0	0
		1.5	0.0	0.0	1.5	0.0	0.0	0.0	0.0	0.0	1.5	0.0	1.5	0.0	0.0	0.0	0.0	0.0	0.0	0.0	0.0
25	RMNA	0	3	4	0	0	0	0	1	0	2	0	1	0	0	0	2	0	0	0	0
		0.0	1.0	1.4	0.0	0.0	0.0	0.0	0.3	0.0	0.7	0.0	0.3	0.0	0.0	0.0	0.7	0.0	0.0	0.0	0.0
26	SANM	0	0	0	0	1	0	0	0	0	0	0	0	0	0	1	0	0	0	0	0
		0.0	0.0	0.0	0.0	0.9	0.0	0.0	0.0	0.0	0.0	0.0	0.0	0.0	0.0	0.9	0.0	0.0	0.0	0.0	0.0
27	SPAN	2	0	6	7	1	0	0	0	0	1	0	0	0	1	0	0	0	0	0	0
		1.2	0.0	3.6	4.2	0.6	0.0	0.0	0.0	0.0	0.6	0.0	0.0	0.0	0.6	0.0	0.0	0.0	0.0	0.0	0.0
28	SWDN	0	0	0	0	0	0	0	0	2	2	0	0	0	0	0	4	0	1	0	0
		0.0	0.0	0.0	0.0	0.0	0.0	0.0	0.0	1.4	1.4	0.0	0.0	0.0	0.0	0.0	2.8	0.0	0.7	0.0	0.0
29	SWTZ	1	0	0	0	0	0	0	0	5	8	0	4	0	0	0	0	0	0	0	0
		0.9	0.0	0.0	0.0	0.0	0.0	0.0	0.0	4.7	7.5	0.0	3.8	0.0	0.0	0.0	0.0	0.0	0.0	0.0	0.0
30	TRKY	0	0	0	0	0	0	0	0	0	0	0	0	0	1	0	0	0	0	0	0
		0.0	0.0	0.0	0.0	0.0	0.0	0.0	0.0	0.0	0.0	0.0	0.0	0.0	0.6	0.0	0.0	0.0	0.0	0.0	0.0
31	USSR	0	0	0	0	0	0	1	0	0	1	0	0	0	1	0	0	0	0	0	0
		0.0	0.0	0.0	0.0	0.0	0.0	1.5	0.0	0.0	1.5	0.0	0.0	0.0	1.5	0.0	0.0	0.0	0.0	0.0	0.0
32	UK	1	3	3	2	0	0	0	0	0	2	0	1	1	1	0	0	0	0	0	0
		0.5	1.6	1.6	1.0	0.0	0.0	0.0	0.0	0.0	1.0	0.0	0.5	0.5	0.5	0.0	0.0	0.0	0.0	0.0	0.0
33	USA	1	1	2	0	0	0	0	0	0	2	0	0	1	0	0	4	0	0	0	0
		0.6	0.6	1.2	0.0	0.0	0.0	0.0	0.0	0.0	1.2	0.0	0.0	0.6	0.0	0.0	2.4	0.0	0.0	0.0	0.0
34	VATC	0	0	1	0	0	0	1	0	0	0	0	0	0	0	0	0	0	0	0	0
		0.0	0.0	0.9	0.0	0.0	0.0	0.9	0.0	0.0	0.0	0.0	0.0	0.0	0.0	0.0	0.0	0.0	0.0	0.0	0.0
35	YGSL	0	0	1	0	0	0	0	1	0	0	0	0	1	0	0	0	0	0	0	0
		0.0	0.0	0.5	0.0	0.0	0.0	0.0	0.5	0.0	0.0	0.0	0.0	0.5	0.0	0.0	0.0	0.0	0.0	0.0	0.0

Table A2.4. *(cont.)*

COUNTRIES	81	82	83	84	85	86	87	88	89	90	91	92	93	94	95	96	97	98	99	100
1 AUST	0	0	0	0	0	0	0	0	0	0	0	0	0	0	0	0	0	2	0	0
	0.0	0.0	0.0	0.0	0.0	0.0	0.0	0.0	0.0	0.0	0.0	0.0	0.0	0.0	0.0	0.0	0.0	4.1	0.0	0.0
2 BLGM	0	0	0	0	0	0	0	0	0	0	0	3	0	0	0	0	12	4	0	0
	0.0	0.0	0.0	0.0	0.0	0.0	0.0	0.0	0.0	0.0	0.0	2.0	0.0	0.0	0.0	0.0	7.9	2.6	0.0	0.0
3 BLGR	0	1	0	0	0	0	0	0	0	0	0	0	0	0	0	0	1	0	2	0
	0.0	1.4	0.0	0.0	0.0	0.0	0.0	0.0	0.0	0.0	0.0	0.0	0.0	0.0	0.0	0.0	1.4	0.0	2.8	0.0
4 CNDA	0	0	0	0	0	0	0	0	0	0	2	0	0	3	0	0	5	0	1	0
	0.0	0.0	0.0	0.0	0.0	0.0	0.0	0.0	0.0	0.0	2.7	0.0	0.0	4.0	0.0	0.0	6.7	0.0	1.3	0.0
5 CYPR	1	1	0	0	0	0	0	0	0	0	0	0	0	0	0	0	2	0	6	0
	0.7	0.7	0.0	0.0	0.0	0.0	0.0	0.0	0.0	0.0	0.0	0.0	0.0	0.0	0.0	0.0	1.5	0.0	4.5	0.0
6 CZCH	0	0	0	0	0	0	0	0	1	0	0	0	0	0	0	0	0	0	1	0
	0.0	0.0	0.0	0.0	0.0	0.0	0.0	0.0	1.0	0.0	0.0	0.0	0.0	0.0	0.0	0.0	0.0	0.0	1.0	0.0
7 DNMK	0	1	0	0	0	0	0	0	0	0	0	0	0	0	0	0	0	3	0	0
	0.0	1.5	0.0	0.0	0.0	0.0	0.0	0.0	0.0	0.0	0.0	0.0	0.0	0.0	0.0	0.0	0.0	4.4	0.0	0.0
8 FNLD	0	0	0	0	0	0	0	0	0	0	0	0	0	0	0	0	0	8	4	0
	0.0	0.0	0.0	0.0	0.0	0.0	0.0	0.0	0.0	0.0	0.0	0.0	0.0	0.0	0.0	0.0	0.0	5.7	2.9	0.0
9 FRNC	0	0	0	0	0	0	0	0	0	0	0	0	0	0	0	0	0	3	0	0
	0.0	0.0	0.0	0.0	0.0	0.0	0.0	0.0	0.0	0.0	0.0	0.0	0.0	0.0	0.0	0.0	0.0	7.1	0.0	0.0
10 FRG	0	1	0	0	0	0	0	0	0	0	3	0	0	0	0	0	2	0	0	0
	0.0	1.0	0.0	0.0	0.0	0.0	0.0	0.0	0.0	0.0	3.1	0.0	0.0	0.0	0.0	0.0	2.1	0.0	0.0	0.0
11 GDR	0	1	0	0	0	0	0	0	0	0	0	0	0	0	0	0	0	2	1	0
	0.0	1.4	0.0	0.0	0.0	0.0	0.0	0.0	0.0	0.0	0.0	0.0	0.0	0.0	0.0	0.0	0.0	2.8	1.4	0.0
12 GRCE	0	0	0	0	0	0	0	0	0	0	1	0	0	0	0	0	0	0	3	0
	0.0	0.0	0.0	0.0	0.0	0.0	0.0	0.0	0.0	0.0	1.4	0.0	0.0	0.0	0.0	0.0	0.0	0.0	4.2	0.0
13 HNGR	0	1	0	0	0	0	0	0	0	0	0	0	0	0	0	0	3	1	2	0
	0.0	1.0	0.0	0.0	0.0	0.0	0.0	0.0	0.0	0.0	0.0	0.0	0.0	0.0	0.0	0.0	3.0	1.0	2.0	0.0
14 ICLD	0	0	0	0	0	0	0	0	0	0	0	0	0	0	0	0	1	0	3	0
	0.0	0.0	0.0	0.0	0.0	0.0	0.0	0.0	0.0	0.0	0.0	0.0	0.0	0.0	0.0	0.0	1.2	0.0	3.6	0.0
15 IRLD	0	1	0	0	0	0	0	0	0	0	2	0	0	0	0	0	0	5	9	0
	0.0	1.0	0.0	0.0	0.0	0.0	0.0	0.0	0.0	0.0	2.1	0.0	0.0	0.0	0.0	0.0	0.0	5.2	9.4	0.0
16 ITLY	0	3	0	0	0	0	0	0	0	0	1	0	0	0	0	0	0	20	0	0
	0.0	2.7	0.0	0.0	0.0	0.0	0.0	0.0	0.0	0.0	0.9	0.0	0.0	0.0	0.0	0.0	0.0	18.0	0.0	0.0
17 LICH	0	1	0	0	0	0	0	0	0	1	0	0	0	0	0	0	0	0	0	0
	0.0	4.3	0.0	0.0	0.0	0.0	0.0	0.0	0.0	4.3	0.0	0.0	0.0	0.0	0.0	0.0	0.0	0.0	0.0	0.0

18	LXBG	0	2	0	0	0	0	0	0	0	1	0	1	0	0	0	0	1	4	1	0
		0.0	1.8	0.0	0.0	0.0	0.0	0.0	0.0	0.0	0.9	0.0	0.9	0.0	0.0	0.0	0.0	0.9	3.5	0.9	0.0
19	MLTA	0	1	0	0	0	0	0	0	0	0	0	0	0	0	0	0	1	2	3	0
		0.0	1.3	0.0	0.0	0.0	0.0	0.0	0.0	0.0	0.0	0.0	0.0	0.0	0.0	0.0	0.0	1.3	2.5	3.8	0.0
20	MNCO	0	0	0	0	0	0	0	0	0	0	0	1	0	0	0	0	0	0	0	0
		0.0	0.0	0.0	0.0	0.0	0.0	0.0	0.0	0.0	0.0	0.0	2.6	0.0	0.0	0.0	0.0	0.0	0.0	0.0	0.0
21	NTHL	0	0	1	0	0	0	2	0	0	1	0	0	0	0	0	0	5	3	1	0
		0.0	0.0	0.8	0.0	0.0	0.0	1.7	0.0	0.0	0.8	0.0	0.0	0.0	0.0	0.0	0.0	4.2	2.5	0.8	0.0
22	NRWY	0	0	0	0	0	0	0	0	0	0	0	0	0	0	0	0	6	5	0	0
		0.0	0.0	0.0	0.0	0.0	0.0	0.0	0.0	0.0	0.0	0.0	0.0	0.0	0.0	0.0	0.0	3.4	2.9	0.0	0.0
23	PLND	0	1	0	0	0	0	0	0	0	0	0	0	0	0	0	0	0	3	0	0
		0.0	1.0	0.0	0.0	0.0	0.0	0.0	0.0	0.0	0.0	0.0	0.0	0.0	0.0	0.0	0.0	0.0	3.0	0.0	0.0
24	PRTG	0	0	0	0	0	0	0	0	0	0	0	0	0	0	0	0	0	0	0	0
		0.0	0.0	0.0	0.0	0.0	0.0	0.0	0.0	0.0	0.0	0.0	0.0	0.0	0.0	0.0	0.0	0.0	0.0	0.0	0.0
25	RMNA	0	0	0	0	0	0	0	0	0	1	0	0	0	1	0	0	0	3	2	0
		0.0	0.0	0.0	0.0	0.0	0.0	0.0	0.0	0.0	0.3	0.0	0.0	0.0	0.3	0.0	0.0	0.0	1.0	0.7	0.0
26	SANM	0	0	0	0	0	0	0	0	0	1	0	2	0	0	0	0	0	0	0	0
		0.0	0.0	0.0	0.0	0.0	0.0	0.0	0.0	0.0	0.9	0.0	1.8	0.0	0.0	0.0	0.0	0.0	0.0	0.0	0.0
27	SPAN	0	1	0	0	0	0	0	0	0	0	4	0	0	0	0	0	7	1	1	0
		0.0	0.6	0.0	0.0	0.0	0.0	0.0	0.0	0.0	0.0	2.4	0.0	0.0	0.0	0.0	0.0	4.2	0.6	0.6	0.0
28	SWDN	1	0	0	0	0	0	0	0	0	0	1	2	0	0	0	0	5	4	1	0
		0.7	0.0	0.0	0.0	0.0	0.0	0.0	0.0	0.0	0.0	0.7	1.4	0.0	0.0	0.0	0.0	3.5	2.8	0.7	0.0
29	SWTZ	0	0	0	0	0	0	0	0	0	0	0	1	0	0	0	0	1	2	0	0
		0.0	0.0	0.0	0.0	0.0	0.0	0.0	0.0	0.0	0.0	0.0	0.9	0.0	0.0	0.0	0.0	0.9	1.9	0.0	0.0
30	TRKY	0	0	0	0	0	0	0	0	0	0	0	0	0	0	0	0	1	0	0	0
		0.0	0.0	0.0	0.0	0.0	0.0	0.0	0.0	0.0	0.0	0.0	0.0	0.0	0.0	0.0	0.0	0.6	0.0	0.0	0.0
31	USSR	0	1	0	0	0	0	0	0	0	0	0	0	0	0	0	0	1	0	0	0
		0.0	1.5	0.0	0.0	0.0	0.0	0.0	0.0	0.0	0.0	0.0	0.0	0.0	0.0	0.0	0.0	1.5	0.0	0.0	0.0
32	UK	0	0	0	0	0	0	0	0	0	2	0	2	3	10	0	0	9	11	11	0
		0.0	0.0	0.0	0.0	0.0	0.0	0.0	0.0	0.0	1.0	0.0	1.0	1.6	5.2	0.0	0.0	4.7	5.7	5.7	0.0
33	USA	2	0	0	1	0	0	0	0	0	0	1	0	0	4	0	0	9	0	0	0
		1.2	0.0	0.0	0.6	0.0	0.0	0.0	0.0	0.0	0.0	0.6	0.0	0.0	2.4	0.0	0.0	5.4	0.0	0.0	0.0
34	VATC	0	0	0	0	0	0	0	0	0	0	0	0	0	0	0	0	0	0	0	0
		0.0	0.0	0.0	0.0	0.0	0.0	0.0	0.0	0.0	0.0	0.0	0.0	0.0	0.0	0.0	0.0	0.0	0.0	0.0	0.0
35	YGSL	1	0	0	0	0	0	0	0	1	1	0	0	0	0	0	0	0	0	1	0
		0.5	0.0	0.0	0.0	0.0	0.0	0.0	0.0	0.5	0.5	0.0	0.0	0.0	0.0	0.0	0.0	0.0	0.0	0.5	0.0

Table A2.4. *(cont.)*

COUNTRIES	101	102	103	104	105	106	107	108	109	110	111	112	113	114	115	116	117	118	119	120
1 AUST	0	0	2	2	0	6	0	2	0	0	0	0	0	0	0	1	7	0	3	0
	0.0	0.0	4.1	4.1	0.0	12.2	0.0	4.1	0.0	0.0	0.0	0.0	0.0	0.0	0.0	2.0	14.3	0.0	6.1	0.0
2 BLGM	0	1	3	4	0	0	0	0	0	0	0	1	0	0	0	1	2	0	2	0
	0.0	0.7	2.0	2.6	0.0	0.0	0.0	0.0	0.0	0.0	0.0	0.7	0.0	0.0	0.0	0.7	1.3	0.0	1.3	0.0
3 BLGR	0	0	5	4	0	0	0	0	0	1	0	0	0	0	0	1	0	0	0	1
	0.0	0.0	7.0	5.6	0.0	0.0	0.0	0.0	0.0	1.4	0.0	0.0	0.0	0.0	0.0	1.4	0.0	0.0	0.0	1.4
4 CNDA	0	0	5	2	0	0	0	3	1	1	0	0	0	0	0	0	5	0	1	2
	0.0	0.0	6.7	2.7	0.0	0.0	0.0	4.0	1.3	1.3	0.0	0.0	0.0	0.0	0.0	0.0	6.7	0.0	1.3	2.7
5 CYPR	3	0	13	2	1	0	3	0	0	2	0	0	0	0	0	0	0	0	2	0
	2.2	0.0	9.7	1.5	0.7	0.0	2.2	0.0	0.0	1.5	0.0	0.0	0.0	0.0	0.0	0.0	0.0	0.0	1.5	0.0
6 CZCH	0	0	16	7	0	0	0	1	0	0	0	0	0	0	0	5	0	0	1	3
	0.0	0.0	15.8	6.9	0.0	0.0	0.0	1.0	0.0	0.0	0.0	0.0	0.0	0.0	0.0	5.0	0.0	0.0	1.0	3.0
7 DNMK	0	0	1	1	0	0	0	0	0	0	0	0	0	0	0	0	0	0	8	0
	0.0	0.0	1.5	1.5	0.0	0.0	0.0	0.0	0.0	0.0	0.0	0.0	0.0	0.0	0.0	0.0	0.0	0.0	11.8	0.0
8 FNLD	1	2	8	3	0	0	0	0	0	0	2	6	0	0	0	0	0	0	0	0
	0.7	1.4	5.7	2.1	0.0	0.0	0.0	0.0	0.0	0.0	1.4	4.3	0.0	0.0	0.0	0.0	0.0	0.0	0.0	0.0
9 FRNC	0	0	3	3	3	0	0	4	0	1	0	0	0	0	0	0	0	0	0	0
	0.0	0.0	7.1	7.1	7.1	0.0	0.0	9.5	0.0	2.4	0.0	0.0	0.0	0.0	0.0	0.0	0.0	0.0	0.0	0.0
10 FRG	0	0	8	7	0	0	0	1	0	0	0	1	0	0	0	0	0	0	17	0
	0.0	0.0	8.3	7.3	0.0	0.0	0.0	1.0	0.0	0.0	0.0	1.0	0.0	0.0	0.0	0.0	0.0	0.0	17.7	0.0
11 GDR	0	0	12	3	0	0	0	0	0	0	0	0	0	0	0	2	0	0	2	0
	0.0	0.0	16.9	4.2	0.0	0.0	0.0	0.0	0.0	0.0	0.0	0.0	0.0	0.0	0.0	2.8	0.0	0.0	2.8	0.0
12 GRCE	0	0	3	3	0	0	0	0	0	0	0	0	0	0	0	0	0	0	0	0
	0.0	0.0	4.2	4.2	0.0	0.0	0.0	0.0	0.0	0.0	0.0	0.0	0.0	0.0	0.0	0.0	0.0	0.0	0.0	0.0
13 HNGR	0	0	8	9	0	0	1	0	0	0	0	0	0	0	0	3	0	0	0	0
	0.0	0.0	8.1	9.1	0.0	0.0	1.0	0.0	0.0	0.0	0.0	0.0	0.0	0.0	0.0	3.0	0.0	0.0	0.0	0.0
14 ICLD	0	0	0	0	0	0	0	0	0	0	0	0	0	0	0	0	0	0	0	0
	0.0	0.0	0.0	0.0	0.0	0.0	0.0	0.0	0.0	0.0	0.0	0.0	0.0	0.0	0.0	0.0	0.0	0.0	0.0	0.0
15 IRLD	0	0	7	5	0	1	0	0	0	0	0	0	0	0	0	1	0	0	3	0
	0.0	0.0	7.3	5.2	0.0	1.0	0.0	0.0	0.0	0.0	0.0	0.0	0.0	0.0	0.0	1.0	0.0	0.0	3.1	0.0
16 ITLY	0	0	5	0	0	0	0	2	1	1	0	2	0	0	0	1	0	0	0	0
	0.0	0.0	4.5	0.0	0.0	0.0	0.0	1.8	0.9	0.9	0.0	1.8	0.0	0.0	0.0	0.9	0.0	0.0	0.0	0.0
17 LICH	0	1	4	0	0	2	0	0	0	0	0	2	1	0	0	0	0	0	0	0
	0.0	4.3	17.4	0.0	0.0	8.7	0.0	0.0	0.0	0.0	0.0	8.7	4.3	0.0	0.0	0.0	0.0	0.0	0.0	0.0

18	LXBG	0	0	6	7	0	0	0	2	5	1	1	0	2	0	0	0	0	0	0	1
		0.0	0.0	5.3	6.1	0.0	0.0	0.0	1.8	4.4	0.9	0.9	0.0	1.8	0.0	0.0	0.0	0.0	0.0	0.0	0.9
19	MLTA	0	0	6	2	0	0	0	0	1	0	0	1	0	0	0	0	0	0	0	2
		0.0	0.0	7.6	2.5	0.0	0.0	0.0	0.0	1.3	0.0	0.0	1.3	0.0	0.0	0.0	0.0	0.0	0.0	0.0	2.5
20	MNCO	0	0	5	5	1	0	0	0	0	0	0	3	0	0	0	0	0	0	0	0
		0.0	0.0	13.2	13.2	2.6	0.0	0.0	0.0	0.0	0.0	0.0	7.9	0.0	0.0	0.0	0.0	0.0	0.0	0.0	0.0
21	NTHL	0	0	7	5	0	0	0	2	1	1	1	1	0	0	0	0	1	0	0	1
		0.0	0.0	5.8	4.2	0.0	0.0	0.0	1.7	0.8	0.8	0.8	0.8	0.0	0.0	0.0	0.0	0.8	0.0	0.0	0.8
22	NRWY	0	1	6	3	0	0	0	1	0	0	0	5	0	0	0	0	0	0	6	5
		0.0	0.6	3.4	1.7	0.0	0.0	0.0	0.6	0.0	0.0	0.0	2.9	0.0	0.0	0.0	0.0	0.0	0.0	3.4	2.9
23	PLND	0	0	21	10	0	0	0	0	0	0	0	0	0	0	0	5	0	0	1	0
		0.0	0.0	21.2	10.1	0.0	0.0	0.0	0.0	0.0	0.0	0.0	0.0	0.0	0.0	0.0	5.1	0.0	0.0	1.0	0.0
24	PRTG	0	0	3	3	0	2	0	0	0	1	1	0	0	0	0	0	2	0	0	0
		0.0	0.0	4.6	4.6	0.0	3.1	0.0	0.0	0.0	1.5	1.5	0.0	0.0	0.0	0.0	0.0	3.1	0.0	0.0	0.0
25	RMNA	0	0	27	10	0	10	0	2	7	3	14	2	1	0	0	0	4	0	0	1
		0.0	0.0	9.4	3.5	0.0	3.5	0.0	0.7	2.4	1.0	4.9	0.7	0.3	0.0	0.0	0.0	1.4	0.0	0.0	0.3
26	SANM	0	2	24	12	0	0	0	0	9	6	0	0	0	0	0	1	0	0	0	0
		0.0	1.8	22.0	11.0	0.0	0.0	0.0	0.0	8.3	5.5	0.0	0.0	0.0	0.0	0.0	0.9	0.0	0.0	0.0	0.0
27	SPAN	0	1	5	0	0	0	0	0	0	3	0	0	0	0	0	0	1	1	0	0
		0.0	0.6	3.0	0.0	0.0	0.0	0.0	0.0	0.0	1.8	0.0	0.0	0.0	0.0	0.0	0.0	0.6	0.6	0.0	0.0
28	SWDN	0	1	7	14	0	1	0	3	0	1	0	3	0	0	0	0	2	0	1	2
		0.0	0.7	5.0	9.9	0.0	0.7	0.0	2.1	0.0	0.7	0.0	2.1	0.0	0.0	0.0	0.0	1.4	0.0	0.7	1.4
29	SWTZ	0	3	2	7	0	0	0	0	1	0	0	0	0	0	0	0	1	0	0	0
		0.0	2.8	1.9	6.6	0.0	0.0	0.0	0.0	0.9	0.0	0.0	0.0	0.0	0.0	0.0	0.0	0.9	0.0	0.0	0.0
30	TRKY	0	0	16	1	0	0	0	0	0	4	4	0	0	0	0	0	3	1	0	0
		0.0	0.0	9.6	0.6	0.0	0.0	0.0	0.0	0.0	2.4	2.4	0.0	0.0	0.0	0.0	0.0	1.8	0.6	0.0	0.0
31	USSR	0	0	15	3	0	0	0	0	0	0	0	1	0	0	0	1	0	0	0	0
		0.0	0.0	22.4	4.5	0.0	0.0	0.0	0.0	0.0	0.0	0.0	1.5	0.0	0.0	0.0	1.5	0.0	0.0	0.0	0.0
32	UK	0	0	7	10	2	0	0	0	1	2	0	5	0	0	0	5	0	0	8	0
		0.0	0.0	3.6	5.2	1.0	0.0	0.0	0.0	0.5	1.0	0.0	2.6	0.0	0.0	0.0	2.6	0.0	0.0	4.1	0.0
33	USA	0	0	12	14	0	0	0	2	9	3	10	2	0	0	0	0	4	1	6	3
		0.0	0.0	7.2	8.4	0.0	0.0	0.0	1.2	5.4	1.8	6.0	1.2	0.0	0.0	0.0	0.0	2.4	0.6	3.6	1.8
34	VATC	0	0	33	5	0	0	0	0	0	7	1	4	0	0	5	0	0	0	0	0
		0.0	0.0	29.2	4.4	0.0	0.0	0.0	0.0	0.0	6.2	0.9	3.5	0.0	0.0	4.4	0.0	0.0	0.0	0.0	0.0
35	YGSL	7	1	16	12	1	1	0	1	2	0	1	1	0	0	0	3	8	0	0	2
		3.8	0.5	8.6	6.5	0.5	0.5	0.0	0.5	1.1	0.0	0.5	0.5	0.0	0.0	0.0	1.6	4.3	0.0	0.0	1.1

Table A2.5. Category Scores and Percentages: The Belgrade Opening Statements

COUNTRIES	1	2	3	4	5	6	7	8	9	10	11	12	13	14	15	16	17	18	19	20
1 AUST	6	5	0	0	0	0	2	1	4	0	6	0	0	16	2	5	6	0	6	1
	4.2	3.5	0.0	0.0	0.0	0.0	1.4	0.7	2.8	0.0	4.2	0.0	0.0	11.3	1.4	3.5	4.2	0.0	4.2	0.7
2 BLGM	4	7	0	0	0	0	0	0	7	0	5	0	0	5	5	3	9	0	9	2
	2.4	4.3	0.0	0.0	0.0	0.0	0.0	0.0	4.3	0.0	3.0	0.0	0.0	3.0	3.0	1.8	5.5	0.0	5.5	1.2
3 BLGR	14	9	5	0	0	0	7	0	2	3	18	0	0	15	6	25	14	0	20	1
	6.9	4.5	2.5	0.0	0.0	0.0	3.5	0.0	1.0	1.5	8.9	0.0	0.0	7.4	3.0	12.4	6.9	0.0	9.9	0.5
4 CNDA	8	6	0	0	0	0	0	1	14	0	5	0	0	6	0	12	6	0	4	4
	6.2	4.7	0.0	0.0	0.0	0.0	0.0	0.8	10.9	0.0	3.9	0.0	0.0	4.7	0.0	9.3	4.7	0.0	3.1	3.1
5 CYPR	10	12	2	0	0	0	5	0	3	0	6	0	0	1	3	1	8	0	5	1
	8.2	9.8	1.6	0.0	0.0	0.0	4.1	0.0	2.5	0.0	4.9	0.0	0.0	0.8	2.5	0.8	6.6	0.0	4.1	0.8
6 CZCH	3	1	3	0	0	0	0	0	0	0	4	0	0	2	4	38	9	0	8	11
	1.2	0.4	1.2	0.0	0.0	0.0	0.0	0.0	0.0	0.0	1.6	0.0	0.0	0.8	1.6	15.5	3.7	0.0	3.3	4.5
7 DNMK	0	22	0	0	0	0	0	0	23	0	4	0	0	5	2	10	0	0	4	4
	0.0	11.7	0.0	0.0	0.0	0.0	0.0	0.0	12.2	0.0	2.1	0.0	0.0	2.7	1.1	5.3	0.0	0.0	2.1	2.1
8 FNLD	17	8	14	1	0	0	0	0	5	0	37	0	0	1	0	19	26	0	35	5
	6.8	3.2	5.6	0.4	0.0	0.0	0.0	0.0	2.0	0.0	14.9	0.0	0.0	0.4	0.0	7.6	10.4	0.0	14.1	2.0
9 FRNC	3	1	2	0	0	0	0	1	7	0	8	0	0	0	0	1	3	0	4	4
	3.5	1.2	2.3	0.0	0.0	0.0	0.0	1.2	8.1	0.0	9.3	0.0	0.0	0.0	0.0	1.2	3.5	0.0	4.7	4.7
10 FRG	2	0	3	2	1	0	1	0	13	1	6	0	0	6	2	5	4	0	7	2
	1.0	0.0	1.6	1.0	0.5	0.0	0.5	0.0	6.8	0.5	3.1	0.0	0.0	3.1	1.0	2.6	2.1	0.0	3.6	1.0
11 GDR	6	11	8	0	6	5	0	7	0	1	12	1	0	4	6	14	6	0	14	2
	2.5	4.5	3.3	0.0	2.5	2.1	0.0	2.9	0.0	0.4	4.9	0.4	0.0	1.6	2.5	5.8	2.5	0.0	5.8	0.8
12 GRCE	6	4	0	0	0	0	0	0	0	0	6	0	0	9	0	0	6	0	9	2
	10.9	7.3	0.0	0.0	0.0	0.0	0.0	0.0	0.0	0.0	10.9	0.0	0.0	16.4	0.0	0.0	10.9	0.0	16.4	3.6
13 HNGR	13	13	3	0	0	0	0	0	6	0	16	0	0	4	9	14	18	0	12	10
	5.1	5.1	1.2	0.0	0.0	0.0	0.0	0.0	2.4	0.0	6.3	0.0	0.0	1.6	3.5	5.5	7.1	0.0	4.7	3.9
14 ICLD	2	4	1	3	0	0	1	1	7	0	3	0	0	0	0	3	2	0	2	5
	2.4	4.8	1.2	3.6	0.0	0.0	1.2	1.2	8.3	0.0	3.6	0.0	0.0	0.0	0.0	3.6	2.4	0.0	2.4	6.0
15 IRLD	2	13	1	0	0	0	0	0	20	0	7	1	0	10	2	28	3	0	13	9
	1.0	6.2	0.5	0.0	0.0	0.0	0.0	0.0	9.5	0.0	3.3	0.5	0.0	4.8	1.0	13.3	1.4	0.0	6.2	4.3
16 ITLY	11	6	1	0	0	0	0	0	4	0	17	0	0	2	1	0	12	0	18	2
	8.4	4.6	0.8	0.0	0.0	0.0	0.0	0.0	3.1	0.0	13.0	0.0	0.0	1.5	0.8	0.0	9.2	0.0	13.7	1.5
17 LICH	1	0	2	0	0	0	0	0	4	0	6	0	0	0	0	0	1	0	3	0
	4.0	0.0	8.0	0.0	0.0	0.0	0.0	0.0	16.0	0.0	24.0	0.0	0.0	0.0	0.0	0.0	4.0	0.0	12.0	0.0

18	LXBG	4	7	0	0	0	0	1	0	14	0	7	0	0	2	0	20	4	0	7	6
		2.4	4.2	0.0	0.0	0.0	0.0	0.6	0.0	8.4	0.0	4.2	0.0	0.0	1.2	0.0	12.0	2.4	0.0	4.2	3.6
19	MLTA	4	1	4	0	0	0	0	0	3	0	7	0	0	3	1	9	4	0	7	1
		1.6	0.4	1.6	0.0	0.0	0.0	0.0	0.0	1.2	0.0	2.9	0.0	0.0	1.2	0.4	3.7	1.6	0.0	2.9	0.4
20	MNCO	1	0	0	0	0	0	0	0	0	0	3	0	0	0	0	0	1	0	1	0
		2.1	0.0	0.0	0.0	0.0	0.0	0.0	0.0	0.0	0.0	6.3	0.0	0.0	0.0	0.0	0.0	2.1	0.0	2.1	0.0
21	NTHL	7	21	0	2	0	0	0	1	20	1	19	1	0	8	2	15	7	0	16	2
		3.2	9.7	0.0	0.9	0.0	0.0	0.0	0.5	9.3	0.5	8.8	0.5	0.0	3.7	0.9	6.9	3.2	0.0	7.4	0.9
22	NRWY	8	1	1	0	0	0	0	1	49	0	12	0	0	7	15	10	14	0	12	14
		2.8	0.4	0.4	0.0	0.0	0.0	0.0	0.4	17.3	0.0	4.2	0.0	0.0	2.5	5.3	3.5	4.9	0.0	4.2	4.9
23	PLND	22	22	4	1	1	1	1	1	16	1	10	1	0	1	0	3	22	0	9	3
		10.7	10.7	1.9	0.5	0.5	0.5	0.5	0.5	7.8	0.5	4.9	0.5	0.0	0.5	0.0	1.5	10.7	0.0	4.4	1.5
24	PRTG	12	6	1	0	0	0	0	0	15	0	25	0	0	3	3	5	15	0	15	0
		4.3	2.1	0.4	0.0	0.0	0.0	0.0	0.0	5.3	0.0	8.9	0.0	0.0	1.1	1.1	1.8	5.3	0.0	5.3	0.0
25	RMNA	44	8	11	15	0	0	8	4	0	0	29	4	0	7	6	66	48	0	29	12
		10.5	1.9	2.6	3.6	0.0	0.0	1.9	1.0	0.0	0.0	6.9	1.0	0.0	1.7	1.4	15.7	11.4	0.0	6.9	2.9
26	SANM	7	8	11	8	0	4	8	8	13	4	3	0	0	1	0	4	7	0	2	0
		5.8	6.7	9.2	6.7	0.0	3.3	6.7	6.7	10.8	3.3	2.5	0.0	0.0	0.8	0.0	3.3	5.8	0.0	1.7	0.0
27	SPAN	12	1	5	0	0	0	0	1	22	0	6	1	0	0	0	14	13	0	4	1
		9.8	0.8	4.1	0.0	0.0	0.0	0.0	0.8	18.0	0.0	4.9	0.8	0.0	0.0	0.0	11.5	10.7	0.0	3.3	0.8
28	SWDN	11	6	0	0	4	3	0	4	31	0	23	0	0	5	3	51	13	0	19	5
		3.7	2.0	0.0	0.0	1.4	1.0	0.0	1.4	10.5	0.0	7.8	0.0	0.0	1.7	1.0	17.3	4.4	0.0	6.5	1.7
29	SWTZ	6	5	12	2	1	0	5	3	9	0	17	0	0	1	2	9	6	0	16	8
		2.6	2.2	5.2	0.9	0.4	0.0	2.2	1.3	3.9	0.0	7.4	0.0	0.0	0.4	0.9	3.9	2.6	0.0	7.0	3.5
30	TRKY	6	8	0	0	0	0	0	1	0	0	12	2	0	6	1	5	6	0	18	6
		3.3	4.4	0.0	0.0	0.0	0.0	0.0	0.6	0.0	0.0	6.6	1.1	0.0	3.3	0.6	2.8	3.3	0.0	9.9	3.3
31	USSR	10	16	4	0	0	0	1	1	2	1	18	0	0	6	3	4	10	0	15	4
		3.8	6.0	1.5	0.0	0.0	0.0	0.4	0.4	0.8	0.4	6.8	0.0	0.0	2.3	1.1	1.5	3.8	0.0	5.6	1.5
32	UK	2	0	1	0	0	0	0	0	3	0	6	0	0	2	0	9	2	0	9	6
		1.6	0.0	0.8	0.0	0.0	0.0	0.0	0.0	2.4	0.0	4.8	0.0	0.0	1.6	0.0	7.3	1.6	0.0	7.3	4.8
33	USA	5	2	2	0	0	0	0	0	47	0	9	0	0	3	4	4	6	0	9	1
		2.4	1.0	1.0	0.0	0.0	0.0	0.0	0.0	22.6	0.0	4.3	0.0	0.0	1.4	1.9	1.9	2.9	0.0	4.3	0.5
34	VATC	3	3	2	1	0	0	3	0	26	0	6	0	0	6	0	7	3	0	4	0
		1.7	1.7	1.1	0.6	0.0	0.0	1.7	0.0	14.6	0.0	3.4	0.0	0.0	3.4	0.0	3.9	1.7	0.0	2.2	0.0
35	YGSL	16	5	27	2	0	3	1	4	25	1	28	0	0	16	24	63	28	0	22	13
		2.9	0.9	5.0	0.4	0.0	0.6	0.2	0.7	4.6	0.2	5.1	0.0	0.0	2.9	4.4	11.6	5.1	0.0	4.0	2.4

Table A2.5. *(cont.)*

COUNTRIES	21	22	23	24	25	26	27	28	29	30	31	32	33	34	35	36	37	38	39	40
1 AUST	1	1	1	1	0	1	0	0	0	0	0	0	0	0	0	0	0	0	0	0
	0.7	0.7	0.7	0.7	0.0	0.7	0.0	0.0	0.0	0.0	0.0	0.0	0.0	0.0	0.0	0.0	0.0	0.0	0.0	0.0
2 BLGM	0	0	0	0	1	2	0	0	0	4	0	0	0	0	0	0	0	0	0	0
	0.0	0.0	0.0	0.0	0.6	1.2	0.0	0.0	0.0	2.4	0.0	0.0	0.0	0.0	0.0	0.0	0.0	0.0	0.0	0.0
3 BLGR	0	0	0	0	0	1	0	0	0	0	0	0	0	0	1	0	0	0	0	1
	0.0	0.0	0.0	0.0	0.0	0.5	0.0	0.0	0.0	0.0	0.0	0.0	0.0	0.0	0.5	0.0	0.0	0.0	0.0	0.5
4 CNDA	0	0	0	0	0	4	0	2	0	0	0	0	0	0	0	0	0	0	0	0
	0.0	0.0	0.0	0.0	0.0	3.1	0.0	1.6	0.0	0.0	0.0	0.0	0.0	0.0	0.0	0.0	0.0	0.0	0.0	0.0
5 CYPR	0	0	0	0	0	1	0	0	0	0	0	0	0	0	0	0	0	0	0	3
	0.0	0.0	0.0	0.0	0.0	0.8	0.0	0.0	0.0	0.0	0.0	0.0	0.0	0.0	0.0	0.0	0.0	0.0	0.0	2.5
6 CZCH	0	3	2	0	0	8	0	0	0	1	0	0	0	0	7	0	1	0	0	1
	0.0	1.2	0.8	0.0	0.0	3.3	0.0	0.0	0.0	0.4	0.0	0.0	0.0	0.0	2.9	0.0	0.4	0.0	0.0	0.4
7 DNMK	0	2	1	0	2	4	0	0	0	1	0	0	1	2	0	0	0	0	0	0
	0.0	1.1	0.5	0.0	1.1	2.1	0.0	0.0	0.0	0.5	0.0	0.0	0.5	1.1	0.0	0.0	0.0	0.0	0.0	0.0
8 FNLD	1	0	0	0	0	5	0	0	0	0	0	0	0	0	3	0	0	0	0	0
	0.4	0.0	0.0	0.0	0.0	2.0	0.0	0.0	0.0	0.0	0.0	0.0	0.0	0.0	1.2	0.0	0.0	0.0	0.0	0.0
9 FRNC	0	1	0	0	0	3	0	0	0	1	0	0	0	0	0	0	0	0	0	0
	0.0	1.2	0.0	0.0	0.0	3.5	0.0	0.0	0.0	1.2	0.0	0.0	0.0	0.0	0.0	0.0	0.0	0.0	0.0	0.0
10 FRG	5	0	0	0	0	6	0	0	0	0	0	0	0	0	0	0	1	0	0	2
	2.6	0.0	0.0	0.0	0.0	3.1	0.0	0.0	0.0	0.0	0.0	0.0	0.0	0.0	0.0	0.0	0.5	0.0	0.0	1.0
11 GDR	0	0	0	0	0	1	0	0	0	1	0	0	0	0	1	0	0	0	0	0
	0.0	0.0	0.0	0.0	0.0	0.4	0.0	0.0	0.0	0.4	0.0	0.0	0.0	0.0	0.4	0.0	0.0	0.0	0.0	0.0
12 GRCE	0	0	0	0	0	2	0	0	0	0	0	0	0	0	0	0	0	0	0	0
	0.0	0.0	0.0	0.0	0.0	3.6	0.0	0.0	0.0	0.0	0.0	0.0	0.0	0.0	0.0	0.0	0.0	0.0	0.0	0.0
13 HNGR	5	4	0	1	0	16	0	0	0	6	0	0	8	7	0	0	0	0	0	0
	2.0	1.6	0.0	0.4	0.0	6.3	0.0	0.0	0.0	2.4	0.0	0.0	3.1	2.8	0.0	0.0	0.0	0.0	0.0	0.0
14 ICLD	0	6	0	0	0	5	0	0	0	0	0	0	0	0	0	0	0	0	0	0
	0.0	7.1	0.0	0.0	0.0	6.0	0.0	0.0	0.0	0.0	0.0	0.0	0.0	0.0	0.0	0.0	0.0	0.0	0.0	0.0
15 IRLD	2	7	7	12	0	4	0	0	0	0	0	0	0	0	0	0	0	0	0	0
	1.0	3.3	3.3	5.7	0.0	1.9	0.0	0.0	0.0	0.0	0.0	0.0	0.0	0.0	0.0	0.0	0.0	0.0	0.0	0.0
16 ITLY	0	0	2	0	0	2	0	0	0	0	0	0	0	0	0	0	0	0	0	0
	0.0	0.0	1.5	0.0	0.0	1.5	0.0	0.0	0.0	0.0	0.0	0.0	0.0	0.0	0.0	0.0	0.0	0.0	0.0	0.0
17 LICH	0	0	0	0	0	0	0	0	0	0	0	0	0	0	0	0	0	0	0	0
	0.0	0.0	0.0	0.0	0.0	0.0	0.0	0.0	0.0	0.0	0.0	0.0	0.0	0.0	0.0	0.0	0.0	0.0	0.0	0.0

18	LXBG	0	2	1	0	0	3	0	0	0	0	0	0	0	0	0	0	0	0	0	1
		0.0	1.2	0.6	0.0	0.0	1.8	0.0	0.0	0.0	0.0	0.0	0.0	0.0	0.0	0.0	0.0	0.0	0.0	0.0	0.6
19	MLTA	0	0	0	0	3	1	3	0	0	0	0	0	0	0	0	0	0	0	0	0
		0.0	0.0	0.0	0.0	1.2	0.4	1.2	0.0	0.0	0.0	0.0	0.0	0.0	0.0	0.0	0.0	0.0	0.0	0.0	0.0
20	MNCO	0	0	0	0	0	0	0	0	0	0	0	0	0	0	6	0	0	0	0	8
		0.0	0.0	0.0	0.0	0.0	0.0	0.0	0.0	0.0	0.0	0.0	0.0	0.0	0.0	12.5	0.0	0.0	0.0	0.0	16.7
21	NTHL	0	1	1	0	0	2	0	0	0	0	0	0	0	0	1	0	0	0	0	1
		0.0	0.5	0.5	0.0	0.0	0.9	0.0	0.0	0.0	0.0	0.0	0.0	0.0	0.0	0.5	0.0	0.0	0.0	0.0	0.5
22	NRWY	0	0	0	0	0	22	0	0	0	4	0	0	0	0	8	0	0	0	0	11
		0.0	0.0	0.0	0.0	0.0	7.8	0.0	0.0	0.0	1.4	0.0	0.0	0.0	0.0	2.8	0.0	0.0	0.0	0.0	3.9
23	PLND	0	2	0	0	0	3	0	0	0	0	0	0	0	0	2	0	0	0	0	0
		0.0	1.0	0.0	0.0	0.0	1.5	0.0	0.0	0.0	0.0	0.0	0.0	0.0	0.0	1.0	0.0	0.0	0.0	0.0	0.0
24	PRTG	0	0	0	0	0	0	0	0	0	0	0	0	0	0	0	0	0	0	0	0
		0.0	0.0	0.0	0.0	0.0	0.0	0.0	0.0	0.0	0.0	0.0	0.0	0.0	0.0	0.0	0.0	0.0	0.0	0.0	0.0
25	RMNA	1	0	0	0	0	16	0	2	0	0	0	1	1	4	7	0	4	0	1	1
		0.2	0.0	0.0	0.0	0.0	3.8	0.0	0.5	0.0	0.0	0.0	0.2	0.2	1.0	1.7	0.0	1.0	0.0	0.2	0.2
26	SANM	0	0	0	0	0	0	0	0	0	0	0	0	0	0	0	0	0	0	0	0
		0.0	0.0	0.0	0.0	0.0	0.0	0.0	0.0	0.0	0.0	0.0	0.0	0.0	0.0	0.0	0.0	0.0	0.0	0.0	0.0
27	SPAN	0	0	0	0	0	1	0	0	0	0	0	0	0	0	1	0	0	0	0	0
		0.0	0.0	0.0	0.0	0.0	0.8	0.0	0.0	0.0	0.0	0.0	0.0	0.0	0.0	0.8	0.0	0.0	0.0	0.0	0.0
28	SWDN	0	0	0	0	0	5	0	0	0	0	0	0	0	0	5	0	0	0	0	1
		0.0	0.0	0.0	0.0	0.0	1.7	0.0	0.0	0.0	0.0	0.0	0.0	0.0	0.0	1.7	0.0	0.0	0.0	0.0	0.3
29	SWTZ	4	4	4	0	5	7	0	0	0	11	0	0	0	0	3	0	0	4	0	4
		1.7	1.7	1.7	0.0	2.2	3.0	0.0	0.0	0.0	4.8	0.0	0.0	0.0	0.0	1.3	0.0	0.0	1.7	0.0	1.7
30	TRKY	6	0	0	0	0	5	2	0	0	0	0	0	0	0	2	0	0	0	0	2
		3.3	0.0	0.0	0.0	0.0	2.8	1.1	0.0	0.0	0.0	0.0	0.0	0.0	0.0	1.1	0.0	0.0	0.0	0.0	1.1
31	USSR	3	1	1	0	0	6	1	0	0	3	0	0	0	0	0	0	0	0	0	9
		1.1	0.4	0.4	0.0	0.0	2.3	0.4	0.0	0.0	1.1	0.0	0.0	0.0	0.0	0.0	0.0	0.0	0.0	0.0	3.4
32	UK	0	3	3	0	0	3	0	0	0	0	0	0	0	2	0	0	0	0	0	0
		0.0	2.4	2.4	0.0	0.0	2.4	0.0	0.0	0.0	0.0	0.0	0.0	0.0	1.6	0.0	0.0	0.0	0.0	0.0	0.0
33	USA	2	2	5	1	0	0	0	0	0	0	0	0	0	0	0	1	0	1	0	0
		1.0	1.0	2.4	0.5	0.0	0.0	0.0	0.0	0.0	0.0	0.0	0.0	0.0	0.0	0.0	0.5	0.0	0.5	0.0	0.0
34	VATC	0	0	0	0	0	0	0	0	0	0	0	0	0	0	1	0	0	0	0	0
		0.0	0.0	0.0	0.0	0.0	0.0	0.0	0.0	0.0	0.0	0.0	0.0	0.0	0.0	0.6	0.0	0.0	0.0	0.0	0.0
35	YGSL	0	0	0	0	0	16	0	0	0	2	0	0	0	0	8	0	0	0	0	0
		0.0	0.0	0.0	0.0	0.0	2.9	0.0	0.0	0.0	0.4	0.0	0.0	0.0	0.0	1.5	0.0	0.0	0.0	0.0	0.0

Table A2.5. *(cont.)*

COUNTRIES	41	42	43	44	45	46	47	48	49	50	51	52	53	54	55	56	57	58	59	60
1 AUST	0	0	0	0	0	6	0	0	0	0	1	0	0	0	0	0	0	8	3	0
	0.0	0.0	0.0	0.0	0.0	4.2	0.0	0.0	0.0	0.0	0.7	0.0	0.0	0.0	0.0	0.0	0.0	5.6	2.1	0.0
2 BLGM	0	0	0	0	0	0	0	0	0	0	5	0	0	1	0	0	0	8	5	0
	0.0	0.0	0.0	0.0	0.0	0.0	0.0	0.0	0.0	0.0	3.0	0.0	0.0	0.6	0.0	0.0	0.0	4.9	3.0	0.0
3 BLGR	0	0	0	0	0	1	0	0	0	0	0	0	0	0	0	0	0	3	2	0
	0.0	0.0	0.0	0.0	0.0	0.5	0.0	0.0	0.0	0.0	0.0	0.0	0.0	0.0	0.0	0.0	0.0	1.5	1.0	0.0
4 CNDA	0	0	0	0	0	0	0	0	0	0	0	0	0	0	0	0	0	10	6	0
	0.0	0.0	0.0	0.0	0.0	0.0	0.0	0.0	0.0	0.0	0.0	0.0	0.0	0.0	0.0	0.0	0.0	7.8	4.7	0.0
5 CYPR	0	0	0	0	0	0	0	0	0	0	3	0	0	3	0	4	0	2	1	0
	0.0	0.0	0.0	0.0	0.0	0.0	0.0	0.0	0.0	0.0	2.5	0.0	0.0	2.5	0.0	3.3	0.0	1.6	0.8	0.0
6 CZCH	0	0	0	0	0	0	1	0	0	0	0	0	0	0	0	0	0	1	6	0
	0.0	0.0	0.0	0.0	0.0	0.0	0.4	0.0	0.0	0.0	0.0	0.0	0.0	0.0	0.0	0.0	0.0	0.4	2.4	0.0
7 DNMK	0	0	0	0	0	0	0	0	0	0	1	0	0	1	0	0	0	2	9	0
	0.0	0.0	0.0	0.0	0.0	0.0	0.0	0.0	0.0	0.0	0.5	0.0	0.0	0.5	0.0	0.0	0.0	1.1	4.8	0.0
8 FNLD	6	0	0	0	0	0	0	0	0	0	0	0	0	0	0	0	0	5	1	0
	2.4	0.0	0.0	0.0	0.0	0.0	0.0	0.0	0.0	0.0	0.0	0.0	0.0	0.0	0.0	0.0	0.0	2.0	0.4	0.0
9 FRNC	9	0	0	0	0	0	0	0	0	0	1	0	0	0	0	0	0	2	3	1
	10.5	0.0	0.0	0.0	0.0	0.0	0.0	0.0	0.0	0.0	1.2	0.0	0.0	0.0	0.0	0.0	0.0	2.3	3.5	1.2
10 FRG	0	0	0	0	0	0	0	0	0	0	4	0	0	0	0	0	0	1	13	4
	0.0	0.0	0.0	0.0	0.0	0.0	0.0	0.0	0.0	0.0	2.1	0.0	0.0	0.0	0.0	0.0	0.0	0.5	6.8	2.1
11 GDR	0	0	0	0	0	0	0	0	0	0	0	0	0	0	0	0	0	0	9	0
	0.0	0.0	0.0	0.0	0.0	0.0	0.0	0.0	0.0	0.0	0.0	0.0	0.0	0.0	0.0	0.0	0.0	0.0	3.7	0.0
12 GRCE	0	0	0	0	0	0	0	0	0	0	0	1	0	1	0	0	0	3	1	0
	0.0	0.0	0.0	0.0	0.0	0.0	0.0	0.0	0.0	0.0	0.0	1.8	0.0	1.8	0.0	0.0	0.0	5.5	1.8	0.0
13 HNGR	0	0	0	0	0	0	1	0	0	0	0	0	0	0	0	0	0	2	0	1
	0.0	0.0	0.0	0.0	0.0	0.0	0.4	0.0	0.0	0.0	0.0	0.0	0.0	0.0	0.0	0.0	0.0	0.8	0.0	0.4
14 ICLD	0	0	0	0	0	0	0	0	0	0	0	0	0	0	0	0	0	0	9	0
	0.0	0.0	0.0	0.0	0.0	0.0	0.0	0.0	0.0	0.0	0.0	0.0	0.0	0.0	0.0	0.0	0.0	0.0	10.7	0.0
15 IRLD	0	0	0	0	0	0	0	0	0	0	0	0	0	0	0	0	0	17	0	0
	0.0	0.0	0.0	0.0	0.0	0.0	0.0	0.0	0.0	0.0	0.0	0.0	0.0	0.0	0.0	0.0	0.0	8.1	0.0	0.0
16 ITLY	0	0	0	0	0	0	0	0	0	0	4	0	0	2	0	0	0	2	2	0
	0.0	0.0	0.0	0.0	0.0	0.0	0.0	0.0	0.0	0.0	3.1	0.0	0.0	1.5	0.0	0.0	0.0	1.5	1.5	0.0
17 LICH	0	0	0	0	0	0	0	0	0	0	0	0	0	0	0	0	0	1	0	0
	0.0	0.0	0.0	0.0	0.0	0.0	0.0	0.0	0.0	0.0	0.0	0.0	0.0	0.0	0.0	0.0	0.0	4.0	0.0	0.0

18	LXBG	0	0	0	0	0	0	0	0	0	0	4	0	0	0	0	0	0	0	2	0
		0.0	0.0	0.0	0.0	0.0	0.0	0.0	0.0	0.0	0.0	2.4	0.0	0.0	0.0	0.0	0.0	0.0	0.0	1.2	0.0
19	MLTA	0	0	0	0	0	0	3	0	0	0	23	1	4	3	15	12	5	1	0	0
		0.0	0.0	0.0	0.0	0.0	0.0	1.2	0.0	0.0	0.0	9.5	0.4	1.6	1.2	6.2	4.9	2.1	0.4	0.0	0.0
20	MNCO	2	12	3	0	0	0	0	0	0	0	0	0	0	0	0	0	0	0	2	0
		4.2	25.0	6.3	0.0	0.0	0.0	0.0	0.0	0.0	0.0	0.0	0.0	0.0	0.0	0.0	0.0	0.0	0.0	4.2	0.0
21	NTHL	0	0	0	0	0	0	0	0	0	0	4	0	0	0	0	0	0	16	13	0
		0.0	0.0	0.0	0.0	0.0	0.0	0.0	0.0	0.0	0.0	1.9	0.0	0.0	0.0	0.0	0.0	0.0	7.4	6.0	0.0
22	NRWY	0	0	8	0	0	0	0	0	0	0	0	0	0	0	0	0	0	5	9	0
		0.0	0.0	2.8	0.0	0.0	0.0	0.0	0.0	0.0	0.0	0.0	0.0	0.0	0.0	0.0	0.0	0.0	1.8	3.2	0.0
23	PLND	0	0	0	0	0	0	1	0	0	0	0	0	0	0	0	0	0	4	2	0
		0.0	0.0	0.0	0.0	0.0	0.0	0.5	0.0	0.0	0.0	0.0	0.0	0.0	0.0	0.0	0.0	0.0	1.9	1.0	0.0
24	PRTG	0	0	0	0	0	0	0	40	0	0	5	0	2	4	0	0	0	2	0	0
		0.0	0.0	0.0	0.0	0.0	0.0	0.0	14.2	0.0	0.0	1.8	0.0	0.7	1.4	0.0	0.0	0.0	0.7	0.0	0.0
25	RMNA	0	0	0	0	0	0	0	0	1	0	5	1	0	0	0	0	0	6	2	0
		0.0	0.0	0.0	0.0	0.0	0.0	0.0	0.0	0.2	0.0	1.2	0.2	0.0	0.0	0.0	0.0	0.0	1.4	0.5	0.0
26	SANM	0	0	0	0	0	0	1	0	0	0	0	0	0	0	0	0	0	0	1	0
		0.0	0.0	0.0	0.0	0.0	0.0	0.8	0.0	0.0	0.0	0.0	0.0	0.0	0.0	0.0	0.0	0.0	0.0	0.8	0.0
27	SPAN	0	0	0	0	0	0	3	3	0	0	1	0	0	1	0	0	0	0	0	0
		0.0	0.0	0.0	0.0	0.0	0.0	2.5	2.5	0.0	0.0	0.8	0.0	0.0	0.8	0.0	0.0	0.0	0.0	0.0	0.0
28	SWDN	1	0	0	0	0	0	0	0	0	0	0	0	0	0	0	0	0	0	3	0
		0.3	0.0	0.0	0.0	0.0	0.0	0.0	0.0	0.0	0.0	0.0	0.0	0.0	0.0	0.0	0.0	0.0	0.0	1.0	0.0
29	SWTZ	0	0	0	0	0	0	0	0	0	0	0	0	0	0	0	0	0	1	0	0
		0.0	0.0	0.0	0.0	0.0	0.0	0.0	0.0	0.0	0.0	0.0	0.0	0.0	0.0	0.0	0.0	0.0	0.4	0.0	0.0
30	TRKY	0	0	0	0	0	17	2	0	0	0	0	0	0	2	0	0	0	2	1	0
		0.0	0.0	0.0	0.0	0.0	9.4	1.1	0.0	0.0	0.0	0.0	0.0	0.0	1.1	0.0	0.0	0.0	1.1	0.6	0.0
31	USSR	0	0	0	0	0	9	0	0	0	0	0	0	0	0	0	0	0	4	1	0
		0.0	0.0	0.0	0.0	0.0	3.4	0.0	0.0	0.0	0.0	0.0	0.0	0.0	0.0	0.0	0.0	0.0	1.5	0.4	0.0
32	UK	0	0	0	0	0	0	0	0	0	0	0	0	0	0	0	0	0	3	2	0
		0.0	0.0	0.0	0.0	0.0	0.0	0.0	0.0	0.0	0.0	0.0	0.0	0.0	0.0	0.0	0.0	0.0	2.4	1.6	0.0
33	USA	0	0	0	0	0	0	0	0	0	0	0	0	0	0	0	0	0	1	1	0
		0.0	0.0	0.0	0.0	0.0	0.0	0.0	0.0	0.0	0.0	0.0	0.0	0.0	0.0	0.0	0.0	0.0	0.5	0.5	0.0
34	VATC	0	0	0	0	0	0	0	0	0	0	1	0	0	0	0	0	0	8	2	0
		0.0	0.0	0.0	0.0	0.0	0.0	0.0	0.0	0.0	0.0	0.6	0.0	0.0	0.0	0.0	0.0	0.0	4.5	1.1	0.0
35	YGSL	3	0	0	0	0	7	0	6	0	3	5	0	0	7	0	0	0	17	0	0
		0.6	0.0	0.0	0.0	0.0	1.3	0.0	1.1	0.0	0.6	0.9	0.0	0.0	1.3	0.0	0.0	0.0	3.1	0.0	0.0

Table A2.5. *(cont.)*

COUNTRIES	61	62	63	64	65	66	67	68	69	70	71	72	73	74	75	76	77	78	79	80
1 AUST	1	0	0	0	0	0	0	0	0	2	0	0	0	0	0	0	0	0	0	0
	0.7	0.0	0.0	0.0	0.0	0.0	0.0	0.0	0.0	1.4	0.0	0.0	0.0	0.0	0.0	0.0	0.0	0.0	0.0	0.0
2 BLGM	0	0	0	0	0	0	0	0	0	3	0	0	0	12	0	0	0	1	0	0
	0.0	0.0	0.0	0.0	0.0	0.0	0.0	0.0	0.0	1.8	0.0	0.0	0.0	7.3	0.0	0.0	0.0	0.6	0.0	0.0
3 BLGR	0	0	0	0	0	0	0	0	1	0	0	0	0	2	0	0	0	0	0	0
	0.0	0.0	0.0	0.0	0.0	0.0	0.0	0.0	0.5	0.0	0.0	0.0	0.0	1.0	0.0	0.0	0.0	0.0	0.0	0.0
4 CNDA	14	0	1	0	0	0	0	0	0	0	0	0	0	0	0	0	0	0	0	0
	10.9	0.0	0.8	0.0	0.0	0.0	0.0	0.0	0.0	0.0	0.0	0.0	0.0	0.0	0.0	0.0	0.0	0.0	0.0	0.0
5 CYPR	0	0	3	0	0	0	0	0	0	1	0	0	0	1	0	0	0	0	0	0
	0.0	0.0	2.5	0.0	0.0	0.0	0.0	0.0	0.0	0.8	0.0	0.0	0.0	0.8	0.0	0.0	0.0	0.0	0.0	0.0
6 CZCH	7	1	2	1	0	0	0	1	7	2	1	3	0	4	0	0	5	1	0	0
	2.9	0.4	0.8	0.4	0.0	0.0	0.0	0.4	2.9	0.8	0.4	1.2	0.0	1.6	0.0	0.0	2.0	0.4	0.0	0.0
7 DNMK	5	0	2	0	0	0	0	0	9	0	0	0	0	3	0	0	0	0	0	0
	2.7	0.0	1.1	0.0	0.0	0.0	0.0	0.0	4.8	0.0	0.0	0.0	0.0	1.6	0.0	0.0	0.0	0.0	0.0	0.0
8 FNLD	0	0	0	0	0	0	0	0	1	0	0	0	0	1	0	0	0	0	0	0
	0.0	0.0	0.0	0.0	0.0	0.0	0.0	0.0	0.4	0.0	0.0	0.0	0.0	0.4	0.0	0.0	0.0	0.0	0.0	0.0
9 FRNC	0	0	0	0	0	0	0	0	0	1	0	1	0	2	0	0	1	0	0	1
	0.0	0.0	0.0	0.0	0.0	0.0	0.0	0.0	0.0	1.2	0.0	1.2	0.0	2.3	0.0	0.0	1.2	0.0	0.0	1.2
10 FRG	4	4	4	4	0	0	0	0	5	7	0	1	0	2	0	4	0	0	3	0
	2.1	2.1	2.1	2.1	0.0	0.0	0.0	0.0	2.6	3.6	0.0	0.5	0.0	1.0	0.0	2.1	0.0	0.0	1.6	0.0
11 GDR	0	0	0	0	0	0	0	0	9	0	0	0	0	9	0	0	0	0	0	0
	0.0	0.0	0.0	0.0	0.0	0.0	0.0	0.0	3.7	0.0	0.0	0.0	0.0	3.7	0.0	0.0	0.0	0.0	0.0	0.0
12 GRCE	0	0	0	0	0	0	0	0	1	0	0	0	0	1	0	0	0	0	0	0
	0.0	0.0	0.0	0.0	0.0	0.0	0.0	0.0	1.8	0.0	0.0	0.0	0.0	1.8	0.0	0.0	0.0	0.0	0.0	0.0
13 HNGR	1	1	1	5	0	0	0	0	0	2	0	0	0	1	1	1	8	2	0	0
	0.4	0.4	0.4	2.0	0.0	0.0	0.0	0.0	0.0	0.8	0.0	0.0	0.0	0.4	0.4	0.4	3.1	0.8	0.0	0.0
14 ICLD	0	0	0	0	0	0	0	0	1	1	0	4	0	0	0	0	0	0	0	0
	0.0	0.0	0.0	0.0	0.0	0.0	0.0	0.0	1.2	1.2	0.0	4.8	0.0	0.0	0.0	0.0	0.0	0.0	0.0	0.0
15 IRLD	0	0	0	0	0	0	0	0	0	0	0	0	0	0	0	0	0	0	0	0
	0.0	0.0	0.0	0.0	0.0	0.0	0.0	0.0	0.0	0.0	0.0	0.0	0.0	0.0	0.0	0.0	0.0	0.0	0.0	0.0
16 ITLY	1	1	0	0	0	0	0	0	0	2	0	0	0	1	0	0	0	0	0	0
	0.8	0.8	0.0	0.0	0.0	0.0	0.0	0.0	0.0	1.5	0.0	0.0	0.0	0.8	0.0	0.0	0.0	0.0	0.0	0.0
17 LICH	0	0	0	0	0	0	0	0	0	0	0	0	0	0	0	0	0	0	0	0
	0.0	0.0	0.0	0.0	0.0	0.0	0.0	0.0	0.0	0.0	0.0	0.0	0.0	0.0	0.0	0.0	0.0	0.0	0.0	0.0

18	LXBG	0	0	1	0	0	0	0	1	1	7	0	0	0	1	0	2	0	0	0	0
		0.0	0.0	0.6	0.0	0.0	0.0	0.0	0.6	0.6	4.2	0.0	0.0	0.0	0.6	0.0	1.2	0.0	0.0	0.0	0.0
19	MLTA	0	0	0	0	0	0	0	0	1	5	4	0	0	0	0	2	0	1	0	0
		0.0	0.0	0.0	0.0	0.0	0.0	0.0	0.0	0.4	2.1	1.6	0.0	0.0	0.0	0.0	0.8	0.0	0.4	0.0	0.0
20	MNCO	0	0	0	0	0	0	0	0	0	0	0	0	0	0	0	0	0	0	0	0
		0.0	0.0	0.0	0.0	0.0	0.0	0.0	0.0	0.0	0.0	0.0	0.0	0.0	0.0	0.0	0.0	0.0	0.0	0.0	0.0
21	NTHL	0	0	0	0	0	0	0	0	3	3	0	0	0	0	0	0	0	0	0	0
		0.0	0.0	0.0	0.0	0.0	0.0	0.0	0.0	1.4	1.4	0.0	0.0	0.0	0.0	0.0	0.0	0.0	0.0	0.0	0.0
22	NRWY	3	3	3	0	0	0	0	0	3	0	0	0	0	3	0	0	0	0	0	0
		1.1	1.1	1.1	0.0	0.0	0.0	0.0	0.0	1.1	0.0	0.0	0.0	0.0	1.1	0.0	0.0	0.0	0.0	0.0	0.0
23	PLND	0	0	0	0	0	0	0	0	1	2	0	0	0	2	0	0	0	0	0	0
		0.0	0.0	0.0	0.0	0.0	0.0	0.0	0.0	0.5	1.0	0.0	0.0	0.0	1.0	0.0	0.0	0.0	0.0	0.0	0.0
24	PRTG	0	0	0	0	0	0	0	0	5	0	0	0	0	2	0	0	0	0	0	0
		0.0	0.0	0.0	0.0	0.0	0.0	0.0	0.0	1.8	0.0	0.0	0.0	0.0	0.7	0.0	0.0	0.0	0.0	0.0	0.0
25	RMNA	0	0	0	0	0	0	0	0	0	0	0	0	0	4	1	0	0	0	0	0
		0.0	0.0	0.0	0.0	0.0	0.0	0.0	0.0	0.0	0.0	0.0	0.0	0.0	1.0	0.2	0.0	0.0	0.0	0.0	0.0
26	SANM	0	0	0	0	0	0	0	0	0	0	0	0	0	1	0	0	1	0	0	0
		0.0	0.0	0.0	0.0	0.0	0.0	0.0	0.0	0.0	0.0	0.0	0.0	0.0	0.8	0.0	0.0	0.8	0.0	0.0	0.0
27	SPAN	0	0	0	0	0	0	0	0	0	0	0	0	0	1	0	0	0	0	0	0
		0.0	0.0	0.0	0.0	0.0	0.0	0.0	0.0	0.0	0.0	0.0	0.0	0.0	0.8	0.0	0.0	0.0	0.0	0.0	0.0
28	SWDN	1	0	0	0	0	0	0	0	3	0	0	3	0	8	0	0	0	0	0	0
		0.3	0.0	0.0	0.0	0.0	0.0	0.0	0.0	1.0	0.0	0.0	1.0	0.0	2.7	0.0	0.0	0.0	0.0	0.0	0.0
29	SWTZ	2	2	0	0	0	0	0	0	5	0	0	0	0	0	0	0	0	0	0	0
		0.9	0.9	0.0	0.0	0.0	0.0	0.0	0.0	2.2	0.0	0.0	0.0	0.0	0.0	0.0	0.0	0.0	0.0	0.0	0.0
30	TRKY	0	0	0	0	0	0	0	0	0	0	1	0	0	1	0	0	0	0	0	0
		0.0	0.0	0.0	0.0	0.0	0.0	0.0	0.0	0.0	0.0	0.6	0.0	0.0	0.6	0.0	0.0	0.0	0.0	0.0	0.0
31	USSR	0	0	6	0	0	0	0	0	0	5	5	0	0	0	0	0	0	0	0	0
		0.0	0.0	2.3	0.0	0.0	0.0	0.0	0.0	0.0	1.9	1.9	0.0	0.0	0.0	0.0	0.0	0.0	0.0	0.0	0.0
32	UK	0	0	0	0	0	0	1	0	0	1	0	0	0	0	0	0	0	0	0	0
		0.0	0.0	0.0	0.0	0.0	0.0	0.8	0.0	0.0	0.8	0.0	0.0	0.0	0.0	0.0	0.0	0.0	0.0	0.0	0.0
33	USA	12	1	8	0	0	0	0	0	0	8	0	1	0	0	0	1	2	0	0	1
		5.8	0.5	3.8	0.0	0.0	0.0	0.0	0.0	0.0	3.8	0.0	0.5	0.0	0.0	0.0	0.5	1.0	0.0	0.0	0.5
34	VATC	4	0	9	0	0	0	0	0	2	2	0	0	0	1	0	0	0	0	0	1
		2.2	0.0	5.1	0.0	0.0	0.0	0.0	0.0	1.1	1.1	0.0	0.0	0.0	0.6	0.0	0.0	0.0	0.0	0.0	0.6
35	YGSL	1	0	0	0	0	0	0	0	4	0	0	0	1	18	0	0	5	0	0	23
		0.2	0.0	0.0	0.0	0.0	0.0	0.0	0.0	0.7	0.0	0.0	0.0	0.2	3.3	0.0	0.0	0.9	0.0	0.0	4.2

Table A2.5. *(cont.)*

	COUNTRIES	81	82	83	84	85	86	87	88	89	90	91	92	93	94	95	96	97	98	99	100
1	AUST	0	0	0	0	0	0	0	0	0	0	0	0	0	0	8	0	8	1	1	0
		0.0	0.0	0.0	0.0	0.0	0.0	0.0	0.0	0.0	0.0	0.0	0.0	0.0	0.0	5.6	0.0	5.6	0.7	0.7	0.0
2	BLGM	0	11	0	0	0	0	0	0	0	0	0	0	0	0	0	0	0	17	5	0
		0.0	6.7	0.0	0.0	0.0	0.0	0.0	0.0	0.0	0.0	0.0	0.0	0.0	0.0	0.0	0.0	0.0	10.4	3.0	0.0
3	BLGR	0	0	0	0	0	0	0	0	0	0	0	0	0	0	1	0	6	0	1	0
		0.0	0.0	0.0	0.0	0.0	0.0	0.0	0.0	0.0	0.0	0.0	0.0	0.0	0.0	0.5	0.0	3.0	0.0	0.5	0.0
4	CNDA	0	0	0	0	0	0	0	0	0	0	0	0	0	0	0	0	0	0	0	0
		0.0	0.0	0.0	0.0	0.0	0.0	0.0	0.0	0.0	0.0	0.0	0.0	0.0	0.0	0.0	0.0	0.0	0.0	0.0	0.0
5	CYPR	0	1	0	0	0	0	0	0	0	0	0	0	0	0	0	0	1	0	9	0
		0.0	0.8	0.0	0.0	0.0	0.0	0.0	0.0	0.0	0.0	0.0	0.0	0.0	0.0	0.0	0.0	0.8	0.0	7.4	0.0
6	CZCH	0	3	0	0	0	0	0	0	0	0	0	0	0	0	0	0	25	6	2	0
		0.0	1.2	0.0	0.0	0.0	0.0	0.0	0.0	0.0	0.0	0.0	0.0	0.0	0.0	0.0	0.0	10.2	2.4	0.8	0.0
7	DNMK	0	3	0	0	0	0	0	0	0	0	0	0	0	0	0	0	8	6	10	0
		0.0	1.6	0.0	0.0	0.0	0.0	0.0	0.0	0.0	0.0	0.0	0.0	0.0	0.0	0.0	0.0	4.3	3.2	5.3	0.0
8	FNLD	0	1	0	0	0	0	0	0	0	0	0	0	0	0	0	0	4	1	7	0
		0.0	0.4	0.0	0.0	0.0	0.0	0.0	0.0	0.0	0.0	0.0	0.0	0.0	0.0	0.0	0.0	1.6	0.4	2.8	0.0
9	FRNC	0	0	0	0	0	0	0	1	0	0	0	0	0	0	0	0	0	0	0	0
		0.0	0.0	0.0	0.0	0.0	0.0	0.0	1.2	0.0	0.0	0.0	0.0	0.0	0.0	0.0	0.0	0.0	0.0	0.0	0.0
10	FRG	0	0	0	0	0	0	0	0	0	0	0	0	0	0	2	0	4	1	4	1
		0.0	0.0	0.0	0.0	0.0	0.0	0.0	0.0	0.0	0.0	0.0	0.0	0.0	0.0	1.0	0.0	2.1	0.5	2.1	0.5
11	GDR	0	8	0	0	0	0	0	0	0	0	0	0	0	0	0	0	25	1	1	0
		0.0	3.3	0.0	0.0	0.0	0.0	0.0	0.0	0.0	0.0	0.0	0.0	0.0	0.0	0.0	0.0	10.3	0.4	0.4	0.0
12	GRCE	0	1	0	0	0	0	0	0	0	0	0	0	0	0	0	0	1	0	0	0
		0.0	1.8	0.0	0.0	0.0	0.0	0.0	0.0	0.0	0.0	0.0	0.0	0.0	0.0	0.0	0.0	1.8	0.0	0.0	0.0
13	HNGR	0	0	0	0	0	0	0	0	0	0	0	0	0	0	0	0	9	1	1	0
		0.0	0.0	0.0	0.0	0.0	0.0	0.0	0.0	0.0	0.0	0.0	0.0	0.0	0.0	0.0	0.0	3.5	0.4	0.4	0.0
14	ICLD	0	0	0	0	0	0	0	0	0	0	0	0	0	0	0	0	1	1	7	0
		0.0	0.0	0.0	0.0	0.0	0.0	0.0	0.0	0.0	0.0	0.0	0.0	0.0	0.0	0.0	0.0	1.2	1.2	8.3	0.0
15	IRLD	0	0	0	0	0	0	0	0	0	0	0	0	0	0	0	0	11	2	3	0
		0.0	0.0	0.0	0.0	0.0	0.0	0.0	0.0	0.0	0.0	0.0	0.0	0.0	0.0	0.0	0.0	5.2	1.0	1.4	0.0
16	ITLY	0	1	0	0	0	0	0	0	0	0	0	0	0	0	0	0	2	3	0	0
		0.0	0.8	0.0	0.0	0.0	0.0	0.0	0.0	0.0	0.0	0.0	0.0	0.0	0.0	0.0	0.0	1.5	2.3	0.0	0.0
17	LICH	0	0	0	0	0	0	0	0	0	0	0	0	0	0	0	0	0	0	0	0
		0.0	0.0	0.0	0.0	0.0	0.0	0.0	0.0	0.0	0.0	0.0	0.0	0.0	0.0	0.0	0.0	0.0	0.0	0.0	0.0

18	LXBG	0	1	0	2	0	0	0	0	0	0	0	0	0	0	0	0	4	6	12	0
		0.0	0.6	0.0	1.2	0.0	0.0	0.0	0.0	0.0	0.0	0.0	0.0	0.0	0.0	0.0	0.0	2.4	3.6	7.2	0.0
19	MLTA	0	0	0	0	0	4	0	0	0	0	0	0	0	0	0	0	7	9	16	0
		0.0	0.0	0.0	0.0	0.0	1.6	0.0	0.0	0.0	0.0	0.0	0.0	0.0	0.0	0.0	0.0	2.9	3.7	6.6	0.0
20	MNCO	0	0	0	0	0	0	0	0	0	0	0	0	0	0	0	0	0	0	0	0
		0.0	0.0	0.0	0.0	0.0	0.0	0.0	0.0	0.0	0.0	0.0	0.0	0.0	0.0	0.0	0.0	0.0	0.0	0.0	0.0
21	NTHL	0	0	0	0	0	0	0	0	0	0	0	0	0	0	0	0	3	5	2	0
		0.0	0.0	0.0	0.0	0.0	0.0	0.0	0.0	0.0	0.0	0.0	0.0	0.0	0.0	0.0	0.0	1.4	2.3	0.9	0.0
22	NRWY	0	0	0	0	0	0	0	0	0	0	0	0	0	0	0	0	8	0	3	0
		0.0	0.0	0.0	0.0	0.0	0.0	0.0	0.0	0.0	0.0	0.0	0.0	0.0	0.0	0.0	0.0	2.8	0.0	1.1	0.0
23	PLND	0	2	0	0	0	0	0	0	0	0	0	0	0	0	0	0	1	1	2	0
		0.0	1.0	0.0	0.0	0.0	0.0	0.0	0.0	0.0	0.0	0.0	0.0	0.0	0.0	0.0	0.0	0.5	0.5	1.0	0.0
24	PRTG	0	2	0	0	0	0	0	0	0	0	0	0	0	0	0	0	5	10	20	0
		0.0	0.7	0.0	0.0	0.0	0.0	0.0	0.0	0.0	0.0	0.0	0.0	0.0	0.0	0.0	0.0	1.8	3.6	7.1	0.0
25	RMNA	0	1	0	0	0	0	0	0	0	0	0	0	0	0	0	0	10	0	6	0
		0.0	0.2	0.0	0.0	0.0	0.0	0.0	0.0	0.0	0.0	0.0	0.0	0.0	0.0	0.0	0.0	2.4	0.0	1.4	0.0
26	SANM	0	0	0	1	0	0	0	0	0	0	0	0	0	0	0	0	2	0	0	0
		0.0	0.0	0.0	0.8	0.0	0.0	0.0	0.0	0.0	0.0	0.0	0.0	0.0	0.0	0.0	0.0	1.7	0.0	0.0	0.0
27	SPAN	0	0	0	0	0	0	0	0	0	0	0	0	0	0	0	0	1	1	0	0
		0.0	0.0	0.0	0.0	0.0	0.0	0.0	0.0	0.0	0.0	0.0	0.0	0.0	0.0	0.0	0.0	0.8	0.8	0.0	0.0
28	SWDN	0	0	0	0	0	0	0	0	0	0	0	0	0	0	0	0	11	1	3	0
		0.0	0.0	0.0	0.0	0.0	0.0	0.0	0.0	0.0	0.0	0.0	0.0	0.0	0.0	0.0	0.0	3.7	0.3	1.0	0.0
29	SWTZ	0	0	0	0	0	0	0	0	0	1	0	0	0	0	0	0	4	0	4	1
		0.0	0.0	0.0	0.0	0.0	0.0	0.0	0.0	0.0	0.4	0.0	0.0	0.0	0.0	0.0	0.0	1.7	0.0	1.7	0.4
30	TRKY	0	1	0	0	0	0	0	0	0	0	0	0	0	0	2	0	4	0	11	0
		0.0	0.6	0.0	0.0	0.0	0.0	0.0	0.0	0.0	0.0	0.0	0.0	0.0	0.0	1.1	0.0	2.2	0.0	6.1	0.0
31	USSR	0	0	0	1	0	7	1	0	0	0	0	0	0	0	9	0	11	4	3	0
		0.0	0.0	0.0	0.4	0.0	2.6	0.4	0.0	0.0	0.0	0.0	0.0	0.0	0.0	3.4	0.0	4.1	1.5	1.1	0.0
32	UK	0	0	0	0	0	0	0	0	0	0	0	0	0	0	6	0	0	6	10	0
		0.0	0.0	0.0	0.0	0.0	0.0	0.0	0.0	0.0	0.0	0.0	0.0	0.0	0.0	4.8	0.0	0.0	4.8	8.1	0.0
33	USA	0	0	0	7	0	0	0	1	0	0	0	0	0	0	0	0	0	2	4	0
		0.0	0.0	0.0	3.4	0.0	0.0	0.0	0.5	0.0	0.0	0.0	0.0	0.0	0.0	0.0	0.0	0.0	1.0	1.9	0.0
34	VATC	0	1	0	0	0	0	0	1	0	0	0	0	0	0	0	4	1	1	0	0
		0.0	0.6	0.0	0.0	0.0	0.0	0.0	0.6	0.0	0.0	0.0	0.0	0.0	0.0	0.0	2.2	0.6	0.6	0.0	0.0
35	YGSL	0	0	4	0	0	1	1	19	0	0	0	0	0	0	0	0	7	0	16	1
		0.0	0.0	0.7	0.0	0.0	0.2	0.2	3.5	0.0	0.0	0.0	0.0	0.0	0.0	0.0	0.0	1.3	0.0	2.9	0.2

Table A2.5. *(cont.)*

COUNTRIES	101	102	103	104	105	106	107	108	109	110	111	112	113	114	115	116	117	118	119	120
1 AUST	1	1	1	4	0	0	0	6	0	0	0	2	0	1	0	1	2	0	0	1
	0.7	0.7	0.7	2.8	0.0	0.0	0.0	4.2	0.0	0.0	0.0	1.4	0.0	0.7	0.0	0.7	1.4	0.0	0.0	0.7
2 BLGM	0	0	2	0	0	0	0	1	0	0	0	0	2	0	0	0	2	0	4	0
	0.0	0.0	1.2	0.0	0.0	0.0	0.0	0.6	0.0	0.0	0.0	0.0	1.2	0.0	0.0	0.0	1.2	0.0	2.4	0.0
3 BLGR	0	0	16	2	0	0	0	4	0	0	0	1	1	0	0	0	0	0	7	4
	0.0	0.0	7.9	1.0	0.0	0.0	0.0	2.0	0.0	0.0	0.0	0.5	0.5	0.0	0.0	0.0	0.0	0.0	3.5	2.0
4 CNDA	0	0	0	3	0	0	0	1	0	0	0	5	4	3	0	0	5	0	3	2
	0.0	0.0	0.0	2.3	0.0	0.0	0.0	0.8	0.0	0.0	0.0	3.9	3.1	2.3	0.0	0.0	3.9	0.0	2.3	1.6
5 CYPR	0	0	6	1	0	0	0	1	0	0	1	1	0	1	0	1	2	2	3	0
	0.0	0.0	4.9	0.8	0.0	0.0	0.0	0.8	0.0	0.0	0.8	0.8	0.0	0.8	0.0	0.8	1.6	1.6	2.5	0.0
6 CZCH	0	0	5	2	0	0	0	0	0	0	0	0	0	1	0	0	0	0	18	1
	0.0	0.0	2.0	0.8	0.0	0.0	0.0	0.0	0.0	0.0	0.0	0.0	0.0	0.4	0.0	0.0	0.0	0.0	7.3	0.4
7 DNMK	0	0	0	4	0	0	0	4	0	0	0	0	2	0	0	0	5	3	0	0
	0.0	0.0	0.0	2.1	0.0	0.0	0.0	2.1	0.0	0.0	0.0	0.0	1.1	0.0	0.0	0.0	2.7	1.6	0.0	0.0
8 FNLD	7	6	2	9	0	0	0	2	0	0	0	6	0	0	0	0	0	0	0	0
	2.8	2.4	0.8	3.6	0.0	0.0	0.0	0.8	0.0	0.0	0.0	2.4	0.0	0.0	0.0	0.0	0.0	0.0	0.0	0.0
9 FRNC	0	0	0	5	0	0	0	4	0	0	0	3	5	1	1	0	1	0	0	2
	0.0	0.0	0.0	5.8	0.0	0.0	0.0	4.7	0.0	0.0	0.0	3.5	5.8	1.2	1.2	0.0	1.2	0.0	0.0	2.3
10 FRG	0	0	8	4	0	2	0	3	1	0	0	0	1	1	0	0	3	0	13	3
	0.0	0.0	4.2	2.1	0.0	1.0	0.0	1.6	0.5	0.0	0.0	0.0	0.5	0.5	0.0	0.0	1.6	0.0	6.8	1.6
11 GDR	0	0	10	1	0	0	0	0	0	0	0	0	0	2	0	1	0	0	32	2
	0.0	0.0	4.1	0.4	0.0	0.0	0.0	0.0	0.0	0.0	0.0	0.0	0.0	0.8	0.0	0.4	0.0	0.0	13.2	0.8
12 GRCE	0	0	0	0	0	0	0	0	0	0	0	0	0	0	0	0	0	0	0	0
	0.0	0.0	0.0	0.0	0.0	0.0	0.0	0.0	0.0	0.0	0.0	0.0	0.0	0.0	0.0	0.0	0.0	0.0	0.0	0.0
13 HNGR	6	0	15	11	0	0	0	2	1	0	0	2	0	0	0	0	0	0	3	0
	2.4	0.0	5.9	4.3	0.0	0.0	0.0	0.8	0.4	0.0	0.0	0.8	0.0	0.0	0.0	0.0	0.0	0.0	1.2	0.0
14 ICLD	0	0	2	0	0	0	0	0	0	1	0	0	0	0	0	0	0	0	0	3
	0.0	0.0	2.4	0.0	0.0	0.0	0.0	0.0	0.0	1.2	0.0	0.0	0.0	0.0	0.0	0.0	0.0	0.0	0.0	3.6
15 IRLD	0	0	0	5	0	0	0	1	0	0	2	1	3	0	0	0	0	1	3	4
	0.0	0.0	0.0	2.4	0.0	0.0	0.0	0.5	0.0	0.0	1.0	0.5	1.4	0.0	0.0	0.0	0.0	0.5	1.4	1.9
16 ITLY	0	0	6	7	0	2	0	2	0	0	0	0	1	0	0	0	0	0	2	7
	0.0	0.0	4.6	5.3	0.0	1.5	0.0	1.5	0.0	0.0	0.0	0.0	0.8	0.0	0.0	0.0	0.0	0.0	1.5	5.3
17 LICH	0	0	2	3	0	0	1	0	0	0	0	0	1	0	0	0	0	0	0	0
	0.0	0.0	8.0	12.0	0.0	0.0	4.0	0.0	0.0	0.0	0.0	0.0	4.0	0.0	0.0	0.0	0.0	0.0	0.0	0.0

18	LXBG	0	0	1	2	0	0	3	8	0	0	0	0	1	0	0	0	0	0	0	2
		0.0	0.0	0.6	1.2	0.0	0.0	1.8	4.8	0.0	0.0	0.0	0.0	0.6	0.0	0.0	0.0	0.0	0.0	0.0	1.2
19	MLTA	6	1	10	7	0	1	0	0	1	0	0	1	0	0	0	1	3	1	12	0
		2.5	0.4	4.1	2.9	0.0	0.4	0.0	0.0	0.4	0.0	0.0	0.4	0.0	0.0	0.0	0.4	1.2	0.4	4.9	0.0
20	MNCO	0	0	6	2	0	0	0	0	0	0	0	0	0	0	0	0	0	0	1	0
		0.0	0.0	12.5	4.2	0.0	0.0	0.0	0.0	0.0	0.0	0.0	0.0	0.0	0.0	0.0	0.0	0.0	0.0	2.1	0.0
21	NTHL	0	0	8	0	1	0	0	0	0	12	3	2	0	0	0	0	2	1	0	0
		0.0	0.0	3.7	0.0	0.5	0.0	0.0	0.0	0.0	5.6	1.4	0.9	0.0	0.0	0.0	0.0	0.9	0.5	0.0	0.0
22	NRWY	3	3	2	2	0	2	0	0	0	0	0	3	1	4	0	0	0	1	2	4
		1.1	1.1	0.7	0.7	0.0	0.7	0.0	0.0	0.0	0.0	0.0	1.1	0.4	1.4	0.0	0.0	0.0	0.4	0.7	1.4
23	PLND	0	0	21	2	0	0	0	2	3	3	1	0	0	0	0	7	0	0	15	0
		0.0	0.0	10.2	1.0	0.0	0.0	0.0	1.0	1.5	1.5	0.5	0.0	0.0	0.0	0.0	3.4	0.0	0.0	7.3	0.0
24	PRTG	4	4	6	4	0	7	0	0	1	1	0	3	0	2	0	0	3	5	4	5
		1.4	1.4	2.1	1.4	0.0	2.5	0.0	0.0	0.4	0.4	0.0	1.1	0.0	0.7	0.0	0.0	1.1	1.8	1.4	1.8
25	RMNA	5	0	9	0	0	0	0	1	0	1	1	5	0	2	0	0	9	2	3	1
		1.2	0.0	2.1	0.0	0.0	0.0	0.0	0.2	0.0	0.2	0.2	1.2	0.0	0.5	0.0	0.0	2.1	0.5	0.7	0.2
26	SANM	0	3	4	0	0	7	0	0	6	0	0	1	0	0	0	0	0	0	1	0
		0.0	2.5	3.3	0.0	0.0	5.8	0.0	0.0	5.0	0.0	0.0	0.8	0.0	0.0	0.0	0.0	0.0	0.0	0.8	0.0
27	SPAN	5	0	2	2	0	0	0	0	8	2	0	0	1	0	0	0	1	1	1	4
		4.1	0.0	1.6	1.6	0.0	0.0	0.0	0.0	6.6	1.6	0.0	0.0	0.8	0.0	0.0	0.0	0.8	0.8	0.8	3.3
28	SWDN	5	2	5	3	0	1	0	2	1	0	1	9	0	1	5	0	0	5	10	5
		1.7	0.7	1.7	1.0	0.0	0.3	0.0	0.7	0.3	0.0	0.3	3.1	0.0	0.3	1.7	0.0	0.0	1.7	3.4	1.7
29	SWTZ	1	1	6	1	1	8	1	18	4	1	3	2	5	0	0	0	0	0	1	1
		0.4	0.4	2.6	0.4	0.4	3.5	0.4	7.8	1.7	0.4	1.3	0.9	2.2	0.0	0.0	0.0	0.0	0.0	0.4	0.4
30	TRKY	0	0	2	4	0	0	0	2	0	1	1	1	0	0	0	0	12	1	5	3
		0.0	0.0	1.1	2.2	0.0	0.0	0.0	1.1	0.0	0.6	0.6	0.6	0.0	0.0	0.0	0.0	6.6	0.6	2.8	1.7
31	USSR	6	0	18	5	0	2	0	1	1	1	0	0	0	6	0	2	0	0	10	1
		2.3	0.0	6.8	1.9	0.0	0.8	0.0	0.4	0.4	0.4	0.0	0.0	0.0	2.3	0.0	0.8	0.0	0.0	3.8	0.4
32	UK	3	3	4	2	0	0	0	0	0	0	0	3	3	0	0	0	0	0	3	1
		2.4	2.4	3.2	1.6	0.0	0.0	0.0	0.0	0.0	0.0	0.0	2.4	2.4	0.0	0.0	0.0	0.0	0.0	2.4	0.8
33	USA	0	0	8	6	0	0	0	2	2	5	5	1	1	0	0	0	0	0	18	0
		0.0	0.0	3.8	2.9	0.0	0.0	0.0	1.0	1.0	2.4	24	0.5	0.5	0.0	0.0	0.0	0.0	0.0	8.7	0.0
34	VATC	0	0	10	2	0	0	0	1	6	3	3	1	1	0	33	0	0	0	0	0
		0.0	0.0	5.6	1.1	0.0	0.0	0.0	0.6	3.4	1.7	1.7	0.6	0.6	0.0	18.5	0.0	0.0	0.0	0.0	0.0
35	YGSL	8	0	4	0	0	0	0	1	2	0	0	4	1	3	0	1	8	5	22	5
		1.5	0.0	0.7	0.0	0.0	0.0	0.0	0.2	0.4	0.0	0.0	0.7	0.2	0.6	0.0	0.2	1.5	0.9	4.0	0.9

Table A2.6. Category Scores and Percentages: The Belgrade Closing Statements

COUNTRIES		1	2	3	4	5	6	7	8	9	10	11	12	13	14	15	16	17	18	19	20
1	AUST	7	5	0	0	0	0	0	0	8	0	6	0	0	2	0	3	7	0	6	0
		11.5	8.2	0.0	0.0	0.0	0.0	0.0	0.0	13.1	0.0	9.8	0.0	0.0	3.3	0.0	4.9	11.5	0.0	9.8	0.0
2	BLGM	1	5	0	0	0	0	0	1	12	0	2	0	0	5	0	3	1	0	2	7
		1.9	9.4	0.0	0.0	0.0	0.0	0.0	1.9	22.6	0.0	3.8	0.0	0.0	9.4	0.0	5.7	1.9	0.0	3.8	13.2
3	BLGR	3	1	1	0	0	0	0	0	6	0	13	0	0	2	0	22	5	0	13	1
		2.9	1.0	1.0	0.0	0.0	0.0	0.0	0.0	5.7	0.0	12.4	0.0	0.0	1.9	0.0	21.0	4.8	0.0	12.4	1.0
4	CNDA	7	0	0	0	0	0	0	1	25	1	6	0	0	1	3	12	7	0	6	1
		6.1	0.0	0.0	0.0	0.0	0.0	0.0	0.9	21.7	0.9	5.2	0.0	0.0	0.9	2.6	10.4	6.1	0.0	5.2	0.9
5	CYPR	1	4	1	1	0	1	2	0	3	0	10	1	0	4	0	0	1	0	10	0
		1.7	6.8	1.7	1.7	0.0	1.7	3.4	0.0	5.1	0.0	16.9	1.7	0.0	6.8	0.0	0.0	1.7	0.0	16.9	0.0
6	CZCH	1	5	0	0	0	0	0	2	12	0	1	0	0	1	0	9	9	0	1	3
		1.5	7.6	0.0	0.0	0.0	0.0	0.0	3.0	18.2	0.0	1.5	0.0	0.0	1.5	0.0	13.6	13.6	0.0	1.5	4.5
7	DNMK	1	1	0	0	0	0	0	2	5	0	1	0	0	4	0	12	1	0	1	2
		1.0	1.0	0.0	0.0	0.0	0.0	0.0	2.0	4.9	0.0	1.0	0.0	0.0	3.9	0.0	11.8	1.0	0.0	1.0	2.0
8	FNLD	3	0	0	0	0	0	0	0	0	0	5	0	0	17	0	9	3	0	5	2
		3.7	0.0	0.0	0.0	0.0	0.0	0.0	0.0	0.0	0.0	6.3	0.0	0.0	21.2	0.0	11.2	3.7	0.0	6.3	2.5
9	FRNC	6	0	0	0	0	0	0	0	6	0	1	0	0	1	0	10	5	0	2	0
		9.4	0.0	0.0	0.0	0.0	0.0	0.0	0.0	9.4	0.0	1.6	0.0	0.0	1.6	0.0	15.6	7.8	0.0	3.1	0.0
10	FRG	0	4	0	0	0	0	3	0	11	1	8	0	0	2	0	0	3	0	8	4
		0.0	4.2	0.0	0.0	0.0	0.0	3.2	0.0	11.6	1.1	8.4	0.0	0.0	2.1	0.0	0.0	3.2	0.0	8.4	4.2
11	GDR	8	1	8	0	0	0	0	4	10	0	3	0	0	3	0	30	30	0	3	3
		4.6	0.6	4.6	0.0	0.0	0.0	0.0	2.3	5.8	0.0	1.7	0.0	0.0	1.7	0.0	17.3	17.3	0.0	1.7	1.7
12	GRCE	1	3	0	0	0	0	1	0	1	0	5	0	0	0	0	0	1	0	5	0
		5.6	16.7	0.0	0.0	0.0	0.0	5.6	0.0	5.6	0.0	27.8	0.0	0.0	0.0	0.0	0.0	5.6	0.0	27.8	0.0
13	HNGR	8	10	0	0	0	0	0	8	6	0	11	0	0	3	0	7	8	0	11	1
		6.2	7.7	0.0	0.0	0.0	0.0	0.0	6.2	4.6	0.0	8.5	0.0	0.0	2.3	0.0	5.4	6.2	0.0	8.5	0.8
14	ICLD	0	0	0	0	0	0	0	0	1	0	2	0	0	0	0	2	0	0	2	0
		0.0	0.0	0.0	0.0	0.0	0.0	0.0	0.0	12.5	0.0	25.0	0.0	0.0	0.0	0.0	25.0	0.0	0.0	25.0	0.0
15	IRLD	2	6	0	0	0	0	0	1	17	0	5	0	0	2	0	0	2	0	7	0
		3.3	10.0	0.0	0.0	0.0	0.0	0.0	1.7	28.3	0.0	8.3	0.0	0.0	3.3	0.0	0.0	3.3	0.0	11.7	0.0
16	ITLY	2	0	0	0	0	0	1	1	14	0	8	0	0	2	0	4	3	0	8	1
		2.4	0.0	0.0	0.0	0.0	0.0	1.2	1.2	17.1	0.0	9.8	0.0	0.0	2.4	0.0	4.9	3.7	0.0	9.8	1.2
17	LICH	0	0	0	0	0	0	0	0	0	0	0	0	0	0	0	0	0	0	4	0
		0.0	0.0	0.0	0.0	0.0	0.0	0.0	0.0	0.0	0.0	0.0	0.0	0.0	0.0	0.0	0.0	0.0	0.0	50.0	0.0

18	LXBG	0	1	0	0	0	0	0	2	6	0	1	0	0	0	0	12	0	0	1	0
		0.0	2.3	0.0	0.0	0.0	0.0	0.0	4.5	13.6	0.0	2.3	0.0	0.0	0.0	0.0	27.3	0.0	0.0	2.3	0.0
19	MLTA	1	0	0	0	0	0	0	0	1	0	2	0	0	0	0	0	1	0	2	0
		3.7	0.0	0.0	0.0	0.0	0.0	0.0	0.0	3.7	0.0	7.4	0.0	0.0	0.0	0.0	0.0	3.7	0.0	7.4	0.0
20	MNCO	1	0	0	0	0	0	0	0	0	0	1	0	0	0	0	0	1	0	1	1
		9.1	0.0	0.0	0.0	0.0	0.0	0.0	0.0	0.0	0.0	9.1	0.0	0.0	0.0	0.0	0.0	9.1	0.0	9.1	9.1
21	NTHL	0	2	0	0	0	0	0	0	6	0	0	0	0	0	0	0	0	0	0	0
		0.0	11.8	0.0	0.0	0.0	0.0	0.0	0.0	35.3	0.0	0.0	0.0	0.0	0.0	0.0	0.0	0.0	0.0	0.0	0.0
22	NRWY	1	5	0	0	0	0	0	0	4	0	2	0	0	1	0	2	1	0	3	0
		3.3	16.7	0.0	0.0	0.0	0.0	0.0	0.0	13.3	0.0	6.7	0.0	0.0	3.3	0.0	6.7	3.3	0.0	10.0	0.0
23	PLND	16	8	1	0	0	0	0	1	8	0	18	0	0	5	0	40	16	0	26	3
		5.9	2.9	0.4	0.0	0.0	0.0	0.0	0.4	2.9	0.0	6.6	0.0	0.0	1.8	0.0	14.7	5.9	0.0	9.5	1.1
24	PRTG	2	1	0	0	0	0	0	0	0	0	3	0	0	1	0	0	2	0	3	1
		7.1	3.6	0.0	0.0	0.0	0.0	0.0	0.0	0.0	0.0	10.7	0.0	0.0	3.6	0.0	0.0	7.1	0.0	10.7	3.6
25	RMNA	8	1	0	0	0	0	0	0	0	0	9	0	0	9	0	11	8	0	9	3
		11.8	1.5	0.0	0.0	0.0	0.0	0.0	0.0	0.0	0.0	13.2	0.0	0.0	13.2	0.0	16.2	11.8	0.0	13.2	4.4
26	SANM	5	2	0	0	0	0	4	1	16	0	5	0	0	1	0	8	5	0	5	0
		5.6	2.2	0.0	0.0	0.0	0.0	4.4	1.1	17.8	0.0	5.6	0.0	0.0	1.1	0.0	8.9	5.6	0.0	5.6	0.0
27	SPAN	3	1	0	0	0	0	0	0	8	0	7	0	0	5	0	9	3	0	9	0
		3.3	1.1	0.0	0.0	0.0	0.0	0.0	0.0	8.7	0.0	7.6	0.0	0.0	5.4	0.0	9.8	3.3	0.0	9.8	0.0
28	SWDN	2	4	1	0	0	0	0	2	9	0	6	0	0	3	1	4	2	0	8	0
		3.1	6.3	1.6	0.0	0.0	0.0	0.0	3.1	14.1	0.0	9.4	0.0	0.0	4.7	1.6	6.3	3.1	0.0	12.5	0.0
29	SWTZ	3	0	0	0	0	0	2	1	10	0	2	0	0	1	0	1	3	0	2	2
		7.1	0.0	0.0	0.0	0.0	0.0	4.8	2.4	23.8	0.0	4.8	0.0	0.0	2.4	0.0	2.4	7.1	0.0	4.8	4.8
30	TRKY	0	2	4	0	0	1	2	0	1	0	8	0	0	2	0	0	0	0	10	0
		0.0	3.3	6.7	0.0	0.0	1.7	3.3	0.0	1.7	0.0	13.3	0.0	0.0	3.3	0.0	0.0	0.0	0.0	16.7	0.0
31	USSR	13	2	0	0	0	0	0	3	9	0	6	0	0	9	4	34	21	4	10	0
		6.8	1.1	0.0	0.0	0.0	0.0	0.0	1.6	4.7	0.0	3.2	0.0	0.0	4.7	2.1	17.9	11.1	2.1	5.3	0.0
32	UK	2	2	0	0	0	0	0	5	34	0	4	0	0	2	0	13	2	0	4	1
		1.8	1.8	0.0	0.0	0.0	0.0	0.0	4.4	29.8	0.0	3.5	0.0	0.0	1.8	0.0	11.4	1.8	0.0	3.5	0.9
33	USA	4	0	4	0	0	0	0	1	41	0	4	0	0	2	5	2	4	0	3	4
		3.1	0.0	3.1	0.0	0.0	0.0	0.0	0.8	31.5	0.0	3.1	0.0	0.0	1.5	3.8	1.5	3.1	0.0	2.3	3.1
34	VATC	2	1	0	0	1	0	4	0	9	0	3	0	0	1	0	3	2	0	3	0
		2.8	1.4	0.0	0.0	1.4	0.0	5.6	0.0	12.5	0.0	4.2	0.0	0.0	1.4	0.0	4.2	2.8	0.0	4.2	0.0
35	YGSL	5	4	0	0	0	0	1	0	0	0	8	0	0	3	0	9	7	0	8	2
		6.0	4.8	0.0	0.0	0.0	0.0	1.2	0.0	0.0	0.0	9.6	0.0	0.0	3.6	0.0	10.8	8.4	0.0	9.6	2.4

Table A2.6. *(cont.)*

COUNTRIES	21	22	23	24	25	26	27	28	29	30	31	32	33	34	35	36	37	38	39	40
1 AUST	0	1	1	0	0	0	0	0	0	0	0	0	0	0	0	0	0	0	0	0
	0.0	1.6	1.6	0.0	0.0	0.0	0.0	0.0	0.0	0.0	0.0	0.0	0.0	0.0	0.0	0.0	0.0	0.0	0.0	0.0
2 BLGM	0	0	0	0	0	7	0	0	0	0	0	0	0	0	0	0	0	0	0	0
	0.0	0.0	0.0	0.0	0.0	13.2	0.0	0.0	0.0	0.0	0.0	0.0	0.0	0.0	0.0	0.0	0.0	0.0	0.0	0.0
3 BLGR	0	0	0	0	0	1	0	0	0	0	0	0	0	0	1	0	0	0	0	2
	0.0	0.0	0.0	0.0	0.0	1.0	0.0	0.0	0.0	0.0	0.0	0.0	0.0	0.0	1.0	0.0	0.0	0.0	0.0	1.9
4 CNDA	0	0	0	0	0	1	0	0	0	0	0	0	0	0	0	0	0	0	0	0
	0.0	0.0	0.0	0.0	0.0	0.9	0.0	0.0	0.0	0.0	0.0	0.0	0.0	0.0	0.0	0.0	0.0	0.0	0.0	0.0
5 CYPR	0	0	0	0	0	0	0	0	0	0	0	0	0	0	0	3	0	0	0	0
	0.0	0.0	0.0	0.0	0.0	0.0	0.0	0.0	0.0	0.0	0.0	0.0	0.0	0.0	0.0	5.1	0.0	0.0	0.0	0.0
6 CZCH	0	2	2	0	0	3	0	0	0	0	0	0	0	0	0	0	0	0	0	0
	0.0	3.0	3.0	0.0	0.0	4.5	0.0	0.0	0.0	0.0	0.0	0.0	0.0	0.0	0.0	0.0	0.0	0.0	0.0	0.0
7 DNMK	0	3	3	0	0	2	0	0	0	4	0	0	0	0	0	0	0	0	0	0
	0.0	2.9	2.9	0.0	0.0	2.0	0.0	0.0	0.0	3.9	0.0	0.0	0.0	0.0	0.0	0.0	0.0	0.0	0.0	0.0
8 FNLD	0	0	0	0	0	2	0	0	0	0	0	0	0	0	0	0	0	0	0	0
	0.0	0.0	0.0	0.0	0.0	2.5	0.0	0.0	0.0	0.0	0.0	0.0	0.0	0.0	0.0	0.0	0.0	0.0	0.0	0.0
9 FRNC	0	0	0	0	0	0	0	0	0	0	0	0	0	0	0	0	0	0	0	0
	0.0	0.0	0.0	0.0	0.0	0.0	0.0	0.0	0.0	0.0	0.0	0.0	0.0	0.0	0.0	0.0	0.0	0.0	0.0	0.0
10 FRG	0	0	0	0	0	4	0	0	0	0	0	0	0	0	0	2	0	0	0	0
	0.0	0.0	0.0	0.0	0.0	4.2	0.0	0.0	0.0	0.0	0.0	0.0	0.0	0.0	0.0	2.1	0.0	0.0	0.0	0.0
11 GDR	4	0	0	0	0	3	0	0	0	1	0	0	0	5	0	0	0	0	0	5
	2.3	0.0	0.0	0.0	0.0	1.7	0.0	0.0	0.0	0.6	0.0	0.0	0.0	2.9	0.0	0.0	0.0	0.0	0.0	2.9
12 GRCE	0	0	0	0	0	0	0	0	0	0	0	0	0	0	0	0	0	0	0	0
	0.0	0.0	0.0	0.0	0.0	0.0	0.0	0.0	0.0	0.0	0.0	0.0	0.0	0.0	0.0	0.0	0.0	0.0	0.0	0.0
13 HNGR	1	0	0	0	0	1	0	0	0	3	0	0	0	0	3	0	4	0	0	2
	0.8	0.0	0.0	0.0	0.0	0.8	0.0	0.0	0.0	2.3	0.0	0.0	0.0	0.0	2.3	0.0	3.1	0.0	0.0	1.5
14 ICLD	0	0	0	0	0	0	0	0	0	0	0	0	0	0	0	0	0	0	0	0
	0.0	0.0	0.0	0.0	0.0	0.0	0.0	0.0	0.0	0.0	0.0	0.0	0.0	0.0	0.0	0.0	0.0	0.0	0.0	0.0
15 IRLD	0	0	0	0	0	0	0	0	0	4	0	0	0	0	0	0	0	0	0	0
	0.0	0.0	0.0	0.0	0.0	0.0	0.0	0.0	0.0	6.7	0.0	0.0	0.0	0.0	0.0	0.0	0.0	0.0	0.0	0.0
16 ITLY	0	0	0	0	0	1	0	0	0	0	0	0	0	1	0	1	0	0	0	0
	0.0	0.0	0.0	0.0	0.0	1.2	0.0	0.0	0.0	0.0	0.0	0.0	0.0	1.2	0.0	1.2	0.0	0.0	0.0	0.0
17 LICH	0	0	0	0	0	0	0	0	0	0	0	0	0	0	0	0	0	0	0	0
	0.0	0.0	0.0	0.0	0.0	0.0	0.0	0.0	0.0	0.0	0.0	0.0	0.0	0.0	0.0	0.0	0.0	0.0	0.0	0.0

18	LXBG	0	0	1	0	0	1	0	0	0	0	0	0	0	0	0	0	0	0	0	0
		0.0	0.0	2.3	0.0	0.0	2.3	0.0	0.0	0.0	0.0	0.0	0.0	0.0	0.0	0.0	0.0	0.0	0.0	0.0	0.0
19	MLTA	0	0	0	0	0	0	0	0	0	0	0	0	0	0	0	0	0	0	0	0
		0.0	0.0	0.0	0.0	0.0	0.0	0.0	0.0	0.0	0.0	0.0	0.0	0.0	0.0	0.0	0.0	0.0	0.0	0.0	0.0
20	MNCO	0	0	0	0	0	1	0	0	0	0	0	0	0	0	1	1	0	0	0	1
		0.0	0.0	0.0	0.0	0.0	9.1	0.0	0.0	0.0	0.0	0.0	0.0	0.0	0.0	9.1	9.1	0.0	0.0	0.0	9.1
21	NTHL	0	0	0	0	0	0	0	0	0	0	0	0	0	0	0	0	0	0	0	0
		0.0	0.0	0.0	0.0	0.0	0.0	0.0	0.0	0.0	0.0	0.0	0.0	0.0	0.0	0.0	0.0	0.0	0.0	0.0	0.0
22	NRWY	0	0	0	0	0	0	0	0	0	0	0	0	0	0	0	0	0	0	0	0
		0.0	0.0	0.0	0.0	0.0	0.0	0.0	0.0	0.0	0.0	0.0	0.0	0.0	0.0	0.0	0.0	0.0	0.0	0.0	0.0
23	PLND	5	0	0	0	0	3	0	0	0	0	0	0	0	0	1	0	0	0	0	1
		1.8	0.0	0.0	0.0	0.0	1.1	0.0	0.0	0.0	0.0	0.0	0.0	0.0	0.0	0.4	0.0	0.0	0.0	0.0	0.4
24	PRTG	0	0	0	0	0	1	0	0	0	0	0	0	0	0	0	0	0	0	0	0
		0.0	0.0	0.0	0.0	0.0	3.6	0.0	0.0	0.0	0.0	0.0	0.0	0.0	0.0	0.0	0.0	0.0	0.0	0.0	0.0
25	RMNA	0	0	0	0	0	3	0	0	0	0	0	0	0	0	2	0	0	0	0	0
		0.0	0.0	0.0	0.0	0.0	4.4	0.0	0.0	0.0	0.0	0.0	0.0	0.0	0.0	2.9	0.0	0.0	0.0	0.0	0.0
26	SANM	0	0	0	0	0	0	0	0	0	0	0	0	0	0	0	0	0	0	0	0
		0.0	0.0	0.0	0.0	0.0	0.0	0.0	0.0	0.0	0.0	0.0	0.0	0.0	0.0	0.0	0.0	0.0	0.0	0.0	0.0
27	SPAN	0	0	0	0	0	0	0	0	0	0	0	0	0	0	0	0	0	0	0	0
		0.0	0.0	0.0	0.0	0.0	0.0	0.0	0.0	0.0	0.0	0.0	0.0	0.0	0.0	0.0	0.0	0.0	0.0	0.0	0.0
28	SWDN	0	0	0	0	0	0	0	0	0	0	0	0	0	0	0	0	0	0	0	1
		0.0	0.0	0.0	0.0	0.0	0.0	0.0	0.0	0.0	0.0	0.0	0.0	0.0	0.0	0.0	0.0	0.0	0.0	0.0	1.6
29	SWTZ	0	0	0	0	0	2	0	0	0	0	0	0	1	1	0	0	0	0	0	0
		0.0	0.0	0.0	0.0	0.0	4.8	0.0	0.0	0.0	0.0	0.0	0.0	2.4	2.4	0.0	0.0	0.0	0.0	0.0	0.0
30	TRKY	0	0	0	0	0	0	0	0	0	0	0	0	0	0	1	1	0	0	0	0
		0.0	0.0	0.0	0.0	0.0	0.0	0.0	0.0	0.0	0.0	0.0	0.0	0.0	0.0	1.7	1.7	0.0	0.0	0.0	0.0
31	USSR	1	0	0	0	0	0	0	0	0	0	0	0	0	0	0	1	0	0	0	6
		0.5	0.0	0.0	0.0	0.0	0.0	0.0	0.0	0.0	0.0	0.0	0.0	0.0	0.0	0.0	0.5	0.0	0.0	0.0	3.2
32	UK	0	1	2	0	0	1	0	0	0	0	0	0	0	0	0	1	0	0	0	0
		0.0	0.9	1.8	0.0	0.0	0.9	0.0	0.0	0.0	0.0	0.0	0.0	0.0	0.0	0.0	0.9	0.0	0.0	0.0	0.0
33	USA	0	3	1	0	0	3	0	0	0	0	0	0	0	0	1	3	0	0	0	0
		0.0	2.3	0.8	0.0	0.0	2.3	0.0	0.0	0.0	0.0	0.0	0.0	0.0	0.0	0.8	2.3	0.0	0.0	0.0	0.0
34	VATC	0	0	0	0	0	0	0	0	0	0	0	0	0	0	0	4	0	0	0	0
		0.0	0.0	0.0	0.0	0.0	0.0	0.0	0.0	0.0	0.0	0.0	0.0	0.0	0.0	0.0	5.6	0.0	0.0	0.0	0.0
35	YGSL	0	0	0	0	0	2	0	0	0	0	0	0	0	0	0	0	0	0	0	0
		0.0	0.0	0.0	0.0	0.0	2.4	0.0	0.0	0.0	0.0	0.0	0.0	0.0	0.0	0.0	0.0	0.0	0.0	0.0	0.0

Table A2.6. *(cont.)*

	COUNTRIES	41	42	43	44	45	46	47	48	49	50	51	52	53	54	55	56	57	58	59	60
1	AUST	0	0	1	0	0	0	0	0	0	0	0	0	0	0	0	0	0	10	1	0
		0.0	0.0	1.6	0.0	0.0	0.0	0.0	0.0	0.0	0.0	0.0	0.0	0.0	0.0	0.0	0.0	0.0	16.4	1.6	0.0
2	BLGM	0	0	0	0	0	0	0	0	0	0	0	0	0	0	0	0	0	4	1	0
		0.0	0.0	0.0	0.0	0.0	0.0	0.0	0.0	0.0	0.0	0.0	0.0	0.0	0.0	0.0	0.0	0.0	7.5	1.9	0.0
3	BLGR	0	0	0	0	0	2	0	0	0	0	0	0	0	0	0	0	0	1	1	0
		0.0	0.0	0.0	0.0	0.0	1.9	0.0	0.0	0.0	0.0	0.0	0.0	0.0	0.0	0.0	0.0	0.0	1.0	1.0	0.0
4	CNDA	0	0	0	0	0	0	0	0	0	0	0	0	0	0	0	0	0	16	2	1
		0.0	0.0	0.0	0.0	0.0	0.0	0.0	0.0	0.0	0.0	0.0	0.0	0.0	0.0	0.0	0.0	0.0	13.9	1.7	0.9
5	CYPR	0	0	0	0	0	0	0	0	0	0	9	0	0	1	0	0	0	0	0	0
		0.0	0.0	0.0	0.0	0.0	0.0	0.0	0.0	0.0	0.0	15.3	0.0	0.0	1.7	0.0	0.0	0.0	0.0	0.0	0.0
6	CZCH	0	0	0	0	0	0	0	0	0	0	0	0	0	0	0	0	0	0	0	0
		0.0	0.0	0.0	0.0	0.0	0.0	0.0	0.0	0.0	0.0	0.0	0.0	0.0	0.0	0.0	0.0	0.0	0.0	0.0	0.0
7	DNMK	0	0	0	0	0	0	0	0	0	0	0	0	0	0	0	0	0	9	7	1
		0.0	0.0	0.0	0.0	0.0	0.0	0.0	0.0	0.0	0.0	0.0	0.0	0.0	0.0	0.0	0.0	0.0	8.8	6.9	1.0
8	FNLD	0	0	0	0	0	0	0	0	0	0	0	0	0	0	0	0	0	4	8	0
		0.0	0.0	0.0	0.0	0.0	0.0	0.0	0.0	0.0	0.0	0.0	0.0	0.0	0.0	0.0	0.0	0.0	5.0	10.0	0.0
9	FRNC	0	0	0	0	0	0	0	0	0	0	0	0	0	0	0	0	0	1	6	0
		0.0	0.0	0.0	0.0	0.0	0.0	0.0	0.0	0.0	0.0	0.0	0.0	0.0	0.0	0.0	0.0	0.0	1.6	9.4	0.0
10	FRG	0	0	0	0	0	0	0	0	0	0	0	0	0	0	0	0	0	5	3	2
		0.0	0.0	0.0	0.0	0.0	0.0	0.0	0.0	0.0	0.0	0.0	0.0	0.0	0.0	0.0	0.0	0.0	5.3	3.2	2.1
11	GDR	0	0	0	0	0	5	0	0	0	0	0	0	0	0	0	0	0	0	3	0
		0.0	0.0	0.0	0.0	0.0	2.9	0.0	0.0	0.0	0.0	0.0	0.0	0.0	0.0	0.0	0.0	0.0	0.0	1.7	0.0
12	GRCE	0	0	0	0	0	0	0	0	0	0	1	0	0	0	0	0	0	0	0	0
		0.0	0.0	0.0	0.0	0.0	0.0	0.0	0.0	0.0	0.0	5.6	0.0	0.0	0.0	0.0	0.0	0.0	0.0	0.0	0.0
13	HNGR	0	0	0	0	0	2	0	0	0	0	0	0	0	0	0	0	0	2	0	0
		0.0	0.0	0.0	0.0	0.0	1.5	0.0	0.0	0.0	0.0	0.0	0.0	0.0	0.0	0.0	0.0	0.0	1.5	0.0	0.0
14	ICLD	0	0	0	0	0	0	0	0	0	0	0	0	0	0	0	0	0	0	0	0
		0.0	0.0	0.0	0.0	0.0	0.0	0.0	0.0	0.0	0.0	0.0	0.0	0.0	0.0	0.0	0.0	0.0	0.0	0.0	0.0
15	IRLD	0	0	0	0	0	0	0	0	0	0	0	0	0	0	0	0	0	2	0	1
		0.0	0.0	0.0	0.0	0.0	0.0	0.0	0.0	0.0	0.0	0.0	0.0	0.0	0.0	0.0	0.0	0.0	3.3	0.0	1.7
16	ITLY	0	0	0	0	0	0	0	1	0	0	8	0	0	0	0	0	0	0	1	0
		0.0	0.0	0.0	0.0	0.0	0.0	0.0	1.2	0.0	0.0	9.8	0.0	0.0	0.0	0.0	0.0	0.0	0.0	1.2	0.0
17	LICH	0	0	0	0	0	0	0	0	0	0	0	0	0	0	0	0	0	4	0	0
		.0	0.0	0.0	0.0	0.0	0.0	0.0	0.0	0.0	0.0	0.0	0.0	0.0	0.0	0.0	0.0	0.0	50.0	0.0	0.0

18	LXBG	0	0	0	0	0	0	0	0	0	0	0	0	0	0	0	0	0	0	6	0
		0.0	0.0	0.0	0.0	0.0	0.0	0.0	0.0	0.0	0.0	0.0	0.0	0.0	0.0	0.0	0.0	0.0	0.0	13.6	0.0
19	MLTA	0	0	0	0	0	0	0	0	0	0	2	0	5	5	0	0	0	0	0	0
		0.0	0.0	0.0	0.0	0.0	0.0	0.0	0.0	0.0	0.0	7.4	0.0	18.5	18.5	0.0	0.0	0.0	0.0	0.0	0.0
20	MNCO	0	1	0	0	0	0	0	0	0	0	0	0	0	0	0	0	0	0	0	0
		0.0	9.1	0.0	0.0	0.0	0.0	0.0	0.0	0.0	0.0	0.0	0.0	0.0	0.0	0.0	0.0	0.0	0.0	0.0	0.0
21	NTHL	0	0	0	0	0	0	0	0	0	0	0	0	0	0	0	0	0	3	3	0
		0.0	0.0	0.0	0.0	0.0	0.0	0.0	0.0	0.0	0.0	0.0	0.0	0.0	0.0	0.0	0.0	0.0	17.6	17.6	0.0
22	NRWY	0	1	0	0	0	0	0	0	0	0	0	0	0	0	0	0	0	5	2	0
		0.0	3.3	0.0	0.0	0.0	0.0	0.0	0.0	0.0	0.0	0.0	0.0	0.0	0.0	0.0	0.0	0.0	16.7	6.7	0.0
23	PLND	0	0	0	0	0	1	0	0	0	0	0	0	0	0	0	0	0	1	5	0
		0.0	0.0	0.0	0.0	0.0	0.4	0.0	0.0	0.0	0.0	0.0	0.0	0.0	0.0	0.0	0.0	0.0	0.4	1.8	0.0
24	PRTG	0	0	0	0	0	0	0	10	0	0	1	0	0	0	0	0	0	0	1	0
		0.0	0.0	0.0	0.0	0.0	0.0	0.0	35.7	0.0	0.0	3.6	0.0	0.0	0.0	0.0	0.0	0.0	0.0	3.6	0.0
25	RMNA	0	0	0	0	0	0	0	0	0	0	0	0	0	0	0	0	0	0	0	0
		0.0	0.0	0.0	0.0	0.0	0.0	0.0	0.0	0.0	0.0	0.0	0.0	0.0	0.0	0.0	0.0	0.0	0.0	0.0	0.0
26	SANM	0	0	0	0	0	0	0	0	0	0	2	0	0	1	0	0	0	3	0	0
		0.0	0.0	0.0	0.0	0.0	0.0	0.0	0.0	0.0	0.0	2.2	0.0	0.0	1.1	0.0	0.0	0.0	3.3	0.0	0.0
27	SPAN	0	0	0	0	0	0	0	4	0	0	1	0	0	0	0	0	0	7	1	0
		0.0	0.0	0.0	0.0	0.0	0.0	0.0	4.3	0.0	0.0	1.1	0.0	0.0	0.0	0.0	0.0	0.0	7.6	1.1	0.0
28	SWDN	0	0	3	0	0	0	0	0	0	0	0	0	0	0	0	0	0	2	0	0
		0.0	0.0	4.7	0.0	0.0	0.0	0.0	0.0	0.0	0.0	0.0	0.0	0.0	0.0	0.0	0.0	0.0	3.1	0.0	0.0
29	SWTZ	0	0	0	0	0	0	0	0	0	0	0	0	0	0	0	0	0	2	0	0
		0.0	0.0	0.0	0.0	0.0	0.0	0.0	0.0	0.0	0.0	0.0	0.0	0.0	0.0	0.0	0.0	0.0	4.8	0.0	0.0
30	TRKY	0	0	0	0	0	0	0	0	0	0	0	0	0	8	0	0	0	2	0	0
		0.0	0.0	0.0	0.0	0.0	0.0	0.0	0.0	0.0	0.0	0.0	0.0	0.0	13.3	0.0	0.0	0.0	3.3	0.0	0.0
31	USSR	0	0	0	0	0	7	0	1	0	0	0	0	4	0	0	0	0	4	1	0
		0.0	0.0	0.0	0.0	0.0	3.7	0.0	0.5	0.0	0.0	0.0	0.0	2.1	0.0	0.0	0.0	0.0	2.1	0.5	0.0
32	UK	0	0	0	0	0	0	0	0	0	0	0	0	0	0	0	0	0	2	4	1
		0.0	0.0	0.0	0.0	0.0	0.0	0.0	0.0	0.0	0.0	0.0	0.0	0.0	0.0	0.0	0.0	0.0	1.8	3.5	0.9
33	USA	0	0	0	0	0	0	0	0	0	0	0	0	0	0	0	0	0	1	3	0
		0.0	0.0	0.0	0.0	0.0	0.0	0.0	0.0	0.0	0.0	0.0	0.0	0.0	0.0	0.0	0.0	0.0	0.8	2.3	0.0
34	VATC	0	0	0	0	0	0	0	1	0	0	0	0	0	5	0	0	0	1	1	0
		0.0	0.0	0.0	0.0	0.0	0.0	0.0	1.4	0.0	0.0	0.0	0.0	0.0	6.9	0.0	0.0	0.0	1.4	1.4	0.0
35	YGSL	0	0	0	0	0	0	0	1	0	0	2	0	2	1	0	0	0	1	1	0
		0.0	0.0	0.0	0.0	0.0	0.0	0.0	1.2	0.0	0.0	2.4	0.0	2.4	1.2	0.0	0.0	0.0	1.2	1.2	0.0

Table A2.6. *(cont.)*

COUNTRIES	61	62	63	64	65	66	67	68	69	70	71	72	73	74	75	76	77	78	79	80
1 AUST	0	0	0	0	0	0	0	0	0	0	0	0	0	0	0	0	0	0	0	0
	0.0	0.0	0.0	0.0	0.0	0.0	0.0	0.0	0.0	0.0	0.0	0.0	0.0	0.0	0.0	0.0	0.0	0.0	0.0	0.0
2 BLGM	0	0	0	0	0	0	0	0	0	0	0	0	0	0	0	0	0	0	0	0
	0.0	0.0	0.0	0.0	0.0	0.0	0.0	0.0	0.0	0.0	0.0	0.0	0.0	0.0	0.0	0.0	0.0	0.0	0.0	0.0
3 BLGR	0	0	0	0	0	0	0	0	1	0	0	0	0	1	0	0	0	0	0	0
	0.0	0.0	0.0	0.0	0.0	0.0	0.0	0.0	1.0	0.0	0.0	0.0	0.0	1.0	0.0	0.0	0.0	0.0	0.0	0.0
4 CNDA	5	0	0	0	0	0	0	0	1	11	0	0	0	1	0	0	0	0	0	0
	4.3	0.0	0.0	0.0	0.0	0.0	0.0	0.0	0.9	9.6	0.0	0.0	0.0	0.9	0.0	0.0	0.0	0.0	0.0	0.0
5 CYPR	0	0	0	0	0	0	0	0	1	0	0	0	0	0	0	0	0	0	1	0
	0.0	0.0	0.0	0.0	0.0	0.0	0.0	0.0	1.7	0.0	0.0	0.0	0.0	0.0	0.0	0.0	0.0	0.0	1.7	0.0
6 CZCH	0	0	0	0	0	0	0	0	0	0	0	0	0	0	0	0	0	0	0	0
	0.0	0.0	0.0	0.0	0.0	0.0	0.0	0.0	0.0	0.0	0.0	0.0	0.0	0.0	0.0	0.0	0.0	0.0	0.0	0.0
7 DNMK	1	1	1	1	0	0	0	0	3	3	0	3	0	0	0	0	0	0	0	0
	1.0	1.0	1.0	1.0	0.0	0.0	0.0	0.0	2.9	2.9	0.0	2.9	0.0	0.0	0.0	0.0	0.0	0.0	0.0	0.0
8 FNLD	0	0	0	0	0	0	0	0	0	1	0	0	0	8	0	0	0	0	0	0
	0.0	0.0	0.0	0.0	0.0	0.0	0.0	0.0	0.0	1.2	0.0	0.0	0.0	10.0	0.0	0.0	0.0	0.0	0.0	0.0
9 FRNC	0	0	0	0	0	0	0	0	6	0	0	0	0	0	0	0	0	0	0	0
	0.0	0.0	0.0	0.0	0.0	0.0	0.0	0.0	9.4	0.0	0.0	0.0	0.0	0.0	0.0	0.0	0.0	0.0	0.0	0.0
10 FRG	1	1	1	0	0	0	0	0	4	1	0	1	0	2	0	0	0	0	0	0
	1.1	1.1	1.1	0.0	0.0	0.0	0.0	0.0	4.2	1.1	0.0	1.1	0.0	2.1	0.0	0.0	0.0	0.0	0.0	0.0
11 GDR	0	0	0	0	0	0	0	0	0	2	0	0	0	2	1	0	1	0	0	0
	0.0	0.0	0.0	0.0	0.0	0.0	0.0	0.0	0.0	1.2	0.0	0.0	0.0	1.2	0.6	0.0	0.6	0.0	0.0	0.0
12 GRCE	0	0	0	0	0	0	0	0	0	0	0	0	0	0	0	0	0	0	0	0
	0.0	0.0	0.0	0.0	0.0	0.0	0.0	0.0	0.0	0.0	0.0	0.0	0.0	0.0	0.0	0.0	0.0	0.0	0.0	0.0
13 HNGR	0	0	0	0	0	0	0	0	0	0	0	0	0	4	0	0	0	0	0	0
	0.0	0.0	0.0	0.0	0.0	0.0	0.0	0.0	0.0	0.0	0.0	0.0	0.0	3.1	0.0	0.0	0.0	0.0	0.0	0.0
14 ICLD	0	0	0	0	0	0	0	0	0	0	0	0	0	0	0	0	0	0	0	0
	0.0	0.0	0.0	0.0	0.0	0.0	0.0	0.0	0.0	0.0	0.0	0.0	0.0	0.0	0.0	0.0	0.0	0.0	0.0	0.0
15 IRLD	1	0	0	0	0	0	0	0	0	0	0	0	0	0	0	0	0	0	0	0
	1.7	0.0	0.0	0.0	0.0	0.0	0.0	0.0	0.0	0.0	0.0	0.0	0.0	0.0	0.0	0.0	0.0	0.0	0.0	0.0
16 ITLY	0	0	6	0	0	0	0	0	1	6	0	0	0	1	0	0	0	0	0	0
	0.0	0.0	7.3	0.0	0.0	0.0	0.0	0.0	1.2	7.3	0.0	0.0	0.0	1.2	0.0	0.0	0.0	0.0	0.0	0.0
17 LICH	0	0	0	0	0	0	0	0	0	0	0	0	0	0	0	0	0	0	0	0
	0.0	0.0	0.0	0.0	0.0	0.0	0.0	0.0	0.0	0.0	0.0	0.0	0.0	0.0	0.0	0.0	0.0	0.0	0.0	0.0

18	LXBG	0	0	0	0	0	0	0	0	1	1	0	1	0	0	0	0	0	0	0	0
		0.0	0.0	0.0	0.0	0.0	0.0	0.0	0.0	2.3	2.3	0.0	2.3	0.0	0.0	0.0	0.0	0.0	0.0	0.0	0.0
19	MLTA	0	0	0	0	0	0	0	0	0	0	0	0	0	0	0	0	0	0	0	0
		0.0	0.0	0.0	0.0	0.0	0.0	0.0	0.0	0.0	0.0	0.0	0.0	0.0	0.0	0.0	0.0	0.0	0.0	0.0	0.0
20	MNCO	0	0	0	0	0	0	0	0	0	0	0	0	0	1	0	0	0	0	0	0
		0.0	0.0	0.0	0.0	0.0	0.0	0.0	0.0	0.0	0.0	0.0	0.0	0.0	9.1	0.0	0.0	0.0	0.0	0.0	0.0
21	NTHL	0	0	0	0	0	0	0	0	3	0	0	0	0	0	0	0	0	0	0	0
		0.0	0.0	0.0	0.0	0.0	0.0	0.0	0.0	17.6	0.0	0.0	0.0	0.0	0.0	0.0	0.0	0.0	0.0	0.0	0.0
22	NRWY	0	0	0	0	0	0	0	0	0	0	0	0	0	0	0	0	0	0	0	0
		0.0	0.0	0.0	0.0	0.0	0.0	0.0	0.0	0.0	0.0	0.0	0.0	0.0	0.0	0.0	0.0	0.0	0.0	0.0	0.0
23	PLND	0	0	0	0	0	0	0	0	0	5	0	0	0	12	0	0	0	0	0	0
		0.0	0.0	0.0	0.0	0.0	0.0	0.0	0.0	0.0	1.8	0.0	0.0	0.0	4.4	0.0	0.0	0.0	0.0	0.0	0.0
24	PRTG	0	0	0	0	0	0	0	0	0	0	0	0	0	0	0	0	0	0	0	0
		0.0	0.0	0.0	0.0	0.0	0.0	0.0	0.0	0.0	0.0	0.0	0.0	0.0	0.0	0.0	0.0	0.0	0.0	0.0	0.0
25	RMNA	0	0	0	0	0	0	0	0	0	0	0	0	0	2	0	0	0	0	0	0
		0.0	0.0	0.0	0.0	0.0	0.0	0.0	0.0	0.0	0.0	0.0	0.0	0.0	2.9	0.0	0.0	0.0	0.0	0.0	0.0
26	SANM	0	0	0	0	0	0	0	0	1	2	0	0	0	0	0	0	0	0	0	0
		0.0	0.0	0.0	0.0	0.0	0.0	0.0	0.0	1.1	2.2	0.0	0.0	0.0	0.0	0.0	0.0	0.0	0.0	0.0	0.0
27	SPAN	1	1	1	0	0	0	0	0	3	0	0	0	0	3	0	0	0	0	0	0
		1.1	1.1	1.1	0.0	0.0	0.0	0.0	0.0	3.3	0.0	0.0	0.0	0.0	3.3	0.0	0.0	0.0	0.0	0.0	0.0
28	SWDN	3	0	1	0	0	0	0	0	0	1	0	0	0	1	0	0	0	1	0	0
		4.7	0.0	1.6	0.0	0.0	0.0	0.0	0.0	0.0	1.6	0.0	0.0	0.0	1.6	0.0	0.0	0.0	1.6	0.0	0.0
29	SWTZ	0	0	0	0	0	0	0	0	1	2	0	0	0	0	0	0	0	0	0	0
		0.0	0.0	0.0	0.0	0.0	0.0	0.0	0.0	2.4	4.8	0.0	0.0	0.0	0.0	0.0	0.0	0.0	0.0	0.0	0.0
30	TRKY	0	0	0	0	0	0	0	0	0	0	0	0	0	0	0	0	0	0	0	0
		0.0	0.0	0.0	0.0	0.0	0.0	0.0	0.0	0.0	0.0	0.0	0.0	0.0	0.0	0.0	0.0	0.0	0.0	0.0	0.0
31	USSR	0	0	0	0	0	0	0	0	1	0	0	0	0	1	0	0	0	1	0	1
		0.0	0.0	0.0	0.0	0.0	0.0	0.0	0.0	0.5	0.0	0.0	0.0	0.0	0.5	0.0	0.0	0.0	0.5	0.0	0.5
32	UK	1	1	1	0	0	0	0	0	0	2	0	1	0	0	0	0	0	0	0	0
		0.9	0.9	0.9	0.0	0.0	0.0	0.0	0.0	0.0	1.8	0.0	0.9	0.0	0.0	0.0	0.0	0.0	0.0	0.0	0.0
33	USA	1	0	1	0	0	0	0	0	0	2	0	2	0	1	0	0	0	1	0	1
		0.8	0.0	0.8	0.0	0.0	0.0	0.0	0.0	0.0	1.5	0.0	1.5	0.0	0.8	0.0	0.0	0.0	0.8	0.0	0.8
34	VATC	1	1	5	0	0	0	0	0	0	0	0	0	0	0	0	0	0	0	0	1
		1.4	1.4	6.9	0.0	0.0	0.0	0.0	0.0	0.0	0.0	0.0	0.0	0.0	0.0	0.0	0.0	0.0	0.0	0.0	1.4
35	YGSL	0	0	0	0	0	0	0	0	0	0	0	0	0	1	0	0	0	0	0	1
		0.0	0.0	0.0	0.0	0.0	0.0	0.0	0.0	0.0	0.0	0.0	0.0	0.0	1.2	0.0	0.0	0.0	0.0	0.0	1.2

Table A2.6. *(cont.)*

COUNTRIES	81	82	83	84	85	86	87	88	89	90	91	92	93	94	95	96	97	98	99	100
1 AUST	0	0	0	0	0	0	0	0	0	0	0	0	0	0	1	0	0	0	0	0
	0.0	0.0	0.0	0.0	0.0	0.0	0.0	0.0	0.0	0.0	0.0	0.0	0.0	0.0	1.6	0.0	0.0	0.0	0.0	0.0
2 BLGM	0	0	0	0	0	0	0	0	0	0	0	0	0	0	0	0	0	0	1	0
	0.0	0.0	0.0	0.0	0.0	0.0	0.0	0.0	0.0	0.0	0.0	0.0	0.0	0.0	0.0	0.0	0.0	0.0	1.9	0.0
3 BLGR	0	0	0	0	0	0	0	0	0	0	0	0	0	0	2	0	8	1	0	0
	0.0	0.0	0.0	0.0	0.0	0.0	0.0	0.0	0.0	0.0	0.0	0.0	0.0	0.0	1.9	0.0	7.6	1.0	0.0	0.0
4 CNDA	0	0	0	0	0	0	0	0	0	0	0	0	0	0	0	0	1	0	0	0
	0.0	0.0	0.0	0.0	0.0	0.0	0.0	0.0	0.0	0.0	0.0	0.0	0.0	0.0	0.0	0.0	0.9	0.0	0.0	0.0
5 CYPR	0	0	0	0	0	0	0	0	0	0	0	0	0	0	1	0	0	0	0	0
	0.0	0.0	0.0	0.0	0.0	0.0	0.0	0.0	0.0	0.0	0.0	0.0	0.0	0.0	1.7	0.0	0.0	0.0	0.0	0.0
6 CZCH	0	0	0	0	0	0	0	0	0	0	0	0	0	0	0	0	1	0	4	0
	0.0	0.0	0.0	0.0	0.0	0.0	0.0	0.0	0.0	0.0	0.0	0.0	0.0	0.0	0.0	0.0	1.5	0.0	6.1	0.0
7 DNMK	0	0	0	0	0	0	0	0	0	0	0	0	0	0	0	0	0	15	0	0
	0.0	0.0	0.0	0.0	0.0	0.0	0.0	0.0	0.0	0.0	0.0	0.0	0.	0.0	0.0	0.0	0.0	14.7	0.0	0.0
8 FNLD	0	1	0	0	0	0	0	0	0	0	0	0	0	0	0	0	1	0	3	0
	0.0	1.2	0.0	0.0	0.0	0.0	0.0	0.0	0.0	0.0	0.0	0.0	0.0	0.0	0.0	0.0	1.2	0.0	3.7	0.0
9 FRNC	0	0	0	0	0	0	0	0	0	0	0	0	0	0	0	0	0	1	0	0
	0.0	0.0	0.0	0.0	0.0	0.0	0.0	0.0	0.0	0.0	0.0	0.0	0.0	0.0	0.0	0.0	0.0	1.6	0.0	0.0
10 FRG	0	2	0	0	0	0	0	0	0	0	0	0	0	0	0	0	0	3	0	0
	0.0	2.1	0.0	0.0	0.0	0.0	0.0	0.0	0.0	0.0	0.0	0.0	0.0	00	0.0	0.0	0.0	3.2	0.0	0.0
11 GDR	0	1	0	1	0	0	0	0	0	0	0	0	0	0	5	0	5	0	0	0
	0.0	0.6	0.0	0.6	0.0	0.0	0.0	0.0	0.0	0.0	0.0	0.0	0.0	0.0	2.9	0.0	2.9	0.0	0.0	0.0
12 GRCE	0	0	0	0	0	0	0	0	0	0	0	0	0	0	0	0	0	0	0	0
	0.0	0.0	0.0	0.0	0.0	0.0	0.0	0.0	0.0	0.0	0.0	0.0	0.0	0.0	0.0	0.0	0.0	0.0	0.0	0.0
13 HNGR	0	0	0	0	0	0	0	6	0	0	0	0	0	0	2	0	5	1	1	0
	0.0	0.0	0.0	0.0	0.0	0.0	0.0	4.6	0.0	0.0	0.0	0.0	0.0	0.0	1.5	0.0	3.8	0.8	0.8	0.0
14 ICLD	0	0	0	0	0	0	0	0	0	0	0	0	0	0	0	0	0	0	0	0
	0.0	0.0	0.0	0.0	0.0	0.0	0.0	0.0	0.0	0.0	0.0	0.0	0.0	0.0	0.0	0.0	0.0	0.0	0.0	0.0
15 IRLD	0	0	0	0	0	0	0	0	0	0	0	0	0	0	0	0	0	4	0	0
	0.0	0.0	0.0	0.0	0.0	0.0	0.0	0.0	0.0	0.0	0.0	0.0	0.0	0.0	0.0	0.0	0.0	6.7	0.0	0.0
16 ITLY	0	0	0	0	0	0	0	0	0	0	0	0	0	0	0	0	0	1	4	0
	0.0	0.0	0.0	0.0	0.0	0.0	0.0	0.0	0.0	0.0	0.0	0.0	0.0	0.0	0.0	0.0	0.0	1.2	4.9	0.0
17 LICH	0	0	0	0	0	0	0	0	0	0	0	0	0	0	0	0	0	0	0	0
	0.0	0.0	0.0	0.0	0.0	0.0	0.0	0.0	0.0	0.0	0.0	0.0	0.0	0.0	0.0	0.0	0.0	0.0	0.0	0.0

18	LXBG	0	0	0	0	0	0	0	0	0	0	0	0	0	0	0	0	4	1	0	0
		0.0	0.0	0.0	0.0	0.0	0.0	0.0	0.0	0.0	0.0	0.0	0.0	0.0	0.0	0.0	0.0	9.1	2.3	0.0	0.0
19	MLTA	0	0	0	0	0	0	0	0	0	0	0	0	0	0	0	0	0	0	0	0
		0.0	0.0	0.0	0.0	0.0	0.0	0.0	0.0	0.0	0.0	0.0	0.0	0.0	0.0	0.0	0.0	0.0	0.0	0.0	0.0
20	MNCO	0	0	0	0	0	0	0	0	0	0	0	0	0	0	0	0	0	0	0	0
		0.0	0.0	0.0	0.0	0.0	0.0	0.0	0.0	0.0	0.0	0.0	0.0	0.0	0.0	0.0	0.0	0.0	0.0	0.0	0.0
21	NTHL	0	0	0	0	0	0	0	0	0	0	0	0	0	0	0	0	0	0	0	0
		0.0	0.0	0.0	0.0	0.0	0.0	0.0	0.0	0.0	0.0	0.0	0.0	0.0	0.0	0.0	0.0	0.0	0.0	0.0	0.0
22	NRWY	0	0	0	0	0	0	0	0	0	0	0	0	0	0	0	0	0	0	1	0
		0.0	0.0	0.0	0.0	0.0	0.0	0.0	0.0	0.0	0.0	0.0	0.0	0.0	0.0	0.0	0.0	0.0	0.0	3.3	0.0
23	PLND	8	15	0	0	0	0	0	0	0	0	0	0	0	0	1	0	8	0	9	0
		2.9	5.5	0.0	0.0	0.0	0.0	0.0	0.0	0.0	0.0	0.0	0.0	0.0	0.0	0.4	0.0	2.9	0.0	3.3	0.0
24	PRTG	0	0	0	0	0	0	0	0	0	0	0	0	0	0	0	0	0	0	0	0
		0.0	0.0	0.0	0.0	0.0	0.0	0.0	0.0	0.0	0.0	0.0	0.0	0.0	0.0	0.0	0.0	0.0	0.0	0.0	0.0
25	RMNA	0	0	0	0	0	0	0	0	0	0	0	0	0	0	0	0	0	0	0	0
		0.0	0.0	0.0	0.0	0.0	0.0	0.0	0.0	0.0	0.0	0.0	0.0	0.0	0.0	0.0	0.0	0.0	0.0	0.0	0.0
26	SANM	0	0	0	0	0	0	0	0	0	0	0	0	0	0	0	0	7	0	0	0
		0.0	0.0	0.0	0.0	0.0	0.0	0.0	0.0	0.0	0.0	0.0	0.0	0.0	0.0	0.0	0.0	7.8	0.0	0.0	0.0
27	SPAN	0	3	0	0	0	0	0	0	0	0	0	0	0	0	0	0	7	0	0	0
		0.0	3.3	0.0	0.0	0.0	0.0	0.0	0.0	0.0	0.0	0.0	0.0	0.0	0.0	0.0	0.0	7.6	0.0	0.0	0.0
28	SWDN	0	1	1	0	0	0	0	0	0	0	0	0	0	0	0	0	0	0	1	0
		0.0	1.6	1.6	0.0	0.0	0.0	0.0	0.0	0.0	0.0	0.0	0.0	0.0	0.0	0.0	0.0	0.0	0.0	1.6	0.0
29	SWTZ	0	0	0	0	0	0	0	0	0	0	0	0	0	0	0	0	0	0	0	0
		0.0	0.0	0.0	0.0	0.0	0.0	0.0	0.0	0.0	0.0	0.0	0.0	0.0	0.0	0.0	0.0	0.0	0.0	0.0	0.0
30	TRKY	0	0	0	0	0	0	0	0	0	0	0	0	0	0	0	0	5	0	0	0
		0.0	0.0	0.0	0.0	0.0	0.0	0.0	0.0	0.0	0.0	0.0	0.0	0.0	0.0	0.0	0.0	8.3	0.0	0.0	0.0
31	USSR	0	1	0	0	0	0	0	1	0	0	0	0	0	0	7	0	1	0	0	0
		0.0	0.5	0.0	0.0	0.0	0.0	0.0	0.5	0.0	0.0	0.0	0.0	0.0	0.0	3.7	0.0	0.5	0.0	0.0	0.0
32	UK	0	0	0	0	0	0	0	0	0	0	0	0	0	0	0	0	4	1	0	0
		0.0	0.0	0.0	0.0	0.0	0.0	0.0	0.0	0.0	0.0	0.0	0.0	0.0	0.0	0.0	0.0	3.5	0.9	0.0	0.0
33	USA	0	0	0	3	0	0	0	0	0	0	0	0	0	0	0	0	1	0	0	0
		0.0	0.0	0.0	2.3	0.0	0.0	0.0	0.0	0.0	0.0	0.0	0.0	0.0	0.0	0.0	0.0	0.8	0.0	0.0	0.0
34	VATC	0	0	0	0	0	0	0	1	0	0	0	0	0	0	0	4	2	0	1	0
		0.0	0.0	0.0	0.0	0.0	0.0	0.0	1.4	0.0	0.0	0.0	0.0	0.0	0.0	0.0	5.6	2.8	0.0	1.4	0.0
35	YGSL	0	0	0	0	0	0	0	1	0	0	0	0	0	0	0	0	1	1	1	0
		0.0	0.0	0.0	0.0	0.0	0.0	0.0	1.2	0.0	0.0	0.0	0.0	0.0	0.0	0.0	0.0	1.2	1.2	1.2	0.0

Table A2.6. *(cont.)*

COUNTRIES	101	102	103	104	105	106	107	108	109	110	111	112	113	114	115	116	117	118	119	120
1 AUST	0	0	1	0	0	0	0	0	0	0	0	0	0	0	0	0	0	0	0	0
	0.0	0.0	1.6	0.0	0.0	0.0	0.0	0.0	0.0	0.0	0.0	0.0	0.0	0.0	0.0	0.0	0.0	0.0	0.0	0.0
2 BLGM	0	0	0	0	0	0	0	0	0	0	0	0	0	0	0	0	0	0	0	0
	0.0	0.0	0.0	0.0	0.0	0.0	0.0	0.0	0.0	0.0	0.0	0.0	0.0	0.0	0.0	0.0	0.0	0.0	0.0	0.0
3 BLGR	0	0	2	3	0	0	0	0	0	0	0	0	0	1	0	0	0	0	0	0
	0.0	0.0	1.9	2.9	0.0	0.0	0.0	0.0	0.0	0.0	0.0	0.0	0.0	1.0	0.0	0.0	0.0	0.0	0.0	0.0
4 CNDA	0	0	0	0	0	0	0	2	0	0	0	0	0	0	0	0	0	0	0	3
	0.0	0.0	0.0	0.0	0.0	0.0	0.0	1.7	0.0	0.0	0.0	0.0	0.0	0.0	0.0	0.0	0.0	0.0	0.0	2.6
5 CYPR	0	0	0	0	0	0	0	0	0	0	0	0	0	0	0	0	0	0	2	0
	0.0	0.0	0.0	0.0	0.0	0.0	0.0	0.0	0.0	0.0	0.0	0.0	0.0	0.0	0.0	0.0	0.0	0.0	3.4	0.0
6 CZCH	0	0	1	4	0	0	0	0	0	0	0	0	0	0	0	0	0	0	0	0
	0.0	0.0	1.5	6.1	0.0	0.0	0.0	0.0	0.0	0.0	0.0	0.0	0.0	0.0	0.0	0.0	0.0	0.0	0.0	0.0
7 DNMK	0	0	0	0	0	0	0	0	0	0	0	0	0	0	0	0	0	0	0	0
	0.0	0.0	0.0	0.0	0.0	0.0	0.0	0.0	0.0	0.0	0.0	0.0	0.0	0.0	0.0	0.0	0.0	0.0	0.0	0.0
8 FNLD	1	1	2	0	0	0	0	0	0	0	0	0	0	0	0	0	0	0	0	0
	1.2	1.2	2.5	0.0	0.0	0.0	0.0	0.0	0.0	0.0	0.0	0.0	0.0	0.0	0.0	0.0	0.0	0.0	0.0	0.0
9 FRNC	0	0	1	7	0	0	0	8	0	0	0	0	0	0	0	0	0	0	0	1
	0.0	0.0	1.6	10.9	0.0	0.0	0.0	12.5	0.0	0.0	0.0	0.0	0.0	0.0	0.0	0.0	0.0	0.0	0.0	1.6
10 FRG	0	0	4	9	0	0	0	1	0	0	0	0	1	1	0	0	0	0	0	0
	0.0	0.0	4.2	9.5	0.0	0.0	0.0	1.1	0.0	0.0	0.0	0.0	1.1	1.1	0.0	0.0	0.0	0.0	0.0	0.0
11 GDR	0	0	11	2	0	0	0	0	0	0	0	0	0	1	0	2	0	0	0	0
	0.0	0.0	6.4	1.2	0.0	0.0	0.0	0.0	0.0	0.0	0.0	0.0	0.0	0.6	0.0	1.2	0.0	0.0	0.0	0.0
12 GRCE	0	0	0	0	0	0	0	0	0	0	0	0	0	0	0	0	0	0	0	0
	0.0	0.0	0.0	0.0	0.0	0.0	0.0	0.0	0.0	0.0	0.0	0.0	0.0	0.0	0.0	0.0	0.0	0.0	0.0	0.0
13 HNGR	0	0	6	0	0	0	0	0	0	0	0	0	0	0	0	1	0	0	0	0
	0.0	0.0	4.6	0.0	0.0	0.0	0.0	0.0	0.0	0.0	0.0	0.0	0.0	0.0	0.0	0.8	0.0	0.0	0.0	0.0
14 ICLD	0	0	1	0	0	0	0	0	0	0	0	0	0	0	0	0	0	0	0	0
	0.0	0.0	12.5	0.0	0.0	0.0	0.0	0.0	0.0	0.0	0.0	0.0	0.0	0.0	0.0	0.0	0.0	0.0	0.0	0.0
15 IRLD	0	0	0	0	0	0	0	0	0	0	0	0	0	0	0	0	0	0	0	2
	0.0	0.0	0.0	0.0	0.0	0.0	0.0	0.0	0.0	0.0	0.0	0.0	0.0	0.0	0.0	0.0	0.0	0.0	0.0	3.3
16 ITLY	0	0	0	0	0	0	0	0	0	0	0	0	1	0	0	0	0	0	0	0
	0.0	0.0	0.0	0.0	0.0	0.0	0.0	0.0	0.0	0.0	0.0	0.0	1.2	0.0	0.0	0.0	0.0	0.0	0.0	0.0
17 LICH	0	0	0	0	0	0	0	0	0	0	0	0	0	0	0	0	0	0	0	0
	0.0	0.0	0.0	0.0	0.0	0.0	0.0	0.0	0.0	0.0	0.0	0.0	0.0	0.0	0.0	0.0	0.0	0.0	0.0	0.0

18	LXBG	0	0	0	0	0	0	0	0	0	0	0	0	0	0	0	0	0	0	0	0
		0.0	0.0	0.0	0.0	0.0	0.0	0.0	0.0	0.0	0.0	0.0	0.0	0.0	0.0	0.0	0.0	0.0	0.0	0.0	0.0
19	MLTA	0	0	3	1	0	0	0	0	0	0	0	0	0	0	0	0	0	0	0	0
		0.0	0.0	11.1	3.7	0.0	0.0	0.0	0.0	0.0	0.0	0.0	0.0	0.0	0.0	0.0	0.0	0.0	0.0	0.0	0.0
20	MNCO	0	0	0	0	0	0	0	0	0	0	0	0	0	0	0	0	0	0	0	0
		0.0	0.0	0.0	0.0	0.0	0.0	0.0	0.0	0.0	0.0	0.0	0.0	0.0	0.0	0.0	0.0	0.0	0.0	0.0	0.0
21	NTHL	0	0	0	0	0	0	0	0	0	0	0	0	0	0	0	0	0	0	0	0
		0.0	0.0	0.0	0.0	0.0	0.0	0.0	0.0	0.0	0.0	0.0	0.0	0.0	0.0	0.0	0.0	0.0	0.0	0.0	0.0
22	NRWY	0	0	0	0	0	0	0	0	0	0	0	0	0	1	0	0	0	0	0	0
		0.0	0.0	0.0	0.0	0.0	0.0	0.0	0.0	0.0	0.0	0.0	0.0	0.0	3.3	0.0	0.0	0.0	0.0	0.0	0.0
23	PLND	0	0	25	1	0	0	0	5	0	6	0	0	0	0	0	1	0	0	0	0
		0.0	0.0	9.2	0.4	0.0	0.0	0.0	1.8	0.0	2.2	0.0	0.0	0.0	0.0	0.0	0.4	0.0	0.0	0.0	0.0
24	PRTG	0	0	1	0	0	0	0	0	0	1	0	0	0	0	0	0	0	0	0	0
		0.0	0.0	3.6	0.0	0.0	0.0	0.0	0.0	0.0	3.6	0.0	0.0	0.0	0.0	0.0	0.0	0.0	0.0	0.0	0.0
25	RMNA	0	0	3	0	0	0	0	0	0	0	0	0	0	0	0	0	0	0	0	0
		0.0	0.0	4.4	0.0	0.0	0.0	0.0	0.0	0.0	0.0	0.0	0.0	0.0	0.0	0.0	0.0	0.0	0.0	0.0	0.0
26	SANM	0	2	10	0	0	0	0	0	0	2	0	0	0	0	0	0	0	0	0	0
		0.0	2.2	11.1	0.0	0.0	0.0	0.0	0.0	0.0	2.2	0.0	0.0	0.0	0.0	0.0	0.0	0.0	0.0	0.0	0.0
27	SPAN	0	0	7	0	0	0	0	0	0	0	0	0	0	0	1	0	0	0	0	0
		0.0	0.0	7.6	0.0	0.0	0.0	0.0	0.0	0.0	0.0	0.0	0.0	0.0	0.0	1.1	0.0	0.0	0.0	0.0	0.0
28	SWDN	0	0	0	0	0	0	0	0	0	0	0	0	3	1	0	0	0	0	1	0
		0.0	0.0	0.0	0.0	0.0	0.0	0.0	0.0	0.0	0.0	0.0	0.0	4.7	1.6	0.0	0.0	0.0	0.0	1.6	0.0
29	SWTZ	0	0	3	2	0	0	0	1	0	0	0	0	0	0	0	0	0	0	0	0
		0.0	0.0	7.1	4.8	0.0	0.0	0.0	2.4	0.0	0.0	0.0	0.0	0.0	0.0	0.0	0.0	0.0	0.0	0.0	0.0
30	TRKY	0	0	5	0	0	0	0	0	0	0	0	0	0	0	0	0	0	0	0	3
		0.0	0.0	8.3	0.0	0.0	0.0	0.0	0.0	0.0	0.0	0.0	0.0	0.0	0.0	0.0	0.0	0.0	0.0	0.0	5.0
31	USSR	0	0	9	7	0	0	0	3	0	0	0	0	0	2	0	6	0	0	0	0
		0.0	0.0	4.7	3.7	0.0	0.0	0.0	1.6	0.0	0.0	0.0	0.0	0.0	1.1	0.0	3.2	0.0	0.0	0.0	0.0
32	UK	0	0	0	10	0	0	0	4	0	0	0	0	2	0	0	0	1	0	0	0
		0.0	0.0	0.0	8.8	0.0	0.0	0.0	3.5	0.0	0.0	0.0	0.0	1.8	0.0	0.0	0.0	0.9	0.0	0.0	0.0
33	USA	0	0	3	0	0	0	0	1	7	6	0	0	0	1	6	0	0	0	3	0
		0.0	0.0	2.3	0.0	0.0	0.0	0.0	0.8	5.4	4.6	0.0	0.0	0.0	0.8	4.6	0.0	0.0	0.0	2.3	0.0
34	VATC	0	0	1	0	0	0	0	0	0	0	0	0	0	0	3	0	0	0	0	0
		0.0	0.0	1.4	0.0	0.0	0.0	0.0	0.0	0.0	0.0	0.0	0.0	0.0	0.0	4.2	0.0	0.0	0.0	0.0	0.0
35	YGSL	1	0	0	4	0	0	0	1	0	0	0	0	0	0	0	0	4	6	0	0
		1.2	0.0	0.0	4.8	0.0	0.0	0.0	1.2	0.0	0.0	0.0	0.0	0.0	0.0	0.0	0.0	4.8	7.2	0.0	0.0

Table A2.7. Category Scores and Percentages: The Madrid Opening Statements

	COUNTRIES	1	2	3	4	5	6	7	8	9	10	11	12	13	14	15	16	17	18	19	20
1	AUST	2	1	0	1	0	0	0	1	6	0	5	0	0	6	0	9	5	0	4	0
		1.4	0.7	0.0	0.7	0.0	0.0	0.0	0.7	4.3	0.0	3.5	0.0	0.0	4.3	0.0	6.4	3.5	0.0	2.8	0.0
2	BLGM	2	3	0	2	0	0	0	2	8	3	4	0	0	4	1	2	1	1	3	0
		2.2	3.2	0.0	2.2	0.0	0.0	0.0	2.2	8.6	3.2	4.3	0.0	0.0	4.3	1.1	2.2	1.1	1.1	3.2	0.0
3	BLGR	2	2	0	2	0	0	0	3	2	0	11	0	0	5	0	7	5	0	4	0
		1.8	1.8	0.0	1.8	0.0	0.0	0.0	2.7	1.8	0.0	9.9	0.0	0.0	4.5	0.0	6.3	4.5	0.0	3.6	0.0
4	CNDA	4	1	4	7	1	2	1	7	22	1	11	3	0	10	0	14	1	0	3	1
		2.4	0.6	2.4	4.2	0.6	1.2	0.6	4.2	13.1	0.6	6.5	1.8	0.0	6.0	0.0	8.3	0.6	0.0	1.8	0.6
5	CYPR	3	8	0	0	0	0	1	0	3	0	9	0	0	2	0	5	3	0	4	0
		3.0	8.0	0.0	0.0	0.0	0.0	1.0	0.0	3.0	0.0	9.0	0.0	0.0	2.0	0.0	5.0	3.0	0.0	4.0	0.0
6	CZCH	8	0	1	0	0	0	4	2	2	0	8	0	0	6	0	13	7	0	9	0
		7.8	0.0	1.0	0.0	0.0	0.0	3.9	2.0	2.0	0.0	7.8	0.0	0.0	5.9	0.0	12.7	6.9	0.0	8.8	0.0
7	DNMK	2	4	0	1	0	0	0	0	8	0	6	0	0	13	0	1	4	0	2	0
		2.0	3.9	0.0	1.0	0.0	0.0	0.0	0.0	7.8	0.0	5.9	0.0	0.0	12.7	0.0	1.0	3.9	0.0	2.0	0.0
8	FNLD	3	4	0	0	0	0	3	0	5	0	4	0	0	11	0	9	4	0	3	0
		2.6	3.4	0.0	0.0	0.0	0.0	2.6	0.0	4.3	0.0	3.4	0.0	0.0	9.5	0.0	7.8	3.4	0.0	2.6	0.0
9	FRNC	1	2	2	2	0	0	1	2	5	1	3	0	0	2	0	1	8	0	2	1
		1.5	3.0	3.0	3.0	0.0	0.0	1.5	3.0	7.5	1.5	4.5	0.0	0.0	3.0	0.0	1.5	11.9	0.0	3.0	1.5
10	FRG	4	3	3	4	0	0	0	2	15	1	36	0	0	17	0	10	11	0	2	0
		1.5	1.1	1.1	1.5	0.0	0.0	0.0	0.8	5.7	0.4	13.7	0.0	0.0	6.5	0.0	3.8	4.2	0.0	0.8	0.0
11	GDR	5	4	2	0	1	0	0	4	1	0	14	4	0	19	0	7	14	0	2	0
		3.1	2.5	1.2	0.0	0.6	0.0	0.0	2.5	0.6	0.0	8.7	2.5	0.0	11.8	0.0	4.3	8.7	0.0	1.2	0.0
12	GRCE	2	4	2	2	1	2	1	2	2	0	6	1	0	4	0	4	6	0	7	4
		1.6	3.1	1.6	1.6	0.8	1.6	0.8	1.6	1.6	0.0	4.7	0.8	0.0	3.1	0.0	3.1	4.7	0.0	5.5	3.1
13	HNGR	12	4	0	0	0	0	3	0	7	0	24	2	0	21	0	3	9	0	2	0
		5.9	2.0	0.0	0.0	0.0	0.0	1.5	0.0	3.5	0.0	11.9	1.0	0.0	10.4	0.0	1.5	4.5	0.0	1.0	0.0
14	ICLD	1	2	0	1	0	0	0	1	2	0	5	0	3	6	0	1	0	0	1	1
		1.8	3.6	0.0	1.8	0.0	0.0	0.0	1.8	3.6	0.0	8.9	0.0	5.4	10.7	0.0	1.8	0.0	0.0	1.8	1.8
15	IRLD	5	3	1	2	0	0	0	3	9	0	5	2	0	14	0	12	1	4	3	7
		4.4	2.6	0.9	1.8	0.0	0.0	0.0	2.6	7.9	0.0	4.4	1.8	0.0	12.3	0.0	10.5	0.9	3.5	2.6	6.1
16	ITLY	5	9	2	1	0	0	0	1	7	0	16	0	0	10	1	4	9	0	6	0
		3.4	6.2	1.4	0.7	0.0	0.0	0.0	0.7	4.8	0.0	11.0	0.0	0.0	6.8	0.7	2.7	6.2	0.0	4.1	0.0
17	LICH	0	1	0	1	0	0	0	0	1	0	3	0	0	1	0	0	1	0	0	0
		0.0	4.8	0.0	4.8	0.0	0.0	0.0	0.0	4.8	0.0	14.3	0.0	0.0	4.8	0.0	0.0	4.8	0.0	0.0	0.0

18	LXBG	2	2	0	1	0	0	0	2	7	0	0	0	0	7	0	4	4	0	3	2
		1.4	1.4	0.0	0.7	0.0	0.0	0.0	1.4	4.9	0.0	0.0	0.0	0.0	4.9	0.0	2.8	2.8	0.0	2.1	1.4
19	MLTA	2	0	0	0	0	0	0	0	0	0	4	0	0	1	0	3	7	0	0	0
		2.7	0.0	0.0	0.0	0.0	0.0	0.0	0.0	0.0	0.0	5.4	0.0	0.0	1.4	0.0	4.1	9.5	0.0	0.0	0.0
20	MNCO	0	0	0	0	0	0	0	0	1	0	0	0	0	0	0	0	1	0	1	0
		0.0	0.0	0.0	0.0	0.0	0.0	0.0	0.0	7.1	0.0	0.0	0.0	0.0	0.0	0.0	0.0	7.1	0.0	7.1	0.0
21	NTHL	1	6	0	1	1	0	0	0	26	0	5	1	3	1	0	4	9	0	2	0
		0.9	5.5	0.0	0.9	0.9	0.0	0.0	0.0	23.6	0.0	4.5	0.9	2.7	0.9	0.0	3.6	8.2	0.0	1.8	0.0
22	NRWY	4	3	1	3	3	0	4	5	10	1	6	0	0	19	1	26	4	0	6	0
		2.2	1.6	0.5	1.6	1.6	0.0	2.2	2.7	5.4	0.5	3.2	0.0	0.0	10.3	0.5	14.1	2.2	0.0	3.2	0.0
23	PLND	3	2	2	1	0	0	1	4	0	0	18	0	0	14	0	19	12	0	4	0
		1.6	1.1	1.1	0.5	0.0	0.0	0.5	2.2	0.0	0.0	9.7	0.0	0.0	7.5	0.0	10.2	6.5	0.0	2.2	0.0
24	PRTG	0	1	1	3	1	1	0	4	8	2	2	1	0	0	0	0	3	0	0	0
		0.0	2.0	2.0	6.1	2.0	2.0	0.0	8.2	16.3	4.1	4.1	2.0	0.0	0.0	0.0	0.0	6.1	0.0	0.0	0.0
25	RMNA	25	1	7	6	0	3	5	9	7	4	41	0	0	30	0	19	6	0	5	0
		7.3	0.3	2.0	1.7	0.0	0.9	1.5	2.6	2.0	1.2	12.0	0.0	0.0	8.7	0.0	5.5	1.7	0.0	1.5	0.0
26	SANM	0	4	0	2	0	1	0	4	2	1	8	0	0	1	0	0	2	0	0	0
		0.0	6.3	0.0	3.1	0.0	1.6	0.0	6.3	3.1	1.6	12.5	0.0	0.0	1.6	0.0	0.0	3.1	0.0	0.0	0.0
27	SPAN	4	6	6	1	0	1	1	0	14	0	26	0	0	20	0	6	18	0	3	1
		1.9	2.8	2.8	0.5	0.0	0.5	0.5	0.0	6.5	0.0	12.1	0.0	0.0	9.3	0.0	2.8	8.4	0.0	1.4	0.5
28	SWDN	1	1	2	1	0	1	1	2	16	0	1	2	0	13	0	36	22	0	7	0
		0.5	0.5	1.0	0.5	0.0	0.5	0.5	1.0	7.7	0.0	0.5	1.0	0.0	6.2	0.0	17.2	10.5	0.0	3.3	0.0
29	SWTZ	10	2	1	14	0	0	12	1	3	3	2	0	0	7	0	16	9	3	0	0
		6.3	1.3	0.6	8.9	0.0	0.0	7.6	0.6	1.9	1.9	1.3	0.0	0.0	4.4	0.0	10.1	5.7	1.9	0.0	0.0
30	TRKY	3	3	0	1	0	0	0	2	2	0	9	0	0	8	0	10	2	0	1	0
		4.1	4.1	0.0	1.4	0.0	0.0	0.0	2.7	2.7	0.0	12.3	0.0	0.0	11.0	0.0	13.7	2.7	0.0	1.4	0.0
31	USSR	1	2	0	3	0	0	0	3	3	0	5	0	0	19	0	11	3	0	3	0
		0.6	1.1	0.0	1.7	0.0	0.0	0.0	1.7	1.7	0.0	2.8	0.0	0.0	10.6	0.0	6.1	1.7	0.0	1.7	0.0
32	UK	4	3	2	4	0	3	3	3	28	2	6	9	0	4	0	4	9	0	4	0
		2.6	2.0	1.3	2.6	0.0	2.0	2.0	2.0	18.4	1.3	3.9	5.9	0.0	2.6	0.0	2.6	5.9	0.0	2.6	0.0
33	USA	3	5	3	2	0	0	0	3	52	2	7	0	0	7	0	5	12	0	3	0
		1.9	3.2	1.9	1.3	0.0	0.0	0.0	1.9	33.3	1.3	4.5	0.0	0.0	4.5	0.0	3.2	7.7	0.0	1.9	0.0
34	VATC	1	1	3	3	0	0	3	1	16	3	10	3	0	5	1	5	3	0	1	0
		0.7	0.7	2.1	2.1	0.0	0.0	2.1	0.7	11.0	2.1	6.9	2.1	0.0	3.4	0.7	3.4	2.1	0.0	0.7	0.0
35	YGSL	3	12	3	3	0	1	0	5	16	2	13	0	0	9	0	9	9	0	0	0
		1.7	6.8	1.7	1.7	0.0	0.6	0.0	2.8	9.0	1.1	7.3	0.0	0.0	5.1	0.0	5.1	5.1	0.0	0.0	0.0

Table A2.7. *(cont.)*

COUNTRIES		21	22	23	24	25	26	27	28	29	30	31	32	33	34	35	36	37	38	39	40
1	AUST	0	0	2	0	0	0	1	0	0	0	0	0	0	0	2	0	0	0	0	0
		0.0	0.0	1.4	0.0	0.0	0.0	0.7	0.0	0.0	0.0	0.0	0.0	0.0	0.0	1.4	0.0	0.0	0.0	0.0	0.0
2	BLGM	2	1	1	0	0	0	0	0	0	0	0	0	0	0	0	0	0	0	0	0
		2.2	1.1	1.1	0.0	0.0	0.0	0.0	0.0	0.0	0.0	0.0	0.0	0.0	0.0	0.0	0.0	0.0	0.0	0.0	0.0
3	BLGR	1	0	0	0	0	0	0	0	0	0	0	0	0	0	0	0	0	0	0	0
		0.9	0.0	0.0	0.0	0.0	0.0	0.0	0.0	0.0	0.0	0.0	0.0	0.0	0.0	0.0	0.0	0.0	0.0	0.0	0.0
4	CNDA	0	0	0	0	0	0	0	0	0	0	0	0	0	0	1	0	0	0	0	4
		0.0	0.0	0.0	0.0	0.0	0.0	0.0	0.0	0.0	0.0	0.0	0.0	0.0	0.0	0.6	0.0	0.0	0.0	0.0	2.4
5	CYPR	0	0	0	0	0	0	0	0	0	0	0	0	0	0	0	0	0	0	0	0
		0.0	0.0	0.0	0.0	0.0	0.0	0.0	0.0	0.0	0.0	0.0	0.0	0.0	0.0	0.0	0.0	0.0	0.0	0.0	0.0
6	CZCH	0	0	0	0	0	0	0	0	0	0	0	0	0	0	0	0	0	0	0	0
		0.0	0.0	0.0	0.0	0.0	0.0	0.0	0.0	0.0	0.0	0.0	0.0	0.0	0.0	0.0	0.0	0.0	0.0	0.0	0.0
7	DNMK	0	1	1	0	0	0	0	0	0	0	0	0	0	0	0	0	0	0	0	1
		0.0	1.0	1.0	0.0	0.0	0.0	0.0	0.0	0.0	0.0	0.0	0.0	0.0	0.0	0.0	0.0	0.0	0.0	0.0	1.0
8	FNLD	3	0	0	0	0	0	0	0	0	9	0	0	0	0	0	0	0	0	0	1
		2.6	0.0	0.0	0.0	0.0	0.0	0.0	0.0	0.0	7.8	0.0	0.0	0.0	0.0	0.0	0.0	0.0	0.0	0.0	0.9
9	FRNC	1	0	0	0	0	0	0	0	0	0	0	0	0	0	0	0	0	0	0	0
		1.5	0.0	0.0	0.0	0.0	0.0	0.0	0.0	0.0	0.0	0.0	0.0	0.0	0.0	0.0	0.0	0.0	0.0	0.0	0.0
10	FRG	0	0	0	0	0	0	0	0	0	0	0	0	0	0	1	0	0	0	0	1
		0.0	0.0	0.0	0.0	0.0	0.0	0.0	0.0	0.0	0.0	0.0	0.0	0.0	0.0	0.4	0.0	0.0	0.0	0.0	0.4
11	GDR	0	0	0	0	0	0	0	0	0	0	0	0	0	0	0	0	0	0	0	0
		0.0	0.0	0.0	0.0	0.0	0.0	0.0	0.0	0.0	0.0	0.0	0.0	0.0	0.0	0.0	0.0	0.0	0.0	0.0	0.0
12	GRCE	0	0	1	0	0	0	0	0	0	0	0	0	0	0	1	0	0	0	0	5
		0.0	0.0	0.8	0.0	0.0	0.0	0.0	0.0	0.0	0.0	0.0	0.0	0.0	0.0	0.8	0.0	0.0	0.0	0.0	3.9
13	HNGR	0	0	0	0	0	0	0	0	0	1	0	0	4	0	0	0	0	0	0	1
		0.0	0.0	0.0	0.0	0.0	0.0	0.0	0.0	0.0	0.5	0.0	0.0	2.0	0.0	0.0	0.0	0.0	0.0	0.0	0.5
14	ICLD	1	3	0	0	0	0	0	0	0	0	0	0	0	0	0	0	0	0	0	0
		1.8	5.4	0.0	0.0	0.0	0.0	0.0	0.0	0.0	0.0	0.0	0.0	0.0	0.0	0.0	0.0	0.0	0.0	0.0	0.0
15	IRLD	0	6	1	0	0	0	0	0	0	0	0	0	0	0	0	0	0	0	0	0
		0.0	5.3	0.9	0.0	0.0	0.0	0.0	0.0	0.0	0.0	0.0	0.0	0.0	0.0	0.0	0.0	0.0	0.0	0.0	0.0
16	ITLY	2	1	1	0	0	0	1	0	0	1	0	0	0	0	2	0	0	0	0	0
		1.4	0.7	0.7	0.0	0.0	0.0	0.7	0.0	0.0	0.7	0.0	0.0	0.0	0.0	1.4	0.0	0.0	0.0	0.0	0.0
17	LICH	0	0	0	0	0	0	0	0	0	0	0	0	0	0	0	0	0	0	0	0
		0.0	0.0	0.0	0.0	0.0	0.0	0.0	0.0	0.0	0.0	0.0	0.0	0.0	0.0	0.0	0.0	0.0	0.0	0.0	0.0

18	LXBG	0	2	1	0	0	0	0	0	0	5	0	0	1	0	0	0	1	0	0	0
		0.0	1.4	0.7	0.0	0.0	0.0	0.0	0.0	0.0	3.5	0.0	0.0	0.7	0.0	0.0	0.0	0.7	0.0	0.0	0.0
19	MLTA	0	0	0	0	0	0	0	0	0	0	0	0	0	0	0	0	0	0	0	0
		0.0	0.0	0.0	0.0	0.0	0.0	0.0	0.0	0.0	0.0	0.0	0.0	0.0	0.0	0.0	0.0	0.0	0.0	0.0	0.0
20	MNCO	0	0	0	0	0	0	0	0	0	0	0	0	0	0	4	0	0	0	0	0
		0.0	0.0	0.0	0.0	0.0	0.0	0.0	0.0	0.0	0.0	0.0	0.0	0.0	0.0	28.6	0.0	0.0	0.0	0.0	0.0
21	NTHL	0	0	0	0	0	0	0	0	0	0	0	0	0	0	0	0	0	0	0	0
		0.0	0.0	0.0	0.0	0.0	0.0	0.0	0.0	0.0	0.0	0.0	0.0	0.0	0.0	0.0	0.0	0.0	0.0	0.0	0.0
22	NRWY	0	0	0	0	0	0	0	0	0	0	0	0	0	0	0	0	0	0	0	4
		0.0	0.0	0.0	0.0	0.0	0.0	0.0	0.0	0.0	0.0	0.0	0.0	0.0	0.0	0.0	0.0	0.0	0.0	0.0	2.2
23	PLND	0	0	0	0	0	0	0	0	0	0	0	0	0	0	0	0	0	0	0	1
		0.0	0.0	0.0	0.0	0.0	0.0	0.0	0.0	0.0	0.0	0.0	0.0	0.0	0.0	0.0	0.0	0.0	0.0	0.0	0.5
24	PRTG	0	0	0	0	0	0	0	0	0	0	0	0	0	0	0	0	0	0	0	0
		0.0	0.0	0.0	0.0	0.0	0.0	0.0	0.0	0.0	0.0	0.0	0.0	0.0	0.0	0.0	0.0	0.0	0.0	0.0	0.0
25	RMNA	0	1	0	0	0	4	0	0	0	0	0	0	0	0	3	0	0	1	0	4
		0.0	0.3	0.0	0.0	0.0	1.2	0.0	0.0	0.0	0.0	0.0	0.0	0.0	0.0	0.9	0.0	0.0	0.3	0.0	1.2
26	SANM	0	0	0	0	0	0	0	0	0	0	0	0	0	0	0	0	0	0	0	0
		0.0	0.0	0.0	0.0	0.0	0.0	0.0	0.0	0.0	0.0	0.0	0.0	0.0	0.0	0.0	0.0	0.0	0.0	0.0	0.0
27	SPAN	0	0	0	0	0	0	0	0	0	0	0	0	0	0	0	0	0	0	0	0
		0.0	0.0	0.0	0.0	0.0	0.0	0.0	0.0	0.0	0.0	0.0	0.0	0.0	0.0	0.0	0.0	0.0	0.0	0.0	0.0
28	SWDN	0	0	0	0	0	0	0	0	0	0	0	0	0	0	0	0	0	0	0	0
		0.0	0.0	0.0	0.0	0.0	0.0	0.0	0.0	0.0	0.0	0.0	0.0	0.0	0.0	0.0	0.0	0.0	0.0	0.0	0.0
29	SWTZ	0	0	0	0	0	0	0	0	0	0	0	0	0	0	0	0	0	0	0	0
		0.0	0.0	0.0	0.0	0.0	0.0	0.0	0.0	0.0	0.0	0.0	0.0	0.0	0.0	0.0	0.0	0.0	0.0	0.0	0.0
30	TRKY	0	0	0	0	0	0	0	0	0	0	0	0	0	0	0	0	0	0	0	0
		0.0	0.0	0.0	0.0	0.0	0.0	0.0	0.0	0.0	0.0	0.0	0.0	0.0	0.0	0.0	0.0	0.0	0.0	0.0	0.0
31	USSR	3	0	0	0	0	0	0	0	0	3	0	0	0	0	2	0	0	0	0	4
		1.7	0.0	0.0	0.0	0.0	0.0	0.0	0.0	0.0	1.7	0.0	0.0	0.0	0.0	1.1	0.0	0.0	0.0	0.0	2.2
32	UK	0	0	0	0	0	0	0	0	0	0	0	0	0	0	0	0	0	0	0	0
		0.0	0.0	0.0	0.0	0.0	0.0	0.0	0.0	0.0	0.0	0.0	0.0	0.0	0.0	0.0	0.0	0.0	0.0	0.0	0.0
33	USA	0	0	0	0	0	0	0	0	0	0	0	0	0	0	0	0	0	0	0	0
		0.0	0.0	0.0	0.0	0.0	0.0	0.0	0.0	0.0	0.0	0.0	0.0	0.0	0.0	0.0	0.0	0.0	0.0	0.0	0.0
34	VATC	0	0	0	0	0	0	0	0	0	0	0	0	0	0	0	0	0	0	0	0
		0.0	0.0	0.0	0.0	0.0	0.0	0.0	0.0	0.0	0.0	0.0	0.0	0.0	0.0	0.0	0.0	0.0	0.0	0.0	0.0
35	YGSL	1	0	0	0	0	0	0	0	0	0	0	0	0	0	1	0	0	0	0	0
		0.6	0.0	0.0	0.0	0.0	0.0	0.0	0.0	0.0	0.0	0.0	0.0	0.0	0.0	0.6	0.0	0.0	0.0	0.0	0.0

Table A2.7. *(cont.)*

COUNTRIES	41	42	43	44	45	46	47	48	49	50	51	52	53	54	55	56	57	58	59	60
1 AUST	0	0	0	0	0	0	0	0	0	0	0	0	0	0	0	0	0	2	2	0
	0.0	0.0	0.0	0.0	0.0	0.0	0.0	0.0	0.0	0.0	0.0	0.0	0.0	0.0	0.0	0.0	0.0	1.4	1.4	0.0
2 BLGM	0	0	0	0	0	0	0	0	0	0	4	1	0	1	0	0	0	8	4	0
	0.0	0.0	0.0	0.0	0.0	0.0	0.0	0.0	0.0	0.0	4.3	1.1	0.0	1.1	0.0	0.0	0.0	8.6	4.3	0.0
3 BLGR	0	0	0	0	0	0	0	0	0	0	1	0	0	0	0	0	0	6	0	0
	0.0	0.0	0.0	0.0	0.0	0.0	0.0	0.0	0.0	0.0	0.9	0.0	0.0	0.0	0.0	0.0	0.0	5.4	0.0	0.0
4 CNDA	0	0	0	0	0	0	0	0	0	0	0	0	0	0	0	0	0	5	3	0
	0.0	0.0	0.0	0.0	0.0	0.0	0.0	0.0	0.0	0.0	0.0	0.0	0.0	0.0	0.0	0.0	0.0	3.0	1.8	0.0
5 CYPR	0	0	0	0	0	0	0	0	0	0	4	0	1	2	0	0	0	1	0	0
	0.0	0.0	0.0	0.0	0.0	0.0	0.0	0.0	0.0	0.0	4.0	0.0	1.0	2.0	0.0	0.0	0.0	1.0	0.0	0.0
6 CZCH	0	0	0	0	0	0	0	0	0	0	0	0	0	0	0	0	0	0	0	0
	0.0	0.0	0.0	0.0	0.0	0.0	0.0	0.0	0.0	0.0	0.0	0.0	0.0	0.0	0.0	0.0	0.0	0.0	0.0	0.0
7 DNMK	0	0	0	0	0	1	0	0	0	1	0	0	0	0	0	0	0	3	7	0
	0.0	0.0	0.0	0.0	0.0	1.0	0.0	0.0	0.0	1.0	0.0	0.0	0.0	0.0	0.0	0.0	0.0	2.9	6.9	0.0
8 FNLD	0	0	0	0	0	0	0	0	0	0	1	0	0	0	0	0	0	1	2	0
	0.0	0.0	0.0	0.0	0.0	0.0	0.0	0.0	0.0	0.0	0.9	0.0	0.0	0.0	0.0	0.0	0.0	0.9	1.7	0.0
9 FRNC	0	0	0	0	0	0	0	0	0	0	0	0	0	0	0	0	0	0	5	1
	0.0	0.0	0.0	0.0	0.0	0.0	0.0	0.0	0.0	0.0	0.0	0.0	0.0	0.0	0.0	0.0	0.0	0.0	7.5	1.5
10 FRG	0	0	0	0	0	0	0	0	0	0	0	0	0	0	0	0	0	5	10	1
	0.0	0.0	0.0	0.0	0.0	0.0	0.0	0.0	0.0	0.0	0.0	0.0	0.0	0.0	0.0	0.0	0.0	1.9	3.8	0.4
11 GDR	0	0	0	0	0	0	0	0	0	0	1	0	0	0	0	0	0	2	3	0
	0.0	0.0	0.0	0.0	0.0	0.0	0.0	0.0	0.0	0.0	0.6	0.0	0.0	0.0	0.0	0.0	0.0	1.2	1.9	0.0
12 GRCE	0	0	0	0	0	5	0	0	0	9	2	0	1	1	0	0	0	1	4	0
	0.0	0.0	0.0	0.0	0.0	3.9	0.0	0.0	0.0	7.0	1.6	0.0	0.8	0.8	0.0	0.0	0.0	0.8	3.1	0.0
13 HNGR	0	0	0	0	0	1	0	0	0	1	1	0	0	0	0	0	0	1	1	0
	0.0	0.0	0.0	0.0	0.0	0.5	0.0	0.0	0.0	0.5	0.5	0.0	0.0	0.0	0.0	0.0	0.0	0.5	0.5	0.0
14 ICLD	0	0	0	0	0	0	0	0	0	0	0	0	0	0	0	0	0	0	5	0
	0.0	0.0	0.0	0.0	0.0	0.0	0.0	0.0	0.0	0.0	0.0	0.0	0.0	0.0	0.0	0.0	0.0	0.0	8.9	0.0
15 IRLD	0	0	0	0	0	0	0	0	0	0	0	0	0	0	0	0	0	8	0	0
	0.0	0.0	0.0	0.0	0.0	0.0	0.0	0.0	0.0	0.0	0.0	0.0	0.0	0.0	0.0	0.0	0.0	7.0	0.0	0.0
16 ITLY	0	0	0	0	0	0	0	2	0	0	10	0	5	0	0	0	0	1	1	1
	0.0	0.0	0.0	0.0	0.0	0.0	0.0	1.4	0.0	0.0	6.8	0.0	3.4	0.0	0.0	0.0	0.0	0.7	0.7	0.7
17 LICH	0	0	0	0	0	0	0	0	0	0	0	0	0	0	0	0	0	1	0	0
	0.0	0.0	0.0	0.0	0.0	0.0	0.0	0.0	0.0	0.0	0.0	0.0	0.0	0.0	0.0	0.0	0.0	4.8	0.0	0.0

18	LXBG	0	0	0	0	0	0	0	0	0	0	2	0	0	0	0	0	0	1	8	0
		0.0	0.0	0.0	0.0	0.0	0.0	0.0	0.0	0.0	0.0	1.4	0.0	0.0	0.0	0.0	0.0	0.0	0.7	5.6	0.0
19	MLTA	0	0	0	0	0	0	0	0	0	0	9	0	8	2	0	0	0	0	0	0
		0.0	0.0	0.0	0.0	0.0	0.0	0.0	0.0	0.0	0.0	12.2	0.0	10.8	2.7	0.0	0.0	0.0	0.0	0.0	0.0
20	MNCO	0	1	0	0	0	0	0	0	0	0	2	0	0	0	0	0	0	0	0	0
		0.0	7.1	0.0	0.0	0.0	0.0	0.0	0.0	0.0	0.0	14.3	0.0	0.0	0.0	0.0	0.0	0.0	0.0	0.0	0.0
21	NTHL	0	0	0	0	0	0	0	0	0	0	0	0	0	0	0	0	0	0	1	0
		0.0	0.0	0.0	0.0	0.0	0.0	0.0	0.0	0.0	0.0	0.0	0.0	0.0	0.0	0.0	0.0	0.0	0.0	0.9	0.0
22	NRWY	0	0	0	0	0	0	0	0	0	0	0	0	0	0	0	0	0	1	1	0
		0.0	0.0	0.0	0.0	0.0	0.0	0.0	0.0	0.0	0.0	0.0	0.0	0.0	0.0	0.0	0.0	0.0	0.5	0.5	0.0
23	PLND	0	0	0	0	0	0	0	0	0	0	0	0	0	0	0	0	0	0	2	0
		0.0	0.0	0.0	0.0	0.0	0.0	0.0	0.0	0.0	0.0	0.0	0.0	0.0	0.0	0.0	0.0	0.0	0.0	1.1	0.0
24	PRTG	0	0	0	0	0	0	0	0	0	0	0	0	0	0	0	0	0	0	1	0
		0.0	0.0	0.0	0.0	0.0	0.0	0.0	0.0	0.0	0.0	0.0	0.0	0.0	0.0	0.0	0.0	0.0	0.0	2.0	0.0
25	RMNA	0	0	0	0	0	4	0	0	0	4	1	0	1	0	0	0	0	0	5	0
		0.0	0.0	0.0	0.0	0.0	1.2	0.0	0.0	0.0	1.2	0.3	0.0	0.3	0.0	0.0	0.0	0.0	0.0	1.5	0.0
26	SANM	0	0	0	0	0	0	0	0	0	0	1	0	0	0	0	0	0	0	0	0
		0.0	0.0	0.0	0.0	0.0	0.0	0.0	0.0	0.0	0.0	1.6	0.0	0.0	0.0	0.0	0.0	0.0	0.0	0.0	0.0
27	SPAN	0	0	0	0	0	0	0	3	0	0	5	0	5	0	0	0	0	0	0	0
		0.0	0.0	0.0	0.0	0.0	0.0	0.0	1.4	0.0	0.0	2.3	0.0	2.3	0.0	0.0	0.0	0.0	0.0	0.0	0.0
28	SWDN	0	0	0	0	0	0	0	0	0	0	0	0	0	0	0	0	0	1	1	0
		0.0	0.0	0.0	0.0	0.0	0.0	0.0	0.0	0.0	0.0	0.0	0.0	0.0	0.0	0.0	0.0	0.0	0.5	0.5	0.0
29	SWTZ	0	0	0	0	0	0	0	0	0	0	0	0	0	0	0	0	0	1	2	0
		0.0	0.0	0.0	0.0	0.0	0.0	0.0	0.0	0.0	0.0	0.0	0.0	0.0	0.0	0.0	0.0	0.0	0.6	1.3	0.0
30	TRKY	0	0	0	0	0	0	0	2	0	0	0	0	0	0	0	0	0	0	1	0
		0.0	0.0	0.0	0.0	0.0	0.0	0.0	2.7	0.0	0.0	0.0	0.0	0.0	0.0	0.0	0.0	0.0	0.0	1.4	0.0
31	USSR	0	0	0	0	0	3	0	0	0	3	0	1	4	0	0	0	0	1	0	0
		0.0	0.0	0.0	0.0	0.0	1.7	0.0	0.0	0.0	1.7	0.0	0.6	2.2	0.0	0.0	0.0	0.0	0.6	0.0	0.0
32	UK	0	0	0	0	0	0	0	0	0	0	0	0	0	0	0	0	0	11	5	0
		0.0	0.0	0.0	0.0	0.0	0.0	0.0	0.0	0.0	0.0	0.0	0.0	0.0	0.0	0.0	0.0	0.0	7.2	3.3	0.0
33	USA	0	0	0	0	0	0	0	0	0	0	0	0	0	0	0	0	0	2	3	1
		0.0	0.0	0.0	0.0	0.0	0.0	0.0	0.0	0.0	0.0	0.0	0.0	0.0	0.0	0.0	0.0	0.0	1.3	1.9	0.6
34	VATC	0	0	0	0	0	0	0	0	0	0	0	0	0	0	0	0	0	4	0	0
		0.0	0.0	0.0	0.0	0.0	0.0	0.0	0.0	0.0	0.0	0.0	0.0	0.0	0.0	0.0	0.0	0.0	2.8	0.0	0.0
35	YGSL	0	0	0	0	0	0	0	1	0	0	6	0	0	0	0	0	0	1	0	0
		0.0	0.0	0.0	0.0	0.0	0.0	0.0	0.6	0.0	0.0	3.4	0.0	0.0	0.0	0.0	0.0	0.0	0.6	0.0	0.0

Table A2.7. *(cont.)*

COUNTRIES	61	62	63	64	65	66	67	68	69	70	71	72	73	74	75	76	77	78	79	80
1 AUST	0	0	1	0	0	0	0	0	2	1	0	6	0	2	0	1	0	0	0	0
	0.0	0.0	0.7	0.0	0.0	0.0	0.0	0.0	1.4	0.7	0.0	4.3	0.0	1.4	0.0	0.7	0.0	0.0	0.0	0.0
2 BLGM	1	0	0	3	0	0	0	0	3	4	0	4	0	1	0	0	0	0	0	0
	1.1	0.0	0.0	3.2	0.0	0.0	0.0	0.0	3.2	4.3	0.0	4.3	0.0	1.1	0.0	0.0	0.0	0.0	0.0	0.0
3 BLGR	0	0	0	0	0	0	1	0	0	0	0	0	0	3	0	2	0	0	0	0
	0.0	0.0	0.0	0.0	0.0	0.0	0.9	0.0	0.0	0.0	0.0	0.0	0.0	2.7	0.0	1.8	0.0	0.0	0.0	0.0
4 CNDA	2	0	5	1	0	0	0	0	1	0	0	0	0	1	0	0	0	0	0	0
	1.2	0.0	3.0	0.6	0.0	0.0	0.0	0.0	0.6	0.0	0.0	0.0	0.0	0.6	0.0	0.0	0.0	0.0	0.0	0.0
5 CYPR	0	0	0	0	0	0	0	0	0	0	0	0	0	0	0	0	0	0	0	0
	0.0	0.0	0.0	0.0	0.0	0.0	0.0	0.0	0.0	0.0	0.0	0.0	0.0	0.0	0.0	0.0	0.0	0.0	0.0	0.0
6 CZCH	0	0	0	0	0	0	0	0	0	0	0	0	0	0	0	0	0	0	0	0
	0.0	0.0	0.0	0.0	0.0	0.0	0.0	0.0	0.0	0.0	0.0	0.0	0.0	0.0	0.0	0.0	0.0	0.0	0.0	0.0
7 DNMK	0	0	0	0	1	0	0	0	6	1	0	1	0	1	0	0	0	0	0	0
	0.0	0.0	0.0	0.0	1.0	0.0	0.0	0.0	5.9	1.0	0.0	1.0	0.0	1.0	0.0	0.0	0.0	0.0	0.0	0.0
8 FNLD	1	1	1	0	0	0	0	0	2	1	0	1	0	4	0	0	0	4	0	0
	0.9	0.9	0.9	0.0	0.0	0.0	0.0	0.0	1.7	0.9	0.0	0.9	0.0	3.4	0.0	0.0	0.0	3.4	0.0	0.0
9 FRNC	0	0	1	0	0	0	0	0	0	0	0	0	0	1	1	1	0	0	2	0
	0.0	0.0	1.5	0.0	0.0	0.0	0.0	0.0	0.0	0.0	0.0	0.0	0.0	1.5	1.5	1.5	0.0	0.0	3.0	0.0
10 FRG	2	0	1	2	1	0	0	1	3	3	0	6	0	2	0	0	1	1	0	0
	0.8	0.0	0.4	0.8	0.4	0.0	0.0	0.4	1.1	1.1	0.0	2.3	0.0	0.8	0.0	0.0	0.4	0.4	0.0	0.0
11 GDR	0	0	0	1	0	0	0	0	2	0	0	0	0	2	0	0	0	0	0	0
	0.0	0.0	0.0	0.6	0.0	0.0	0.0	0.0	1.2	0.0	0.0	0.0	0.0	1.2	0.0	0.0	0.0	0.0	0.0	0.0
12 GRCE	0	0	0	0	0	0	0	0	1	0	0	2	0	2	0	0	0	0	0	0
	0.0	0.0	0.0	0.0	0.0	0.0	0.0	0.0	0.8	0.0	0.0	1.6	0.0	1.6	0.0	0.0	0.0	0.0	0.0	0.0
13 HNGR	1	1	2	4	0	0	0	0	2	0	0	1	0	2	1	0	0	0	0	0
	0.5	0.5	1.0	2.0	0.0	0.0	0.0	0.0	1.0	0.0	0.0	0.5	0.0	1.0	0.5	0.0	0.0	0.0	0.0	0.0
14 ICLD	1	0	1	0	0	0	0	0	4	0	0	0	0	4	0	0	0	0	0	0
	1.8	0.0	1.8	0.0	0.0	0.0	0.0	0.0	7.1	0.0	0.0	0.0	0.0	7.1	0.0	0.0	0.0	0.0	0.0	0.0
15 IRLD	0	0	0	0	0	0	0	0	0	0	0	0	0	0	0	0	0	0	0	0
	0.0	0.0	0.0	0.0	0.0	0.0	0.0	0.0	0.0	0.0	0.0	0.0	0.0	0.0	0.0	0.0	0.0	0.0	0.0	0.0
16 ITLY	1	1	0	0	0	0	0	0	1	1	0	2	0	1	2	0	0	0	0	0
	0.7	0.7	0.0	0.0	0.0	0.0	0.0	0.0	0.7	0.7	0.0	1.4	0.0	0.7	1.4	0.0	0.0	0.0	0.0	0.0
17 LICH	0	0	0	0	0	0	0	0	0	0	0	0	0	0	0	0	0	0	0	0
	0.0	0.0	0.0	0.0	0.0	0.0	0.0	0.0	0.0	0.0	0.0	0.0	0.0	0.0	0.0	0.0	0.0	0.0	0.0	0.0

18	LXBG	0	0	0	0	0	0	0	0	1	0	0	2	0	1	0	1	0	0	0	0
		0.0	0.0	0.0	0.0	0.0	0.0	0.0	0.0	0.7	0.0	0.0	1.4	0.0	0.7	0.0	0.7	0.0	0.0	0.0	0.0
19	MLTA	0	0	0	0	0	0	0	0	0	0	0	0	0	0	0	0	0	0	0	0
		0.0	0.0	0.0	0.0	0.0	0.0	0.0	0.0	0.0	0.0	0.0	0.0	0.0	0.0	0.0	0.0	0.0	0.0	0.0	0.0
20	MNCO	0	0	0	0	0	0	0	0	0	0	0	0	0	0	0	0	0	0	0	0
		0.0	0.0	0.0	0.0	0.0	0.0	0.0	0.0	0.0	0.0	0.0	0.0	0.0	0.0	0.0	0.0	0.0	0.0	0.0	0.0
21	NTHL	0	0	0	0	0	0	0	0	3	3	0	0	0	0	0	0	0	0	0	0
		0.0	0.0	0.0	0.0	0.0	0.0	0.0	0.0	2.7	2.7	0.0	0.0	0.0	0.0	0.0	0.0	0.0	0.0	0.0	0.0
22	NRWY	4	0	3	3	0	0	1	0	1	0	0	0	0	0	0	0	0	0	0	0
		2.2	0.0	1.6	1.6	0.0	0.0	0.5	0.0	0.5	0.0	0.0	0.0	0.0	0.0	0.0	0.0	0.0	0.0	0.0	0.0
23	PLND	0	0	0	0	0	0	0	0	1	0	0	0	0	3	0	0	0	0	0	0
		0.0	0.0	0.0	0.0	0.0	0.0	0.0	0.0	0.5	0.0	0.0	0.0	0.0	1.6	0.0	0.0	0.0	0.0	0.0	0.0
24	PRTG	1	1	1	0	0	0	0	0	0	1	0	0	0	0	0	0	0	0	0	0
		2.0	2.0	2.0	0.0	0.0	0.0	0.0	0.0	0.0	2.0	0.0	0.0	0.0	0.0	0.0	0.0	0.0	0.0	0.0	0.0
25	RMNA	0	0	0	0	0	0	0	0	4	1	0	0	0	9	0	0	0	0	1	0
		0.0	0.0	0.0	0.0	0.0	0.0	0.0	0.0	1.2	0.3	0.0	0.0	0.0	2.6	0.0	0.0	0.0	0.0	0.3	0.0
26	SANM	0	0	0	0	0	0	0	0	0	0	0	0	0	0	0	0	0	0	0	0
		0.0	0.0	0.0	0.0	0.0	0.0	0.0	0.0	0.0	0.0	0.0	0.0	0.0	0.0	0.0	0.0	0.0	0.0	0.0	0.0
27	SPAN	0	0	0	0	0	0	0	0	1	0	0	1	0	2	1	1	0	0	0	0
		0.0	0.0	0.0	0.0	0.0	0.0	0.0	0.0	0.5	0.0	0.0	0.5	0.0	0.9	0.5	0.5	0.0	0.0	0.0	0.0
28	SWDN	3	0	0	0	0	0	0	0	1	0	0	3	0	0	0	0	0	0	0	0
		1.4	0.0	0.0	0.0	0.0	0.0	0.0	0.0	0.5	0.0	0.0	1.4	0.0	0.0	0.0	0.0	0.0	0.0	0.0	0.0
29	SWTZ	6	0	1	0	0	0	0	0	5	2	0	2	0	0	0	0	0	0	0	0
		3.8	0.0	0.6	0.0	0.0	0.0	0.0	0.0	3.2	1.3	0.0	1.3	0.0	0.0	0.0	0.0	0.0	0.0	0.0	0.0
30	TRKY	0	0	0	0	0	0	0	0	2	0	0	0	0	1	0	0	0	0	0	0
		0.0	0.0	0.0	0.0	0.0	0.0	0.0	0.0	2.7	0.0	0.0	0.0	0.0	1.4	0.0	0.0	0.0	0.0	0.0	0.0
31	USSR	1	1	0	0	0	0	0	0	1	0	0	0	0	2	0	0	0	0	0	0
		0.6	0.6	0.0	0.0	0.0	0.0	0.0	0.0	0.6	0.0	0.0	0.0	0.0	1.1	0.0	0.0	0.0	0.0	0.0	0.0
32	UK	1	0	0	0	0	0	3	0	11	0	0	0	0	0	0	0	0	0	0	0
		0.7	0.0	0.0	0.0	0.0	0.0	2.0	0.0	7.2	0.0	0.0	0.0	0.0	0.0	0.0	0.0	0.0	0.0	0.0	0.0
33	USA	1	0	0	0	0	0	0	0	2	0	0	0	0	0	0	0	0	0	0	0
		0.6	0.0	0.0	0.0	0.0	0.0	0.0	0.0	1.3	0.0	0.0	0.0	0.0	0.0	0.0	0.0	0.0	0.0	0.0	0.0
34	VATC	4	4	4	4	4	0	0	0	1	0	0	0	0	1	0	0	0	0	0	1
		2.8	2.8	2.8	2.8	2.8	0.0	0.0	0.0	0.7	0.0	0.0	0.0	0.0	0.7	0.0	0.0	0.0	0.0	0.0	0.7
35	YGSL	0	0	0	0	0	0	0	0	1	0	0	0	0	0	0	0	0	0	0	0
		0.0	0.0	0.0	0.0	0.0	0.0	0.0	0.0	0.6	0.0	0.0	0.0	0.0	0.0	0.0	0.0	0.0	0.0	0.0	0.0

Table A2.7. *(cont.)*

	COUNTRIES	81	82	83	84	85	86	87	88	89	90	91	92	93	94	95	96	97	98	99	100
1	AUST	0	1	0	0	0	0	0	0	0	0	0	0	0	0	4	0	11	0	0	0
		0.0	0.7	0.0	0.0	0.0	0.0	0.0	0.0	0.0	0.0	0.0	0.0	0.0	0.0	2.8	0.0	7.8	0.0	0.0	0.0
2	BLGM	0	0	0	0	0	0	0	0	0	0	0	0	0	0	0	0	0	0	0	0
		0.0	0.0	0.0	0.0	0.0	0.0	0.0	0.0	0.0	0.0	0.0	0.0	0.0	0.0	0.0	0.0	0.0	0.0	0.0	0.0
3	BLGR	0	1	0	0	1	0	0	0	0	2	0	0	0	4	0	0	4	0	1	0
		0.0	0.9	0.0	0.0	0.9	0.0	0.0	0.0	0.0	1.8	0.0	0.0	0.0	3.6	0.0	0.0	3.6	0.0	0.9	0.0
4	CNDA	0	0	0	0	0	0	0	0	0	1	0	0	0	0	8	0	0	0	1	0
		0.0	0.0	0.0	0.0	0.0	0.0	0.0	0.0	0.0	0.6	0.0	0.0	0.0	0.0	4.8	0.0	0.0	0.0	0.6	0.0
5	CYPR	0	0	0	0	0	0	0	0	0	0	0	0	0	0	1	0	5	0	1	0
		0.0	0.0	0.0	0.0	0.0	0.0	0.0	0.0	0.0	0.0	0.0	0.0	0.0	0.0	1.0	0.0	5.0	0.0	1.0	0.0
6	CZCH	0	0	0	0	0	0	0	0	0	4	0	0	0	0	0	0	4	0	0	0
		0.0	0.0	0.0	0.0	0.0	0.0	0.0	0.0	0.0	3.9	0.0	0.0	0.0	0.0	0.0	0.0	3.9	0.0	0.0	0.0
7	DNMK	0	1	0	0	0	0	0	0	0	0	0	0	0	0	4	0	4	0	0	0
		0.0	1.0	0.0	0.0	0.0	0.0	0.0	0.0	0.0	0.0	0.0	0.0	0.0	0.0	3.9	0.0	3.9	0.0	0.0	0.0
8	FNLD	0	2	0	0	3	1	0	0	0	0	0	0	0	1	1	0	5	0	1	0
		0.0	1.7	0.0	0.0	2.6	0.9	0.0	0.0	0.0	0.0	0.0	0.0	0.0	0.9	0.9	0.0	4.3	0.0	0.9	0.0
9	FRNC	0	0	0	0	0	0	0	0	0	0	0	0	0	0	0	0	2	0	0	0
		0.0	0.0	0.0	0.0	0.0	0.0	0.0	0.0	0.0	0.0	0.0	0.0	0.0	0.0	0.0	0.0	3.0	0.0	0.0	0.0
10	FRG	0	1	1	0	1	0	0	0	0	1	0	1	0	0	3	0	11	3	1	0
		0.0	0.4	0.4	0.0	0.4	0.0	0.0	0.0	0.0	0.4	0.0	0.4	0.0	0.0	1.1	0.0	4.2	1.1	0.4	0.0
11	GDR	0	1	0	0	0	0	0	0	0	2	0	0	0	0	0	0	7	0	0	0
		0.0	0.6	0.0	0.0	0.0	0.0	0.0	0.0	0.0	1.2	0.0	0.0	0.0	0.0	0.0	0.0	4.3	0.0	0.0	0.0
12	GRCE	0	0	0	0	3	0	0	0	0	1	0	0	0	0	6	0	1	0	3	0
		0.0	0.0	0.0	0.0	2.3	0.0	0.0	0.0	0.0	0.8	0.0	0.0	0.0	0.0	4.7	0.0	0.8	0.0	2.3	0.0
13	HNGR	0	1	0	0	2	0	0	0	0	0	0	0	0	2	2	0	13	3	0	0
		0.0	0.5	0.0	0.0	1.0	0.0	0.0	0.0	0.0	0.0	0.0	0.0	0.0	1.0	1.0	0.0	6.4	1.5	0.0	0.0
14	ICLD	0	0	0	0	0	0	0	0	0	0	0	0	0	0	0	0	0	0	1	0
		0.0	0.0	0.0	0.0	0.0	0.0	0.0	0.0	0.0	0.0	0.0	0.0	0.0	0.0	0.0	0.0	0.0	0.0	1.8	0.0
15	IRLD	0	0	0	0	0	0	0	0	0	0	0	0	0	0	1	0	4	0	1	0
		0.0	0.0	0.0	0.0	0.0	0.0	0.0	0.0	0.0	0.0	0.0	0.0	0.0	0.0	0.9	0.0	3.5	0.0	0.9	0.0
16	ITLY	0	0	0	0	2	0	0	0	0	0	0	1	0	0	0	0	5	0	1	0
		0.0	0.0	0.0	0.0	1.4	0.0	0.0	0.0	0.0	0.0	0.0	0.7	0.0	0.0	0.0	0.0	3.4	0.0	0.7	0.0
17	LICH	0	0	0	0	0	0	0	0	0	1	0	1	0	0	0	0	0	0	0	0
		0.0	0.0	0.0	0.0	0.0	0.0	0.0	0.0	0.0	4.8	0.0	4.8	0.0	0.0	0.0	0.0	0.0	0.0	0.0	0.0

18	LXBG	0	1	0	0	0	0	0	0	0	0	0	0	0	0	0	0	5	25	0	0
		0.0	0.7	0.0	0.0	0.0	0.0	0.0	0.0	0.0	0.0	0.0	0.0	0.0	0.0	0.0	0.0	3.5	17.5	0.0	0.0
19	MLTA	0	0	0	0	0	0	0	0	0	0	0	0	0	0	0	0	0	0	0	0
		0.0	0.0	0.0	0.0	0.0	0.0	0.0	0.0	0.0	0.0	0.0	0.0	0.0	0.0	0.0	0.0	0.0	0.0	0.0	0.0
20	MNCO	0	0	0	0	0	0	0	0	0	0	0	0	0	0	0	0	1	0	0	0
		0.0	0.0	0.0	0.0	0.0	0.0	0.0	0.0	0.0	0.0	0.0	0.0	0.0	0.0	0.0	0.0	7.1	0.0	0.0	0.0
21	NTHL	0	0	0	0	0	0	0	0	0	1	0	0	0	0	0	0	0	0	0	0
		0.0	0.0	0.0	0.0	0.0	0.0	0.0	0.0	0.0	0.9	0.0	0.0	0.0	0.0	0.0	0.0	0.0	0.0	0.0	0.0
22	NRWY	0	0	0	0	0	0	0	0	0	0	0	0	0	1	0	0	12	0	0	0
		0.0	0.0	0.0	0.0	0.0	0.0	0.0	0.0	0.0	0.0	0.0	0.0	0.0	0.5	0.0	0.0	6.5	0.0	0.0	0.0
23	PLND	0	1	0	0	1	0	0	0	0	0	0	0	0	3	1	0	11	0	0	0
		0.0	0.5	0.0	0.0	0.5	0.0	0.0	0.0	0.0	0.0	0.0	0.0	0.0	1.6	0.5	0.0	5.9	0.0	0.0	0.0
24	PRTG	0	0	0	0	0	0	0	0	0	0	0	0	0	0	0	0	0	0	2	0
		0.0	0.0	0.0	0.0	0.0	0.0	0.0	0.0	0.0	0.0	0.0	0.0	0.0	0.0	0.0	0.0	0.0	0.0	4.1	0.0
25	RMNA	0	4	0	0	3	0	0	0	0	1	0	1	0	8	6	0	10	0	0	0
		0.0	1.2	0.0	0.0	0.9	0.0	0.0	0.0	0.0	0.3	0.0	0.3	0.0	2.3	1.7	0.0	2.9	0.0	0.0	0.0
26	SANM	0	0	0	0	0	0	0	0	0	0	0	4	0	0	0	0	1	0	0	0
		0.0	0.0	0.0	0.0	0.0	0.0	0.0	0.0	0.0	0.0	0.0	6.3	0.0	0.0	0.0	0.0	1.6	0.0	0.0	0.0
27	SPAN	0	0	0	0	0	0	0	0	0	0	0	3	0	0	1	0	7	0	1	0
		0.0	0.0	0.0	0.0	0.0	0.0	0.0	0.0	0.0	0.0	0.0	1.4	0.0	0.0	0.5	0.0	3.3	0.0	0.5	0.0
28	SWDN	0	0	0	0	0	0	0	0	0	1	0	0	0	16	1	0	17	0	1	0
		0.0	0.0	0.0	0.0	0.0	0.0	0.0	0.0	0.0	0.5	0.0	0.0	0.0	7.7	0.5	0.0	8.1	0.0	0.5	0.0
29	SWTZ	0	0	0	0	0	0	0	0	0	0	0	0	0	0	0	0	4	0	0	0
		0.0	0.0	0.0	0.0	0.0	0.0	0.0	0.0	0.0	0.0	0.0	0.0	0.0	0.0	0.0	0.0	2.5	0.0	0.0	0.0
30	TRKY	0	0	0	0	0	0	0	0	0	0	0	1	0	1	1	0	2	0	1	0
		0.0	0.0	0.0	0.0	0.0	0.0	0.0	0.0	0.0	0.0	0.0	1.4	0.0	1.4	1.4	0.0	2.7	0.0	1.4	0.0
31	USSR	0	1	0	0	4	0	0	0	0	1	0	0	0	4	7	0	14	0	1	0
		0.0	0.6	0.0	0.0	2.2	0.0	0.0	0.0	0.0	0.6	0.0	0.0	0.0	2.2	3.9	0.0	7.8	0.0	0.6	0.0
32	UK	0	0	0	0	0	0	0	0	0	1	0	2	0	0	0	0	0	0	3	0
		0.0	0.0	0.0	0.0	0.0	0.0	0.0	0.0	0.0	0.7	0.0	1.3	0.0	0.0	0.0	0.0	0.0	0.0	2.0	0.0
33	USA	0	0	0	0	0	0	0	0	0	1	0	1	0	5	0	0	6	0	0	0
		0.0	0.0	0.0	0.0	0.0	0.0	0.0	0.0	0.0	0.6	0.0	0.6	0.0	3.2	0.0	0.0	3.8	0.0	0.0	0.0
34	VATC	0	0	0	0	1	0	0	0	0	1	0	0	0	0	0	1	0	0	1	0
		0.0	0.0	0.0	0.0	0.7	0.0	0.0	0.0	0.0	0.7	0.0	0.0	0.0	0.0	0.0	0.7	0.0	0.0	0.7	0.0
35	YGSL	0	0	0	0	0	0	0	0	0	2	0	0	0	1	0	0	4	0	2	0
		0.0	0.0	0.0	0.0	0.0	0.0	0.0	0.0	0.0	1.1	0.0	0.0	0.0	0.6	0.0	0.0	2.3	0.0	1.1	0.0

Table A2.7. *(cont.)*

COUNTRIES		101	102	103	104	105	106	107	108	109	110	111	112	113	114	115	116	117	118	119	120
1	AUST	4	5	4	9	0	2	0	3	1	0	0	1	0	5	1	0	5	0	1	1
		2.8	3.5	2.8	6.4	0.0	1.4	0.0	2.1	0.7	0.0	0.0	0.7	0.0	3.5	0.7	0.0	3.5	0.0	0.7	0.7
2	BLGM	1	4	2	3	0	0	0	0	0	1	0	1	0	3	0	0	1	0	0	3
		1.1	4.3	2.2	3.2	0.0	0.0	0.0	0.0	0.0	1.1	0.0	1.1	0.0	3.2	0.0	0.0	1.1	0.0	0.0	3.2
3	BLGR	0	0	14	3	0	0	2	0	0	0	0	2	0	8	0	0	0	0	1	0
		0.0	0.0	12.6	2.7	0.0	0.0	1.8	0.0	0.0	0.0	0.0	1.8	0.0	7.2	0.0	0.0	0.0	0.0	0.9	0.0
4	CNDA	0	0	2	4	0	0	2	13	0	0	0	1	0	0	0	0	2	3	2	4
		0.0	0.0	1.2	2.4	0.0	0.0	1.2	7.7	0.0	0.0	0.0	0.6	0.0	0.0	0.0	0.0	1.2	1.8	1.2	2.4
5	CYPR	2	2	8	6	0	0	4	2	2	5	0	0	0	5	0	0	0	4	0	0
		2.0	2.0	8.0	6.0	0.0	0.0	4.0	2.0	2.0	5.0	0.0	0.0	0.0	5.0	0.0	0.0	0.0	4.0	0.0	0.0
6	CZCH	0	0	17	9	0	0	0	0	0	0	0	1	1	1	0	0	0	1	0	0
		0.0	0.0	16.7	8.8	0.0	0.0	0.0	0.0	0.0	0.0	0.0	1.0	1.0	1.0	0.0	0.0	0.0	1.0	0.0	0.0
7	DNMK	0	0	0	5	0	0	0	0	0	0	0	3	1	9	0	0	0	0	1	0
		0.0	0.0	0.0	4.9	0.0	0.0	0.0	0.0	0.0	0.0	0.0	2.9	1.0	8.8	0.0	0.0	0.0	0.0	1.0	0.0
8	FNLD	1	2	1	1	0	0	0	0	0	0	1	1	0	7	0	0	0	0	1	0
		0.9	1.7	0.9	0.9	0.0	0.0	0.0	0.0	0.0	0.0	0.9	0.9	0.0	6.0	0.0	0.0	0.0	0.0	0.9	0.0
9	FRNC	0	1	2	3	0	0	0	2	0	1	0	0	0	2	1	0	0	0	0	3
		0.0	1.5	3.0	4.5	0.0	0.0	0.0	3.0	0.0	1.5	0.0	0.0	0.0	3.0	1.5	0.0	0.0	0.0	0.0	4.5
10	FRG	2	1	16	13	0	0	2	2	1	0	3	7	0	2	0	0	9	1	9	5
		0.8	0.4	6.1	4.9	0.0	0.0	0.8	0.8	0.4	0.0	1.1	2.7	0.0	0.8	0.0	0.0	3.4	0.4	3.4	1.9
11	GDR	0	0	18	7	0	0	0	0	0	1	0	1	1	5	0	2	0	0	9	1
		0.0	0.0	11.2	4.3	0.0	0.0	0.0	0.0	0.0	0.6	0.0	0.6	0.6	3.1	0.0	1.2	0.0	0.0	5.6	0.6
12	GRCE	0	0	10	0	0	0	1	0	0	0	0	0	1	5	0	0	0	0	1	0
		0.0	0.0	7.8	0.0	0.0	0.0	0.8	0.0	0.0	0.0	0.0	0.0	0.8	3.9	0.0	0.0	0.0	0.0	0.8	0.0
13	HNGR	0	0	10	8	0	0	1	3	0	0	0	2	2	12	0	0	0	0	9	0
		0.0	0.0	5.0	4.0	0.0	0.0	0.5	1.5	0.0	0.0	0.0	1.0	1.0	5.9	0.0	0.0	0.0	0.0	4.5	0.0
14	ICLD	0	0	2	1	0	1	0	0	0	0	0	0	2	5	0	0	0	0	0	0
		0.0	0.0	3.6	1.8	0.0	1.8	0.0	0.0	0.0	0.0	0.0	0.0	3.6	8.9	0.0	0.0	0.0	0.0	0.0	0.0
15	IRLD	0	0	5	3	0	0	1	1	0	0	0	1	0	0	0	0	0	0	1	1
		0.0	0.0	4.4	2.6	0.0	0.0	0.9	0.9	0.0	0.0	0.0	0.9	0.0	0.0	0.0	0.0	0.0	0.0	0.9	0.9
16	ITLY	0	1	1	1	0	1	0	1	0	0	1	1	3	0	1	0	1	0	3	4
		0.0	0.7	0.7	0.7	0.0	0.7	0.0	0.7	0.0	0.0	0.7	0.7	2.1	0.0	0.7	0.0	0.7	0.0	2.1	2.7
17	LICH	2	0	1	1	0	0	0	0	0	0	0	0	1	3	0	0	1	0	1	0
		9.5	0.0	4.8	4.8	0.0	0.0	0.0	0.0	0.0	0.0	0.0	0.0	4.8	14.3	0.0	0.0	4.8	0.0	4.8	0.0

18	LXBG	1	1	3	2	0	0	1	0	0	0	2	0	2	5	0	0	0	0	4	1
		0.7	0.7	2.1	1.4	0.0	0.0	0.7	0.0	0.0	0.0	1.4	0.0	1.4	3.5	0.0	0.0	0.0	0.0	2.8	0.7
19	MLTA	3	5	17	6	0	0	0	0	0	0	0	1	0	1	0	0	0	0	2	2
		4.1	6.8	23.0	8.1	0.0	0.0	0.0	0.0	0.0	0.0	0.0	1.4	0.0	1.4	0.0	0.0	0.0	0.0	2.7	2.7
20	MNCO	0	0	1	0	0	0	0	0	0	0	0	0	0	0	0	0	0	0	1	0
		0.0	0.0	7.1	0.0	0.0	0.0	0.0	0.0	0.0	0.0	0.0	0.0	0.0	0.0	0.0	0.0	0.0	0.0	7.1	0.0
21	NTHL	0	0	4	6	0	0	2	8	11	1	0	1	0	7	0	0	0	0	1	1
		0.0	0.0	3.6	5.5	0.0	0.0	1.8	7.3	10.0	0.9	0.0	0.9	0.0	6.4	0.0	0.0	0.0	0.0	0.9	0.9
22	NRWY	0	0	2	11	0	0	0	1	0	1	0	2	1	17	4	0	0	0	3	4
		0.0	0.0	1.1	5.9	0.0	0.0	0.0	0.5	0.0	0.5	0.0	1.1	0.5	9.2	2.2	0.0	0.0	0.0	1.6	2.2
23	PLND	1	1	4	16	0	1	0	0	0	6	1	1	0	11	0	2	0	0	5	3
		0.5	0.5	2.2	8.6	0.0	0.5	0.0	0.0	0.0	3.2	0.5	0.5	0.0	5.9	0.0	1.1	0.0	0.0	2.7	1.6
24	PRTG	2	2	0	2	0	1	0	0	1	0	0	0	2	1	1	0	0	0	0	1
		4.1	4.1	0.0	4.1	0.0	2.0	0.0	0.0	2.0	0.0	0.0	0.0	4.1	2.0	2.0	0.0	0.0	0.0	0.0	2.0
25	RMNA	0	0	19	7	0	1	6	2	2	0	8	3	1	11	0	0	2	1	5	2
		0.0	0.0	5.5	2.0	0.0	0.3	1.7	0.6	0.6	0.0	2.3	0.9	0.3	3.2	0.0	0.0	0.6	0.3	1.5	0.6
26	SANM	0	2	6	5	0	2	3	1	2	1	5	1	0	0	0	0	1	1	1	0
		0.0	3.1	9.4	7.8	0.0	3.1	4.7	1.6	3.1	1.6	7.8	1.6	0.0	0.0	0.0	0.0	1.6	1.6	1.6	0.0
27	SPAN	0	0	19	10	0	1	2	3	2	1	4	4	0	10	0	1	0	0	5	3
		0.0	0.0	8.9	4.7	0.0	0.5	0.9	1.4	0.9	0.5	1.9	1.9	0.0	4.7	0.0	0.5	0.0	0.0	2.3	1.4
28	SWDN	2	3	4	4	0	1	0	6	1	0	0	0	0	12	4	0	0	0	0	2
		1.0	1.4	1.9	1.9	0.0	0.5	0.0	2.9	0.5	0.0	0.0	0.0	0.0	5.7	1.9	0.0	0.0	0.0	0.0	1.0
29	SWTZ	4	3	7	7	0	0	14	1	0	1	0	1	1	7	0	0	0	0	0	2
		2.5	1.9	4.4	4.4	0.0	0.0	8.9	0.6	0.0	0.6	0.0	0.6	0.6	4.4	0.0	0.0	0.0	0.0	0.0	1.3
30	TRKY	0	0	1	2	0	0	0	0	0	0	0	1	0	2	0	0	2	0	0	3
		0.0	0.0	1.4	2.7	0.0	0.0	0.0	0.0	0.0	0.0	0.0	1.4	0.0	2.7	0.0	0.0	2.7	0.0	0.0	4.1
31	USSR	1	0	19	6	0	0	0	0	0	0	0	3	0	1	0	0	0	0	13	0
		0.6	0.0	10.6	3.4	0.0	0.0	0.0	0.0	0.0	0.0	0.0	1.7	0.0	0.6	0.0	0.0	0.0	0.0	7.3	0.0
32	UK	0	0	5	2	0	0	0	3	2	1	0	1	1	2	3	0	0	0	1	3
		0.0	0.0	3.3	1.3	0.0	0.0	0.0	2.0	1.3	0.7	0.0	0.7	0.7	1.3	2.0	0.0	0.0	0.0	0.7	2.0
33	USA	0	0	6	1	0	1	0	1	3	3	1	0	0	1	3	0	0	0	4	0
		0.0	0.0	3.8	0.6	0.0	0.6	0.0	0.6	1.9	1.9	0.6	0.0	0.0	0.6	1.9	0.0	0.0	0.0	2.6	0.0
34	VATC	0	0	6	10	0	1	6	1	3	5	2	2	0	1	14	1	0	0	0	0
		0.0	0.0	4.1	6.9	0.0	0.7	4.1	0.7	2.1	3.4	1.4	1.4	0.0	0.7	9.7	0.7	0.0	0.0	0.0	0.0
35	YGSL	6	4	8	19	0	2	0	1	0	1	2	6	0	1	0	2	2	1	1	2
		3.4	2.3	4.5	10.7	0.0	1.1	0.0	0.6	0.0	0.6	1.1	3.4	0.0	0.6	0.0	1.1	1.1	0.6	0.6	1.1

A2.3 THE MAJOR ISSUES OF EAST–WEST RELATIONS: HIGHEST-SCORING CATEGORIES IN RANK-ORDER FOR INDIVIDUAL COUNTRIES

Table A2.8. Rank-Order of Categories: The 1973 Helsinki Statements

AUSTRIA

RANK	CODE	CATEGORY	%	CUMULATIVE %
1.	1	BASKET ONE: QUESTIONS RELATING TO SECURITY IN EUROPE	8.33	8.33
2.	11	COOPERATION AMONG STATES AS A PRINCIPLE OF INTERNATIONAL RELATIONS	8.33	16.67
3.	103	PEACE	8.33	25.00
4.	104	CONFLICT AND CONFRONTATION	8.33	33.33
5.	9	RESPECT FOR HUMAN RIGHTS AND FUNDAMENTAL FREEDOMS	7.41	40.74
6.	2	GENERAL REMARKS CONCERNING THE DECLARATION ON PRINCIPLES GUIDING RELATIONS	6.48	47.22
7.	17	QUESTIONS RELATING TO SECURITY	4.63	51.85
8.	14	DOCUMENT ON CONFIDENCE-BUILDING MEASURES AND CERTAIN ASPECTS OF SECURITY AND DISARMAMENT	3.70	55.56
9.	102	NEUTRALITY	3.70	59.26
10.	108	IDEOLOGY AND IDEAS	3.70	62.96

BELGIUM

RANK	CODE	CATEGORY	%	CUMULATIVE %
1.	19	BASKET TWO: COOPERATION IN THE FIELD OF ECONOMICS, SCIENCE, TECHNOLOGY, AND THE ENVIRONMENT	9.93	9.93
2.	16	QUESTIONS RELATING TO DISARMAMENT	7.09	17.02
3.	11	COOPERATION AMONG STATES AS A PRINCIPLE OF INTERNATIONAL RELATIONS	4.96	21.99
4.	58	BASKET THREE: COOPERATION IN HUMANITARIAN AND OTHER FIELDS	4.96	26.95
5.	14	DOCUMENT ON CONFIDENCE-BUILDING MEASURES AND CERTAIN ASPECTS OF SECURITY AND DISARMAMENT	4.26	31.21
6.	101	NON-ALIGNMENT	4.26	35.46
7.	102	NEUTRALITY	4.26	39.72
8.	1	BASKET ONE: QUESTIONS RELATING TO SECURITY IN EUROPE	3.55	43.26
9.	2	GENERAL REMARKS CONCERNING THE DECLARATION ON PRINCIPLES GUIDING RELATIONS	3.55	46.81
10.	76	CULTURAL EXCHANGE	3.55	50.35

BULGARIA

RANK	CODE	CATEGORY	%	CUMULATIVE %
1.	1	BASKET ONE: QUESTIONS RELATING TO SECURITY IN EUROPE	15.00	15.00
2.	11	COOPERATION AMONG STATES AS A PRINCIPLE OF INTERNATIONAL RELATIONS	10.00	25.00
3.	103	PEACE	10.00	35.00
4.	5	INVIOLABILITY OF FRONTIERS	6.00	41.00
5.	19	BASKET TWO: COOPERATION IN THE FIELD OF ECONOMICS, SCIENCE, TECHNOLOGY, AND THE ENVIRONMENT	6.00	47.00
6.	6	TERRITORIAL INTEGRITY OF STATES	5.00	52.00
7.	14	DOCUMENT ON CONFIDENCE-BUILDING MEASURES AND CERTAIN ASPECTS OF SECURITY AND DISARMAMENT	4.00	56.00
8.	114	POLITICAL COOPERATION AND POLITICAL DISCUSSIONS	4.00	60.00
9.	59	GENERAL REMARKS CONCERNING HUMAN CONTACTS	3.00	63.00
10.	70	IMPROVEMENT OF THE CIRCULATION, ACCESS TO, AND EXCHANGE OF INFORMATION	3.00	66.00

CANADA

RANK	CODE	CATEGORY	%	CUMULATIVE %
1.	11	COOPERATION AMONG STATES AS A PRINCIPLE OF INTERNATIONAL RELATIONS	9.33	9.33
2.	59	GENERAL REMARKS CONCERNING HUMAN CONTACTS	9.33	18.67
3.	1	BASKET ONE: QUESTIONS RELATING TO SECURITY IN EUROPE	6.67	25.33
4.	2	GENERAL REMARKS CONCERNING THE DECLARATION ON PRINCIPLES GUIDING RELATIONS	6.67	32.00
5.	14	DOCUMENT ON CONFIDENCE-BUILDING MEASURES AND CERTAIN ASPECTS OF SECURITY AND DISARMAMENT	6.67	38.67
6.	114	POLITICAL COOPERATION AND POLITICAL DISCUSSIONS	6.67	45.33
7.	17	QUESTIONS RELATING TO SECURITY	5.33	50.67
8.	21	GENERAL PROVISIONS CONCERNING THE EXPANSION OF MUTUAL TRADE	5.33	56.00
9.	107	JUDICIAL SYSTEMS AND LEGAL INSTITUTIONS	5.33	61.33
10.	19	BASKET TWO: COOPERATION IN THE FIELD OF ECONOMICS, SCIENCE, TECHNOLOGY, AND THE ENVIRONMENT	4.00	65.33

Table A2.8. *(cont.)*

CYPRUS

RANK	CODE	CATEGORY	%	CUMULATIVE %
1.	1	BASKET ONE: QUESTIONS RELATING TO SECURITY IN EUROPE	10.92	10.92
2.	11	COOPERATION AMONG STATES AS A PRINCIPLE OF INTERNATIONAL RELATIONS	9.24	20.17
3.	103	PEACE	8.40	28.57
4.	7	PEACEFUL SETTLEMENT OF DISPUTES	5.88	34.45
5.	51	SECTION ON THE MEDITERRANEAN: GENERAL REMARKS	5.88	40.34
6.	2	GENERAL REMARKS CONCERNING THE DECLARATION ON PRINCIPLES GUIDING RELATIONS	5.04	45.38
7.	4	REFRAINING FROM THE THREAT OR USE OF FORCE	5.04	50.42
8.	8	NON-INTERVENTION IN INTERNAL AFFAIRS	5.04	55.46
9.	19	BASKET TWO: COOPERATION IN THE FIELD OF ECONOMICS, SCIENCE, TECHNOLOGY, AND THE ENVIRONMENT	5.04	60.50
10.	14	DOCUMENT ON CONFIDENCE-BUILDING MEASURES AND CERTAIN ASPECTS OF SECURITY AND DISARMAMENT	4.20	64.71

CZECHOSLOVAKIA

RANK	CODE	CATEGORY	%	CUMULATIVE %
1.	11	COOPERATION AMONG STATES AS A PRINCIPLE OF INTERNATIONAL RELATIONS	14.29	14.29
2.	103	PEACE	14.29	28.57
3.	1	BASKET ONE: QUESTIONS RELATING TO SECURITY IN EUROPE	7.14	35.71
4.	19	BASKET TWO: COOPERATION IN THE FIELD OF ECONOMICS, SCIENCE, TECHNOLOGY, AND THE ENVIRONMENT	7.14	42.86
5.	35	COOPERATION IN SCIENCE AND TECHNOLOGY	6.25	49.11
6.	108	IDEOLOGY AND IDEAS	6.25	55.36
7.	85	COOPERATION IN THE FIELD OF SCIENTIFIC RESEARCH	3.57	58.93
8.	5	INVIOLABILITY OF FRONTIERS	2.68	61.61
9.	95	ENERGY PROBLEMS	2.68	64.29
10.	97	INTERNATIONAL CONFERENCES	2.68	66.96

RANK	CODE	CATEGORY	%	CUMULATIVE %
1.	11	COOPERATION AMONG STATES AS A PRINCIPLE OF INTERNATIONAL RELATIONS	10.00	10.00
2.	14	DOCUMENT ON CONFIDENCE-BUILDING MEASURES AND CERTAIN ASPECTS OF SECURITY AND DISARMAMENT	8.75	18.75
3.	58	BASKET THREE: COOPERATION IN HUMANITARIAN AND OTHER FIELDS	8.75	27.50
4.	59	GENERAL REMARKS CONCERNING HUMAN CONTACTS	7.50	35.00
5.	119	SPECIFIC INTERNATIONAL AGREEMENTS	6.25	41.25
6.	2	GENERAL REMARKS CONCERNING THE DECLARATION ON PRINCIPLES GUIDING RELATIONS	5.00	46.25
7.	16	QUESTIONS RELATING TO DISARMAMENT	5.00	51.25
8.	17	QUESTIONS RELATING TO SECURITY	5.00	56.25
9.	104	CONFLICT AND CONFRONTATION	5.00	61.25
10.	5	INVIOLABILITY OF FRONTIERS	3.75	65.00

FINLAND

RANK	CODE	CATEGORY	%	CUMULATIVE %
1.	1	BASKET ONE: QUESTIONS RELATING TO SECURITY IN EUROPE	14.52	14.52
2.	11	COOPERATION AMONG STATES AS A PRINCIPLE OF INTERNATIONAL RELATIONS	12.90	27.42
3.	102	NEUTRALITY	6.45	33.87
4.	103	PEACE	6.45	40.32
5.	112	RESPONSIBILITY	6.45	46.77
6.	3	SOVEREIGN EQUALITY, RESPECT FOR THE RIGHTS INHERENT IN SOVEREIGNTY	5.65	52.42
7.	16	QUESTIONS RELATING TO DISARMAMENT	5.65	58.06
8.	21	GENERAL PROVISIONS CONCERNING THE EXPANSION OF MUTUAL TRADE	5.65	63.71
9.	108	IDEOLOGY AND IDEAS	5.65	69.35
10.	19	BASKET TWO: COOPERATION IN THE FIELD OF ECONOMICS, SCIENCE, TECHNOLOGY, AND THE ENVIRONMENT	4.03	73.39

FRANCE

RANK	CODE	CATEGORY	%	CUMULATIVE %
1.	1	BASKET ONE: QUESTIONS RELATING TO SECURITY IN EUROPE	13.75	13.75
2.	104	CONFLICT AND CONFRONTATION	8.75	22.50
3.	103	PEACE	7.50	30.00
4.	14	DOCUMENT ON CONFIDENCE-BUILDING MEASURES AND CERTAIN ASPECTS OF SECURITY AND DISARMAMENT	6.25	36.25
5.	113	PUBLIC OPINION	6.25	42.50
6.	11	COOPERATION AMONG STATES AS A PRINCIPLE OF INTERNATIONAL RELATIONS	5.00	47.50
7.	119	SPECIFIC INTERNATIONAL AGREEMENTS	5.00	52.50
8.	19	BASKET TWO: COOPERATION IN THE FIELD OF ECONOMICS, SCIENCE, TECHNOLOGY, AND THE ENVIRONMENT	3.75	56.25
9.	109	FREEDOM	3.75	60.00
10.	111	WELFARE AND PROSPERITY	3.75	63.75

Table A2.8. *(cont.)*

FEDERAL REPUBLIC OF GERMANY

RANK	CODE	CATEGORY	%	CUMULATIVE %
1.	11	COOPERATION AMONG STATES AS A PRINCIPLE OF INTERNATIONAL RELATIONS	14.65	14.65
2.	108	IDEOLOGY AND IDEAS	6.37	21.02
3.	85	COOPERATION IN THE FIELD OF SCIENTIFIC RESEARCH	5.73	26.75
4.	119	SPECIFIC INTERNATIONAL AGREEMENTS	5.10	31.85
5.	14	DOCUMENT ON CONFIDENCE-BUILDING MEASURES AND CERTAIN ASPECTS OF SECURITY AND DISARMAMENT	4.46	36.31
6.	114	POLITICAL COOPERATION AND POLITICAL DISCUSSIONS	4.46	40.76
7.	4	REFRAINING FROM THE THREAT OR USE OF FORCE	3.82	44.59
8.	17	QUESTIONS RELATING TO SECURITY	3.82	48.41
9.	19	BASKET TWO: COOPERATION IN THE FIELD OF ECONOMICS, SCIENCE, TECHNOLOGY, AND THE ENVIRONMENT	3.82	52.23
10.	69	COOPERATION IN THE FIELD OF INFORMATION EXCHANGE	3.82	56.05

GERMAN DEMOCRATIC REPUBLIC

RANK	CODE	CATEGORY	%	CUMULATIVE %
1.	119	SPECIFIC INTERNATIONAL AGREEMENTS	12.77	12.77
2.	11	COOPERATION AMONG STATES AS A PRINCIPLE OF INTERNATIONAL RELATIONS	12.06	24.82
3.	103	PEACE	10.64	35.46
4.	5	INVIOLABILITY OF FRONTIERS	8.51	43.97
5.	1	BASKET ONE: QUESTIONS RELATING TO SECURITY IN EUROPE	7.80	51.77
6.	6	TERRITORIAL INTEGRITY OF STATES	7.09	58.87
7.	99	UN AND UN SPECIAL ORGANISATIONS	4.96	63.83
8.	108	IDEOLOGY AND IDEAS	4.26	68.09
9.	14	DOCUMENT ON CONFIDENCE-BUILDING MEASURES AND CERTAIN ASPECTS OF SECURITY AND DISARMAMENT	2.84	70.92
10.	17	QUESTIONS RELATING TO SECURITY	2.84	73.76

RANK	CODE	CATEGORY	%	CUMULATIVE %
1.	11	COOPERATION AMONG STATES AS A PRINCIPLE OF INTERNATIONAL RELATIONS	14.02	14.02
2.	1	BASKET ONE: QUESTIONS RELATING TO SECURITY IN EUROPE	11.21	25.23
3.	14	DOCUMENT ON CONFIDENCE-BUILDING MEASURES AND CERTAIN ASPECTS OF SECURITY AND DISARMAMENT	8.41	33.64
4.	103	PEACE	8.41	42.06
5.	104	CONFLICT AND CONFRONTATION	8.41	50.47
6.	2	GENERAL REMARKS CONCERNING THE DECLARATION ON PRINCIPLES GUIDING RELATIONS	4.67	55.14
7.	4	REFRAINING FROM THE THREAT OR USE OF FORCE	3.74	58.88
8.	108	IDEOLOGY AND IDEAS	3.74	62.62
9.	19	BASKET TWO: COOPERATION IN THE FIELD OF ECONOMICS, SCIENCE, TECHNOLOGY, AND THE ENVIRONMENT	2.80	65.42
10.	107	JUDICIAL SYSTEMS AND LEGAL INSTITUTIONS	2.80	68.22

HUNGARY

RANK	CODE	CATEGORY	%	CUMULATIVE %
1.	11	COOPERATION AMONG STATES AS A PRINCIPLE OF INTERNATIONAL RELATIONS	14.14	14.14
2.	104	CONFLICT AND CONFRONTATION	11.11	25.25
3.	1	BASKET ONE: QUESTIONS RELATING TO SECURITY IN EUROPE	9.09	34.34
4.	19	BASKET TWO: COOPERATION IN THE FIELD OF ECONOMICS, SCIENCE, TECHNOLOGY, AND THE ENVIRONMENT	8.08	42.42
5.	20	GENERAL REMARKS CONCERNING COMMERCIAL EXCHANGES	8.08	50.51
6.	114	POLITICAL COOPERATION AND POLITICAL DISCUSSIONS	6.06	56.57
7.	16	QUESTIONS RELATING TO DISARMAMENT	5.05	61.62
8.	108	IDEOLOGY AND IDEAS	5.05	66.67
9.	119	SPECIFIC INTERNATIONAL AGREEMENTS	5.05	71.72
10.	40	COOPERATION IN THE FIELD OF ENVIRONMENT	4.04	75.76

ICELAND

RANK	CODE	CATEGORY	%	CUMULATIVE %
1.	16	QUESTIONS RELATING TO DISARMAMENT	12.96	12.96
2.	14	DOCUMENT ON CONFIDENCE-BUILDING MEASURES AND CERTAIN ASPECTS OF SECURITY AND DISARMAMENT	11.11	24.07
3.	59	GENERAL REMARKS CONCERNING HUMAN CONTACTS	9.26	33.33
4.	1	BASKET ONE: QUESTIONS RELATING TO SECURITY IN EUROPE	7.41	40.74
5.	11	COOPERATION AMONG STATES AS A PRINCIPLE OF INTERNATIONAL RELATIONS	7.41	48.15
6.	40	COOPERATION IN THE FIELD OF ENVIRONMENT	7.41	55.56
7.	103	PEACE	7.41	62.96
8.	19	BASKET TWO: COOPERATION IN THE FIELD OF ECONOMICS, SCIENCE, TECHNOLOGY, AND THE ENVIRONMENT	5.56	68.52
9.	17	QUESTIONS RELATING TO SECURITY	3.70	72.22
10.	35	COOPERATION IN SCIENCE AND TECHNOLOGY	3.70	75.93

Table A2.8. *(cont.)*

IRELAND

RANK	CODE	CATEGORY	%	CUMULATIVE %
1.	1	BASKET ONE: QUESTIONS RELATING TO SECURITY IN EUROPE	7.77	7.77
2.	11	COOPERATION AMONG STATES AS A PRINCIPLE OF INTERNATIONAL RELATIONS	7.77	15.54
3.	2	GENERAL REMARKS CONCERNING THE DECLARATION ON PRINCIPLES GUIDING RELATIONS	4.66	20.21
4.	14	DOCUMENT ON CONFIDENCE-BUILDING MEASURES AND CERTAIN ASPECTS OF SECURITY AND DISARMAMENT	4.66	24.87
5.	99	UN AND UN SPECIAL ORGANISATIONS	4.66	29.53
6.	108	IDEOLOGY AND IDEAS	4.66	34.20
7.	112	RESPONSIBILITY	4.66	38.86
8.	104	CONFLICT AND CONFRONTATION	4.15	43.01
9.	120	STABILITY, STRATEGIC AND POLITICAL BALANCE	4.15	47.15
10.	16	QUESTIONS RELATING TO DISARMAMENT	3.63	50.78

ITALY

RANK	CODE	CATEGORY	%	CUMULATIVE %
1.	11	COOPERATION AMONG STATES AS A PRINCIPLE OF INTERNATIONAL RELATIONS	11.70	11.70
2.	1	BASKET ONE: QUESTIONS RELATING TO SECURITY IN EUROPE	9.57	21.28
3.	103	PEACE	8.51	29.79
4.	14	DOCUMENT ON CONFIDENCE-BUILDING MEASURES AND CERTAIN ASPECTS OF SECURITY AND DISARMAMENT	6.38	36.17
5.	17	QUESTIONS RELATING TO SECURITY	4.26	40.43
6.	40	COOPERATION IN THE FIELD OF ENVIRONMENT	4.26	44.68
7.	114	POLITICAL COOPERATION AND POLITICAL DISCUSSIONS	4.26	48.94
8.	119	SPECIFIC INTERNATIONAL AGREEMENTS	4.26	53.19
9.	70	IMPROVEMENT OF THE CIRCULATION, ACCESS TO, AND EXCHANGE OF INFORMATION	3.19	56.38
10.	3	SOVEREIGN EQUALITY, RESPECT FOR THE RIGHTS INHERENT IN SOVEREIGNTY	2.13	58.51

LIECHTENSTEIN

RANK	CODE	CATEGORY	%	CUMULATIVE %
1.	11	COOPERATION AMONG STATES AS A PRINCIPLE OF INTERNATIONAL RELATIONS	15.38	15.38
2.	1	BASKET ONE: QUESTIONS RELATING TO SECURITY IN EUROPE	11.54	26.92
3.	3	SOVEREIGN EQUALITY, RESPECT FOR THE RIGHTS INHERENT IN SOVEREIGNTY	7.69	34.62
4.	4	REFRAINING FROM THE THREAT OR USE OF FORCE	7.69	42.31
5.	14	DOCUMENT ON CONFIDENCE-BUILDING MEASURES AND CERTAIN ASPECTS OF SECURITY AND DISARMAMENT	7.69	50.00
6.	19	BASKET TWO: COOPERATION IN THE FIELD OF ECONOMICS, SCIENCE, TECHNOLOGY, AND THE ENVIRONMENT	7.69	57.69
7.	103	PEACE	7.69	65.38
8.	104	CONFLICT AND CONFRONTATION	7.69	73.08
9.	7	PEACEFUL SETTLEMENT OF DISPUTES	3.85	76.92
10.	12	FULFILLMENT IN GOOD FAITH OF OBLIGATIONS UNDER INTERNATIONAL LAW	3.85	80.77

LUXEMBOURG

RANK	CODE	CATEGORY	%	CUMULATIVE %
1.	14	DOCUMENT ON CONFIDENCE-BUILDING MEASURES AND CERTAIN ASPECTS OF SECURITY AND DISARMAMENT	7.84	7.84
2.	104	CONFLICT AND CONFRONTATION	7.84	15.69
3.	114	POLITICAL COOPERATION AND POLITICAL DISCUSSIONS	7.84	23.53
4.	1	BASKET ONE: QUESTIONS RELATING TO SECURITY IN EUROPE	6.86	30.39
5.	17	QUESTIONS RELATING TO SECURITY	6.86	37.25
6.	11	COOPERATION AMONG STATES AS A PRINCIPLE OF INTERNATIONAL RELATIONS	5.88	43.14
7.	19	BASKET TWO: COOPERATION IN THE FIELD OF ECONOMICS, SCIENCE, TECHNOLOGY, AND THE ENVIRONMENT	4.90	48.04
8.	70	IMPROVEMENT OF THE CIRCULATION, ACCESS TO, AND EXCHANGE OF INFORMATION	4.90	52.94
9.	103	PEACE	4.90	57.84
10.	59	GENERAL REMARKS CONCERNING HUMAN CONTACTS	3.92	61.76

MALTA

RANK	CODE	CATEGORY	%	CUMULATIVE %
1.	1	BASKET ONE: QUESTIONS RELATING TO SECURITY IN EUROPE	20.00	20.00
2.	11	COOPERATION AMONG STATES AS A PRINCIPLE OF INTERNATIONAL RELATIONS	13.85	33.85
3.	51	SECTION ON THE MEDITERRANEAN: GENERAL REMARKS	12.31	46.15
4.	19	BASKET TWO: COOPERATION IN THE FIELD OF ECONOMICS, SCIENCE, TECHNOLOGY, AND THE ENVIRONMENT	7.69	53.85
5.	16	QUESTIONS RELATING TO DISARMAMENT	6.15	60.00
6.	104	CONFLICT AND CONFRONTATION	6.15	66.15
7.	7	PEACEFUL SETTLEMENT OF DISPUTES	4.62	70.77
8.	103	PEACE	4.62	75.38
9.	14	DOCUMENT ON CONFIDENCE-BUILDING MEASURES AND CERTAIN ASPECTS OF SECURITY AND DISARMAMENT	3.08	78.46
10.	76	CULTURAL EXCHANGE	3.08	81.54

Table A2.8. *(cont.)*

MONACO

RANK	CODE	CATEGORY	%	CUMULATIVE %
1.	1	BASKET ONE: QUESTIONS RELATING TO SECURITY IN EUROPE	15.00	15.00
2.	40	COOPERATION IN THE FIELD OF ENVIRONMENT	15.00	30.00
3.	51	SECTION ON THE MEDITERRANEAN: GENERAL REMARKS	15.00	45.00
4.	35	COOPERATION IN SCIENCE AND TECHNOLOGY	10.00	55.00
5.	103	PEACE	10.00	65.00
6.	119	SPECIFIC INTERNATIONAL AGREEMENTS	10.00	75.00
7.	11	COOPERATION AMONG STATES AS A PRINCIPLE OF INTERNATIONAL RELATIONS	5.00	80.00
8.	17	QUESTIONS RELATING TO SECURITY	5.00	85.00
9.	47	PROMOTION OF TOURISM	5.00	90.00
10.	76	CULTURAL EXCHANGE	5.00	95.00

NETHERLANDS

RANK	CODE	CATEGORY	%	CUMULATIVE %
1.	1	BASKET ONE: QUESTIONS RELATING TO SECURITY IN EUROPE	10.81	10.81
2.	14	DOCUMENT ON CONFIDENCE-BUILDING MEASURES AND CERTAIN ASPECTS OF SECURITY AND DISARMAMENT	9.01	19.82
3.	2	GENERAL REMARKS CONCERNING THE DECLARATION ON PRINCIPLES GUIDING RELATIONS	7.21	27.03
4.	97	INTERNATIONAL CONFERENCES	5.41	32.43
5.	10	EQUAL RIGHTS AND SELF-DETERMINATION OF PEOPLES	4.50	36.94
6.	12	FULFILLMENT IN GOOD FAITH OF OBLIGATIONS UNDER INTERNATIONAL LAW	4.50	41.44
7.	75	PROMOTION OF MUTUAL KNOWLEDGE	4.50	45.95
8.	99	UN AND UN SPECIAL ORGANISATIONS	4.50	50.45
9.	103	PEACE	4.50	54.95
10.	61	REUNIFICATION OF FAMILIES	3.60	58.56

NORWAY

RANK	CODE	CATEGORY	%	CUMULATIVE %
1.	40	COOPERATION IN THE FIELD OF ENVIRONMENT	14.19	14.19
2.	11	COOPERATION AMONG STATES AS A PRINCIPLE OF INTERNATIONAL RELATIONS	9.46	23.65
3.	1	BASKET ONE: QUESTIONS RELATING TO SECURITY IN EUROPE	7.43	31.08
4.	14	DOCUMENT ON CONFIDENCE-BUILDING MEASURES AND CERTAIN ASPECTS OF SECURITY AND DISARMAMENT	6.76	37.84
5.	67	EXPANSION OF CONTACTS AMONG GOVERNMENTAL AND NON-GOVERNMENTAL INSTITUTIONS	6.76	44.59
6.	65	MEETINGS AMONG YOUNG PEOPLE	5.41	50.00
7.	114	POLITICAL COOPERATION AND POLITICAL DISCUSSIONS	4.05	54.05
8.	21	GENERAL PROVISIONS CONCERNING THE EXPANSION OF MUTUAL TRADE	3.38	57.43
9.	26	INDUSTRIAL COOPERATION AND PROJECTS OF COMMON INTEREST	2.70	60.14
10.	35	COOPERATION IN SCIENCE AND TECHNOLOGY	2.70	62.84

POLAND

RANK	CODE	CATEGORY	%	CUMULATIVE %
1.	11	COOPERATION AMONG STATES AS A PRINCIPLE OF INTERNATIONAL RELATIONS	10.78	10.78
2.	1	BASKET ONE: QUESTIONS RELATING TO SECURITY IN EUROPE	10.18	20.96
3.	114	POLITICAL COOPERATION AND POLITICAL DISCUSSIONS	6.59	27.54
4.	17	QUESTIONS RELATING TO SECURITY	5.99	33.53
5.	19	BASKET TWO: COOPERATION IN THE FIELD OF ECONOMICS, SCIENCE, TECHNOLOGY, AND THE ENVIRONMENT	5.99	39.52
6.	103	PEACE	5.39	44.91
7.	5	INVIOLABILITY OF FRONTIERS	4.79	49.70
8.	6	TERRITORIAL INTEGRITY OF STATES	4.19	53.89
9.	97	INTERNATIONAL CONFERENCES	4.19	58.08
10.	104	CONFLICT AND CONFRONTATION	3.59	61.68

PORTUGAL

RANK	CODE	CATEGORY	%	CUMULATIVE %
1.	11	COOPERATION AMONG STATES AS A PRINCIPLE OF INTERNATIONAL RELATIONS	12.75	12.75
2.	1	BASKET ONE: QUESTIONS RELATING TO SECURITY IN EUROPE	11.76	24.51
3.	103	PEACE	9.80	34.31
4.	108	IDEOLOGY AND IDEAS	6.86	41.18
5.	2	GENERAL REMARKS CONCERNING THE DECLARATION ON PRINCIPLES GUIDING RELATIONS	5.88	47.06
6.	58	BASKET THREE: COOPERATION IN HUMANITARIAN AND OTHER FIELDS	5.88	52.94
7.	119	SPECIFIC INTERNATIONAL AGREEMENTS	5.88	58.82
8.	17	QUESTIONS RELATING TO SECURITY	4.90	63.73
9.	104	CONFLICT AND CONFRONTATION	4.90	68.63
10.	14	DOCUMENT ON CONFIDENCE-BUILDING MEASURES AND CERTAIN ASPECTS OF SECURITY AND DISARMAMENT	2.94	71.57

Table A2.8. *(cont.)*

ROMANIA

RANK	CODE	CATEGORY	%	CUMULATIVE %
1.	11	COOPERATION AMONG STATES AS A PRINCIPLE OF INTERNATIONAL RELATIONS	11.17	11.17
2.	1	BASKET ONE: QUESTIONS RELATING TO SECURITY IN EUROPE	9.04	20.21
3.	103	PEACE	8.51	28.72
4.	14	DOCUMENT ON CONFIDENCE-BUILDING MEASURES AND CERTAIN ASPECTS OF SECURITY AND DISARMAMENT	7.98	36.70
5.	111	WELFARE AND PROSPERITY	6.38	43.09
6.	16	QUESTIONS RELATING TO DISARMAMENT	5.32	48.40
7.	104	CONFLICT AND CONFRONTATION	3.72	52.13
8.	2	GENERAL REMARKS CONCERNING THE DECLARATION ON PRINCIPLES GUIDING RELATIONS	3.19	55.32
9.	3	SOVEREIGN EQUALITY, RESPECT FOR THE RIGHTS INHERENT IN SOVEREIGNTY	3.19	58.51
10.	30	PROVISIONS CONCERNING TRADE AND INDUSTRIAL COOPERATION	2.66	61.17

SAN MARINO

RANK	CODE	CATEGORY	%	CUMULATIVE %
1.	103	PEACE	24.35	24.35
2.	11	COOPERATION AMONG STATES AS A PRINCIPLE OF INTERNATIONAL RELATIONS	8.70	33.04
3.	2	GENERAL REMARKS CONCERNING THE DECLARATION ON PRINCIPLES GUIDING RELATIONS	6.96	40.00
4.	102	NEUTRALITY	6.96	46.96
5.	40	COOPERATION IN THE FIELD OF ENVIRONMENT	5.22	52.17
6.	109	FREEDOM	5.22	57.39
7.	3	SOVEREIGN EQUALITY, RESPECT FOR THE RIGHTS INHERENT IN SOVEREIGNTY	3.48	60.87
8.	4	REFRAINING FROM THE THREAT OR USE OF FORCE	3.48	64.35
9.	9	RESPECT FOR HUMAN RIGHTS AND FUNDAMENTAL FREEDOMS	3.48	67.83
10.	16	QUESTIONS RELATING TO DISARMAMENT	2.61	70.43

SPAIN

RANK	CODE	CATEGORY	%	CUMULATIVE %
1.	11	COOPERATION AMONG STATES AS A PRINCIPLE OF INTERNATIONAL RELATIONS	11.59	11.59
2.	1	BASKET ONE: QUESTIONS RELATING TO SECURITY IN EUROPE	10.14	21.74
3.	51	SECTION ON THE MEDITERRANEAN: GENERAL REMARKS	7.25	28.99
4.	103	PEACE	6.52	35.51
5.	17	QUESTIONS RELATING TO SECURITY	5.07	40.58
6.	14	DOCUMENT ON CONFIDENCE-BUILDING MEASURES AND CERTAIN ASPECTS OF SECURITY AND DISARMAMENT	4.35	44.93
7.	19	BASKET TWO: COOPERATION IN THE FIELD OF ECONOMICS, SCIENCE, TECHNOLOGY, AND THE ENVIRONMENT	4.35	49.28
8.	104	CONFLICT AND CONFRONTATION	4.35	53.62
9.	47	PROMOTION OF TOURISM	3.62	57.25
10.	74	COOPERATION AND EXCHANGES IN THE FIELD OF CULTURE	3.62	60.87

SWEDEN

RANK	CODE	CATEGORY	%	CUMULATIVE %
1.	11	COOPERATION AMONG STATES AS A PRINCIPLE OF INTERNATIONAL RELATIONS	12.50	12.50
2.	16	QUESTIONS RELATING TO DISARMAMENT	7.24	19.74
3.	104	CONFLICT AND CONFRONTATION	7.24	26.97
4.	14	DOCUMENT ON CONFIDENCE-BUILDING MEASURES AND CERTAIN ASPECTS OF SECURITY AND DISARMAMENT	4.61	31.58
5.	99	UN AND UN SPECIAL ORGANISATIONS	4.61	36.18
6.	103	PEACE	4.61	40.79
7.	17	QUESTIONS RELATING TO SECURITY	3.95	44.74
8.	19	BASKET TWO: COOPERATION IN THE FIELD OF ECONOMICS, SCIENCE, TECHNOLOGY, AND THE ENVIRONMENT	3.95	48.68
9.	70	IMPROVEMENT OF THE CIRCULATION, ACCESS TO, AND EXCHANGE OF INFORMATION	3.95	52.63
10.	97	INTERNATIONAL CONFERENCES	3.95	56.58

SWITZERLAND

RANK	CODE	CATEGORY	%	CUMULATIVE %
1.	1	BASKET ONE: QUESTIONS RELATING TO SECURITY IN EUROPE	11.67	11.67
2.	107	JUDICIAL SYSTEMS AND LEGAL INSTITUTIONS	10.00	21.67
3.	7	PEACEFUL SETTLEMENT OF DISPUTES	8.33	30.00
4.	102	NEUTRALITY	8.33	38.33
5.	104	CONFLICT AND CONFRONTATION	8.33	46.67
6.	11	COOPERATION AMONG STATES AS A PRINCIPLE OF INTERNATIONAL RELATIONS	6.67	53.33
7.	4	REFRAINING FROM THE THREAT OR USE OF FORCE	5.00	58.33
8.	119	SPECIFIC INTERNATIONAL AGREEMENTS	5.00	63.33
9.	2	GENERAL REMARKS CONCERNING THE DECLARATION ON PRINCIPLES GUIDING RELATIONS	3.33	66.67
10.	12	FULFILLMENT IN GOOD FAITH OF OBLIGATIONS UNDER INTERNATIONAL LAW	3.33	70.00

Table A2.8. *(cont.)*

TURKEY

RANK	CODE	CATEGORY	%	CUMULATIVE %
1.	1	BASKET ONE: QUESTIONS RELATING TO SECURITY IN EUROPE	9.22	9.22
2.	2	GENERAL REMARKS CONCERNING THE DECLARATION ON PRINCIPLES GUIDING RELATIONS	9.22	18.44
3.	11	COOPERATION AMONG STATES AS A PRINCIPLE OF INTERNATIONAL RELATIONS	7.09	25.53
4.	103	PEACE	7.09	32.62
5.	19	BASKET TWO: COOPERATION IN THE FIELD OF ECONOMICS, SCIENCE, TECHNOLOGY, AND THE ENVIRONMENT	6.38	39.01
6.	48	ECONOMIC AND SOCIAL ASPECTS OF MIGRANT LABOUR	6.38	45.39
7.	53	INCREASING MUTUAL CONFIDENCE, SECURITY, STABILITY IN THE MEDITERRANEAN	6.38	51.77
8.	40	COOPERATION IN THE FIELD OF ENVIRONMENT	5.67	57.45
9.	14	DOCUMENT ON CONFIDENCE-BUILDING MEASURES AND CERTAIN ASPECTS OF SECURITY AND DISARMAMENT	4.26	61.70
10.	51	SECTION ON THE MEDITERRANEAN: GENERAL REMARKS	4.26	65.96

UNION OF THE SOVIET SOCIALIST REPUBLICS

RANK	CODE	CATEGORY	%	CUMULATIVE %
1.	103	PEACE	21.20	21.20
2.	11	COOPERATION AMONG STATES AS A PRINCIPLE OF INTERNATIONAL RELATIONS	9.68	30.88
3.	1	BASKET ONE: QUESTIONS RELATING TO SECURITY IN EUROPE	8.76	39.63
4.	104	CONFLICT AND CONFRONTATION	6.45	46.08
5.	14	DOCUMENT ON CONFIDENCE-BUILDING MEASURES AND CERTAIN ASPECTS OF SECURITY AND DISARMAMENT	5.99	52.07
6.	119	SPECIFIC INTERNATIONAL AGREEMENTS	5.99	58.06
7.	2	GENERAL REMARKS CONCERNING THE DECLARATION ON PRINCIPLES GUIDING RELATIONS	5.07	63.13
8.	108	IDEOLOGY AND IDEAS	3.69	66.82
9.	114	POLITICAL COOPERATION AND POLITICAL DISCUSSIONS	3.69	70.51
10.	17	QUESTIONS RELATING TO SECURITY	2.76	73.27

UNITED KINGDOM

RANK	CODE	CATEGORY	%	CUMULATIVE %
1.	14	DOCUMENT ON CONFIDENCE-BUILDING MEASURES AND CERTAIN ASPECTS OF SECURITY AND DISARMAMENT	19.40	19.40
2.	1	BASKET ONE: QUESTIONS RELATING TO SECURITY IN EUROPE	13.43	32.84
3.	59	GENERAL REMARKS CONCERNING HUMAN CONTACTS	8.96	41.79
4.	104	CONFLICT AND CONFRONTATION	7.46	49.25
5.	103	PEACE	5.97	55.22
6.	11	COOPERATION AMONG STATES AS A PRINCIPLE OF INTERNATIONAL RELATIONS	4.48	59.70
7.	20	GENERAL REMARKS CONCERNING COMMERCIAL EXCHANGES	4.48	64.18
8.	97	INTERNATIONAL CONFERENCES	4.48	68.66
9.	120	STABILITY, STRATEGIC AND POLITICAL BALANCE	4.48	73.13
10.	17	QUESTIONS RELATING TO SECURITY	2.99	76.12

UNITED STATES OF AMERICA

RANK	CODE	CATEGORY	%	CUMULATIVE %
1.	103	PEACE	8.47	8.47
2.	14	DOCUMENT ON CONFIDENCE-BUILDING MEASURES AND CERTAIN ASPECTS OF SECURITY AND DISARMAMENT	7.63	16.10
3.	59	GENERAL REMARKS CONCERNING HUMAN CONTACTS	7.63	23.73
4.	1	BASKET ONE: QUESTIONS RELATING TO SECURITY IN EUROPE	6.78	30.51
5.	104	CONFLICT AND CONFRONTATION	6.78	37.29
6.	4	REFRAINING FROM THE THREAT OR USE OF FORCE	5.93	43.22
7.	70	IMPROVEMENT OF THE CIRCULATION, ACCESS TO, AND EXCHANGE OF INFORMATION	5.93	49.15
8.	9	RESPECT FOR HUMAN RIGHTS AND FUNDAMENTAL FREEDOMS	4.24	53.39
9.	78	DEVELOPMENT OF CONTACTS AND COOPERATION IN THE FIELD OF CULTURE	4.24	57.63
10.	83	EXPANSION AND IMPROVEMENT OF COOPERATION AND LINKS IN THE FIELD OF EDUCATION	4.24	61.86

VATICAN (HOLY SEE)

RANK	CODE	CATEGORY	%	CUMULATIVE %
1.	103	PEACE	18.45	18.45
2.	1	BASKET ONE: QUESTIONS RELATING TO SECURITY IN EUROPE	17.48	35.92
3.	11	COOPERATION AMONG STATES AS A PRINCIPLE OF INTERNATIONAL RELATIONS	8.74	44.66
4.	120	STABILITY, STRATEGIC AND POLITICAL BALANCE	6.80	51.46
5.	110	JUSTICE	5.83	57.28
6.	2	GENERAL REMARKS CONCERNING THE DECLARATION ON PRINCIPLES GUIDING RELATIONS	4.85	62.14
7.	14	DOCUMENT ON CONFIDENCE-BUILDING MEASURES AND CERTAIN ASPECTS OF SECURITY AND DISARMAMENT	3.88	66.02
8.	119	SPECIFIC INTERNATIONAL AGREEMENTS	3.88	69.90
9.	4	REFRAINING FROM THE THREAT OR USE OF FORCE	2.91	72.82
10.	104	CONFLICT AND CONFRONTATION	2.91	75.73

Table A2.8. *(cont.)*

YUGOSLAVIA

RANK	CODE	CATEGORY	%	CUMULATIVE %
1.	1	BASKET ONE: QUESTIONS RELATING TO SECURITY IN EUROPE	18.66	18.66
2.	11	COOPERATION AMONG STATES AS A PRINCIPLE OF INTERNATIONAL RELATIONS	8.96	27.61
3.	103	PEACE	7.46	35.07
4.	2	GENERAL REMARKS CONCERNING THE DECLARATION ON PRINCIPLES GUIDING RELATIONS	5.22	40.30
5.	3	SOVEREIGN EQUALITY, RESPECT FOR THE RIGHTS INHERENT IN SOVEREIGNTY	4.48	44.78
6.	19	BASKET TWO: COOPERATION IN THE FIELD OF ECONOMICS, SCIENCE, TECHNOLOGY, AND THE ENVIRONMENT	4.48	49.25
7.	101	NON-ALIGNMENT	4.48	53.73
8.	104	CONFLICT AND CONFRONTATION	4.48	58.21
9.	99	UN AND UN SPECIAL ORGANISATIONS	3.73	61.94
10.	106	DEMOCRACY AND DEMOCRATIC INSTITUTIONS	3.73	65.67

Table A2.9. Rank-Order of Categories: The 1975 Helsinki Statements

AUSTRIA

RANK	CODE	CATEGORY	%	CUMULATIVE %
1.	11	COOPERATION AMONG STATES AS A PRINCIPLE OF INTERNATIONAL RELATIONS	17.02	17.02
2.	19	BASKET TWO: COOPERATION IN THE FIELD OF ECONOMICS, SCIENCE, TECHNOLOGY, AND THE ENVIRONMENT	17.02	34.04
3.	117	REMARKS CONCERNING DEVELOPING COUNTRIES	14.89	48.94
4.	106	DEMOCRACY AND DEMOCRATIC INSTITUTIONS	12.77	61.70
5.	119	SPECIFIC INTERNATIONAL AGREEMENTS	6.38	68.09
6.	2	GENERAL REMARKS CONCERNING THE DECLARATION ON PRINCIPLES GUIDING RELATIONS	4.26	72.34
7.	98	INTERNATIONAL ORGANISATIONS OTHER THAN UN	4.26	76.60
8.	103	PEACE	4.26	80.85
9.	104	CONFLICT AND CONFRONTATION	4.26	85.11
10.	108	IDEOLOGY AND IDEAS	4.26	89.36

BELGIUM

RANK	CODE	CATEGORY	%	CUMULATIVE %
1.	17	QUESTIONS RELATING TO SECURITY	11.85	11.85
2.	1	BASKET ONE: QUESTIONS RELATING TO SECURITY IN EUROPE	10.37	22.22
3.	16	QUESTIONS RELATING TO DISARMAMENT	8.89	31.11
4.	97	INTERNATIONAL CONFERENCES	8.89	40.00
5.	11	COOPERATION AMONG STATES AS A PRINCIPLE OF INTERNATIONAL RELATIONS	7.41	47.41
6.	19	BASKET TWO: COOPERATION IN THE FIELD OF ECONOMICS, SCIENCE, TECHNOLOGY, AND THE ENVIRONMENT	5.93	53.33
7.	2	GENERAL REMARKS CONCERNING THE DECLARATION ON PRINCIPLES GUIDING RELATIONS	3.70	57.04
8.	8	NON-INTERVENTION IN INTERNAL AFFAIRS	3.70	60.74
9.	4	REFRAINING FROM THE THREAT OR USE OF FORCE	2.96	63.70
10.	7	PEACEFUL SETTLEMENT OF DISPUTES	2.96	66.67

Table A2.9. *(cont.)*

BULGARIA

RANK	CODE	CATEGORY	%	CUMULATIVE %
1.	19	BASKET TWO: COOPERATION IN THE FIELD OF ECONOMICS, SCIENCE, TECHNOLOGY, AND THE ENVIRONMENT	13.24	13.24
2.	11	COOPERATION AMONG STATES AS A PRINCIPLE OF INTERNATIONAL RELATIONS	11.76	25.00
3.	17	QUESTIONS RELATING TO SECURITY	10.29	35.29
4.	1	BASKET ONE: QUESTIONS RELATING TO SECURITY IN EUROPE	8.82	44.12
5.	16	QUESTIONS RELATING TO DISARMAMENT	7.35	51.47
6.	103	PEACE	7.35	58.82
7.	104	CONFLICT AND CONFRONTATION	5.88	64.71
8.	33	SPECIFIC BILATERAL ARRANGEMENTS CONCERNING TRADE AND INDUSTRIAL COOPERATION	4.41	69.12
9.	20	GENERAL REMARKS CONCERNING COMMERCIAL EXCHANGES	2.94	72.06
10.	25	OTHER ASPECTS OF COMMERCIAL EXCHANGE	2.94	75.00

CANADA

RANK	CODE	CATEGORY	%	CUMULATIVE %
1.	1	BASKET ONE: QUESTIONS RELATING TO SECURITY IN EUROPE	10.14	10.14
2.	20	GENERAL REMARKS CONCERNING COMMERCIAL EXCHANGES	10.14	20.29
3.	17	QUESTIONS RELATING TO SECURITY	8.70	28.99
4.	16	QUESTIONS RELATING TO DISARMAMENT	7.25	36.23
5.	97	INTERNATIONAL CONFERENCES	7.25	43.48
6.	103	PEACE	7.25	50.72
7.	117	REMARKS CONCERNING DEVELOPING COUNTRIES	7.25	57.97
8.	19	BASKET TWO: COOPERATION IN THE FIELD OF ECONOMICS, SCIENCE, TECHNOLOGY, AND THE ENVIRONMENT	5.80	63.77
9.	11	COOPERATION AMONG STATES AS A PRINCIPLE OF INTERNATIONAL RELATIONS	4.35	68.12
10.	94	DANGERS OF NUCLEAR PROLIFERATION	4.35	72.46

RANK	CODE	CATEGORY	%	CUMULATIVE %
1.	2	GENERAL REMARKS CONCERNING THE DECLARATION ON PRINCIPLES GUIDING RELATIONS	15.08	15.08
2.	103	PEACE	10.32	25.40
3.	1	BASKET ONE: QUESTIONS RELATING TO SECURITY IN EUROPE	9.52	34.92
4.	17	QUESTIONS RELATING TO SECURITY	9.52	44.44
5.	4	REFRAINING FROM THE THREAT OR USE OF FORCE	6.35	50.79
6.	6	TERRITORIAL INTEGRITY OF STATES	4.76	55.56
7.	99	UN AND UN SPECIAL ORGANISATIONS	4.76	60.32
8.	3	SOVEREIGN EQUALITY, RESPECT FOR THE RIGHTS INHERENT IN SOVEREIGNTY	3.97	64.29
9.	9	RESPECT FOR HUMAN RIGHTS AND FUNDAMENTAL FREEDOMS	2.38	66.67
10.	11	COOPERATION AMONG STATES AS A PRINCIPLE OF INTERNATIONAL RELATIONS	2.38	69.05

CZECHOSLOVAKIA

RANK	CODE	CATEGORY	%	CUMULATIVE %
1.	103	PEACE	16.00	16.00
2.	11	COOPERATION AMONG STATES AS A PRINCIPLE OF INTERNATIONAL RELATIONS	8.00	24.00
3.	17	QUESTIONS RELATING TO SECURITY	8.00	32.00
4.	19	BASKET TWO: COOPERATION IN THE FIELD OF ECONOMICS, SCIENCE, TECHNOLOGY, AND THE ENVIRONMENT	8.00	40.00
5.	1	BASKET ONE: QUESTIONS RELATING TO SECURITY IN EUROPE	7.00	47.00
6.	2	GENERAL REMARKS CONCERNING THE DECLARATION ON PRINCIPLES GUIDING RELATIONS	7.00	54.00
7.	104	CONFLICT AND CONFRONTATION	7.00	61.00
8.	20	GENERAL REMARKS CONCERNING COMMERCIAL EXCHANGES	5.00	66.00
9.	116	PEACEFUL COEXISTENCE	5.00	71.00
10.	4	REFRAINING FROM THE THREAT OR USE OF FORCE	3.00	74.00

DENMARK

RANK	CODE	CATEGORY	%	CUMULATIVE %
1.	58	BASKET THREE: COOPERATION IN HUMANITARIAN AND OTHER FIELDS	18.46	18.46
2.	17	QUESTIONS RELATING TO SECURITY	15.38	33.85
3.	119	SPECIFIC INTERNATIONAL AGREEMENTS	12.31	46.15
4.	19	BASKET TWO: COOPERATION IN THE FIELD OF ECONOMICS, SCIENCE, TECHNOLOGY, AND THE ENVIRONMENT	7.69	53.85
5.	1	BASKET ONE: QUESTIONS RELATING TO SECURITY IN EUROPE	6.15	60.00
6.	11	COOPERATION AMONG STATES AS A PRINCIPLE OF INTERNATIONAL RELATIONS	6.15	66.15
7.	14	DOCUMENT ON CONFIDENCE-BUILDING MEASURES AND CERTAIN ASPECTS OF SECURITY AND DISARMAMENT	6.15	72.31
8.	20	GENERAL REMARKS CONCERNING COMMERCIAL EXCHANGES	4.62	76.92
9.	98	INTERNATIONAL ORGANISATIONS OTHER THAN UN	4.62	81.54
10.	59	GENERAL REMARKS CONCERNING HUMAN CONTACTS	3.08	84.62

Table A2.9. *(cont.)*

FINLAND

RANK	CODE	CATEGORY	%	CUMULATIVE %
1.	17	QUESTIONS RELATING TO SECURITY	14.06	14.06
2.	1	BASKET ONE: QUESTIONS RELATING TO SECURITY IN EUROPE	13.28	27.34
3.	11	COOPERATION AMONG STATES AS A PRINCIPLE OF INTERNATIONAL RELATIONS	12.50	39.84
4.	19	BASKET TWO: COOPERATION IN THE FIELD OF ECONOMICS, SCIENCE, TECHNOLOGY, AND THE ENVIRONMENT	10.94	50.78
5.	3	SOVEREIGN EQUALITY, RESPECT FOR THE RIGHTS INHERENT IN SOVEREIGNTY	8.59	59.38
6.	2	GENERAL REMARKS CONCERNING THE DECLARATION ON PRINCIPLES GUIDING RELATIONS	7.81	67.19
7.	98	INTERNATIONAL ORGANISATIONS OTHER THAN UN	6.25	73.44
8.	103	PEACE	6.25	79.69
9.	112	RESPONSIBILITY	4.69	84.38
10.	99	UN AND UN SPECIAL ORGANISATIONS	3.13	87.50

FRANCE

RANK	CODE	CATEGORY	%	CUMULATIVE %
1.	17	QUESTIONS RELATING TO SECURITY	15.38	15.38
2.	1	BASKET ONE: QUESTIONS RELATING TO SECURITY IN EUROPE	12.82	28.21
3.	108	IDEOLOGY AND IDEAS	10.26	38.46
4.	98	INTERNATIONAL ORGANISATIONS OTHER THAN UN	7.69	46.15
5.	103	PEACE	7.69	53.85
6.	104	CONFLICT AND CONFRONTATION	7.69	61.54
7.	105	DEFENCE	7.69	69.23
8.	11	COOPERATION AMONG STATES AS A PRINCIPLE OF INTERNATIONAL RELATIONS	5.13	74.36
9.	70	IMPROVEMENT OF THE CIRCULATION, ACCESS TO, AND EXCHANGE OF INFORMATION	5.13	79.49
10.	3	SOVEREIGN EQUALITY, RESPECT FOR THE RIGHTS INHERENT IN SOVEREIGNTY	2.56	82.05

FEDERAL REPUBLIC OF GERMANY

RANK	CODE	CATEGORY	%	CUMULATIVE %
1.	119	SPECIFIC INTERNATIONAL AGREEMENTS	18.09	18.09
2.	20	GENERAL REMARKS CONCERNING COMMERCIAL EXCHANGES	8.51	26.60
3.	103	PEACE	8.51	35.11
4.	104	CONFLICT AND CONFRONTATION	7.45	42.55
5.	16	QUESTIONS RELATING TO DISARMAMENT	6.38	48.94
6.	12	FULFILLMENT IN GOOD FAITH OF OBLIGATIONS UNDER INTERNATIONAL LAW	5.32	54.26
7.	2	GENERAL REMARKS CONCERNING THE DECLARATION ON PRINCIPLES GUIDING RELATIONS	4.26	58.51
8.	3	SOVEREIGN EQUALITY, RESPECT FOR THE RIGHTS INHERENT IN SOVEREIGNTY	4.26	62.77
9.	11	COOPERATION AMONG STATES AS A PRINCIPLE OF INTERNATIONAL RELATIONS	4.26	67.02
10.	19	BASKET TWO: COOPERATION IN THE FIELD OF ECONOMICS, SCIENCE, TECHNOLOGY, AND THE ENVIRONMENT	3.19	70.21

GERMAN DEMOCRATIC REPUBLIC

RANK	CODE	CATEGORY	%	CUMULATIVE %
1.	103	PEACE	17.65	17.65
2.	1	BASKET ONE: QUESTIONS RELATING TO SECURITY IN EUROPE	14.71	32.35
3.	17	QUESTIONS RELATING TO SECURITY	14.71	47.06
4.	5	INVIOLABILITY OF FRONTIERS	5.88	52.94
5.	2	GENERAL REMARKS CONCERNING THE DECLARATION ON PRINCIPLES GUIDING RELATIONS	4.41	57.35
6.	3	SOVEREIGN EQUALITY, RESPECT FOR THE RIGHTS INHERENT IN SOVEREIGNTY	4.41	61.76
7.	16	QUESTIONS RELATING TO DISARMAMENT	4.41	66.18
8.	104	CONFLICT AND CONFRONTATION	4.41	70.59
9.	11	COOPERATION AMONG STATES AS A PRINCIPLE OF INTERNATIONAL RELATIONS	2.94	73.53
10.	19	BASKET TWO: COOPERATION IN THE FIELD OF ECONOMICS, SCIENCE, TECHNOLOGY, AND THE ENVIRONMENT	2.94	76.47

GREECE

RANK	CODE	CATEGORY	%	CUMULATIVE %
1.	2	GENERAL REMARKS CONCERNING THE DECLARATION ON PRINCIPLES GUIDING RELATIONS	34.78	34.78
2.	5	INVIOLABILITY OF FRONTIERS	5.80	40.58
3.	3	SOVEREIGN EQUALITY, RESPECT FOR THE RIGHTS INHERENT IN SOVEREIGNTY	4.35	44.93
4.	4	REFRAINING FROM THE THREAT OR USE OF FORCE	4.35	49.28
5.	11	COOPERATION AMONG STATES AS A PRINCIPLE OF INTERNATIONAL RELATIONS	4.35	53.62
6.	17	QUESTIONS RELATING TO SECURITY	4.35	57.97
7.	19	BASKET TWO: COOPERATION IN THE FIELD OF ECONOMICS, SCIENCE, TECHNOLOGY, AND THE ENVIRONMENT	4.35	62.32
8.	99	UN AND UN SPECIAL ORGANISATIONS	4.35	66.67
9.	103	PEACE	4.35	71.01
10.	104	CONFLICT AND CONFRONTATION	4.35	75.36

Table A2.9. *(cont.)*

HUNGARY

RANK	CODE	CATEGORY	%	CUMULATIVE %
1.	104	CONFLICT AND CONFRONTATION	9.68	9.68
2.	103	PEACE	8.60	18.28
3.	16	QUESTIONS RELATING TO DISARMAMENT	7.53	25.81
4.	20	GENERAL REMARKS CONCERNING COMMERCIAL EXCHANGES	7.53	33.33
5.	2	GENERAL REMARKS CONCERNING THE DECLARATION ON PRINCIPLES GUIDING RELATIONS	6.45	39.78
6.	1	BASKET ONE: QUESTIONS RELATING TO SECURITY IN EUROPE	5.38	45.16
7.	17	QUESTIONS RELATING TO SECURITY	5.38	50.54
8.	3	SOVEREIGN EQUALITY, RESPECT FOR THE RIGHTS INHERENT IN SOVEREIGNTY	4.30	54.84
9.	11	COOPERATION AMONG STATES AS A PRINCIPLE OF INTERNATIONAL RELATIONS	4.30	59.14
10.	74	COOPERATION AND EXCHANGES IN THE FIELD OF CULTURE	4.30	63.44

ICELAND

RANK	CODE	CATEGORY	%	CUMULATIVE %
1.	20	GENERAL REMARKS CONCERNING COMMERCIAL EXCHANGES	7.59	7.59
2.	63	TRAVEL FOR PERSONAL OR PROFESSIONAL REASONS	7.59	15.19
3.	58	BASKET THREE: COOPERATION IN HUMANITARIAN AND OTHER FIELDS	6.33	21.52
4.	69	COOPERATION IN THE FIELD OF INFORMATION EXCHANGE	6.33	27.85
5.	74	COOPERATION AND EXCHANGES IN THE FIELD OF CULTURE	6.33	34.18
6.	77	ACCESS TO THE CULTURE OF OTHER PARTICIPATING STATES	6.33	40.51
7.	1	BASKET ONE: QUESTIONS RELATING TO SECURITY IN EUROPE	5.06	45.57
8.	16	QUESTIONS RELATING TO DISARMAMENT	5.06	50.63
9.	17	QUESTIONS RELATING TO SECURITY	5.06	55.70
10.	19	BASKET TWO: COOPERATION IN THE FIELD OF ECONOMICS, SCIENCE, TECHNOLOGY, AND THE ENVIRONMENT	5.06	60.76

RANK	CODE	CATEGORY	%	CUMULATIVE %
1.	19	BASKET TWO: COOPERATION IN THE FIELD OF ECONOMICS, SCIENCE, TECHNOLOGY, AND THE ENVIRONMENT	14.63	14.63
2.	99	UN AND UN SPECIAL ORGANISATIONS	10.98	25.61
3.	11	COOPERATION AMONG STATES AS A PRINCIPLE OF INTERNATIONAL RELATIONS	9.76	35.37
4.	103	PEACE	8.54	43.90
5.	2	GENERAL REMARKS CONCERNING THE DECLARATION ON PRINCIPLES GUIDING RELATIONS	7.32	51.22
6.	9	RESPECT FOR HUMAN RIGHTS AND FUNDAMENTAL FREEDOMS	6.10	57.32
7.	59	GENERAL REMARKS CONCERNING HUMAN CONTACTS	6.10	63.41
8.	98	INTERNATIONAL ORGANISATIONS OTHER THAN UN	6.10	69.51
9.	104	CONFLICT AND CONFRONTATION	6.10	75.61
10.	58	BASKET THREE: COOPERATION IN HUMANITARIAN AND OTHER FIELDS	4.88	80.49

ITALY

RANK	CODE	CATEGORY	%	CUMULATIVE %
1.	98	INTERNATIONAL ORGANISATIONS OTHER THAN UN	21.98	21.98
2.	9	RESPECT FOR HUMAN RIGHTS AND FUNDAMENTAL FREEDOMS	8.79	30.77
3.	2	GENERAL REMARKS CONCERNING THE DECLARATION ON PRINCIPLES GUIDING RELATIONS	5.49	36.26
4.	11	COOPERATION AMONG STATES AS A PRINCIPLE OF INTERNATIONAL RELATIONS	5.49	41.76
5.	19	BASKET TWO: COOPERATION IN THE FIELD OF ECONOMICS, SCIENCE, TECHNOLOGY, AND THE ENVIRONMENT	5.49	47.25
6.	103	PEACE	5.49	52.75
7.	1	BASKET ONE: QUESTIONS RELATING TO SECURITY IN EUROPE	4.40	57.14
8.	17	QUESTIONS RELATING TO SECURITY	4.40	61.54
9.	59	GENERAL REMARKS CONCERNING HUMAN CONTACTS	4.40	65.93
10.	20	GENERAL REMARKS CONCERNING COMMERCIAL EXCHANGES	3.30	69.23

LIECHTENSTEIN

RANK	CODE	CATEGORY	%	CUMULATIVE %
1.	103	PEACE	17.39	17.39
2.	19	BASKET TWO: COOPERATION IN THE FIELD OF ECONOMICS, SCIENCE, TECHNOLOGY, AND THE ENVIRONMENT	13.04	30.43
3.	3	SOVEREIGN EQUALITY, RESPECT FOR THE RIGHTS INHERENT IN SOVEREIGNTY	8.70	39.13
4.	106	DEMOCRACY AND DEMOCRATIC INSTITUTIONS	8.70	47.83
5.	112	RESPONSIBILITY	8.70	56.52
6.	1	BASKET ONE: QUESTIONS RELATING TO SECURITY IN EUROPE	4.35	60.87
7.	2	GENERAL REMARKS CONCERNING THE DECLARATION ON PRINCIPLES GUIDING RELATIONS	4.35	65.22
8.	11	COOPERATION AMONG STATES AS A PRINCIPLE OF INTERNATIONAL RELATIONS	4.35	69.57
9.	59	GENERAL REMARKS CONCERNING HUMAN CONTACTS	4.35	73.91
10.	70	IMPROVEMENT OF THE CIRCULATION, ACCESS TO, AND EXCHANGE OF INFORMATION	4.35	78.26

Table A2.9. *(cont.)*

LUXEMBOURG

RANK	CODE	CATEGORY	%	CUMULATIVE %
1.	1	BASKET ONE: QUESTIONS RELATING TO SECURITY IN EUROPE	9.26	9.26
2.	2	GENERAL REMARKS CONCERNING THE DECLARATION ON PRINCIPLES GUIDING RELATIONS	9.26	18.52
3.	17	QUESTIONS RELATING TO SECURITY	8.33	26.85
4.	104	CONFLICT AND CONFRONTATION	6.48	33.33
5.	19	BASKET TWO: COOPERATION IN THE FIELD OF ECONOMICS, SCIENCE, TECHNOLOGY, AND THE ENVIRONMENT	5.56	38.89
6.	103	PEACE	5.56	44.44
7.	9	RESPECT FOR HUMAN RIGHTS AND FUNDAMENTAL FREEDOMS	4.63	49.07
8.	11	COOPERATION AMONG STATES AS A PRINCIPLE OF INTERNATIONAL RELATIONS	4.63	53.70
9.	109	FREEDOM	4.63	58.33
10.	7	PEACEFUL SETTLEMENT OF DISPUTES	3.70	62.04

MALTA

RANK	CODE	CATEGORY	%	CUMULATIVE %
1.	54	COOPERATION WITH NON-PARTICIPATING MEDITERRANEAN COUNTRIES	8.22	8.22
2.	103	PEACE	8.22	16.44
3.	1	BASKET ONE: QUESTIONS RELATING TO SECURITY IN EUROPE	6.85	23.29
4.	14	DOCUMENT ON CONFIDENCE-BUILDING MEASURES AND CERTAIN ASPECTS OF SECURITY AND DISARMAMENT	6.85	30.14
5.	17	QUESTIONS RELATING TO SECURITY	6.85	36.99
6.	20	GENERAL REMARKS CONCERNING COMMERCIAL EXCHANGES	6.85	43.84
7.	51	SECTION ON THE MEDITERRANEAN: GENERAL REMARKS	5.48	49.32
8.	57	OTHER ASPECTS OF COOPERATION IN THE MEDITERRANEAN	5.48	54.79
9.	11	COOPERATION AMONG STATES AS A PRINCIPLE OF INTERNATIONAL RELATIONS	4.11	58.90
10.	99	UN AND UN SPECIAL ORGANISATIONS	4.11	63.01

MONACO

RANK	CODE	CATEGORY	%	CUMULATIVE %
1.	42	FIELDS OF COOPERATION IN THE FIELD OF ENVIRONMENT	23.68	23.68
2.	40	COOPERATION IN THE FIELD OF ENVIRONMENT	13.16	36.84
3.	103	PEACE	13.16	50.00
4.	104	CONFLICT AND CONFRONTATION	13.16	63.16
5.	112	RESPONSIBILITY	7.89	71.05
6.	1	BASKET ONE: QUESTIONS RELATING TO SECURITY IN EUROPE	5.26	76.32
7.	17	QUESTIONS RELATING TO SECURITY	5.26	81.58
8.	41	AIMS OF COOPERATION IN THE FIELD OF ENVIRONMENT	5.26	86.84
9.	56	ENVIRONMENTAL QUESTIONS CONCERNING THE MEDITERRANEAN	2.63	89.47
10.	59	GENERAL REMARKS CONCERNING HUMAN CONTACTS	2.63	92.11

NETHERLANDS

RANK	CODE	CATEGORY	%	CUMULATIVE %
1.	11	COOPERATION AMONG STATES AS A PRINCIPLE OF INTERNATIONAL RELATIONS	10.81	10.81
2.	19	BASKET TWO: COOPERATION IN THE FIELD OF ECONOMICS, SCIENCE, TECHNOLOGY, AND THE ENVIRONMENT	8.11	18.92
3.	2	GENERAL REMARKS CONCERNING THE DECLARATION ON PRINCIPLES GUIDING RELATIONS	7.21	26.13
4.	103	PEACE	6.31	32.43
5.	16	QUESTIONS RELATING TO DISARMAMENT	5.41	37.84
6.	17	QUESTIONS RELATING TO SECURITY	4.50	42.34
7.	59	GENERAL REMARKS CONCERNING HUMAN CONTACTS	4.50	46.85
8.	76	CULTURAL EXCHANGE	4.50	51.35
9.	97	INTERNATIONAL CONFERENCES	4.50	55.86
10.	104	CONFLICT AND CONFRONTATION	4.50	60.36

NORWAY

RANK	CODE	CATEGORY	%	CUMULATIVE %
1.	11	COOPERATION AMONG STATES AS A PRINCIPLE OF INTERNATIONAL RELATIONS	11.66	11.66
2.	19	BASKET TWO: COOPERATION IN THE FIELD OF ECONOMICS, SCIENCE, TECHNOLOGY, AND THE ENVIRONMENT	11.66	23.31
3.	9	RESPECT FOR HUMAN RIGHTS AND FUNDAMENTAL FREEDOMS	11.04	34.36
4.	17	QUESTIONS RELATING TO SECURITY	10.43	44.79
5.	1	BASKET ONE: QUESTIONS RELATING TO SECURITY IN EUROPE	8.59	53.37
6.	16	QUESTIONS RELATING TO DISARMAMENT	7.36	60.74
7.	97	INTERNATIONAL CONFERENCES	3.68	64.42
8.	103	PEACE	3.68	68.10
9.	119	SPECIFIC INTERNATIONAL AGREEMENTS	3.68	71.78
10.	2	GENERAL REMARKS CONCERNING THE DECLARATION ON PRINCIPLES GUIDING RELATIONS	3.07	74.85

Table A2.9. *(cont.)*

POLAND

RANK	CODE	CATEGORY	%	CUMULATIVE %
1.	103	PEACE	21.88	21.88
2.	19	BASKET TWO: COOPERATION IN THE FIELD OF ECONOMICS, SCIENCE, TECHNOLOGY, AND THE ENVIRONMENT	12.50	34.38
3.	11	COOPERATION AMONG STATES AS A PRINCIPLE OF INTERNATIONAL RELATIONS	11.46	45.83
4.	104	CONFLICT AND CONFRONTATION	10.42	56.25
5.	2	GENERAL REMARKS CONCERNING THE DECLARATION ON PRINCIPLES GUIDING RELATIONS	5.21	61.46
6.	3	SOVEREIGN EQUALITY, RESPECT FOR THE RIGHTS INHERENT IN SOVEREIGNTY	5.21	66.67
7.	116	PEACEFUL COEXISTENCE	5.21	71.87
8.	17	QUESTIONS RELATING TO SECURITY	4.17	76.04
9.	1	BASKET ONE: QUESTIONS RELATING TO SECURITY IN EUROPE	3.13	79.17
10.	98	INTERNATIONAL ORGANISATIONS OTHER THAN UN	3.13	82.29

PORTUGAL

RANK	CODE	CATEGORY	%	CUMULATIVE %
1.	11	COOPERATION AMONG STATES AS A PRINCIPLE OF INTERNATIONAL RELATIONS	12.31	12.31
2.	17	QUESTIONS RELATING TO SECURITY	9.23	21.54
3.	19	BASKET TWO: COOPERATION IN THE FIELD OF ECONOMICS, SCIENCE, TECHNOLOGY, AND THE ENVIRONMENT	9.23	30.77
4.	1	BASKET ONE: QUESTIONS RELATING TO SECURITY IN EUROPE	6.15	36.92
5.	2	GENERAL REMARKS CONCERNING THE DECLARATION ON PRINCIPLES GUIDING RELATIONS	6.15	43.08
6.	51	SECTION ON THE MEDITERRANEAN: GENERAL REMARKS	4.62	47.69
7.	103	PEACE	4.62	52.31
8.	104	CONFLICT AND CONFRONTATION	4.62	56.92
9.	3	SOVEREIGN EQUALITY, RESPECT FOR THE RIGHTS INHERENT IN SOVEREIGNTY	3.08	60.00
10.	8	NON-INTERVENTION IN INTERNAL AFFAIRS	3.08	63.08

ROMANIA

RANK	CODE	CATEGORY	%	CUMULATIVE %
1.	103	PEACE	9.61	9.61
2.	19	BASKET TWO: COOPERATION IN THE FIELD OF ECONOMICS, SCIENCE, TECHNOLOGY, AND THE ENVIRONMENT	9.25	18.86
3.	17	QUESTIONS RELATING TO SECURITY	8.90	27.76
4.	11	COOPERATION AMONG STATES AS A PRINCIPLE OF INTERNATIONAL RELATIONS	8.19	35.94
5.	16	QUESTIONS RELATING TO DISARMAMENT	7.83	43.77
6.	1	BASKET ONE: QUESTIONS RELATING TO SECURITY IN EUROPE	7.47	51.25
7.	3	SOVEREIGN EQUALITY, RESPECT FOR THE RIGHTS INHERENT IN SOVEREIGNTY	4.98	56.23
8.	111	WELFARE AND PROSPERITY	4.98	61.21
9.	2	GENERAL REMARKS CONCERNING THE DECLARATION ON PRINCIPLES GUIDING RELATIONS	4.27	65.48
10.	104	CONFLICT AND CONFRONTATION	3.56	69.04

SAN MARINO

RANK	CODE	CATEGORY	%	CUMULATIVE %
1.	103	PEACE	22.02	22.02
2.	104	CONFLICT AND CONFRONTATION	11.01	33.03
3.	11	COOPERATION AMONG STATES AS A PRINCIPLE OF INTERNATIONAL RELATIONS	10.09	43.12
4.	9	RESPECT FOR HUMAN RIGHTS AND FUNDAMENTAL FREEDOMS	8.26	51.38
5.	19	BASKET TWO: COOPERATION IN THE FIELD OF ECONOMICS, SCIENCE, TECHNOLOGY, AND THE ENVIRONMENT	8.26	59.63
6.	109	FREEDOM	8.26	67.89
7.	110	JUSTICE	5.50	73.39
8.	2	GENERAL REMARKS CONCERNING THE DECLARATION ON PRINCIPLES GUIDING RELATIONS	4.59	77.98
9.	16	QUESTIONS RELATING TO DISARMAMENT	1.83	79.82
10.	40	COOPERATION IN THE FIELD OF ENVIRONMENT	1.83	81.65

SPAIN

RANK	CODE	CATEGORY	%	CUMULATIVE %
1.	17	QUESTIONS RELATING TO SECURITY	9.49	9.49
2.	1	BASKET ONE: QUESTIONS RELATING TO SECURITY IN EUROPE	7.59	17.09
3.	2	GENERAL REMARKS CONCERNING THE DECLARATION ON PRINCIPLES GUIDING RELATIONS	6.33	23.42
4.	3	SOVEREIGN EQUALITY, RESPECT FOR THE RIGHTS INHERENT IN SOVEREIGNTY	5.70	29.11
5.	11	COOPERATION AMONG STATES AS A PRINCIPLE OF INTERNATIONAL RELATIONS	5.70	34.81
6.	16	QUESTIONS RELATING TO DISARMAMENT	5.70	40.51
7.	19	BASKET TWO: COOPERATION IN THE FIELD OF ECONOMICS, SCIENCE, TECHNOLOGY, AND THE ENVIRONMENT	4.43	44.94
8.	64	IMPROVEMENT OF THE CONDITIONS FOR TOURISM ON AN INDIVIDUAL OR COLLECTIVE BASIS	4.43	49.37
9.	97	INTERNATIONAL CONFERENCES	4.43	53.80
10.	51	SECTION ON THE MEDITERRANEAN: GENERAL REMARKS	3.80	57.59

Table A2.9. *(cont.)*

SWEDEN

RANK	CODE	CATEGORY	%	CUMULATIVE %
1.	104	CONFLICT AND CONFRONTATION	10.69	10.69
2.	1	BASKET ONE: QUESTIONS RELATING TO SECURITY IN EUROPE	9.16	19.85
3.	17	QUESTIONS RELATING TO SECURITY	9.16	29.01
4.	19	BASKET TWO: COOPERATION IN THE FIELD OF ECONOMICS, SCIENCE, TECHNOLOGY, AND THE ENVIRONMENT	7.63	36.64
5.	11	COOPERATION AMONG STATES AS A PRINCIPLE OF INTERNATIONAL RELATIONS	6.87	43.51
6.	16	QUESTIONS RELATING TO DISARMAMENT	6.87	50.38
7.	103	PEACE	5.34	55.73
8.	2	GENERAL REMARKS CONCERNING THE DECLARATION ON PRINCIPLES GUIDING RELATIONS	3.82	59.54
9.	97	INTERNATIONAL CONFERENCES	3.82	63.36
10.	20	GENERAL REMARKS CONCERNING COMMERCIAL EXCHANGES	3.05	66.41

SWITZERLAND

RANK	CODE	CATEGORY	%	CUMULATIVE %
1.	3	SOVEREIGN EQUALITY, RESPECT FOR THE RIGHTS INHERENT IN SOVEREIGNTY	8.74	8.74
2.	2	GENERAL REMARKS CONCERNING THE DECLARATION ON PRINCIPLES GUIDING RELATIONS	7.77	16.50
3.	7	PEACEFUL SETTLEMENT OF DISPUTES	7.77	24.27
4.	70	IMPROVEMENT OF THE CIRCULATION, ACCESS TO, AND EXCHANGE OF INFORMATION	7.77	32.04
5.	104	CONFLICT AND CONFRONTATION	6.80	38.83
6.	1	BASKET ONE: QUESTIONS RELATING TO SECURITY IN EUROPE	5.83	44.66
7.	9	RESPECT FOR HUMAN RIGHTS AND FUNDAMENTAL FREEDOMS	5.83	50.49
8.	17	QUESTIONS RELATING TO SECURITY	5.83	56.31
9.	20	GENERAL REMARKS CONCERNING COMMERCIAL EXCHANGES	4.85	61.16
10.	69	COOPERATION IN THE FIELD OF INFORMATION EXCHANGE	4.85	66.02

TURKEY

RANK	CODE	CATEGORY	%	CUMULATIVE %
1.	2	GENERAL REMARKS CONCERNING THE DECLARATION ON PRINCIPLES GUIDING RELATIONS	17.47	17.47
2.	9	RESPECT FOR HUMAN RIGHTS AND FUNDAMENTAL FREEDOMS	10.24	27.71
3.	17	QUESTIONS RELATING TO SECURITY	10.24	37.95
4.	103	PEACE	9.64	47.59
5.	11	COOPERATION AMONG STATES AS A PRINCIPLE OF INTERNATIONAL RELATIONS	9.04	56.63
6.	1	BASKET ONE: QUESTIONS RELATING TO SECURITY IN EUROPE	5.42	62.05
7.	20	GENERAL REMARKS CONCERNING COMMERCIAL EXCHANGES	4.22	66.26
8.	4	REFRAINING FROM THE THREAT OR USE OF FORCE	3.01	69.28
9.	51	SECTION ON THE MEDITERRANEAN: GENERAL REMARKS	3.01	72.29
10.	3	SOVEREIGN EQUALITY, RESPECT FOR THE RIGHTS INHERENT IN SOVEREIGNTY	2.41	74.70

UNION OF THE SOVIET SOCIALIST REPUBLICS

RANK	CODE	CATEGORY	%	CUMULATIVE %
1.	103	PEACE	22.73	22.73
2.	11	COOPERATION AMONG STATES AS A PRINCIPLE OF INTERNATIONAL RELATIONS	9.09	31.82
3.	17	QUESTIONS RELATING TO SECURITY	9.09	40.91
4.	16	QUESTIONS RELATING TO DISARMAMENT	7.58	48.48
5.	19	BASKET TWO: COOPERATION IN THE FIELD OF ECONOMICS, SCIENCE, TECHNOLOGY, AND THE ENVIRONMENT	7.58	56.06
6.	1	BASKET ONE: QUESTIONS RELATING TO SECURITY IN EUROPE	6.06	62.12
7.	2	GENERAL REMARKS CONCERNING THE DECLARATION ON PRINCIPLES GUIDING RELATIONS	6.06	68.18
8.	3	SOVEREIGN EQUALITY, RESPECT FOR THE RIGHTS INHERENT IN SOVEREIGNTY	4.55	72.73
9.	104	CONFLICT AND CONFRONTATION	4.55	77.27
10.	8	NON-INTERVENTION IN INTERNAL AFFAIRS	3.03	80.30

UNITED KINGDOM

RANK	CODE	CATEGORY	%	CUMULATIVE %
1.	16	QUESTIONS RELATING TO DISARMAMENT	9.26	9.26
2.	98	INTERNATIONAL ORGANISATIONS OTHER THAN UN	6.79	16.05
3.	99	UN AND UN SPECIAL ORGANISATIONS	6.79	22.84
4.	94	DANGERS OF NUCLEAR PROLIFERATION	6.17	29.01
5.	104	CONFLICT AND CONFRONTATION	6.17	35.19
6.	97	INTERNATIONAL CONFERENCES	5.56	40.74
7.	3	SOVEREIGN EQUALITY, RESPECT FOR THE RIGHTS INHERENT IN SOVEREIGNTY	4.94	45.68
8.	119	SPECIFIC INTERNATIONAL AGREEMENTS	4.94	50.62
9.	103	PEACE	4.32	54.94
10.	15	PRIOR NOTIFICATION OF MILITARY MANOEUVRES	3.70	58.64

Table A2.9. *(cont.)*

UNITED STATES OF AMERICA

RANK	CODE	CATEGORY	%	CUMULATIVE %
1.	104	CONFLICT AND CONFRONTATION	8.92	8.92
2.	16	QUESTIONS RELATING TO DISARMAMENT	7.64	16.56
3.	103	PEACE	7.64	24.20
4.	111	WELFARE AND PROSPERITY	6.37	30.57
5.	2	GENERAL REMARKS CONCERNING THE DECLARATION ON PRINCIPLES GUIDING RELATIONS	5.73	36.31
6.	97	INTERNATIONAL CONFERENCES	5.73	42.04
7.	109	FREEDOM	5.73	47.77
8.	9	RESPECT FOR HUMAN RIGHTS AND FUNDAMENTAL FREEDOMS	5.10	52.87
9.	119	SPECIFIC INTERNATIONAL AGREEMENTS	3.82	56.69
10.	17	QUESTIONS RELATING TO SECURITY	3.18	59.87

VATICAN (HOLY SEE)

RANK	CODE	CATEGORY	%	CUMULATIVE %
1.	103	PEACE	29.20	29.20
2.	19	BASKET TWO: COOPERATION IN THE FIELD OF ECONOMICS, SCIENCE, TECHNOLOGY, AND THE ENVIRONMENT	7.96	37.17
3.	9	RESPECT FOR HUMAN RIGHTS AND FUNDAMENTAL FREEDOMS	7.08	44.25
4.	11	COOPERATION AMONG STATES AS A PRINCIPLE OF INTERNATIONAL RELATIONS	7.08	51.33
5.	1	BASKET ONE: QUESTIONS RELATING TO SECURITY IN EUROPE	6.19	57.52
6.	17	QUESTIONS RELATING TO SECURITY	6.19	63.72
7.	110	JUSTICE	6.19	69.91
8.	104	CONFLICT AND CONFRONTATION	4.42	74.34
9.	115	FREEDOM OF RELIGION OR BELIEF	4.42	78.76
10.	2	GENERAL REMARKS CONCERNING THE DECLARATION ON PRINCIPLES GUIDING RELATIONS	3.54	82.30

YUGOSLAVIA

RANK	CODE	CATEGORY	%	CUMULATIVE %
1.	3	SOVEREIGN EQUALITY, RESPECT FOR THE RIGHTS INHERENT IN SOVEREIGNTY	9.73	9.73
2.	17	QUESTIONS RELATING TO SECURITY	9.73	19.46
3.	103	PEACE	8.65	28.11
4.	1	BASKET ONE: QUESTIONS RELATING TO SECURITY IN EUROPE	7.57	35.68
5.	11	COOPERATION AMONG STATES AS A PRINCIPLE OF INTERNATIONAL RELATIONS	7.57	43.24
6.	19	BASKET TWO: COOPERATION IN THE FIELD OF ECONOMICS, SCIENCE, TECHNOLOGY, AND THE ENVIRONMENT	7.03	50.27
7.	16	QUESTIONS RELATING TO DISARMAMENT	6.49	56.76
8.	104	CONFLICT AND CONFRONTATION	6.49	63.24
9.	117	REMARKS CONCERNING DEVELOPING COUNTRIES	4.32	67.57

Table A2.10. Rank-Order of Categories: The Belgrade Opening Statements

AUSTRIA

RANK	CODE	CATEGORY	%	CUMULATIVE %
1.	14	DOCUMENT ON CONFIDENCE-BUILDING MEASURES AND CERTAIN ASPECTS OF SECURITY AND DISARMAMENT	12.90	12.90
2.	58	BASKET THREE: COOPERATION IN HUMANITARIAN AND OTHER FIELDS	6.45	19.35
3.	95	ENERGY PROBLEMS	6.45	25.81
4.	97	INTERNATIONAL CONFERENCES	6.45	32.26
5.	1	BASKET ONE: QUESTIONS RELATING TO SECURITY IN EUROPE	4.84	37.10
6.	11	COOPERATION AMONG STATES AS A PRINCIPLE OF INTERNATIONAL RELATIONS	4.84	41.94
7.	17	QUESTIONS RELATING TO SECURITY	4.84	46.77
8.	19	BASKET TWO: COOPERATION IN THE FIELD OF ECONOMICS, SCIENCE, TECHNOLOGY, AND THE ENVIRONMENT	4.84	51.61
9.	46	DEVELOPMENT OF TRANSPORT	4.84	56.45
10.	108	IDEOLOGY AND IDEAS	4.84	61.29

BELGIUM

RANK	CODE	CATEGORY	%	CUMULATIVE %
1.	98	INTERNATIONAL ORGANISATIONS OTHER THAN UN	11.97	11.97
2.	74	COOPERATION AND EXCHANGES IN THE FIELD OF CULTURE	8.45	20.42
3.	82	COOPERATION AND EXCHANGES IN THE FIELD OF EDUCATION	7.75	28.17
4.	17	QUESTIONS RELATING TO SECURITY	6.34	34.51
5.	19	BASKET TWO: COOPERATION IN THE FIELD OF ECONOMICS, SCIENCE, TECHNOLOGY, AND THE ENVIRONMENT	6.34	40.85
6.	58	BASKET THREE: COOPERATION IN HUMANITARIAN AND OTHER FIELDS	5.63	46.48
7.	2	GENERAL REMARKS CONCERNING THE DECLARATION ON PRINCIPLES GUIDING RELATIONS	4.93	51.41
8.	9	RESPECT FOR HUMAN RIGHTS AND FUNDAMENTAL FREEDOMS	4.93	56.34
9.	11	COOPERATION AMONG STATES AS A PRINCIPLE OF INTERNATIONAL RELATIONS	3.52	59.86
10.	14	DOCUMENT ON CONFIDENCE-BUILDING MEASURES AND CERTAIN ASPECTS OF SECURITY AND DISARMAMENT	3.52	63.38

Table A2.10. *(cont.)*

BULGARIA

RANK	CODE	CATEGORY	%	CUMULATIVE %
1.	16	QUESTIONS RELATING TO DISARMAMENT	12.89	12.89
2.	19	BASKET TWO: COOPERATION IN THE FIELD OF ECONOMICS, SCIENCE, TECHNOLOGY, AND THE ENVIRONMENT	10.31	23.20
3.	11	COOPERATION AMONG STATES AS A PRINCIPLE OF INTERNATIONAL RELATIONS	9.28	32.47
4.	103	PEACE	8.25	40.72
5.	14	DOCUMENT ON CONFIDENCE-BUILDING MEASURES AND CERTAIN ASPECTS OF SECURITY AND DISARMAMENT	7.73	48.45
6.	1	BASKET ONE: QUESTIONS RELATING TO SECURITY IN EUROPE	7.22	55.67
7.	17	QUESTIONS RELATING TO SECURITY	7.22	62.89
8.	2	GENERAL REMARKS CONCERNING THE DECLARATION ON PRINCIPLES GUIDING RELATIONS	4.64	67.53
9.	7	PEACEFUL SETTLEMENT OF DISPUTES	3.61	71.13
10.	119	SPECIFIC INTERNATIONAL AGREEMENTS	3.61	74.74

CANADA

RANK	CODE	CATEGORY	%	CUMULATIVE %
1.	9	RESPECT FOR HUMAN RIGHTS AND FUNDAMENTAL FREEDOMS	10.85	10.85
2.	61	REUNIFICATION OF FAMILIES	10.85	21.71
3.	16	QUESTIONS RELATING TO DISARMAMENT	9.30	31.01
4.	58	BASKET THREE: COOPERATION IN HUMANITARIAN AND OTHER FIELDS	7.75	38.76
5.	1	BASKET ONE: QUESTIONS RELATING TO SECURITY IN EUROPE	6.20	44.96
6.	2	GENERAL REMARKS CONCERNING THE DECLARATION ON PRINCIPLES GUIDING RELATIONS	4.65	49.61
7.	14	DOCUMENT ON CONFIDENCE-BUILDING MEASURES AND CERTAIN ASPECTS OF SECURITY AND DISARMAMENT	4.65	54.26
8.	17	QUESTIONS RELATING TO SECURITY	4.65	58.91
9.	59	GENERAL REMARKS CONCERNING HUMAN CONTACTS	4.65	63.57
10.	11	COOPERATION AMONG STATES AS A PRINCIPLE OF INTERNATIONAL RELATIONS	3.88	67.44

CYPRUS

RANK	CODE	CATEGORY	%	CUMULATIVE %
1.	2	GENERAL REMARKS CONCERNING THE DECLARATION ON PRINCIPLES GUIDING RELATIONS	11.01	11.01
2.	1	BASKET ONE: QUESTIONS RELATING TO SECURITY IN EUROPE	9.17	20.18
3.	99	UN AND UN SPECIAL ORGANISATIONS	8.26	28.44
4.	17	QUESTIONS RELATING TO SECURITY	7.34	35.78
5.	11	COOPERATION AMONG STATES AS A PRINCIPLE OF INTERNATIONAL RELATIONS	5.50	41.28
6.	103	PEACE	5.50	46.79
7.	7	PEACEFUL SETTLEMENT OF DISPUTES	4.59	51.38
8.	19	BASKET TWO: COOPERATION IN THE FIELD OF ECONOMICS, SCIENCE, TECHNOLOGY, AND THE ENVIRONMENT	4.59	55.96
9.	56	ENVIRONMENTAL QUESTIONS CONCERNING THE MEDITERRANEAN	3.67	59.63
10.	9	RESPECT FOR HUMAN RIGHTS AND FUNDAMENTAL FREEDOMS	2.75	62.39

CZECHOSLOVAKIA

RANK	CODE	CATEGORY	%	CUMULATIVE %
1.	16	QUESTIONS RELATING TO DISARMAMENT	17.92	17.92
2.	97	INTERNATIONAL CONFERENCES	11.79	29.72
3.	119	SPECIFIC INTERNATIONAL AGREEMENTS	8.49	38.21
4.	20	GENERAL REMARKS CONCERNING COMMERCIAL EXCHANGES	5.19	43.40
5.	17	QUESTIONS RELATING TO SECURITY	4.25	47.64
6.	19	BASKET TWO: COOPERATION IN THE FIELD OF ECONOMICS, SCIENCE, TECHNOLOGY, AND THE ENVIRONMENT	3.77	51.42
7.	26	INDUSTRIAL COOPERATION AND PROJECTS OF COMMON INTEREST	3.77	55.19
8.	35	COOPERATION IN SCIENCE AND TECHNOLOGY	3.30	58.49
9.	61	REUNIFICATION OF FAMILIES	3.30	61.79
10.	69	COOPERATION IN THE FIELD OF INFORMATION EXCHANGE	3.30	65.09

DENMARK

RANK	CODE	CATEGORY	%	CUMULATIVE %
1.	9	RESPECT FOR HUMAN RIGHTS AND FUNDAMENTAL FREEDOMS	14.02	14.02
2.	2	GENERAL REMARKS CONCERNING THE DECLARATION ON PRINCIPLES GUIDING RELATIONS	13.41	27.44
3.	16	QUESTIONS RELATING TO DISARMAMENT	6.10	33.54
4.	99	UN AND UN SPECIAL ORGANISATIONS	6.10	39.63
5.	59	GENERAL REMARKS CONCERNING HUMAN CONTACTS	5.49	45.12
6.	69	COOPERATION IN THE FIELD OF INFORMATION EXCHANGE	5.49	50.61
7.	97	INTERNATIONAL CONFERENCES	4.88	55.49
8.	98	INTERNATIONAL ORGANISATIONS OTHER THAN UN	3.66	59.15
9.	14	DOCUMENT ON CONFIDENCE-BUILDING MEASURES AND CERTAIN ASPECTS OF SECURITY AND DISARMAMENT	3.05	62.20
10.	61	REUNIFICATION OF FAMILIES	3.05	65.24

Table A2.10. *(cont.)*

FINLAND

RANK	CODE	CATEGORY	%	CUMULATIVE %
1.	11	COOPERATION AMONG STATES AS A PRINCIPLE OF INTERNATIONAL RELATIONS	15.68	15.68
2.	19	BASKET TWO: COOPERATION IN THE FIELD OF ECONOMICS, SCIENCE, TECHNOLOGY, AND THE ENVIRONMENT	14.83	30.51
3.	17	QUESTIONS RELATING TO SECURITY	11.02	41.53
4.	16	QUESTIONS RELATING TO DISARMAMENT	8.05	49.58
5.	1	BASKET ONE: QUESTIONS RELATING TO SECURITY IN EUROPE	7.20	56.78
6.	3	SOVEREIGN EQUALITY, RESPECT FOR THE RIGHTS INHERENT IN SOVEREIGNTY	5.93	62.71
7.	104	CONFLICT AND CONFRONTATION	3.81	66.53
8.	2	GENERAL REMARKS CONCERNING THE DECLARATION ON PRINCIPLES GUIDING RELATIONS	3.39	69.92
9.	99	UN AND UN SPECIAL ORGANISATIONS	2.97	72.88
10.	101	NON-ALIGNMENT	2.97	75.85

FRANCE

RANK	CODE	CATEGORY	%	CUMULATIVE %
1.	41	AIMS OF COOPERATION IN THE FIELD OF ENVIRONMENT	10.71	10.71
2.	11	COOPERATION AMONG STATES AS A PRINCIPLE OF INTERNATIONAL RELATIONS	9.52	20.24
3.	9	RESPECT FOR HUMAN RIGHTS AND FUNDAMENTAL FREEDOMS	8.33	28.57
4.	104	CONFLICT AND CONFRONTATION	5.95	34.52
5.	113	PUBLIC OPINION	5.95	40.48
6.	19	BASKET TWO: COOPERATION IN THE FIELD OF ECONOMICS, SCIENCE, TECHNOLOGY, AND THE ENVIRONMENT	4.76	45.24
7.	20	GENERAL REMARKS CONCERNING COMMERCIAL EXCHANGES	4.76	50.00
8.	108	IDEOLOGY AND IDEAS	4.76	54.76
9.	1	BASKET ONE: QUESTIONS RELATING TO SECURITY IN EUROPE	3.57	58.33
10.	17	QUESTIONS RELATING TO SECURITY	3.57	61.90

FEDERAL REPUBLIC OF GERMANY

RANK	CODE	CATEGORY	%	CUMULATIVE %
1.	9	RESPECT FOR HUMAN RIGHTS AND FUNDAMENTAL FREEDOMS	7.22	7.22
2.	59	GENERAL REMARKS CONCERNING HUMAN CONTACTS	7.22	14.44
3.	119	SPECIFIC INTERNATIONAL AGREEMENTS	7.22	21.67
4.	103	PEACE	4.44	26.11
5.	19	BASKET TWO: COOPERATION IN THE FIELD OF ECONOMICS, SCIENCE, TECHNOLOGY, AND THE ENVIRONMENT	3.89	30.00
6.	70	IMPROVEMENT OF THE CIRCULATION, ACCESS TO, AND EXCHANGE OF INFORMATION	3.89	33.89
7.	11	COOPERATION AMONG STATES AS A PRINCIPLE OF INTERNATIONAL RELATIONS	3.33	37.22
8.	14	DOCUMENT ON CONFIDENCE-BUILDING MEASURES AND CERTAIN ASPECTS OF SECURITY AND DISARMAMENT	3.33	40.56
9.	26	INDUSTRIAL COOPERATION AND PROJECTS OF COMMON INTEREST	3.33	43.89
10.	16	QUESTIONS RELATING TO DISARMAMENT	2.78	46.67

GERMAN DEMOCRATIC REPUBLIC

RANK	CODE	CATEGORY	%	CUMULATIVE %
1.	119	SPECIFIC INTERNATIONAL AGREEMENTS	14.81	14.81
2.	97	INTERNATIONAL CONFERENCES	11.57	26.39
3.	16	QUESTIONS RELATING TO DISARMAMENT	6.48	32.87
4.	19	BASKET TWO: COOPERATION IN THE FIELD OF ECONOMICS, SCIENCE, TECHNOLOGY, AND THE ENVIRONMENT	6.48	39.35
5.	11	COOPERATION AMONG STATES AS A PRINCIPLE OF INTERNATIONAL RELATIONS	5.56	44.91
6.	2	GENERAL REMARKS CONCERNING THE DECLARATION ON PRINCIPLES GUIDING RELATIONS	5.09	50.00
7.	103	PEACE	4.63	54.63
8.	59	GENERAL REMARKS CONCERNING HUMAN CONTACTS	4.17	58.80
9.	69	COOPERATION IN THE FIELD OF INFORMATION EXCHANGE	4.17	62.96
10.	74	COOPERATION AND EXCHANGES IN THE FIELD OF CULTURE	4.17	67.13

GREECE

RANK	CODE	CATEGORY	%	CUMULATIVE %
1.	14	DOCUMENT ON CONFIDENCE-BUILDING MEASURES AND CERTAIN ASPECTS OF SECURITY AND DISARMAMENT	16.67	16.67
2.	19	BASKET TWO: COOPERATION IN THE FIELD OF ECONOMICS, SCIENCE, TECHNOLOGY, AND THE ENVIRONMENT	16.67	33.33
3.	1	BASKET ONE: QUESTIONS RELATING TO SECURITY IN EUROPE	11.11	44.44
4.	11	COOPERATION AMONG STATES AS A PRINCIPLE OF INTERNATIONAL RELATIONS	11.11	55.56
5.	17	QUESTIONS RELATING TO SECURITY	11.11	66.67
6.	2	GENERAL REMARKS CONCERNING THE DECLARATION ON PRINCIPLES GUIDING RELATIONS	7.41	74.07
7.	58	BASKET THREE: COOPERATION IN HUMANITARIAN AND OTHER FIELDS	5.56	79.63
8.	20	GENERAL REMARKS CONCERNING COMMERCIAL EXCHANGES	3.70	83.33
9.	26	INDUSTRIAL COOPERATION AND PROJECTS OF COMMON INTEREST	3.70	87.04
10.	52	DEVELOPMENT OF GOOD NEIGHBOURLY RELATIONS IN THE MEDITERRANEAN	1.85	88.89

Table A2.10. *(cont.)*

HUNGARY

RANK	CODE	CATEGORY	%	CUMULATIVE %
1.	17	QUESTIONS RELATING TO SECURITY	7.41	7.41
2.	11	COOPERATION AMONG STATES AS A PRINCIPLE OF INTERNATIONAL RELATIONS	6.58	13.99
3.	26	INDUSTRIAL COOPERATION AND PROJECTS OF COMMON INTEREST	6.58	20.58
4.	103	PEACE	6.17	26.75
5.	16	QUESTIONS RELATING TO DISARMAMENT	5.76	32.51
6.	1	BASKET ONE: QUESTIONS RELATING TO SECURITY IN EUROPE	5.35	37.86
7.	2	GENERAL REMARKS CONCERNING THE DECLARATION ON PRINCIPLES GUIDING RELATIONS	5.35	43.21
8.	19	BASKET TWO: COOPERATION IN THE FIELD OF ECONOMICS, SCIENCE, TECHNOLOGY, AND THE ENVIRONMENT	4.94	48.15
9.	104	CONFLICT AND CONFRONTATION	4.53	52.67
10.	20	GENERAL REMARKS CONCERNING COMMERCIAL EXCHANGES	4.12	56.79

ICELAND

RANK	CODE	CATEGORY	%	CUMULATIVE %
1.	59	GENERAL REMARKS CONCERNING HUMAN CONTACTS	12.00	12.00
2.	9	RESPECT FOR HUMAN RIGHTS AND FUNDAMENTAL FREEDOMS	9.33	21.33
3.	99	UN AND UN SPECIAL ORGANISATIONS	9.33	30.67
4.	22	BUSINESS CONTACTS AND FACILITIES	8.00	38.67
5.	20	GENERAL REMARKS CONCERNING COMMERCIAL EXCHANGES	6.67	45.33
6.	26	INDUSTRIAL COOPERATION AND PROJECTS OF COMMON INTEREST	6.67	52.00
7.	2	GENERAL REMARKS CONCERNING THE DECLARATION ON PRINCIPLES GUIDING RELATIONS	5.33	57.33
8.	72	IMPROVEMENT OF WORKING CONDITIONS FOR JOURNALISTS	5.33	62.67
9.	4	REFRAINING FROM THE THREAT OR USE OF FORCE	4.00	66.67
10.	11	COOPERATION AMONG STATES AS A PRINCIPLE OF INTERNATIONAL RELATIONS	4.00	70.67

IRELAND

RANK	CODE	CATEGORY	%	CUMULATIVE %
1.	16	QUESTIONS RELATING TO DISARMAMENT	14.43	14.43
2.	9	RESPECT FOR HUMAN RIGHTS AND FUNDAMENTAL FREEDOMS	10.31	24.74
3.	58	BASKET THREE: COOPERATION IN HUMANITARIAN AND OTHER FIELDS	8.76	33.51
4.	2	GENERAL REMARKS CONCERNING THE DECLARATION ON PRINCIPLES GUIDING RELATIONS	6.70	40.21
5.	19	BASKET TWO: COOPERATION IN THE FIELD OF ECONOMICS, SCIENCE, TECHNOLOGY, AND THE ENVIRONMENT	6.70	46.91
6.	24	MARKETING AND TRADE PROMOTION	6.19	53.09
7.	97	INTERNATIONAL CONFERENCES	5.67	58.76
8.	14	DOCUMENT ON CONFIDENCE-BUILDING MEASURES AND CERTAIN ASPECTS OF SECURITY AND DISARMAMENT	5.15	63.92
9.	20	GENERAL REMARKS CONCERNING COMMERCIAL EXCHANGES	4.64	68.56
10.	11	COOPERATION AMONG STATES AS A PRINCIPLE OF INTERNATIONAL RELATIONS	3.61	72.16

ITALY

RANK	CODE	CATEGORY	%	CUMULATIVE %
1.	19	BASKET TWO: COOPERATION IN THE FIELD OF ECONOMICS, SCIENCE, TECHNOLOGY, AND THE ENVIRONMENT	14.29	14.29
2.	11	COOPERATION AMONG STATES AS A PRINCIPLE OF INTERNATIONAL RELATIONS	13.49	27.78
3.	17	QUESTIONS RELATING TO SECURITY	9.52	37.30
4.	1	BASKET ONE: QUESTIONS RELATING TO SECURITY IN EUROPE	8.73	46.03
5.	104	CONFLICT AND CONFRONTATION	5.56	51.59
6.	120	STABILITY, STRATEGIC AND POLITICAL BALANCE	5.56	57.14
7.	2	GENERAL REMARKS CONCERNING THE DECLARATION ON PRINCIPLES GUIDING RELATIONS	4.76	61.90
8.	103	PEACE	4.76	66.67
9.	9	RESPECT FOR HUMAN RIGHTS AND FUNDAMENTAL FREEDOMS	3.17	69.84
10.	51	SECTION ON THE MEDITERRANEAN: GENERAL REMARKS	3.17	73.02

LIECHTENSTEIN

RANK	CODE	CATEGORY	%	CUMULATIVE %
1.	11	COOPERATION AMONG STATES AS A PRINCIPLE OF INTERNATIONAL RELATIONS	24.00	24.00
2.	9	RESPECT FOR HUMAN RIGHTS AND FUNDAMENTAL FREEDOMS	16.00	40.00
3.	19	BASKET TWO: COOPERATION IN THE FIELD OF ECONOMICS, SCIENCE, TECHNOLOGY, AND THE ENVIRONMENT	12.00	52.00
4.	104	CONFLICT AND CONFRONTATION	12.00	64.00
5.	3	SOVEREIGN EQUALITY, RESPECT FOR THE RIGHTS INHERENT IN SOVEREIGNTY	8.00	72.00
6.	103	PEACE	8.00	80.00
7.	1	BASKET ONE: QUESTIONS RELATING TO SECURITY IN EUROPE	4.00	84.00
8.	17	QUESTIONS RELATING TO SECURITY	4.00	88.00
9.	58	BASKET THREE: COOPERATION IN HUMANITARIAN AND OTHER FIELDS	4.00	92.00
10.	107	JUDICIAL SYSTEMS AND LEGAL INSTITUTIONS	4.00	96.00

Table A2.10. *(cont.)*

LUXEMBOURG

RANK	CODE	CATEGORY	%	CUMULATIVE %
1.	16	QUESTIONS RELATING TO DISARMAMENT	14.29	14.29
2.	9	RESPECT FOR HUMAN RIGHTS AND FUNDAMENTAL FREEDOMS	10.00	24.29
3.	99	UN AND UN SPECIAL ORGANISATIONS	8.57	32.86
4.	108	IDEOLOGY AND IDEAS	5.71	38.57
5.	2	GENERAL REMARKS CONCERNING THE DECLARATION ON PRINCIPLES GUIDING RELATIONS	5.00	43.57
6.	11	COOPERATION AMONG STATES AS A PRINCIPLE OF INTERNATIONAL RELATIONS	5.00	48.57
7.	19	BASKET TWO: COOPERATION IN THE FIELD OF ECONOMICS, SCIENCE, TECHNOLOGY, AND THE ENVIRONMENT	5.00	53.57
8.	70	IMPROVEMENT OF THE CIRCULATION, ACCESS TO, AND EXCHANGE OF INFORMATION	5.00	58.57
9.	20	GENERAL REMARKS CONCERNING COMMERCIAL EXCHANGES	4.29	62.86
10.	98	INTERNATIONAL ORGANISATIONS OTHER THAN UN	4.29	67.14

MALTA

RANK	CODE	CATEGORY	%	CUMULATIVE %
1.	51	SECTION ON THE MEDITERRANEAN: GENERAL REMARKS	10.90	10.90
2.	99	UN AND UN SPECIAL ORGANISATIONS	7.58	18.48
3.	55	ECONOMIC DEVELOPMENT IN THE MEDITERRANEAN AREA	7.11	25.59
4.	56	ENVIRONMENTAL QUESTIONS CONCERNING THE MEDITERRANEAN	5.69	31.28
5.	119	SPECIFIC INTERNATIONAL AGREEMENTS	5.69	36.97
6.	103	PEACE	4.74	41.71
7.	16	QUESTIONS RELATING TO DISARMAMENT	4.27	45.97
8.	98	INTERNATIONAL ORGANISATIONS OTHER THAN UN	4.27	50.24
9.	11	COOPERATION AMONG STATES AS A PRINCIPLE OF INTERNATIONAL RELATIONS	3.32	53.55
10.	19	BASKET TWO: COOPERATION IN THE FIELD OF ECONOMICS, SCIENCE, TECHNOLOGY, AND THE ENVIRONMENT	3.32	56.87

MONACO

RANK	CODE	CATEGORY	%	CUMULATIVE %
1.	42	FIELDS OF COOPERATION IN THE FIELD OF ENVIRONMENT	25.00	25.00
2.	40	COOPERATION IN THE FIELD OF ENVIRONMENT	16.67	41.67
3.	35	COOPERATION IN SCIENCE AND TECHNOLOGY	12.50	54.17
4.	103	PEACE	12.50	66.67
5.	11	COOPERATION AMONG STATES AS A PRINCIPLE OF INTERNATIONAL RELATIONS	6.25	72.92
6.	43	FORMS AND METHODS OF COOPERATION IN THE FIELD OF ENVIRONMENT	6.25	79.17
7.	41	AIMS OF COOPERATION IN THE FIELD OF ENVIRONMENT	4.17	83.33
8.	59	GENERAL REMARKS CONCERNING HUMAN CONTACTS	4.17	87.50
9.	104	CONFLICT AND CONFRONTATION	4.17	91.67
10.	1	BASKET ONE: QUESTIONS RELATING TO SECURITY IN EUROPE	2.08	93.75

NETHERLANDS

RANK	CODE	CATEGORY	%	CUMULATIVE %
1.	2	GENERAL REMARKS CONCERNING THE DECLARATION ON PRINCIPLES GUIDING RELATIONS	10.19	10.19
2.	9	RESPECT FOR HUMAN RIGHTS AND FUNDAMENTAL FREEDOMS	9.71	19.90
3.	11	COOPERATION AMONG STATES AS A PRINCIPLE OF INTERNATIONAL RELATIONS	9.22	29.13
4.	19	BASKET TWO: COOPERATION IN THE FIELD OF ECONOMICS, SCIENCE, TECHNOLOGY, AND THE ENVIRONMENT	7.77	36.89
5.	58	BASKET THREE: COOPERATION IN HUMANITARIAN AND OTHER FIELDS	7.77	44.66
6.	16	QUESTIONS RELATING TO DISARMAMENT	7.28	51.94
7.	59	GENERAL REMARKS CONCERNING HUMAN CONTACTS	6.31	58.25
8.	110	JUSTICE	5.83	64.08
9.	14	DOCUMENT ON CONFIDENCE-BUILDING MEASURES AND CERTAIN ASPECTS OF SECURITY AND DISARMAMENT	3.88	67.96
10.	103	PEACE	3.88	71.84

NORWAY

RANK	CODE	CATEGORY	%	CUMULATIVE %
1.	9	RESPECT FOR HUMAN RIGHTS AND FUNDAMENTAL FREEDOMS	18.56	18.56
2.	26	INDUSTRIAL COOPERATION AND PROJECTS OF COMMON INTEREST	8.33	26.89
3.	15	PRIOR NOTIFICATION OF MILITARY MANOEUVRES	5.68	32.58
4.	17	QUESTIONS RELATING TO SECURITY	5.30	37.88
5.	20	GENERAL REMARKS CONCERNING COMMERCIAL EXCHANGES	5.30	43.18
6.	11	COOPERATION AMONG STATES AS A PRINCIPLE OF INTERNATIONAL RELATIONS	4.55	47.73
7.	19	BASKET TWO: COOPERATION IN THE FIELD OF ECONOMICS, SCIENCE, TECHNOLOGY, AND THE ENVIRONMENT	4.55	52.27
8.	40	COOPERATION IN THE FIELD OF ENVIRONMENT	4.17	56.44
9.	16	QUESTIONS RELATING TO DISARMAMENT	3.79	60.23
10.	59	GENERAL REMARKS CONCERNING HUMAN CONTACTS	3.41	63.64

Table A2.10. *(cont.)*

POLAND

RANK	CODE	CATEGORY	%	CUMULATIVE %
1.	1	BASKET ONE: QUESTIONS RELATING TO SECURITY IN EUROPE	11.11	11.11
2.	2	GENERAL REMARKS CONCERNING THE DECLARATION ON PRINCIPLES GUIDING RELATIONS	11.11	22.22
3.	17	QUESTIONS RELATING TO SECURITY	11.11	33.33
4.	103	PEACE	10.61	43.94
5.	9	RESPECT FOR HUMAN RIGHTS AND FUNDAMENTAL FREEDOMS	8.08	52.02
6.	119	SPECIFIC INTERNATIONAL AGREEMENTS	7.58	59.60
7.	11	COOPERATION AMONG STATES AS A PRINCIPLE OF INTERNATIONAL RELATIONS	5.05	64.65
8.	19	BASKET TWO: COOPERATION IN THE FIELD OF ECONOMICS, SCIENCE, TECHNOLOGY, AND THE ENVIRONMENT	4.55	69.19
9.	116	PEACEFUL COEXISTENCE	3.54	72.73
10.	3	SOVEREIGN EQUALITY, RESPECT FOR THE RIGHTS INHERENT IN SOVEREIGNTY	2.02	74.75

PORTUGAL

RANK	CODE	CATEGORY	%	CUMULATIVE %
1.	48	ECONOMIC AND SOCIAL ASPECTS OF MIGRANT LABOUR	16.26	16.26
2.	11	COOPERATION AMONG STATES AS A PRINCIPLE OF INTERNATIONAL RELATIONS	10.16	26.42
3.	99	UN AND UN SPECIAL ORGANISATIONS	8.13	34.55
4.	9	RESPECT FOR HUMAN RIGHTS AND FUNDAMENTAL FREEDOMS	6.10	40.65
5.	17	QUESTIONS RELATING TO SECURITY	6.10	46.75
6.	19	BASKET TWO: COOPERATION IN THE FIELD OF ECONOMICS, SCIENCE, TECHNOLOGY, AND THE ENVIRONMENT	6.10	52.85
7.	1	BASKET ONE: QUESTIONS RELATING TO SECURITY IN EUROPE	4.88	57.72
8.	98	INTERNATIONAL ORGANISATIONS OTHER THAN UN	4.07	61.79
9.	106	DEMOCRACY AND DEMOCRATIC INSTITUTIONS	2.85	64.63
10.	2	GENERAL REMARKS CONCERNING THE DECLARATION ON PRINCIPLES GUIDING RELATIONS	2.44	67.07

ROMANIA

RANK	CODE	CATEGORY	%	CUMULATIVE %
1.	16	QUESTIONS RELATING TO DISARMAMENT	16.30	16.30
2.	17	QUESTIONS RELATING TO SECURITY	11.85	28.15
3.	1	BASKET ONE: QUESTIONS RELATING TO SECURITY IN EUROPE	10.86	39.01
4.	11	COOPERATION AMONG STATES AS A PRINCIPLE OF INTERNATIONAL RELATIONS	7.16	46.17
5.	19	BASKET TWO: COOPERATION IN THE FIELD OF ECONOMICS, SCIENCE, TECHNOLOGY, AND THE ENVIRONMENT	7.16	53.33
6.	26	INDUSTRIAL COOPERATION AND PROJECTS OF COMMON INTEREST	3.95	57.28
7.	4	REFRAINING FROM THE THREAT OR USE OF FORCE	3.70	60.99
8.	20	GENERAL REMARKS CONCERNING COMMERCIAL EXCHANGES	2.96	63.95
9.	3	SOVEREIGN EQUALITY, RESPECT FOR THE RIGHTS INHERENT IN SOVEREIGNTY	2.72	66.67
10.	97	INTERNATIONAL CONFERENCES	2.47	69.14

SAN MARINO

RANK	CODE	CATEGORY	%	CUMULATIVE %
1.	9	RESPECT FOR HUMAN RIGHTS AND FUNDAMENTAL FREEDOMS	11.11	11.11
2.	3	SOVEREIGN EQUALITY, RESPECT FOR THE RIGHTS INHERENT IN SOVEREIGNTY	9.40	20.51
3.	2	GENERAL REMARKS CONCERNING THE DECLARATION ON PRINCIPLES GUIDING RELATIONS	6.84	27.35
4.	4	REFRAINING FROM THE THREAT OR USE OF FORCE	6.84	34.19
5.	7	PEACEFUL SETTLEMENT OF DISPUTES	6.84	41.03
6.	8	NON-INTERVENTION IN INTERNAL AFFAIRS	6.84	47.86
7.	1	BASKET ONE: QUESTIONS RELATING TO SECURITY IN EUROPE	5.98	53.85
8.	17	QUESTIONS RELATING TO SECURITY	5.98	59.83
9.	106	DEMOCRACY AND DEMOCRATIC INSTITUTIONS	5.98	65.81
10.	109	FREEDOM	5.13	70.94

SPAIN

RANK	CODE	CATEGORY	%	CUMULATIVE %
1.	9	RESPECT FOR HUMAN RIGHTS AND FUNDAMENTAL FREEDOMS	18.33	18.33
2.	16	QUESTIONS RELATING TO DISARMAMENT	11.67	30.00
3.	17	QUESTIONS RELATING TO SECURITY	10.83	40.83
4.	1	BASKET ONE: QUESTIONS RELATING TO SECURITY IN EUROPE	10.00	50.83
5.	109	FREEDOM	6.67	57.50
6.	11	COOPERATION AMONG STATES AS A PRINCIPLE OF INTERNATIONAL RELATIONS	5.00	62.50
7.	3	SOVEREIGN EQUALITY, RESPECT FOR THE RIGHTS INHERENT IN SOVEREIGNTY	4.17	66.67
8.	101	NON-ALIGNMENT	4.17	70.83
9.	19	BASKET TWO: COOPERATION IN THE FIELD OF ECONOMICS, SCIENCE, TECHNOLOGY, AND THE ENVIRONMENT	3.33	74.17
10.	120	STABILITY, STRATEGIC AND POLITICAL BALANCE	3.33	77.50

Table A2.10. *(cont.)*

SWEDEN

RANK	CODE	CATEGORY	%	CUMULATIVE %
1.	16	QUESTIONS RELATING TO DISARMAMENT	18.35	18.35
2.	9	RESPECT FOR HUMAN RIGHTS AND FUNDAMENTAL FREEDOMS	11.15	29.50
3.	11	COOPERATION AMONG STATES AS A PRINCIPLE OF INTERNATIONAL RELATIONS	8.27	37.77
4.	19	BASKET TWO: COOPERATION IN THE FIELD OF ECONOMICS, SCIENCE, TECHNOLOGY, AND THE ENVIRONMENT	6.83	44.60
5.	17	QUESTIONS RELATING TO SECURITY	4.68	49.28
6.	1	BASKET ONE: QUESTIONS RELATING TO SECURITY IN EUROPE	3.96	53.24
7.	97	INTERNATIONAL CONFERENCES	3.96	57.19
8.	119	SPECIFIC INTERNATIONAL AGREEMENTS	3.60	60.79
9.	112	RESPONSIBILITY	3.24	64.03
10.	74	COOPERATION AND EXCHANGES IN THE FIELD OF CULTURE	2.88	66.91

SWITZERLAND

RANK	CODE	CATEGORY	%	CUMULATIVE %
1.	108	IDEOLOGY AND IDEAS	8.11	8.11
2.	11	COOPERATION AMONG STATES AS A PRINCIPLE OF INTERNATIONAL RELATIONS	7.66	15.77
3.	19	BASKET TWO: COOPERATION IN THE FIELD OF ECONOMICS, SCIENCE, TECHNOLOGY, AND THE ENVIRONMENT	7.21	22.97
4.	3	SOVEREIGN EQUALITY, RESPECT FOR THE RIGHTS INHERENT IN SOVEREIGNTY	5.41	28.38
5.	30	PROVISIONS CONCERNING TRADE AND INDUSTRIAL COOPERATION	4.95	33.33
6.	9	RESPECT FOR HUMAN RIGHTS AND FUNDAMENTAL FREEDOMS	4.05	37.39
7.	16	QUESTIONS RELATING TO DISARMAMENT	4.05	41.44
8.	20	GENERAL REMARKS CONCERNING COMMERCIAL EXCHANGES	3.60	45.04
9.	106	DEMOCRACY AND DEMOCRATIC INSTITUTIONS	3.60	48.65
10.	26	INDUSTRIAL COOPERATION AND PROJECTS OF COMMON INTEREST	3.15	51.80

TURKEY

RANK	CODE	CATEGORY	%	CUMULATIVE %
1.	19	BASKET TWO: COOPERATION IN THE FIELD OF ECONOMICS, SCIENCE, TECHNOLOGY, AND THE ENVIRONMENT	10.98	10.98
2.	46	DEVELOPMENT OF TRANSPORT	10.37	21.34
3.	11	COOPERATION AMONG STATES AS A PRINCIPLE OF INTERNATIONAL RELATIONS	7.32	28.66
4.	117	REMARKS CONCERNING DEVELOPING COUNTRIES	7.32	35.98
5.	99	UN AND UN SPECIAL ORGANISATIONS	6.71	42.68
6.	2	GENERAL REMARKS CONCERNING THE DECLARATION ON PRINCIPLES GUIDING RELATIONS	4.88	47.56
7.	1	BASKET ONE: QUESTIONS RELATING TO SECURITY IN EUROPE	3.66	51.22
8.	14	DOCUMENT ON CONFIDENCE-BUILDING MEASURES AND CERTAIN ASPECTS OF SECURITY AND DISARMAMENT	3.66	54.88
9.	17	QUESTIONS RELATING TO SECURITY	3.66	58.54
10.	20	GENERAL REMARKS CONCERNING COMMERCIAL EXCHANGES	3.66	62.20

UNION OF THE SOVIET SOCIALIST REPUBLICS

RANK	CODE	CATEGORY	%	CUMULATIVE %
1.	11	COOPERATION AMONG STATES AS A PRINCIPLE OF INTERNATIONAL RELATIONS	7.56	7.56
2.	103	PEACE	7.56	15.13
3.	2	GENERAL REMARKS CONCERNING THE DECLARATION ON PRINCIPLES GUIDING RELATIONS	6.72	21.85
4.	19	BASKET TWO: COOPERATION IN THE FIELD OF ECONOMICS, SCIENCE, TECHNOLOGY, AND THE ENVIRONMENT	6.30	28.15
5.	97	INTERNATIONAL CONFERENCES	4.62	32.77
6.	1	BASKET ONE: QUESTIONS RELATING TO SECURITY IN EUROPE	4.20	36.97
7.	17	QUESTIONS RELATING TO SECURITY	4.20	41.18
8.	119	SPECIFIC INTERNATIONAL AGREEMENTS	4.20	45.38
9.	40	COOPERATION IN THE FIELD OF ENVIRONMENT	3.78	49.16
10.	46	DEVELOPMENT OF TRANSPORT	3.78	52.94

UNITED KINGDOM

RANK	CODE	CATEGORY	%	CUMULATIVE %
1.	99	UN AND UN SPECIAL ORGANISATIONS	9.80	9.80
2.	16	QUESTIONS RELATING TO DISARMAMENT	8.82	18.63
3.	19	BASKET TWO: COOPERATION IN THE FIELD OF ECONOMICS, SCIENCE, TECHNOLOGY, AND THE ENVIRONMENT	8.82	27.45
4.	11	COOPERATION AMONG STATES AS A PRINCIPLE OF INTERNATIONAL RELATIONS	5.88	33.33
5.	20	GENERAL REMARKS CONCERNING COMMERCIAL EXCHANGES	5.88	39.22
6.	95	ENERGY PROBLEMS	5.88	45.10
7.	98	INTERNATIONAL ORGANISATIONS OTHER THAN UN	5.88	50.98
8.	103	PEACE	3.92	54.90
9.	9	RESPECT FOR HUMAN RIGHTS AND FUNDAMENTAL FREEDOMS	2.94	57.84
10.	22	BUSINESS CONTACTS AND FACILITIES	2.94	60.78

Table A2.10. *(cont.)*

UNITED STATES OF AMERICA

RANK	CODE	CATEGORY	%	CUMULATIVE %
1.	9	RESPECT FOR HUMAN RIGHTS AND FUNDAMENTAL FREEDOMS	23.27	23.27
2.	119	SPECIFIC INTERNATIONAL AGREEMENTS	8.91	32.18
3.	61	REUNIFICATION OF FAMILIES	5.94	38.12
4.	11	COOPERATION AMONG STATES AS A PRINCIPLE OF INTERNATIONAL RELATIONS	4.46	42.57
5.	19	BASKET TWO: COOPERATION IN THE FIELD OF ECONOMICS, SCIENCE, TECHNOLOGY, AND THE ENVIRONMENT	4.46	47.03
6.	63	TRAVEL FOR PERSONAL OR PROFESSIONAL REASONS	3.96	50.99
7.	70	IMPROVEMENT OF THE CIRCULATION, ACCESS TO, AND EXCHANGE OF INFORMATION	3.96	54.95
8.	103	PEACE	3.96	58.91
9.	84	ACCESS TO EDUCATION SYSTEMS AND EXCHANGES OF STUDENTS	3.47	62.38
10.	17	QUESTIONS RELATING TO SECURITY	2.97	65.35

VATICAN (HOLY SEE)

RANK	CODE	CATEGORY	%	CUMULATIVE %
1.	115	FREEDOM OF RELIGION OR BELIEF	20.25	20.25
2.	9	RESPECT FOR HUMAN RIGHTS AND FUNDAMENTAL FREEDOMS	15.95	36.20
3.	103	PEACE	6.13	42.33
4.	63	TRAVEL FOR PERSONAL OR PROFESSIONAL REASONS	5.52	47.85
5.	58	BASKET THREE: COOPERATION IN HUMANITARIAN AND OTHER FIELDS	4.91	52.76
6.	16	QUESTIONS RELATING TO DISARMAMENT	4.29	57.06
7.	11	COOPERATION AMONG STATES AS A PRINCIPLE OF INTERNATIONAL RELATIONS	3.68	60.74
8.	14	DOCUMENT ON CONFIDENCE-BUILDING MEASURES AND CERTAIN ASPECTS OF SECURITY AND DISARMAMENT	3.68	64.42
9.	109	FREEDOM	3.68	68.10
10.	19	BASKET TWO: COOPERATION IN THE FIELD OF ECONOMICS, SCIENCE, TECHNOLOGY, AND THE ENVIRONMENT	2.45	70.55

YUGOSLAVIA

RANK	CODE	CATEGORY	%	CUMULATIVE %
1.	16	QUESTIONS RELATING TO DISARMAMENT	12.19	12.19
2.	11	COOPERATION AMONG STATES AS A PRINCIPLE OF INTERNATIONAL RELATIONS	5.42	17.60
3.	17	QUESTIONS RELATING TO SECURITY	5.42	23.02
4.	3	SOVEREIGN EQUALITY, RESPECT FOR THE RIGHTS INHERENT IN SOVEREIGNTY	5.22	28.24
5.	9	RESPECT FOR HUMAN RIGHTS AND FUNDAMENTAL FREEDOMS	4.84	33.08
6.	15	PRIOR NOTIFICATION OF MILITARY MANOEUVRES	4.64	37.72
7.	80	CULTURAL CONTRIBUTIONS OF NATIONAL MINORITIES	4.45	42.17
8.	19	BASKET TWO: COOPERATION IN THE FIELD OF ECONOMICS, SCIENCE, TECHNOLOGY, AND THE ENVIRONMENT	4.26	46.42
9.	119	SPECIFIC INTERNATIONAL AGREEMENTS	4.26	50.68
10.	88	THE ROLE OF NATIONAL MINORITIES IN THE FIELD OF EDUCATION	3.68	54.35

Table A2.11. Rank-Order of Categories: The Belgrade Closing Statements

AUSTRIA

RANK	CODE	CATEGORY	%	CUMULATIVE %
1.	58	BASKET THREE: COOPERATION IN HUMANITARIAN AND OTHER FIELDS	16.67	16.67
2.	9	RESPECT FOR HUMAN RIGHTS AND FUNDAMENTAL FREEDOMS	13.33	30.00
3.	1	BASKET ONE: QUESTIONS RELATING TO SECURITY IN EUROPE	11.67	41.67
4.	17	QUESTIONS RELATING TO SECURITY	11.67	53.33
5.	11	COOPERATION AMONG STATES AS A PRINCIPLE OF INTERNATIONAL RELATIONS	10.00	63.33
6.	19	BASKET TWO: COOPERATION IN THE FIELD OF ECONOMICS, SCIENCE, TECHNOLOGY, AND THE ENVIRONMENT	10.00	73.33
7.	2	GENERAL REMARKS CONCERNING THE DECLARATION ON PRINCIPLES GUIDING RELATIONS	8.33	81.67
8.	16	QUESTIONS RELATING TO DISARMAMENT	5.00	86.67
9.	14	DOCUMENT ON CONFIDENCE-BUILDING MEASURES AND CERTAIN ASPECTS OF SECURITY AND DISARMAMENT	3.33	90.00
10.	22	BUSINESS CONTACTS AND FACILITIES	1.67	91.67

BELGIUM

RANK	CODE	CATEGORY	%	CUMULATIVE %
1.	9	RESPECT FOR HUMAN RIGHTS AND FUNDAMENTAL FREEDOMS	23.08	23.08
2.	20	GENERAL REMARKS CONCERNING COMMERCIAL EXCHANGES	13.46	36.54
3.	26	INDUSTRIAL COOPERATION AND PROJECTS OF COMMON INTEREST	13.46	50.00
4.	2	GENERAL REMARKS CONCERNING THE DECLARATION ON PRINCIPLES GUIDING RELATIONS	9.62	59.62
5.	14	DOCUMENT ON CONFIDENCE-BUILDING MEASURES AND CERTAIN ASPECTS OF SECURITY AND DISARMAMENT	9.62	69.23
6.	58	BASKET THREE: COOPERATION IN HUMANITARIAN AND OTHER FIELDS	7.69	76.92
7.	16	QUESTIONS RELATING TO DISARMAMENT	5.77	82.69
8.	11	COOPERATION AMONG STATES AS A PRINCIPLE OF INTERNATIONAL RELATIONS	3.85	86.54
9.	19	BASKET TWO: COOPERATION IN THE FIELD OF ECONOMICS, SCIENCE, TECHNOLOGY, AND THE ENVIRONMENT	3.85	90.38
10.	1	BASKET ONE: QUESTIONS RELATING TO SECURITY IN EUROPE	1.92	92.31

Table A2.11. *(cont.)*

BULGARIA

RANK	CODE	CATEGORY	%	CUMULATIVE %
1.	16	QUESTIONS RELATING TO DISARMAMENT	23.40	23.40
2.	11	COOPERATION AMONG STATES AS A PRINCIPLE OF INTERNATIONAL RELATIONS	13.83	37.23
3.	19	BASKET TWO: COOPERATION IN THE FIELD OF ECONOMICS, SCIENCE, TECHNOLOGY, AND THE ENVIRONMENT	13.83	51.06
4.	97	INTERNATIONAL CONFERENCES	8.51	59.57
5.	9	RESPECT FOR HUMAN RIGHTS AND FUNDAMENTAL FREEDOMS	6.38	65.96
6.	17	QUESTIONS RELATING TO SECURITY	5.32	71.28
7.	1	BASKET ONE: QUESTIONS RELATING TO SECURITY IN EUROPE	3.19	74.47
8.	104	CONFLICT AND CONFRONTATION	3.19	77.66
9.	14	DOCUMENT ON CONFIDENCE-BUILDING MEASURES AND CERTAIN ASPECTS OF SECURITY AND DISARMAMENT	2.13	79.79
10.	40	COOPERATION IN THE FIELD OF ENVIRONMENT	2.13	81.91

CANADA

RANK	CODE	CATEGORY	%	CUMULATIVE %
1.	9	RESPECT FOR HUMAN RIGHTS AND FUNDAMENTAL FREEDOMS	21.93	21.93
2.	58	BASKET THREE: COOPERATION IN HUMANITARIAN AND OTHER FIELDS	14.04	35.96
3.	16	QUESTIONS RELATING TO DISARMAMENT	10.53	46.49
4.	70	IMPROVEMENT OF THE CIRCULATION, ACCESS TO, AND EXCHANGE OF INFORMATION	9.65	56.14
5.	1	BASKET ONE: QUESTIONS RELATING TO SECURITY IN EUROPE	6.14	62.28
6.	17	QUESTIONS RELATING TO SECURITY	6.14	68.42
7.	11	COOPERATION AMONG STATES AS A PRINCIPLE OF INTERNATIONAL RELATIONS	5.26	73.68
8.	19	BASKET TWO: COOPERATION IN THE FIELD OF ECONOMICS, SCIENCE, TECHNOLOGY, AND THE ENVIRONMENT	5.26	78.95
9.	61	REUNIFICATION OF FAMILIES	4.39	83.33
10.	15	PRIOR NOTIFICATION OF MILITARY MANOEUVRES	2.63	85.96

CYPRUS

RANK	CODE	CATEGORY	%	CUMULATIVE %
1.	11	COOPERATION AMONG STATES AS A PRINCIPLE OF INTERNATIONAL RELATIONS	17.54	17.54
2.	19	BASKET TWO: COOPERATION IN THE FIELD OF ECONOMICS, SCIENCE, TECHNOLOGY, AND THE ENVIRONMENT	17.54	35.09
3.	51	SECTION ON THE MEDITERRANEAN: GENERAL REMARKS	15.79	50.88
4.	2	GENERAL REMARKS CONCERNING THE DECLARATION ON PRINCIPLES GUIDING RELATIONS	7.02	57.89
5.	14	DOCUMENT ON CONFIDENCE-BUILDING MEASURES AND CERTAIN ASPECTS OF SECURITY AND DISARMAMENT	7.02	64.91
6.	9	RESPECT FOR HUMAN RIGHTS AND FUNDAMENTAL FREEDOMS	5.26	70.18
7.	36	POSSIBILITIES FOR IMPROVING COOPERATION IN SCIENCE AND TECHNOLOGY	5.26	75.44
8.	7	PEACEFUL SETTLEMENT OF DISPUTES	3.51	78.95
9.	119	SPECIFIC INTERNATIONAL AGREEMENTS	3.51	82.46
10.	1	BASKET ONE: QUESTIONS RELATING TO SECURITY IN EUROPE	1.75	84.21

CZECHOSLOVAKIA

RANK	CODE	CATEGORY	%	CUMULATIVE %
1.	9	RESPECT FOR HUMAN RIGHTS AND FUNDAMENTAL FREEDOMS	19.67	19.67
2.	16	QUESTIONS RELATING TO DISARMAMENT	14.75	34.43
3.	17	QUESTIONS RELATING TO SECURITY	14.75	49.18
4.	2	GENERAL REMARKS CONCERNING THE DECLARATION ON PRINCIPLES GUIDING RELATIONS	8.20	57.38
5.	99	UN AND UN SPECIAL ORGANISATIONS	6.56	63.93
6.	104	CONFLICT AND CONFRONTATION	6.56	70.49
7.	20	GENERAL REMARKS CONCERNING COMMERCIAL EXCHANGES	4.92	75.41
8.	26	INDUSTRIAL COOPERATION AND PROJECTS OF COMMON INTEREST	4.92	80.33
9.	8	NON-INTERVENTION IN INTERNAL AFFAIRS	3.28	83.61
10.	22	BUSINESS CONTACTS AND FACILITIES	3.28	86.89

DENMARK

RANK	CODE	CATEGORY	%	CUMULATIVE %
1.	98	INTERNATIONAL ORGANISATIONS OTHER THAN UN	17.24	17.24
2.	16	QUESTIONS RELATING TO DISARMAMENT	13.79	31.03
3.	58	BASKET THREE: COOPERATION IN HUMANITARIAN AND OTHER FIELDS	10.34	41.38
4.	59	GENERAL REMARKS CONCERNING HUMAN CONTACTS	8.05	49.43
5.	9	RESPECT FOR HUMAN RIGHTS AND FUNDAMENTAL FREEDOMS	5.75	55.17
6.	14	DOCUMENT ON CONFIDENCE-BUILDING MEASURES AND CERTAIN ASPECTS OF SECURITY AND DISARMAMENT	4.60	59.77
7.	30	PROVISIONS CONCERNING TRADE AND INDUSTRIAL COOPERATION	4.60	64.37
8.	22	BUSINESS CONTACTS AND FACILITIES	3.45	67.82
9.	23	ECONOMIC AND COMMERCIAL INFORMATION	3.45	71.26
10.	69	COOPERATION IN THE FIELD OF INFORMATION EXCHANGE	3.45	74.71

Table A2.11. *(cont.)*

FINLAND

RANK	CODE	CATEGORY	%	CUMULATIVE %
1.	14	DOCUMENT ON CONFIDENCE-BUILDING MEASURES AND CERTAIN ASPECTS OF SECURITY AND DISARMAMENT	22.37	22.37
2.	16	QUESTIONS RELATING TO DISARMAMENT	11.84	34.21
3.	59	GENERAL REMARKS CONCERNING HUMAN CONTACTS	10.53	44.74
4.	74	COOPERATION AND EXCHANGES IN THE FIELD OF CULTURE	10.53	55.26
5.	11	COOPERATION AMONG STATES AS A PRINCIPLE OF INTERNATIONAL RELATIONS	6.58	61.84
6.	19	BASKET TWO: COOPERATION IN THE FIELD OF ECONOMICS, SCIENCE, TECHNOLOGY, AND THE ENVIRONMENT	6.58	68.42
7.	58	BASKET THREE: COOPERATION IN HUMANITARIAN AND OTHER FIELDS	5.26	73.68
8.	1	BASKET ONE: QUESTIONS RELATING TO SECURITY IN EUROPE	3.95	77.63
9.	17	QUESTIONS RELATING TO SECURITY	3.95	81.58
10.	99	UN AND UN SPECIAL ORGANISATIONS	3.95	85.53

FRANCE

RANK	CODE	CATEGORY	%	CUMULATIVE %
1.	16	QUESTIONS RELATING TO DISARMAMENT	16.13	16.13
2.	108	IDEOLOGY AND IDEAS	12.90	29.03
3.	104	CONFLICT AND CONFRONTATION	11.29	40.32
4.	1	BASKET ONE: QUESTIONS RELATING TO SECURITY IN EUROPE	9.68	50.00
5.	9	RESPECT FOR HUMAN RIGHTS AND FUNDAMENTAL FREEDOMS	9.68	59.68
6.	59	GENERAL REMARKS CONCERNING HUMAN CONTACTS	9.68	69.35
7.	69	COOPERATION IN THE FIELD OF INFORMATION EXCHANGE	9.68	79.03
8.	17	QUESTIONS RELATING TO SECURITY	8.06	87.10
9.	19	BASKET TWO: COOPERATION IN THE FIELD OF ECONOMICS, SCIENCE, TECHNOLOGY, AND THE ENVIRONMENT	3.23	90.32
10.	11	COOPERATION AMONG STATES AS A PRINCIPLE OF INTERNATIONAL RELATIONS	1.61	91.94

FEDERAL REPUBLIC OF GERMANY

RANK	CODE	CATEGORY	%	CUMULATIVE %
1.	9	RESPECT FOR HUMAN RIGHTS AND FUNDAMENTAL FREEDOMS	11.96	11.96
2.	104	CONFLICT AND CONFRONTATION	9.78	21.74
3.	11	COOPERATION AMONG STATES AS A PRINCIPLE OF INTERNATIONAL RELATIONS	8.70	30.43
4.	19	BASKET TWO: COOPERATION IN THE FIELD OF ECONOMICS, SCIENCE, TECHNOLOGY, AND THE ENVIRONMENT	8.70	39.13
5.	58	BASKET THREE: COOPERATION IN HUMANITARIAN AND OTHER FIELDS	5.43	44.57
6.	2	GENERAL REMARKS CONCERNING THE DECLARATION ON PRINCIPLES GUIDING RELATIONS	4.35	48.91
7.	20	GENERAL REMARKS CONCERNING COMMERCIAL EXCHANGES	4.35	53.26
8.	26	INDUSTRIAL COOPERATION AND PROJECTS OF COMMON INTEREST	4.35	57.61
9.	69	COOPERATION IN THE FIELD OF INFORMATION EXCHANGE	4.35	61.96
10.	103	PEACE	4.35	66.30

GERMAN DEMOCRATIC REPUBLIC

RANK	CODE	CATEGORY	%	CUMULATIVE %
1.	16	QUESTIONS RELATING TO DISARMAMENT	18.40	18.40
2.	17	QUESTIONS RELATING TO SECURITY	18.40	36.81
3.	103	PEACE	6.75	43.56
4.	9	RESPECT FOR HUMAN RIGHTS AND FUNDAMENTAL FREEDOMS	6.13	49.69
5.	1	BASKET ONE: QUESTIONS RELATING TO SECURITY IN EUROPE	4.91	54.60
6.	3	SOVEREIGN EQUALITY, RESPECT FOR THE RIGHTS INHERENT IN SOVEREIGNTY	4.91	59.51
7.	34	OTHER ASPECTS OF TRADE AND INDUSTRIAL COOPERATION	3.07	62.58
8.	40	COOPERATION IN THE FIELD OF ENVIRONMENT	3.07	65.64
9.	46	DEVELOPMENT OF TRANSPORT	3.07	68.71
10.	95	ENERGY PROBLEMS	3.07	71.78

GREECE

RANK	CODE	CATEGORY	%	CUMULATIVE %
1.	11	COOPERATION AMONG STATES AS A PRINCIPLE OF INTERNATIONAL RELATIONS	27.78	27.78
2.	19	BASKET TWO: COOPERATION IN THE FIELD OF ECONOMICS, SCIENCE, TECHNOLOGY, AND THE ENVIRONMENT	27.78	55.56
3.	2	GENERAL REMARKS CONCERNING THE DECLARATION ON PRINCIPLES GUIDING RELATIONS	16.67	72.22
4.	1	BASKET ONE: QUESTIONS RELATING TO SECURITY IN EUROPE	5.56	77.78
5.	7	PEACEFUL SETTLEMENT OF DISPUTES	5.56	83.33
6.	9	RESPECT FOR HUMAN RIGHTS AND FUNDAMENTAL FREEDOMS	5.56	88.89
7.	17	QUESTIONS RELATING TO SECURITY	5.56	94.44
8.	51	SECTION ON THE MEDITERRANEAN: GENERAL REMARKS	5.56	100.00
9.				
10.				

Table A2.11. *(cont.)*

HUNGARY

RANK	CODE	CATEGORY	%	CUMULATIVE %
1.	11	COOPERATION AMONG STATES AS A PRINCIPLE OF INTERNATIONAL RELATIONS	9.40	9.40
2.	19	BASKET TWO: COOPERATION IN THE FIELD OF ECONOMICS, SCIENCE, TECHNOLOGY, AND THE ENVIRONMENT	9.40	18.80
3.	2	GENERAL REMARKS CONCERNING THE DECLARATION ON PRINCIPLES GUIDING RELATIONS	8.55	27.35
4.	1	BASKET ONE: QUESTIONS RELATING TO SECURITY IN EUROPE	6.84	34.19
5.	8	NON-INTERVENTION IN INTERNAL AFFAIRS	6.84	41.03
6.	17	QUESTIONS RELATING TO SECURITY	6.84	47.86
7.	16	QUESTIONS RELATING TO DISARMAMENT	5.98	53.85
8.	9	RESPECT FOR HUMAN RIGHTS AND FUNDAMENTAL FREEDOMS	5.13	58.97
9.	88	THE ROLE OF NATIONAL MINORITIES IN THE FIELD OF EDUCATION	5.13	64.10
10.	103	PEACE	5.13	69.23

ICELAND

RANK	CODE	CATEGORY	%	CUMULATIVE %
1.	11	COOPERATION AMONG STATES AS A PRINCIPLE OF INTERNATIONAL RELATIONS	25.00	25.00
2.	16	QUESTIONS RELATING TO DISARMAMENT	25.00	50.00
3.	19	BASKET TWO: COOPERATION IN THE FIELD OF ECONOMICS, SCIENCE, TECHNOLOGY, AND THE ENVIRONMENT	25.00	75.00
4.	9	RESPECT FOR HUMAN RIGHTS AND FUNDAMENTAL FREEDOMS	12.50	87.50
5.	103	PEACE	12.50	100.00
6.				
7.				
8.				
9.				
10.				

IRELAND

RANK	CODE	CATEGORY	%	CUMULATIVE %
1.	9	RESPECT FOR HUMAN RIGHTS AND FUNDAMENTAL FREEDOMS	30.36	30.36
2.	19	BASKET TWO: COOPERATION IN THE FIELD OF ECONOMICS, SCIENCE, TECHNOLOGY, AND THE ENVIRONMENT	12.50	42.86
3.	2	GENERAL REMARKS CONCERNING THE DECLARATION ON PRINCIPLES GUIDING RELATIONS	10.71	53.57
4.	11	COOPERATION AMONG STATES AS A PRINCIPLE OF INTERNATIONAL RELATIONS	8.93	62.50
5.	30	PROVISIONS CONCERNING TRADE AND INDUSTRIAL COOPERATION	7.14	69.64
6.	98	INTERNATIONAL ORGANISATIONS OTHER THAN UN	7.14	76.79
7.	1	BASKET ONE: QUESTIONS RELATING TO SECURITY IN EUROPE	3.57	80.36
8.	14	DOCUMENT ON CONFIDENCE-BUILDING MEASURES AND CERTAIN ASPECTS OF SECURITY AND DISARMAMENT	3.57	83.93
9.	17	QUESTIONS RELATING TO SECURITY	3.57	87.50
10.	58	BASKET THREE: COOPERATION IN HUMANITARIAN AND OTHER FIELDS	3.57	91.07

ITALY

RANK	CODE	CATEGORY	%	CUMULATIVE %
1.	9	RESPECT FOR HUMAN RIGHTS AND FUNDAMENTAL FREEDOMS	18.18	18.18
2.	11	COOPERATION AMONG STATES AS A PRINCIPLE OF INTERNATIONAL RELATIONS	10.39	28.57
3.	19	BASKET TWO: COOPERATION IN THE FIELD OF ECONOMICS, SCIENCE, TECHNOLOGY, AND THE ENVIRONMENT	10.39	38.96
4.	51	SECTION ON THE MEDITERRANEAN: GENERAL REMARKS	10.39	49.35
5.	63	TRAVEL FOR PERSONAL OR PROFESSIONAL REASONS	7.79	57.14
6.	70	IMPROVEMENT OF THE CIRCULATION, ACCESS TO, AND EXCHANGE OF INFORMATION	7.79	64.93
7.	16	QUESTIONS RELATING TO DISARMAMENT	5.19	70.13
8.	99	UN AND UN SPECIAL ORGANISATIONS	5.19	75.32
9.	17	QUESTIONS RELATING TO SECURITY	3.90	79.22
10.	1	BASKET ONE: QUESTIONS RELATING TO SECURITY IN EUROPE	2.60	81.82

LIECHTENSTEIN

RANK	CODE	CATEGORY	%	CUMULATIVE %
1.	19	BASKET TWO: COOPERATION IN THE FIELD OF ECONOMICS, SCIENCE, TECHNOLOGY, AND THE ENVIRONMENT	50.00	50.00
2.	58	BASKET THREE: COOPERATION IN HUMANITARIAN AND OTHER FIELDS	50.00	100.00
3.				
4.				
5.				
6.				
7.				
8.				
9.				
10.				

Table A2.11. *(cont.)*

LUXEMBOURG

RANK	CODE	CATEGORY	%	CUMULATIVE %
1.	16	QUESTIONS RELATING TO DISARMAMENT	30.77	30.77
2.	9	RESPECT FOR HUMAN RIGHTS AND FUNDAMENTAL FREEDOMS	15.38	46.15
3.	59	GENERAL REMARKS CONCERNING HUMAN CONTACTS	15.38	61.54
4.	97	INTERNATIONAL CONFERENCES	10.26	71.79
5.	8	NON-INTERVENTION IN INTERNAL AFFAIRS	5.13	76.92
6.	2	GENERAL REMARKS CONCERNING THE DECLARATION ON PRINCIPLES GUIDING RELATIONS	2.56	79.49
7.	11	COOPERATION AMONG STATES AS A PRINCIPLE OF INTERNATIONAL RELATIONS	2.56	82.05
8.	19	BASKET TWO: COOPERATION IN THE FIELD OF ECONOMICS, SCIENCE, TECHNOLOGY, AND THE ENVIRONMENT	2.56	84.62
9.	23	ECONOMIC AND COMMERCIAL INFORMATION	2.56	87.18
10.	26	INDUSTRIAL COOPERATION AND PROJECTS OF COMMON INTEREST	2.56	89.74

MALTA

RANK	CODE	CATEGORY	%	CUMULATIVE %
1.	53	INCREASING MUTUAL CONFIDENCE, SECURITY, STABILITY IN THE MEDITERRANEAN	21.74	21.74
2.	54	COOPERATION WITH NON-PARTICIPATING MEDITERRANEAN COUNTRIES	21.74	43.48
3.	103	PEACE	13.04	56.52
4.	11	COOPERATION AMONG STATES AS A PRINCIPLE OF INTERNATIONAL RELATIONS	8.70	65.22
5.	19	BASKET TWO: COOPERATION IN THE FIELD OF ECONOMICS, SCIENCE, TECHNOLOGY, AND THE ENVIRONMENT	8.70	73.91
6.	51	SECTION ON THE MEDITERRANEAN: GENERAL REMARKS	8.70	82.61
7.	1	BASKET ONE: QUESTIONS RELATING TO SECURITY IN EUROPE	4.35	86.96
8.	9	RESPECT FOR HUMAN RIGHTS AND FUNDAMENTAL FREEDOMS	4.35	91.30
9.	17	QUESTIONS RELATING TO SECURITY	4.35	95.65
10.	104	CONFLICT AND CONFRONTATION	4.35	100.00

MONACO

RANK	CODE	CATEGORY	%	CUMULATIVE %
1.	1	BASKET ONE: QUESTIONS RELATING TO SECURITY IN EUROPE	9.09	9.09
2.	11	COOPERATION AMONG STATES AS A PRINCIPLE OF INTERNATIONAL RELATIONS	9.09	18.18
3.	17	QUESTIONS RELATING TO SECURITY	9.09	27.27
4.	19	BASKET TWO: COOPERATION IN THE FIELD OF ECONOMICS, SCIENCE, TECHNOLOGY, AND THE ENVIRONMENT	9.09	36.36
5.	20	GENERAL REMARKS CONCERNING COMMERCIAL EXCHANGES	9.09	45.45
6.	26	INDUSTRIAL COOPERATION AND PROJECTS OF COMMON INTEREST	9.09	54.55
7.	35	COOPERATION IN SCIENCE AND TECHNOLOGY	9.09	63.64
8.	36	POSSIBILITIES FOR IMPROVING COOPERATION IN SCIENCE AND TECHNOLOGY	9.09	72.73
9.	40	COOPERATION IN THE FIELD OF ENVIRONMENT	9.09	81.82
10.	42	FIELDS OF COOPERATION IN THE FIELD OF ENVIRONMENT	9.09	90.91

NETHERLANDS

RANK	CODE	CATEGORY	%	CUMULATIVE %
1.	9	RESPECT FOR HUMAN RIGHTS AND FUNDAMENTAL FREEDOMS	35.29	35.29
2.	58	BASKET THREE: COOPERATION IN HUMANITARIAN AND OTHER FIELDS	17.65	52.94
3.	59	GENERAL REMARKS CONCERNING HUMAN CONTACTS	17.65	70.59
4.	69	COOPERATION IN THE FIELD OF INFORMATION EXCHANGE	17.65	88.24
5.	2	GENERAL REMARKS CONCERNING THE DECLARATION ON PRINCIPLES GUIDING RELATIONS	11.76	100.00
6.				
7.				
8.				
9.				
10.				

NORWAY

RANK	CODE	CATEGORY	%	CUMULATIVE %
1.	2	GENERAL REMARKS CONCERNING THE DECLARATION ON PRINCIPLES GUIDING RELATIONS	17.24	17.24
2.	58	BASKET THREE: COOPERATION IN HUMANITARIAN AND OTHER FIELDS	17.24	34.48
3.	9	RESPECT FOR HUMAN RIGHTS AND FUNDAMENTAL FREEDOMS	13.79	48.28
4.	19	BASKET TWO: COOPERATION IN THE FIELD OF ECONOMICS, SCIENCE, TECHNOLOGY, AND THE ENVIRONMENT	10.34	58.62
5.	11	COOPERATION AMONG STATES AS A PRINCIPLE OF INTERNATIONAL RELATIONS	6.90	65.52
6.	16	QUESTIONS RELATING TO DISARMAMENT	6.90	72.41
7.	59	GENERAL REMARKS CONCERNING HUMAN CONTACTS	6.90	79.31
8.	1	BASKET ONE: QUESTIONS RELATING TO SECURITY IN EUROPE	3.45	82.76
9.	14	DOCUMENT ON CONFIDENCE-BUILDING MEASURES AND CERTAIN ASPECTS OF SECURITY AND DISARMAMENT	3.45	86.21
10.	17	QUESTIONS RELATING TO SECURITY	3.45	89.66

Table A2.11. *(cont.)*

POLAND

RANK	CODE	CATEGORY	%	CUMULATIVE %
1.	16	QUESTIONS RELATING TO DISARMAMENT	15.69	15.69
2.	19	BASKET TWO: COOPERATION IN THE FIELD OF ECONOMICS, SCIENCE, TECHNOLOGY, AND THE ENVIRONMENT	10.20	25.88
3.	103	PEACE	9.80	35.69
4.	11	COOPERATION AMONG STATES AS A PRINCIPLE OF INTERNATIONAL RELATIONS	7.06	42.75
5.	1	BASKET ONE: QUESTIONS RELATING TO SECURITY IN EUROPE	6.27	49.02
6.	17	QUESTIONS RELATING TO SECURITY	6.27	55.29
7.	82	COOPERATION AND EXCHANGES IN THE FIELD OF EDUCATION	5.88	61.18
8.	74	COOPERATION AND EXCHANGES IN THE FIELD OF CULTURE	4.71	65.88
9.	99	UN AND UN SPECIAL ORGANISATIONS	3.53	69.41
10.	2	GENERAL REMARKS CONCERNING THE DECLARATION ON PRINCIPLES GUIDING RELATIONS	3.14	72.55

PORTUGAL

RANK	CODE	CATEGORY	%	CUMULATIVE %
1.	48	ECONOMIC AND SOCIAL ASPECTS OF MIGRANT LABOUR	35.71	35.71
2.	11	COOPERATION AMONG STATES AS A PRINCIPLE OF INTERNATIONAL RELATIONS	10.71	46.43
3.	19	BASKET TWO: COOPERATION IN THE FIELD OF ECONOMICS, SCIENCE, TECHNOLOGY, AND THE ENVIRONMENT	10.71	57.14
4.	1	BASKET ONE: QUESTIONS RELATING TO SECURITY IN EUROPE	7.14	64.29
5.	17	QUESTIONS RELATING TO SECURITY	7.14	71.43
6.	2	GENERAL REMARKS CONCERNING THE DECLARATION ON PRINCIPLES GUIDING RELATIONS	3.57	75.00
7.	14	DOCUMENT ON CONFIDENCE-BUILDING MEASURES AND CERTAIN ASPECTS OF SECURITY AND DISARMAMENT	3.57	78.57
8.	20	GENERAL REMARKS CONCERNING COMMERCIAL EXCHANGES	3.57	82.14
9.	26	INDUSTRIAL COOPERATION AND PROJECTS OF COMMON INTEREST	3.57	85.71
10.	51	SECTION ON THE MEDITERRANEAN: GENERAL REMARKS	3.57	89.29

ROMANIA

RANK	CODE	CATEGORY	%	CUMULATIVE %
1.	16	QUESTIONS RELATING TO DISARMAMENT	16.18	16.18
2.	11	COOPERATION AMONG STATES AS A PRINCIPLE OF INTERNATIONAL RELATIONS	13.24	29.41
3.	14	DOCUMENT ON CONFIDENCE-BUILDING MEASURES AND CERTAIN ASPECTS OF SECURITY AND DISARMAMENT	13.24	42.65
4.	19	BASKET TWO: COOPERATION IN THE FIELD OF ECONOMICS, SCIENCE, TECHNOLOGY, AND THE ENVIRONMENT	13.24	55.88
5.	1	BASKET ONE: QUESTIONS RELATING TO SECURITY IN EUROPE	11.76	67.65
6.	17	QUESTIONS RELATING TO SECURITY	11.76	79.41
7.	20	GENERAL REMARKS CONCERNING COMMERCIAL EXCHANGES	4.41	83.82
8.	26	INDUSTRIAL COOPERATION AND PROJECTS OF COMMON INTEREST	4.41	88.24
9.	103	PEACE	4.41	92.65
10.	35	COOPERATION IN SCIENCE AND TECHNOLOGY	2.94	95.59

SAN MARINO

RANK	CODE	CATEGORY	%	CUMULATIVE %
1.	9	RESPECT FOR HUMAN RIGHTS AND FUNDAMENTAL FREEDOMS	19.51	19.51
2.	103	PEACE	12.20	31.71
3.	16	QUESTIONS RELATING TO DISARMAMENT	9.76	41.46
4.	97	INTERNATIONAL CONFERENCES	8.54	50.00
5.	1	BASKET ONE: QUESTIONS RELATING TO SECURITY IN EUROPE	6.10	56.10
6.	11	COOPERATION AMONG STATES AS A PRINCIPLE OF INTERNATIONAL RELATIONS	6.10	62.20
7.	17	QUESTIONS RELATING TO SECURITY	6.10	68.29
8.	19	BASKET TWO: COOPERATION IN THE FIELD OF ECONOMICS, SCIENCE, TECHNOLOGY, AND THE ENVIRONMENT	6.10	74.39
9.	7	PEACEFUL SETTLEMENT OF DISPUTES	4.88	79.27
10.	58	BASKET THREE: COOPERATION IN HUMANITARIAN AND OTHER FIELDS	3.66	82.93

SPAIN

RANK	CODE	CATEGORY	%	CUMULATIVE %
1.	16	QUESTIONS RELATING TO DISARMAMENT	10.59	10.59
2.	19	BASKET TWO: COOPERATION IN THE FIELD OF ECONOMICS, SCIENCE, TECHNOLOGY, AND THE ENVIRONMENT	10.59	21.18
3.	9	RESPECT FOR HUMAN RIGHTS AND FUNDAMENTAL FREEDOMS	9.41	30.59
4.	11	COOPERATION AMONG STATES AS A PRINCIPLE OF INTERNATIONAL RELATIONS	8.24	38.82
5.	58	BASKET THREE: COOPERATION IN HUMANITARIAN AND OTHER FIELDS	8.24	47.06
6.	97	INTERNATIONAL CONFERENCES	8.24	55.29
7.	103	PEACE	8.24	63.53
8.	14	DOCUMENT ON CONFIDENCE-BUILDING MEASURES AND CERTAIN ASPECTS OF SECURITY AND DISARMAMENT	5.88	69.41
9.	48	ECONOMIC AND SOCIAL ASPECTS OF MIGRANT LABOUR	4.71	74.12
10.	1	BASKET ONE: QUESTIONS RELATING TO SECURITY IN EUROPE	3.53	77.65

Table A2.11. *(cont.)*

SWEDEN

RANK	CODE	CATEGORY	%	CUMULATIVE %
1.	9	RESPECT FOR HUMAN RIGHTS AND FUNDAMENTAL FREEDOMS	14.29	14.29
2.	19	BASKET TWO: COOPERATION IN THE FIELD OF ECONOMICS, SCIENCE, TECHNOLOGY, AND THE ENVIRONMENT	12.70	26.98
3.	11	COOPERATION AMONG STATES AS A PRINCIPLE OF INTERNATIONAL RELATIONS	9.52	36.51
4.	2	GENERAL REMARKS CONCERNING THE DECLARATION ON PRINCIPLES GUIDING RELATIONS	6.35	42.86
5.	16	QUESTIONS RELATING TO DISARMAMENT	6.35	49.21
6.	14	DOCUMENT ON CONFIDENCE-BUILDING MEASURES AND CERTAIN ASPECTS OF SECURITY AND DISARMAMENT	4.76	53.97
7.	43	FORMS AND METHODS OF COOPERATION IN THE FIELD OF ENVIRONMENT	4.76	58.73
8.	61	REUNIFICATION OF FAMILIES	4.76	63.49
9.	113	PUBLIC OPINION	4.76	68.25
10.	1	BASKET ONE: QUESTIONS RELATING TO SECURITY IN EUROPE	3.17	71.43

SWITZERLAND

RANK	CODE	CATEGORY	%	CUMULATIVE %
1.	9	RESPECT FOR HUMAN RIGHTS AND FUNDAMENTAL FREEDOMS	23.81	23.81
2.	1	BASKET ONE: QUESTIONS RELATING TO SECURITY IN EUROPE	7.14	30.95
3.	17	QUESTIONS RELATING TO SECURITY	7.14	38.10
4.	103	PEACE	7.14	45.24
5.	7	PEACEFUL SETTLEMENT OF DISPUTES	4.76	50.00
6.	11	COOPERATION AMONG STATES AS A PRINCIPLE OF INTERNATIONAL RELATIONS	4.76	54.76
7.	19	BASKET TWO: COOPERATION IN THE FIELD OF ECONOMICS, SCIENCE, TECHNOLOGY, AND THE ENVIRONMENT	4.76	59.52
8.	20	GENERAL REMARKS CONCERNING COMMERCIAL EXCHANGES	4.76	64.29
9.	26	INDUSTRIAL COOPERATION AND PROJECTS OF COMMON INTEREST	4.76	69.05
10.	58	BASKET THREE: COOPERATION IN HUMANITARIAN AND OTHER FIELDS	4.76	73.81

TURKEY

RANK	CODE	CATEGORY	%	CUMULATIVE %
1.	19	BASKET TWO: COOPERATION IN THE FIELD OF ECONOMICS, SCIENCE, TECHNOLOGY, AND THE ENVIRONMENT	18.18	18.18
2.	11	COOPERATION AMONG STATES AS A PRINCIPLE OF INTERNATIONAL RELATIONS	14.55	32.73
3.	54	COOPERATION WITH NON-PARTICIPATING MEDITERRANEAN COUNTRIES	14.55	47.27
4.	97	INTERNATIONAL CONFERENCES	9.09	56.36
5.	103	PEACE	9.09	65.45
6.	3	SOVEREIGN EQUALITY, RESPECT FOR THE RIGHTS INHERENT IN SOVEREIGNTY	7.27	72.73
7.	120	STABILITY, STRATEGIC AND POLITICAL BALANCE	5.45	78.18
8.	2	GENERAL REMARKS CONCERNING THE DECLARATION ON PRINCIPLES GUIDING RELATIONS	3.64	81.82
9.	7	PEACEFUL SETTLEMENT OF DISPUTES	3.64	85.45
10.	14	DOCUMENT ON CONFIDENCE-BUILDING MEASURES AND CERTAIN ASPECTS OF SECURITY AND DISARMAMENT	3.64	89.09

UNION OF THE SOVIET SOCIALIST REPUBLICS

RANK	CODE	CATEGORY	%	CUMULATIVE %
1.	16	QUESTIONS RELATING TO DISARMAMENT	18.78	18.78
2.	17	QUESTIONS RELATING TO SECURITY	11.60	30.39
3.	1	BASKET ONE: QUESTIONS RELATING TO SECURITY IN EUROPE	7.18	37.57
4.	19	BASKET TWO: COOPERATION IN THE FIELD OF ECONOMICS, SCIENCE, TECHNOLOGY, AND THE ENVIRONMENT	5.52	43.09
5.	9	RESPECT FOR HUMAN RIGHTS AND FUNDAMENTAL FREEDOMS	4.97	48.07
6.	14	DOCUMENT ON CONFIDENCE-BUILDING MEASURES AND CERTAIN ASPECTS OF SECURITY AND DISARMAMENT	4.97	53.04
7.	103	PEACE	4.97	58.01
8.	46	DEVELOPMENT OF TRANSPORT	3.87	61.88
9.	95	ENERGY PROBLEMS	3.87	65.75
10.	104	CONFLICT AND CONFRONTATION	3.87	69.61

UNITED KINGDOM

RANK	CODE	CATEGORY	%	CUMULATIVE %
1.	9	RESPECT FOR HUMAN RIGHTS AND FUNDAMENTAL FREEDOMS	31.19	31.19
2.	16	QUESTIONS RELATING TO DISARMAMENT	11.93	43.12
3.	104	CONFLICT AND CONFRONTATION	9.17	52.29
4.	8	NON-INTERVENTION IN INTERNAL AFFAIRS	4.59	56.88
5.	11	COOPERATION AMONG STATES AS A PRINCIPLE OF INTERNATIONAL RELATIONS	3.67	60.55
6.	19	BASKET TWO: COOPERATION IN THE FIELD OF ECONOMICS, SCIENCE, TECHNOLOGY, AND THE ENVIRONMENT	3.67	64.22
7.	59	GENERAL REMARKS CONCERNING HUMAN CONTACTS	3.67	67.89
8.	97	INTERNATIONAL CONFERENCES	3.67	71.56
9.	108	IDEOLOGY AND IDEAS	3.67	75.23
10.	1	BASKET ONE: QUESTIONS RELATING TO SECURITY IN EUROPE	1.83	77.06

Table A2.11. *(cont.)*

UNITED STATES OF AMERICA

RANK	CODE	CATEGORY	%	CUMULATIVE %
1.	9	RESPECT FOR HUMAN RIGHTS AND FUNDAMENTAL FREEDOMS	31.78	31.78
2.	109	FREEDOM	5.43	37.21
3.	110	JUSTICE	4.65	41.86
4.	115	FREEDOM OF RELIGION OR BELIEF	4.65	46.51
5.	15	PRIOR NOTIFICATION OF MILITARY MANOEUVRES	3.88	50.39
6.	1	BASKET ONE: QUESTIONS RELATING TO SECURITY IN EUROPE	3.10	53.49
7.	3	SOVEREIGN EQUALITY, RESPECT FOR THE RIGHTS INHERENT IN SOVEREIGNTY	3.10	56.59
8.	11	COOPERATION AMONG STATES AS A PRINCIPLE OF INTERNATIONAL RELATIONS	3.10	59.69
9.	17	QUESTIONS RELATING TO SECURITY	3.10	62.79
10.	20	GENERAL REMARKS CONCERNING COMMERCIAL EXCHANGES	3.10	65.89

VATICAN (HOLY SEE)

RANK	CODE	CATEGORY	%	CUMULATIVE %
1.	9	RESPECT FOR HUMAN RIGHTS AND FUNDAMENTAL FREEDOMS	14.75	14.75
2.	54	COOPERATION WITH NON-PARTICIPATING MEDITERRANEAN COUNTRIES	8.20	22.95
3.	63	TRAVEL FOR PERSONAL OR PROFESSIONAL REASONS	8.20	31.15
4.	7	PEACEFUL SETTLEMENT OF DISPUTES	6.56	37.70
5.	36	POSSIBILITIES FOR IMPROVING COOPERATION IN SCIENCE AND TECHNOLOGY	6.56	44.26
6.	96	EFFECTIVE EXERCISE OF THE FREEDOM OF RELIGION	6.56	50.82
7.	11	COOPERATION AMONG STATES AS A PRINCIPLE OF INTERNATIONAL RELATIONS	4.92	55.74
8.	16	QUESTIONS RELATING TO DISARMAMENT	4.92	60.66
9.	19	BASKET TWO: COOPERATION IN THE FIELD OF ECONOMICS, SCIENCE, TECHNOLOGY, AND THE ENVIRONMENT	4.92	65.57
10.	115	FREEDOM OF RELIGION OR BELIEF	4.92	70.49

YUGOSLAVIA

RANK	CODE	CATEGORY	%	CUMULATIVE %
1.	16	QUESTIONS RELATING TO DISARMAMENT	11.39	11.39
2.	11	COOPERATION AMONG STATES AS A PRINCIPLE OF INTERNATIONAL RELATIONS	10.13	21.52
3.	19	BASKET TWO: COOPERATION IN THE FIELD OF ECONOMICS, SCIENCE, TECHNOLOGY, AND THE ENVIRONMENT	10.13	31.65
4.	17	QUESTIONS RELATING TO SECURITY	8.86	40.51
5.	118	REMARKS CONCERNING THE NEW ECONOMIC ORDER	7.59	48.10
6.	1	BASKET ONE: QUESTIONS RELATING TO SECURITY IN EUROPE	6.33	54.43
7.	2	GENERAL REMARKS CONCERNING THE DECLARATION ON PRINCIPLES GUIDING RELATIONS	5.06	59.49
8.	104	CONFLICT AND CONFRONTATION	5.06	64.56
9.	117	REMARKS CONCERNING DEVELOPING COUNTRIES	5.06	69.62

Table A2.12. Rank-Order of Categories: The Madrid Opening Statements

AUSTRIA

RANK	CODE	CATEGORY	%	CUMULATIVE %
1.	97	INTERNATIONAL CONFERENCES	9.17	9.17
2.	16	QUESTIONS RELATING TO DISARMAMENT	7.50	16.67
3.	104	CONFLICT AND CONFRONTATION	7.50	24.17
4.	9	RESPECT FOR HUMAN RIGHTS AND FUNDAMENTAL FREEDOMS	5.00	29.17
5.	14	DOCUMENT ON CONFIDENCE-BUILDING MEASURES AND CERTAIN ASPECTS OF SECURITY AND DISARMAMENT	5.00	34.17
6.	72	IMPROVEMENT OF WORKING CONDITIONS FOR JOURNALISTS	5.00	39.17
7.	11	COOPERATION AMONG STATES AS A PRINCIPLE OF INTERNATIONAL RELATIONS	4.17	43.33
8.	17	QUESTIONS RELATING TO SECURITY	4.17	47.50
9.	102	NEUTRALITY	4.17	51.67
10.	114	POLITICAL COOPERATION AND POLITICAL DISCUSSIONS	4.17	55.83

BELGIUM

RANK	CODE	CATEGORY	%	CUMULATIVE %
1.	9	RESPECT FOR HUMAN RIGHTS AND FUNDAMENTAL FREEDOMS	8.60	8.60
2.	58	BASKET THREE: COOPERATION IN HUMANITARIAN AND OTHER FIELDS	8.60	17.20
3.	11	COOPERATION AMONG STATES AS A PRINCIPLE OF INTERNATIONAL RELATIONS	4.30	21.51
4.	14	DOCUMENT ON CONFIDENCE-BUILDING MEASURES AND CERTAIN ASPECTS OF SECURITY AND DISARMAMENT	4.30	25.81
5.	51	SECTION ON THE MEDITERRANEAN: GENERAL REMARKS	4.30	30.11
6.	59	GENERAL REMARKS CONCERNING HUMAN CONTACTS	4.30	34.41
7.	70	IMPROVEMENT OF THE CIRCULATION, ACCESS TO, AND EXCHANGE OF INFORMATION	4.30	38.71
8.	72	IMPROVEMENT OF WORKING CONDITIONS FOR JOURNALISTS	4.30	43.01
9.	102	NEUTRALITY	4.30	47.31
10.	2	GENERAL REMARKS CONCERNING THE DECLARATION ON PRINCIPLES GUIDING RELATIONS	3.23	50.54

Table A2.12. *(cont.)*

BULGARIA

RANK	CODE	CATEGORY	%	CUMULATIVE %
1.	103	PEACE	14.00	14.00
2.	11	COOPERATION AMONG STATES AS A PRINCIPLE OF INTERNATIONAL RELATIONS	11.00	25.00
3.	114	POLITICAL COOPERATION AND POLITICAL DISCUSSIONS	8.00	33.00
4.	16	QUESTIONS RELATING TO DISARMAMENT	7.00	40.00
5.	58	BASKET THREE: COOPERATION IN HUMANITARIAN AND OTHER FIELDS	6.00	46.00
6.	14	DOCUMENT ON CONFIDENCE-BUILDING MEASURES AND CERTAIN ASPECTS OF SECURITY AND DISARMAMENT	5.00	51.00
7.	17	QUESTIONS RELATING TO SECURITY	5.00	56.00
8.	19	BASKET TWO: COOPERATION IN THE FIELD OF ECONOMICS, SCIENCE, TECHNOLOGY, AND THE ENVIRONMENT	4.00	60.00
9.	94	DANGERS OF NUCLEAR PROLIFERATION	4.00	64.00
10.	97	INTERNATIONAL CONFERENCES	4.00	68.00

CANADA

RANK	CODE	CATEGORY	%	CUMULATIVE %
1.	9	RESPECT FOR HUMAN RIGHTS AND FUNDAMENTAL FREEDOMS	13.84	13.84
2.	16	QUESTIONS RELATING TO DISARMAMENT	8.81	22.64
3.	108	IDEOLOGY AND IDEAS	8.18	30.82
4.	11	COOPERATION AMONG STATES AS A PRINCIPLE OF INTERNATIONAL RELATIONS	6.92	37.74
5.	14	DOCUMENT ON CONFIDENCE-BUILDING MEASURES AND CERTAIN ASPECTS OF SECURITY AND DISARMAMENT	6.29	44.03
6.	95	ENERGY PROBLEMS	5.03	49.06
7.	4	REFRAINING FROM THE THREAT OR USE OF FORCE	4.40	53.46
8.	8	NON-INTERVENTION IN INTERNAL AFFAIRS	4.40	57.86
9.	58	BASKET THREE: COOPERATION IN HUMANITARIAN AND OTHER FIELDS	3.14	61.01
10.	63	TRAVEL FOR PERSONAL OR PROFESSIONAL REASONS	3.14	64.15

CYPRUS

RANK	CODE	CATEGORY	%	CUMULATIVE %
1.	11	COOPERATION AMONG STATES AS A PRINCIPLE OF INTERNATIONAL RELATIONS	9.68	9.68
2.	2	GENERAL REMARKS CONCERNING THE DECLARATION ON PRINCIPLES GUIDING RELATIONS	8.60	18.28
3.	103	PEACE	8.60	26.88
4.	104	CONFLICT AND CONFRONTATION	6.45	33.33
5.	16	QUESTIONS RELATING TO DISARMAMENT	5.38	38.71
6.	97	INTERNATIONAL CONFERENCES	5.38	44.09
7.	110	JUSTICE	5.38	49.46
8.	114	POLITICAL COOPERATION AND POLITICAL DISCUSSIONS	5.38	54.84
9.	19	BASKET TWO: COOPERATION IN THE FIELD OF ECONOMICS, SCIENCE, TECHNOLOGY, AND THE ENVIRONMENT	4.30	59.14
10.	51	SECTION ON THE MEDITERRANEAN: GENERAL REMARKS	4.30	63.44

CZECHOSLOVAKIA

RANK	CODE	CATEGORY	%	CUMULATIVE %
1.	103	PEACE	17.35	17.35
2.	16	QUESTIONS RELATING TO DISARMAMENT	13.27	30.61
3.	19	BASKET TWO: COOPERATION IN THE FIELD OF ECONOMICS, SCIENCE, TECHNOLOGY, AND THE ENVIRONMENT	9.18	39.80
4.	104	CONFLICT AND CONFRONTATION	9.18	48.98
5.	1	BASKET ONE: QUESTIONS RELATING TO SECURITY IN EUROPE	8.16	57.14
6.	11	COOPERATION AMONG STATES AS A PRINCIPLE OF INTERNATIONAL RELATIONS	8.16	65.31
7.	17	QUESTIONS RELATING TO SECURITY	7.14	72.45
8.	14	DOCUMENT ON CONFIDENCE-BUILDING MEASURES AND CERTAIN ASPECTS OF SECURITY AND DISARMAMENT	6.12	78.57
9.	7	PEACEFUL SETTLEMENT OF DISPUTES	4.08	82.65
10.	90	GOOD-NEIGHBOURLY RELATIONS	4.08	86.73

DENMARK

RANK	CODE	CATEGORY	%	CUMULATIVE %
1.	14	DOCUMENT ON CONFIDENCE-BUILDING MEASURES AND CERTAIN ASPECTS OF SECURITY AND DISARMAMENT	13.83	13.83
2.	114	POLITICAL COOPERATION AND POLITICAL DISCUSSIONS	9.57	23.40
3.	9	RESPECT FOR HUMAN RIGHTS AND FUNDAMENTAL FREEDOMS	8.51	31.91
4.	59	GENERAL REMARKS CONCERNING HUMAN CONTACTS	7.45	39.36
5.	11	COOPERATION AMONG STATES AS A PRINCIPLE OF INTERNATIONAL RELATIONS	6.38	45.74
6.	69	COOPERATION IN THE FIELD OF INFORMATION EXCHANGE	6.38	52.13
7.	104	CONFLICT AND CONFRONTATION	5.32	57.45
8.	2	GENERAL REMARKS CONCERNING THE DECLARATION ON PRINCIPLES GUIDING RELATIONS	4.26	61.70
9.	17	QUESTIONS RELATING TO SECURITY	4.26	65.96
10.	95	ENERGY PROBLEMS	4.26	70.21

Table A2.12. *(cont.)*

FINLAND

RANK	CODE	CATEGORY	%	CUMULATIVE %
1.	14	DOCUMENT ON CONFIDENCE-BUILDING MEASURES AND CERTAIN ASPECTS OF SECURITY AND DISARMAMENT	10.28	10.28
2.	16	QUESTIONS RELATING TO DISARMAMENT	8.41	18.69
3.	30	PROVISIONS CONCERNING TRADE AND INDUSTRIAL COOPERATION	8.41	27.10
4.	114	POLITICAL COOPERATION AND POLITICAL DISCUSSIONS	6.54	33.64
5.	9	RESPECT FOR HUMAN RIGHTS AND FUNDAMENTAL FREEDOMS	4.67	38.32
6.	97	INTERNATIONAL CONFERENCES	4.67	42.99
7.	2	GENERAL REMARKS CONCERNING THE DECLARATION ON PRINCIPLES GUIDING RELATIONS	3.74	46.73
8.	11	COOPERATION AMONG STATES AS A PRINCIPLE OF INTERNATIONAL RELATIONS	3.74	50.47
9.	17	QUESTIONS RELATING TO SECURITY	3.74	54.21
10.	74	COOPERATION AND EXCHANGES IN THE FIELD OF CULTURE	3.74	57.94

FRANCE

RANK	CODE	CATEGORY	%	CUMULATIVE %
1.	17	QUESTIONS RELATING TO SECURITY	12.70	12.70
2.	9	RESPECT FOR HUMAN RIGHTS AND FUNDAMENTAL FREEDOMS	7.94	20.63
3.	59	GENERAL REMARKS CONCERNING HUMAN CONTACTS	7.94	28.57
4.	11	COOPERATION AMONG STATES AS A PRINCIPLE OF INTERNATIONAL RELATIONS	4.76	33.33
5.	104	CONFLICT AND CONFRONTATION	4.76	38.10
6.	120	STABILITY, STRATEGIC AND POLITICAL BALANCE	4.76	42.86
7.	2	GENERAL REMARKS CONCERNING THE DECLARATION ON PRINCIPLES GUIDING RELATIONS	3.17	46.03
8.	3	SOVEREIGN EQUALITY, RESPECT FOR THE RIGHTS INHERENT IN SOVEREIGNTY	3.17	49.21
9.	4	REFRAINING FROM THE THREAT OR USE OF FORCE	3.17	52.38
10.	8	NON-INTERVENTION IN INTERNAL AFFAIRS	3.17	55.56

FEDERAL REPUBLIC OF GERMANY

RANK	CODE	CATEGORY	%	CUMULATIVE %
1.	11	COOPERATION AMONG STATES AS A PRINCIPLE OF INTERNATIONAL RELATIONS	14.69	14.69
2.	14	DOCUMENT ON CONFIDENCE-BUILDING MEASURES AND CERTAIN ASPECTS OF SECURITY AND DISARMAMENT	6.94	21.63
3.	103	PEACE	6.53	28.16
4.	9	RESPECT FOR HUMAN RIGHTS AND FUNDAMENTAL FREEDOMS	6.12	34.29
5.	104	CONFLICT AND CONFRONTATION	5.31	39.59
6.	17	QUESTIONS RELATING TO SECURITY	4.49	44.08
7.	97	INTERNATIONAL CONFERENCES	4.49	48.57
8.	16	QUESTIONS RELATING TO DISARMAMENT	4.08	52.65
9.	59	GENERAL REMARKS CONCERNING HUMAN CONTACTS	4.08	56.73
10.	117	REMARKS CONCERNING DEVELOPING COUNTRIES	3.67	60.41

GERMAN DEMOCRATIC REPUBLIC

RANK	CODE	CATEGORY	%	CUMULATIVE %
1.	14	DOCUMENT ON CONFIDENCE-BUILDING MEASURES AND CERTAIN ASPECTS OF SECURITY AND DISARMAMENT	13.29	13.29
2.	103	PEACE	12.59	25.87
3.	11	COOPERATION AMONG STATES AS A PRINCIPLE OF INTERNATIONAL RELATIONS	9.79	35.66
4.	17	QUESTIONS RELATING TO SECURITY	9.79	45.45
5.	119	SPECIFIC INTERNATIONAL AGREEMENTS	6.29	51.75
6.	16	QUESTIONS RELATING TO DISARMAMENT	4.90	56.64
7.	97	INTERNATIONAL CONFERENCES	4.90	61.54
8.	104	CONFLICT AND CONFRONTATION	4.90	66.43
9.	1	BASKET ONE: QUESTIONS RELATING TO SECURITY IN EUROPE	3.50	69.93
10.	114	POLITICAL COOPERATION AND POLITICAL DISCUSSIONS	3.50	73.43

GREECE

RANK	CODE	CATEGORY	%	CUMULATIVE %
1.	103	PEACE	8.55	8.55
2.	50	OTHER ASPECTS OF COOPERATION IN VARIOUS FIELDS	7.69	16.24
3.	19	BASKET TWO: COOPERATION IN THE FIELD OF ECONOMICS, SCIENCE, TECHNOLOGY, AND THE ENVIRONMENT	5.98	22.22
4.	11	COOPERATION AMONG STATES AS A PRINCIPLE OF INTERNATIONAL RELATIONS	5.13	27.35
5.	17	QUESTIONS RELATING TO SECURITY	5.13	32.48
6.	95	ENERGY PROBLEMS	5.13	37.61
7.	40	COOPERATION IN THE FIELD OF ENVIRONMENT	4.27	41.88
8.	46	DEVELOPMENT OF TRANSPORT	4.27	46.15
9.	114	POLITICAL COOPERATION AND POLITICAL DISCUSSIONS	4.27	50.43
10.	2	GENERAL REMARKS CONCERNING THE DECLARATION ON PRINCIPLES GUIDING RELATIONS	3.42	53.85

Table A2.12. *(cont.)*

HUNGARY

RANK	CODE	CATEGORY	%	CUMULATIVE %
1.	11	COOPERATION AMONG STATES AS A PRINCIPLE OF INTERNATIONAL RELATIONS	13.19	13.19
2.	14	DOCUMENT ON CONFIDENCE-BUILDING MEASURES AND CERTAIN ASPECTS OF SECURITY AND DISARMAMENT	11.54	24.73
3.	97	INTERNATIONAL CONFERENCES	7.14	31.87
4.	1	BASKET ONE: QUESTIONS RELATING TO SECURITY IN EUROPE	6.59	38.46
5.	114	POLITICAL COOPERATION AND POLITICAL DISCUSSIONS	6.59	45.05
6.	103	PEACE	5.49	50.55
7.	17	QUESTIONS RELATING TO SECURITY	4.95	55.49
8.	119	SPECIFIC INTERNATIONAL AGREEMENTS	4.95	60.44
9.	104	CONFLICT AND CONFRONTATION	4.40	64.84
10.	9	RESPECT FOR HUMAN RIGHTS AND FUNDAMENTAL FREEDOMS	3.85	68.68

ICELAND

RANK	CODE	CATEGORY	%	CUMULATIVE %
1.	14	DOCUMENT ON CONFIDENCE-BUILDING MEASURES AND CERTAIN ASPECTS OF SECURITY AND DISARMAMENT	10.91	10.91
2.	11	COOPERATION AMONG STATES AS A PRINCIPLE OF INTERNATIONAL RELATIONS	9.09	20.00
3.	59	GENERAL REMARKS CONCERNING HUMAN CONTACTS	9.09	29.09
4.	114	POLITICAL COOPERATION AND POLITICAL DISCUSSIONS	9.09	38.18
5.	69	COOPERATION IN THE FIELD OF INFORMATION EXCHANGE	7.27	45.45
6.	74	COOPERATION AND EXCHANGES IN THE FIELD OF CULTURE	7.27	52.73
7.	13	OTHER ASPECTS CONCERNING THE DECLARATION ON PRINCIPLES GUIDING RELATIONS	5.45	58.18
8.	22	BUSINESS CONTACTS AND FACILITIES	5.45	63.64
9.	2	GENERAL REMARKS CONCERNING THE DECLARATION ON PRINCIPLES GUIDING RELATIONS	3.64	67.27
10.	9	RESPECT FOR HUMAN RIGHTS AND FUNDAMENTAL FREEDOMS	3.64	70.91

IRELAND

RANK	CODE	CATEGORY	%	CUMULATIVE %
1.	14	DOCUMENT ON CONFIDENCE-BUILDING MEASURES AND CERTAIN ASPECTS OF SECURITY AND DISARMAMENT	13.33	13.33
2.	16	QUESTIONS RELATING TO DISARMAMENT	11.43	24.76
3.	9	RESPECT FOR HUMAN RIGHTS AND FUNDAMENTAL FREEDOMS	8.57	33.33
4.	58	BASKET THREE: COOPERATION IN HUMANITARIAN AND OTHER FIELDS	7.62	40.95
5.	20	GENERAL REMARKS CONCERNING COMMERCIAL EXCHANGES	6.67	47.62
6.	22	BUSINESS CONTACTS AND FACILITIES	5.71	53.33
7.	1	BASKET ONE: QUESTIONS RELATING TO SECURITY IN EUROPE	4.76	58.10
8.	11	COOPERATION AMONG STATES AS A PRINCIPLE OF INTERNATIONAL RELATIONS	4.76	62.86
9.	103	PEACE	4.76	67.62
10.	18	OTHER ASPECTS CONCERNING CONFIDENCE-BUILDING MEASURES, SECURITY, DISARMAMENT	3.81	71.43

ITALY

RANK	CODE	CATEGORY	%	CUMULATIVE %
1.	11	COOPERATION AMONG STATES AS A PRINCIPLE OF INTERNATIONAL RELATIONS	11.76	11.76
2.	14	DOCUMENT ON CONFIDENCE-BUILDING MEASURES AND CERTAIN ASPECTS OF SECURITY AND DISARMAMENT	7.35	19.12
3.	51	SECTION ON THE MEDITERRANEAN: GENERAL REMARKS	7.35	26.47
4.	2	GENERAL REMARKS CONCERNING THE DECLARATION ON PRINCIPLES GUIDING RELATIONS	6.62	33.09
5.	17	QUESTIONS RELATING TO SECURITY	6.62	39.71
6.	9	RESPECT FOR HUMAN RIGHTS AND FUNDAMENTAL FREEDOMS	5.15	44.85
7.	19	BASKET TWO: COOPERATION IN THE FIELD OF ECONOMICS, SCIENCE, TECHNOLOGY, AND THE ENVIRONMENT	4.41	49.26
8.	1	BASKET ONE: QUESTIONS RELATING TO SECURITY IN EUROPE	3.68	52.94
9.	53	INCREASING MUTUAL CONFIDENCE, SECURITY, STABILITY IN THE MEDITERRANEAN	3.68	56.62
10.	97	INTERNATIONAL CONFERENCES	3.68	60.29

LIECHTENSTEIN

RANK	CODE	CATEGORY	%	CUMULATIVE %
1.	11	COOPERATION AMONG STATES AS A PRINCIPLE OF INTERNATIONAL RELATIONS	14.29	14.29
2.	114	POLITICAL COOPERATION AND POLITICAL DISCUSSIONS	14.29	28.57
3.	101	NON-ALIGNMENT	9.52	38.10
4.	2	GENERAL REMARKS CONCERNING THE DECLARATION ON PRINCIPLES GUIDING RELATIONS	4.76	42.86
5.	4	REFRAINING FROM THE THREAT OR USE OF FORCE	4.76	47.62
6.	9	RESPECT FOR HUMAN RIGHTS AND FUNDAMENTAL FREEDOMS	4.76	52.38
7.	14	DOCUMENT ON CONFIDENCE-BUILDING MEASURES AND CERTAIN ASPECTS OF SECURITY AND DISARMAMENT	4.76	57.14
8.	17	QUESTIONS RELATING TO SECURITY	4.76	61.90
9.	58	BASKET THREE: COOPERATION IN HUMANITARIAN AND OTHER FIELDS	4.76	66.67
10.	90	GOOD-NEIGHBOURLY RELATIONS	4.76	71.43

Table A2.12. *(cont.)*

LUXEMBOURG

RANK	CODE	CATEGORY	%	CUMULATIVE %
1.	98	INTERNATIONAL ORGANISATIONS OTHER THAN UN	22.32	22.32
2.	59	GENERAL REMARKS CONCERNING HUMAN CONTACTS	7.14	29.46
3.	9	RESPECT FOR HUMAN RIGHTS AND FUNDAMENTAL FREEDOMS	6.25	35.71
4.	14	DOCUMENT ON CONFIDENCE-BUILDING MEASURES AND CERTAIN ASPECTS OF SECURITY AND DISARMAMENT	6.25	41.96
5.	30	PROVISIONS CONCERNING TRADE AND INDUSTRIAL COOPERATION	4.46	46.43
6.	97	INTERNATIONAL CONFERENCES	4.46	50.89
7.	114	POLITICAL COOPERATION AND POLITICAL DISCUSSIONS	4.46	55.36
8.	16	QUESTIONS RELATING TO DISARMAMENT	3.57	58.93
9.	17	QUESTIONS RELATING TO SECURITY	3.57	62.50
10.	119	SPECIFIC INTERNATIONAL AGREEMENTS	3.57	66.07

MALTA

RANK	CODE	CATEGORY	%	CUMULATIVE %
1.	103	PEACE	23.29	23.29
2.	51	SECTION ON THE MEDITERRANEAN: GENERAL REMARKS	12.33	35.62
3.	53	INCREASING MUTUAL CONFIDENCE, SECURITY, STABILITY IN THE MEDITERRANEAN	10.96	46.58
4.	17	QUESTIONS RELATING TO SECURITY	9.59	56.16
5.	104	CONFLICT AND CONFRONTATION	8.22	64.38
6.	102	NEUTRALITY	6.85	71.23
7.	11	COOPERATION AMONG STATES AS A PRINCIPLE OF INTERNATIONAL RELATIONS	5.48	76.71
8.	16	QUESTIONS RELATING TO DISARMAMENT	4.11	80.82
9.	101	NON-ALIGNMENT	4.11	84.93
10.	1	BASKET ONE: QUESTIONS RELATING TO SECURITY IN EUROPE	2.74	87.67

MONACO

RANK	CODE	CATEGORY	%	CUMULATIVE %
1.	35	COOPERATION IN SCIENCE AND TECHNOLOGY	30.77	30.77
2.	51	SECTION ON THE MEDITERRANEAN: GENERAL REMARKS	15.38	46.15
3.	9	RESPECT FOR HUMAN RIGHTS AND FUNDAMENTAL FREEDOMS	7.69	53.85
4.	17	QUESTIONS RELATING TO SECURITY	7.69	61.54
5.	19	BASKET TWO: COOPERATION IN THE FIELD OF ECONOMICS, SCIENCE, TECHNOLOGY, AND THE ENVIRONMENT	7.69	69.23
6.	42	FIELDS OF COOPERATION IN THE FIELD OF ENVIRONMENT	7.69	76.92
7.	97	INTERNATIONAL CONFERENCES	7.69	84.62
8.	103	PEACE	7.69	92.31
9.	119	SPECIFIC INTERNATIONAL AGREEMENTS	7.69	100.00
10.				

NETHERLANDS

RANK	CODE	CATEGORY	%	CUMULATIVE %
1.	9	RESPECT FOR HUMAN RIGHTS AND FUNDAMENTAL FREEDOMS	23.64	23.64
2.	109	FREEDOM	10.00	33.64
3.	17	QUESTIONS RELATING TO SECURITY	8.18	41.82
4.	108	IDEOLOGY AND IDEAS	7.27	49.09
5.	114	POLITICAL COOPERATION AND POLITICAL DISCUSSIONS	6.36	55.45
6.	2	GENERAL REMARKS CONCERNING THE DECLARATION ON PRINCIPLES GUIDING RELATIONS	5.45	60.91
7.	104	CONFLICT AND CONFRONTATION	5.45	66.36
8.	11	COOPERATION AMONG STATES AS A PRINCIPLE OF INTERNATIONAL RELATIONS	4.55	70.91
9.	16	QUESTIONS RELATING TO DISARMAMENT	3.64	74.55
10.	103	PEACE	3.64	78.18

NORWAY

RANK	CODE	CATEGORY	%	CUMULATIVE %
1.	16	QUESTIONS RELATING TO DISARMAMENT	15.03	15.03
2.	14	DOCUMENT ON CONFIDENCE-BUILDING MEASURES AND CERTAIN ASPECTS OF SECURITY AND DISARMAMENT	10.98	26.01
3.	114	POLITICAL COOPERATION AND POLITICAL DISCUSSIONS	9.83	35.84
4.	97	INTERNATIONAL CONFERENCES	6.94	42.77
5.	104	CONFLICT AND CONFRONTATION	6.36	49.13
6.	9	RESPECT FOR HUMAN RIGHTS AND FUNDAMENTAL FREEDOMS	5.78	54.91
7.	11	COOPERATION AMONG STATES AS A PRINCIPLE OF INTERNATIONAL RELATIONS	3.47	58.38
8.	19	BASKET TWO: COOPERATION IN THE FIELD OF ECONOMICS, SCIENCE, TECHNOLOGY, AND THE ENVIRONMENT	3.47	61.85
9.	8	NON-INTERVENTION IN INTERNAL AFFAIRS	2.89	64.74
10.	1	BASKET ONE: QUESTIONS RELATING TO SECURITY IN EUROPE	2.31	67.05

Table A2.12. *(cont.)*

POLAND

RANK	CODE	CATEGORY	%	CUMULATIVE %
1.	16	QUESTIONS RELATING TO DISARMAMENT	12.18	12.18
2.	11	COOPERATION AMONG STATES AS A PRINCIPLE OF INTERNATIONAL RELATIONS	11.54	23.72
3.	104	CONFLICT AND CONFRONTATION	10.26	33.97
4.	14	DOCUMENT ON CONFIDENCE-BUILDING MEASURES AND CERTAIN ASPECTS OF SECURITY AND DISARMAMENT	8.97	42.95
5.	17	QUESTIONS RELATING TO SECURITY	7.69	50.64
6.	97	INTERNATIONAL CONFERENCES	7.05	57.69
7.	114	POLITICAL COOPERATION AND POLITICAL DISCUSSIONS	7.05	64.74
8.	110	JUSTICE	3.85	68.59
9.	119	SPECIFIC INTERNATIONAL AGREEMENTS	3.21	71.79
10.	8	NON-INTERVENTION IN INTERNAL AFFAIRS	2.56	74.36

PORTUGAL

RANK	CODE	CATEGORY	%	CUMULATIVE %
1.	9	RESPECT FOR HUMAN RIGHTS AND FUNDAMENTAL FREEDOMS	17.02	17.02
2.	8	NON-INTERVENTION IN INTERNAL AFFAIRS	8.51	25.53
3.	4	REFRAINING FROM THE THREAT OR USE OF FORCE	6.38	31.91
4.	17	QUESTIONS RELATING TO SECURITY	6.38	38.30
5.	10	EQUAL RIGHTS AND SELF-DETERMINATION OF PEOPLES	4.26	42.55
6.	11	COOPERATION AMONG STATES AS A PRINCIPLE OF INTERNATIONAL RELATIONS	4.26	46.81
7.	99	UN AND UN SPECIAL ORGANISATIONS	4.26	51.06
8.	101	NON-ALIGNMENT	4.26	55.32
9.	102	NEUTRALITY	4.26	59.57
10.	104	CONFLICT AND CONFRONTATION	4.26	63.83

ROMANIA

RANK	CODE	CATEGORY	%	CUMULATIVE %
1.	11	COOPERATION AMONG STATES AS A PRINCIPLE OF INTERNATIONAL RELATIONS	13.06	13.06
2.	14	DOCUMENT ON CONFIDENCE-BUILDING MEASURES AND CERTAIN ASPECTS OF SECURITY AND DISARMAMENT	9.55	22.61
3.	1	BASKET ONE: QUESTIONS RELATING TO SECURITY IN EUROPE	7.96	30.57
4.	16	QUESTIONS RELATING TO DISARMAMENT	6.05	36.62
5.	103	PEACE	6.05	42.68
6.	114	POLITICAL COOPERATION AND POLITICAL DISCUSSIONS	3.50	46.18
7.	97	INTERNATIONAL CONFERENCES	3.18	49.36
8.	8	NON-INTERVENTION IN INTERNAL AFFAIRS	2.87	52.23
9.	74	COOPERATION AND EXCHANGES IN THE FIELD OF CULTURE	2.87	55.10
10.	94	DANGERS OF NUCLEAR PROLIFERATION	2.55	57.64

SAN MARINO

RANK	CODE	CATEGORY	%	CUMULATIVE %
1.	11	COOPERATION AMONG STATES AS A PRINCIPLE OF INTERNATIONAL RELATIONS	12.90	12.90
2.	103	PEACE	9.68	22.58
3.	104	CONFLICT AND CONFRONTATION	8.06	30.65
4.	111	WELFARE AND PROSPERITY	8.06	38.71
5.	2	GENERAL REMARKS CONCERNING THE DECLARATION ON PRINCIPLES GUIDING RELATIONS	6.45	45.16
6.	8	NON-INTERVENTION IN INTERNAL AFFAIRS	6.45	51.61
7.	92	SOLIDARITY AMONG COUNTRIES	6.45	58.06
8.	107	JUDICIAL SYSTEMS AND LEGAL INSTITUTIONS	4.84	62.90
9.	4	REFRAINING FROM THE THREAT OR USE OF FORCE	3.23	66.13
10.	9	RESPECT FOR HUMAN RIGHTS AND FUNDAMENTAL FREEDOMS	3.23	69.35

SPAIN

RANK	CODE	CATEGORY	%	CUMULATIVE %
1.	11	COOPERATION AMONG STATES AS A PRINCIPLE OF INTERNATIONAL RELATIONS	12.81	12.81
2.	14	DOCUMENT ON CONFIDENCE-BUILDING MEASURES AND CERTAIN ASPECTS OF SECURITY AND DISARMAMENT	9.85	22.66
3.	103	PEACE	9.36	32.02
4.	17	QUESTIONS RELATING TO SECURITY	8.87	40.89
5.	9	RESPECT FOR HUMAN RIGHTS AND FUNDAMENTAL FREEDOMS	6.90	47.78
6.	104	CONFLICT AND CONFRONTATION	4.93	52.71
7.	114	POLITICAL COOPERATION AND POLITICAL DISCUSSIONS	4.93	57.64
8.	97	INTERNATIONAL CONFERENCES	3.45	61.08
9.	2	GENERAL REMARKS CONCERNING THE DECLARATION ON PRINCIPLES GUIDING RELATIONS	2.96	64.04
10.	3	SOVEREIGN EQUALITY, RESPECT FOR THE RIGHTS INHERENT IN SOVEREIGNTY	2.96	67.00

Table A2.12. *(cont.)*

SWEDEN

RANK	CODE	CATEGORY	%	CUMULATIVE %
1.	16	QUESTIONS RELATING TO DISARMAMENT	18.95	18.95
2.	17	QUESTIONS RELATING TO SECURITY	11.58	30.53
3.	97	INTERNATIONAL CONFERENCES	8.95	39.47
4.	9	RESPECT FOR HUMAN RIGHTS AND FUNDAMENTAL FREEDOMS	8.42	47.89
5.	94	DANGERS OF NUCLEAR PROLIFERATION	8.42	56.32
6.	14	DOCUMENT ON CONFIDENCE-BUILDING MEASURES AND CERTAIN ASPECTS OF SECURITY AND DISARMAMENT	6.84	63.16
7.	114	POLITICAL COOPERATION AND POLITICAL DISCUSSIONS	6.32	69.47
8.	19	BASKET TWO: COOPERATION IN THE FIELD OF ECONOMICS, SCIENCE, TECHNOLOGY, AND THE ENVIRONMENT	3.68	73.16
9.	108	IDEOLOGY AND IDEAS	3.16	76.32
10.	103	PEACE	2.11	78.42

SWITZERLAND

RANK	CODE	CATEGORY	%	CUMULATIVE %
1.	16	QUESTIONS RELATING TO DISARMAMENT	10.39	10.39
2.	4	REFRAINING FROM THE THREAT OR USE OF FORCE	9.09	19.48
3.	107	JUDICIAL SYSTEMS AND LEGAL INSTITUTIONS	9.09	28.57
4.	7	PEACEFUL SETTLEMENT OF DISPUTES	7.79	36.36
5.	1	BASKET ONE: QUESTIONS RELATING TO SECURITY IN EUROPE	6.49	42.86
6.	17	QUESTIONS RELATING TO SECURITY	5.84	48.70
7.	14	DOCUMENT ON CONFIDENCE-BUILDING MEASURES AND CERTAIN ASPECTS OF SECURITY AND DISARMAMENT	4.55	53.25
8.	103	PEACE	4.55	57.79
9.	104	CONFLICT AND CONFRONTATION	4.55	62.34
10.	114	POLITICAL COOPERATION AND POLITICAL DISCUSSIONS	4.55	66.88

TURKEY

RANK	CODE	CATEGORY	%	CUMULATIVE %
1.	16	QUESTIONS RELATING TO DISARMAMENT	15.63	15.63
2.	11	COOPERATION AMONG STATES AS A PRINCIPLE OF INTERNATIONAL RELATIONS	14.06	29.69
3.	14	DOCUMENT ON CONFIDENCE-BUILDING MEASURES AND CERTAIN ASPECTS OF SECURITY AND DISARMAMENT	12.50	42.19
4.	1	BASKET ONE: QUESTIONS RELATING TO SECURITY IN EUROPE	4.69	46.88
5.	2	GENERAL REMARKS CONCERNING THE DECLARATION ON PRINCIPLES GUIDING RELATIONS	4.69	51.56
6.	120	STABILITY, STRATEGIC AND POLITICAL BALANCE	4.69	56.25
7.	8	NON-INTERVENTION IN INTERNAL AFFAIRS	3.13	59.38
8.	9	RESPECT FOR HUMAN RIGHTS AND FUNDAMENTAL FREEDOMS	3.13	62.50
9.	17	QUESTIONS RELATING TO SECURITY	3.13	65.63
10.	48	ECONOMIC AND SOCIAL ASPECTS OF MIGRANT LABOUR	3.13	68.75

UNION OF THE SOVIET SOCIALIST REPUBLICS

RANK	CODE	CATEGORY	%	CUMULATIVE %
1.	14	DOCUMENT ON CONFIDENCE-BUILDING MEASURES AND CERTAIN ASPECTS OF SECURITY AND DISARMAMENT	12.10	12.10
2.	103	PEACE	12.10	24.20
3.	97	INTERNATIONAL CONFERENCES	8.92	33.12
4.	119	SPECIFIC INTERNATIONAL AGREEMENTS	8.28	41.40
5.	16	QUESTIONS RELATING TO DISARMAMENT	7.01	48.41
6.	95	ENERGY PROBLEMS	4.46	52.87
7.	104	CONFLICT AND CONFRONTATION	3.82	56.69
8.	11	COOPERATION AMONG STATES AS A PRINCIPLE OF INTERNATIONAL RELATIONS	3.18	59.87
9.	40	COOPERATION IN THE FIELD OF ENVIRONMENT	2.55	62.42
10.	53	INCREASING MUTUAL CONFIDENCE, SECURITY, STABILITY IN THE MEDITERRANEAN	2.55	64.97

UNITED KINGDOM

RANK	CODE	CATEGORY	%	CUMULATIVE %
1.	9	RESPECT FOR HUMAN RIGHTS AND FUNDAMENTAL FREEDOMS	18.79	18.79
2.	58	BASKET THREE: COOPERATION IN HUMANITARIAN AND OTHER FIELDS	7.38	26.17
3.	69	COOPERATION IN THE FIELD OF INFORMATION EXCHANGE	7.38	33.56
4.	12	FULFILLMENT IN GOOD FAITH OF OBLIGATIONS UNDER INTERNATIONAL LAW	6.04	39.60
5.	17	QUESTIONS RELATING TO SECURITY	6.04	45.64
6.	11	COOPERATION AMONG STATES AS A PRINCIPLE OF INTERNATIONAL RELATIONS	4.03	49.66
7.	59	GENERAL REMARKS CONCERNING HUMAN CONTACTS	3.36	53.02
8.	103	PEACE	3.36	56.38
9.	1	BASKET ONE: QUESTIONS RELATING TO SECURITY IN EUROPE	2.68	59.06
10.	4	REFRAINING FROM THE THREAT OR USE OF FORCE	2.68	61.74

Table A2.12 *(cont.)*

UNITED STATES OF AMERICA

RANK	CODE	CATEGORY	%	CUMULATIVE %
1.	9	RESPECT FOR HUMAN RIGHTS AND FUNDAMENTAL FREEDOMS	34.67	34.67
2.	17	QUESTIONS RELATING TO SECURITY	8.00	42.67
3.	11	COOPERATION AMONG STATES AS A PRINCIPLE OF INTERNATIONAL RELATIONS	4.67	47.33
4.	14	DOCUMENT ON CONFIDENCE-BUILDING MEASURES AND CERTAIN ASPECTS OF SECURITY AND DISARMAMENT	4.67	52.00
5.	97	INTERNATIONAL CONFERENCES	4.00	56.00
6.	103	PEACE	4.00	60.00
7.	2	GENERAL REMARKS CONCERNING THE DECLARATION ON PRINCIPLES GUIDING RELATIONS	3.33	63.33
8.	16	QUESTIONS RELATING TO DISARMAMENT	3.33	66.67
9.	94	DANGERS OF NUCLEAR PROLIFERATION	3.33	70.00
10.	119	SPECIFIC INTERNATIONAL AGREEMENTS	2.67	72.67

VATICAN (HOLY SEE)

RANK	CODE	CATEGORY	%	CUMULATIVE %
1.	9	RESPECT FOR HUMAN RIGHTS AND FUNDAMENTAL FREEDOMS	11.27	11.27
2.	115	FREEDOM OF RELIGION OR BELIEF	9.86	21.13
3.	11	COOPERATION AMONG STATES AS A PRINCIPLE OF INTERNATIONAL RELATIONS	7.04	28.17
4.	104	CONFLICT AND CONFRONTATION	7.04	35.21
5.	103	PEACE	4.23	39.44
6.	107	JUDICIAL SYSTEMS AND LEGAL INSTITUTIONS	4.23	43.66
7.	14	DOCUMENT ON CONFIDENCE-BUILDING MEASURES AND CERTAIN ASPECTS OF SECURITY AND DISARMAMENT	3.52	47.18
8.	16	QUESTIONS RELATING TO DISARMAMENT	3.52	50.70
9.	110	JUSTICE	3.52	54.23
10.	58	BASKET THREE: COOPERATION IN HUMANITARIAN AND OTHER FIELDS	2.82	57.04

YUGOSLAVIA

RANK	CODE	CATEGORY	%	CUMULATIVE %
1.	104	CONFLICT AND CONFRONTATION	11.66	11.66
2.	9	RESPECT FOR HUMAN RIGHTS AND FUNDAMENTAL FREEDOMS	9.82	21.47
3.	11	COOPERATION AMONG STATES AS A PRINCIPLE OF INTERNATIONAL RELATIONS	7.98	29.45
4.	2	GENERAL REMARKS CONCERNING THE DECLARATION ON PRINCIPLES GUIDING RELATIONS	7.36	36.81
5.	14	DOCUMENT ON CONFIDENCE-BUILDING MEASURES AND CERTAIN ASPECTS OF SECURITY AND DISARMAMENT	5.52	42.33
6.	16	QUESTIONS RELATING TO DISARMAMENT	5.52	47.85
7.	17	QUESTIONS RELATING TO SECURITY	5.52	53.37
8.	103	PEACE	4.91	58.28
9.	51	SECTION ON THE MEDITERRANEAN: GENERAL REMARKS	3.68	61.96
10.	101	NON-ALIGNMENT	3.68	65.64

A2.4 THE FACTOR ANALYSIS OF THE CONTENT-ANALYTICAL DATA

Methodological and Technical Considerations

There are various methods of multivariate data reduction. After considerable experimentation, the authors of this study selected factor analysis since it appeared to be the most appropriate for this purpose (see also Iker and Harway 1969; Iker 1974, 1974/75; and Iker and Klein 1974).

Factor analysis requires a matrix of similarities between variables or objects. In the context of this study, similarities between *categories* had to be computed. In most cases, a matrix of product-moment correlation coefficients is used. For the computation of a similarity matrix between the categories of the analysis, the basic sampling unit is what has been called the *associational sequence.* This is a fraction of text devoted to one single issue in a speech, with an average length of 120 to 210 words. Each of these associational sequences constitutes a "case" for computing measures of similarity.* The categories of this study are treated as "variables." Each of the thirty-five statements made at Helsinki, Belgrade, and Madrid contains around ten associational sequences, on the average.

The selection of an appropriate measure of similarity proved to be extremely difficult, however. Usually, product-moment correlation coefficients or Euclidian distances are used as measures of association or similarity. For the following reasons, these measures lead to serious distortions in the case of this analysis: Both correlation coefficients and Euclidian distances treat combined scores of zero from two categories within one single associational sequence as an evidence of close connection between these categories. This is due of course to the formulas for the correlation coefficient and the Euclidian distance:

$$r_{12} = \frac{\Sigma\,(X_1 - \overline{X}_1)\,(X_2 - \overline{X}_2)}{\sqrt{\Sigma\,(X_1 - \overline{X}_1)^2\,\Sigma(X_2 - \overline{X}_2)^2}}$$

$$d_{12} = \sqrt{\Sigma\,(X_1 - X_2)^2}$$

In the case of the product-moment correlation coefficient (r), the product of the deviation of scores for two categories (X_1 and X_2) from their respective means ($\overline{X}_1$ and $\overline{X}_2$) is summed up and divided by the square root of the sum of the squared deviations. Obviously scores of zero on both categories result in an increase in the correlation coefficient (because the square root of the sum of

*The associational sequence is selected as the context unit in this part of the study because complete statements as units of analysis yield misleading measures of proximity: due to the use of a highly standardized diplomatic language, practically all categories would be highly related with each other. See also in A2.1 the section on the WORDS System and assertion analysis.

the squared and multiplied deviations is equal to the sum of the product of deviations in the nominator of the formula), if the mean is nonzero. The same is true for the Euclidian distance, which is computed by taking the square root of the sum of the squared differences between scores. Scores of zero on both categories would contribute nothing to the distance, therefore counting as a close association of two categories.

The theoretical consequences are as follows: The use of correlation coefficients or Euclidian distances would implicitly support the assumption that the combined absence of two categories within one associational sequence would be valued the same as the combined occurrence of these categories. In other words, if in an associational sequence the concepts of industrial cooperation (No. 27) and human contacts (No. 59), for instance, do not occur, this combined nonoccurrence would be treated as an evidence of close connection. This is certainly not the case, however.

A different measure of association was proposed by Weymann (1973). The focus here is not on the occurrence of a category in a specific context but rather the sequence of the occurrence of a set of categories in the text. Categories that follow each other are regarded as closely connected, whereby the first category of a pair of categories is supposed to be a *stimulus* followed by a special *response* represented by the second category. For the calculation of measures of similarity, those categories are regarded as highly associated, which, as stimuli, share a high number of common responses. The formula would be as follows:

$$P_{12} = \frac{\Sigma\, f(R_1,\ R_2)}{\sqrt{N_1 N_2}}$$

Where R_1 and R_2 are responses; f is a function that selects the smaller of the two arguments. Then all response categories from the pair of stimulus categories 1 and 2 in this case are added together. The terms N_1 and N_2 are the total number of responses to stimuli 1 and 2, respectively. During various tests, including the factor analysis of the resulting matrix of similarities, it turned out, however, that the requirements of the just cited formula are much too rigid for this kind of study. Most categories were reported to be highly unconnected even though they were found in the same associational sequence. Thus a different solution had to be found. The computation of fractions of common scores for each pair of categories seems to meet these requirements. The common formula is:

$$s_{12} = \Sigma\, f\left(\frac{X_1}{\Sigma X_1}, \frac{X_2}{\Sigma X_2}\right)$$

For each associational sequence and each pair of categories in this associational sequence, the fraction of common scores is computed.

The term *f* is a function selecting the smaller of the two arguments. Values are then summed up for all association sequences. The resulting index is constrained to values ranging from zero to one. For the needs of this study, this index proved to be more valuable than the more sophisticated measures discussed previously.

Factor-analytical solutions cannot be expected for the complete set of 120 categories in the analysis. Since most of the categories achieved only very low scores, the attempt to place all of them into the factor structure would destroy the pattern rather than contribute to the search for a solution, especially when rotating the initial solution into a simple structure since those solutions that fit all categories best are preferred. Keeping this in mind, the authors selected a subset of forty categories with high scores. These categories represent 78.9 percent of the total sum of scores for all categories and all association sequences.*

The matrix of similarities for this set of forty categories is factor analyzed according to the principal-factor algorithm. The resulting initial solution is rotated into a simple structure against a varimax criterion. This is the procedure adopted by Iker in his approach. The result is a set of 10 factors representing *dimensions of the concept of East-West relations,* as perceived by the actors. Each dimension can be regarded as a synthetically constructed *new category* representing a set of highly associated categories gleaned from those initial forty categories for which values were computed. In a table containing measures of association between the original categories and the factors extracted from the data, that is, so-called factor loadings, the exact content of each dimension is defined. The inferred factor structure is optimal in the sense that further changes would not increase the factor loading of one category

*The selection of only the 40 most frequent categories entering the computations for the extraction of factors, thereby disregarding the rest of 80 other categories, could cause concern with some readers. Some details on this decision must suffice in order to explain why the factor analysis was not run on the complete set of 120 categories. Suppose there are two categories with very low frequency but very closely related since they are mentioned in one or two associational sequences of one of the delegations. The proximity between these two categories will be very high, due to the formula selected. Since these two categories are unconnected with other categories and very closely related to each other, they will emerge from the factor analysis as one single factor, even though the total amount of attention on these two categories is negligible. Experimenting with the complete set of 120 categories and the respective 7140-cell matrix of proximities as an input to the factor analysis, it turned out that the resulting factor structure would be virutally dominated by marginal categories loading high on factors also negligible from the point of view of attention devoted to these factors by the delegations in their statements. The reason is simply that the formula rewards low frequency of categories that are highly associated. The selection of the most frequent categories proved to be a good solution to this problem for several reasons. First, it ensures a reasonable distribution of category scores, and second, the selected categories account for the vast majority of attention also in single statements. This criterion for the selection of categories might seem rigid; but other solutions as, for example, the technique applied by Iker (1974/75) in his SELECT procedure (see also section A2.1) appear to be not applicable due to the characteristics of the proximity measure adopted.

without reducing the factor loading in another one. In the case of orthogonal rotation, factors are supposed to represent highly independent dimensions. Correlations between factors would remain around zero. For well-known reasons, factor analysis requires a covariance matrix or a matrix of correlation coefficients as input. In this analysis, although a matrix of cooccurrence measures is employed, factor analysis was preferred to multidimensional scaling because of its advantages in controlling the extraction of factors. This is justified since the task of factor analysis in this case is "purely heuristic,"* namely, the construction of an empirical taxonomy guiding the aggregation of categories. Consequently, factor scores were not computed in the usual way but by simply adding up the scores of the highest loading categories for each factor, respectively.

*Cf. Jae-On Kim and Charles W. Mueller, *Factor Analysis: Statistical Methods and Practical Issues* (Beverly Hills and London: Sage, 1978), p. 73.

Table A2.13. Varimax Rotated-Factor Matrix: The 1973 Helsinki Statements

Categories	Factor Loadings									
	FACTOR 1	FACTOR 2	FACTOR 3	FACTOR 4	FACTOR 5	FACTOR 6	FACTOR 7	FACTOR 8	FACTOR 9	FACTOR 10
1	0.55028	0.15717	0.05017	0.00924	0.21389	0.11323	0.00247	-0.01758	0.18946	0.03569
2	0.13695	0.35045	0.01880	0.02251	-0.00145	0.03885	0.14057	-0.01977	0.38329	-0.01419
3	0.26595	0.51165	0.04771	0.01120	-0.00336	-0.03388	0.02420	0.04424	0.06881	-0.01769
4	0.06118	0.63875	-0.01270	-0.00346	0.06500	0.06846	0.03096	-0.00623	-0.00589	0.00886
5	0.04952	0.29185	0.00200	0.00088	-0.00926	-0.00414	-0.00103	0.02110	0.15973	-0.00384
7	0.03869	0.31047	0.00237	0.00256	0.04900	0.06534	0.15780	-0.00714	0.06859	0.00837
8	0.00080	0.61231	0.01445	0.00984	0.02950	-0.02617	0.13204	0.00421	-0.02650	-0.00035
9	0.02857	0.14369	0.08457	-0.00747	-0.04073	0.05524	0.67566	0.00063	0.10235	-0.00716
11	0.47529	0.09740	0.15435	0.08449	0.38963	-0.05342	0.09438	0.10632	0.10123	0.11081
14	0.20049	0.01688	0.10077	0.02387	0.15561	0.55522	0.01640	0.00129	0.03754	0.02058
15	0.03893	-0.00538	-0.01003	0.00058	-0.02577	0.32292	-0.00155	-0.00768	0.00636	-0.00004
16	0.05091	0.00803	-0.02488	-0.01175	0.24087	0.55509	0.00032	0.01779	0.04068	-0.01427
17	0.23159	0.09070	0.00005	0.01769	0.15696	0.28719	0.12126	0.00303	-0.03718	-0.00505
19	0.14316	0.01711	0.03746	0.24292	0.05709	0.01317	0.05226	0.61381	-0.02909	0.14876
20	0.04708	-0.01833	-0.00355	-0.01824	0.00366	0.01897	0.02595	0.40457	-0.01981	-0.00394
26	0.04129	-0.00382	-0.00529	0.00644	-0.00427	-0.01929	-0.00153	0.05936	-0.01797	0.39786
46	0.00956	-0.01296	-0.00516	0.72420	-0.00681	0.02337	0.01463	-0.03885	0.00447	0.26031
48	-0.01783	0.00150	0.00973	0.09149	-0.00454	0.02237	0.00052	-0.01906	0.01373	0.51354
51	0.15084	0.00279	-0.00071	-0.01467	0.03120	0.03846	-0.00090	0.01580	0.05951	0.01786
58	0.07906	-0.01450	0.20072	0.01345	0.03074	0.01939	0.18041	0.06796	0.01968	0.02377
59	-0.01425	0.01096	0.61643	-0.01858	0.08196	0.05693	0.09627	0.03081	0.04369	0.04555
69	0.05234	-0.01878	0.32017	0.00785	0.01128	-0.01592	0.01916	-0.01252	-0.02261	-0.01225
70	0.01066	0.02659	0.63377	-0.01275	-0.02503	0.06542	0.03752	-0.01876	0.00451	-0.00481
74	0.09404	0.04800	0.50385	0.04684	0.02237	-0.05037	-0.07074	0.04916	-0.00372	-0.02253
94	0.02742	0.02530	-0.01167	0.00092	0.18163	0.07765	-0.00133	-0.02182	-0.05059	-0.00130
95	-0.01322	-0.00709	0.01892	0.56601	0.05134	-0.01674	0.01614	0.02835	0.00761	-0.05581
97	0.00914	-0.01164	0.02366	-0.00934	0.39247	0.04236	-0.01896	0.06543	0.05714	-0.00529
98	0.11197	0.02130	0.02531	-0.01276	0.05941	-0.01496	-0.01508	0.21926	0.06443	-0.01407
99	0.13035	0.14367	-0.01270	-0.00191	0.05007	0.02654	-0.02937	0.01950	0.53887	-0.00746
103	0.54260	0.18522	0.07509	0.00902	0.13229	0.08660	0.09347	-0.00523	0.06979	-0.00211
104	0.29687	0.08313	0.0706[illegible]	-0.02485	0.23558	0.14786	0.04738	0.07737	0.07945	-0.00238
108	0.26301	0.10428	0.10829	0.06513	0.18125	-0.06073	0.18402	0.17756	-0.01449	0.00937
109	0.22925	0.02950	0.08205	-0.01861	-0.06774	0.04499	0.18362	0.02743	-0.03438	-0.03054
111	0.31990	0.02290	0.06197	0.09785	-0.06768	-0.00237	-0.03910	0.16014	-0.07135	0.05801
112	0.27890	0.01091	0.00438	0.04037	-0.04038	0.05882	-0.01594	0.12793	0.03493	-0.03641
114	0.13870	0.01845	0.04916	0.00999	0.55177	0.09106	-0.00067	0.01439	0.04066	-0.01658
115	0.02015	0.25092	-0.01596	-0.00021	0.02761	-0.02678	0.52225	-0.00541	-0.08117	0.00360
117	0.13214	0.05067	0.02593	0.34836	-0.06344	0.02271	-0.04216	0.22876	-0.00908	0.02525
119	0.13009	0.06813	0.03338	-0.00362	0.18817	0.17270	-0.00102	0.03413	0.15655	-0.00496
120	0.29476	0.03971	0.00250	-0.00345	0.09969	0.18806	0.01646	0.07637	-0.01634	-0.01373

Table A2.14. Varimax Rotated-Factor Matrix: The 1975 Helsinki Statements

Categories	Factor Loadings									
	FACTOR 1	FACTOR 2	FACTOR 3	FACTOR 4	FACTOR 5	FACTOR 6	FACTOR 7	FACTOR 8	FACTOR 9	FACTOR 10
1	0.18707	0.04854	0.19253	0.87770	0.00492	0.09039	0.06457	0.15115	0.05864	0.03432
2	0.46325	0.07968	0.07435	0.10723	-0.00611	-0.01606	0.07423	0.06337	0.01548	0.07199
3	0.45839	0.04930	0.13425	0.13255	0.03876	-0.01183	0.10165	0.03291	0.01667	0.00541
4	0.80503	-0.02320	0.01185	-0.00897	-0.07423	0.02757	-0.04437	0.00870	0.01187	-0.08966
5	0.46315	-0.00031	0.07540	-0.00818	0.12884	-0.03749	-0.01658	-0.02019	-0.01064	-0.01951
7	0.25788	-0.00604	-0.01126	0.07213	-0.01729	0.11730	-0.00622	0.00726	0.00043	-0.05900
8	0.59939	-0.00502	0.01360	0.01748	0.11196	0.07548	-0.03013	-0.05875	-0.02164	0.00241
9	0.21289	0.15514	0.02505	-0.01280	0.03526	0.00030	0.15712	0.03438	-0.01953	0.15252
11	0.11768	0.10487	0.88458	0.23155	0.08465	-0.00930	0.08541	0.08199	0.02939	-0.02528
14	0.02504	0.00882	0.03626	0.04470	0.00409	0.07710	-0.00709	0.00792	0.65160	0.00407
15	0.01399	0.01072	-0.00671	0.07101	-0.00353	0.17249	0.00181	-0.05386	0.47905	0.01689
16	0.06263	0.01261	0.06487	0.09496	-0.00095	0.72480	0.07816	0.05519	0.16467	0.00639
17	0.17276	0.04344	0.18688	0.85880	0.00580	0.14532	0.09954	0.10445	0.20906	0.03513
19	0.09073	0.12804	0.84674	0.21585	0.11073	-0.02885	0.07618	0.11831	0.02730	-0.00201
20	0.01267	0.15535	0.12259	0.05590	0.23493	-0.01598	0.02496	0.27175	0.11148	-0.17043
26	0.05785	0.00315	0.01530	0.02001	0.70580	-0.00722	-0.00471	0.00562	-0.00565	0.10917
46	0.12743	0.02595	-0.01199	-0.02984	0.75946	0.00073	-0.00895	-0.01766	-0.01698	0.25755
48	-0.00090	0.04400	-0.00016	-0.00362	-0.00452	0.00090	0.00419	-0.00411	0.00022	0.01131
51	0.01163	-0.00427	0.05314	0.13857	0.00291	0.00085	-0.01786	0.09524	-0.01342	-0.00762
58	0.01591	0.35195	0.06726	0.02156	-0.00308	0.02440	0.15198	-0.01280	-0.02019	-0.01639
59	0.07648	0.68496	0.07593	0.02702	0.08159	-0.03922	-0.06472	0.05400	0.06545	0.21615
69	0.03129	0.66397	-0.04892	0.02324	0.00614	0.00735	-0.02125	0.01601	-0.02784	-0.12997
70	0.06683	0.53670	0.03594	-0.01706	0.05290	0.00422	-0.03553	0.00572	0.00804	0.39992
74	-0.00205	0.74117	0.03802	0.06829	0.02988	-0.00505	-0.01877	0.03336	0.03821	-0.19047
94	0.00239	-0.01027	-0.01873	0.01383	-0.01602	0.08333	-0.01133	0.23170	-0.02418	0.05055
95	-0.00000	-0.00000	-0.00000	0.00000	0.00000	0.00000	-0.00000	0.00000	-0.00000	0.00000
97	0.06220	0.00229	0.00672	0.04354	0.00829	0.69016	-0.03382	0.18897	0.18650	-0.02138
98	0.03766	0.00295	0.19151	0.11581	0.01442	0.00205	-0.00162	0.04692	0.05575	-0.01702
99	0.22917	0.01205	0.04410	0.00567	-0.03272	-0.01064	-0.01905	0.16422	0.08305	0.00817
103	0.22168	0.03118	0.33341	0.28390	-0.06483	0.05248	0.11226	0.26350	-0.00373	0.08081
104	0.16112	0.02449	0.30105	0.09904	-0.03800	0.10641	0.08805	0.12959	0.00626	0.03236
108	0.08023	0.14389	0.10510	0.01250	0.09862	-0.01383	0.15337	-0.01193	0.02866	0.43179
109	0.04957	0.04517	0.04606	0.06287	-0.04394	0.00281	0.66633	0.02588	-0.00985	0.16390
111	0.02136	0.03295	0.05408	0.02464	0.01108	0.00891	0.67746	0.12849	0.00645	-0.02580
112	0.01204	0.01381	0.07035	0.13820	-0.02881	0.04215	-0.02752	0.42487	-0.03491	0.09127
114	0.00000	-0.00000	-0.00000	0.00000	-0.00000	0.00000	-0.00000	0.00000	-0.00000	-0.00000
115	-0.00018	-0.00215	0.03987	-0.00704	-0.00430	0.00270	-0.00207	0.00076	-0.00420	0.00222
117	0.00985	-0.00190	0.10061	0.01543	0.04719	0.04213	0.14215	0.28584	0.00590	-0.09699
119	0.02845	0.00775	0.08409	0.03121	-0.02415	0.12741	-0.05000	0.14889	-0.01652	0.06446

Categories	Factor Loadings									
	FACTOR 1	FACTOR 2	FACTOR 3	FACTOR 4	FACTOR 5	FACTOR 6	FACTOR 7	FACTOR 8	FACTOR 9	FACTOR 10
1	0.32186	0.02744	0.84366	0.01223	0.21126	-0.00256	0.10909	0.07948	0.04068	0.08511
2	0.21923	-0.00182	0.08351	0.02207	0.09504	0.00036	0.10156	0.09472	0.00891	0.14036
3	0.19079	0.04906	0.09718	0.04868	0.12456	0.01371	0.18666	0.36459	0.05403	0.14264
4	0.07271	0.03863	0.06819	-0.00117	0.00100	-0.00446	0.75153	0.16711	0.03434	0.00698
5	0.03122	-0.01121	0.03137	-0.00687	0.01795	-0.00470	-0.04512	0.59465	-0.01631	0.02692
7	0.06022	-0.00577	0.06247	0.02413	0.09289	-0.00089	0.59823	0.05163	0.01012	0.01701
8	0.03118	0.00472	0.02306	0.02002	0.00231	-0.00210	0.23089	0.66624	-0.02996	0.07697
9	0.04274	0.00899	0.03467	0.12500	0.03495	0.00493	0.05577	0.03143	0.01410	0.52175
11	0.87220	0.06354	0.22294	0.10945	0.11816	0.06289	0.03396	0.03224	0.13801	0.05480
14	0.06402	0.00022	0.05036	0.02549	0.44798	-0.00534	0.09222	0.00751	-0.00132	0.07250
15	-0.06755	-0.01771	0.07865	-0.00419	0.54899	-0.00775	0.00701	-0.02755	0.02022	-0.01018
16	-0.00701	0.00500	0.05831	-0.00739	0.50579	-0.00556	0.04236	0.00778	0.01564	-0.02431
17	0.25127	0.01547	0.84757	0.01364	0.36664	-0.00347	0.08860	0.06648	0.04303	0.04887
19	0.80542	0.13523	0.22614	0.08564	0.10448	0.06296	0.03685	0.04386	0.20161	0.04172
20	0.03925	0.87871	0.02806	0.09097	0.05652	-0.01242	0.00623	0.01324	0.17411	0.01285
26	0.02517	0.92015	0.03481	0.07323	0.05111	0.04462	0.00862	0.01079	0.12798	0.01101
46	0.02807	0.06169	-0.00808	-0.00238	0.01750	0.82580	-0.00720	0.01344	0.05858	-0.00955
48	0.02295	0.04662	-0.02196	0.01254	-0.00099	0.04559	-0.00396	-0.00126	0.12484	0.03554
51	0.05853	0.02974	0.07680	-0.00615	0.03000	-0.02010	0.00591	0.00820	0.29202	0.00647
58	0.10351	0.06760	0.02629	0.37409	0.02004	0.02120	0.03917	-0.01085	-0.01750	0.21380
59	0.00989	-0.00350	0.02057	0.64243	0.05891	-0.00292	-0.01872	-0.00228	-0.00110	0.07472
69	0.01365	-0.02377	0.01002	0.65002	0.02730	-0.00313	0.00709	0.00515	0.08072	-0.05797
70	0.02558	0.00575	-0.01602	0.26765	0.01266	-0.00300	-0.00721	0.02822	-0.01882	0.06763
74	0.04659	0.09894	0.01216	0.62039	0.02681	0.00239	0.03139	0.00034	0.05056	-0.01775
94	-0.00000	0.00000	0.00000	-0.00000	-0.00000	0.00000	-0.00000	0.00000	-0.00000	0.00000
95	0.03068	0.04881	0.00451	0.00332	0.00286	0.64257	-0.00115	-0.00537	0.01960	0.00855
97	0.02143	0.12249	-0.00480	0.09757	0.32390	0.01103	0.00413	0.03283	0.14291	-0.03411
98	-0.01049	0.05364	0.02779	-0.02780	0.07071	-0.04040	-0.00425	0.01295	0.62230	0.03801
99	0.01196	0.25277	0.01234	0.08283	0.04688	0.07963	0.01035	0.02305	0.48794	-0.00434
103	0.25168	-0.00314	0.28991	0.01929	0.17497	-0.01746	0.05550	0.07809	0.05885	0.26499
104	0.19154	-0.01437	0.07671	0.01699	0.25955	-0.01212	0.02299	-0.01850	0.01487	0.11361
108	0.14898	0.01786	-0.01811	0.07526	0.06130	-0.00951	0.04264	0.04139	-0.02913	0.11004
109	0.04960	-0.01075	0.02417	0.03934	0.02896	0.00067	-0.02271	0.03408	-0.00772	0.38112
111	0.11574	0.01287	0.01616	-0.02116	0.01327	-0.00976	-0.00744	0.05318	0.03024	0.27877
112	0.13486	0.02445	0.06907	0.01153	0.12340	0.02410	0.03158	0.04862	0.00213	0.12539
114	0.06740	0.06285	0.01843	0.00623	0.18991	0.02904	0.00444	0.02211	-0.00434	0.08632
115	-0.02003	-0.00453	-0.00182	0.02390	0.00162	0.00320	-0.00630	-0.00400	0.01157	0.18742
117	0.09371	0.23501	-0.01777	-0.00325	0.08965	0.09236	0.00667	0.00373	0.11657	-0.00668
119	0.11886	0.04334	-0.01780	0.09041	0.23173	0.03183	-0.02935	0.15743	0.11683	0.05239
120	0.14220	0.01318	0.08586	0.01075	0.30219	-0.00942	-0.03479	0.02547	0.00554	-0.01812

Table A2.16. Varimax Rotated-Factor Matrix: The Belgrade Closing Statements

Categories	Factor Loadings									
	FACTOR 1	FACTOR 2	FACTOR 3	FACTOR 4	FACTOR 5	FACTOR 6	FACTOR 7	FACTOR 8	FACTOR 9	FACTOR 10
1	0.86036	0.00572	-0.00940	0.25985	0.03091	0.07884	0.03017	0.03781	0.04699	0.02894
2	-0.03837	0.04587	0.01842	0.12289	0.13485	0.24649	0.03504	0.19178	-0.01614	0.16055
3	0.04257	-0.00623	0.05293	0.00513	0.06418	-0.03303	0.08642	0.63278	0.23673	-0.01631
4	-0.00868	0.00147	-0.01322	-0.01771	-0.02246	0.05102	-0.02248	0.33230	-0.02429	0.02432
5	-0.01860	-0.00291	0.00065	0.01257	0.00423	0.01096	-0.00102	-0.00335	0.01634	0.52802
7	0.05282	-0.00420	-0.01192	0.03603	-0.03253	0.11371	-0.03057	0.20574	-0.08612	-0.00369
8	0.05552	-0.02076	0.00269	0.04605	0.14274	0.00589	0.08880	0.25591	0.02611	0.00125
9	0.01546	-0.01507	0.01223	0.03506	0.29937	0.15481	0.16574	0.14145	-0.02760	0.19492
11	0.38279	0.04113	0.02814	0.86579	0.06474	0.06668	0.02460	0.05632	0.01495	-0.01301
14	0.12923	0.08855	0.02890	0.04032	0.10089	0.44485	0.00431	-0.06612	0.21267	-0.01206
15	0.05685	0.01406	0.00318	-0.00720	-0.00317	0.04670	-0.00870	-0.06176	0.42684	0.00196
16	0.28768	0.04299	0.00569	-0.02191	0.01417	0.50191	0.00810	-0.13406	0.27502	-0.02263
17	0.90050	0.02703	-0.01611	0.14638	0.03012	0.18783	0.02441	-0.01288	0.08211	0.02204
19	0.33556	0.06634	0.06953	0.90292	0.06996	0.07096	0.02332	0.03932	0.01675	-0.01135
20	0.02869	0.97968	0.03546	0.03890	0.08456	0.00987	0.01626	0.01508	-0.04297	0.01164
26	0.02728	0.97868	0.03608	0.03785	0.11275	0.00974	0.01586	0.01163	-0.04407	0.00823
46	-0.00399	0.07694	0.97814	0.03022	-0.01982	0.06537	-0.03777	0.03221	-0.03008	0.00104
48	-0.00206	0.06919	-0.01034	0.00994	0.09790	0.05762	-0.00069	-0.03282	0.02032	-0.00035
51	0.05263	0.02860	-0.00743	0.05123	0.02450	0.01529	-0.00982	0.02387	-0.02725	-0.00613
58	0.00125	-0.00599	-0.01073	0.08313	0.35644	0.12783	0.00624	-0.00535	-0.01649	0.07715
59	0.01469	0.03269	0.00844	-0.00629	0.83565	-0.01240	-0.03517	0.03601	0.01127	-0.05232
69	0.02234	0.04428	0.02673	-0.02429	0.54089	-0.01069	-0.00888	-0.03978	-0.01637	0.01703
70	0.06137	0.02345	-0.00477	0.04830	0.35262	0.01805	-0.01314	0.09067	-0.00899	-0.03415
74	0.10387	0.14349	-0.00601	0.03535	0.48191	-0.04078	-0.03647	0.04982	0.00810	-0.01803
94	0.00000	0.00000	0.00000	-0.00000	-0.00000	-0.00000	-0.00000	0.00000	-0.00000	0.00000
95	-0.00419	0.07000	0.95268	0.02469	-0.00019	0.06794	-0.03510	0.02285	-0.02698	0.00297
97	0.07951	0.10444	0.26291	0.05026	-0.02077	0.25550	-0.00411	-0.07633	0.17121	-0.02420
98	0.00617	0.06526	-0.00771	0.06864	0.04995	0.07339	0.00818	-0.01509	0.00590	0.00130
99	0.01634	0.18644	0.04415	0.02630	0.03936	0.08670	0.01094	-0.00981	0.06964	-0.00434
103	0.42630	0.01657	0.01928	0.17819	0.13468	0.05405	0.03197	0.14611	0.09115	0.00550
104	0.04872	-0.01645	0.05702	0.03582	-0.01276	0.48428	-0.01343	0.11494	-0.05800	-0.02240
108	0.05165	0.00583	-0.01464	0.01452	0.07985	0.14244	0.01337	0.07278	-0.06630	0.03116
109	0.02407	-0.01560	0.03142	-0.03534	0.02562	-0.01270	0.76228	0.03011	0.00414	-0.00614
111	0.00000	0.00000	-0.00000	0.00000	-0.00000	0.00000	0.00000	-0.00000	-0.00000	-0.00000
112	-0.00000	-0.00000	0.00000	-0.00000	0.00000	0.00000	0.00000	-0.00000	0.00000	0.00000
114	0.03458	-0.01013	0.07121	0.01422	-0.00109	0.27447	0.00069	0.04313	0.01713	-0.01286
115	-0.01394	-0.01224	0.00504	0.00273	0.08340	-0.00345	0.00311	-0.02848	0.01812	0.55138
117	-0.05547	0.06008	-0.02840	-0.00425	0.03582	0.31319	-0.00073	0.03803	-0.03274	-0.01474
119	0.01280	-0.01265	0.02237	0.04193	0.01196	-0.01336	0.59531	0.04899	0.01282	-0.01275

Categories	Factor Loadings									
	FACTOR 1	FACTOR 2	FACTOR 3	FACTOR 4	FACTOR 5	FACTOR 6	FACTOR 7	FACTOR 8	FACTOR 9	FACTOR 10
1	0.20051	0.09966	-0.00543	0.36272	-0.01260	-0.04274	-0.02918	0.22443	-0.01658	-0.19421
2	0.02217	0.27856	0.03252	0.22056	-0.01548	0.04763	0.20148	0.01941	-0.05951	-0.08881
3	0.05436	0.39203	0.01837	0.16518	-0.00595	0.03735	0.02513	0.00113	0.24352	0.07358
4	0.05502	0.74939	-0.00782	0.07059	-0.00930	0.00166	0.04071	-0.02429	0.29405	0.01880
5	-0.01533	0.37802	0.01084	-0.01040	-0.00053	-0.01450	-0.01458	0.02675	-0.02089	0.00715
7	0.10051	0.11256	-0.00418	0.07096	0.02642	-0.01320	0.01008	-0.00633	0.63378	-0.03893
8	0.01103	0.66297	0.05338	0.04963	0.00147	0.03304	0.11763	-0.00338	0.05100	-0.03517
9	0.03798	0.07720	0.18842	0.00686	0.00744	-0.02031	0.47771	0.06716	0.08043	-0.03612
11	0.14346	0.08432	0.07916	0.55373	0.02251	0.15997	0.06915	0.23035	0.07344	-0.19796
14	0.58038	0.08514	-0.00483	0.09954	0.00168	-0.01963	0.02617	0.00064	-0.05867	0.11429
15	0.09297	0.03834	0.00390	0.08911	0.00413	-0.04107	-0.02154	-0.02710	-0.05081	0.13819
16	0.78970	0.05044	0.02596	0.02361	0.00409	-0.01459	0.01393	-0.00219	-0.01796	0.05850
17	0.35246	0.08600	0.06093	0.30573	0.02425	-0.02027	0.09314	0.22867	0.03193	0.33799
19	0.02759	0.04388	0.13400	0.08240	0.06794	0.57930	0.09475	0.14250	-0.03442	0.01483
20	0.00407	0.00017	-0.01306	-0.02471	0.16331	0.33353	-0.00803	0.05649	0.02351	0.05555
26	-0.00802	0.00870	0.01353	-0.00263	0.66470	-0.03489	-0.00339	0.02983	-0.02386	-0.03472
46	-0.00468	0.00774	-0.01952	0.01652	0.80703	0.14335	-0.01381	0.05311	0.01995	0.04261
48	0.00630	-0.00508	0.05176	0.02287	-0.00440	0.16359	0.00722	-0.02146	-0.00206	-0.04775
51	0.01209	0.00012	-0.01582	0.16720	0.01588	0.02170	-0.00677	0.02646	0.02368	0.01269
58	0.02569	0.01648	0.35796	0.00620	0.00056	0.05206	0.12468	0.06175	0.00742	0.00868
59	-0.00204	0.04377	0.67161	0.01887	-0.00413	0.03722	0.00970	0.02488	-0.00162	-0.01998
69	0.00710	0.00377	0.67500	0.04719	-0.00042	0.10528	0.08496	-0.06309	-0.00075	0.01099
70	0.01645	-0.00832	0.43083	-0.01791	0.02191	-0.07100	0.08184	0.01246	0.00753	0.02883
74	0.00553	0.02429	0.51719	0.09358	-0.03621	0.27318	-0.06169	0.11932	-0.02659	-0.04581
94	0.27384	0.00264	-0.00690	0.05324	0.00384	0.01248	-0.00926	0.06489	0.05124	0.17353
95	0.03332	-0.00291	0.00709	0.13758	0.41710	0.29745	0.01064	-0.04240	0.04995	0.01188
97	0.57211	-0.00840	-0.00316	0.01696	0.02510	0.06092	0.00214	0.03895	0.06630	-0.16188
98	0.06774	-0.00309	0.00001	0.01069	-0.01107	0.08498	-0.00178	0.11720	-0.00650	-0.04426
99	0.10245	0.34971	-0.00568	0.06757	0.02429	0.01261	-0.00604	0.04560	-0.08810	0.04060
103	0.13188	0.12700	0.05154	0.34289	0.00425	-0.00436	0.12443	0.50660	0.02732	0.15697
104	0.13751	0.14090	0.05505	0.41200	-0.00079	-0.02798	0.08382	0.06989	0.07991	0.09179
108	0.00290	0.02964	0.10011	0.10328	-0.01716	0.05987	0.21913	0.01806	0.01227	0.04065
109	-0.00356	-0.01043	0.04210	0.08224	0.00198	0.01676	0.46850	0.02557	-0.00947	0.07536
111	-0.00184	0.00136	0.08203	0.07300	0.05706	0.08101	0.07899	0.34527	-0.01107	0.01289
112	0.01169	-0.00186	0.04211	0.32303	0.02221	0.03496	0.04663	0.05317	-0.00904	0.03379
114	0.36472	0.04216	0.05500	0.13969	-0.02378	0.09375	0.01719	0.07111	0.10697	-0.02609
115	0.00482	0.03117	-0.01438	-0.00470	0.00289	0.00423	0.36522	0.01563	-0.02611	-0.06103
117	-0.02195	0.02543	0.00679	0.28101	0.01261	0.10317	0.03723	-0.20206	-0.02347	0.05310
119	0.17694	0.09196	0.00205	0.12864	-0.00423	0.20861	0.00818	0.16345	0.00708	0.02702
120	0.12372	0.17592	-0.00254	0.31010	-0.00296	-0.03668	0.08715	-0.07449	-0.01289	0.10655

Table A2.18. Varimax Rotated-Factor Matrix for All Five Sets of Statements

Categories	Factor Loadings									
	FACTOR 1	FACTOR 2	FACTOR 3	FACTOR 4	FACTOR 5	FACTOR 6	FACTOR 7	FACTOR 8	FACTOR 9	FACTOR 10
1	0.02924	0.16723	0.18140	-0.00600	0.24412	0.55171	-0.02686	0.28873	0.13484	0.00005
2	0.04504	0.30341	0.03449	-0.00968	0.08263	0.07261	0.00269	0.11040	0.11495	0.15188
3	0.03955	0.42918	0.02748	0.00822	0.04304	0.08331	0.00918	0.19197	0.11000	0.06165
4	-0.01234	0.72980	0.06352	0.03286	0.01229	0.01079	-0.00816	0.00360	-0.03029	0.00101
5	0.00153	0.33241	-0.02451	-0.02195	-0.01435	0.00689	0.00042	0.04495	0.09971	0.01010
7	0.00161	0.31624	0.09933	0.01672	0.05297	0.03396	0.00456	0.00827	-0.05336	0.01000
8	0.04743	0.54273	0.01526	0.00165	0.00118	-0.00488	0.01130	0.02241	0.00446	0.07493
9	0.15419	0.10531	0.02974	0.00006	0.02464	0.01108	0.00393	0.04836	0.03089	0.51054
11	0.10590	0.12655	0.11030	0.01457	0.77794	0.16757	0.04492	0.31268	0.16421	0.02025
14	0.03756	0.04701	0.46337	0.00956	0.03107	0.08051	-0.00410	0.07910	0.00658	0.02654
15	0.00507	-0.00678	0.28408	0.00339	-0.04213	0.14138	-0.00983	-0.02516	0.02534	0.01792
16	-0.00697	0.01493	0.64474	0.00232	-0.00331	0.08598	-0.01365	0.00435	0.04335	0.04217
17	0.03689	0.11989	0.30925	0.02097	0.15483	0.78112	-0.00173	0.17383	0.06547	0.05151
19	0.09867	0.06711	0.03400	0.11731	0.58430	0.20405	0.09279	0.20390	0.20182	0.05920
20	0.07823	-0.00187	0.03131	0.79376	0.04924	0.02406	0.01891	0.06146	0.18019	-0.00646
26	0.05810	0.00674	0.02425	0.77139	0.01417	0.01052	0.07874	0.01004	0.17792	0.01089
46	-0.00479	0.00661	0.01288	0.06424	0.01257	0.00281	0.75500	0.03401	0.05464	-0.00131
48	0.03648	-0.00499	0.00716	0.04717	0.03202	-0.01199	0.05098	-0.02693	0.09634	0.03566
51	-0.00036	0.01979	0.01290	0.01540	0.05128	0.08390	-0.00342	0.06593	0.14960	-0.03190
58	0.33603	0.02053	0.02691	0.03611	0.09297	0.01649	0.01019	0.02319	0.00729	0.18613
59	0.69482	0.02826	0.03522	0.00524	0.01402	0.01267	-0.00561	0.01364	0.02493	0.05307
69	0.57054	0.00941	0.01705	0.00074	-0.00741	-0.00115	0.01463	0.00087	0.05124	0.02593
70	0.40033	0.02465	0.01137	0.00088	0.00389	0.00338	-0.00229	0.05580	-0.02305	0.05244
74	0.57573	0.01313	0.01263	0.08365	0.04923	0.01926	0.00601	0.06620	0.05823	-0.05591
94	-0.00654	0.00827	0.17439	-0.00075	-0.01185	0.01836	0.01533	0.06803	-0.02458	-0.01417
95	0.01485	0.01159	0.04394	0.04071	0.05024	-0.01148	0.67437	0.03593	-0.00221	-0.00117
97	0.02216	0.01544	0.45704	0.06496	0.02792	-0.02610	0.06127	0.00063	0.14147	-0.00615
98	-0.00101	0.00666	0.04194	0.05495	0.05066	0.03505	-0.02310	0.04321	0.31505	0.01771
99	0.02869	0.13700	0.06196	0.14268	-0.02170	-0.00581	0.03483	0.03390	0.43206	-0.01540
103	0.05645	0.16859	0.13030	-0.02223	0.11402	0.22718	-0.01439	0.46410	0.09580	0.05769
104	0.03682	0.13705	0.21229	-0.01846	0.10878	0.02210	-0.00636	0.33284	0.01319	-0.00547
108	0.10229	0.07812	0.03802	0.01762	0.11455	-0.02641	-0.00006	0.20335	-0.03667	0.11588
109	0.02413	0.00363	-0.01165	-0.00882	-0.03255	0.03534	-0.00296	0.25878	0.00289	0.35531
111	0.02045	-0.01131	-0.00964	0.02938	0.01029	0.02253	0.01795	0.33084	0.00825	0.13025
112	0.01940	0.02389	0.06865	0.00785	0.03821	0.04858	0.01647	0.26227	0.05322	-0.00262
114	0.03572	0.05002	0.29691	-0.00415	0.09753	-0.04004	0.00304	0.11787	0.00666	-0.00597
115	0.01199	0.04297	0.00280	-0.00178	0.01153	-0.00456	-0.00133	0.00795	-0.00420	0.24653
117	0.00285	0.01820	0.04178	0.14808	0.05729	-0.01908	0.09562	0.17110	0.06895	-0.02170
119	0.04363	0.07577	0.18867	0.00356	0.05944	-0.02097	0.01798	0.12803	0.14419	0.01421

Table A2.19. Factor Scores: The 1973 Helsinki Statements

COUNTRY	FACTOR 1	FACTOR 2	FACTOR 3	FACTOR 4	FACTOR 5	FACTOR 6	FACTOR 7	FACTOR 8	FACTOR 9	FACTOR 10
AUST	48.89	2.22	5.56	1.11	4.44	15.56	8.89	3.33	10.00	0.0
BLGM	29.00	6.00	13.00	5.00	5.00	17.00	4.00	15.00	6.00	0.0
BLGR	52.56	8.97	12.82	0.0	7.69	6.41	0.0	8.97	1.28	1.28
CNDA	36.67	3.33	15.00	3.33	11.67	16.67	0.0	5.00	8.33	0.0
CYPR	45.28	19.81	.94	1.89	5.66	10.38	0.0	5.66	10.38	0.0
CZCH	60.98	4.88	4.88	4.88	7.32	4.88	0.0	10.98	1.22	0.0
DNMK	23.29	9.59	20.55	0.0	9.59	20.55	4.11	6.85	5.48	0.0
FNLD	62.24	8.16	4.08	2.04	2.04	12.24	0.0	5.10	4.08	0.0
FRNC	56.72	10.45	2.99	0.0	7.46	13.43	0.0	7.46	1.49	0.0
FRG	46.43	8.93	8.04	.89	13.39	11.61	.89	5.36	4.46	0.0
GDR	46.28	14.88	2.48	.83	19.01	7.44	0.0	2.48	6.61	0.0
GRCE	62.64	5.49	4.40	4.40	2.20	9.89	0.0	3.30	7.69	0.0
HNGR	52.94	0.0	4.71	0.0	12.94	9.41	0.0	18.82	1.18	0.0
ICLD	40.00	0.0	11.11	0.0	4.44	33.33	0.0	6.67	4.44	0.0
IRLD	49.68	5.16	5.16	4.52	7.74	12.26	.65	3.23	11.61	0.0
ITLY	50.00	8.33	9.72	0.0	11.11	16.67	1.39	0.0	2.78	0.0
LICH	54.17	20.83	8.33	0.0	0.0	8.33	0.0	8.33	0.0	0.0
LXBG	35.48	12.90	9.68	0.0	12.90	17.20	3.23	5.38	3.23	0.0
MLTA	65.57	8.20	3.28	0.0	3.28	11.48	0.0	8.20	0.0	0.0
MNCO	69.23	0.0	0.0	0.0	15.38	7.69	0.0	0.0	7.69	0.0
NTHL	38.16	6.58	3.95	3.95	9.21	14.47	2.63	3.95	17.11	0.0
NRWY	42.86	5.95	8.33	3.57	11.90	15.48	2.38	2.38	2.38	4.76
PLND	44.60	7.91	8.63	1.44	15.83	12.95	0.0	7.19	1.44	0.0
PRTG	53.06	7.14	9.18	0.0	10.20	11.22	0.0	3.06	6.12	0.0
RMNA	51.92	8.97	3.21	3.21	6.41	17.95	0.0	2.56	5.77	0.0
SANM	61.11	13.33	1.11	0.0	1.11	7.78	6.67	0.0	8.89	0.0
SPAN	57.01	.93	9.35	.93	1.87	14.02	0.0	5.61	5.61	4.67
SWDN	36.72	5.47	8.59	7.03	9.38	18.75	0.0	4.69	9.38	0.0
SWTZ	53.66	21.95	7.32	0.0	7.32	4.88	0.0	0.0	4.88	0.0
TRKY	44.35	6.09	.87	4.35	4.35	8.70	0.0	7.83	15.65	7.83
USSR	55.78	7.04	4.02	0.0	12.06	11.06	1.01	2.51	6.53	0.0
UK	43.33	0.0	11.67	0.0	8.33	26.67	0.0	6.67	3.33	0.0
USA	35.79	13.68	18.95	0.0	7.37	14.74	5.26	0.0	4.21	0.0
VATC	66.67	9.68	2.15	1.08	4.30	6.45	3.23	1.08	5.38	0.0
YGSL	57.89	7.02	2.63	2.63	6.14	6.14	.88	5.26	10.53	.88
MEAN	49.4560	7.9971	7.0477	1.6304	7.9731	12.9619	1.2915	5.2257	5.8617	.5549

Table A2.20. Factor Scores: The 1975 Helsinki Statements

COUNTRY	FACTOR 1	FACTOR 2	FACTOR 3	FACTOR 4	FACTOR 5	FACTOR 6	FACTOR 7	FACTOR 8	FACTOR 9	FACTOR 10
AUST	7.69	2.56	56.41	0.0	0.0	0.0	0.0	28.21	0.0	5.13
BLGM	19.35	6.45	23.39	25.00	0.0	19.35	0.0	4.84	1.61	0.0
BLGR	9.09	3.64	47.27	23.64	0.0	10.91	0.0	3.64	0.0	1.82
CNDA	6.25	1.56	21.88	20.31	0.0	15.63	1.56	25.00	0.0	7.81
CYPR	43.00	3.00	21.00	26.00	0.0	2.00	0.0	5.00	0.0	0.0
CZCH	14.46	3.61	46.99	18.07	1.20	3.61	0.0	7.23	0.0	4.82
DNMK	1.64	27.87	22.95	22.95	0.0	0.0	0.0	18.03	6.56	0.0
FNLD	20.00	3.20	39.20	28.00	0.0	2.40	1.60	5.60	0.0	0.0
FRNC	3.03	12.12	36.36	33.33	0.0	3.03	0.0	0.0	0.0	12.12
FRG	12.82	5.13	28.21	3.85	0.0	10.26	0.0	33.33	5.13	1.28
GDR	19.67	1.64	34.43	32.79	0.0	4.92	0.0	6.56	0.0	0.0
GRCE	61.54	0.0	18.46	9.23	0.0	3.08	0.0	3.08	4.62	0.0
HNGR	20.00	15.00	31.25	12.50	0.0	12.50	0.0	8.75	0.0	0.0
ICLD	14.29	37.50	12.50	14.29	0.0	8.93	0.0	10.71	1.79	0.0
IRLD	27.63	14.47	48.68	5.26	0.0	0.0	0.0	3.95	0.0	0.0
ITLY	20.99	13.58	43.21	12.35	0.0	0.0	1.23	6.17	0.0	2.47
LICH	18.75	12.50	50.00	6.25	0.0	0.0	0.0	12.50	0.0	0.0
LXBG	25.00	7.29	29.17	19.79	0.0	3.13	6.25	0.0	6.25	3.13
MLTA	7.55	5.66	28.30	26.42	0.0	5.66	1.89	11.32	9.43	3.77
MNCO	0.0	5.56	55.56	22.22	0.0	0.0	0.0	16.67	0.0	0.0
NTHL	14.29	9.89	39.56	8.79	0.0	12.09	2.20	6.59	3.30	3.30
NRWY	15.79	3.29	34.21	20.39	0.0	11.84	0.0	7.24	3.29	3.95
PLND	16.67	3.57	67.86	8.33	0.0	1.19	0.0	2.38	0.0	0.0
PRTG	20.75	3.77	37.74	24.53	0.0	0.0	1.89	5.66	5.66	0.0
RMNA	16.80	2.87	36.48	19.67	0.0	9.02	8.61	3.28	2.05	1.23
SANM	17.24	1.15	64.37	4.60	0.0	2.30	10.34	0.0	0.0	0.0
SPAN	27.73	3.36	18.49	27.73	0.0	13.45	0.0	2.52	6.72	0.0
SWDN	10.17	5.93	37.29	20.34	0.0	11.86	0.0	8.47	1.69	4.24
SWTZ	37.36	18.68	18.68	13.19	1.10	3.30	1.10	6.59	0.0	0.0
TRKY	40.69	.69	24.83	21.38	0.0	1.38	2.76	6.90	1.38	0.0
USSR	14.75	4.92	47.54	16.39	0.0	9.84	0.0	4.92	1.64	0.0
UK	18.94	3.79	25.00	6.06	0.0	18.18	.76	21.97	5.30	0.0
USA	18.18	2.27	24.24	6.06	1.52	15.91	14.39	13.64	0.0	3.79
VATC	15.79	1.05	57.89	17.89	0.0	2.11	1.05	4.21	0.0	0.0
YGSL	24.07	0.0	33.95	19.75	0.0	7.41	1.85	8.64	2.47	1.85
MEAN	18.9138	7.0739	36.0951	17.0674	.1091	6.4360	1.6424	8.9598	1.9682	1.7343

Table A2.21. Factor Scores: The Belgrade Opening Statements

COUNTRY	FACTOR 1	FACTOR 2	FACTOR 3	FACTOR 4	FACTOR 5	FACTOR 6	FACTOR 7	FACTOR 8	FACTOR 9	FACTOR 10
AUST	21.55	3.45	11.21	11.21	31.90	12.07	1.72	.86	2.59	3.45
BLGM	18.03	4.92	12.30	22.95	13.93	0.0	0.0	0.0	22.13	5.74
BLGR	27.66	1.06	23.40	4.26	34.57	1.06	3.72	2.66	.53	1.06
CNDA	19.44	12.04	12.96	14.81	26.85	0.0	0.0	.93	0.0	12.96
CYPR	27.17	4.35	26.09	5.43	11.96	0.0	5.43	2.17	13.04	4.35
CZCH	7.60	11.11	9.94	11.70	53.22	0.0	0.0	1.75	4.68	0.0
DNMK	24.46	9.35	0.0	16.55	20.86	0.0	0.0	0.0	12.23	16.55
FNLD	41.51	4.72	21.23	3.77	15.57	0.0	.47	6.60	3.77	2.36
FRNC	31.75	12.70	9.52	12.70	14.29	0.0	0.0	4.76	1.59	12.70
FRG	11.51	7.91	10.07	20.14	27.34	1.44	2.16	2.88	6.47	10.07
GDR	18.69	1.52	11.11	13.64	43.43	0.0	0.0	10.61	1.01	0.0
GRCE	37.25	7.84	23.53	11.76	19.61	0.0	0.0	0.0	0.0	0.0
HNGR	24.46	14.13	25.00	2.72	27.17	0.0	0.0	1.63	1.09	3.80
ICLD	14.06	15.63	9.38	17.19	10.94	0.0	6.25	3.13	12.50	10.94
IRLD	21.74	8.07	3.11	10.56	39.13	0.0	0.0	.62	3.11	13.66
ITLY	37.07	3.45	25.00	6.03	18.10	0.0	0.0	.86	6.03	3.45
LICH	39.13	0.0	17.39	4.35	13.04	0.0	0.0	8.70	0.0	17.39
LXBG	23.20	7.20	7.20	8.80	24.00	0.0	.80	0.0	17.60	11.20
MLTA	11.35	3.55	12.77	4.96	27.66	0.0	0.0	2.84	34.04	2.84
MNCO	23.53	0.0	47.06	11.76	17.65	0.0	0.0	0.0	0.0	0.0
NTHL	31.18	3.23	11.83	18.82	15.05	0.0	1.08	.54	5.91	12.37
NRWY	13.08	16.82	11.21	9.35	24.30	0.0	0.0	.93	1.40	22.90
PLND	24.16	3.37	36.52	6.18	12.36	0.0	1.12	3.37	1.69	11.24
PRTG	22.58	1.38	15.21	4.15	14.29	0.0	0.0	.46	34.56	7.37
RMNA	19.62	10.08	27.52	3.27	25.89	0.0	6.27	4.09	3.00	.27
SANM	14.58	0.0	18.75	2.08	8.33	0.0	16.67	19.79	0.0	19.79
SPAN	10.48	2.86	25.71	.95	20.95	0.0	0.0	5.71	4.76	28.57
SWDN	23.51	3.98	11.55	5.58	35.46	0.0	0.0	3.19	1.59	15.14
SWTZ	36.48	9.43	11.32	3.77	11.95	0.0	4.40	10.06	2.52	10.06
TRKY	28.87	16.20	9.86	2.82	19.72	13.38	0.0	.70	7.75	.70
USSR	26.60	5.32	20.21	5.32	24.47	9.57	.53	2.66	3.72	1.60
UK	21.43	10.71	9.52	7.14	20.24	7.14	0.0	1.19	19.05	3.57
USA	15.33	.67	12.67	6.67	23.33	0.0	0.0	1.33	4.00	36.00
VATC	10.87	0.0	11.59	10.87	11.59	0.0	2.90	1.45	1.45	49.28
YGSL	14.32	8.83	11.46	9.31	33.41	1.67	.72	7.40	6.44	6.44
MEAN	22.6930	6.4536	16.0913	8.9019	22.6447	1.3240	1.5498	3.2537	6.8646	10.2234

Table A2.22. Factor Scores: The Belgrade Closing Statements

COUNTRY	FACTOR 1	FACTOR 2	FACTOR 3	FACTOR 4	FACTOR 5	FACTOR 6	FACTOR 7	FACTOR 8	FACTOR 9	FACTOR 10
AUST	26.32	0.0	1.75	21.05	33.33	17.54	0.0	0.0	0.0	0.0
BLGM	3.85	28.85	0.0	7.69	32.69	25.00	0.0	1.92	0.0	0.0
BLGR	11.11	2.22	13.33	28.89	11.11	32.22	0.0	1.11	0.0	0.0
CNDA	13.08	1.87	.93	11.21	52.34	14.02	0.0	.93	5.61	0.0
CYPR	4.88	0.0	2.44	48.78	9.76	19.51	4.88	9.76	0.0	0.0
CZCH	19.30	17.54	1.75	3.51	21.05	33.33	0.0	3.51	0.0	0.0
DNMK	3.70	7.41	0.0	3.70	50.00	31.48	0.0	3.70	0.0	0.0
FNLD	10.96	9.59	1.37	13.70	28.77	35.62	0.0	0.0	0.0	0.0
FRNC	19.67	0.0	0.0	4.92	31.15	42.62	0.0	0.0	1.64	0.0
FRG	9.09	10.39	0.0	20.78	33.77	22.08	0.0	3.90	0.0	0.0
GDR	34.51	4.23	10.56	4.23	11.97	26.06	0.0	8.45	0.0	0.0
GRCE	11.76	0.0	0.0	58.82	5.88	17.65	0.0	5.88	0.0	0.0
HNGR	22.92	3.13	9.38	22.92	12.50	20.83	0.0	8.33	0.0	0.0
ICLD	12.50	0.0	0.0	50.00	12.50	25.00	0.0	0.0	0.0	0.0
IRLD	8.70	0.0	0.0	26.09	41.30	17.39	0.0	2.17	4.35	0.0
ITLY	8.62	10.34	0.0	27.59	39.66	10.34	0.0	3.45	0.0	0.0
LICH	0.0	0.0	0.0	50.00	50.00	0.0	0.0	0.0	0.0	0.0
LXBG	0.0	2.78	11.11	5.56	38.89	36.11	0.0	5.56	0.0	0.0
MLTA	45.45	0.0	0.0	36.36	9.09	9.09	0.0	0.0	0.0	0.0
MNCO	28.57	28.57	0.0	28.57	14.29	0.0	0.0	0.0	0.0	0.0
NTHL	0.0	0.0	0.0	0.0	88.24	11.76	0.0	0.0	0.0	0.0
NRWY	7.14	3.57	0.0	17.86	39.29	32.14	0.0	0.0	0.0	0.0
PLND	26.15	6.88	4.59	20.18	14.22	27.06	0.0	.92	0.0	0.0
PRTG	31.25	12.50	0.0	37.50	6.25	12.50	0.0	0.0	0.0	0.0
RMNA	28.79	9.09	0.0	27.27	3.03	31.82	0.0	0.0	0.0	0.0
SANM	26.67	0.0	9.33	13.33	29.33	14.67	0.0	6.67	0.0	0.0
SPAN	17.57	0.0	9.46	21.62	29.73	20.27	0.0	0.0	0.0	1.35
SWDN	8.16	2.04	0.0	28.57	26.53	24.49	2.04	6.12	2.04	0.0
SWTZ	22.50	10.00	0.0	10.00	37.50	12.50	0.0	7.50	0.0	0.0
TRKY	11.36	0.0	11.36	40.91	6.82	9.09	0.0	13.64	6.82	0.0
USSR	27.92	0.0	9.74	10.39	10.39	37.01	0.0	1.95	2.60	0.0
UK	4.12	2.06	4.12	8.25	43.30	32.99	0.0	5.15	0.0	0.0
USA	10.38	6.60	.94	6.60	45.28	5.66	9.43	4.72	4.72	5.66
VATC	13.16	2.63	5.26	15.79	28.95	13.16	0.0	10.53	0.0	10.53
YGSL	19.05	7.94	1.59	25.40	4.76	39.68	0.0	1.59	0.0	0.0
MEAN	15.6916	5.4351	3.1153	21.6584	27.2473	21.7347	.4672	3.3558	.7934	.5011

Table A2.23. Factor Scores: The Madrid Opening Statements

COUNTRY	FACTOR 1	FACTOR 2	FACTOR 3	FACTOR 4	FACTOR 5	FACTOR 6	FACTOR 7	FACTOR 8	FACTOR 9	FACTOR 10
AUST	31.25	3.75	11.25	28.75	0.0	6.25	13.75	5.00	0.0	0.0
BLGM	14.49	10.14	28.99	26.09	0.0	4.35	11.59	2.90	0.0	1.45
BLGR	34.12	8.24	10.59	22.35	0.0	5.88	2.35	16.47	0.0	0.0
CNDA	20.00	16.00	8.00	20.80	0.0	4.80	28.00	1.60	.80	0.0
CYPR	22.73	12.12	1.52	33.33	0.0	6.06	10.61	12.12	1.52	0.0
CZCH	30.68	3.41	0.0	29.55	0.0	10.23	2.27	19.32	4.55	0.0
DNMK	34.62	6.41	23.08	20.51	1.28	3.85	10.26	0.0	0.0	0.0
FNLD	45.71	5.71	14.29	14.29	0.0	5.71	7.14	2.86	4.29	0.0
FRNC	25.49	15.69	11.76	19.61	0.0	5.88	15.69	3.92	1.96	0.0
FRG	20.30	6.09	11.68	37.56	0.0	5.58	9.14	9.64	0.0	0.0
GDR	36.29	8.87	7.26	23.39	0.0	8.87	.81	14.52	0.0	0.0
GRCE	24.36	14.10	10.26	12.82	6.41	15.38	2.56	12.82	1.28	0.0
HNGR	33.81	2.88	4.32	33.81	.72	7.91	7.19	7.19	2.16	0.0
ICLD	28.57	9.52	30.95	16.67	0.0	4.76	4.76	4.76	0.0	0.0
IRLD	31.76	10.59	9.41	17.65	0.0	12.94	11.76	5.88	0.0	0.0
ITLY	22.55	12.75	4.90	37.25	0.0	10.78	8.82	1.96	0.0	.98
LICH	31.25	12.50	6.25	31.25	0.0	6.25	6.25	6.25	0.0	0.0
LXBG	31.25	7.81	17.19	10.94	0.0	14.06	10.94	7.81	0.0	0.0
MLTA	21.82	0.0	0.0	43.64	0.0	3.64	0.0	30.91	0.0	0.0
MNCO	14.29	0.0	0.0	28.57	0.0	28.57	14.29	14.29	0.0	0.0
NTHL	20.59	7.84	6.86	13.73	0.0	2.94	44.12	3.92	0.0	0.0
NRWY	46.85	10.49	2.10	18.88	0.0	6.29	10.49	1.40	2.80	.70
PLND	45.38	6.92	4.62	31.54	0.0	6.92	0.0	3.85	.77	0.0
PRTG	12.90	32.26	6.45	16.13	0.0	0.0	32.26	0.0	0.0	0.0
RMNA	28.68	8.91	7.36	31.40	3.10	3.88	4.26	10.47	1.94	0.0
SANM	6.52	21.74	0.0	34.78	0.0	2.17	10.87	23.91	0.0	0.0
SPAN	30.51	7.34	1.69	29.38	0.0	6.78	10.73	12.99	.56	0.0
SWDN	63.87	3.87	1.94	5.16	0.0	4.52	17.42	2.58	.65	0.0
SWTZ	34.82	16.07	8.93	19.64	0.0	0.0	3.57	6.25	10.71	0.0
TRKY	38.98	10.17	6.78	33.90	0.0	5.08	3.39	1.69	0.0	0.0
USSR	35.85	7.55	3.77	14.15	2.83	15.09	2.83	17.92	0.0	0.0
UK	15.45	9.76	21.95	13.01	0.0	4.07	29.27	4.07	2.44	0.0
USA	22.39	9.70	5.22	8.21	0.0	5.22	44.03	5.22	0.0	0.0
VATC	14.29	8.16	6.12	23.47	0.0	1.02	34.69	8.16	3.06	1.02
YGSL	21.64	17.16	1.49	38.06	0.0	1.49	12.69	7.46	0.0	0.0
MEAN	28.4021	9.8440	8.4849	24.0072	.4098	6.7787	12.5374	8.2894	1.1279	.1186

Table A2.24. Factor Scores for All Five Sets of Statements

COUNTRY	FACTOR 1	FACTOR 2	FACTOR 3	FACTOR 4	FACTOR 5	FACTOR 6	FACTOR 7	FACTOR 8	FACTOR 9	FACTOR 10
AUST	9.82	7.05	21.41	.76	15.37	11.84	5.04	19.14	2.52	7.05
BLGM	16.03	10.90	17.95	4.27	13.68	11.54	0.0	9.62	8.33	7.69
BLGR	6.76	7.95	27.24	1.59	22.27	14.31	1.19	15.31	1.39	1.99
CNDA	14.16	8.25	19.87	3.81	10.99	11.63	1.69	16.07	.42	13.11
CYPR	2.61	23.04	12.59	1.19	15.91	15.20	.48	14.49	11.16	3.33
CZCH	5.76	7.00	27.78	6.58	14.61	12.76	.82	19.14	2.67	2.88
DNMK	22.38	9.79	23.08	3.96	8.86	6.29	1.17	6.99	8.39	9.09
FNLD	8.35	10.39	17.38	2.56	23.85	18.57	.34	12.27	4.60	1.70
FRNC	11.87	7.55	11.87	3.60	10.79	17.99	0.0	25.54	2.52	8.27
FRG	13.49	7.94	21.27	3.81	16.35	5.40	.95	20.95	3.02	6.83
GDR	7.20	13.17	30.93	1.68	11.03	15.93	1.68	14.70	1.99	1.68
GRCE	6.35	21.27	13.02	3.17	19.68	12.38	4.44	14.29	4.44	.95
HNGR	5.47	9.29	23.71	7.13	17.41	14.43	1.16	16.09	1.99	3.32
ICLD	23.15	9.26	18.06	7.87	13.43	8.80	0.0	8.33	6.02	5.09
IRLD	8.80	10.11	22.10	3.75	14.98	6.74	.19	15.92	7.49	9.93
ITLY	8.82	8.60	11.76	2.04	21.27	14.25	0.0	11.76	12.90	8.60
LICH	11.49	13.79	8.05	0.0	29.89	8.05	0.0	21.84	0.0	6.90
LXBG	10.36	10.59	21.85	2.70	9.23	10.59	0.0	12.39	13.29	9.01
MLTA	3.72	3.41	17.03	2.17	12.69	13.31	0.0	21.98	23.84	1.86
MNCO	6.35	0.0	7.94	3.17	12.70	20.63	0.0	38.10	9.52	1.59
NTHL	13.71	11.60	15.40	1.90	14.35	9.28	.21	14.14	4.43	14.98
NRWY	6.64	6.32	28.44	6.32	15.01	11.85	0.0	10.27	1.42	13.74
PLND	7.23	9.99	22.08	1.71	17.87	16.43	.53	18.00	2.50	3.68
PRTG	6.08	10.85	11.38	.79	20.63	16.14	0.0	15.61	11.38	7.14
RMNA	4.15	11.91	23.56	3.52	17.69	18.41	1.08	16.06	1.99	1.62
SANM	2.52	21.66	8.56	0.0	13.35	8.06	0.0	27.20	1.26	17.38
SPAN	5.48	9.93	20.38	1.37	15.92	17.29	.34	14.73	5.14	9.42
SWDN	5.42	6.81	32.22	1.94	15.00	11.94	.97	13.61	2.50	9.58
SWTZ	9.17	22.37	13.65	5.59	10.96	12.53	0.0	17.00	1.34	7.38
TRKY	2.41	17.07	13.86	3.61	19.28	11.45	4.62	18.07	5.62	4.02
USSR	4.38	9.45	27.26	1.78	12.74	12.74	5.75	22.19	1.37	2.33
UK	10.60	7.60	22.40	4.00	8.40	8.00	1.20	14.80	8.80	14.20
USA	7.22	8.83	19.74	1.77	7.06	8.03	.16	16.53	1.28	29.37
VATC	5.56	10.04	9.19	0.0	11.54	10.04	0.0	25.21	1.50	26.92
YGSL	5.37	13.42	22.26	4.25	13.87	14.43	.78	15.44	4.59	5.59
MEAN	8.5396	10.7769	19.0066	2.9819	15.1044	12.4927	.9944	16.9649	5.1891	7.9494

Attention Distribution on Master Dimensions

See tables A2.25 through A2.29, on the following pages.

Table A2.25. The 1973 Helsinki Statements: Percentage Distribution of Attention on Dimensions of East–West Relations

COUNTRY GROUP	COUNTRY	DISARMAMENT AND SECURITY	PEACE AND CONFLICT	ECONOMIC COOPERATION	HUMAN RIGHTS AND CONTACTS	SOVEREIGNTY AND INDEPENDENCE
NATO						
	BLGM	26.73	21.78	21.78	18.81	10.89
	CNDA	36.67	20.00	16.67	15.00	11.67
	DNMK	31.08	10.81	17.57	25.68	14.86
	FRNC	37.31	31.34	13.43	7.46	10.45
	FRG	24.58	23.73	25.42	14.41	11.86
	GRCE	24.73	35.48	22.58	6.45	10.75
	ICLD	46.67	22.22	15.56	13.33	2.22
	ITLY	40.28	20.83	15.28	13.89	9.72
	LXBG	37.63	23.66	11.83	12.90	13.98
	NTHL	38.46	25.64	8.97	10.26	16.67
	NRWY	40.48	16.67	23.81	10.71	8.33
	PRTG	33.67	27.55	16.33	9.18	13.27
	TRKY	26.42	33.02	20.75	.94	18.87
	UK	50.00	25.00	11.67	11.67	1.67
	USA	30.53	24.21	3.16	24.21	17.89
MEAN		35.0155	24.1299	16.3203	12.9939	11.5403
WTO						
	BLGR	32.91	21.52	22.78	13.92	8.86
	CZCH	21.69	31.33	34.94	6.02	6.02
	GDR	35.54	28.93	17.36	2.48	15.70
	HNGR	32.94	25.88	35.29	4.71	1.18
	PLND	41.01	20.14	20.86	9.35	8.63
	RMNA	35.03	31.21	17.20	3.82	12.74
	USSR	32.66	36.68	13.07	5.03	12.56

N+N						
	AUST	30.00	31.11	14.44	14.44	10.00
	CYPR	28.30	29.25	16.04	.94	25.47
	FNLD	32.00	30.00	22.00	6.00	10.00
	IRLD	29.49	39.74	12.82	7.05	10.90
	LICH	20.83	20.83	25.00	12.50	20.83
	MLTA	36.07	29.51	22.95	3.28	8.20
	SANM	10.00	42.22	11.11	14.44	22.22
	SWDN	32.03	25.78	24.22	8.59	9.38
	SWTZ	29.27	26.83	9.76	7.32	26.83
	YGSL	34.21	28.95	15.79	7.89	13.16
MEAN		28.2198	30.4221	17.4129	8.2468	15.6984
OTHER						
	MNCO	46.15	46.15	7.69	0.0	0.0
	SPAN	29.52	32.38	24.76	9.52	3.81
	VATC	30.11	38.71	10.75	5.38	15.05
MEAN		35.2617	39.0815	14.4023	4.9667	6.2878
MEAN		32.7141	27.9744	17.8183	9.6460	11.8472

Table A2.26. The 1975 Helsinki Statements: Percentage Distribution of Attention on Dimensions of East–West Relations

COUNTRY GROUP	COUNTRY	DISARMAMENT AND SECURITY	PEACE AND CONFLICT	ECONOMIC COOPERATION	HUMAN RIGHTS AND CONTACTS	SOVEREIGNTY AND INDEPENDENCE
NATO						
	BLGM	46.77	12.10	15.32	9.68	16.13
	CNDA	42.19	28.13	21.88	3.13	4.69
	DNMK	42.62	8.20	19.67	27.87	1.64
	FRNC	36.36	39.39	9.09	12.12	3.03
	FRG	41.03	21.79	19.23	5.13	12.82
	GRCE	15.38	15.38	12.31	0.0	56.92
	ICLD	25.00	5.36	23.21	37.50	8.93
	ITLY	9.88	38.27	16.05	24.69	11.11
	LXBG	29.17	22.92	11.46	17.71	18.75
	NTHL	24.18	24.18	27.47	15.38	8.79
	NRWY	39.47	16.45	25.00	15.13	3.95
	PRTG	24.53	22.64	28.30	5.66	18.87
	TRKY	20.69	20.00	17.93	12.41	28.97
	UK	43.18	33.33	8.33	4.55	10.61
	USA	29.55	35.61	7.58	15.15	12.12
MEAN		31.3331	22.9161	17.5224	13.7405	14.4879
WTO						
	BLGR	34.55	21.82	34.55	3.64	5.45
	CZCH	22.89	33.73	26.51	3.61	13.25
	GDR	40.98	29.51	9.84	1.64	18.03
	HNGR	25.00	25.00	17.50	15.00	17.50
	PLND	10.71	40.48	28.57	3.57	16.67
	RMNA	30.33	27.46	20.49	6.56	15.16
	USSR	27.87	31.15	21.31	4.92	14.75
MEAN		27.4759	29.8777	22.6803	5.5624	14.4036

N+N						
	AUST	7.69	38.46	43.59	2.56	7.69
	CYPR	28.00	23.00	9.00	6.00	34.00
	FNLD	30.40	24.80	24.80	3.20	16.80
	IRLD	7.89	35.53	26.32	21.05	9.21
	LICH	6.25	37.50	25.00	12.50	18.75
	MLTA	33.96	37.74	18.87	7.55	1.89
	SANM	4.60	43.68	22.99	21.84	6.90
	SWDN	34.75	30.51	19.49	7.63	7.63
	SWTZ	16.48	13.19	13.19	26.37	30.77
	YGSL	29.63	25.93	19.75	1.23	23.46
MEAN		19.9656	31.0323	22.2993	10.9938	15.7089
OTHER						
	MNCO	22.22	72.22	0.0	5.56	0.0
	SPAN	42.86	11.76	15.13	3.36	26.89
	VATC	16.00	46.00	17.00	14.00	7.00
MEAN		27.0264	43.3290	10.7087	7.6390	11.2969
MEAN		26.9447	28.3770	19.3348	10.7971	14.5464

Table A2.27. The Belgrade Opening Statements: Percentage Distribution of Attention on Dimensions of East–West Relations

COUNTRY GROUP	COUNTRY	DISARMAMENT AND SECURITY	PEACE AND CONFLICT	ECONOMIC COOPERATION	HUMAN RIGHTS AND CONTACTS	SOVEREIGNTY AND INDEPENDENCE
NATO						
	BLGM	24.59	26.23	14.75	28.69	5.74
	CNDA	35.19	14.81	15.74	27.78	6.48
	DNMK	17.99	21.58	11.51	33.09	15.83
	FRNC	12.70	25.40	30.16	25.40	6.35
	FRG	26.62	21.58	16.55	30.22	5.04
	GRCE	43.14	0.0	37.25	11.76	7.84
	ICLD	12.50	20.31	23.44	28.13	15.63
	ITLY	25.86	25.00	33.62	9.48	6.03
	LXBG	27.20	28.00	18.40	20.00	6.40
	NTHL	22.58	13.98	20.97	29.57	12.90
	NRWY	31.78	6.54	28.04	32.24	1.40
	PRTG	27.68	31.64	22.60	14.12	3.95
	TRKY	23.24	25.35	42.25	2.82	6.34
	UK	21.43	30.95	35.71	10.71	1.19
	USA	26.67	18.67	12.67	39.33	2.67
MEAN		25.2768	20.6699	24.2442	22.8898	6.9193
WTO						
	BLGR	46.28	14.89	22.34	5.32	11.17
	CZCH	58.48	9.36	18.13	11.70	2.34
	GDR	47.98	7.58	14.65	13.64	16.16
	HNGR	38.04	17.39	29.35	6.52	8.70
	PLND	35.96	16.29	14.04	16.85	16.85
	RMNA	50.68	10.08	23.43	3.27	12.53
	USSR	31.91	17.02	32.45	6.91	11.70

N+N						
	AUST	37.93	16.38	24.14	14.66	6.90
	CYPR	30.43	26.09	14.13	8.70	20.65
	FNLD	31.60	12.74	38.68	6.13	10.85
	IRLD	36.65	11.18	20.50	22.98	8.70
	LICH	8.70	21.74	39.13	21.74	8.70
	MLTA	28.37	48.94	11.35	7.80	3.55
	SANM	22.92	5.21	5.21	21.87	44.79
	SWDN	41.83	11.55	20.72	20.32	5.58
	SWTZ	18.24	22.01	30.19	11.95	17.61
	YGSL	43.34	10.41	20.82	15.98	9.44
MEAN		30.0010	18.6244	22.4860	15.2129	13.6758
OTHER						
	MNCO	17.65	47.06	23.53	11.76	0.0
	SPAN	40.20	10.78	11.76	30.39	6.86
	VATC	14.49	13.77	7.25	57.97	6.52
MEAN		24.1120	23.8704	14.1802	33.3759	4.4615
MEAN		30.3094	18.8719	22.4415	18.8519	9.5254

Table A2.28. The Belgrade Closing Statements: Percentage Distribution of Attention on Dimensions of East–West Relations

COUNTRY GROUP	COUNTRY	DISARMAMENT AND SECURITY	PEACE AND CONFLICT	ECONOMIC COOPERATION	HUMAN RIGHTS AND CONTACTS	SOVEREIGNTY AND INDEPENDENCE
NATO						
	BLGM	19.23	1.92	34.62	32.69	11.54
	CNDA	28.97	4.67	13.08	52.34	.93
	DNMK	26.09	21.74	8.70	39.13	4.35
	FRNC	35.48	29.03	4.84	30.65	0.0
	FRG	7.50	21.25	30.00	32.50	8.75
	GRCE	11.11	5.56	55.56	5.56	22.22
	ICLD	25.00	12.50	50.00	12.50	0.0
	ITLY	16.42	19.40	26.87	34.33	2.99
	LXBG	43.24	2.70	8.11	37.84	8.11
	NTHL	0.0	0.0	0.0	88.24	11.76
	NRWY	21.43	3.57	17.86	39.29	17.86
	PRTG	29.41	11.76	47.06	5.88	5.88
	TRKY	15.91	18.18	40.91	6.82	18.18
	UK	23.47	16.33	10.20	42.86	7.14
	USA	20.75	3.77	13.21	57.55	4.72
MEAN		21.6013	11.4931	24.0666	34.5434	8.2955
WTO						
	BLGR	45.05	6.59	35.16	10.99	2.20
	CZCH	36.84	15.79	14.04	21.05	12.28
	GDR	54.23	9.15	15.49	11.97	9.15
	HNGR	31.96	8.25	28.87	12.37	18.56
	PLND	38.99	18.35	23.85	14.22	4.59
	RMNA	54.55	4.55	36.36	3.03	1.52
	USSR	54.55	12.34	19.48	10.39	3.25
MEAN		45.1661	10.7167	24.7509	12.0035	7.3627

N+N						
	AUST	33.33	1.75	22.81	33.33	8.77
	CYPR	16.00	18.00	42.00	8.00	16.00
	FNLD	45.21	6.85	19.18	28.77	0.0
	IRLD	12.00	12.00	24.00	38.00	14.00
	LICH	0.0	0.0	50.00	50.00	0.0
	MLTA	15.38	46.15	30.77	7.69	0.0
	SANM	33.77	15.58	12.99	28.57	9.09
	SWDN	28.57	2.04	28.57	26.53	14.29
	SWTZ	20.00	15.00	20.00	37.50	7.50
	YGSL	37.88	19.70	30.30	4.55	7.58
MEAN		24.2140	13.7080	28.0616	26.2940	7.7224
OTHER						
	MNCO	28.57	0.0	57.14	14.29	0.0
	SPAN	36.00	10.67	21.33	30.67	1.33
	VATC	26.32	5.26	15.79	36.84	15.79
MEAN		30.2957	5.3099	31.4219	27.2648	5.7076
MEAN		27.8060	11.4407	25.9753	27.0546	7.7234

Table A2.29. The Madrid Opening Statements: Percentage Distribution of Attention on Dimensions of East–West Relations

COUNTRY GROUP	COUNTRY	DISARMAMENT AND SECURITY	PEACE AND CONFLICT	ECONOMIC COOPERATION	HUMAN RIGHTS AND CONTACTS	SOVEREIGNTY AND INDEPENDENCE
NATO						
	BLGM	18.84	20.29	10.14	40.58	10.14
	CNDA	24.80	20.80	12.00	25.60	16.80
	DNMK	38.46	10.26	11.54	33.33	6.41
	FRNC	27.45	19.61	11.76	23.53	17.65
	FRG	26.90	27.92	19.29	19.80	6.09
	GRCE	28.21	15.38	28.21	12.82	15.38
	ICLD	30.95	7.14	16.67	35.71	9.52
	ITLY	32.00	20.00	22.00	13.00	13.00
	LXBG	40.63	15.63	7.81	28.13	7.81
	NTHL	22.55	19.61	6.86	43.14	7.84
	NRWY	52.45	13.99	8.39	11.89	13.29
	PRTG	12.90	9.68	6.45	38.71	32.26
	TRKY	45.61	15.79	17.54	10.53	10.53
	UK	19.51	11.38	8.13	48.78	12.20
	USA	27.61	6.72	7.46	48.51	9.70
MEAN		29.9251	15.6123	12.9510	28.9366	12.5750
WTO						
	BLGR	37.65	23.53	17.65	12.94	8.24
	CZCH	39.77	30.68	19.32	2.27	7.95
	GDR	47.58	22.58	12.90	8.06	8.87
	HNGR	48.92	17.27	19.42	9.35	5.04
	PLND	51.54	19.23	16.92	4.62	7.69
	RMNA	40.31	17.05	20.93	10.85	10.85
	USSR	49.06	26.42	10.38	6.60	7.55
MEAN		44.9752	22.3940	16.7891	7.8147	8.0270

N+N						
	AUST	35.00	28.75	11.25	21.25	3.75
	CYPR	27.27	30.30	19.70	9.09	13.64
	FNLD	51.43	7.14	10.00	21.43	10.00
	IRLD	38.82	12.94	17.65	20.00	10.59
	LICH	37.50	18.75	18.75	12.50	12.50
	MLTA	29.09	63.64	7.27	0.0	0.0
	SANM	8.70	43.48	17.39	8.70	21.74
	SWDN	64.52	10.32	5.16	15.48	4.52
	SWTZ	43.75	16.07	1.79	11.61	26.79
	YGSL	24.81	34.59	9.77	13.53	17.29
MEAN		36.0889	26.5982	11.8729	13.3590	12.0809
OTHER						
	MNCO	28.57	42.86	14.29	14.29	0.0
	SPAN	36.21	27.59	17.24	10.92	8.05
	VATC	16.33	21.43	11.22	39.80	11.22
MEAN		27.0349	30.6240	14.2505	21.6670	6.4235
MEAN		34.4485	21.3942	13.5220	19.6383	10.9970

A2.5 THE CLUSTER ANALYSIS OF THE CONTENT-ANALYTICAL DATA

Methodological and Technical Considerations

The identification of groups of nations or the detection of clusters of nations on the basis of content-analytical data requires the solution of some technical problems discussed in this section. For the application of any technique of multivariate data reduction (factor analysis, cluster analysis, multidimensional scaling, and so on), a matrix of measures of association is required, that is, either a matrix of distances or a matrix of proximities. On the basis of extensive tests with several methods of multivariate reduction and selected measures of distance and proximity, it turned out that cluster analysis meets best the requirements of this study. Extensive experimentation with various measures of distance (share of common attention distribution regarding all 120 categories, Euclidian distances, correlation coefficients, and so on) lead to the conclusion that the computation of measures of proximity over the complete range of 120 categories and the subsequent analysis of these data by means of multivariate reduction yields no meaningful results. The reason is that there is a heavy concentration of attention on selected categories and no even distribution over the complete range of categories. Consequently, the distribution of attention on the ten dimensions of East–West relations presented in Chapter 2 (see also Tables A2.19-A2.25 with the factor scores was employed as the data bases. With the ten dimensions as "cases," Pearson product-moment correlation coefficients were computed between countries (following tables) and subsequently cluster analyzed.

The software used is the HICLUS program incorporated in the *Multidimensional Scaling Programs Library* (Edinburgh Version, October 1975) and the authors' own programs for the output of the results. HICLUS is a version of *Johnson's Hierarchical Clustering Schemes* (1967).

There are two algorithms available for grouping objects or items, the diameter and the connectedness methods. Both versions have advantages and disadvantages. The *diameter method* builds groups by adding an object to a group if the maximum distance between the object and any member of the group is smaller than the distance between the object and other objects not included in this group. The *connectedness method* adds an object to a group if the distance between the object and any member of the group is smaller than the distance between the object and the other objects not included in the group. Extensive experimentation (Phillips 1968) has shown that the diameter method tends to split objects close in space into different groups. Therefore Rummel (1972, p. 304) suggests that the connectedness method be used. The connectedness method, however, tends to construct a small number of highly homogeneous groups leaving the rest of objects (and sometimes the overwhelming majority) as residual items that enter the cluster only at a considerably higher level in the process of clustering.

Results for both methods are presented in this study in the form of combined dendrograms (the connectedness method at the left side, the diameter method at the right side of each table). The dendrograms are line-printer output and very easy to read. Countries close in distance are indicated by joined bars of "X." The length of the bars indicates the proximity of countries.

Measures of Association between Countries for the Five Sets of Statements
(for explanations, see the preceding section on cluster analysis)

See tables on following pages.

Table A2.30. The 1973 Helsinki Statements: Correlations Between Countries

	AUST	BLGM	BLGR	CNDA	CYPR	CZCH	DNMK	FNLD	FRNC	FRG
AUST	1.0000	0.7074	0.7659	0.7605	0.6367	0.7776	0.3212	0.9098	0.9438	0.6940
BLGM	0.7074	1.0000	0.7733	0.9090	0.5573	0.7591	0.8072	0.7819	0.6510	0.9777
BLGR	0.7659	0.7733	1.0000	0.9057	0.5438	0.8207	0.5825	0.9156	0.7662	0.7986
CNDA	0.7605	0.9090	0.9057	1.0000	0.6127	0.7194	0.8053	0.8544	0.7824	0.8845
CYPR	0.6367	0.5573	0.5438	0.6127	1.0000	0.5070	0.3775	0.6794	0.6374	0.6212
CZCH	0.7776	0.7591	0.8207	0.7194	0.5070	1.0000	0.3013	0.9277	0.7193	0.8347
DNMK	0.3212	0.8072	0.5825	0.8053	0.3775	0.3013	1.0000	0.4075	0.3265	0.7345
FNLD	0.9098	0.7819	0.9156	0.8544	0.6794	0.9277	0.4075	1.0000	0.8970	0.8246
FRNC	0.9438	0.6510	0.7662	0.7824	0.6374	0.7193	0.3265	0.8970	1.0000	0.6267
FRG	0.6940	0.9777	0.7986	0.8845	0.6212	0.8347	0.7345	0.8246	0.6267	1.0000
GDR	0.8225	0.8108	0.7191	0.8434	0.8550	0.7299	0.5356	0.8665	0.8576	0.8249
GRCE	0.9033	0.7651	0.8273	0.7894	0.6772	0.9351	0.3402	0.9709	0.8710	0.8171
HNGR	0.6924	0.8112	0.7761	0.7676	0.4257	0.8598	0.4539	0.8377	0.7331	0.8247
ICLD	0.6831	0.8404	0.7088	0.8761	0.4138	0.5956	0.7059	0.7117	0.7346	0.7740
IRLD	0.9166	0.7538	0.7251	0.7872	0.7253	0.7679	0.3925	0.8895	0.9096	0.7621
ITLY	0.7745	0.7969	0.8333	0.9219	0.6577	0.5970	0.6966	0.8018	0.7947	0.7634
LICH	0.7199	0.7481	0.7976	0.7386	0.7619	0.8115	0.4790	0.8412	0.6356	0.8163
LXBG	0.8164	0.8372	0.7928	0.9465	0.7275	0.6028	0.7305	0.8147	0.8557	0.7917
MLTA	0.6608	0.4946	0.7385	0.6053	0.6898	0.6521	0.2179	0.7692	0.6327	0.5802
MNCO	0.4306	0.0218	0.3153	0.2134	0.3841	0.1709	-0.1401	0.3706	0.4543	0.0569
NTHL	0.7448	0.6216	0.5657	0.7664	0.7786	0.3763	0.5548	0.6573	0.8215	0.5657
NRWY	0.6946	0.8700	0.8078	0.9150	0.5505	0.6900	0.7167	0.7993	0.7682	0.8348
PLND	0.7715	0.8292	0.9028	0.9381	0.6446	0.7423	0.6564	0.8806	0.7977	0.8303
PRTG	0.9124	0.8149	0.9162	0.9215	0.7257	0.8373	0.5402	0.9710	0.9209	0.8280
RMNA	0.8867	0.8439	0.7737	0.8786	0.7328	0.8054	0.5278	0.9162	0.9206	0.8405
SANM	0.7852	0.5319	0.4280	0.4541	0.5564	0.6460	0.1245	0.6688	0.7041	0.5353
SPAN	0.7247	0.5863	0.8625	0.6847	0.5182	0.7918	0.2646	0.8513	0.6830	0.6608
SWDN	0.7222	0.9189	0.7687	0.9008	0.6327	0.7955	0.6728	0.8392	0.7269	0.9314
SWTZ	0.7725	0.5971	0.6986	0.7352	0.8178	0.6005	0.4314	0.7834	0.7985	0.6139
TRKY	0.7945	0.6459	0.6738	0.6826	0.9343	0.7538	0.2967	0.8579	0.7769	0.7268
USSR	0.9240	0.7650	0.7462	0.8109	0.6683	0.8016	0.4069	0.9099	0.9523	0.7561
UK	0.6570	0.6681	0.6650	0.8123	0.3419	0.4578	0.5987	0.6481	0.7841	0.5788
USA	0.6207	0.7159	0.5414	0.7835	0.4909	0.3367	0.7614	0.5298	0.6379	0.6196
VATC	0.9300	0.5714	0.7284	0.6767	0.6341	0.7720	0.1846	0.8908	0.9328	0.5860
YGSL	0.8815	0.5196	0.8335	0.6930	0.7111	0.7331	0.2054	0.8990	0.8612	0.5658

	GDR	GRCE	HNGR	ICLD	IRLD	ITLY	LICH	LXBG	MLTA	MNCO
AUST	0.8225	0.9033	0.6924	0.6831	0.9166	0.7745	0.7199	0.8164	0.6608	0.4306
BLGM	0.8108	0.7651	0.8112	0.8404	0.7538	0.7969	0.7481	0.8372	0.4946	0.0218
BLGR	0.7191	0.8273	0.7761	0.7088	0.7251	0.8333	0.7976	0.7928	0.7385	0.3153
CNDA	0.8434	0.7894	0.7676	0.8761	0.7872	0.9219	0.7386	0.9465	0.6053	0.2134
CYPR	0.8550	0.6772	0.4257	0.4138	0.7253	0.6577	0.7619	0.7275	0.6898	0.3841
CZCH	0.7299	0.9351	0.8598	0.5956	0.7679	0.5970	0.8115	0.6028	0.6521	0.1709
DNMK	0.5356	0.3402	0.4539	0.7059	0.3925	0.6966	0.4790	0.7305	0.2179	-0.1401
FNLD	0.8665	0.9709	0.8377	0.7117	0.8895	0.8018	0.8412	0.8147	0.7692	0.3706
FRNC	0.8576	0.8710	0.7331	0.7346	0.9096	0.7947	0.6356	0.8557	0.6327	0.4543
FRG	0.8249	0.8171	0.8247	0.7740	0.7621	0.7634	0.8163	0.7917	0.5802	0.0569
GDR	1.0000	0.8534	0.7686	0.7885	0.9048	0.8487	0.7464	0.9141	0.6959	0.3610
GRCE	0.8534	1.0000	0.7935	0.6402	0.9265	0.6919	0.8209	0.7578	0.6728	0.3047
HNGR	0.7686	0.7935	1.0000	0.8211	0.7412	0.7134	0.6086	0.6859	0.6307	0.2362
ICLD	0.7885	0.6402	0.8211	1.0000	0.7348	0.8947	0.4287	0.8746	0.5422	0.3215
IRLD	0.9048	0.9265	0.7412	0.7348	1.0000	0.7651	0.6624	0.8458	0.6624	0.4702
ITLY	0.8487	0.6919	0.7134	0.8947	0.7651	1.0000	0.6278	0.9506	0.7599	0.4896
LICH	0.7464	0.8209	0.6086	0.4287	0.6624	0.6278	1.0000	0.6728	0.6184	0.0350
LXBG	0.9141	0.7578	0.6859	0.8746	0.8458	0.9506	0.6728	1.0000	0.6171	0.3452
MLTA	0.6959	0.6728	0.6307	0.5422	0.6624	0.7599	0.6184	0.6171	1.0000	0.7535
MNCO	0.3610	0.3047	0.2362	0.3215	0.4702	0.4896	0.0350	0.3452	0.7535	1.0000
NTHL	0.8700	0.6256	0.4739	0.7291	0.8018	0.8377	0.5075	0.9284	0.5275	0.4380
NRWY	0.8543	0.7033	0.8885	0.9402	0.7217	0.9078	0.6235	0.8906	0.6215	0.2406
PLND	0.8645	0.7730	0.8208	0.8856	0.7647	0.9681	0.7129	0.9110	0.7969	0.4199
PRTG	0.8970	0.9434	0.7736	0.7529	0.9139	0.8564	0.8284	0.9077	0.7036	0.3438
RMNA	0.9669	0.9182	0.8250	0.8251	0.9426	0.8275	0.7371	0.9140	0.6175	0.2913
SANM	0.6240	0.7776	0.4296	0.2799	0.7340	0.3211	0.6865	0.5121	0.2202	-0.0381
SPAN	0.6360	0.7879	0.7351	0.5895	0.7343	0.7232	0.6307	0.6081	0.9088	0.6514
SWDN	0.9056	0.8191	0.8613	0.8998	0.8282	0.8487	0.6749	0.8658	0.6442	0.2529
SWTZ	0.7920	0.7943	0.4363	0.4348	0.7675	0.6385	0.8197	0.7880	0.4744	0.1571
TRKY	0.9124	0.8786	0.6176	0.5057	0.8642	0.6798	0.8320	0.7472	0.7550	0.4072
USSR	0.8985	0.9384	0.7711	0.7314	0.9539	0.7330	0.7101	0.8504	0.5407	0.2748
UK	0.7071	0.5770	0.7138	0.9329	0.7196	0.8378	0.2757	0.8460	0.4613	0.4143
USA	0.6488	0.5549	0.3666	0.6565	0.6815	0.6601	0.4729	0.8279	0.1443	0.0038
VATC	0.7652	0.9166	0.6137	0.5060	0.8732	0.6103	0.7304	0.7176	0.5446	0.3147
YGSL	0.7394	0.8340	0.5854	0.4970	0.7735	0.7467	0.7779	0.7218	0.8269	0.5565

Table A2.30. *(cont.)*

	NTHL	NRWY	PLND	PRTG	RMNA	SANM	SPAN	SWDN	SWTZ	TRKY
AUST	0.7448	0.6946	0.7715	0.9124	0.8867	0.7852	0.7247	0.7222	0.7725	0.7945
BLGM	0.6216	0.8700	0.8292	0.8149	0.8439	0.5319	0.5863	0.9189	0.5971	0.6459
BLGR	0.5657	0.8078	0.9028	0.9162	0.7737	0.4280	0.8625	0.7687	0.6986	0.6738
CNDA	0.7664	0.9150	0.9381	0.9215	0.8786	0.4541	0.6847	0.9008	0.7352	0.6826
CYPR	0.7786	0.5505	0.6446	0.7257	0.7328	0.5564	0.5182	0.6327	0.8178	0.9343
CZCH	0.3763	0.6900	0.7423	0.8373	0.8054	0.6460	0.7918	0.7955	0.6005	0.7538
DNMK	0.5548	0.7167	0.6564	0.5402	0.5278	0.1245	0.2646	0.6728	0.4314	0.2967
FNLD	0.6573	0.7993	0.8806	0.9710	0.9162	0.6688	0.8513	0.8392	0.7834	0.8579
FRNC	0.8215	0.7682	0.7977	0.9209	0.9206	0.7041	0.6830	0.7269	0.7985	0.7769
FRG	0.5657	0.8348	0.8303	0.8280	0.8405	0.5353	0.6608	0.9314	0.6139	0.7268
GDR	0.8700	0.8543	0.8645	0.8970	0.9669	0.6240	0.6360	0.9056	0.7920	0.9124
GRCE	0.6256	0.7033	0.7730	0.9434	0.9182	0.7776	0.7879	0.8191	0.7943	0.8786
HNGR	0.4739	0.8885	0.8208	0.7736	0.8250	0.4296	0.7351	0.8613	0.4363	0.6176
ICLD	0.7291	0.9402	0.8856	0.7529	0.8251	0.2799	0.5895	0.8998	0.4348	0.5057
IRLD	0.8018	0.7217	0.7647	0.9139	0.9426	0.7340	0.7343	0.8282	0.7675	0.8642
ITLY	0.8377	0.9078	0.9681	0.8564	0.8275	0.3211	0.7232	0.8487	0.6385	0.6798
LICH	0.5075	0.6235	0.7129	0.8284	0.7371	0.6865	0.6307	0.6749	0.8197	0.8320
LXBG	0.9284	0.8906	0.9110	0.9077	0.9140	0.5121	0.6081	0.8658	0.7880	0.7472
MLTA	0.5275	0.6215	0.7969	0.7036	0.6175	0.2202	0.9088	0.6442	0.4744	0.7550
MNCO	0.4380	0.2406	0.4199	0.3438	0.2913	-0.0381	0.6514	0.2529	0.1571	0.4072
NTHL	1.0000	0.7236	0.7433	0.7813	0.8313	0.5055	0.4318	0.7000	0.7840	0.7320
NRWY	0.7236	1.0000	0.9426	0.8226	0.8656	0.3439	0.6319	0.9070	0.5642	0.6219
PLND	0.7433	0.9426	1.0000	0.8927	0.8583	0.3442	0.7894	0.9011	0.6413	0.7222
PRTG	0.7813	0.8226	0.8927	1.0000	0.9434	0.6791	0.7838	0.8472	0.8679	0.8524
RMNA	0.8313	0.8656	0.8583	0.9434	1.0000	0.7076	0.6546	0.9123	0.8026	0.8580
SANM	0.5055	0.3439	0.3442	0.6791	0.7076	1.0000	0.3168	0.4506	0.7687	0.7001
SPAN	0.4318	0.6319	0.7894	0.7838	0.6546	0.3168	1.0000	0.6779	0.4822	0.6827
SWDN	0.7000	0.9070	0.9011	0.8472	0.9123	0.4506	0.6779	1.0000	0.5906	0.7496
SWTZ	0.7840	0.5642	0.6413	0.8679	0.8026	0.7687	0.4822	0.5906	1.0000	0.8412
TRKY	0.7320	0.6219	0.7222	0.8524	0.8580	0.7001	0.6827	0.7496	0.8412	1.0000
USSR	0.7870	0.7639	0.7612	0.9366	0.9718	0.8119	0.6340	0.8107	0.8317	0.8277
UK	0.7710	0.8528	0.7974	0.7256	0.7715	0.2477	0.5425	0.7561	0.4628	0.4236
USA	0.7969	0.5991	0.5676	0.7038	0.7096	0.5557	0.2499	0.6208	0.7274	0.4761
VATC	0.6794	0.5743	0.6460	0.8969	0.8514	0.8585	0.6434	0.6077	0.8698	0.8077
YGSL	0.6550	0.6070	0.7764	0.8791	0.7500	0.5984	0.8233	0.5870	0.7964	0.8211

	USSR	UK	USA	VATC	YGSL
AUST	0.9240	0.6570	0.6207	0.9300	0.8815
BLGM	0.7650	0.6681	0.7159	0.5714	0.5196
BLGR	0.7462	0.6650	0.5414	0.7284	0.8335
CNDA	0.8109	0.8123	0.7835	0.6767	0.6930
CYPR	0.6683	0.3419	0.4909	0.6341	0.7111
CZCH	0.8016	0.4578	0.3367	0.7720	0.7331
DNMK	0.4069	0.5987	0.7614	0.1846	0.2054
FNLD	0.9099	0.6481	0.5298	0.8908	0.8990
FRNC	0.9523	0.7841	0.6379	0.9328	0.8612
FRG	0.7561	0.5788	0.6196	0.5860	0.5658
GDR	0.8985	0.7071	0.6488	0.7652	0.7394
GRCE	0.9384	0.5770	0.5549	0.9166	0.8340
HNGR	0.7711	0.7138	0.3666	0.6137	0.5854
ICLD	0.7314	0.9329	0.6565	0.5060	0.4970
IRLD	0.9539	0.7196	0.6815	0.8732	0.7735
ITLY	0.7330	0.8378	0.6601	0.6103	0.7467
LICH	0.7101	0.2757	0.4729	0.7304	0.7779
LXBG	0.8504	0.8460	0.8279	0.7176	0.7218
MLTA	0.5407	0.4613	0.1443	0.5446	0.8269
MNCO	0.2748	0.4143	0.0038	0.3147	0.5565
NTHL	0.7870	0.7710	0.7969	0.6794	0.6550
NRWY	0.7639	0.8528	0.5991	0.5743	0.6070
PLND	0.7612	0.7974	0.5676	0.6460	0.7764
PRTG	0.9366	0.7256	0.7038	0.8969	0.8791
RMNA	0.9718	0.7715	0.7096	0.8514	0.7500
SANM	0.8119	0.2477	0.5557	0.8585	0.5984
SPAN	0.6340	0.5425	0.2499	0.6434	0.8233
SWDN	0.8107	0.7561	0.6208	0.6077	0.5870
SWTZ	0.8317	0.4628	0.7274	0.8698	0.7964
TRKY	0.8277	0.4236	0.4761	0.8077	0.8211
USSR	1.0000	0.7286	0.7129	0.9343	0.7720
UK	0.7286	1.0000	0.6931	0.5493	0.5027
USA	0.7129	0.6931	1.0000	0.5841	0.4047
VATC	0.9343	0.5493	0.5841	1.0000	0.8760
YGSL	0.7720	0.5027	0.4047	0.8760	1.0000

Table A2.31. The 1975 Helsinki Statements: Correlations Between Countries

	AUST	BLGM	BLGR	CNDA	CYPR	CZCH	DNMK	FNLD	FRNC	FRG
AUST	1.0000	0.5848	0.3680	0.6704	0.1303	0.7348	-0.1494	0.5370	0.7066	0.3361
BLGM	0.5848	1.0000	0.1842	0.8194	0.4020	0.4492	0.0553	0.5551	0.3520	0.2818
BLGR	0.3680	0.1842	1.0000	0.2852	0.5164	0.5782	0.2280	0.4213	0.2594	0.5720
CNDA	0.6704	0.8194	0.2852	1.0000	0.3289	0.5015	0.0987	0.5705	0.5285	0.0287
CYPR	0.1303	0.4020	0.5164	0.3289	1.0000	0.5837	0.4494	0.3904	0.2141	0.5150
CZCH	0.7348	0.4492	0.5782	0.5015	0.5837	1.0000	0.0655	0.7074	0.7462	0.3641
DNMK	-0.1494	0.0553	0.2280	0.0987	0.4494	0.0655	1.0000	0.2560	0.3770	0.2164
FNLD	0.5370	0.5551	0.4213	0.5705	0.3904	0.7074	0.2560	1.0000	0.6823	-0.0198
FRNC	0.7066	0.3520	0.2594	0.5285	0.2141	0.7462	0.3770	0.6823	1.0000	0.0722
FRG	0.3361	0.2818	0.5720	0.0287	0.5150	0.3641	0.2164	-0.0198	0.0722	1.0000
GDR	0.7650	0.5495	0.2035	0.4498	0.2931	0.7732	0.1970	0.7798	0.8405	0.2529
GRCE	0.2639	0.7609	-0.0560	0.3757	0.3990	0.2569	-0.2167	0.3899	-0.0679	0.2108
HNGR	0.5174	0.6498	0.3196	0.5000	0.7760	0.7337	0.3848	0.4405	0.5754	0.6035
ICLD	-0.4131	0.0782	-0.0828	0.1061	0.5164	-0.0968	0.8323	0.0415	0.1138	-0.0109
IRLD	0.3054	0.4709	0.5661	0.7864	0.3631	0.3635	0.1337	0.4590	0.2534	-0.0680
ITLY	0.2983	0.4904	-0.0671	0.7835	-0.1040	0.0332	0.0027	0.3207	0.2598	-0.4324
LICH	0.5810	0.5337	0.5528	0.6432	0.6909	0.8714	0.0071	0.5463	0.5290	0.2730
LXBG	0.7664	0.6574	0.2727	0.6341	0.4701	0.7062	0.1720	0.7486	0.6644	0.2586
MLTA	0.6862	0.3309	0.4492	0.4364	0.0861	0.5594	0.3172	0.4512	0.7481	0.3971
MNCO	0.7957	0.2780	0.3092	0.4412	0.2222	0.8144	-0.0559	0.3312	0.7859	0.2902
NTHL	0.4749	0.3754	0.9012	0.4909	0.7808	0.7466	0.3597	0.5316	0.4342	0.5811
NRWY	0.4152	0.0843	0.7777	0.2265	0.4022	0.4941	0.4202	0.5913	0.4261	0.3833
PLND	0.6768	0.5394	0.6625	0.6390	0.6010	0.9158	-0.0819	0.6375	0.5453	0.3043
PRTG	0.5374	0.6023	0.6082	0.5906	0.6189	0.7881	0.1941	0.9330	0.5435	0.1878
RMNA	0.7745	0.5573	0.6787	0.5762	0.5874	0.9124	0.1742	0.8081	0.7007	0.4333
SANM	0.6676	0.1699	0.5615	0.4733	0.3300	0.7045	-0.3021	0.2897	0.3816	0.2023
SPAN	0.3332	0.6588	0.2390	0.3010	0.4187	0.3189	0.3295	0.6430	0.2501	0.4173
SWDN	0.7693	0.4318	0.6877	0.4917	0.5368	0.9025	0.3401	0.6958	0.8190	0.5318
SWTZ	0.1641	0.6150	-0.2463	0.4333	0.5900	0.2976	0.1336	0.3492	0.1682	0.0266
TRKY	0.5891	0.6074	0.1009	0.4754	0.4266	0.6148	-0.1977	0.6765	0.3468	0.0968
USSR	0.7502	0.5356	0.6508	0.5243	0.6591	0.9672	0.1417	0.6742	0.6946	0.5315
UK	0.3979	0.4148	0.4304	0.1995	0.1560	0.1124	0.1933	-0.0503	0.0648	0.8432
USA	0.7504	0.3065	0.4780	0.3031	0.3454	0.6120	-0.1277	0.0787	0.3641	0.7325
VATC	0.8347	0.2882	0.5170	0.5362	0.3151	0.8660	-0.1670	0.4832	0.6790	0.2329
YGSL	0.7333	0.6461	0.5003	0.5022	0.5884	0.8850	0.0476	0.7900	0.6039	0.4424

	GDR	GRCE	HNGR	ICLD	IRLD	ITLY	LICH	LXBG	MLTA	MNCO
AUST	0.7650	0.2639	0.5174	-0.4131	0.3054	0.2983	0.5810	0.7664	0.6862	0.7957
BLGM	0.5495	0.7609	0.6498	0.0782	0.4709	0.4904	0.5337	0.6574	0.3309	0.2780
BLGR	0.2035	-0.0560	0.3196	-0.0828	0.5661	-0.0671	0.5528	0.2727	0.4492	0.3092
CNDA	0.4498	0.3757	0.5000	0.1061	0.7864	0.7835	0.6432	0.6341	0.4364	0.4412
CYPR	0.2931	0.3990	0.7760	0.5164	0.3631	-0.1040	0.6909	0.4701	0.0861	0.2222
CZCH	0.7732	0.2569	0.7337	-0.0968	0.3635	0.0332	0.8714	0.7062	0.5594	0.8144
DNMK	0.1970	-0.2167	0.3848	0.8323	0.1337	0.0027	0.0071	0.1720	0.3172	-0.0559
FNLD	0.7798	0.3899	0.4405	0.0415	0.4590	0.3207	0.5463	0.7486	0.4512	0.3312
FRNC	0.8405	-0.0679	0.5754	0.1138	0.2534	0.2598	0.5290	0.6644	0.7481	0.7859
FRG	0.2529	0.2108	0.6035	-0.0109	-0.0680	-0.4324	0.2730	0.2586	0.3971	0.2902
GDR	1.0000	0.3861	0.6665	-0.0721	0.0290	0.0650	0.4883	0.8538	0.6209	0.6516
GRCE	0.3861	1.0000	0.4521	-0.0683	0.0562	0.0740	0.3368	0.5526	-0.1851	-0.0505
HNGR	0.6665	0.4521	1.0000	0.3686	0.1918	0.0	0.7018	0.6488	0.4679	0.6029
ICLD	-0.0721	-0.0683	0.3686	1.0000	0.1592	0.1216	0.0398	-0.0215	-0.0415	-0.2050
IRLD	0.0290	0.0562	0.1918	0.1592	1.0000	0.7155	0.5921	0.2413	0.2699	0.1798
ITLY	0.0650	0.0740	0.0	0.1216	0.7155	1.0000	0.1690	0.1792	0.2842	0.0598
LICH	0.4883	0.3368	0.7018	0.0398	0.5921	0.1690	1.0000	0.6027	0.2647	0.7024
LXBG	0.8538	0.5526	0.6488	-0.0215	0.2413	0.1792	0.6027	1.0000	0.3732	0.5239
MLTA	0.6209	-0.1851	0.4679	-0.0415	0.2699	0.2842	0.2647	0.3732	1.0000	0.6165
MNCO	0.6516	-0.0505	0.6029	-0.2050	0.1798	0.0598	0.7024	0.5239	0.6165	1.0000
NTHL	0.3848	0.1223	0.6238	0.1538	0.6173	0.0269	0.7735	0.5318	0.4436	0.4650
NRWY	0.4318	-0.0645	0.2233	-0.0226	0.3413	-0.0747	0.3211	0.5516	0.4371	0.2147
PLND	0.5467	0.3325	0.6275	-0.1453	0.6148	0.1838	0.9638	0.6171	0.3824	0.7045
PRTG	0.6861	0.5000	0.5471	0.0267	0.5499	0.2103	0.7234	0.7679	0.3455	0.3463
RMNA	0.8042	0.3682	0.6755	-0.1061	0.4195	0.0571	0.7894	0.8568	0.5345	0.6511
SANM	0.2853	0.0137	0.2965	-0.3846	0.4975	0.1365	0.7718	0.4698	0.2544	0.7047
SPAN	0.6366	0.7112	0.5000	0.1128	0.0189	-0.0325	0.1605	0.6818	0.2432	-0.0559
SWDN	0.8084	0.1127	0.7260	-0.0056	0.3336	0.0033	0.7060	0.7430	0.7419	0.7610
SWTZ	0.4055	0.7672	0.6205	0.4004	0.0729	0.1573	0.4375	0.6160	-0.2134	0.0958
TRKY	0.6946	0.7793	0.4888	-0.2079	0.1394	0.1200	0.5512	0.8579	0.0545	0.3194
USSR	0.7686	0.3405	0.8000	-0.0608	0.3562	-0.0362	0.8714	0.7655	0.5408	0.7719
UK	0.1946	0.1510	0.3963	-0.0852	0.0341	-0.0740	0.0095	0.1705	0.5541	0.1567
USA	0.4485	0.1647	0.5691	-0.3430	0.0537	-0.2126	0.5534	0.5406	0.4282	0.7283
VATC	0.5950	0.0423	0.4760	-0.3410	0.4060	0.1425	0.8043	0.6384	0.4966	0.8879
YGSL	0.8542	0.6012	0.7319	-0.1479	0.2416	-0.0249	0.7428	0.8696	0.4251	0.5853

Table A2.31. *(cont.)*

	NTHL	NRWY	PLND	PRTG	RMNA	SANM	SPAN	SWDN	SWTZ	TRKY
AUST	0.4749	0.4152	0.6768	0.5374	0.7745	0.6676	0.3332	0.7693	0.1641	0.5891
BLGM	0.3754	0.0843	0.5394	0.6023	0.5573	0.1699	0.6588	0.4318	0.6150	0.6074
BLGR	0.9012	0.7777	0.6625	0.6082	0.6787	0.5615	0.2390	0.6877	-0.2463	0.1009
CNDA	0.4909	0.2265	0.6390	0.5906	0.5762	0.4733	0.3010	0.4917	0.4333	0.4754
CYPR	0.7808	0.4022	0.6010	0.6189	0.5874	0.3300	0.4187	0.5368	0.5900	0.4266
CZCH	0.7466	0.4941	0.9158	0.7881	0.9124	0.7045	0.3189	0.9025	0.2976	0.6148
DNMK	0.3597	0.4202	-0.0819	0.1941	0.1742	-0.3021	0.3295	0.3401	0.1336	-0.1977
FNLD	0.5316	0.5913	0.6375	0.9330	0.8081	0.2897	0.6430	0.6958	0.3492	0.6765
FRNC	0.4342	0.4261	0.5453	0.5435	0.7007	0.3816	0.2501	0.8190	0.1682	0.3468
FRG	0.5811	0.3833	0.3043	0.1878	0.4333	0.2023	0.4173	0.5318	0.0266	0.0968
GDR	0.3848	0.4318	0.5467	0.6861	0.8042	0.2853	0.6366	0.8084	0.4055	0.6946
GRCE	0.1223	-0.0645	0.3325	0.5000	0.3682	0.0137	0.7112	0.1127	0.7672	0.7793
HNGR	0.6238	0.2233	0.6275	0.5471	0.6755	0.2965	0.5000	0.7260	0.6205	0.4888
ICLD	0.1538	-0.0226	-0.1453	0.0267	-0.1061	-0.3846	0.1128	-0.0056	0.4004	-0.2079
IRLD	0.6173	0.3413	0.6148	0.5499	0.4195	0.4975	0.0189	0.3336	0.0729	0.1394
ITLY	0.0269	-0.0747	0.1838	0.2103	0.0571	0.1365	-0.0325	0.0033	0.1573	0.1200
LICH	0.7735	0.3211	0.9638	0.7234	0.7894	0.7718	0.1605	0.7060	0.4375	0.5512
LXBG	0.5318	0.5516	0.6171	0.7679	0.8568	0.4698	0.6818	0.7430	0.6160	0.8579
MLTA	0.4436	0.4371	0.3824	0.3455	0.5345	0.2544	0.2432	0.7419	-0.2134	0.0545
MNCO	0.4650	0.2147	0.7045	0.3463	0.6511	0.7047	-0.0559	0.7610	0.0958	0.3194
NTHL	1.0000	0.7517	0.8010	0.7373	0.8186	0.6523	0.3352	0.8100	0.1433	0.3349
NRWY	0.7517	1.0000	0.4308	0.6533	0.7242	0.4333	0.4557	0.7143	-0.1078	0.3047
PLND	0.8010	0.4308	1.0000	0.7978	0.8599	0.8089	0.2238	0.7682	0.2939	0.5844
PRTG	0.7373	0.6533	0.7978	1.0000	0.8961	0.4663	0.6479	0.7405	0.4195	0.7388
RMNA	0.8186	0.7242	0.8599	0.8961	1.0000	0.6536	0.5701	0.9332	0.3197	0.7002
SANM	0.6523	0.4333	0.8089	0.4663	0.6536	1.0000	-0.1541	0.5853	0.0452	0.4272
SPAN	0.3352	0.4557	0.2238	0.6479	0.5701	-0.1541	1.0000	0.4526	0.4981	0.6292
SWDN	0.8100	0.7143	0.7682	0.7405	0.9332	0.5853	0.4526	1.0000	0.1486	0.4662
SWTZ	0.1433	-0.1078	0.2939	0.4195	0.3197	0.0452	0.4981	0.1486	1.0000	0.7138
TRKY	0.3349	0.3047	0.5844	0.7388	0.7002	0.4272	0.6292	0.4662	0.7138	1.0000
USSR	0.8222	0.5666	0.9051	0.7980	0.9541	0.6805	0.4454	0.9359	0.3403	0.6226
UK	0.3540	0.2755	0.0890	0.0409	0.2568	0.0009	0.4277	0.3801	-0.1425	-0.0629
USA	0.5767	0.3880	0.5781	0.2604	0.6289	0.7036	0.1684	0.6724	0.0997	0.3683
VATC	0.6454	0.4678	0.8523	0.5691	0.7962	0.9257	0.0092	0.7848	0.1059	0.5113
YGSL	0.6494	0.5782	0.8074	0.8768	0.9440	0.5211	0.6854	0.8350	0.4887	0.8323

	USSR	UK	USA	VATC	YGSL
AUST	0.7502	0.3979	0.7504	0.8347	0.7333
BLGM	0.5356	0.4148	0.3065	0.2882	0.6461
BLGR	0.6508	0.4304	0.4780	0.5170	0.5003
CNDA	0.5243	0.1995	0.3031	0.5362	0.5022
CYPR	0.6591	0.1560	0.3454	0.3151	0.5884
CZCH	0.9672	0.1124	0.6120	0.8660	0.8850
DNMK	0.1417	0.1933	-0.1277	-0.1670	0.0476
FNLD	0.6742	-0.0503	0.0787	0.4832	0.7900
FRNC	0.6946	0.0648	0.3641	0.6790	0.6039
FRG	0.5315	0.8432	0.7325	0.2329	0.4424
GDR	0.7686	0.1946	0.4485	0.5950	0.8542
GRCE	0.3405	0.1510	0.1647	0.0423	0.6012
HNGR	0.8000	0.3963	0.5691	0.4760	0.7319
ICLD	-0.0608	-0.0852	-0.3430	-0.3410	-0.1479
IRLD	0.3562	0.0341	0.0537	0.4060	0.2416
ITLY	-0.0362	-0.0740	-0.2126	0.1425	-0.0249
LICH	0.8714	0.0095	0.5534	0.8043	0.7428
LXBG	0.7655	0.1705	0.5406	0.6384	0.8696
MLTA	0.5408	0.5541	0.4282	0.4966	0.4251
MNCO	0.7719	0.1567	0.7283	0.8879	0.5853
NTHL	0.8222	0.3540	0.5767	0.6454	0.6694
NRWY	0.5666	0.2755	0.3880	0.4678	0.5392
PLND	0.9051	0.0890	0.5781	0.8523	0.8074
PRTG	0.7980	0.0409	0.2604	0.5691	0.8768
RMNA	0.9541	0.2568	0.6289	0.7962	0.9440
SANM	0.6805	0.0009	0.7036	0.9257	0.5211
SPAN	0.4454	0.4277	0.1684	0.0092	0.6854
SWDN	0.9359	0.3801	0.6724	0.7848	0.8350
SWTZ	0.3403	-0.1425	0.0997	0.1059	0.4887
TRKY	0.6226	-0.0629	0.3683	0.5113	0.8323
USSR	1.0000	0.2844	0.7138	0.8279	0.9236
UK	0.2844	1.0000	0.5687	0.0619	0.2407
USA	0.7138	0.5687	1.0000	0.7401	0.5869
VATC	0.8279	0.0619	0.7401	1.0000	0.6881
YGSL	0.9236	0.2407	0.5869	0.6881	1.0000

Table A2.32. The Belgrade Opening Statements: Correlations Between Countries

	AUST	BLGM	BLGR	CNDA	CYPR	CZCH	DNMK	FNLD	FRNC	FRG
AUST	1.0000	0.7517	0.8010	0.7373	0.8186	0.6523	0.3352	0.8100	0.1433	0.3349
BLGM	0.7517	1.0000	0.4308	0.6533	0.7242	0.4333	0.4557	0.7143	-0.1078	0.3047
BLGR	0.8010	0.4308	1.0000	0.7978	0.8599	0.8089	0.2238	0.7682	0.2939	0.5844
CNDA	0.7373	0.6533	0.7978	1.0000	0.8961	0.4663	0.6479	0.7405	0.4195	0.7388
CYPR	0.8186	0.7242	0.8599	0.8961	1.0000	0.6536	0.5701	0.9332	0.3197	0.7002
CZCH	0.6523	0.4333	0.8089	0.4663	0.6536	1.0000	-0.1541	0.5853	0.0452	0.4272
DNMK	0.3352	0.4557	0.2238	0.6479	0.5701	-0.1541	1.0000	0.4526	0.4981	0.6292
FNLD	0.8100	0.7143	0.7682	0.7405	0.9332	0.5853	0.4526	1.0000	0.1486	0.4662
FRNC	0.1433	-0.1078	0.2939	0.4195	0.3197	0.0452	0.4981	0.1486	1.0000	0.7138
FRG	0.3349	0.3047	0.5844	0.7388	0.7002	0.4272	0.6292	0.4662	0.7138	1.0000
GDR	0.4949	0.4234	0.0449	0.1641	0.2709	-0.1196	0.5697	0.3226	0.1230	-0.0066
GRCE	0.5609	0.7280	0.1562	0.5824	0.4443	-0.1300	0.5939	0.4516	0.0960	0.1445
HNGR	0.6636	0.6880	0.4094	0.5206	0.6646	0.2532	0.5442	0.7527	0.0366	0.3309
ICLD	-0.0736	-0.3895	-0.0473	-0.0486	-0.2107	-0.1137	-0.0040	-0.2520	0.5812	0.1683
IRLD	0.4449	0.4429	-0.0654	-0.0360	0.1233	0.0171	0.3032	0.1967	-0.0654	-0.1226
ITLY	0.8143	0.7869	0.7572	0.8793	0.8326	0.5493	0.3452	0.7955	0.0673	0.4165
LICH	0.7443	0.6678	0.7487	0.7266	0.6743	0.7833	0.0681	0.5169	0.1064	0.4653
LXBG	0.3499	0.3635	-0.0229	-0.0198	0.0797	0.0727	0.1641	0.1842	-0.2825	-0.2194
MLTA	0.2335	0.1900	0.1059	0.0606	0.1332	0.0491	0.1572	0.2332	-0.3522	-0.2103
MNCO	0.7984	0.4793	0.8695	0.5663	0.7708	0.8026	-0.0224	0.8427	0.0529	0.2621
NTHL	0.6614	0.5259	0.2854	0.4372	0.3702	0.2009	0.3625	0.2980	0.4195	0.1956
NRWY	0.1327	0.4056	-0.3125	-0.2338	-0.1111	0.0487	-0.0885	-0.0110	-0.2275	-0.1658
PLND	0.4518	0.6376	0.4365	0.7054	0.7903	0.3129	0.7178	0.7191	0.5233	0.7915
PRTG	0.5785	0.7182	0.4115	0.5839	0.5295	0.3510	0.2883	0.5147	-0.2357	0.1318
RMNA	0.4890	0.6993	0.1667	0.5493	0.5733	-0.1187	0.8289	0.6113	0.1172	0.3244
SANM	0.0054	0.0676	0.1412	0.3797	0.3085	0.0646	0.6419	0.0402	0.7660	0.8296
SPAN	0.1602	0.6607	-0.0355	0.2064	0.3487	0.2695	0.2912	0.3159	0.0093	0.3813
SWDN	0.5838	0.7538	0.0840	0.1956	0.3677	0.2071	0.3802	0.4161	-0.1583	0.0289
SWTZ	0.8185	0.5604	0.8320	0.8042	0.8095	0.6760	0.4607	0.6572	0.4035	0.7104
TRKY	0.6745	0.4963	0.6266	0.4985	0.5629	0.4080	0.1496	0.5910	-0.3647	-0.0018
USSR	0.7044	0.6577	0.4608	0.5619	0.6383	0.1930	0.6003	0.6196	-0.0369	0.2092
UK	0.4116	0.3061	0.1724	0.0763	0.0782	0.1092	-0.1013	0.2132	-0.6387	-0.4600
USA	0.3056	0.5244	0.0503	-0.0347	0.1867	0.5315	-0.1154	0.1760	-0.1404	0.0947
VATC	0.0206	0.2194	-0.0865	-0.1759	-0.0306	0.4358	-0.2544	-0.1079	0.0586	0.1532
YGSL	0.4078	0.5415	-0.1214	0.0826	0.1985	-0.1785	0.5286	0.2900	-0.0894	-0.0936

	GDR	GRCE	HNGR	ICLD	IRLD	ITLY	LICH	LXBG	MLTA	MNCO
AUST	0.4949	0.5609	0.6636	-0.0736	0.4449	0.8143	0.7443	0.3499	0.2335	0.7984
BLGM	0.4234	0.7280	0.6880	-0.3895	0.4429	0.7869	0.6678	0.3635	0.1900	0.4793
BLGR	0.0449	0.1562	0.4094	-0.0473	-0.0654	0.7572	0.7487	-0.0229	0.1059	0.8695
CNDA	0.1641	0.5824	0.5206	-0.0486	-0.0360	0.8793	0.7266	-0.0198	0.0606	0.5663
CYPR	0.2709	0.4443	0.6646	-0.2107	0.1233	0.8326	0.6743	0.0797	0.1332	0.7708
CZCH	-0.1196	-0.1300	0.2532	-0.1137	0.0171	0.5493	0.7833	0.0727	0.0491	0.8026
DNMK	0.5697	0.5939	0.5442	-0.0040	0.3032	0.3452	0.0681	0.1641	0.1572	-0.0224
FNLD	0.3226	0.4516	0.7527	-0.2520	0.1967	0.7955	0.5169	0.1842	0.2332	0.8427
FRNC	0.1230	0.0960	0.0366	0.5812	-0.0654	0.0673	0.1064	-0.2825	-0.3522	0.0529
FRG	-0.0066	0.1445	0.3309	0.1683	-0.1226	0.4165	0.4653	-0.2194	-0.2103	0.2621
GDR	1.0000	0.5236	0.5736	-0.0527	0.8990	0.0787	-0.0649	0.5567	0.3091	0.0648
GRCE	0.5236	1.0000	0.6381	-0.1191	0.3891	0.6470	0.3643	0.1604	-0.0243	0.1525
HNGR	0.5736	0.6381	1.0000	-0.1554	0.5486	0.5500	0.2886	0.2894	0.1022	0.4517
ICLD	-0.0527	-0.1191	-0.1554	1.0000	0.0043	-0.1986	-0.1093	0.1544	-0.0113	-0.1862
IRLD	0.8990	0.3891	0.5486	0.0043	1.0000	-0.0196	0.0	0.6838	0.2891	0.0202
ITLY	0.0787	0.6470	0.5500	-0.1986	-0.0196	1.0000	0.8143	0.0720	0.1187	0.7243
LICH	-0.0649	0.3643	0.2886	-0.1093	0.0	0.8143	1.0000	-0.0144	-0.1025	0.6364
LXBG	0.5567	0.1604	0.2894	0.1544	0.6838	0.0720	-0.0144	1.0000	0.8403	0.0484
MLTA	0.3091	-0.0243	0.1022	-0.0113	0.2891	0.1187	-0.1025	0.8403	1.0000	0.1299
MNCO	0.0648	0.1525	0.4517	-0.1862	0.0202	0.7243	0.6364	0.0484	0.1299	1.0000
NTHL	0.5945	0.5782	0.2383	0.2970	0.5578	0.4198	0.4769	0.4050	0.1070	0.2519
NRWY	0.3215	0.2945	0.4278	0.0757	0.6510	-0.0456	0.0884	0.3935	-0.1129	-0.1195
PLND	0.2320	0.4658	0.5934	-0.0715	0.1110	0.5577	0.3823	-0.0333	-0.1059	0.3674
PRTG	0.1336	0.4495	0.2805	-0.1535	0.1257	0.7266	0.5542	0.5874	0.6595	0.3851
RMNA	0.6778	0.8119	0.8447	-0.2186	0.5159	0.4847	0.1099	0.2994	0.1790	0.1398
SANM	0.1646	0.0284	0.0724	0.2630	0.0710	-0.0451	0.1196	-0.1561	-0.2616	-0.2097
SPAN	0.1085	0.2731	0.3696	-0.2300	0.2838	0.2471	0.3084	0.1907	-0.0766	0.0363
SWDN	0.7975	0.5386	0.6703	-0.2361	0.9105	0.2736	0.2653	0.6440	0.2785	0.1805
SWTZ	0.3186	0.3774	0.6390	0.1157	0.2896	0.6708	0.7442	0.1261	0.0041	0.5981
TRKY	0.3017	0.3674	0.5253	-0.5526	0.1875	0.6197	0.4624	0.1302	0.2787	0.6179
USSR	0.7423	0.6254	0.7108	-0.4850	0.5631	0.5165	0.3335	0.2394	0.2021	0.3993
UK	0.2725	0.2291	0.2631	-0.1478	0.3264	0.3220	0.1458	0.6901	0.7542	0.2563
USA	0.2010	-0.0082	0.1829	-0.1002	0.5158	0.0965	0.4007	0.4467	0.0872	0.1836
VATC	-0.0722	-0.2315	-0.1387	0.0957	0.2519	-0.1226	0.3083	0.1693	-0.1754	-0.0148
YGSL	0.9352	0.5893	0.6468	-0.1387	0.9266	0.0840	-0.0877	0.6443	-0.3407	-0.0415

Table A2.32. *(cont.)*

	NTHL	NRWY	PLND	PRTG	RMNA	SANM	SPAN	SWDN	SWTZ	TRKY
AUST	0.6614	0.1327	0.4518	0.5785	0.4890	0.0054	0.1602	0.5838	0.8185	0.6745
BLGM	0.5259	0.4056	0.6376	0.7182	0.6993	0.0676	0.6607	0.7538	0.5604	0.4963
BLGR	0.2854	-0.3125	0.4365	0.4115	0.1667	0.1412	-0.0355	0.0840	0.8320	0.6266
CNDA	0.4372	-0.2338	0.7054	0.5839	0.5493	0.3797	0.2064	0.1956	0.8042	0.4985
CYPR	0.3702	-0.1111	0.7903	0.5295	0.5733	0.3085	0.3487	0.3677	0.8095	0.5629
CZCH	0.2009	0.0487	0.3129	0.3510	-0.1187	0.0646	0.2695	0.2071	0.6760	0.4080
DNMK	0.3625	-0.0885	0.7178	0.2883	0.8289	0.6419	0.2912	0.3802	0.4607	0.1496
FNLD	0.2980	-0.0110	0.7191	0.5147	0.6113	0.0402	0.3159	0.4161	0.6572	0.5910
FRNC	0.4195	-0.2275	0.5233	-0.2357	0.1172	0.7660	0.0093	-0.1583	0.4035	-0.3647
FRG	0.1956	-0.1658	0.7915	0.1318	0.3244	0.8296	0.3813	0.0289	0.7104	-0.0018
GDR	0.5945	0.3215	0.2320	0.1336	0.6778	0.1646	0.1085	0.7975	0.3186	0.3017
GRCE	0.5782	0.2945	0.4658	0.4495	0.8119	0.0284	0.2731	0.5386	0.3774	0.3674
HNGR	0.2383	0.4278	0.5934	0.2805	0.8447	0.0724	0.3696	0.6703	0.6390	0.5253
ICLD	0.2970	0.0757	-0.0715	-0.1535	-0.2186	0.2630	-0.2300	-0.2361	0.1157	-0.5526
IRLD	0.5578	0.6510	0.1110	0.1257	0.5159	0.0710	0.2838	0.9105	0.2896	0.1875
ITLY	0.4198	-0.0456	0.5577	0.7266	0.4847	-0.0451	0.2471	0.2736	0.6708	0.6197
LICH	0.4769	0.0884	0.3823	0.5542	0.1099	0.1196	0.3084	0.2653	0.7442	0.4624
LXBG	0.4050	0.3935	-0.0333	0.5874	0.2994	-0.1561	0.1907	0.6440	0.1261	0.1302
MLTA	0.1070	-0.1129	-0.1059	0.6595	0.1790	-0.2616	-0.0766	0.2785	0.0041	0.2787
MNCO	0.2519	-0.1195	0.3674	0.3851	0.1398	-0.2097	0.0363	0.1805	0.5981	0.6179
NTHL	1.0000	0.2669	0.3272	0.4056	0.3346	0.2521	0.2109	0.5620	0.4604	0.0538
NRWY	0.2669	1.0000	0.1112	0.0185	0.2707	-0.0560	0.6119	0.6881	0.0766	-0.1745
PLND	0.3272	0.1112	1.0000	0.3052	0.6614	0.5987	0.6790	0.3518	0.5416	0.0349
PRTG	0.4056	0.0185	0.3052	1.0000	0.3726	-0.1342	0.3144	0.3806	0.3472	0.4190
RMNA	0.3346	0.2707	0.6614	0.3726	1.0000	0.2294	0.4056	0.6493	0.4217	0.3769
SANM	0.2521	-0.0560	0.5987	-0.1342	0.2294	1.0000	0.3760	0.0872	0.4165	-0.3454
SPAN	0.2109	0.6119	0.6790	0.3144	0.4056	0.3760	1.0000	0.5648	0.1866	-0.1982
SWDN	0.5620	0.6881	0.3518	0.3806	0.6493	0.0872	0.5648	1.0000	0.4025	0.3201
SWTZ	0.4604	0.0766	0.5416	0.3472	0.4217	0.4165	0.1866	0.4025	1.0000	0.5103
TRKY	0.0538	-0.1745	0.0349	0.4190	0.3769	-0.3454	-0.1982	0.3201	0.5103	1.0000
USSR	0.3708	0.0346	0.3669	0.3336	0.7456	0.0866	0.0923	0.6626	0.5808	0.7910
UK	0.1047	0.0784	-0.3576	0.6268	0.1786	-0.6402	-0.2497	0.3378	0.1153	0.6287
USA	0.3857	0.6993	0.2684	0.2814	0.0295	0.1495	0.7607	0.6663	0.2283	-0.1125
VATC	0.2886	0.5840	0.1796	0.0214	-0.2650	0.3003	0.6807	0.3480	0.0745	-0.4401
YGSL	0.4930	0.5483	0.2519	0.2297	0.7557	0.0709	0.3242	0.8964	0.2163	0.2489

	USSR	UK	USA	VATC	YGSL
AUST	0.7044	0.4116	0.3056	0.0206	0.4078
BLGM	0.6577	0.3061	0.5244	0.2194	0.5415
BLGR	0.4608	0.1724	0.0503	-0.0865	-0.1214
CNDA	0.5619	0.0763	-0.0347	-0.1759	0.0826
CYPR	0.6383	0.0782	0.1867	-0.0306	0.1985
CZCH	0.1930	0.1092	0.5315	0.4358	-0.1785
DNMK	0.6003	-0.1013	-0.1154	-0.2544	0.5286
FNLD	0.6196	0.2132	0.1760	-0.1079	0.2900
FRNC	-0.0369	-0.6387	-0.1404	0.0586	-0.0894
FRG	0.2092	-0.4600	0.0947	0.1532	-0.0936
GDR	0.7423	0.2725	0.2010	-0.0722	0.9352
GRCE	0.6254	0.2291	-0.0082	-0.2315	0.5893
HNGR	0.7108	0.2631	0.1829	-0.1387	0.6468
ICLD	-0.4850	-0.1478	-0.1002	0.0957	-0.1387
IRLD	0.5631	0.3264	0.5158	0.2519	0.9266
ITLY	0.5165	0.3220	0.0965	-0.1226	0.0840
LICH	0.3335	0.1458	0.4007	0.3083	-0.0877
LXBG	0.2394	0.6901	0.4467	0.1693	0.6443
MLTA	0.2021	0.7542	0.0872	-0.1754	0.3407
MNCO	0.3993	0.2563	0.1836	-0.0148	-0.0415
NTHL	0.3708	0.1047	0.3857	0.2886	0.4930
NRWY	0.0346	0.0784	0.6993	0.5840	0.5483
PLND	0.3669	-0.3576	0.2684	0.1796	0.2519
PRTG	0.3336	0.6268	0.2814	0.0214	0.2297
RMNA	0.7456	0.1786	0.0295	-0.2650	0.7557
SANM	0.0866	-0.6402	0.1495	0.3003	0.0709
SPAN	0.0923	-0.2497	0.7607	0.6807	0.3242
SWDN	0.6626	0.3378	0.6663	0.3480	0.8964
SWTZ	0.5808	0.1153	0.2283	0.0745	0.2163
TRKY	0.7910	0.6287	-0.1125	-0.4401	0.2489
USSR	1.0000	0.3614	0.0439	-0.2938	0.6773
UK	0.3614	1.0000	0.0085	-0.3178	0.3431
USA	0.0439	0.0085	1.0000	0.9039	0.3324
VATC	-0.2938	-0.3178	0.9039	1.0000	0.0225
YGSL	0.6773	0.3431	0.3324	0.0225	1.0000

Table A2.33. The Belgrade Closing Statements: Correlations Between Countries

	AUST	BLGM	BLGR	CNDA	CYPR	CZCH	DNMK	FNLD	FRNC	FRG
AUST	1.0000	0.2135	0.2652	0.2639	0.2758	0.1400	0.6031	0.4577	0.0427	-0.5175
BLGM	0.2135	1.0000	-0.3477	0.1215	0.5050	0.3864	0.3528	-0.5229	-0.0986	-0.1196
BLGR	0.2652	-0.3477	1.0000	0.4978	0.0552	-0.0190	0.2853	0.5554	0.4321	-0.3245
CNDA	0.2639	0.1215	0.4978	1.0000	0.3640	-0.0233	-0.0606	0.1418	-0.0776	-0.0344
CYPR	0.2758	0.5050	0.0552	0.3640	1.0000	-0.1623	0.6223	0.1420	-0.4395	-0.5445
CZCH	0.1400	0.3864	-0.0190	-0.0233	-0.1623	1.0000	-0.0079	-0.5440	0.6455	-0.0361
DNMK	0.6031	0.3528	0.2853	-0.0606	0.6223	-0.0079	1.0000	0.4115	-0.0611	-0.8502
FNLD	0.4577	-0.5229	0.5554	0.1418	0.1420	-0.5440	0.4115	1.0000	-0.1621	-0.3578
FRNC	0.0427	-0.0986	0.4321	-0.0776	-0.4395	0.6455	-0.0611	-0.1621	1.0000	0.1532
FRG	-0.5175	-0.1196	-0.3245	-0.0344	-0.5445	-0.0361	-0.8502	-0.3578	0.1532	1.0000
GDR	0.3238	0.3137	0.2289	0.6208	0.3717	-0.1605	0.0070	0.1942	-0.1958	0.2028
GRCE	0.1578	0.6860	-0.1668	0.2216	0.3487	0.5484	0.2697	-0.4350	0.1825	-0.1815
HNGR	0.5268	0.2796	-0.1171	-0.3017	0.2176	0.5677	0.4612	-0.0481	0.1918	-0.4674
ICLD	0.4580	0.4752	-0.1428	0.5180	0.3203	0.2456	-0.0045	-0.1504	-0.3503	-0.0823
IRLD	-0.3292	-0.0433	0.5464	0.2515	-0.1837	0.3681	-0.0578	-0.0795	0.4761	0.0180
ITLY	-0.3492	0.4067	-0.2048	-0.1095	-0.1703	0.5465	-0.2997	-0.5587	0.5376	0.5936
LICH	0.0925	0.1812	0.0639	0.0871	-0.5327	0.6384	-0.3708	-0.5142	0.7314	0.4261
LXBG	-0.1457	0.2554	0.0012	0.4233	0.2034	0.2344	-0.3254	-0.3010	-0.1374	0.2480
MLTA	-0.0151	0.0064	0.3525	0.2573	0.1167	-0.0913	0.0808	0.0560	0.4477	0.1327
MNCO	0.1107	0.0046	0.5190	0.0481	-0.4479	0.2355	0.1420	0.0751	0.5402	-0.0390
NTHL	0.2896	0.6635	-0.4565	-0.2653	0.0636	0.5157	0.1191	-0.5249	0.1062	0.0350
NRWY	0.2744	0.6074	-0.1735	0.3263	-0.0169	0.7663	-0.1838	-0.5616	0.2951	0.2228
PLND	0.0053	0.1132	0.5364	0.8666	0.1266	0.0205	-0.2602	-0.0352	0.1909	0.2886
PRTG	0.0353	0.0141	0.5216	0.3885	-0.3328	0.2522	-0.0746	-0.0025	0.5826	0.1748
RMNA	-0.1671	0.0054	0.5726	0.7433	-0.0573	-0.0030	-0.2606	0.0201	0.1537	0.2423
SANM	-0.0611	0.6931	0.0425	0.6155	0.6721	0.1299	0.0879	-0.3535	-0.1437	0.0387
SPAN	-0.1632	0.3496	0.2075	0.6120	0.0795	0.2867	-0.3837	-0.4474	0.2274	0.4200
SWDN	-0.2154	0.5054	0.0128	0.5143	0.0945	0.6241	-0.2893	-0.6266	0.2938	0.2667
SWTZ	0.2122	0.8273	0.0124	0.0222	0.5643	0.2367	0.6344	-0.3090	0.0777	-0.3839
TRKY	-0.0014	0.0262	0.3888	0.6245	0.0021	0.4662	-0.2390	-0.2897	0.5266	0.0817
USSR	-0.1623	0.1073	0.2489	0.7695	0.2812	-0.4088	-0.2559	0.0428	-0.4185	0.2203
UK	-0.1961	0.7149	-0.1971	0.1597	0.7140	0.1989	0.2241	-0.5026	-0.1584	-0.1235
USA	-0.2764	0.7859	-0.3640	-0.1524	0.5322	0.2764	0.2826	-0.5736	-0.1443	-0.1231
VATC	-0.1553	0.8203	-0.2890	0.2515	0.5372	0.4429	0.1210	-0.5920	-0.0922	-0.0232
YGSL	0.0595	-0.0516	0.6832	0.8420	0.0422	0.0131	-0.1529	0.1593	0.3011	0.1682

	GDR	GRCE	HNGR	ICLD	IRLD	ITLY	LICH	LXBG	MLTA	MNCO
AUST	0.3238	0.1578	0.5268	0.4580	-0.3292	-0.3492	0.0925	-0.1457	-0.0151	0.1107
BLGM	0.3137	0.6860	0.2796	0.4752	-0.0433	0.4067	0.1812	0.2554	0.0064	0.0046
BLGR	0.2289	-0.1668	-0.1171	-0.1428	0.5464	-0.2048	0.0639	0.0012	0.3525	0.5190
CNDA	0.6208	0.2216	-0.3017	0.5180	0.2515	-0.1095	0.0871	0.4233	0.2573	0.0481
CYPR	0.3717	0.3487	0.2176	0.3203	-0.1837	-0.1703	-0.5327	0.2034	0.1167	-0.4479
CZCH	-0.1605	0.5484	0.5677	0.2456	0.3681	0.5465	0.6384	0.2344	-0.0913	0.2355
DNMK	0.0070	0.2697	0.4612	-0.0045	-0.0578	-0.2997	-0.3708	-0.3254	0.0808	0.1420
FNLD	0.1942	-0.4350	-0.0481	-0.1504	-0.0795	-0.5587	-0.5142	-0.3010	0.0560	0.0751
FRNC	-0.1958	0.1825	0.1918	-0.3503	0.4761	0.5376	0.7314	-0.1374	0.4477	0.5402
FRG	0.2028	-0.1815	-0.4674	-0.0823	0.0180	0.5936	0.4261	0.2480	0.1327	-0.0390
GDR	1.0000	-0.1411	-0.0348	0.6387	-0.0977	0.0763	0.0690	0.6519	-0.0142	-0.0885
GRCE	-0.1411	1.0000	0.1117	0.1310	0.2500	0.4471	0.1894	-0.1418	0.3438	0.1080
HNGR	-0.0348	0.1117	1.0000	0.3504	-0.2892	-0.0100	0.1067	0.1550	-0.4014	-0.2277
ICLD	0.6387	0.1310	0.3504	1.0000	-0.2289	-0.1249	0.1238	0.6918	-0.5059	-0.2461
IRLD	-0.0977	0.2500	-0.2892	-0.2289	1.0000	0.3752	0.1700	0.1234	0.1589	0.6551
ITLY	0.0763	0.4471	-0.0100	-0.1249	0.3752	1.0000	0.5086	0.2080	0.3079	0.1525
LICH	0.0690	0.1894	0.1067	0.1238	0.1700	0.5086	1.0000	0.1344	0.2295	0.4373
LXBG	0.6519	-0.1418	0.1550	0.6918	0.1234	0.2080	0.1344	1.0000	-0.4306	-0.2769
MLTA	-0.0142	0.3438	-0.4014	-0.5059	0.1589	0.3079	0.2295	-0.4306	1.0000	0.2074
MNCO	-0.0885	0.1080	-0.2277	-0.2461	0.6551	0.1525	0.4373	-0.2769	0.2074	1.0000
NTHL	0.2327	0.1681	0.6751	0.5076	-0.3733	0.3118	0.4628	0.3541	-0.3370	-0.1153
NRWY	0.3845	0.4785	0.3932	0.7033	0.0871	0.5066	0.6730	0.5590	-0.1612	0.0584
PLND	0.6729	0.0859	-0.4357	0.3192	0.4001	0.2016	0.3592	0.4996	0.4008	0.2408
PRTG	-0.0047	0.3826	-0.4633	-0.2356	0.6966	0.3467	0.4947	-0.2506	0.5645	0.8196
RMNA	0.4410	0.0931	-0.6113	0.1475	0.7103	0.1727	0.2173	0.3564	0.2553	0.5147
SANM	0.6045	0.4809	-0.1048	0.4548	0.1917	0.3616	0.0277	0.5851	0.2354	-0.1635
SPAN	0.6461	0.0991	-0.1682	0.4558	0.3051	0.4407	0.5332	0.7622	0.1507	0.0868
SWDN	0.1944	0.6729	-0.1171	0.3357	0.5616	0.6361	0.4500	0.4798	0.1773	0.1486
SWTZ	0.1932	0.5073	0.2653	0.1271	0.0621	0.2383	0.1042	0.0395	0.2319	0.1993
TRKY	-0.0037	0.4932	-0.1597	0.0516	0.4168	0.2784	0.5116	0.1082	0.5550	0.1504
USSR	0.6743	-0.1049	-0.6153	0.4054	0.1927	-0.1208	-0.1249	0.5323	0.0608	-0.0015
UK	0.2983	0.4070	0.2024	0.2830	0.0192	0.3450	-0.0937	0.5057	0.0642	-0.3645
USA	0.0734	0.4710	0.2252	0.1455	0.1246	0.4446	-0.1137	0.3300	-0.0895	-0.1603
VATC	0.1853	0.7653	0.1020	0.3611	0.2719	0.5404	0.0157	0.4069	0.0305	-0.1421
YGSL	0.4354	0.2039	-0.5309	0.0788	0.5678	0.1528	0.2757	0.1732	0.5521	0.4248

Table A2.33. *(cont.)*

	NTHL	NRWY	PLND	PRTG	RMNA	SANM	SPAN	SWDN	SWTZ	TRKY
AUST	0.2896	0.2744	0.0053	0.0353	-0.1671	-0.0611	-0.1632	-0.2154	0.2122	-0.0014
BLGM	0.6635	0.6074	0.1132	0.0141	0.0054	0.6931	0.3496	0.5054	0.8273	0.0262
BLGR	-0.4565	-0.1735	0.5364	0.5216	0.5726	0.0425	0.2075	0.0128	0.0124	0.3888
CNDA	-0.2653	0.3263	0.8666	0.3885	0.7433	0.6155	0.6120	0.5143	0.0222	0.6245
CYPR	0.0636	-0.0169	0.1266	-0.3328	-0.0573	0.6721	0.0795	0.0945	0.5643	0.0021
CZCH	0.5157	0.7663	0.0205	0.2522	-0.0030	0.1299	0.2867	0.6241	0.2367	0.4662
DNMK	0.1191	-0.1838	-0.2602	-0.0746	-0.2606	0.0879	-0.3837	-0.2893	0.6344	-0.2390
FNLD	-0.5249	-0.5616	-0.0352	-0.0025	0.0201	-0.3535	-0.4474	-0.6266	-0.3090	-0.2897
FRNC	0.1062	0.2951	0.1909	0.5826	0.1537	-0.1437	0.2274	0.2938	0.0777	0.5266
FRG	0.0350	0.2228	0.2886	0.1748	0.2423	0.0387	0.4200	0.2667	-0.3839	0.0817
GDR	0.2327	0.3845	0.6729	-0.0047	0.4410	0.6045	0.6461	0.1944	0.1932	-0.0037
GRCE	0.1681	0.4785	0.0859	0.3826	0.0931	0.4809	0.0991	0.6729	0.5073	0.4932
HNGR	0.6751	0.3932	-0.4357	-0.4633	-0.6113	-0.1048	-0.1682	-0.1171	0.2653	-0.1597
ICLD	0.5076	0.7033	0.3192	-0.2356	0.1475	0.4548	0.4558	0.3357	0.1271	0.0516
IRLD	-0.3733	0.0871	0.4001	0.6966	0.7103	0.1917	0.3051	0.5616	0.0621	0.4168
ITLY	0.3118	0.5066	0.2016	0.3467	0.1727	0.3616	0.4407	0.6361	0.2383	0.2784
LICH	0.4628	0.6730	0.3592	0.4947	0.2173	0.0277	0.5332	0.4500	0.1042	0.5116
LXBG	0.3541	0.5590	0.4996	-0.2506	0.3564	0.5851	0.7622	0.4798	0.0395	0.1082
MLTA	-0.3370	-0.1612	0.4008	0.5645	0.2553	0.2354	0.1507	0.1773	0.2319	0.5550
MNCO	-0.1153	0.0584	0.2408	0.8196	0.5147	-0.1635	0.0868	0.1486	0.1993	0.1504
NTHL	1.0000	0.6769	-0.1694	-0.3309	-0.3983	0.1994	0.2659	0.1362	0.5050	-0.1983
NRWY	0.6769	1.0000	0.3550	0.1715	0.1882	0.4483	0.6192	0.7105	0.2537	0.4044
PLND	-0.1694	0.3550	1.0000	0.5366	0.8672	0.6438	0.8487	0.5822	0.0980	0.6273
PRTG	-0.3309	0.1715	0.5366	1.0000	0.7102	0.0933	0.2763	0.4691	0.0793	0.5744
RMNA	-0.3983	0.1882	0.8672	0.7102	1.0000	0.4687	0.6543	0.5794	-0.0024	0.4980
SANM	0.1994	0.4483	0.6438	0.0933	0.4687	1.0000	0.7273	0.6876	0.5899	0.3668
SPAN	0.2659	0.6192	0.8487	0.2763	0.6543	0.7273	1.0000	0.7039	0.2479	0.5136
SWDN	0.1362	0.7105	0.5822	0.4691	0.5794	0.6876	0.7039	1.0000	0.2501	0.6978
SWTZ	0.5050	0.2537	0.0980	0.0793	-0.0024	0.5899	0.2479	0.2501	1.0000	0.0011
TRKY	-0.1983	0.4044	0.6273	0.5744	0.4980	0.3668	0.5136	0.6978	0.0011	1.0000
USSR	-0.2797	0.0670	0.7882	0.1883	0.7680	0.6292	0.6374	0.3442	0.0231	0.1958
UK	0.4109	0.3092	0.2087	-0.2813	0.0197	0.8386	0.4860	0.4725	0.7095	0.1148
USA	0.4766	0.2686	-0.0711	-0.2265	-0.0833	0.6501	0.2634	0.4173	0.7561	-0.1264
VATC	0.3265	0.5406	0.2166	0.0515	0.1980	0.8105	0.4273	0.7746	0.5910	0.2657
YGSL	-0.4562	0.1775	0.9051	0.7652	0.8984	0.4469	0.5863	0.5300	-0.0157	0.7052

	USSR	UK	USA	VATC	YGSL
AUST	-0.1623	-0.1961	-0.2764	-0.1553	0.0595
BLGM	0.1073	0.7149	0.7859	0.8203	-0.0516
BLGR	0.2489	-0.1971	-0.3640	-0.2890	0.6832
CNDA	0.7695	0.1597	-0.1524	0.2515	0.8420
CYPR	0.2812	0.7140	0.5322	0.5372	0.0422
CZCH	-0.4088	0.1989	0.2764	0.4429	0.0131
DNMK	-0.2559	0.2241	0.2826	0.1210	-0.1529
FNLD	0.0428	-0.5026	-0.5736	-0.5920	0.1593
FRNC	-0.4185	-0.1584	-0.1443	-0.0922	0.3011
FRG	0.2203	-0.1235	-0.1231	-0.0232	0.1682
GDR	0.6743	0.2983	0.0734	0.1853	0.4354
GRCE	-0.1049	0.4070	0.4710	0.7653	0.2039
HNGR	-0.6153	0.2024	0.2252	0.1020	-0.5309
ICLD	0.4054	0.2830	0.1455	0.3611	0.0788
IRLD	0.1927	0.0192	0.1246	0.2719	0.5678
ITLY	-0.1208	0.3450	0.4446	0.5404	0.1528
LICH	-0.1249	-0.0937	-0.1137	0.0157	0.2757
LXBG	0.5323	0.5057	0.3300	0.4069	0.1732
MLTA	0.0608	0.0642	-0.0895	0.0305	0.5521
MNCO	-0.0015	-0.3645	-0.1603	-0.1421	0.4248
NTHL	-0.2797	0.4109	0.4766	0.3265	-0.4562
NRWY	0.0670	0.3092	0.2686	0.5406	0.1775
PLND	0.7882	0.2087	-0.0711	0.2166	0.9051
PRTG	0.1883	-0.2813	-0.2265	0.0515	0.7652
RMNA	0.7680	0.0197	-0.0833	0.1980	0.8984
SANM	0.6292	0.8386	0.6501	0.8105	0.4469
SPAN	0.6374	0.4860	0.2634	0.4273	0.5863
SWDN	0.3442	0.4725	0.4173	0.7746	0.5300
SWTZ	0.0231	0.7095	0.7561	0.5910	-0.0157
TRKY	0.1958	0.1148	-0.1264	0.2657	0.7052
USSR	1.0000	0.2534	0.0416	0.2232	0.6432
UK	0.2534	1.0000	0.8931	0.8100	-0.0394
USA	0.0416	0.8931	1.0000	0.8364	-0.2539
VATC	0.2232	0.8100	0.8364	1.0000	0.1110
YGSL	0.6432	-0.0394	-0.2539	0.1110	1.0000

Table A2.34. The Madrid Opening Statements: Correlations Between Countries

	AUST	BLGM	BLGR	CNDA	CYPR	CZCH	DNMK	FNLD	FRNC	FRG
AUST	1.0000	0.7273	0.6876	0.5899	0.3668	0.6292	0.8386	0.6501	0.8105	0.4469
BLGM	0.7273	1.0000	0.7039	0.2479	0.5136	0.6374	0.4860	0.2634	0.4273	0.5863
BLGR	0.6876	0.7039	1.0000	0.2501	0.6978	0.3442	0.4725	0.4173	0.7746	0.5300
CNDA	0.5899	0.2479	0.2501	1.0000	0.0011	0.0231	0.7095	0.7561	0.5910	-0.0157
CYPR	0.3668	0.5136	0.6978	0.0011	1.0000	0.1958	0.1148	-0.1264	0.2657	0.7052
CZCH	0.6292	0.6374	0.3442	0.0231	0.1958	1.0000	0.2534	0.0416	0.2232	0.6432
DNMK	0.8386	0.4860	0.4725	0.7095	0.1148	0.2534	1.0000	0.8931	0.8100	-0.0394
FNLD	0.6501	0.2634	0.4173	0.7561	-0.1264	0.0416	0.8931	1.0000	0.8364	-0.2539
FRNC	0.8105	0.4273	0.7746	0.5910	0.2657	0.2232	0.8100	0.8364	1.0000	0.1110
FRG	0.4469	0.5863	0.5300	-0.0157	0.7052	0.6432	-0.0394	-0.2539	0.1110	1.0000
GDR	0.7171	0.6858	0.2623	0.3283	0.4315	0.6654	0.5334	0.1380	0.2106	0.5498
GRCE	0.4294	0.6435	0.2883	0.3398	0.2394	0.0916	0.3915	0.1721	0.2169	0.0764
HNGR	0.6306	0.7847	0.4618	0.0492	0.6645	0.7139	0.2996	-0.1004	0.1590	0.7684
ICLD	0.8134	0.5456	0.5052	0.4441	0.5138	0.4063	0.7586	0.4333	0.6056	0.3227
IRLD	0.6377	0.4755	0.4893	0.1692	0.7823	0.4636	0.3615	0.0033	0.3301	0.7335
ITLY	0.5763	0.4804	0.2904	0.1656	0.6109	0.6800	0.2314	-0.1202	0.1179	0.8094
LICH	0.6710	0.9016	0.4846	0.1834	0.2796	0.6652	0.4616	0.1996	0.3232	0.4032
LXBG	0.6729	0.8138	0.5451	-0.0221	0.3113	0.7958	0.3803	0.1268	0.3610	0.5311
MLTA	0.6139	0.2901	0.2787	0.5937	0.3541	0.3420	0.3880	0.1845	0.3986	0.4074
MNCO	0.6468	0.6870	0.3817	0.3434	0.6727	0.5146	0.4294	0.0457	0.1992	0.6528
NTHL	0.8122	0.3453	0.3572	0.8214	0.0718	0.2188	0.9512	0.8594	0.7696	-0.0394
NRWY	0.7094	0.6644	0.4772	-0.0188	0.3518	0.7830	0.4865	0.1811	0.3966	0.5074
PLND	0.6356	0.7395	0.4682	-0.0620	0.5454	0.8530	0.2650	-0.0847	0.1934	0.7862
PRTG	0.4871	-0.0637	0.3658	0.5826	0.1044	-0.1489	0.6000	0.6271	0.7560	-0.2049
RMNA	0.6597	0.7438	0.5544	0.0293	0.6744	0.8028	0.2669	-0.0791	0.2523	0.8386
SANM	0.3104	0.0183	0.0821	0.2798	0.5760	0.0148	0.2610	-0.0416	0.1153	0.3200
SPAN	0.7446	0.6049	0.4311	0.2474	0.6097	0.7109	0.4485	0.0923	0.3183	0.7670
SWDN	0.7476	0.6822	0.4403	0.0737	0.1664	0.8780	0.5097	0.2814	0.4249	0.4894
SWTZ	0.5063	0.3176	0.2401	0.0281	0.2495	0.5959	0.1929	-0.0782	0.2435	0.4334
TRKY	0.6949	0.7910	0.5852	-0.0154	0.6091	0.8028	0.3512	0.0069	0.3138	0.7521
USSR	0.5943	0.6305	0.2780	-0.0734	0.3903	0.7704	0.3746	-0.0168	0.1409	0.5440
UK	0.6734	0.4542	0.4126	0.8054	0.0456	0.0724	0.7532	0.7215	0.6930	-0.1162
USA	0.7920	0.3371	0.5051	0.7337	-0.0195	0.2069	0.9305	0.9620	0.9151	-0.1147
VATC	0.7824	0.3505	0.4330	0.7576	0.2506	0.1225	0.9425	0.8094	0.7725	-0.0145
[illegible]	[illegible]	[illegible]	[illegible]	[illegible]	[illegible]	[illegible]	[illegible]	[illegible]	[illegible]	0.4230

	GDR	GRCE	HNGR	ICLD	IRLD	ITLY	LICH	LXBG	MLTA	MNCO
AUST	0.7171	0.4294	0.6306	0.8134	0.6377	0.5763	0.6710	0.6729	0.6139	0.6468
BLGM	0.6858	0.6435	0.7847	0.5456	0.4755	0.4804	0.9016**	0.8138	0.2901	0.6870
BLGR	0.2623	0.2883	0.4618	0.5052	0.4893	0.2904	0.4846	0.5451	0.2787	0.3817
CNDA	0.3283	0.3398	0.0492	0.4441	0.1692	0.1656	0.1834	-0.0221	0.5937	0.3434
CYPR	0.4315	0.2394	0.6645	0.5138	0.7823	0.6109	0.2796	0.3113	0.3541	0.6727
CZCH	0.6654	0.0916	0.7139	0.4063	0.4636	0.6800	0.6652	0.7958	0.3420	0.5146
DNMK	0.5334	0.3915	0.2996	0.7586	0.3615	0.2314	0.4616	0.3803	0.3880	0.4294
FNLD	0.1380	0.1721	-0.1004	0.4333	0.0033	-0.1202	0.1996	0.1268	0.1845	0.0457
FRNC	0.2106	0.2169	0.1590	0.6056	0.3301	0.1179	0.3232	0.3610	0.3986	0.1992
FRG	0.5498	0.0764	0.7684	0.3227	0.7335	0.8094	0.4032	0.5311	0.4074	0.6528
GDR	1.0000	0.5142	0.8996	0.7931	0.7712	0.8477	0.7126	0.6447	0.6019	0.9330
GRCE	0.5142	1.0000	0.4845	0.5011	0.2353	0.1446	0.7452	0.4536	0.4465	0.5421
HNGR	0.8996	0.4845	1.0000	0.7099	0.8170	0.8571	0.7677	0.7811	0.5069	0.8988
ICLD	0.7931	0.5011	0.7099	1.0000	0.7713	0.6337	0.5974	0.5849	0.6909	0.7544
IRLD	0.7712	0.2353	0.8170	0.7713	1.0000	0.9054	0.3610	0.4367	0.6331	0.8562
ITLY	0.8477	0.1446	0.8571	0.6337	0.9054	1.0000	0.4071	0.4763	0.6359	0.8733
LICH	0.7126	0.7452	0.7677	0.5974	0.3610	0.4071	1.0000	0.9092	0.3679	0.6097
LXBG	0.6447	0.4536	0.7811	0.5849	0.4367	0.4763	0.9092	1.0000	0.2900	0.5000
MLTA	0.6019	0.4465	0.5069	0.6909	0.6331	0.6359	0.3679	0.2900	1.0000	0.6461
MNCO	0.9330	0.5421	0.8988	0.7544	0.8562	0.8733	0.6097	0.5000	0.6461	1.0000
NTHL	0.5288	0.3388	0.2336	0.7277	0.3951	0.3009	0.3208	0.2124	0.5511	0.4530
NRWY	0.7241	0.2570	0.7955	0.7292	0.6015	0.6093	0.7536	0.9197	0.3141	0.5544
PLND	0.8143	0.2762	0.9459	0.6330	0.7382	0.8199	0.7442	0.8716	0.3975	0.7414
PRTG	0.0423	0.1923	-0.0888	0.5726	0.2331	-0.0055	0.0026	-0.0069	0.5996	0.0582
RMNA	0.8127	0.3157	0.9601	0.6838	0.8102	0.8648	0.7159	0.8164	0.5273	0.8054
SANM	0.5709	0.1731	0.4720	0.6592	0.8037	0.6911	-0.0184	-0.0526	0.6687	0.6969
SPAN	0.9012	0.2283	0.8891	0.7620	0.9274	0.9627	0.5254	0.5989	0.6122	0.8886
SWDN	0.6792	0.1958	0.7044	0.6002	0.4641	0.5509	0.7573	0.9153	0.2683	0.4647
SWTZ	0.5598	0.3076	0.6300	0.6534	0.5487	0.5752	0.5574	0.6892	0.7032	0.4475
TRKY	0.7980	0.3540	0.9449	0.7083	0.7497	0.7703	0.7887	0.9032	0.4196	0.7432
USSR	0.8582	0.2933	0.8911	0.7104	0.6802	0.7481	0.7225	0.8276	0.3318	0.7130
UK	0.3557	0.7138	0.1653	0.5749	0.1469	0.0390	0.5041	0.2579	0.6102	0.3482
USA	0.2785	0.2222	0.0626	0.5898	0.1919	0.0608	0.3016	0.2687	0.3668	0.1783
VATC	0.5357	0.3625	0.2857	0.8013	0.4959	0.3278	0.2937	0.1890	0.5375	0.5148
YGSL	0.7845	0.2561	0.6642	0.8441	0.8877	0.8155	0.2803	0.3132	0.7467	0.7761

Table A2.34. *(cont.)*

	NTHL	NRWY	PLND	PRTG	RMNA	SANM	SPAN	SWDN	SWTZ	TRKY
AUST	0.8122	0.7094	0.6356	0.4871	0.6597	0.3104	0.7446	0.7476	0.5063	0.6949
BLGM	0.3453	0.6644	0.7395	-0.0637	0.7438	0.0183	0.6049	0.6822	0.3176	0.7910
BLGR	0.3572	0.4772	0.4682	0.3658	0.5544	0.0821	0.4311	0.4403	0.2401	0.5852
CNDA	0.8214	-0.0188	-0.0620	0.5826	0.0293	0.2798	0.2474	0.0737	0.0281	-0.0154
CYPR	0.0718	0.3518	0.5454	0.1044	0.6744	0.5760	0.6097	0.1664	0.2495	0.6091
CZCH	0.2188	0.7830	0.8530	-0.1489	0.8028	0.0148	0.7109	0.8780	0.5959	0.8028
DNMK	0.9512	0.4865	0.2650	0.6000	0.2669	0.2610	0.4485	0.5097	0.1929	0.3512
FNLD	0.8594	0.1811	-0.0847	0.6271	-0.0791	-0.0416	0.0923	0.2814	-0.0782	0.0069
FRNC	0.7696	0.3966	0.1934	0.7560	0.2523	0.1153	0.3183	0.4249	0.2435	0.3138
FRG	-0.0394	0.5074	0.7862	-0.2049	0.8386	0.3200	0.7670	0.4894	0.4334	0.7521
GDR	0.5288	0.7241	0.8143	0.0423	0.8127	0.5709	0.9012	0.6792	0.5598	0.7980
GRCE	0.3388	0.2570	0.2762	0.1923	0.3157	0.1731	0.2283	0.1958	0.3076	0.3540
HNGR	0.2336	0.7955	0.9459	-0.0888	0.9601	0.4720	0.8891	0.7044	0.6300	0.9449
ICLD	0.7277	0.7292	0.6330	0.5726	0.6838	0.6592	0.7620	0.6002	0.6534	0.7083
IRLD	0.3951	0.6015	0.7382	0.2331	0.8102	0.8037	0.9274	0.4641	0.5487	0.7497
ITLY	0.3009	0.6093	0.8199	-0.0055	0.8648	0.6911	0.9627	0.5509	0.5752	0.7703
LICH	0.3208	0.7536	0.7442	0.0026	0.7159	-0.0184	0.5254	0.7573	0.5574	0.7887
LXBG	0.2124	0.9197	0.8716	-0.0069	0.8164	-0.0526	0.5989	0.9153	0.6892	0.9032
MLTA	0.5511	0.3141	0.3975	0.5996	0.5273	0.6687	0.6122	0.2683	0.7032	0.4196
MNCO	0.4530	0.5544	0.7414	0.0582	0.8054	0.6969	0.8886	0.4647	0.4475	0.7432
NTHL	1.0000	0.3386	0.1712	0.6802	0.2061	0.4002	0.4665	0.3799	0.2032	0.2348
NRWY	0.3386	1.0000	0.9040	0.0949	0.8412	0.1831	0.7399	0.9516	0.7227	0.9255
PLND	0.1712	0.9040	1.0000	-0.1295	0.9748	0.2964	0.8661	0.8564	0.6875	0.9843
PRTG	0.6802	0.0949	-0.1295	1.0000	-0.0182	0.3931	0.0978	0.0301	0.3627	-0.0149
RMNA	0.2061	0.8412	0.9748	-0.0182	1.0000	0.4107	0.8905	0.7694	0.7081	0.9750
SANM	0.4002	0.1831	0.2964	0.3931	0.4107	1.0000	0.6430	-0.0049	0.3721	0.3029
SPAN	0.4665	0.7399	0.8661	0.0978	0.8905	0.6430	1.0000	0.6881	0.5833	0.8457
SWDN	0.3799	0.9516	0.8564	0.0301	0.7694	-0.0049	0.6881	1.0000	0.6385	0.8556
SWTZ	0.2032	0.7227	0.6875	0.3627	0.7081	0.3721	0.5833	0.6385	1.0000	0.6984
TRKY	0.2348	0.9255	0.9843	-0.0149	0.9750	0.3029	0.8457	0.8556	0.6984	1.0000
USSR	0.2655	0.9345	0.9350	-0.0890	0.8725	0.3495	0.8208	0.8595	0.6756	0.9192
UK	0.7879	0.1539	0.0316	0.6838	0.1114	0.1691	0.1749	0.1917	0.2402	0.1347
USA	0.9176	0.3416	0.0881	0.7217	0.1054	0.0922	0.2697	0.4214	0.1504	0.1797
VATC	0.9690	0.3468	0.1868	0.7108	0.2442	0.5248	0.4949	0.3179	0.1906	0.2723
YGSL	0.5707	0.5447	0.5751	0.4274	0.6281	0.8912	0.8401	0.4125	0.6310	0.5766

	USSR	UK	USA	VATC	YGSL
AUST	0.5943	0.6734	0.7920	0.7824	0.6094
BLGM	0.6305	0.4542	0.3371	0.3505	0.2442
BLGR	0.2780	0.4126	0.5051	0.4330	0.1922
CNDA	-0.0734	0.8054	0.7337	0.7576	0.3149
CYPR	0.3903	0.0456	-0.0195	0.2506	0.4780
CZCH	0.7704	0.0724	0.2069	0.1225	0.3575
DNMK	0.3746	0.7532	0.9305	0.9425	0.4804
FNLD	-0.0168	0.7215	0.9620	0.8094	0.1214
FRNC	0.1409	0.6930	0.9151	0.7725	0.3029
FRG	0.5440	-0.1162	-0.1147	-0.0145	0.4230
GDR	0.8582	0.3557	0.2785	0.5357	0.7845
GRCE	0.2933	0.7138	0.2222	0.3625	0.2561
HNGR	0.8911	0.1653	0.0626	0.2857	0.6642
ICLD	0.7104	0.5749	0.5898	0.8013	0.8441
IRLD	0.6802	0.1469	0.1919	0.4959	0.8877
ITLY	0.7481	0.0390	0.0608	0.3278	0.8155
LICH	0.7225	0.5041	0.3016	0.2937	0.2803
LXBG	0.8276	0.2579	0.2687	0.1890	0.3132
MLTA	0.3318	0.6102	0.3668	0.5375	0.7467
MNCO	0.7130	0.3482	0.1783	0.5148	0.7761
NTHL	0.2655	0.7879	0.9176	0.9690	0.5707
NRWY	0.9345	0.1539	0.3416	0.3468	0.5447
PLND	0.9350	0.0316	0.0881	0.1868	0.5751
PRTG	-0.0890	0.6838	0.7217	0.7108	0.4274
RMNA	0.8725	0.1114	0.1054	0.2442	0.6281
SANM	0.3495	0.1691	0.0922	0.5248	0.8912
SPAN	0.8208	0.1749	0.2697	0.4949	0.8401
SWDN	0.8595	0.1917	0.4214	0.3179	0.4125
SWTZ	0.6756	0.2402	0.1504	0.1906	0.6310
TRKY	0.9192	0.1347	0.1797	0.2723	0.5766
USSR	1.0000	0.0459	0.1399	0.2886	0.6448
UK	0.0459	1.0000	0.7643	0.7484	0.2824
USA	0.1399	0.7643	1.0000	0.8691	0.3095
VATC	0.2886	0.7484	0.8691	1.0000	0.6344
YGSL	0.6448	0.2824	0.3095	0.6344	1.0000

Appendix A3

The Structure and Dynamics of East–West Relations: Additional Tables

A3.2 DISARMAMENT AND SECURITY

See tables on following pages.

Table A3.1. Military Expenditure of NATO Countries (in millions of US dollars, prices and exchange rates of 1978)

Year	Countries														
YEAR	NATO	BLGM	CNDA	DNMK	FRNC	FRG	GRCE	ITLY	LXBG	NTHL	NRWY	PRTG	TRKY	UK	USA
1960	150501	1582	3422	741	12623	11654	437	3231	19	2168	603	397	987	12636	100001
1961	156976	1600	3511	759	13107	12393	422	3341	20	2542	656	636	1086	12688	104215
1962	170961	1708	3663	928	13565	15729	430	3672	25	2700	722	722	1144	12953	113000
1963	171425	1765	3409	932	13272	17661	441	4084	24	2757	754	707	1141	13087	111391
1964	168800	1887	3540	965	13691	16952	458	4181	30	3006	765	767	1240	13557	107761
1965	168115	1839	3167	1026	13888	16715	495	4344	30	2896	885	768	1318	13552	107192
1966	186872	1867	3248	1010	14295	16427	538	4698	30	2815	880	811	1268	13427	125558
1967	211513	1958	3487	1009	15045	17087	693	4589	25	3122	908	995	1281	13825	147489
1968	213547	2028	3288	1076	15072	15150	809	4667	22	3081	964	1049	1354	13521	151466
1969	206916	2039	3102	1058	14396	16622	915	4579	22	3225	1017	971	1351	12672	144947
1970	194021	2174	3256	1038	14480	16827	990	4831	23	3349	1018	1061	1448	12654	130872
1971	187046	2211	3273	1137	14663	18001	1044	5457	19	3452	1045	1112	1655	13322	120655
1972	191043	2333	3279	1130	15023	19255	1114	6027	21	3558	1043	1097	1683	14375	121105
1973	186168	2419	3276	1074	15573	20010	1112	6018	23	3614	1052	1014	1806	14201	114976
1974	186851	2517	3515	1177	15505	20885	1065	6025	25	3781	1080	1215	1894	14501	113666
1975	185885	2758	3468	1277	16194	20791	1705	5607	26	3965	1171	836	2908	14950	110229
1976	180902	2902	3702	1260	16898	20641	1665	5580	28	3922	1200	653	3420	14770	104261
1977	186671	2978	3939	1266	17670	20561	2015	5990	28	4373	1223	616	3320	14155	108537
1978	189715	3175	4087	1315	18623	21417	2071	6246	30	4228	1307	623	2728	14618	109247
1979	191803	3246	3875	1322	19112	21730	1882	6642	31	4482	1340	631	2368	15281	109861
1980	193911	3305	3745	1322	19498	22003	1673	6324	35	4333	1365	674	2211	16187	111236

Table A3.2. Military Expenditure of WTO Countries (in millions of US dollars, prices and exchange rates of 1978)

	Countries							
YEAR	WTO	BLGR	CZCH	GDR	HNGR	PLND	RMNA	USSR
1960	51425	208	1025	456	235	1177	324	48000
1961	63655	252	1110	456	256	1333	348	59900
1962	70448	299	1265	1231	373	1405	375	65500
1963	77144	345	1263	1277	493	1570	396	71800
1964	73840	302	1192	1323	468	1640	415	68500
1965	71377	267	1181	1414	437	1726	452	65900
1966	74759	279	1302	1460	396	1851	471	69000
1967	81119	287	1471	1642	412	1915	492	74900
1968	92383	297	1578	2196	507	2161	544	85100
1969	98839	340	1605	2385	574	2349	586	91000
1970	100837	365	1645	2605	703	2364	655	92500
1971	102753	399	1721	2745	721	2586	681	93900
1972	104440	440	1739	2864	668	2621	708	95400
1973	106441	475	1831	3058	651	2807	719	96900
1974	108303	538	1948	3172	712	2838	795	98300
1975	110424	611	2008	3364	766	3001	874	99800
1976	112403	664	2115	3444	721	3208	951	101300
1977	114144	597	2148	3560	750	3412	977	102700
1978	115774	624	2105	3738	819	3218	1070	104200
1979	117643	666	2115	4123	780	3195	1064	105700
1980	.	.		4470	.	.	.	107300

Table A3.3. Military Expenditure of Neutral and Nonaligned Countries (in millions of US dollars, prices and exchange rates of 1978)

				Countries					
YEAR	N+N	AUST	FNLD	IRLD	SPAN	SWDN	SWTZ	YGSL	CYP
1960	5813	309	254	76	966	1888	1080	1240	
1961	6246	298	294	79	981	1981	1259	1354	
1962	6808	314	411	81	1145	2131	1391	1335	
1963	7023	384	326	81	1179	2273	1450	1330	
1964	7459	482	322	90	1198	2390	1570	1393	1
1965	7499	399	329	93	1189	2530	1584	1358	1
1966	7774	458	324	89	1401	2555	1664	1269	1
1967	7852	478	316	90	1573	2490	1623	1266	1
1968	7988	480	362	93	1569	2492	1546	1433	1
1969	8273	494	331	97	1630	2627	1649	1433	1
1970	8493	490	350	110	1662	2696	1697	1474	1
1971	8691	472	381	121	1718	2739	1766	1477	1
1972	9245	506	435	144	1868	2811	1799	1666	1
1973	9410	511	442	152	2042	2822	1743	1683	1
1974	10023	575	455	167	2217	2844	1737	2006	2
1975	10487	642	490	182	2308	2925	1638	2279	2
1976	10958	657	499	169	2472	2919	1856	2363	2
1977	10922	679	462	174	2478	2932	1753	2414	3
1978	11014	741	485	182	2461	2980	1762	2379	2
1979	11403	767	473	200	2672	3067	1843	2363	1
1980	.	765	532	206	2784	2908	1814	2605	

Table A3.4. Rates of Change of Military Expenditure of NATO Countries (percent of previous year)

Year	Countries														
YEAR	NATO	CNDA	BLGM	DNMK	FRNC	FRG	GRCE	ITLY	LXBG	NTHL	NRWY	PRTG	TRKY	UK	USA
1961	4.30	2.60	1.14	2.43	3.83	6.34	-3.43	3.40	5.26	17.25	8.79	60.20	10.03	.41	4.21
1962	8.91	4.33	6.75	22.27	3.49	26.92	1.90	9.91	25.00	6.22	10.06	13.52	5.34	2.09	8.43
1963	.27	-6.93	3.34	.43	-2.16	12.28	2.56	11.22	-4.00	2.11	4.43	-2.08	- .26	1.03	-1.42
1964	-1.53	3.84	6.91	3.54	3.16	-4.01	3.85	2.38	25.00	9.03	1.46	8.49	8.68	3.59	-3.26
1965	- .41	-10.5	-2.54	6.32	1.44	-1.40	8.08	3.90	0.0	-3.66	15.69	.13	6.29	- .04	- .53
1966	11.16	2.56	1.52	-1.56	2.93	-1.72	8.69	8.15	0.0	-2.80	- .56	5.60	-3.79	- .92	17.13
1967	13.19	7.36	4.87	- .10	5.25	4.02	28.81	-2.32	-16.7	10.91	3.18	22.69	1.03	2.96	17.47
1968	.96	-5.71	3.58	6.64	.18	-11.3	16.74	1.70	-12.0	-1.31	6.17	5.43	5.70	-2.20	2.70
1969	-3.11	-5.66	.54	-1.67	-4.49	9.72	13.10	-1.89	0.0	4.67	5.50	-7.44	- .22	-6.28	-4.30
1970	-6.23	4.96	6.62	-1.89	.58	1.23	8.20	5.50	4.55	3.84	.10	9.27	7.18	- .14	-9.71
1971	-3.60	.52	1.70	9.54	1.26	6.98	5.45	12.96	-18.3	3.08	2.65	4.81	14.30	5.28	-7.81
1972	2.14	.18	5.52	- .62	2.46	6.97	6.70	10.45	11.17	3.07	- .19	-1.35	1.69	7.90	.37
1973	-2.55	- .09	3.69	-4.96	3.66	3.92	- .18	- .15	9.57	1.57	.86	-7.57	7.31	-1.21	-5.06
1974	.37	7.30	4.05	9.59	- .44	4.37	-4.23	.12	7.86	4.62	2.66	19.82	4.87	2.11	-1.14
1975	- .52	-1.34	9.57	8.50	4.44	- .45	60.09	-6.94	6.48	4.87	8.43	-31.2	53.54	3.10	-3.02
1976	-2.68	6.75	5.22	-1.33	4.35	- .72	-2.35	- .48	7.22	-1.08	2.48	-21.9	17.61	-1.20	-5.41
1977	3.19	6.40	2.62	.48	4.57	- .39	21.02	7.35	-2.13	11.50	1.92	-5.67	-2.92	-4.16	4.10
1978	1.63	3.76	6.62	3.87	5.39	4.16	2.78	4.27	8.70	-3.32	6.87	1.14	-17.8	3.27	.65
1979	1.10	-5.19	2.24	.53	2.63	1.46	-9.13	6.34	3.00	6.01	2.52	1.28	-13.2	4.54	.56
1980	1.10	-3.35	1.82	0.0	2.02	1.26	-11.1	-4.79	12.30	-3.32	1.87	6.81	-6.63	5.93	1.25

Table A3.5. Rates of Change of Military Expenditure of WTO Countries (percent of previous year)

Year	Countries							
YEAR	WTO	BLGR	CZCH	GDR	HNGR	PLND	RMNA	USSR
1961	23.78	21.15	8.29	0.0	8.94	13.25	7.41	24.7
1962	10.67	18.65	13.96	170.0	45.70	5.40	7.76	9.3
1963	9.50	15.38	- .16	3.74	32.17	11.74	5.60	9.6
1964	-4.28	-12.5	-5.62	3.60	-5.07	4.46	4.80	-4.6
1965	-3.34	-11.6	- .92	6.88	-6.62	5.24	8.92	-3.8
1966	4.74	4.49	10.25	3.25	-9.38	7.24	4.20	4.7
1967	8.51	2.87	12.98	12.47	4.04	3.46	4.46	8.5
1968	13.89	3.48	7.27	33.74	23.06	12.85	10.57	13.6
1969	6.99	14.48	1.71	8.61	13.21	8.70	7.72	6.9
1970	2.02	7.35	2.49	9.22	22.47	.64	11.77	1.6
1971	1.90	9.32	4.62	5.37	2.56	9.39	3.97	1.5
1972	1.64	10.28	1.05	4.34	-7.35	1.35	3.96	1.6
1973	1.92	7.95	5.29	6.77	-2.54	7.10	1.55	1.5
1974	1.75	13.26	6.39	3.73	9.37	1.10	10.57	1.4
1975	1.96	13.57	3.08	6.05	7.58	5.74	9.94	1.5
1976	1.79	8.67	5.33	2.38	-5.87	6.90	8.81	1.5
1977	1.55	-10.1	1.56	3.37	4.02	6.36	2.73	1.3
1978	1.43	4.52	-2.00	5.00	9.20	-5.69	9.52	1.4
1979	1.61	6.73	.48	10.30	-4.76	- .71	- .56	1.4
1980	.	.	.	8.42	.	.	.	1.5

Table A3.6. Rates of Change of Military Expenditure of Neutral and Nonaligned Countries (percent of previous year)

Year	Countries								
YEAR	N+N	AUST	FNLD	IRLD	SPAN	SWDN	SWTZ	YGSL	CYPR
1961	7.45	-3.56	15.75	3.95	1.55	4.93	16.57	9.19	
1962	9.00	5.37	39.80	2.53	16.72	7.57	10.48	-1.40	
1963	3.16	22.29	-20.7	0.0	2.97	6.66	4.24	- .37	
1964	6.21	25.52	-1.23	11.11	1.61	5.15	8.28	4.74	
1965	.54	-17.2	2.17	3.33	- .75	5.86	.89	-2.51	21.43
1966	3.67	14.79	-1.52	-4.30	17.83	.99	5.05	-6.55	-17.6
1967	1.00	4.37	-2.47	1.12	12.28	-2.54	-2.46	- .24	14.29
1968	1.73	.42	14.56	3.33	- .25	.08	-4.74	13.19	-18.8
1969	3.57	2.92	-8.56	4.30	3.89	5.42	6.66	0.0	-7.69
1970	2.66	- .81	5.74	13.40	1.96	2.63	2.91	2.86	16.67
1971	2.33	-3.67	8.86	10.00	3.37	1.59	4.07	.20	20.00
1972	6.38	7.20	14.17	19.01	8.73	2.63	1.87	12.80	-2.38
1973	1.78	.99	1.61	5.56	9.31	.39	-3.11	1.02	-7.32
1974	6.51	12.52	2.94	9.87	8.57	.78	- .34	19.19	42.76
1975	4.63	11.65	7.69	8.98	4.10	2.85	-5.70	13.61	6.45
1976	4.49	2.34	1.84	-7.14	7.11	- .21	13.31	3.69	-2.60
1977	- .32	3.35	-7.41	2.96	.24	.45	-5.55	2.16	32.89
1978	.84	9.13	4.98	4.60	- .69	1.64	.51	-1.45	-20.4
1979	3.53	3.51	-2.47	9.89	8.57	2.92	4.60	- .67	-26.1
1980	.	- .26	12.47	3.00	4.19	-5.18	-1.57	10.24	.

Table A3.7. US and USSR Strategic Nuclear Forces

YEAR	BOMBERS USA	BOMBERS USSR	SUBMARINES USA	SUBMARINES USSR	SLBM USA	SLBM USSR	ICBM USA	ICBM USSR	DELIVERY SYSTEMS USA	DELIVERY SYSTEMS USSR	NUCLEAR WARHEADS USA	NUCLEAR WARHEADS USSR
1960	450	130	2	0	32	0	9	0	491	130	1391	390
1961	600	140	5	0	80	0	63	20	743	160	1943	440
1962	630	140	9	2	144	6	294	50	1068	196	2328	476
1963	630	140	14	4	224	12	414	100	1268	252	2528	532
1964	630	140	26	6	416	18	834	200	1880	358	3396	638
1965	630	150	31	8	496	24	854	270	1980	444	3656	744
1966	600	160	37	11	592	33	904	300	2096	493	4064	813
1967	540	150	41	12	656	36	1054	460	2250	646	4226	946
1968	560	150	41	18	656	39	1054	1050	2270	1239	4286	1539
1969	550	150	41	19	656	109	1054	1050	2260	1309	4256	1609
1970	505	140	41	20	656	205	1054	1500	2215	1845	4141	2125
1971	479	156	41	21	656	360	1054	1527	2189	2043	4600	2100
1972	430	156	41	27	656	459	1054	1527	2140	2142	5700	2500
1973	430	156	41	34	656	567	1054	1547	2140	2270	6784	2200
1974	390	156	41	41	656	655	1054	1567	2100	2378	7650	2500
1975	369	156	41	46	656	715	1054	1587	2079	2458	8500	2500
1976	348	156	41	52	656	811	1054	1547	2058	2514	8400	3300
1977	348	156	41	57	656	891	1054	1447	2058	2494	8500	4000
1978	348	156	41	59	656	923	1054	1400	2058	2479	9000	4500
1979	348	156	41	60	656	939	1054	1398	2058	2493	9200	5000
1980	348	156	37	62	600	950	1054	1398	2002	2504	9200	6000

Table A3.8. Eurostrategic Weapons of NATO and WTO

YEAR	MRBM/IRBM NATO	MRBM/IRBM WTO	SLBM NATO	SLBM WTO	BOMBER NATO	BOMBER WTO	TOTAL SYSTEMS NATO	TOTAL SYSTEMS WTO
1960	60	0	0	0	0	1000	60	1000
1961	60	200	0	0	0	1000	60	1200
1962	105	700	0	0	0	1000	105	1700
1963	0	750	0	0	0	1000	0	1750
1964	0	725	0	0	0	1000	0	1725
1965	0	725	0	0	0	900	0	1625
1966	0	725	0	0	80	900	80	1625
1967	0	725	0	0	80	800	80	1525
1968	0	750	16	0	80	750	96	1500
1969	0	700	32	0	50	750	82	1450
1970	0	700	48	0	50	725	98	1425
1971	0	700	64	78	50	700	114	1478
1972	0	600	64	60	131	700	195	1360
1973	0	600	64	60	128	700	192	1360
1974	0	600	64	57	128	700	192	1357
1975	0	600	64	57	128	670	192	1327
1976	0	600	64	54	128	650	192	1304
1977	0	620	64	54	206	476	270	1150
1978	0	690	64	54	204	491	268	1235
1979	0	710	64	60	204	503	268	1273
1980	0	600	64	60	204	518	268	1178

A.3.3 COOPERATIVE AND CONFLICTIVE INTERACTIONS

Table A3.9. Cooperative Interactions in Europe: Time Series for Selected Dyads (index values computed on the basis of COPDAB data)

ACTOR:	USA	USA	USA	USA	USA	USA	USA	USA	USA	UK	UK	UK	UK	UK	UK	UK	UK	UK
TARGET:	UK	FRNC	SWTZ	FRG	GDR	PLND	CZCH	YGSL	USSR	USA	FRNC	SWTZ	FRG	GDR	PLND	CZCH	YGSL	USSR
1960	300	74	0	155	6	176	0	94	48	295	69	94	171	0	27	0	20	105
1961	398	678	27	681	43	93	33	130	419	463	220	6	364	6	6	6	0	126
1962	668	195	108	381	24	68	6	54	430	664	122	14	316	27	0	0	0	125
1963	545	270	0	394	16	55	33	47	286	498	130	0	124	27	0	0	0	146
1964	287	204	27	177	18	33	0	47	235	284	53	0	94	0	54	81	0	259
1965	123	70	0	67	20	39	27	97	66	140	18	14	131	0	12	6	22	97
1966	232	92	20	273	20	20	12	57	345	229	116	16	132	6	33	39	6	94
1967	442	197	6	220	27	88	12	85	493	335	182	10	150	6	75	20	6	222
1968	184	32	70	128	6	91	60	45	269	192	6	33	167	0	14	30	0	108
1969	268	167	40	279	33	33	46	37	377	242	71	39	192	43	14	0	0	182
1970	318	89	37	191	24	0	0	28	413	321	124	37	148	60	10	0	12	135
1971	150	208	10	142	14	78	0	6	538	207	110	0	53	14	6	0	0	78
1972	247	103	0	91	0	141	0	55	513	137	173	0	122	6	0	0	12	14
1973	299	161	77	346	97	131	79	82	1193	190	354	100	424	40	20	34	111	109
1974	81	145	0	126	67	92	69	109	618	53	60	0	57	0	27	0	0	33
1975	262	209	14	184	42	143	28	56	537	256	167	6	156	56	52	42	28	114
1976	112	70	95	135	54	58	14	69	227	74	187	0	197	14	27	0	0	0
1977	286	133	14	173	41	34	14	112	542	248	118	41	160	41	14	14	12	163
1978	309	305	39	309	12	0	0	51	467	315	257	6	260	6	6	6	0	48

ACTOR:	FRNC	FRNC	FRNC	FRNC	FRNC	FRNC	FRNC	FRNC	FRNC	SWTZ	SWTZ	SWTZ	SWTZ	SWTZ	SWTZ	SWTZ	SWTZ	SWTZ
TARGET:	USA	UK	SWTZ	FRG	GDR	PLND	CZCH	YGSL	USSR	USA	UK	FRNC	FRG	GDR	PLND	CZCH	YGSL	USSR
1960	90	89	0	233	6	0	0	0	65	0	94	0	47	0	0	0	0	0
1961	444	177	16	434	6	12	6	0	62	6	41	51	20	0	0	0	0	0
1962	174	119	45	259	0	0	0	0	28	54	31	31	31	0	0	0	0	0
1963	292	67	0	270	6	33	6	27	59	0	31	0	10	0	0	0	0	0
1964	73	153	26	244	16	27	27	20	103	0	6	36	27	0	0	6	0	0
1965	44	26	0	194	20	43	27	0	96	0	0	0	0	0	0	0	0	0
1966	40	76	16	421	0	75	82	20	283	73	57	16	20	0	0	0	0	14
1967	221	212	0	515	18	105	57	6	142	10	0	0	0	0	0	0	0	27
1968	118	36	0	498	0	0	46	0	153	61	26	0	20	0	0	0	0	0
1969	133	126	45	514	16	14	0	27	170	117	66	66	66	0	0	16	0	14
1970	216	122	20	658	91	24	6	41	218	10	51	16	47	0	0	0	0	6
1971	183	86	0	470	14	0	0	0	187	20	0	0	0	10	0	0	0	0
1972	149	91	27	359	27	33	27	0	85	0	0	54	54	14	0	0	0	0
1973	207	505	111	458	65	20	20	132	270	82	135	121	123	0	0	0	14	0
1974	141	43	0	77	0	0	0	0	130	10	0	0	0	0	0	0	0	0
1975	189	178	0	255	42	97	38	42	200	37	6	0	0	0	10	0	0	6
1976	78	200	31	178	0	54	0	0	14	27	14	14	41	27	0	0	0	0
1977	125	154	41	142	14	41	14	0	91	14	41	41	41	14	14	14	0	14
1978	292	321	6	366	6	20	6	6	33	33	6	6	12	0	0	0	0	14

Table A3.9. *(cont.)*

ACTOR: TARGET:	FRG USA	FRG UK	FRG FRNC	FRG SWTZ	FRG GDR	FRG PLND	FRG CZCH	FRG YGSL	FRG USSR	GDR USA	GDR UK	GDR FRNC	GDR SWTZ	GDR FRG	GDR PLND	GDR CZCH	GDR YGSL	GDR USSR
1960	145	161	187	94	55	0	6	0	66	10	0	0	0	53	14	27	27	44
1961	612	365	367	6	12	27	0	0	53	24	6	6	0	20	108	40	6	107
1962	373	332	259	14	0	0	0	0	12	36	37	10	0	30	59	120	0	298
1963	189	77	286	6	6	54	6	6	33	6	27	6	0	6	108	67	0	94
1964	214	165	268	0	34	27	6	0	96	16	6	12	0	18	33	33	14	135
1965	77	108	137	0	69	47	0	0	12	6	0	33	0	36	80	47	0	257
1966	230	124	406	16	64	88	32	6	70	20	16	0	6	62	202	87	88	283
1967	264	151	522	0	42	22	84	51	120	16	6	6	0	66	243	155	46	200
1968	192	145	419	33	33	14	18	34	65	20	0	0	0	27	126	98	0	168
1969	236	202	534	99	12	70	33	75	144	6	33	0	0	18	384	250	0	401
1970	196	116	568	37	122	134	6	47	243	12	12	18	0	198	75	118	0	253
1971	228	63	485	0	92	0	6	0	94	0	0	0	0	72	124	77	0	143
1972	159	69	387	27	122	75	0	6	103	6	0	0	14	100	71	53	0	45
1973	265	429	426	81	193	95	46	142	262	62	46	67	14	126	72	20	20	200
1974	159	61	69	0	236	109	38	54	154	67	0	0	0	141	142	111	6	173
1975	168	188	229	0	148	69	28	28	166	42	56	42	0	97	218	155	18	406
1976	166	184	185	27	92	61	0	0	20	81	14	28	27	66	14	28	14	58
1977	144	139	144	41	74	84	20	16	79	41	41	14	14	96	124	102	14	184
1978	442	368	413	14	132	6	24	0	51	57	6	6	0	72	32	24	0	54

ACTOR:	PLND	PLND	PLND	PLND	PLND	PLND	PLND	PLND	PLND	CZCH	CZCH	CZCH	CZCH	CZCH	CZCH	CZCH	CZCH	CZCH
TARGET:	USA	UK	FRNC	SWTZ	FRG	GDR	CZCH	YGSL	USSR	USA	UK	FRNC	SWTZ	FRG	GDR	PLND	YGSL	USSR
1960	101	27	0	0	0	27	14	82	142	6	0	0	0	0	0	41	41	85
1961	33	18	12	0	0	125	73	115	195	0	6	6	0	6	77	73	14	67
1962	27	0	0	0	0	83	53	34	200	0	0	0	0	0	100	53	6	189
1963	53	0	33	0	27	100	91	33	128	12	0	6	0	6	67	91	94	197
1964	66	66	27	0	33	39	101	60	122	0	54	41	0	6	14	88	107	187
1965	0	0	47	0	41	74	75	20	273	6	0	27	0	6	47	81	6	206
1966	88	33	81	6	66	167	83	33	349	53	53	65	6	16	40	101	6	231
1967	101	65	86	0	37	191	125	59	291	18	6	78	0	98	101	131	46	222
1968	53	14	0	0	27	171	93	27	179	22	0	0	0	6	134	46	101	786
1969	0	14	14	0	34	352	327	6	421	16	0	0	14	30	256	343	24	697
1970	0	0	30	0	142	88	78	27	94	0	0	0	0	20	106	80	0	347
1971	12	27	0	0	0	133	125	0	309	0	0	0	0	6	76	87	0	185
1972	146	0	47	0	106	80	78	33	68	0	0	0	0	0	33	68	0	52
1973	46	16	16	0	117	96	22	42	215	28	6	6	0	55	6	26	32	85
1974	106	27	0	0	55	142	97	0	166	28	0	0	0	48	97	70	54	98
1975	56	42	110	0	42	218	191	28	330	28	42	38	0	14	193	220	28	346
1976	0	0	41	0	14	14	14	14	56	0	0	0	0	0	14	14	14	34
1977	14	14	55	14	52	140	126	0	224	14	34	14	14	20	118	126	0	140
1978	0	6	6	0	6	32	46	6	66	0	6	6	0	46	32	46	0	46

Table A3.9. *(cont.)*

ACTOR: TARGET:	YGSL USA	YGSL UK	YGSL FRNC	YGSL SWTZ	YGSL FRG	YGSL GDR	YGSL PLND	YGSL CZCH	YGSL USSR	USSR USA	USSR UK	USSR FRNC	USSR SWTZ	USSR FRG	USSR GDR	USSR PLND	USSR CZCH	USSR YGSL
1960	20	34	0	0	10	27	82	41	101	0	0	0	0	0	14	0	27	0
1961	54	6	0	0	27	14	109	14	89	44	0	0	0	0	0	33	0	58
1962	60	0	0	0	0	0	20	0	200	138	0	12	0	0	45	39	39	0
1963	24	0	0	0	6	0	33	108	101	103	6	6	0	6	20	0	26	20
1964	78	0	0	0	0	20	39	61	121	133	31	0	0	14	6	10	81	27
1965	27	12	0	0	0	6	6	20	169	36	10	10	0	0	39	20	48	136
1966	40	6	0	6	0	43	33	6	146	193	10	55	0	0	14	10	0	33
1967	34	12	34	0	39	63	70	49	158	44	0	51	0	6	59	57	14	6
1968	61	0	0	0	10	14	27	147	81	40	0	27	0	6	10	0	42	14
1969	6	0	41	0	84	0	6	6	40	70	0	6	0	33	122	100	167	6
1970	28	14	41	0	61	0	27	0	40	30	0	6	0	38	14	0	55	0
1971	67	0	0	0	0	0	0	0	70	179	0	43	0	14	0	28	0	0
1972	27	6	0	0	6	0	41	0	20	54	0	0	0	20	0	0	0	16
1973	76	107	109	14	128	6	18	12	123	168	0	38	0	40	54	28	34	30
1974	95	6	0	0	68	6	0	54	121	64	6	6	0	14	34	14	42	0
1975	42	28	28	0	14	42	42	28	136	52	24	56	0	42	84	97	56	28
1976	41	0	0	0	0	14	14	14	14	51	0	14	0	0	0	14	0	0
1977	116	6	14	0	6	0	14	14	60	248	84	37	41	72	83	97	83	27
1978	46	14	0	0	6	0	6	0	39	145	38	0	6	0	26	20	20	27

Table A3.10. Conflictive Interactions in Europe: Time Series for Selected Dyads (index values computed on the basis of COPDAB data)

ACTOR:	USA	USA	USA	USA	USA	USA	USA	USA	USA	UK	UK	UK	UK	UK	UK	UK	UK	UK
TARGET:	UK	FRNC	SWTZ	FRG	GDR	PLND	CZCH	YGSL	USSR	USA	FRNC	SWTZ	FRG	GDR	PLND	CZCH	YGSL	USSR
1960	6	67	29	28	38	6	16	0	583	28	28	0	28	22	0	16	0	191
1961	50	58	0	0	227	80	58	28	939	46	44	0	50	32	0	0	0	523
1962	52	44	0	12	160	58	16	29	1070	100	0	0	6	60	0	0	16	530
1963	44	105	0	28	48	48	29	0	264	82	6	0	0	32	0	22	0	61
1964	109	271	0	22	51	74	29	64	158	30	12	0	6	0	0	0	0	318
1965	6	89	0	16	16	0	0	16	205	91	6	0	6	0	6	0	0	139
1966	98	370	16	46	112	117	51	16	517	96	44	6	50	64	0	0	0	134
1967	130	44	0	28	38	0	22	41	551	52	108	0	54	22	0	0	0	164
1968	16	90	0	61	109	45	47	0	334	41	0	0	0	45	32	0	0	226
1969	22	28	0	44	57	16	45	0	356	28	60	0	6	48	0	0	6	111
1970	32	22	0	18	66	0	29	0	791	30	0	0	0	22	0	0	0	183
1971	58	74	58	58	0	0	0	0	428	50	32	0	0	0	0	0	0	128
1972	0	44	0	16	22	0	16	0	265	12	28	0	22	0	0	0	0	0
1973	34	22	0	28	38	0	6	16	597	129	57	0	0	22	0	0	0	12
1974	6	67	0	0	6	0	0	0	214	0	6	0	0	6	0	0	0	16
1975	0	16	0	6	0	29	0	0	206	0	6	0	6	0	0	0	0	16
1976	12	28	0	0	6	0	0	29	182	32	0	0	16	0	0	0	0	16
1977	18	56	0	40	6	6	99	0	693	77	67	0	6	0	0	48	6	34
1978	18	0	0	28	29	0	0	0	1202	24	0	0	22	29	0	0	0	147

Table A3.10. *(cont.)*

ACTOR:	FRNC	FRNC	FRNC	FRNC	FRNC	FRNC	FRNC	FRNC	FRNC	SWTZ	SWTZ	SWTZ	SWTZ	SWTZ	SWTZ	SWTZ	SWTZ	SWTZ
TARGET:	USA	UK	SWTZ	FRG	GDR	PLND	CZCH	YGSL	USSR	USA	UK	FRNC	FRG	GDR	PLND	CZCH	YGSL	USSR
1960	38	0	0	32	67	0	0	29	121	0	0	0	0	0	0	0	0	58
1961	36	35	0	12	32	0	0	29	476	0	0	0	0	0	0	16	0	0
1962	177	6	0	12	16	6	0	0	226	0	0	16	0	0	0	0	0	0
1963	150	96	0	44	16	0	0	0	44	0	0	0	18	0	0	0	0	0
1964	146	16	0	86	0	0	0	0	38	0	0	29	0	0	0	0	0	0
1965	226	6	0	125	0	0	0	0	6	0	0	0	0	0	0	0	0	0
1966	305	105	0	85	102	16	16	0	105	0	0	0	0	0	0	0	0	0
1967	265	191	0	50	22	0	0	0	70	16	6	0	16	0	0	0	0	16
1968	78	61	0	22	29	0	0	0	262	0	0	0	0	0	0	0	0	0
1969	18	22	0	38	77	0	0	0	6	12	0	0	0	0	0	0	0	22
1970	54	53	0	44	69	0	0	0	106	0	0	0	0	0	0	58	0	35
1971	128	6	0	44	0	0	0	0	0	51	0	0	0	0	0	0	0	0
1972	51	0	0	0	16	0	0	0	22	6	0	0	0	0	0	0	0	0
1973	325	6	0	18	22	0	0	0	114	6	0	0	0	0	0	0	0	0
1974	83	6	0	22	6	0	0	0	29	0	0	0	0	0	0	0	0	0
1975	44	0	0	0	0	0	0	29	0	0	0	0	0	29	0	0	0	0
1976	45	0	0	32	0	0	0	6	102	0	0	0	0	0	0	0	0	29
1977	169	44	0	54	0	0	32	0	178	0	0	0	58	0	0	0	0	0
1978	41	0	0	16	29	0	0	0	136	0	0	0	0	0	0	0	0	0

ACTOR:	FRG	FRG	FRG	FRG	FRG	FRG	FRG	FRG	FRG	GDR	GDR	GDR	GDR	GDR	GDR	GDR	GDR	GDR
TARGET:	USA	UK	FRNC	SWTZ	GDR	PLND	CZCH	YGSL	USSR	USA	UK	FRNC	SWTZ	FRG	PLND	CZCH	YGSL	USSR
1960	57	6	54	0	239	0	0	0	189	111	79	35	0	323	0	0	0	0
1961	130	0	0	0	120	0	0	0	187	185	48	38	0	175	29	0	0	0
1962	82	12	18	0	280	0	29	0	263	448	192	126	0	482	0	0	0	34
1963	28	0	96	0	32	0	0	0	99	16	16	16	0	32	0	0	0	0
1964	48	22	112	0	50	0	0	0	54	166	0	16	0	32	0	0	0	71
1965	57	45	48	0	176	0	0	44	73	76	16	0	0	192	0	0	0	0
1966	118	6	153	0	98	0	0	44	83	106	0	0	0	213	0	0	0	0
1967	106	18	80	0	102	12	6	50	127	93	0	32	0	455	0	0	0	16
1968	98	0	51	0	141	0	57	16	132	28	0	0	0	210	0	150	0	0
1969	68	0	12	0	77	32	29	0	95	16	0	0	0	222	0	6	0	16
1970	30	35	6	0	74	0	29	0	78	64	106	0	0	795	0	0	0	6
1971	79	0	22	0	16	0	0	0	0	22	0	0	0	111	0	0	0	0
1972	29	0	0	0	0	29	35	6	45	16	0	0	0	16	16	0	0	0
1973	222	0	24	6	79	0	6	0	88	32	0	0	44	95	0	0	0	6
1974	35	0	16	0	83	16	0	0	51	0	0	0	0	109	0	0	0	0
1975	6	0	0	0	57	0	0	0	0	0	0	0	0	61	0	0	0	0
1976	0	0	12	0	51	0	0	44	6	0	0	0	0	90	0	0	0	0
1977	72	0	16	0	137	0	0	0	44	32	0	0	29	130	0	0	0	29
1978	34	6	0	0	90	0	0	0	6	0	0	0	0	148	0	0	0	0

Table A3.10. *(cont.)*

ACTOR:	PLND	PLND	PLND	PLND	PLND	PLND	PLND	PLND	PLND	CZCH	CZCH	CZCH	CZCH	CZCH	CZCH	CZCH	CZCH	CZCH
TARGET:	USA	UK	FRNC	SWTZ	FRG	GDR	CZCH	YGSL	USSR	USA	UK	FRNC	SWTZ	FRG	GDR	PLND	YGSL	USSR
1960	28	0	29	0	16	0	0	74	0	22	0	0	0	32	0	0	0	0
1961	83	0	32	0	110	0	0	16	29	235	0	0	0	61	0	0	87	0
1962	22	0	0	0	51	0	0	0	0	22	32	0	0	0	0	0	0	0
1963	29	0	0	0	0	0	0	0	0	0	45	0	0	29	0	0	0	0
1964	141	0	0	0	45	0	0	0	0	101	58	0	0	0	0	0	0	0
1965	141	6	0	0	0	0	0	0	0	29	0	0	0	0	0	0	0	0
1966	320	0	0	0	38	0	0	0	0	246	0	0	0	60	0	0	0	0
1967	105	6	16	0	50	0	0	0	0	78	0	44	74	51	0	0	0	0
1968	66	0	0	0	38	0	206	6	0	51	29	0	0	32	44	44	0	224
1969	12	0	0	0	48	0	0	6	0	140	72	0	0	51	0	0	29	192
1970	0	0	0	0	35	0	0	0	0	167	61	0	0	76	0	0	0	0
1971	16	0	0	0	16	0	0	0	0	58	0	0	0	6	0	0	29	6
1972	6	0	0	0	0	0	0	0	0	0	0	0	0	6	0	0	0	0
1973	6	0	0	0	0	0	0	0	6	0	0	0	0	44	0	0	0	6
1974	0	0	0	0	16	0	0	0	0	0	0	0	0	58	0	0	0	0
1975	0	0	0	0	6	0	0	0	0	108	0	0	0	0	0	0	0	0
1976	0	0	0	0	0	0	0	0	0	0	0	0	0	0	0	0	0	0
1977	16	0	0	0	0	0	6	0	0	99	38	16	0	58	0	0	0	0
1978	0	0	0	0	0	0	0	0	6	29	0	0	0	16	0	0	0	0

ACTOR:	YGSL	YGSL	YGSL	YGSL	YGSL	YGSL	YGSL	YGSL	YGSL	USSR	USSR	USSR	USSR	USSR	USSR	USSR	USSR	USSR
TARGET:	USA	UK	FRNC	SWTZ	FRG	GDR	PLND	CZCH	USSR	USA	UK	FRNC	SWTZ	FRG	GDR	PLND	CZCH	YGSL
1960	32	0	0	0	48	0	6	16	0	420	0	108	0	80	0	0	0	0
1961	76	0	0	0	6	0	0	16	0	448	6	189	0	166	6	0	0	0
1962	0	0	0	0	16	0	0	0	29	1518	0	80	0	111	0	0	0	0
1963	0	6	0	0	0	0	0	0	0	223	0	0	0	32	0	0	0	0
1964	16	0	0	0	0	0	0	0	0	319	0	16	0	61	0	0	0	0
1965	40	0	0	0	16	0	0	0	0	381	16	0	0	54	0	0	0	0
1966	51	0	0	0	16	0	0	0	12	753	0	0	0	118	0	0	16	0
1967	76	0	0	0	0	0	0	0	12	384	0	6	0	76	0	0	0	0
1968	54	0	0	0	16	16	22	0	76	280	16	0	0	109	0	0	118	0
1969	0	16	0	0	0	0	0	0	76	178	0	0	0	82	0	0	32	0
1970	16	16	0	0	0	0	0	0	38	231	6	32	0	0	0	0	0	0
1971	0	0	0	0	0	0	0	16	16	216	0	0	0	0	0	0	0	0
1972	0	0	0	0	16	0	0	0	0	124	16	0	0	0	0	0	0	0
1973	16	6	0	0	0	0	0	0	6	96	0	0	0	0	0	0	0	0
1974	38	29	0	0	0	0	0	0	0	68	0	16	0	16	0	0	0	0
1975	29	0	16	0	0	0	0	0	61	22	0	0	0	0	0	0	0	0
1976	28	0	0	0	6	0	0	29	32	162	16	16	0	0	0	0	0	0
1977	67	0	29	0	45	0	0	0	67	410	29	29	0	0	0	0	6	0
1978	32	0	0	0	0	0	0	0	70	212	32	16	0	16	0	0	0	0

Table A3.11. Proximity Between Nations: Cooperation, 1960–1964

	AUST	BLGM	BLGR	CNDA	CYPR	CZCH	DNMK	FNLD	FRNC	FRG	GDR	GRCE	HNGR	IRLD	ITLY	LXBG	MLTA	NTHL	NRWY	PLND	PRTG	RMNA	SPAN	SWDN	SWTZ	TRKY	USSR	UK	USA	YGSL	
AUST	****	.034	.007	.026	.0	.028	.039	.0	.018	.036	.003	.024	.057	.040	.035	.019	.0	.034	.072	.027	.061	.040	.043	.076	.070	.015	.016	.046	.045	.006	AUST
BLGM	.034	****	.001	.026	.0	.014	.016	.0	.109	.113	.002	.028	.012	.038	.131	.150	.0	.140	.026	.005	.025	.005	.038	.043	.042	.007	.007	.023	.034	.001	BLGM
BLGR	.007	.001	****	.032	.035	.072	.012	.0	.016	.011	.061	.044	.097	.0	.032	.0	.0	.005	.015	.067	.0	.108	.0	.001	.0	.008	.129	.013	.025	.130	BLGR
CNDA	.026	.026	.032	****	.0	.016	.010	.030	.046	.059	.0	.028	.018	.057	.027	.026	.220	.035	.024	.036	.029	.0	.037	.040	.023	.016	.034	.075	.132	.0	CNDA
CYPR	.0	.0	.035	.0	****	.051	.0	.0	.0	.036	.028	.097	.044	.006	.0	.0	.0	.0	.0	.015	.0	.0	.0	.0	.0	.037	.087	.099	.087	.0	CYPR
CZCH	.028	.014	.072	.016	.051	****	.0	.0	.013	.005	.134	.031	.142	.0	.002	.010	.0	.009	.0	.128	.0	.059	.0	.0	.001	.002	.140	.021	.012	.109	CZCH
DNMK	.039	.016	.012	.010	.0	.0	****	.022	.006	.037	.0	.012	.0	.032	.010	.009	.0	.015	.051	.005	.031	.0	.023	.042	.035	.0	.002	.029	.022	.0	DNMK
FNLD	.0	.0	.0	.030	.0	.0	.022	****	.004	.0	.006	.0	.005	.0	.0	.0	.0	.0	.053	.005	.0	.006	.0	.046	.0	.0	.181	.056	.105	.057	FNLD
FRNC	.018	.109	.016	.046	.0	.013	.006	.004	****	.184	.012	.012	.015	.0	.101	.106	.0	.102	.008	.018	.010	.045	.060	.025	.038	.012	.025	.087	.153	.008	FRNC
FRG	.036	.113	.011	.059	.036	.005	.037	.0	.184	****	.039	.039	.012	.047	.108	.111	.0	.130	.060	.019	.053	.022	.067	.038	.045	.035	.019	.137	.174	.007	FRG
GDR	.003	.002	.061	.0	.028	.134	.0	.006	.012	.039	****	.0	.066	.0	.012	.0	.0	.0	.008	.160	.0	.060	.0	.0	.0	.0	.128	.024	.034	.029	GDR
GRCE	.024	.028	.044	.028	.097	.031	.012	.0	.012	.039	.0	****	.081	.042	.023	.020	.0	.018	.028	.006	.032	.034	.026	.025	.027	.041	.006	.045	.083	.016	GRCE
HNGR	.057	.012	.097	.018	.044	.142	.0	.005	.015	.012	.066	.081	****	.0	.0	.010	.0	.009	.0	.108	.0	.074	.0	.0	.0	.006	.061	.031	.029	.054	HNGR
IRLD	.040	.038	.0	.057	.006	.0	.032	.0	.0	.047	.0	.042	.0	****	.034	.036	.0	.027	.044	.0	.049	.0	.042	.042	.043	.019	.0	.032	.027	.0	IRLD
ITLY	.035	.131	.032	.027	.0	.002	.010	.0	.101	.108	.012	.023	.0	.034	****	.141	.0	.140	.036	.022	.038	.018	.033	.032	.040	.012	.027	.039	.074	.004	ITLY
LXBG	.019	.150	.0	.026	.0	.010	.009	.0	.106	.111	.0	.020	.010	.036	.141	****	.0	.145	.023	.0	.027	.0	.021	.021	.022	.008	.0	.010	.006	.0	LXBG
MLTA	.0	.0	.0	.220	.0	.0	.0	.0	.0	.0	.0	.0	.0	.0	.0	.0	****	.0	.0	.0	.0	.0	.0	.0	.0	.0	.0	.285	.0	.0	MLTA
NTHL	.034	.140	.005	.035	.0	.009	.015	.0	.102	.130	.0	.018	.009	.027	.140	.145	.0	****	.026	.0	.025	.0	.040	.034	.043	.007	.009	.022	.040	.0	NTHL
NRWY	.072	.026	.015	.024	.0	.0	.051	.053	.008	.060	.008	.028	.0	.044	.036	.023	.0	.026	****	.013	.068	.0	.036	.081	.066	.011	.023	.052	.023	.0	NRWY
PLND	.027	.005	.067	.036	.015	.128	.005	.005	.018	.019	.160	.006	.108	.0	.022	.0	.0	.0	.013	****	.0	.061	.0	.004	.0	.0	.107	.024	.078	.125	PLND
PRTG	.061	.025	.0	.029	.0	.0	.031	.0	.010	.053	.0	.032	.0	.049	.038	.027	.0	.025	.068	.0	****	.0	.053	.064	.067	.014	.0	.053	.040	.0	PRTG
RMNA	.040	.005	.108	.0	.0	.059	.0	.006	.045	.022	.060	.034	.074	.0	.018	.0	.0	.0	.0	.061	.0	****	.0	.0	.0	.001	.074	.020	.058	.123	RMNA
SPAN	.043	.038	.0	.037	.0	.0	.023	.0	.060	.067	.0	.026	.0	.042	.033	.021	.0	.040	.036	.0	.053	.0	****	.049	.053	.010	.0	.058	.093	.0	SPAN
SWDN	.076	.043	.001	.040	.0	.0	.042	.046	.025	.038	.0	.025	.0	.042	.032	.021	.0	.034	.081	.004	.064	.0	.049	****	.085	.016	.018	.072	.038	.0	SWDN
SWTZ	.070	.042	.0	.023	.0	.001	.035	.0	.038	.045	.0	.027	.0	.043	.040	.022	.0	.043	.066	.0	.067	.0	.053	.085	****	.017	.0	.058	.040	.0	SWTZ
TRKY	.015	.007	.008	.016	.037	.002	.0	.0	.012	.035	.0	.041	.006	.019	.012	.008	.0	.007	.011	.0	.014	.001	.010	.016	.017	****	.015	.043	.088	.012	TRKY
USSR	.016	.007	.129	.034	.087	.140	.002	.181	.025	.019	.128	.006	.061	.0	.027	.0	.0	.009	.023	.107	.0	.074	.0	.018	.0	.015	****	.054	.160	.118	USSR
UK	.046	.023	.013	.075	.099	.021	.029	.056	.087	.137	.024	.045	.031	.032	.039	.010	.285	.022	.052	.024	.053	.020	.058	.072	.058	.043	.054	****	.263	.009	UK
USA	.045	.034	.025	.132	.087	.012	.022	.105	.153	.174	.034	.083	.029	.027	.074	.006	.0	.040	.023	.078	.040	.058	.093	.038	.040	.088	.160	.263	****	.089	USA
YGSL	.006	.001	.130	.0	.0	.109	.0	.057	.008	.007	.029	.016	.054	.0	.004	.0	.0	.0	.0	.125	.0	.123	.0	.0	.0	.012	.118	.009	.089	****	YGSL
	AUST	BLGM	BLGR	CNDA	CYPR	CZCH	DNMK	FNLD	FRNC	FRG	GDR	GRCE	HNGR	IRLD	ITLY	LXBG	MLTA	NTHL	NRWY	PLND	PRTG	RMNA	SPAN	SWDN	SWTZ	TRKY	USSR	UK	USA	YGSL	

0 = No relationship
1 = Exclusive Bilateral Relationship

Table 3.12. Proximity Between Nations: Cooperation, 1965–1969

	AUST	BLGM	BLGR	CNDA	CYPR	CZCH	DNMK	FNLD	FRNC	FRG	GDR	GRCE	HNGR	IRLD	ITLY	LXBG	MLTA	NTHL	NRWY	PLND	PRTG	RMNA	SPAN	SWDN	SWTZ	TRKY	USSR	UK	USA	YGSL	
AUST I	****	.013	.047	.0	.0	.053	.003	.047	.014	.034	.004	.0	.084	.0	.019	.002	.0	.005	.009	.053	.0	.071	.0	.005	.0	.0	.060	.006	.047	.039	I AUST
BLGM I	.013	****	.017	.018	.0	.007	.004	.022	.155	.154	.0	.003	.002	.009	.161	.181	.0	.182	.005	.011	.0	.009	.002	.029	.035	.0	.003	.025	.022	.002	I BLGM
BLGR I	.047	.017	****	.022	.0	.074	.037	.020	.064	.023	.061	.013	.107	.0	.020	.0	.0	.0	.040	.075	.0	.114	.0	.019	.008	.043	.118	.038	.011	.070	I BLGR
CNDA I	.0	.018	.022	****	.030	.006	.0	.030	.062	.037	.0	.003	.001	.0	.038	.001	.086	.038	.0	.021	.0	.023	.0	.045	.049	.007	.027	.081	.162	.002	I CNDA
CYPR I	.0	.0	.0	.030	****	.046	.0	.0	.004	.004	.0	.259	.0	.0	.004	.0	.106	.0	.006	.0	.0	.0	.037	.0	.0	.055	.040	.070	.028	.004	I CYPR
CZCH I	.053	.007	.074	.006	.046	****	.013	.005	.029	.023	.146	.002	.150	.0	.012	.005	.0	.009	.009	.144	.0	.069	.019	.009	.010	.002	.176	.015	.023	.064	I CZCH
DNMK I	.003	.004	.037	.0	.0	.013	****	.059	.010	.024	.006	.0	.007	.0	.004	.002	.0	.002	.060	.007	.0	.011	.0	.057	.003	.0	.002	.004	.024	.005	I DNMK
FNLD I	.047	.022	.020	.030	.0	.005	.059	****	.019	.026	.0	.039	.005	.183	.015	.020	.0	.020	.188	.003	.100	.021	.045	.107	.038	.011	.079	.024	.009	.010	I FNLD
FRNC I	.014	.155	.064	.062	.004	.029	.010	.019	****	.184	.009	.002	.019	.009	.137	.157	.0	.148	.003	.035	.042	.031	.053	.030	.035	.014	.053	.060	.062	.016	I FRNC
FRG I	.034	.154	.023	.037	.004	.023	.024	.026	.184	****	.039	.0	.023	.036	.145	.156	.0	.166	.012	.032	.160	.038	.013	.040	.064	.015	.021	.099	.106	.037	I FRG
GDR I	.004	.0	.061	.0	.0	.146	.006	.0	.009	.039	****	.0	.100	.0	.001	.0	.0	.001	.0	.239	.0	.041	.0	.002	.002	.0	.146	.013	.018	.045	I GDR
GRCE I	.0	.003	.013	.003	.259	.002	.0	.039	.002	.0	.0	****	.0	.0	.053	.0	.0	.006	.0	.018	.0	.071	.0	.0	.0	.079	.005	.123	.087	.040	I GRCE
HNGR I	.084	.002	.107	.001	.0	.150	.007	.005	.019	.023	.100	.0	****	.0	.007	.0	.0	.008	.0	.090	.0	.109	.0	.015	.019	.0	.117	.006	.028	.082	I HNGR
IRLD I	.0	.009	.0	.0	.0	.0	.0	.183	.009	.036	.0	.0	.0	****	.009	.009	.0	.009	.0	.0	.0	.0	.0	.0	.0	.0	.021	.239	.0	.0	I IRLD
ITLY I	.019	.161	.020	.038	.004	.012	.004	.015	.137	.145	.001	.053	.007	.009	****	.159	.0	.164	.006	.015	.0	.008	.002	.038	.050	.028	.029	.071	.059	.017	I ITLY
LXBG I	.002	.181	.0	.001	.0	.005	.002	.020	.157	.156	.0	.0	.0	.009	.159	****	.0	.175	.003	.002	.0	.006	.002	.002	.005	.0	.000	.006	.004	.0	I LXBG
MLTA I	.0	.0	.0	.086	.106	.0	.0	.0	.0	.0	.0	.0	.0	.0	.0	.0	****	.0	.0	.0	.0	.058	.065	.0	.0	.0	.0	.173	.0	.059	I MLTA
NTHL I	.005	.182	.0	.038	.0	.009	.002	.020	.148	.166	.001	.006	.008	.009	.164	.175	.0	****	.003	.005	.018	.009	.002	.050	.046	.0	.002	.047	.024	.005	I NTHL
NRWY I	.009	.005	.040	.0	.006	.009	.060	.188	.003	.012	.0	.0	.0	.0	.006	.003	.0	.003	****	.031	.0	.023	.0	.145	.0	.0	.014	.008	.071	.021	I NRWY
PLND I	.053	.011	.075	.021	.0	.144	.007	.003	.035	.032	.239	.018	.090	.0	.015	.002	.0	.005	.031	****	.0	.043	.008	.028	.002	.003	.127	.026	.043	.044	I PLND
PRTG I	.0	.0	.0	.0	.0	.0	.0	.100	.042	.160	.0	.0	.0	.0	.0	.0	.0	.018	.0	.0	****	.0	.090	.0	.0	.0	.0	.030	.111	.0	I PRTG
RMNA I	.071	.009	.114	.023	.0	.069	.011	.021	.031	.038	.041	.071	.109	.0	.008	.006	.058	.009	.023	.043	.0	****	.046	.006	.008	.021	.104	.026	.062	.110	I RMNA
SPAN I	.0	.002	.0	.0	.037	.019	.0	.045	.053	.013	.0	.0	.0	.0	.002	.002	.065	.002	.0	.008	.090	.046	****	.0	.0	.0	.031	.051	.232	.022	I SPAN
SWDN I	.005	.029	.019	.045	.0	.009	.057	.107	.030	.040	.002	.0	.015	.0	.038	.002	.0	.050	.145	.028	.0	.006	.0	****	.059	.0	.025	.057	.053	.003	I SWDN
SWTZ I	.0	.035	.008	.049	.0	.010	.003	.038	.035	.064	.002	.0	.019	.0	.050	.005	.0	.046	.0	.002	.0	.008	.0	.059	****	.008	.012	.070	.101	.002	I SWTZ
TRKY I	.0	.0	.043	.007	.055	.002	.0	.011	.014	.015	.0	.079	.0	.0	.028	.0	.0	.0	.0	.003	.0	.021	.0	.0	.008	****	.017	.051	.084	.0	I TRKY
USSR I	.060	.003	.118	.027	.040	.176	.002	.079	.053	.021	.146	.005	.117	.021	.029	.000	.0	.002	.014	.127	.0	.104	.031	.025	.012	.017	****	.045	.126	.109	I USSR
UK I	.006	.025	.038	.081	.070	.015	.004	.024	.060	.099	.013	.123	.006	.239	.071	.006	.173	.047	.008	.026	.030	.026	.051	.057	.070	.051	.045	****	.186	.010	I UK
USA I	.047	.022	.011	.162	.028	.023	.024	.009	.062	.106	.018	.087	.028	.0	.059	.004	.0	.024	.071	.043	.111	.062	.232	.053	.101	.084	.126	.186	****	.067	I USA
YGSL I	.039	.002	.070	.002	.004	.064	.005	.010	.016	.037	.045	.040	.082	.0	.017	.0	.059	.005	.021	.044	.0	.110	.022	.003	.002	.0	.109	.010	.067	****	I YGSL
	AUST	BLGM	BLGR	CNDA	CYPR	CZCH	DNMK	FNLD	FRNC	FRG	GDR	GRCE	HNGR	IRLD	ITLY	LXBG	MLTA	NTHL	NRWY	PLND	PRTG	RMNA	SPAN	SWDN	SWTZ	TRKY	USSR	UK	USA	YGSL	

0 = No relationship
1 = Exclusive Bilateral Relationship

Table A3.13. Proximity Between Nations: Cooperation, 1970–1974

	AUST	BLGM	BLGR	CNDA	CYPR	CZCH	DNMK	FNLD	FRNC	FRG	GDR	GRCE	HNGR	IRLD	ITLY	LXBG	MLTA	NTHL	NRWY	PLND	PRTG	RMNA	SPAN	SWDN	SWTZ	TRKY	USSR	UK	USA	YGSL
AUST	****	.039	.003	.013	.0	.017	.011	.008	.056	.060	.014	.017	.010	.023	.063	.036	.0	.056	.016	.003	.015	.009	.013	.025	.013	.0	.028	.039	.035	.011
BLGM	.039	****	.002	.038	.035	.006	.036	.027	.136	.129	.008	.017	.009	.075	.147	.143	.054	.144	.045	.017	.029	.008	.055	.040	.052	.014	.004	.063	.034	.039
BLGR	.003	.002	****	.002	.027	.112	.007	.032	.005	.021	.096	.028	.117	.0	.009	.0	.0	.009	.007	.105	.009	.135	.017	.002	.0	.017	.076	.004	.021	.016
CNDA	.013	.038	.002	****	.009	.002	.003	.0	.075	.036	.001	.0	.002	.003	.027	.014	.013	.038	.019	.015	.0	.009	.0	.050	.012	.0	.044	.085	.109	.006
CYPR	.0	.035	.027	.009	****	.0	.013	.0	.034	.036	.013	.165	.0	.014	.044	.035	.059	.034	.0	.0	.0	.0	.0	.0	.0	.032	.027	.036	.034	.0
CZCH	.017	.006	.112	.002	.0	****	.001	.008	.007	.026	.114	.004	.163	.0	.005	.004	.0	.003	.003	.122	.014	.071	.003	.002	.0	.007	.121	.005	.026	.031
DNMK	.011	.036	.007	.003	.013	.001	****	.023	.034	.038	.007	.007	.001	.036	.034	.033	.0	.040	.038	.010	.011	.002	.018	.029	.020	.0	.007	.033	.009	.017
FNLD	.008	.027	.032	.0	.0	.008	.023	****	.042	.058	.050	.005	.017	.022	.031	.035	.0	.041	.045	.021	.013	.004	.003	.050	.004	.0	.099	.026	.014	.007
FRNC	.056	.136	.005	.075	.034	.007	.034	.042	****	.141	.024	.052	.013	.080	.133	.129	.038	.132	.042	.015	.048	.043	.093	.063	.059	.022	.050	.087	.076	.041
FRG	.060	.129	.021	.036	.036	.026	.038	.058	.141	****	.116	.038	.019	.071	.133	.125	.054	.132	.036	.072	.042	.021	.040	.068	.061	.035	.053	.079	.087	.063
GDR	.014	.008	.096	.001	.013	.114	.007	.050	.024	.116	****	.023	.083	.0	.008	.005	.021	.009	.022	.137	.011	.090	.010	.021	.011	.0	.089	.018	.033	.007
GRCE	.017	.017	.028	.0	.165	.004	.007	.005	.052	.038	.023	****	.004	.003	.013	.007	.0	.017	.017	.023	.023	.024	.016	.011	.0	.030	.017	.019	.109	.020
HNGR	.010	.009	.117	.002	.0	.163	.001	.017	.013	.019	.083	.004	****	.0	.001	.004	.0	.009	.002	.101	.008	.088	.004	.015	.0	.0	.104	.011	.048	.029
IRLD	.023	.075	.0	.003	.014	.0	.036	.022	.080	.071	.0	.003	.0	****	.082	.079	.0	.072	.025	.0	.015	.0	.017	.019	.024	.006	.002	.110	.003	.032
ITLY	.063	.147	.009	.027	.044	.005	.034	.031	.133	.133	.008	.013	.001	.082	****	.139	.073	.137	.039	.002	.033	.008	.057	.051	.062	.014	.025	.069	.045	.039
LXBG	.036	.143	.0	.014	.035	.004	.033	.035	.129	.125	.005	.007	.004	.079	.139	****	.054	.138	.022	.009	.035	.006	.023	.036	.031	.014	.003	.049	.012	.035
MLTA	.0	.054	.0	.013	.059	.0	.0	.0	.038	.054	.021	.0	.0	.0	.073	.054	****	.038	.0	.0	.0	.0	.0	.0	.0	.0	.0	.135	.004	.0
NTHL	.056	.144	.009	.038	.034	.003	.040	.041	.132	.132	.009	.017	.009	.072	.137	.138	.038	****	.047	.010	.050	.009	.047	.062	.068	.014	.004	.066	.037	.043
NRWY	.016	.045	.007	.019	.0	.003	.038	.045	.042	.036	.022	.017	.002	.025	.039	.022	.0	.047	****	.005	.022	.003	.020	.065	.029	.0	.028	.056	.013	.011
PLND	.003	.017	.105	.015	.0	.122	.010	.021	.015	.072	.137	.023	.101	.0	.002	.009	.0	.010	.005	****	.010	.082	.003	.024	.0	.008	.084	.014	.074	.033
PRTG	.015	.029	.009	.0	.0	.014	.011	.013	.048	.042	.011	.023	.008	.015	.033	.035	.0	.050	.022	.010	****	.037	.019	.015	.014	.0	.020	.037	.084	.025
RMNA	.009	.008	.135	.009	.0	.071	.002	.004	.043	.021	.090	.024	.088	.0	.008	.006	.0	.009	.003	.082	.037	****	.003	.0	.0	.0	.072	.011	.090	.028
SPAN	.013	.055	.017	.0	.0	.003	.018	.003	.093	.040	.010	.016	.004	.017	.057	.023	.0	.047	.020	.003	.019	.003	****	.024	.044	.0	.020	.034	.075	.010
SWDN	.025	.040	.002	.050	.0	.002	.029	.050	.063	.068	.021	.011	.015	.019	.051	.036	.0	.062	.065	.024	.015	.0	.024	****	.032	.0	.026	.045	.040	.010
SWTZ	.013	.052	.0	.012	.0	.0	.020	.004	.059	.061	.011	.0	.0	.024	.062	.031	.0	.068	.029	.0	.014	.0	.044	.032	****	.0	.001	.059	.044	.007
TRKY	.0	.014	.017	.0	.032	.007	.0	.0	.022	.035	.0	.030	.0	.006	.014	.014	.0	.014	.0	.008	.0	.0	.0	.0	.0	****	.009	.023	.086	.0
USSR	.028	.004	.076	.044	.027	.121	.007	.099	.050	.053	.089	.017	.104	.002	.025	.003	.0	.004	.028	.084	.020	.072	.020	.026	.001	.009	****	.021	.235	.057
UK	.039	.063	.004	.085	.036	.005	.033	.026	.087	.079	.018	.019	.011	.110	.069	.049	.135	.066	.056	.014	.037	.011	.034	.045	.059	.023	.021	****	.125	.038
USA	.035	.034	.021	.109	.034	.026	.009	.014	.076	.087	.033	.109	.048	.003	.045	.012	.004	.037	.013	.074	.084	.090	.075	.040	.044	.086	.235	.125	****	.077
YGSL	.011	.039	.016	.006	.0	.031	.017	.007	.041	.063	.007	.020	.029	.032	.039	.035	.0	.043	.011	.033	.025	.028	.010	.010	.007	.0	.057	.038	.077	****

0 = No relationship
1 = Exclusive Bilateral Relationship

Table A3.14. Proximities Between Nations: Cooperation in Europe, 1975–1978

	AUST	BLGM	BLGR	CNDA	CYPR	CZCH	DNMK	FNLD	FRNC	FRG	GDR	GRCE	HNGR	IRLD	ITLY	LXBG	MLTA	NTHL	NRWY	PLND	PRTG	RMNA	SPAN	SWDN	SWTZ	TRKY	USSR	UK	USA	YGSL	
AUST	****	.031	.010	.015	.014	.043	.016	.025	.030	.042	.023	.013	.015	.026	.032	.036	.021	.031	.027	.009	.014	.009	.025	.030	.006	.013	.019	.030	.049	.012	AUST
BLGM	.031	****	.008	.038	.013	.008	.045	.024	.082	.084	.006	.054	.006	.081	.084	.091	.015	.094	.064	.008	.049	.005	.022	.029	.029	.020	.010	.083	.043	.007	BLGM
BLGR	.010	.008	****	.004	.010	.125	.001	.009	.017	.015	.104	.009	.121	.002	.011	.006	.016	.006	.005	.109	.006	.140	.019	.007	.0	.004	.104	.018	.011	.026	BLGR
CNDA	.015	.038	.004	****	.044	.009	.018	.032	.064	.082	.022	.038	.005	.015	.059	.040	.046	.047	.049	.015	.043	.008	.019	.039	.031	.017	.014	.066	.142	.011	CNDA
CYPR	.014	.013	.010	.044	****	.010	.0	.038	.013	.027	.033	.038	.010	.0	.010	.009	.104	.008	.009	.009	.010	.009	.015	.034	.028	.042	.024	.032	.086	.049	CYPR
CZCH	.043	.008	.125	.009	.010	****	.001	.017	.015	.019	.108	.005	.120	.002	.011	.006	.016	.010	.005	.131	.005	.112	.019	.014	.010	.004	.095	.018	.012	.027	CZCH
DNMK	.016	.045	.001	.018	.0	.001	****	.011	.040	.039	.001	.026	.001	.048	.043	.047	.0	.044	.032	.001	.024	.001	.004	.009	.014	.0	.001	.040	.013	.003	DNMK
FNLD	.025	.024	.009	.032	.038	.017	.011	****	.016	.047	.027	.015	.009	.024	.027	.027	.020	.024	.024	.008	.016	.008	.030	.046	.032	.012	.090	.017	.037	.011	FNLD
FRNC	.030	.082	.017	.064	.013	.015	.040	.016	****	.125	.016	.052	.026	.070	.091	.082	.015	.081	.054	.047	.044	.014	.027	.033	.042	.020	.036	.107	.090	.020	FRNC
FRG	.042	.084	.015	.082	.027	.019	.039	.047	.125	****	.078	.056	.011	.073	.100	.080	.022	.083	.061	.035	.055	.012	.029	.053	.052	.028	.033	.105	.103	.015	FRG
GDR	.023	.006	.104	.022	.033	.108	.001	.027	.016	.078	****	.009	.106	.002	.017	.005	.016	.010	.004	.116	.010	.102	.010	.032	.028	.004	.102	.024	.037	.026	GDR
GRCE	.013	.054	.009	.038	.038	.005	.026	.015	.052	.056	.009	****	.005	.017	.055	.053	.016	.052	.052	.004	.048	.006	.017	.013	.006	.059	.005	.049	.093	.019	GRCE
HNGR	.015	.006	.121	.005	.010	.120	.001	.009	.026	.011	.106	.005	****	.001	.008	.006	.017	.006	.005	.111	.006	.113	.018	.007	.0	.002	.093	.012	.030	.024	HNGR
IRLD	.026	.081	.002	.015	.0	.002	.048	.024	.070	.073	.002	.017	.001	****	.081	.088	.0	.082	.027	.002	.013	.002	.007	.020	.026	.005	.002	.087	.003	.0	IRLD
ITLY	.032	.084	.011	.059	.010	.011	.043	.027	.091	.100	.017	.055	.008	.081	****	.082	.015	.086	.068	.014	.052	.012	.027	.036	.033	.023	.024	.102	.059	.055	ITLY
LXBG	.036	.091	.006	.040	.009	.006	.047	.027	.082	.080	.005	.053	.006	.088	.082	****	.015	.092	.061	.005	.049	.005	.018	.025	.025	.019	.005	.080	.024	.007	LXBG
MLTA	.021	.015	.016	.046	.104	.016	.0	.020	.015	.022	.016	.016	.017	.0	.015	.015	****	.015	.016	.016	.017	.016	.021	.018	.0	.008	.016	.049	.015	.057	MLTA
NTHL	.031	.094	.006	.047	.008	.010	.044	.024	.081	.083	.010	.052	.006	.082	.086	.092	.015	****	.061	.008	.047	.005	.015	.035	.039	.019	.019	.077	.042	.007	NTHL
NRWY	.027	.064	.005	.049	.009	.005	.032	.024	.054	.061	.004	.052	.005	.027	.068	.061	.016	.061	****	.004	.054	.005	.022	.044	.009	.022	.004	.067	.044	.008	NRWY
PLND	.009	.008	.109	.015	.009	.131	.001	.008	.047	.035	.116	.004	.111	.002	.014	.005	.016	.008	.004	****	.015	.108	.017	.013	.013	.002	.111	.018	.032	.032	PLND
PRTG	.014	.049	.006	.043	.010	.005	.024	.016	.044	.055	.010	.048	.006	.013	.052	.049	.017	.047	.054	.015	****	.023	.051	.014	.014	.022	.011	.038	.068	.020	PRTG
RMNA	.009	.005	.140	.008	.009	.112	.001	.008	.014	.012	.102	.006	.113	.002	.012	.005	.016	.005	.005	.108	.023	****	.028	.007	.0	.004	.088	.026	.079	.034	RMNA
SPAN	.025	.022	.019	.019	.015	.019	.004	.030	.027	.029	.010	.017	.018	.007	.027	.018	.021	.015	.022	.017	.051	.028	****	.027	.006	.009	.012	.018	.094	.030	SPAN
SWDN	.030	.029	.007	.039	.034	.014	.009	.046	.033	.053	.032	.013	.007	.020	.036	.025	.018	.035	.044	.013	.014	.007	.027	****	.041	.007	.031	.046	.039	.010	SWDN
SWTZ	.006	.029	.0	.031	.028	.010	.014	.032	.042	.052	.028	.006	.0	.026	.033	.025	.0	.039	.009	.013	.014	.0	.006	.041	****	.002	.027	.036	.082	.0	SWTZ
TRKY	.013	.020	.004	.017	.042	.004	.0	.012	.020	.028	.004	.059	.002	.005	.023	.019	.008	.019	.022	.002	.022	.004	.009	.007	.002	****	.033	.021	.065	.010	TRKY
USSR	.019	.010	.104	.014	.024	.095	.001	.090	.036	.033	.102	.005	.093	.002	.024	.005	.016	.019	.004	.111	.011	.088	.012	.031	.027	.033	****	.040	.163	.076	USSR
UK	.030	.083	.018	.066	.032	.018	.040	.017	.107	.105	.024	.049	.012	.087	.102	.080	.049	.077	.067	.018	.038	.026	.018	.046	.036	.021	.040	****	.116	.019	UK
USA	.049	.043	.011	.142	.086	.012	.013	.037	.090	.103	.037	.093	.030	.003	.059	.024	.015	.042	.044	.032	.068	.079	.094	.039	.082	.065	.163	.116	****	.116	USA
YGSL	.012	.007	.026	.011	.049	.027	.003	.011	.020	.015	.026	.019	.024	.0	.055	.007	.057	.007	.008	.032	.020	.034	.030	.010	.0	.010	.076	.019	.116	****	YGSL
	AUST	BLGM	BLGR	CNDA	CYPR	CZCH	DNMK	FNLD	FRNC	FRG	GDR	GRCE	HNGR	IRLD	ITLY	LXBG	MLTA	NTHL	NRWY	PLND	PRTG	RMNA	SPAN	SWDN	SWTZ	TRKY	USSR	UK	USA	YGSL	

0 = No relationship
1 = Exclusive Bilateral Relationship

Table A3.15. Proximity Between Nations: Conflict, 1960–1964

	AUST	BLGM	BLGR	CNDA	CYPR	CZCH	DNMK	FNLD	FRNC	FRG	GDR	GRCE	HNGR	IRLD	ITLY	LXBG	MLTA	NTHL	NRWY	PLND	PRTG	RMNA	SPAN	SWDN	SWTZ	TRKY	USSR	UK	USA	YGSL	
AUST	****	.0	.0	.0	.0	.122	.0	.0	.0	.0	.043	.0	.0	.0	.384	.0	.0	.0	.0	.0	.0	.0	.0	.0	.0	.0	.021	.0	.052	.0	AUST
BLGM	.0	****	.0	.0	.0	.0	.0	.0	.071	.059	.0	.004	.0	.0	.097	.151	.0	.149	.0	.049	.0	.0	.0	.0	.013	.0	.028	.011	.121	.052	BLGM
BLGR	.0	.0	****	.0	.0	.0	.054	.0	.072	.0	.0	.117	.0	.0	.104	.0	.0	.0	.0	.0	.0	.0	.0	.0	.0	.028	.0	.011	.204	.141	BLGR
CNDA	.0	.0	.0	****	.0	.029	.0	.0	.009	.0	.0	.0	.0	.0	.0	.0	.0	.0	.0	.029	.0	.0	.0	.0	.0	.0	.114	.013	.330	.0	CNDA
CYPR	.0	.0	.0	.0	****	.0	.0	.0	.019	.0	.0	.209	.0	.0	.0	.0	.0	.0	.0	.0	.0	.023	.0	.0	.0	.145	.002	.240	.076	.0	CYPR
CZCH	.122	.0	.0	.029	.0	****	.0	.0	.0	.077	.0	.0	.0	.0	.0	.0	.0	.0	.0	.0	.0	.025	.0	.029	.041	.0	.0	.100	.263	.125	CZCH
DNMK	.0	.0	.054	.0	.0	.0	****	.0	.043	.0	.047	.0	.0	.0	.0	.0	.0	.0	.0	.027	.0	.0	.0	.0	.0	.0	.109	.0	.0	.0	DNMK
FNLD	.0	.0	.0	.0	.0	.0	.0	****	.0	.0	.251	.118	.0	.0	.0	.0	.0	.0	.0	.0	.0	.0	.0	.0	.0	.0	.060	.084	.031	.0	FNLD
FRNC	.0	.071	.072	.009	.019	.0	.043	.0	****	.101	.083	.0	.0	.0	.160	.086	.0	.095	.0	.032	.062	.0	.174	.017	.081	.0	.197	.061	.165	.040	FRNC
FRG	.0	.059	.0	.0	.0	.077	.0	.0	.101	****	.390	.012	.021	.0	.051	.086	.0	.088	.0	.094	.0	.0	.011	.006	.032	.004	.183	.028	.061	.050	FRG
GDR	.043	.0	.0	.0	.0	.0	.047	.251	.083	.390	****	.0	.0	.0	.0	.0	.0	.004	.0	.026	.0	.036	.0	.136	.0	.0	.014	.124	.222	.0	GDR
GRCE	.0	.004	.117	.0	.209	.0	.0	.118	.0	.012	.0	****	.0	.0	.0	.0	.0	.0	.0	.0	.0	.0	.0	.025	.0	.332	.081	.057	.054	.021	GRCE
HNGR	.0	.0	.0	.0	.0	.0	.0	.0	.0	.021	.0	.0	****	.0	.029	.0	.0	.0	.0	.0	.0	.0	.0	.0	.0	.0	.020	.048	.407	.0	HNGR
IRLD	.0	.0	.0	.0	.0	.0	.0	.0	.0	.0	.0	.0	.0	****	.0	.0	.0	.0	.0	.0	.0	.0	.0	.0	.0	.0	.250	.037	.215	.0	IRLD
ITLY	.384	.097	.104	.0	.0	.0	.0	.0	.160	.051	.0	.0	.029	.0	****	.155	.0	.094	.0	.0	.0	.0	.0	.0	.0	.0	.022	.0	.052	.0	ITLY
LXBG	.0	.151	.0	.0	.0	.0	.0	.0	.086	.086	.0	.0	.0	.0	.155	****	.0	.153	.0	.0	.0	.0	.0	.0	.0	.0	.0	.0	.026	.0	LXBG
MLTA	.0	.0	.0	.0	.0	.0	.0	.0	.0	.0	.0	.0	.0	.0	.0	.0	****	.0	.0	.0	.0	.0	.0	.0	.0	.0	.0	.0	.0	.0	MLTA
NTHL	.0	.149	.0	.0	.0	.0	.0	.0	.095	.088	.004	.0	.0	.0	.094	.153	.0	****	.0	.0	.082	.0	.0	.0	.0	.0	.034	.007	.094	.0	NTHL
NRWY	.0	.0	.0	.0	.0	.0	.0	.0	.0	.0	.0	.0	.0	.0	.0	.0	.0	.0	****	.0	.0	.0	.0	.039	.0	.0	.353	.0	.141	.0	NRWY
PLND	.0	.049	.0	.029	.0	.0	.027	.0	.032	.094	.026	.0	.0	.0	.0	.0	.0	.0	.0	****	.0	.0	.0	.0	.0	.0	.010	.0	.333	.090	PLND
PRTG	.0	.0	.0	.0	.0	.0	.0	.0	.062	.0	.0	.0	.0	.0	.0	.0	.0	.082	.0	.0	****	.0	.0	.0	.0	.0	.022	.068	.310	.0	PRTG
RMNA	.0	.0	.0	.0	.023	.025	.0	.0	.0	.0	.036	.0	.0	.0	.0	.0	.0	.0	.0	.0	.0	****	.0	.0	.0	.101	.054	.113	.129	.050	RMNA
SPAN	.0	.0	.0	.0	.0	.0	.0	.0	.174	.011	.0	.0	.0	.0	.0	.0	.0	.0	.0	.0	.0	.0	****	.0	.023	.0	.093	.0	.224	.0	SPAN
SWDN	.0	.0	.0	.0	.0	.029	.0	.0	.017	.006	.136	.025	.0	.0	.0	.0	.0	.0	.039	.0	.0	.0	.0	****	.0	.0	.107	.018	.177	.0	SWDN
SWTZ	.0	.013	.0	.0	.0	.041	.0	.0	.081	.032	.0	.0	.0	.0	.0	.0	.0	.0	.0	.0	.0	.0	.023	.0	****	.0	.099	.0	.251	.0	SWTZ
TRKY	.0	.0	.028	.0	.145	.0	.0	.0	.0	.004	.0	.332	.0	.0	.0	.0	.0	.0	.0	.0	.0	.101	.0	.0	.0	****	.018	.001	.015	.0	TRKY
USSR	.021	.028	.0	.114	.002	.0	.109	.060	.197	.183	.014	.081	.020	.250	.022	.0	.0	.034	.353	.010	.022	.054	.093	.107	.099	.018	****	.215	.509	.019	USSR
UK	.0	.011	.011	.013	.240	.100	.0	.084	.061	.028	.124	.057	.048	.037	.0	.0	.0	.007	.0	.0	.068	.113	.0	.018	.0	.001	.215	****	.093	.016	UK
USA	.052	.121	.204	.330	.076	.263	.0	.031	.165	.061	.222	.054	.407	.215	.052	.026	.0	.094	.141	.333	.310	.129	.224	.177	.251	.015	.509	.093	****	.157	USA
YGSL	.0	.052	.141	.0	.0	.125	.0	.0	.040	.050	.0	.021	.0	.0	.0	.0	.0	.0	.0	.090	.0	.050	.0	.0	.0	.0	.019	.016	.157	****	YGSL
	AUST	BLGM	BLGR	CNDA	CYPR	CZCH	DNMK	FNLD	FRNC	FRG	GDR	GRCE	HNGR	IRLD	ITLY	LXBG	MLTA	NTHL	NRWY	PLND	PRTG	RMNA	SPAN	SWDN	SWTZ	TRKY	USSR	UK	USA	YGSL	

0 = No relationship
1 = Exclusive Bilateral Relationship

Table A3.16. Proximity Between Nations: Conflict, 1965–1969

	AUST	BLGM	BLGR	CNDA	CYPR	CZCH	DNMK	FNLD	FRNC	FRG	GDR	GRCE	HNGR	IRLD	ITLY	LXBG	MLTA	NTHL	NRWY	PLND	PRTG	RMNA	SPAN	SWDN	SWTZ	TRKY	USSR	UK	USA	YGSL	
AUST	****	.0	.040	.0	.0	.237	.0	.0	.0	.0	.0	.0	.233	.0	.0	.0	.0	.0	.0	.0	.0	.0	.0	.0	.0	.0	.020	.010	.010	.020	AUST
BLGM	.0	****	.0	.0	.0	.0	.0	.0	.227	.028	.017	.017	.0	.0	.087	.065	.0	.043	.0	.0	.026	.0	.0	.0	.0	.0	.065	.012	.067	.0	BLGM
BLGR	.040	.0	****	.0	.0	.152	.0	.0	.021	.020	.0	.054	.0	.0	.0	.0	.0	.0	.035	.0	.0	.045	.0	.0	.0	.0	.0	.015	.125	.182	BLGR
CNDA	.0	.0	.0	****	.021	.0	.0	.0	.264	.0	.0	.0	.073	.0	.0	.0	.0	.0	.104	.005	.0	.0	.0	.0	.0	.0	.086	.008	.117	.031	CNDA
CYPR	.0	.0	.0	.021	****	.0	.0	.0	.006	.0	.0	.133	.039	.0	.0	.0	.0	.0	.0	.0	.0	.0	.0	.0	.0	.195	.071	.056	.129	.0	CYPR
CZCH	.237	.0	.152	.0	.0	****	.0	.0	.018	.074	.065	.0	.112	.0	.0	.0	.0	.0	.0	.117	.0	.027	.0	.0	.193	.0	.132	.028	.146	.023	CZCH
DNMK	.0	.0	.0	.0	.0	.0	****	.0	.071	.015	.0	.086	.0	.0	.0	.0	.0	.0	.0	.016	.0	.0	.0	.0	.0	.0	.0	.040	.039	.0	DNMK
FNLD	.0	.0	.0	.0	.0	.0	.0	****	.0	.0	.251	.0	.0	.0	.0	.0	.0	.0	.0	.0	.0	.0	.0	.0	.0	.0	.037	.0	.215	.0	FNLD
FRNC	.0	.227	.021	.264	.006	.018	.071	.0	****	.134	.063	.039	.003	.0	.146	.221	.0	.239	.093	.017	.052	.040	.015	.003	.0	.016	.054	.131	.218	.0	FRNC
FRG	.0	.028	.020	.0	.0	.074	.015	.0	.134	****	.428	.024	.040	.110	.043	.047	.0	.037	.0	.082	.024	.010	.016	.0	.047	.0	.149	.038	.087	.134	FRG
GDR	.0	.017	.0	.0	.0	.065	.0	.251	.063	.428	****	.0	.003	.0	.0	.0	.0	.0	.077	.0	.0	.154	.0	.008	.0	.0	.005	.054	.124	.008	GDR
GRCE	.0	.017	.054	.0	.133	.0	.086	.0	.039	.024	.0	****	.0	.0	.104	.045	.0	.020	.027	.0	.062	.0	.0	.011	.0	.207	.072	.084	.104	.058	GRCE
HNGR	.233	.0	.0	.073	.039	.112	.0	.0	.003	.040	.003	.0	****	.0	.050	.0	.0	.0	.0	.0	.0	.076	.0	.0	.016	.0	.010	.040	.211	.025	HNGR
IRLD	.0	.0	.0	.0	.0	.0	.0	.0	.0	.110	.0	.0	.0	****	.0	.0	.0	.0	.0	.0	.0	.0	.0	.0	.0	.0	.0	.412	.0	.0	IRLD
ITLY	.0	.087	.0	.0	.0	.0	.0	.0	.146	.043	.0	.104	.050	.0	****	.142	.0	.083	.0	.015	.0	.0	.0	.0	.0	.0	.127	.008	.040	.016	ITLY
LXBG	.0	.065	.0	.0	.0	.0	.0	.0	.221	.047	.0	.045	.0	.0	.142	****	.0	.067	.0	.0	.0	.0	.0	.0	.0	.0	.0	.0	.0	.0	LXBG
MLTA	.0	.0	.0	.0	.0	.0	.0	.0	.0	.0	.0	.0	.0	.0	.0	.0	****	.0	.0	.0	.0	.0	.0	.0	.0	.0	.0	.510	.0	.0	MLTA
NTHL	.0	.043	.0	.0	.0	.0	.0	.0	.239	.037	.0	.020	.0	.0	.083	.067	.0	****	.0	.072	.0	.0	.0	.0	.0	.0	.0	.023	.058	.0	NTHL
NRWY	.0	.0	.035	.104	.0	.0	.0	.0	.093	.0	.077	.027	.0	.0	.0	.0	.0	.0	****	.0	.0	.0	.0	.0	.0	.0	.100	.0	.112	.0	NRWY
PLND	.0	.0	.0	.005	.0	.117	.016	.0	.017	.082	.0	.0	.0	.0	.015	.0	.0	.072	.0	****	.010	.088	.0	.028	.0	.0	.0	.032	.275	.031	PLND
PRTG	.0	.026	.0	.0	.0	.0	.0	.0	.052	.024	.0	.062	.0	.0	.0	.0	.0	.0	.0	.010	****	.0	.103	.166	.0	.0	.004	.180	.070	.0	PRTG
RMNA	.0	.0	.045	.0	.0	.027	.0	.0	.040	.010	.154	.0	.076	.0	.0	.0	.0	.0	.0	.088	.0	****	.0	.0	.0	.0	.142	.0	.079	.016	RMNA
SPAN	.0	.0	.0	.0	.0	.0	.0	.0	.015	.016	.0	.0	.0	.0	.0	.0	.0	.0	.0	.0	.103	.0	****	.0	.0	.0	.010	.441	.088	.0	SPAN
SWDN	.0	.0	.0	.0	.0	.0	.0	.0	.003	.0	.008	.011	.0	.0	.0	.0	.0	.0	.0	.028	.166	.0	.0	****	.0	.0	.025	.008	.327	.044	SWDN
SWTZ	.0	.0	.0	.0	.0	.193	.0	.0	.0	.047	.0	.0	.016	.0	.0	.0	.0	.0	.0	.0	.0	.0	.0	.0	****	.0	.110	.033	.121	.0	SWTZ
TRKY	.0	.0	.0	.0	.195	.0	.0	.0	.016	.0	.0	.207	.0	.0	.0	.0	.0	.0	.0	.0	.0	.0	.0	.0	.0	****	.025	.0	.015	.0	TRKY
USSR	.020	.065	.0	.086	.071	.132	.0	.037	.054	.149	.005	.072	.010	.0	.127	.0	.0	.0	.100	.0	.004	.142	.010	.025	.110	.025	****	.132	.436	.069	USSR
UK	.010	.012	.015	.008	.056	.028	.040	.0	.131	.038	.054	.084	.040	.412	.008	.0	.510	.023	.0	.032	.180	.0	.441	.008	.033	.0	.132	****	.094	.012	UK
USA	.010	.067	.125	.117	.129	.146	.039	.215	.218	.087	.124	.104	.211	.0	.040	.0	.0	.058	.112	.275	.070	.079	.088	.327	.121	.015	.436	.094	****	.134	USA
YGSL	.020	.0	.182	.031	.0	.023	.0	.0	.0	.134	.008	.058	.025	.0	.016	.0	.0	.0	.0	.031	.0	.016	.0	.044	.0	.0	.069	.012	.134	****	YGSL
	AUST	BLGM	BLGR	CNDA	CYPR	CZCH	DNMK	FNLD	FRNC	FRG	GDR	GRCE	HNGR	IRLD	ITLY	LXBG	MLTA	NTHL	NRWY	PLND	PRTG	RMNA	SPAN	SWDN	SWTZ	TRKY	USSR	UK	USA	YGSL	

0 = No relationship
1 = Exclusive Bilateral Relationship

Table A3.17. Proximity Between Nations: Conflict, 1970–1974

	AUST	BLGM	BLGR	CNDA	CYPR	CZCH	DNMK	FNLD	FRNC	FRG	GDR	GRCE	HNGR	IRLD	ITLY	LXBG	MLTA	NTHL	NRWY	PLND	PRTG	RMNA	SPAN	SWDN	SWTZ	TRKY	USSR	UK	USA	YGSL	
AUST	****	.0	.0	.0	.0	.033	.0	.0	.017	.0	.048	.0	.025	.0	.038	.0	.0	.0	.0	.248	.0	.009	.0	.0	.0	.0	.007	.0	.239	.092	AUST
BLGM	.0	****	.0	.0	.0	.0	.0	.0	.076	.091	.0	.0	.020	.0	.050	.077	.0	.056	.0	.0	.070	.008	.009	.0	.0	.0	.057	.029	.165	.0	BLGM
BLGR	.0	.0	****	.0	.0	.0	.0	.0	.057	.0	.0	.0	.075	.0	.0	.0	.0	.0	.0	.0	.0	.0	.0	.0	.0	.161	.011	.0	.057	.219	BLGR
CNDA	.0	.0	.0	****	.0	.076	.026	.0	.122	.0	.0	.0	.0	.0	.0	.0	.0	.0	.0	.035	.0	.0	.0	.0	.0	.0	.078	.038	.279	.0	CNDA
CYPR	.0	.0	.0	.0	****	.0	.0	.0	.0	.0	.0	.506	.0	.0	.024	.0	.0	.0	.0	.0	.0	.0	.0	.0	.0	.091	.0	.043	.080	.0	CYPR
CZCH	.033	.0	.0	.076	.0	****	.019	.0	.0	.155	.0	.018	.061	.0	.067	.0	.0	.036	.0	.0	.0	.052	.0	.078	.127	.029	.005	.036	.131	.083	CZCH
DNMK	.0	.0	.0	.026	.0	.019	****	.183	.030	.008	.0	.025	.029	.0	.0	.0	.0	.0	.107	.0	.0	.011	.0	.0	.0	.0	.0	.0	.008	.0	DNMK
FNLD	.0	.0	.0	.0	.0	.0	.183	****	.142	.0	.0	.0	.058	.0	.0	.0	.0	.0	.171	.0	.0	.022	.0	.089	.0	.0	.091	.0	.008	.0	FNLD
FRNC	.017	.076	.057	.122	.0	.0	.030	.142	****	.062	.061	.045	.019	.0	.081	.099	.017	.081	.016	.0	.067	.031	.181	.032	.0	.054	.078	.082	.194	.0	FRNC
FRG	.0	.091	.0	.0	.0	.155	.008	.0	.062	****	.475	.052	.020	.0	.042	.082	.0	.073	.017	.186	.111	.026	.050	.005	.015	.0	.068	.022	.112	.025	FRG
GDR	.048	.0	.0	.0	.0	.0	.0	.0	.061	.475	****	.0	.045	.0	.0	.0	.0	.0	.0	.032	.0	.0	.0	.0	.110	.0	.003	.076	.092	.0	GDR
GRCE	.0	.0	.0	.0	.506	.018	.025	.0	.045	.052	.0	****	.020	.0	.006	.0	.0	.007	.050	.0	.005	.008	.0	.055	.0	.083	.021	.004	.121	.0	GRCE
HNGR	.025	.020	.075	.0	.0	.061	.029	.058	.019	.020	.045	.020	****	.0	.107	.024	.0	.022	.051	.039	.019	.204	.0	.0	.0	.0	.019	.014	.043	.082	HNGR
IRLD	.0	.0	.0	.0	.0	.0	.0	.0	.0	.0	.0	.0	.0	****	.0	.0	.0	.0	.0	.0	.0	.0	.0	.0	.0	.0	.0	.548	.041	.0	IRLD
ITLY	.038	.050	.0	.0	.024	.067	.0	.0	.081	.042	.0	.006	.107	.0	****	.076	.0	.053	.0	.063	.066	.0	.0	.0	.0	.0	.078	.025	.133	.108	ITLY
LXBG	.0	.077	.0	.0	.0	.0	.0	.0	.099	.082	.0	.0	.024	.0	.076	****	.0	.082	.0	.0	.082	.009	.0	.0	.0	.0	.0	.030	.102	.0	LXBG
MLTA	.0	.0	.0	.0	.0	.0	.0	.0	.017	.0	.0	.0	.0	.0	.0	.0	****	.0	.0	.0	.0	.0	.0	.0	.0	.0	.0	.526	.0	.0	MLTA
NTHL	.0	.056	.0	.0	.0	.036	.0	.0	.081	.073	.0	.007	.022	.0	.053	.082	.0	****	.018	.0	.092	.009	.0	.0	.0	.0	.032	.021	.186	.0	NTHL
NRWY	.0	.0	.0	.0	.0	.0	.107	.171	.016	.017	.0	.050	.051	.0	.0	.0	.0	.018	****	.0	.018	.019	.0	.093	.0	.0	.017	.017	.056	.0	NRWY
PLND	.248	.0	.0	.035	.0	.0	.0	.0	.0	.186	.032	.0	.039	.0	.063	.0	.0	.0	.0	****	.0	.0	.0	.0	.0	.0	.008	.0	.039	.0	PLND
PRTG	.0	.070	.0	.0	.0	.0	.0	.0	.067	.111	.0	.005	.019	.0	.066	.082	.0	.092	.018	.0	****	.007	.022	.092	.0	.0	.023	.098	.036	.0	PRTG
RMNA	.009	.008	.0	.0	.0	.052	.011	.022	.031	.026	.0	.008	.204	.0	.0	.009	.0	.009	.019	.0	.007	****	.0	.0	.0	.0	.073	.005	.202	.0	RMNA
SPAN	.0	.009	.0	.0	.0	.0	.0	.0	.181	.050	.0	.0	.0	.0	.0	.0	.0	.0	.0	.0	.022	.0	****	.104	.084	.0	.049	.055	.061	.070	SPAN
SWDN	.0	.0	.0	.0	.0	.078	.0	.089	.032	.005	.0	.055	.0	.0	.0	.0	.0	.0	.093	.0	.092	.0	.104	****	.0	.0	.046	.024	.233	.0	SWDN
SWTZ	.0	.0	.0	.0	.0	.127	.0	.0	.0	.015	.110	.0	.0	.0	.0	.0	.0	.0	.0	.0	.0	.0	.084	.0	****	.0	.049	.0	.226	.0	SWTZ
TRKY	.0	.0	.161	.0	.091	.029	.0	.0	.054	.0	.0	.083	.0	.0	.0	.0	.0	.0	.0	.0	.0	.0	.0	.0	.0	****	.010	.033	.088	.0	TRKY
USSR	.007	.057	.011	.078	.0	.005	.0	.091	.078	.068	.003	.021	.019	.0	.078	.0	.0	.032	.017	.008	.023	.073	.049	.046	.049	.010	****	.093	.522	.050	USSR
UK	.0	.029	.0	.038	.043	.036	.0	.0	.082	.022	.076	.004	.014	.548	.025	.030	.526	.021	.017	.0	.098	.005	.055	.024	.0	.033	.093	****	.095	.054	UK
USA	.239	.165	.057	.279	.080	.131	.008	.008	.194	.112	.092	.121	.043	.041	.133	.102	.0	.186	.056	.039	.036	.202	.061	.233	.226	.088	.522	.095	****	.086	USA
YGSL	.092	.0	.219	.0	.0	.083	.0	.0	.0	.025	.0	.0	.082	.0	.108	.0	.0	.0	.0	.0	.0	.0	.070	.0	.0	.0	.050	.054	.086	****	YGSL
	AUST	BLGM	BLGR	CNDA	CYPR	CZCH	DNMK	FNLD	FRNC	FRG	GDR	GRCE	HNGR	IRLD	ITLY	LXBG	MLTA	NTHL	NRWY	PLND	PRTG	RMNA	SPAN	SWDN	SWTZ	TRKY	USSR	UK	USA	YGSL	

0 = No relationship
1 = Exclusive Bilateral Relationship

Table A3.18. Proximities Between Nations: Conflict in Europe, 1975–1978

	AUST	BLGM	BLGR	CNDA	CYPR	CZCH	DNMK	FNLD	FRNC	FRG	GDR	GRCE	HNGR	IRLD	ITLY	LXBG	MLTA	NTHL	NRWY	PLND	PRTG	RMNA	SPAN	SWDN	SWTZ	TRKY	USSR	UK	USA	YGSL
AUST	****	.0	.0	.0	.0	.165	.0	.0	.0	.125	.054	.0	.0	.0	.0	.0	.0	.0	.0	.106	.0	.0	.058	.0	.0	.0	.029	.0	.0	.124
BLGM	.0	****	.0	.0	.0	.0	.0	.0	.144	.147	.0	.0	.0	.0	.0	.0	.0	.0	.0	.0	.0	.0	.0	.0	.0	.0	.136	.065	.042	.0
BLGR	.0	.0	****	.0	.0	.0	.0	.0	.085	.0	.0	.0	.0	.0	.0	.0	.0	.0	.0	.180	.0	.066	.073	.0	.0	.0	.0	.040	.0	.255
CNDA	.0	.0	.0	****	.0	.0	.0	.0	.017	.006	.007	.0	.0	.0	.0	.0	.0	.0	.044	.0	.0	.0	.0	.0	.0	.0	.291	.029	.219	.0
CYPR	.0	.0	.0	.0	****	.0	.0	.047	.0	.005	.0	.162	.0	.0	.109	.0	.0	.0	.0	.0	.072	.0	.0	.0	.0	.136	.010	.100	.208	.0
CZCH	.165	.0	.0	.0	.0	****	.0	.0	.051	.061	.0	.0	.0	.0	.092	.0	.0	.042	.148	.028	.0	.043	.008	.0	.0	.0	.006	.091	.242	.034
DNMK	.0	.0	.0	.0	.0	.0	****	.0	.0	.0	.0	.0	.0	.0	.0	.0	.0	.0	.0	.0	.0	.0	.100	.0	.0	.0	.040	.166	.0	.0
FNLD	.0	.0	.0	.0	.047	.0	.0	****	.0	.0	.0	.0	.0	.0	.0	.0	.0	.0	.0	.0	.0	.0	.0	.0	.0	.0	.156	.035	.032	.0
FRNC	.0	.144	.085	.017	.0	.051	.0	.0	****	.074	.020	.0	.0	.0	.103	.0	.0	.015	.012	.0	.0	.0	.021	.0	.0	.027	.167	.103	.168	.125
FRG	.125	.147	.0	.006	.005	.061	.0	.0	.074	****	.556	.009	.0	.0	.249	.0	.0	.095	.0	.025	.0	.0	.036	.0	.097	.0	.027	.032	.068	.132
GDR	.054	.0	.0	.007	.0	.0	.0	.0	.020	.556	****	.0	.0	.0	.028	.0	.0	.0	.0	.0	.0	.039	.034	.0	.319	.0	.014	.023	.041	.0
GRCE	.0	.0	.0	.0	.162	.0	.0	.0	.0	.009	.0	****	.0	.0	.0	.0	.0	.0	.0	.0	.0	.0	.017	.0	.0	.233	.100	.059	.189	.0
HNGR	.0	.0	.0	.0	.0	.0	.0	.0	.0	.0	.0	.0	****	.0	.0	.0	.0	.0	.0	.0	.0	.114	.0	.0	.0	.0	.069	.0	.353	.0
IRLD	.0	.0	.0	.0	.0	.0	.0	.0	.0	.0	.0	.0	.0	****	.0	.0	.0	.0	.0	.0	.0	.0	.0	.0	.0	.0	.0	.514	.023	.0
ITLY	.0	.0	.0	.0	.109	.092	.0	.0	.103	.249	.028	.0	.0	.0	****	.0	.0	.0	.0	.0	.0	.0	.0	.0	.0	.0	.034	.029	.091	.0
LXBG	.0	.0	.0	.0	.0	.0	.0	.0	.0	.0	.0	.0	.0	.0	.0	****	.0	.0	.0	.0	.0	.0	.0	.0	.0	.0	.185	.070	.251	.0
MLTA	.0	.0	.0	.0	.0	.0	.0	.0	.0	.0	.0	.0	.0	.0	.0	.0	****	.0	.0	.0	.0	.0	.0	.0	.0	.0	.0	.0	.0	.0
NTHL	.0	.0	.0	.0	.0	.042	.0	.0	.015	.095	.0	.0	.0	.0	.0	.0	.0	****	.0	.0	.0	.0	.042	.0	.0	.0	.247	.084	.024	.0
NRWY	.0	.0	.0	.044	.0	.148	.0	.0	.012	.0	.0	.0	.0	.0	.0	.0	.0	.0	****	.0	.0	.0	.033	.0	.0	.0	.254	.080	.0	.0
PLND	.106	.0	.180	.0	.0	.028	.0	.0	.0	.025	.0	.0	.0	.0	.0	.0	.0	.0	.0	****	.0	.090	.0	.0	.0	.0	.024	.0	.198	.0
PRTG	.0	.0	.0	.0	.072	.0	.0	.0	.0	.0	.0	.0	.0	.0	.0	.0	.0	.0	.0	.0	****	.0	.117	.0	.0	.0	.097	.0	.269	.0
RMNA	.0	.0	.066	.0	.0	.043	.0	.0	.0	.0	.039	.0	.114	.0	.0	.0	.0	.0	.0	.090	.0	****	.0	.0	.179	.0	.103	.062	.108	.0
SPAN	.058	.0	.073	.0	.0	.008	.100	.0	.021	.036	.034	.017	.0	.0	.0	.0	.0	.042	.033	.0	.117	.0	****	.136	.0	.0	.167	.161	.012	.0
SWDN	.0	.0	.0	.0	.0	.0	.0	.0	.0	.0	.0	.0	.0	.0	.0	.0	.0	.0	.0	.0	.0	.0	.136	****	.0	.0	.068	.034	.054	.0
SWTZ	.0	.0	.0	.0	.0	.0	.0	.0	.0	.097	.319	.0	.0	.0	.0	.0	.0	.0	.0	.0	.0	.179	.0	.0	****	.0	.044	.0	.0	.0
TRKY	.0	.0	.0	.0	.136	.0	.0	.0	.027	.0	.0	.233	.0	.0	.0	.0	.0	.0	.0	.0	.0	.0	.0	.0	.0	****	.010	.0	.046	.0
USSR	.029	.136	.0	.291	.010	.006	.040	.156	.167	.027	.014	.100	.069	.0	.034	.185	.0	.247	.254	.024	.097	.103	.167	.068	.044	.010	****	.129	.564	.113
UK	.0	.065	.040	.029	.100	.091	.166	.035	.103	.032	.023	.059	.0	.514	.029	.070	.0	.084	.080	.0	.0	.062	.161	.034	.0	.0	.129	****	.079	.013
USA	.0	.042	.0	.219	.208	.242	.0	.032	.168	.068	.041	.189	.353	.023	.091	.251	.0	.024	.0	.198	.269	.108	.012	.054	.0	.046	.564	.079	****	.139
YGSL	.124	.0	.255	.0	.0	.034	.0	.0	.125	.132	.0	.0	.0	.0	.0	.0	.0	.0	.0	.0	.0	.0	.0	.0	.0	.0	.113	.013	.139	****

0 = No relationship
1 = Exclusive Bilateral Relationship

Table A3.19. Interblock Affinities in UN Voting Behavior (correlation coefficients; values for 1964 interpolated)

	USA WITH USSR	UK WITH USSR	FRNC WITH USSR	FRG WITH USSR
1960	-.52	-.65	-.59	.
1961	-.61	-.64	-.47	.
1962	-.68	-.67	-.64	.
1963	-.44	-.53	-.29	.
1964	-.39	-.47	-.21	.
1965	-.33	-.41	-.10	.
1966	-.46	-.41	.03	.
1967	-.33	-.24	.31	.
1968	-.54	-.50	-.14	.
1969	-.14	-.16	-.07	.
1970	-.61	-.50	-.44	.
1971	-.35	.04	.14	.
1972	-.26	-.13	.08	.
1973	-.09	-.27	-.14	-.31
1974	-.09	-.26	-.15	-.22
1975	-.42	-.35	-.36	-.37
1976	-.23	-.22	-.19	-.23
1977	-.29	-.31	-.13	-.31

Table A3.20. Intrablock Affinities in UN Voting Behavior (correlation coefficients; values for 1964 interpolated)

	USA WITH UK	USA WITH FRG	USA WITH FRNC	USA WITH BLGM	USA WITH NRWY	USA WITH NTHL	USA WITH ITLY	UK WITH FRNC	UK WITH FRG	FRNC WITH FRG
1960	.90	9.99	.80	.79	.74	.90	.88	.81	.	.
1961	.90	9.99	.69	.80	.75	.94	.89	.66	.	.
1962	.91	9.99	.73	.97	.76	.94	.94	.66	.	.
1963	.78	9.99	.75	.85	.64	.81	.81	.73	.	.
1964	.80	9.99	.65	.88	.68	.85	.84	.68	.	.
1965	.83	9.99	.55	.91	.71	.88	.86	.62	.	.
1966	.81	9.99	.52	.92	.76	.90	.90	.55	.	.
1967	.89	9.99	.34	.95	.56	.86	.83	.46	.	.
1968	.82	9.99	.23	.86	.69	.84	.88	.46	.	.
1969	.78	9.99	.58	.90	.71	.83	.75	.59	.	.
1970	.84	9.99	.64	.84	.71	.82	.79	.73	.	.
1971	.58	9.99	.44	.68	.33	.60	.67	.86	.	.
1972	.81	9.99	.62	.74	.58	.68	.74	.74	.	.
1973	.81	.69	.75	.71	.57	.67	.72	.86	.82	.75
1974	.68	.71	.50	.71	.59	.72	.60	.60	.86	.54
1975	.82	.83	.75	.80	.58	.74	.71	.80	.95	.81
1976	.72	.73	.56	.61	.47	.56	.66	.81	.96	.81
1977	.76	.75	.68	.74	.65	.73	.68	.80	.94	.80

Table A3.21. UN Voting Affinities among Neutral and Nonaligned Nations (correlation coefficients; values for 1964 interpolated)

	SWDN WITH YGSL	SWDN WITH FNLD	SWDN WITH AUST	FNLD WITH YGSL	FNLD WITH AUST	YGSL WITH AUST
1960	-.01	.78	.67	.20	.60	-.21
1961	-.24	.88	.77	-.06	.71	-.27
1962	-.45	.82	.77	-.23	.73	-.50
1963	-.04	.93	.88	.01	.80	-.10
1964	0.0	.93	.86	.06	.84	-.10
1965	.04	.92	.84	.10	.87	-.09
1966	-.06	.84	.86	.19	.72	-.22
1967	-.05	.91	.79	.08	.75	-.16
1968	-.03	.88	.88	.18	.86	-.01
1969	-.02	.84	.62	.15	.56	.09
1970	-.19	.91	.82	-.05	.78	-.35
1971	.55	.84	.75	.55	.78	.40
1972	.31	.91	.84	.24	.86	.12
1973	.11	.78	.71	.22	.63	.06
1974	.07	.75	.80	.25	.65	-.13
1975	.26	.80	.80	.42	.78	.29
1976	.28	.80	.90	.33	.77	.27
1977	.38	.79	.82	.38	.75	.39

Table A3.22. UN Voting Affinities of Neutral and Nonaligned Nations with the USA and the USSR (correlation coefficients; values for 1964 interpolated)

	AUST WITH USA	AUST WITH USSR	SWDN WITH USA	SWDN WITH USSR	FNLD WITH USA	FNLD WITH USSR	YGSL WITH USA	YGSL WITH USSR
1960	.76	-.30	.51	-.16	.30	.05	-.47	.87
1961	.69	-.50	.70	-.46	.61	-.29	-.45	.73
1962	.82	-.53	.66	-.45	.62	-.31	-.62	.88
1963	.72	-.21	.62	-.31	.59	-.26	-.40	.54
1964	.75	-.18	.65	-.19	.61	-.12	-.37	.63
1965	.77	-.15	.67	-.06	.62	.02	-.33	.72
1966	.84	-.23	.72	-.09	.48	.19	-.46	.70
1967	.69	-.07	.56	.15	.52	.29	-.55	.71
1968	.68	-.50	.58	.01	.46	-.24	-.35	.43
1969	.56	-.01	.60	-.13	.47	-.06	-.21	.72
1970	.80	-.44	.70	-.29	.62	-.18	-.50	.72
1971	.49	.10	.31	.22	.27	.31	-.24	.66
1972	.61	.06	.52	.02	.56	.04	-.06	.15
1973	.68	-.19	.47	-.19	.42	-.10	0.0	.46
1974	.56	-.21	.50	-.09	.31	.05	-.30	.53
1975	.57	-.08	.51	-.04	.36	.04	-.22	.55
1976	.43	-.03	.41	-.07	.38	-.04	-.14	.32
1977	.61	.01	.54	.04	.48	.02	-.12	.47

A3.4 ECONOMIC COOPERATION: ADDITIONAL TABLES

Table A3.23. Commercial Exchange Between Selected East–West Pairs of Countries (monthly average exports in millions of US dollars at current prices)

YEAR	USA TO USSR	USSR TO USA	FRG TO USSR	USSR TO FRG	UK TO USSR	USSR TO UK	FRNC TO USSR	USSR TO FRNC	EEC TO CMEA	CMEA TO EEC
1960	3.30	1.90	15.45	13.21	12.41	17.49	9.63	7.89	82.61	83.10
1961	3.80	1.90	17.00	11.86	16.20	19.86	9.16	8.11	51.55	89.95
1962	1.67	1.36	17.23	15.53	13.42	19.63	11.51	9.22	98.04	99.88
1963	1.91	1.77	12.80	13.64	14.90	21.22	5.35	11.76	90.10	113.70
1964	12.20	1.79	16.13	14.20	9.27	22.63	5.34	11.76	101.10	113.30
1965	3.70	3.60	12.21	17.54	10.71	27.75	6.00	12.17	118.00	130.90
1966	3.48	4.13	11.28	20.44	11.76	29.32	6.30	14.30	139.20	149.80
1967	5.03	3.43	16.50	22.07	14.86	28.19	12.94	15.59	175.10	167.40
1968	4.79	4.84	22.78	24.36	20.79	31.62	21.37	15.23	198.10	176.60
1969	8.79	4.29	33.81	27.85	19.43	39.43	22.01	17.06	278.70	283.10
1970	9.87	6.03	35.20	28.47	20.43	44.01	22.76	16.96	314.10	318.30
1971	13.48	4.80	38.39	30.53	18.06	41.76	21.29	21.64	349.50	352.60
1972	45.57	7.96	59.35	35.06	18.87	46.80	28.03	24.25	445.50	424.30
1973	99.19	17.83	98.55	59.42	19.86	67.31	48.00	36.07	669.70	605.20
1974	50.77	29.19	154.67	101.89	21.44	77.38	55.02	48.97	997.20	794.90
1975	153.08	21.21	235.37	107.91	38.60	74.11	95.38	64.10	1209.80	863.10
1976	192.30	18.40	223.70	141.80	36.00	99.38	93.27	76.28	1165.20	1043.20
1977	135.60	19.60	232.40	154.40	50.54	113.54	124.63	96.34	1255.40	1106.07
1978	187.70	45.00	261.70	207.40	67.70	110.10	121.00	101.70	1422.90	1349.30
1979	300.60	72.80	301.60	324.40	74.10	146.30	167.10	149.20	1659.30	1837.10
1980	.	37.80	364.40	331.40	88.30	152.40	205.40	297.10	.	.

Table A3.24. Exports as Percentage of Total Exports for Selected East-West Pairs

YEAR	USA TO USSR	USSR TO USA	FRG TO USSR	USSR TO FRG	UK TO USSR	USSR TO UK	FRNC TO USSR	USSR TO FRNC	EEC TO CMEA	CMEA TO EEC
1960	.20	.41	1.62	2.85	1.45	3.77	1.68	1.70	3.33	7.68
1961	.22	.38	1.61	2.37	1.81	3.97	1.52	1.62	1.91	7.64
1962	.09	.23	1.56	2.65	1.46	3.35	1.88	1.57	3.43	7.61
1963	.10	.29	1.05	2.25	1.51	3.50	.79	1.94	2.88	7.92
1964	.56	.28	1.19	2.22	.87	3.53	.71	1.84	2.85	7.39
1965	.16	.53	.82	2.57	.94	4.07	.72	1.79	2.96	7.85
1966	.14	.56	.67	2.78	.96	3.98	.70	1.94	3.17	8.60
1967	.19	.43	.91	2.74	1.24	3.50	1.36	1.94	3.74	8.69
1968	.17	.55	1.10	2.75	1.63	3.57	2.02	1.72	3.70	8.40
1969	.28	.44	1.40	2.87	1.33	4.06	1.76	1.76	4.41	12.19
1970	.27	.57	1.24	2.67	1.27	4.13	1.52	1.59	4.25	12.33
1971	.37	.42	1.18	2.65	.97	3.63	1.25	1.88	4.15	12.52
1972	1.10	.62	1.54	2.74	.93	3.66	1.31	1.89	3.49	12.73
1973	1.67	1.00	1.75	3.32	.78	3.76	1.60	2.02	3.81	13.72
1974	.62	1.28	2.08	4.46	.66	3.39	1.44	2.14	4.35	14.56
1975	1.71	.76	3.14	3.89	1.06	2.67	2.19	2.31	4.90	13.22
1976	2.01	.59	2.63	4.58	.93	3.21	2.01	2.46	4.30	14.69
1977	1.35	.52	2.36	4.11	1.05	3.02	2.35	2.56	3.97	13.38
1978	1.24	1.03	2.21	4.77	1.13	2.53	1.90	2.34	3.72	14.27
1979	2.51	1.35	2.11	6.01	.98	2.71	2.05	2.77	3.47	16.20

Table A3.25. Imports as Percentage of Total Imports for Selected East-West Pairs

YEAR	USSR FROM USA	USA FROM USSR	USSR FROM FRG	FRG FROM USSR	USSR FROM UK	UK FROM USSR	USSR FROM FRNC	FRNC FROM USSR	CMEA FROM EEC	EEC FROM CMEA
1960	.70	.16	3.29	1.56	2.65	1.43	2.05	1.51	7.49	3.37
1961	.78	.16	3.50	1.30	3.34	1.94	1.89	1.46	4.38	3.36
1962	.31	.10	3.21	1.52	2.50	1.87	2.14	1.47	7.58	3.36
1963	.32	.12	2.18	1.26	2.53	1.89	.91	1.62	6.13	3.38
1964	1.89	.12	2.50	1.17	1.44	1.70	.83	1.40	6.29	3.03
1965	.55	.20	1.82	1.20	1.59	1.92	.89	1.41	6.85	3.21
1966	.53	.20	1.71	1.36	1.78	2.11	.96	1.44	7.84	3.35
1967	.71	.15	2.32	1.53	2.09	1.91	1.82	1.51	9.07	3.66
1968	.61	.18	2.91	1.45	2.65	2.00	2.73	1.31	9.45	3.42
1969	1.02	.14	3.93	1.34	2.26	2.37	2.56	1.18	12.07	4.49
1970	1.01	.18	3.60	1.15	2.09	2.43	2.33	1.06	11.89	4.31
1971	1.30	.13	3.69	1.07	1.74	2.09	2.05	1.22	12.21	4.26
1972	3.41	.17	4.44	1.06	1.41	2.02	2.10	1.10	12.63	3.32
1973	5.64	.31	5.60	1.31	1.13	2.08	2.73	1.16	14.29	3.37
1974	2.45	.35	7.46	1.77	1.03	1.71	2.65	1.11	16.88	3.25
1975	4.97	.26	7.64	1.74	1.25	1.67	3.10	1.42	15.77	3.45
1976	6.05	.18	7.04	1.94	1.13	2.13	2.94	1.30	14.46	3.65
1977	3.99	.16	6.83	1.84	1.49	2.14	3.66	1.64	14.23	3.43
1978	4.46	.31	6.21	2.06	1.61	1.68	2.87	1.49	13.76	3.52
1979	6.24	.42	6.26	2.47	1.54	1.71	3.47	1.68	14.17	3.67

Table A3.26. SITC-7 Commercial Exchange Between Selected East-West Pairs of Countries (in millions of US dollars at current prices)

YEAR	USA TO USSR	USSR TO USA	FRG TO USSR	USSR TO FRG	UK TO USSR	USSR TO UK	FRNC TO USSR	USSR TO FRNC	EEC TO CMEA	CMEA TO EEC
1960	19	.010	82	1.032	56	.264	56	.624	309	36
1961	16	0.0	115	1.882	76	2.667	57	.813	393	44
1962	4	.001	67	1.329	57	.654	70	.525	416	47
1963	1	0.0	78	.601	61	1.138	29	.554	378	42
1964	5	.035	129	1.279	43	1.775	32	1.414	461	55
1965	5	.007	79	2.870	50	1.851	27	1.884	494	66
1966	4	.018	82	1.700	75	2.861	32	2.395	647	57
1967	11	.133	83	2.520	76	4.995	78	4.916	944	76
1968	15	.191	116	11.83	129	5.909	152	6.272	993	110
1969	42	.092	200	4.405	113	5.027	144	4.674	1195	133
1970	45	.085	164	17.26	101	5.542	142	7.378	1183	193
1971	63	.120	169	12.39	84	8.863	138	8.403	1285	218
1972	68	.461	367	13.55	96	14.70	117	9.576	1738	272
1973	204	.154	570	29.25	104	25.69	168	15.92	2981	526
1974	225	1.892	759	5.930	69	29.23	290	21.30	3931	590
1975	547	5.345	1350	37.13	210	35.15	574	36.22	5950	802
1976	605	4.153	1397	56.68	205	31.77	411	39.66	5662	896
1977	374	3.112	1504	33.78	191	40.68	577	38.19	6184	1029
1978	283	3.477	1523	37.99	291	54.27	617	47.43	6770	1298
1979	362	4.813	1399	56.24	287	76.94	821	58.52	6914	1440

Table A3.27. SITC-3 Commercial Exchange Between Selected East-West Pairs of Countries (in millions of US dollars at current prices)

YEAR	EEC TO CMEA	CMEA TO EEC	USA TO USSR	USSR TO USA	UK TO USSR	USSR TO UK	FRG TO USSR	USSR TO FRG	FRNC TO USSR	USSR TO FRNC
1960	2.65	220.28	0.0	0.0	0.0	4.12	.01	27.17	.02	52.54
1961	1.91	224.84	.00	0.0	.12	3.40	.00	18.38	.06	49.23
1962	1.89	247.99	0.0	0.0	.12	3.13	.01	20.33	.05	47.61
1963	3.46	297.22	1.96	0.0	.15	3.73	.00	15.18	.15	73.34
1964	5.75	316.25	.30	0.0	.28	1.33	.05	53.22	.03	77.96
1965	4.68	300.91	.00	0.0	.73	1.39	.04	45.24	.01	81.85
1966	3.56	352.07	0.0	.00	.40	.99	.10	59.72	.01	90.33
1967	6.00	449.37	.20	.00	.34	1.14	.60	73.85	.01	90.90
1968	7.26	489.33	.01	.00	.48	.57	.19	84.14	.05	84.76
1969	15.28	427.20	.35	1.18	.58	.46	.09	77.25	.05	83.39
1970	32.82	526.97	.77	2.81	.86	.23	.20	98.03	.02	86.62
1971	48.63	696.22	.03	.65	1.04	3.52	.62	125.63	.08	130.73
1972	61.95	734.93	0.0	7.46	.78	6.62	.78	132.21	.21	113.45
1973	85.59	1264.95	.03	76.52	.90	17.38	.40	296.74	.15	166.20
1974	90.92	2554.42	1.34	105.81	1.45	65.36	.90	654.83	.54	158.12
1975	128.68	3454.18	4.43	96.20	3.52	151.85	1.01	764.67	.67	360.19
1976	125.42	4604.81	1.27	54.48	1.68	391.48	1.32	1007.14	.13	423.42
1977	102.50	4827.68	16.86	64.06	1.94	489.98	2.03	1036.32	.36	549.03
1978	140.87	5835.96	30.51	48.08	1.41	511.42	10.94	1518.59	2.82	606.00
1979	325.34	9160.27	23.44	16.66	3.69	515.67	13.02	2679.35	3.77	1076.54

Table A3.28. SITC-7 Exports as Percentage of Total Exports to Respective Countries for Selected East–West Pairs

YEAR	EEC TO CMEA	USA TO USSR	FRG TO USSR	FRNC TO USSR	UK TO USSR	CMEA TO EEC	USSR TO USA	USSR TO FRG	USSR TO FRNC	USSR TO UK
1960	31.17	47.98	44.23	48.46	37.60	3.61	.04	.65	.66	.13
1961	63.53	35.09	56.37	51.86	39.09	4.08	0.0	1.32	.84	1.12
1962	35.36	19.96	32.40	50.68	35.39	3.92	.01	.71	.47	.28
1963	34.96	4.36	50.78	45.17	34.12	3.08	0.0	.37	.39	.45
1964	38.00	3.42	66.65	49.94	38.66	4.05	.16	.75	1.00	.65
1965	34.89	11.26	53.92	37.50	38.90	4.20	.02	1.36	1.29	.56
1966	38.73	9.58	60.58	42.33	53.15	3.17	.04	.69	1.40	.81
1967	44.93	18.22	41.92	50.23	42.62	3.78	.32	.95	2.63	1.48
1968	41.77	26.10	42.43	59.27	51.71	5.19	.33	4.05	3.43	1.56
1969	35.73	39.82	49.30	54.52	48.46	3.91	.18	1.32	2.28	1.06
1970	31.39	37.99	38.83	51.99	41.20	5.05	.12	5.05	3.63	1.05
1971	30.64	38.95	36.68	54.02	38.76	5.15	.21	3.38	3.24	1.77
1972	32.51	12.44	51.53	34.78	42.40	5.34	.48	3.22	3.29	2.62
1973	37.09	17.14	48.20	29.17	43.64	7.24	.07	4.10	3.68	3.18
1974	32.85	36.93	40.89	43.92	26.82	6.19	.54	.49	3.62	3.15
1975	40.98	29.78	47.80	50.15	45.34	7.74	2.10	2.87	4.71	3.95
1976	40.49	26.22	52.04	36.72	47.45	7.16	1.88	3.33	4.33	2.66
1977	41.05	22.98	53.93	38.58	31.49	7.75	1.32	1.82	3.30	2.99
1978	39.65	12.56	48.50	42.49	35.82	8.02	.64	1.53	3.89	4.11
1979	34.72	10.04	38.65	40.94	32.28	6.53	.55	1.44	3.27	4.38

Table A3.29. SITC-3 Exports as Percentage of Total Exports to Respective Countries for Selected East–West Pairs

YEAR	EEC TO CMEA	USA TO USSR	FRG TO USSR	FRNC TO USSR	UK TO USSR	CMEA TO EEC	USSR TO USA	USSR TO FRG	USSR TO FRNC	USSR TO UK
1960	.27	0.0	.01	.02	0.0	22.09	0.0	17.14	55.49	1.96
1961	.31	.00	.00	.06	.06	20.83	0.0	12.91	50.59	1.43
1962	.16	0.0	.01	.04	.07	20.69	0.0	10.91	43.03	1.33
1963	.32	8.56	.00	.24	.09	21.78	0.0	9.27	51.97	1.46
1964	.47	.20	.03	.05	.25	23.26	0.0	31.23	55.24	.49
1965	.33	.00	.03	.01	.57	19.16	0.0	21.49	56.05	.42
1966	.21	0.0	.07	.01	.28	19.59	.00	24.35	52.64	.28
1967	.29	.32	.30	.00	.19	22.37	.01	27.88	48.59	.34
1968	.31	.03	.07	.02	.19	23.09	.01	28.78	46.38	.15
1969	.46	.33	.02	.02	.25	12.58	2.29	23.11	40.73	.10
1970	.87	.65	.05	.01	.35	13.80	3.88	28.69	42.56	.04
1971	1.16	.02	.13	.03	.48	16.45	1.13	34.29	50.34	.70
1972	1.16	0.0	.11	.06	.34	14.43	7.81	31.42	38.99	1.18
1973	1.06	.00	.03	.03	.38	17.42	35.77	41.62	38.40	2.15
1974	.76	.22	.05	.08	.57	26.78	30.21	53.56	26.91	7.04
1975	.89	.24	.04	.06	.76	33.35	37.80	59.05	46.83	17.07
1976	.90	.06	.05	.01	.39	36.78	24.68	59.19	46.26	32.83
1977	.68	1.04	.07	.02	.32	36.37	27.24	55.93	47.49	35.96
1978	.83	1.35	.35	.19	.17	36.04	8.90	61.02	49.66	38.71
1979	1.63	.65	.36	.19	.41	41.55	1.91	68.83	60.13	29.37

Table A3.30. Trade Between CSCE Countries, 1965 (monthly averages in millions of US dollars, current prices and exchange rates)

	AUST	BLGM	BLGR	CNDA	CZCH	DNMK	FNLD	FRNC	FRG	GDR	GRCE	HNGR	ICLD	IRLD	
AUST	0.0	1.76	2.11	0.95	3.09	2.17	1.08	3.15	35.43	2.37	1.70	3.53	0.02	0.13	AUST
BLGM	3.04	0.0	0.39	5.55	1.91	6.91	3.13	71.55	112.78	1.00	3.43	0.92	0.21	1.74	BLGM
BLGR	0.98	0.21	0.0	0.04	7.43	0.07	0.13	0.61	3.44	7.81	1.50	1.84	0.00	0.00	BLGR
CNDA	1.17	7.29	0.57	0.0	2.69	0.77	0.39	9.62	18.97	1.17	0.63	0.65	0.45	2.27	CNDA
CZCH	3.17	1.73	6.37	1.23	0.0	1.21	0.92	2.23	7.01	21.89	0.90	11.21	0.23	0.13	CZCH
DNMK	2.16	2.43	0.19	1.55	0.92	0.0	4.01	4.98	30.86	2.05	0.88	0.56	1.03	0.88	DNMK
FNLD	0.34	4.19	0.11	0.21	0.69	5.91	0.0	5.90	14.78	1.07	1.14	0.67	0.26	1.27	FNLD
FRNC	7.32	82.85	1.97	7.40	2.95	8.74	5.59	0.0	163.38	5.75	8.01	1.73	0.14	2.49	FRNC
FRG	73.13	105.26	4.60	16.15	8.38	49.74	24.37	159.33	0.0	17.44	16.29	6.39	1.42	5.57	FRG
GDR	2.19	2.18	7.05	0.12	23.99	1.99	1.27	1.33	17.90	0.0	0.70	10.93	0.24	0.27	GDR
GRCE	0.56	0.57	0.63	0.14	0.70	0.12	0.21	1.40	8.15	0.79	0.0	0.56	0.00	0.05	GRCE
HNGR	2.61	0.65	1.64	0.12	14.28	0.56	0.42	1.33	5.99	10.34	0.80	0.0	0.03	0.02	HNGR
ICLD	0.02	0.21	0.0	0.05	0.23	0.89	0.35	0.19	0.99	0.14	0.08	0.0	0.0	0.10	ICLD
IRLD	0.04	0.66	0.0	0.53	0.05	0.09	0.03	1.56	3.13	0.05	0.11	0.01	0.01	0.0	IRLD
ITLY	14.46	21.00	2.59	6.19	3.03	6.90	4.27	60.51	136.73	1.18	8.59	4.31	0.11	1.07	ITLY
NTHL	5.66	80.34	0.98	4.34	1.28	11.04	4.43	43.36	142.15	1.66	2.77	0.90	0.59	2.36	NTHL
NRWY	0.74	2.20	0.40	2.59	0.85	8.91	2.27	4.20	17.94	0.84	0.86	0.46	0.71	0.33	NRWY
PLND	3.79	1.13	3.82	0.91	17.38	2.70	2.63	2.60	9.07	11.68	0.82	7.36	0.25	0.67	PLND
PRTG	0.55	1.40	0.02	0.85	0.13	1.05	0.27	2.37	4.92	0.05	0.27	0.08	0.04	0.21	PRTG
RMNA	1.71	0.29	0.77	0.02	7.86	0.08	0.32	2.40	6.03	6.06	0.74	3.24	0.07	0.03	RMNA
SPAN	0.57	2.58	0.25	1.02	0.31	1.41	0.47	11.08	16.90	0.18	0.25	0.20	0.08	0.67	SPAN
SWDN	3.07	12.51	0.49	4.28	1.57	31.01	16.68	17.45	51.45	2.68	3.14	0.79	0.60	1.26	SWDN
SWTZ	9.68	8.39	0.58	3.39	1.57	4.81	2.88	20.28	43.68	0.70	1.77	0.93	0.09	0.41	SWTZ
TRKY	0.86	1.87	0.45	0.08	0.91	0.99	0.27	2.33	6.62	0.77	0.65	0.91	0.00	0.07	TRKY
USSR	4.39	3.86	49.05	0.76	79.56	2.88	19.27	12.17	17.54	100.42	3.04	46.12	1.01	0.26	USSR
UK	9.58	40.48	0.90	47.74	3.39	31.17	17.04	43.54	64.30	1.93	8.63	1.80	1.59	43.86	UK
USA	7.70	45.83	0.30	466.19	2.30	20.04	6.31	90.68	191.33	1.05	9.39	0.77	1.47	6.97	USA
YGSL	2.32	0.78	1.71	0.23	5.98	0.38	0.08	1.63	9.87	6.52	2.00	2.27	0.00	0.05	YGSL
	AUST	BLGM	BLGR	CNDA	CZCH	DNMK	FNLD	FRNC	FRG	GDR	GRCE	HNGR	ICLD	IRLD	

Table A3.30. *(cont.)*

	ITLY	NTHL	NRWY	PLND	PRTG	RMNA	SPAN	SWDN	SWTZ	TRKY	USSR	UK	USA	YGSL	
AUST I	13.49	5.40	1.22	2.66	0.60	1.83	1.22	4.25	9.06	0.90	4.76	5.72	5.53	3.25	I AUST
BLGM I	17.28	121.99	4.44	1.15	2.55	0.52	6.46	10.67	11.44	0.64	1.90	28.83	41.23	1.28	I BLGM
BLGR I	2.59	0.31	0.12	3.31	0.03	1.09	0.60	0.23	0.18	0.32	51.25	1.26	0.14	1.84	I BLGR
CNDA I	7.61	5.46	6.90	2.44	0.45	0.05	3.04	3.11	3.29	0.18	15.24	107.08	401.11	0.67	I CNDA
CZCH I	3.03	2.33	0.97	20.34	0.21	5.80	0.53	1.82	1.64	0.71	86.20	4.06	1.33	5.88	I CZCH
DNMK I	7.24	4.39	10.05	1.49	0.71	0.20	2.85	22.83	4.44	0.44	2.57	45.49	12.56	0.45	I DNMK
FNLD I	4.27	7.57	1.36	2.74	0.19	0.27	1.51	8.13	0.74	0.41	106.95	27.13	6.97	0.11	I FNLD
FRNC I	59.84	38.19	8.04	2.97	5.62	3.65	27.22	15.11	44.52	1.80	6.00	44.52	51.22	3.87	I FRNC
FRG I	90.11	147.14	29.13	7.62	12.18	9.64	35.25	78.63	92.36	7.06	12.21	61.91	111.38	11.60	I FRG
GDR I	1.18	2.73	0.99	22.61	0.03	5.21	0.57	2.08	0.64	0.78	20.11	2.80	0.54	5.26	I GDR
GRCE I	1.39	0.92	0.14	1.04	0.19	0.27	0.19	0.46	0.51	0.02	2.24	2.61	4.13	1.11	I GRCE
HNGR I	4.31	1.05	0.31	8.81	0.02	2.34	0.20	1.05	1.67	0.77	42.90	1.59	0.17	2.56	I HNGR
ICLD I	0.56	0.19	0.21	0.24	0.15	0.06	0.25	0.77	0.03	0.00	0.57	2.26	1.66	0.0	I ICLD
IRLD I	0.47	1.33	0.10	0.09	0.07	0.0	0.55	0.26	0.34	0.02	0.18	39.75	4.92	0.0	I IRLD
ITLY I	0.0	24.92	3.71	5.10	3.86	5.10	15.20	12.85	31.36	3.07	15.11	33.79	51.65	11.91	I ITLY
NTHL I	23.72	0.0	8.35	1.08	1.88	0.36	9.57	19.69	11.11	1.13	2.44	63.26	20.90	1.71	I NTHL
NRWY I	3.42	4.11	0.0	1.04	0.57	0.14	1.45	19.87	1.21	0.17	1.54	24.66	11.86	0.39	I NRWY
PLND I	5.10	1.26	0.88	0.0	0.34	3.09	1.48	3.19	1.11	0.52	64.99	11.32	5.46	4.76	I PLND
PRTG I	1.38	1.16	0.48	0.10	0.0	0.14	1.50	1.78	0.93	0.18	0.0	9.67	5.12	0.0	I PRTG
RMNA I	5.10	0.48	0.09	3.72	0.32	0.0	0.59	0.61	0.46	0.31	36.71	2.62	0.14	1.34	I RMNA
SPAN I	2.87	3.15	1.52	0.62	2.04	0.33	0.0	2.43	2.72	0.12	0.17	17.25	11.04	0.29	I SPAN
SWDN I	10.59	17.08	38.65	2.57	1.80	0.61	6.22	0.0	6.97	0.59	4.19	50.09	20.16	1.20	I SWDN
SWTZ I	14.36	9.48	3.10	1.21	2.58	0.68	7.21	8.26	0.0	1.04	1.27	20.04	25.57	1.63	I SWTZ
TRKY I	3.59	0.84	0.35	0.77	1.41	0.20	0.80	1.05	0.80	0.0	1.56	4.26	6.82	0.47	I TRKY
USSR I	15.11	4.41	2.35	60.70	0.01	33.84	1.76	6.03	1.01	1.39	0.0	27.75	3.60	8.99	I USSR
UK I	28.35	40.48	22.20	5.89	9.69	2.26	23.04	53.56	22.29	4.65	10.71	0.0	116.95	4.75	I UK
USA I	82.38	63.79	12.88	2.94	5.97	0.53	43.89	34.65	26.03	13.51	3.70	157.17	0.0	12.41	I USA
YGSL I	11.91	0.90	0.07	5.25	0.0	1.03	0.29	0.88	0.90	0.35	15.71	3.38	5.16	0.0	I YGSL
	ITLY	NTHL	NRWY	PLND	PRTG	RMNA	SPAN	SWDN	SWTZ	TRKY	USSR	UK	USA	YGSL	

Table A3.31. Trade Between CSCE Countries, 1970 (monthly averages in millions of US dollars, current prices and exchange rates)

	AUST	BLGM	BLGR	CNDA	CZCH	DNMK	FNLD	FRNC	FRG	GDR	GRCE	HNGR	ICLD	IRLD	
AUST	0.0	2.84	2.22	3.64	5.15	5.53	3.22	5.72	52.36	2.18	2.33	6.70	0.04	0.28	AUST
BLGM	5.51	0.0	0.82	4.10	1.77	10.58	4.16	178.85	236.46	1.31	4.70	1.61	0.25	1.94	BLGM
BLGR	0.92	0.41	0.0	0.09	7.59	0.37	0.47	1.58	5.39	14.17	0.81	4.06	0.00	0.06	BLGR
CNDA	1.28	12.63	0.27	0.0	0.56	2.09	1.00	17.08	42.10	0.03	1.48	0.56	0.03	2.10	CNDA
CZCH	5.62	1.61	8.02	2.19	0.0	3.73	1.06	3.31	16.56	38.09	1.09	16.50	0.21	0.28	CZCH
DNMK	4.03	3.46	0.22	2.44	1.15	0.0	6.48	6.68	34.23	1.41	1.23	0.93	1.76	1.64	DNMK
FNLD	1.54	4.06	0.33	2.05	1.10	10.71	0.0	8.50	21.97	1.57	1.59	0.83	0.36	1.63	FNLD
FRNC	10.42	162.11	3.98	12.64	4.76	15.92	7.48	0.0	316.43	4.97	11.27	3.89	0.36	4.23	FRNC
FRG	121.96	220.79	5.47	29.60	24.08	68.91	36.24	351.70	0.0	55.18	30.28	11.87	1.17	9.22	FRG
GDR	2.32	2.68	13.12	0.29	37.13	2.97	1.41	3.52	45.64	0.0	0.55	21.76	0.06	0.13	GDR
GRCE	1.08	2.12	1.21	0.40	1.11	0.55	0.26	3.68	15.01	1.03	0.0	1.00	0.00	0.05	GRCE
HNGR	4.96	0.87	2.11	0.73	15.19	2.07	0.93	2.26	11.16	18.47	0.77	0.0	0.00	0.06	HNGR
ICLD	0.06	0.18	0.0	0.01	0.09	0.88	0.35	0.14	1.72	0.06	0.72	0.10	0.0	0.03	ICLD
IRLD	0.15	2.28	0.00	1.05	0.06	0.19	0.09	3.30	3.77	0.00	0.08	0.14	0.01	0.0	IRLD
ITLY	19.33	35.66	4.13	11.54	6.22	11.36	4.69	147.14	246.76	2.21	13.65	7.68	0.25	2.59	ITLY
NTHL	8.59	138.38	0.63	6.28	2.69	14.63	6.49	94.01	303.01	3.26	5.45	2.96	0.78	3.56	NTHL
NRWY	1.41	5.13	0.08	3.92	0.59	14.41	5.22	6.82	39.14	0.62	2.79	0.44	0.73	0.65	NRWY
PLND	4.83	2.08	5.38	0.96	22.47	1.83	3.28	5.66	16.95	24.40	0.72	12.06	0.19	1.52	PLND
PRTG	1.27	2.25	0.03	1.12	0.26	2.39	1.57	4.01	6.16	0.05	0.22	0.04	0.04	0.45	PRTG
RMNA	2.40	0.67	2.39	0.41	11.30	1.13	0.69	4.44	13.21	8.72	1.48	5.07	0.00	0.16	RMNA
SPAN	1.07	5.28	0.56	2.75	0.87	2.76	1.02	22.38	27.57	0.66	1.48	0.75	0.08	0.92	SPAN
SWDN	7.66	19.65	0.74	8.46	3.00	58.34	35.35	32.66	71.59	6.46	5.92	2.01	0.67	2.22	SWDN
SWTZ	21.86	10.59	1.03	6.44	3.60	8.54	5.02	42.55	70.27	2.14	2.45	2.02	0.19	0.93	SWTZ
TRKY	1.56	1.63	0.40	0.12	0.96	1.26	0.10	4.84	10.23	0.82	0.50	1.36	0.00	0.15	TRKY
USSR	6.63	6.41	79.60	0.73	100.73	13.16	27.60	16.96	28.47	162.10	3.02	69.14	0.93	0.31	USSR
UK	20.04	54.72	2.22	58.76	4.08	50.75	28.86	81.19	96.56	3.38	14.07	3.80	1.86	69.92	UK
USA	10.11	83.17	5.53	787.86	1.88	27.29	11.41	158.10	274.38	2.71	9.66	2.36	1.06	9.13	USA
YGSL	4.15	1.03	1.84	0.58	7.43	0.64	0.49	4.19	22.24	4.26	2.60	3.98	0.00	0.12	YGSL
	AUST	BLGM	BLGR	CNDA	CZCH	DNMK	FNLD	FRNC	FRG	GDR	GRCE	HNGR	ICLD	IRLD	

Vertical: exporters
Horizontal: importers

	ITLY	NTHL	NRWY	PLND	PRTG	RMNA	SPAN	SWDN	SWTZ	TRKY	USSR	UK	USA	YGSL	
AUST I	22.29	6.60	3.36	3.72	2.03	3.90	2.23	10.92	24.18	0.83	6.84	15.92	9.96	12.65	I AUST
BLGM I	47.28	188.49	7.44	2.17	3.59	2.00	9.20	19.79	19.09	1.41	4.53	39.36	58.02	3.33	I BLGM
BLGR I	4.52	0.75	0.23	6.63	0.04	3.57	0.51	0.32	0.34	0.37	90.05	1.66	0.20	2.74	I BLGR
CNDA I	17.87	15.31	14.59	1.21	0.95	0.28	6.10	4.92	3.77	1.26	8.10	136.55	924.26	1.46	I CNDA
CZCH I	6.28	2.90	1.24	25.87	0.11	13.21	0.90	2.66	2.75	1.08	102.82	4.56	1.99	12.62	I CZCH
DNMK I	8.92	7.25	19.20	3.14	1.66	0.42	2.18	45.24	6.89	0.35	2.21	55.27	23.84	0.79	I DNMK
FNLD I	5.62	9.15	7.33	2.29	0.86	0.44	2.45	29.82	3.54	0.58	23.54	39.00	9.53	0.31	I FNLD
FRNC I	164.37	83.83	9.06	6.77	9.13	6.84	39.47	24.19	65.00	2.65	22.76	73.65	78.51	9.16	I FRNC
FRG I	247.02	302.82	44.29	94.98	19.96	16.43	49.92	110.47	161.43	13.68	122.88	109.79	260.80	47.26	I FRG
GDR I	2.95	3.80	0.66	33.30	0.02	9.59	0.39	3.90	1.13	0.94	144.16	3.22	0.78	6.19	I GDR
GRCE I	5.86	2.03	0.98	0.90	0.26	0.75	0.90	1.27	1.04	0.01	2.88	3.92	4.35	3.48	I GRCE
HNGR I	10.15	1.95	0.49	11.54	0.15	3.98	0.46	1.92	2.68	0.90	66.82	2.13	0.52	4.09	I HNGR
ICLD I	0.46	0.09	0.21	0.15	0.52	0.0	0.60	0.83	0.32	0.00	0.84	1.79	3.91	0.01	I ICLD
IRLD I	1.26	1.43	0.24	0.43	0.06	0.01	0.51	0.53	0.76	0.04	0.00	68.25	11.22	0.11	I IRLD
ITLY I	0.0	48.46	5.78	6.01	7.00	6.58	20.59	17.35	50.71	5.84	25.66	49.84	109.67	31.50	I ITLY
NTHL I	53.51	0.0	10.08	2.40	3.27	1.81	11.00	26.21	18.64	1.84	3.79	91.82	43.98	4.14	I NTHL
NRWY I	5.39	6.78	0.0	1.22	0.78	0.04	2.03	34.02	2.65	0.19	2.07	39.73	11.85	0.57	I NRWY
PLND I	10.06	2.39	1.48	0.0	0.36	6.40	1.49	4.79	1.31	2.37	105.08	12.61	8.16	4.31	I PLND
PRTG I	2.36	1.70	1.23	0.09	0.0	0.17	1.58	4.70	1.99	0.08	0.0	17.28	7.93	0.0	I PRTG
RMNA I	11.25	1.20	0.18	5.96	0.10	0.0	0.94	1.00	0.73	0.69	43.89	4.64	1.12	2.96	I RMNA
SPAN I	12.54	7.45	1.90	1.38	5.70	0.90	0.0	4.32	4.71	0.37	0.49	25.31	29.80	1.43	I SPAN
SWDN I	17.73	25.02	62.00	3.27	3.39	1.71	8.95	0.0	16.83	0.79	10.95	74.21	33.38	3.34	I SWDN
SWTZ I	27.99	13.71	6.00	2.33	4.55	2.19	8.93	14.55	0.0	3.71	4.15	39.77	38.23	10.76	I SWTZ
TRKY I	4.99	1.57	0.59	0.67	0.54	0.33	0.63	0.97	1.40	0.0	2.45	3.12	5.82	0.63	I TRKY
USSR I	23.46	4.84	2.57	113.44	0.08	41.73	0.81	12.98	2.22	3.23	0.0	44.01	6.03	16.10	I USSR
UK I	47.14	63.68	37.99	11.94	18.34	5.82	28.00	80.57	41.89	7.34	20.43	0.0	182.98	14.88	I UK
USA I	128.57	109.02	22.28	5.83	8.94	5.53	74.71	50.79	45.88	14.33	1.87	234.65	0.0	13.34	I USA
YGSL I	22.21	1.84	0.30	4.74	0.01	2.49	0.51	1.71	2.23	0.27	20.13	4.35	8.00	0.0	I YGSL
	ITLY	NTHL	NRWY	PLND	PRTG	RMNA	SPAN	SWDN	SWTZ	TRKY	USSR	UK	USA	YGSL	

Vertical: exporters
Horizontal: importers

Table A3.32. Trade Between CSCE Countries, 1975 (monthly averages in millions of US dollars, current prices and exchange rates)

	AUST	BLGM	BLGR	CNDA	CZCH	DNMK	FNLD	FRNC	FRG	GDR	GRCE	HNGR	ICLD	IRLD	
AUST	0.0	9.75	5.57	4.63	15.83	13.88	9.19	17.39	127.40	9.67	6.55	22.50	0.22	0.97	AUST
BLGM	16.91	0.0	3.17	11.69	5.68	30.50	12.73	428.74	532.50	6.23	12.45	3.76	1.05	5.77	BLGM
BLGR	2.08	0.90	0.0	0.31	17.74	0.52	0.53	3.01	7.80	27.24	1.78	8.48	0.01	0.02	BLGR
CNDA	3.33	26.40	0.21	0.0	0.82	3.71	2.09	38.68	59.50	0.35	3.83	0.56	0.08	3.27	CNDA
CZCH	15.98	4.20	15.39	3.81	0.0	3.37	2.59	8.71	39.10	85.73	2.57	41.00	0.34	0.97	CZCH
DNMK	6.77	12.94	0.93	6.43	2.51	0.0	18.83	25.33	94.90	2.23	3.10	2.30	4.11	2.52	DNMK
FNLD	3.85	7.98	0.50	2.37	2.52	22.35	0.0	18.20	39.80	3.64	2.34	2.47	0.96	3.55	FNLD
FRNC	31.89	447.14	10.25	39.98	13.30	32.53	26.26	0.0	751.40	14.80	26.52	13.82	1.07	16.14	FRNC
FRG	313.19	563.85	34.70	64.40	56.70	169.91	90.24	847.75	0.0	124.65	70.24	47.80	4.36	22.35	FRG
GDR	5.81	6.76	29.85	0.44	92.58	5.06	4.70	13.62	106.20	0.0	3.23	61.87	0.08	0.41	GDR
GRCE	2.30	4.63	2.76	1.39	2.51	1.05	0.23	17.67	57.20	2.01	0.0	0.98	0.00	0.14	GRCE
HNGR	11.54	2.14	7.47	1.23	42.59	2.20	2.35	7.69	30.50	54.97	1.01	0.0	0.02	0.19	HNGR
ICLD	0.13	0.27	0.01	0.04	0.35	1.06	0.39	0.25	1.80	0.02	0.45	0.01	0.0	0.01	ICLD
IRLD	0.67	7.36	0.08	2.59	0.12	0.99	0.55	12.71	22.70	0.08	0.39	0.08	0.04	0.0	IRLD
ITLY	63.20	99.72	10.95	31.04	10.18	22.54	13.90	395.84	583.70	7.28	36.51	15.87	0.56	7.97	ITLY
NTHL	23.84	430.23	2.94	12.98	7.52	50.25	16.83	285.03	871.20	10.63	17.86	7.20	2.77	10.23	NTHL
NRWY	3.79	13.99	0.34	9.28	1.95	41.84	16.54	24.44	63.40	4.00	4.94	0.75	4.25	1.58	NRWY
PLND	12.24	10.34	22.41	3.35	68.77	15.26	13.99	29.37	48.50	79.05	3.20	25.61	0.38	2.53	PLND
PRTG	2.76	5.50	0.41	2.35	0.31	4.47	3.15	12.66	18.60	0.29	1.98	0.15	0.19	1.13	PRTG
RMNA	5.39	2.30	8.05	1.58	19.49	2.68	0.92	14.59	33.60	22.46	2.46	13.88	0.00	0.20	RMNA
SPAN	4.03	22.94	0.69	8.36	2.08	7.16	7.39	105.12	76.10	1.35	9.43	1.18	0.38	2.25	SPAN
SWDN	19.96	45.29	3.14	21.70	6.20	122.48	101.42	78.55	144.30	12.85	9.55	6.27	2.45	6.77	SWDN
SWTZ	52.69	57.94	3.16	14.64	8.71	16.41	14.06	128.45	165.40	5.98	6.93	8.53	0.37	2.28	SWTZ
TRKY	3.39	2.73	0.57	0.28	0.35	2.72	0.34	7.25	26.30	0.63	0.06	1.07	0.01	0.44	TRKY
USSR	26.53	25.01	237.91	2.33	233.29	14.19	105.81	64.10	107.90	344.27	8.57	191.49	4.21	3.31	USSR
UK	31.25	158.37	4.40	100.08	9.41	88.35	54.99	213.61	228.40	6.01	21.36	8.21	4.39	154.43	UK
USA	22.89	162.42	2.50	1925.98	4.40	51.83	35.04	340.71	479.10	1.40	32.69	6.30	3.73	22.93	USA
YGSL	6.81	3.83	4.58	1.55	20.36	1.33	0.69	9.90	54.20	15.77	2.15	7.20	0.06	0.08	YGSL
	AUST	BLGM	BLGR	CNDA	CZCH	DNMK	FNLD	FRNC	FRG	GDR	GRCE	HNGR	ICLD	IRLD	

Vertical: exporters
Horizontal: importers

Table A3.32. *(cont.)*

	ITLY	NTHL	NRWY	PLND	PRTG	RMNA	SPAN	SWDN	SWTZ	TRKY	USSR	UK	USA	YGSL	
AUST	49.75	17.82	9.29	27.64	2.90	7.40	5.92	27.93	48.18	4.98	18.06	37.83	20.20	26.39	AUST
BLGM	101.29	405.09	20.88	18.22	9.29	5.00	28.38	55.46	35.93	10.62	29.43	176.08	99.90	8.30	BLGM
BLGR	5.44	0.53	0.22	15.49	0.03	9.26	1.47	0.66	0.77	2.18	213.53	1.37	1.70	5.52	BLGR
CNDA	46.37	25.57	15.64	9.36	1.33	5.07	11.98	9.51	7.12	4.89	33.50	159.03	1847.50	4.72	CNDA
CZCH	10.53	7.18	3.14	61.79	0.16	22.70	2.25	6.45	5.51	2.04	230.39	10.95	2.90	26.52	CZCH
DNMK	35.00	20.03	46.67	11.26	3.25	0.85	8.38	106.20	12.02	2.41	5.39	115.61	39.30	3.51	DNMK
FNLD	6.32	12.52	23.32	5.85	1.70	0.28	5.97	83.67	6.12	0.92	94.47	73.77	12.50	0.44	FNLD
FRNC	426.67	223.86	30.34	51.99	24.31	16.93	112.94	63.16	153.81	22.03	95.38	301.33	180.30	29.23	FRNC
FRG	547.52	737.59	126.79	108.50	36.39	55.20	138.93	288.66	308.89	83.71	235.40	369.43	450.70	119.78	FRG
GDR	7.26	6.52	2.71	78.52	0.14	26.31	2.42	13.47	1.93	1.08	305.32	7.16	0.90	18.62	GDR
GRCE	20.41	8.67	2.36	2.91	0.24	3.46	6.42	4.53	1.69	0.04	7.28	11.91	9.20	6.37	GRCE
HNGR	17.83	5.65	1.22	26.54	0.05	14.20	1.13	4.57	4.31	1.43	197.25	4.82	2.90	9.47	HNGR
ICLD	0.67	0.11	0.47	0.32	3.02	0.01	1.35	0.68	0.35	0.00	2.70	3.00	7.10	0.27	ICLD
IRLD	7.42	7.22	0.67	0.58	0.16	0.02	3.50	2.89	2.03	0.21	1.98	169.44	14.80	0.38	IRLD
ITLY	0.0	101.94	12.49	33.73	15.98	17.94	69.30	39.83	109.45	29.70	85.28	149.19	204.70	72.41	ITLY
NTHL	149.93	0.0	36.69	15.63	11.40	5.08	36.33	70.38	44.48	11.53	17.45	344.72	90.70	9.91	NTHL
NRWY	12.78	20.10	0.0	5.25	3.70	0.95	5.98	99.39	5.33	1.63	8.02	108.46	33.60	2.28	NRWY
PLND	25.54	11.81	5.79	0.0	0.78	18.88	10.45	16.31	3.30	2.47	270.06	21.14	20.30	16.59	PLND
PRTG	6.01	4.32	4.58	0.31	0.0	0.57	4.45	13.46	5.12	0.68	1.51	37.31	13.30	0.07	PRTG
RMNA	20.37	9.07	0.52	16.97	1.18	0.0	8.93	5.50	2.74	4.96	77.29	6.62	11.10	9.67	RMNA
SPAN	23.60	28.27	4.76	6.76	13.69	3.04	0.0	12.41	12.61	2.59	6.23	57.91	70.50	3.60	SPAN
SWDN	42.63	56.70	155.39	34.27	7.82	4.19	28.32	0.0	30.24	3.18	24.46	164.14	73.90	9.37	SWDN
SWTZ	73.03	37.51	14.46	14.78	9.50	5.50	31.04	36.13	0.0	23.38	15.12	130.75	73.20	17.00	SWTZ
TRKY	8.59	3.66	0.95	0.88	1.56	0.55	2.64	4.72	3.09	0.0	6.14	6.29	12.10	0.76	TRKY
USSR	73.04	25.07	7.05	282.69	4.61	81.10	11.91	43.81	10.11	6.13	0.0	74.11	21.20	67.22	USSR
UK	106.10	167.98	78.20	33.58	27.84	7.49	72.35	164.57	68.08	27.86	38.60	0.0	314.40	19.78	UK
USA	279.01	289.54	57.34	48.60	39.62	15.90	215.43	98.51	83.89	34.43	153.10	433.70	0.0	34.64	USA
YGSL	28.39	5.19	1.35	15.15	0.08	8.53	1.15	3.15	3.18	1.47	84.36	4.47	21.70	0.0	YGSL
	ITLY	NTHL	NRWY	PLND	PRTG	RMNA	SPAN	SWDN	SWTZ	TRKY	USSR	UK	USA	YGSL	

Vertical: exporters
Horizontal: importers

Table A3.33. Measures of Proximity Between CSCE Nations: Trade, 1965

	AUST	BLGM	BLGR	CNDA	CZCH	DNMK	FNLD	FRNC	FRG	GDR	GRCE	HNGR	ICLD	IRLD	ITLY	NTHL	NRWY	PLND	PRTG	RMNA	SPAN	SWDN	SWTZ	TRKY	USSR	UK	USA	YGSL
AUST	****	.011	.015	.005	.020	.014	.006	.022	.212	.015	.015	.026	.001	.001	.066	.026	.007	.021	.009	.018	.007	.020	.055	.014	.021	.032	.027	.027
BLGM	.011	****	.002	.013	.007	.017	.016	.151	.168	.007	.018	.005	.010	.010	.042	.215	.016	.005	.024	.003	.021	.032	.032	.017	.006	.063	.069	.007
BLGR	.015	.002	****	.002	.057	.001	.001	.008	.025	.065	.016	.018	.000	.000	.018	.004	.003	.031	.000	.011	.004	.003	.003	.007	.335	.007	.001	.021
CNDA	.005	.013	.002	****	.007	.004	.001	.014	.022	.002	.004	.002	.012	.011	.014	.009	.021	.006	.009	.000	.009	.009	.010	.002	.014	.117	.567	.003
CZCH	.020	.007	.057	.007	****	.006	.005	.009	.023	.130	.011	.092	.012	.001	.011	.006	.006	.105	.002	.060	.003	.007	.008	.012	.296	.012	.005	.051
DNMK	.014	.017	.001	.004	.006	****	.029	.024	.124	.012	.005	.004	.049	.005	.027	.028	.061	.012	.013	.001	.014	.116	.023	.011	.010	.132	.051	.004
FNLD	.006	.016	.001	.001	.005	.029	****	.024	.078	.008	.007	.004	.016	.006	.019	.025	.014	.017	.004	.003	.006	.065	.011	.005	.233	.084	.025	.001
FRNC	.022	.151	.008	.014	.009	.024	.024	****	.205	.012	.041	.008	.008	.017	.117	.076	.027	.011	.047	.021	.086	.040	.093	.027	.017	.067	.091	.018
FRG	.212	.168	.025	.022	.023	.124	.078	.205	****	.062	.127	.031	.058	.035	.172	.210	.095	.028	.096	.052	.109	.132	.168	.088	.021	.071	.132	.069
GDR	.015	.007	.065	.002	.130	.012	.008	.012	.062	****	.011	.082	.010	.002	.005	.009	.006	.107	.001	.052	.003	.011	.003	.012	.217	.009	.003	.053
GRCE	.015	.018	.016	.004	.011	.005	.007	.041	.127	.011	****	.011	.002	.001	.044	.019	.006	.014	.005	.008	.003	.017	.013	.006	.031	.054	.068	.025
HNGR	.026	.005	.018	.002	.092	.004	.004	.008	.031	.082	.011	****	.001	.000	.025	.006	.003	.062	.001	.030	.002	.006	.009	.014	.250	.009	.002	.026
ICLD	.001	.010	.000	.012	.012	.049	.016	.008	.058	.010	.002	.001	****	.003	.017	.019	.024	.012	.006	.004	.009	.034	.003	.000	.038	.094	.076	.000
IRLD	.001	.010	.000	.011	.001	.005	.006	.017	.035	.002	.001	.000	.003	****	.007	.016	.002	.004	.003	.000	.008	.007	.004	.001	.002	.362	.049	.000
ITLY	.066	.042	.018	.014	.011	.027	.019	.117	.172	.005	.044	.025	.017	.007	****	.052	.017	.021	.031	.037	.038	.032	.071	.045	.032	.055	.105	.084
NTHL	.026	.215	.004	.009	.006	.028	.025	.076	.210	.009	.019	.006	.019	.016	.052	****	.029	.005	.019	.003	.029	.048	.033	.013	.007	.089	.060	.009
NRWY	.007	.016	.003	.021	.006	.061	.014	.027	.095	.006	.006	.003	.024	.002	.017	.029	****	.007	.008	.001	.012	.152	.013	.004	.009	.105	.052	.002
PLND	.021	.005	.031	.006	.105	.012	.017	.011	.028	.107	.014	.062	.012	.004	.021	.005	.007	****	.003	.031	.007	.013	.006	.010	.248	.031	.015	.045
PRTG	.009	.024	.000	.009	.002	.013	.004	.047	.096	.001	.005	.001	.006	.003	.031	.019	.008	.003	****	.004	.029	.024	.023	.018	.000	.122	.067	.0
RMNA	.018	.003	.011	.000	.060	.001	.003	.021	.052	.052	.008	.030	.004	.000	.037	.003	.001	.031	.004	****	.005	.005	.005	.005	.253	.017	.002	.014
SPAN	.007	.021	.004	.009	.003	.014	.006	.086	.109	.003	.003	.002	.009	.008	.038	.029	.012	.007	.029	.005	****	.023	.029	.007	.004	.097	.102	.003
SWDN	.020	.032	.003	.009	.007	.116	.065	.040	.132	.011	.017	.006	.034	.007	.032	.048	.152	.013	.024	.005	.023	****	.029	.012	.013	.119	.056	.008
SWTZ	.055	.032	.003	.010	.008	.023	.011	.093	.168	.003	.013	.009	.003	.004	.071	.033	.013	.006	.023	.005	.029	.029	****	.013	.004	.060	.068	.010
TRKY	.014	.017	.007	.002	.012	.011	.005	.027	.088	.012	.006	.014	.000	.001	.045	.013	.004	.010	.018	.005	.007	.012	.013	****	.020	.058	.130	.008
USSR	.021	.006	.335	.014	.296	.010	.233	.017	.021	.217	.031	.250	.038	.002	.032	.007	.009	.248	.000	.253	.004	.013	.004	.020	****	.032	.005	.087
UK	.032	.063	.007	.117	.012	.132	.084	.067	.071	.009	.054	.009	.094	.362	.055	.089	.105	.031	.122	.017	.097	.119	.060	.058	.032	****	.155	.027
USA	.027	.069	.001	.567	.005	.051	.025	.091	.132	.003	.068	.002	.076	.049	.105	.060	.052	.015	.067	.002	.102	.056	.068	.130	.005	.155	****	.055
YGSL	.027	.007	.021	.003	.051	.004	.001	.018	.069	.053	.025	.026	.000	.000	.084	.009	.002	.045	.0	.014	.003	.008	.010	.008	.087	.027	.055	****

0 = No relationship
1 = Exclusive Bilateral Relationship

Table A3.34. Measures of Proximity Between CSCE Nations: Trade, 1970

	AUST	BLGM	BLGR	CNDA	CZCH	DNMK	FNLD	FRNC	FRG	GDR	GRCE	HNGR	ICLD	IRLD	ITLY	NTHL	NRWY	PLND	PRTG	RMNA	SPAN	SWDN	SWTZ	TRKY	USSR	UK	USA	YGSL	
AUST	****	.011	.009	.007	.021	.018	.011	.020	.191	.008	.013	.029	.002	.001	.055	.020	.010	.016	.014	.019	.007	.029	.076	.014	.018	.045	.023	.042	AUST
BLGM	.011	****	.003	.009	.004	.016	.013	.176	.190	.004	.021	.004	.009	.011	.048	.191	.018	.005	.021	.006	.021	.031	.026	.015	.007	.050	.061	.007	BLGM
BLGR	.009	.003	****	.001	.041	.002	.002	.011	.020	.066	.011	.019	.000	.000	.017	.003	.001	.030	.000	.021	.003	.002	.003	.005	.344	.008	.011	.015	BLGR
CNDA	.007	.009	.001	****	.003	.005	.005	.013	.025	.000	.005	.002	.001	.008	.015	.011	.023	.002	.008	.001	.012	.010	.009	.006	.004	.086	.614	.003	CNDA
CZCH	.021	.004	.041	.003	****	.008	.005	.009	.042	.123	.009	.074	.007	.001	.015	.007	.004	.084	.002	.069	.004	.008	.010	.011	.250	.010	.004	.049	CZCH
DNMK	.018	.016	.002	.005	.008	****	.037	.024	.098	.007	.007	.007	.058	.006	.023	.025	.068	.009	.018	.004	.010	.141	.023	.009	.017	.119	.051	.004	DNMK
FNLD	.011	.013	.002	.005	.005	.037	****	.024	.082	.006	.007	.005	.015	.006	.016	.025	.030	.012	.012	.004	.008	.116	.016	.004	.082	.103	.030	.002	FNLD
FRNC	.020	.176	.011	.013	.009	.024	.024	****	.214	.008	.043	.010	.011	.019	.152	.088	.021	.013	.044	.024	.083	.040	.086	.037	.021	.067	.079	.022	FRNC
FRG	.191	.190	.020	.025	.042	.098	.082	.214	****	.083	.134	.035	.057	.031	.191	.237	.103	.095	.083	.059	.095	.108	.157	.109	.061	.068	.127	.110	FRG
GDR	.008	.004	.066	.000	.123	.007	.006	.008	.083	****	.007	.086	.003	.000	.005	.007	.002	.088	.000	.048	.002	.012	.004	.009	.312	.006	.003	.024	GDR
GRCE	.013	.021	.011	.005	.009	.007	.007	.043	.134	.007	****	.009	.014	.001	.060	.022	.015	.007	.003	.011	.010	.021	.012	.004	.021	.051	.041	.030	GRCE
HNGR	.029	.004	.019	.002	.074	.007	.005	.010	.035	.086	.009	****	.002	.001	.031	.008	.002	.053	.001	.030	.003	.008	.010	.014	.236	.010	.004	.025	HNGR
ICLD	.002	.009	.000	.001	.007	.058	.015	.011	.057	.003	.014	.002	****	.001	.014	.019	.021	.007	.012	.000	.013	.031	.010	.000	.036	.075	.094	.000	ICLD
IRLD	.001	.011	.000	.008	.001	.006	.006	.019	.031	.000	.001	.001	.001	****	.010	.013	.003	.006	.003	.001	.005	.008	.005	.001	.001	.362	.052	.001	IRLD
ITLY	.055	.048	.017	.015	.015	.023	.016	.152	.191	.005	.060	.031	.014	.010	****	.057	.016	.018	.032	.039	.047	.027	.068	.052	.029	.048	.096	.098	ITLY
NTHL	.020	.191	.003	.011	.007	.025	.025	.088	.237	.007	.022	.008	.019	.013	.057	****	.023	.005	.017	.007	.027	.039	.028	.016	.005	.078	.061	.010	NTHL
NRWY	.010	.018	.001	.023	.004	.068	.030	.021	.103	.002	.015	.002	.021	.003	.016	.023	****	.005	.010	.001	.009	.151	.015	.005	.007	.106	.041	.002	NRWY
PLND	.016	.005	.030	.002	.084	.009	.012	.013	.095	.088	.007	.053	.007	.006	.018	.005	.005	****	.002	.034	.006	.011	.005	.015	.248	.026	.014	.022	PLND
PRTG	.014	.021	.000	.008	.002	.018	.012	.044	.083	.000	.003	.001	.012	.003	.032	.017	.010	.002	****	.001	.032	.033	.025	.005	.000	.131	.060	.000	PRTG
RMNA	.019	.006	.021	.001	.069	.004	.004	.024	.059	.048	.011	.030	.000	.001	.039	.007	.001	.034	.001	****	.006	.006	.007	.006	.189	.022	.013	.019	RMNA
SPAN	.007	.021	.003	.012	.004	.010	.008	.083	.095	.002	.010	.003	.013	.005	.047	.027	.009	.006	.032	.006	****	.021	.024	.006	.002	.076	.126	.005	SPAN
SWDN	.029	.031	.002	.010	.008	.141	.116	.040	.108	.012	.021	.008	.031	.008	.027	.039	.151	.011	.033	.006	.021	****	.034	.009	.019	.110	.052	.010	SWDN
SWTZ	.076	.026	.003	.009	.010	.023	.016	.086	.157	.004	.012	.010	.010	.005	.068	.028	.015	.005	.025	.007	.024	.034	****	.025	.006	.068	.061	.026	SWTZ
TRKY	.014	.015	.005	.006	.011	.009	.004	.037	.109	.009	.004	.014	.000	.001	.052	.016	.005	.015	.005	.006	.006	.009	.025	****	.027	.047	.088	.006	TRKY
USSR	.018	.007	.344	.004	.250	.017	.082	.021	.061	.312	.021	.236	.036	.001	.029	.005	.007	.248	.000	.189	.002	.019	.006	.027	****	.034	.003	.072	USSR
UK	.045	.050	.008	.086	.010	.119	.103	.067	.068	.006	.051	.010	.075	.362	.048	.078	.106	.026	.131	.022	.076	.110	.068	.047	.034	****	.145	.031	UK
USA	.023	.061	.011	.614	.004	.051	.030	.079	.127	.003	.041	.004	.094	.052	.096	.061	.041	.014	.060	.013	.126	.052	.061	.088	.003	.145	****	.035	USA
YGSL	.042	.007	.015	.003	.049	.004	.002	.022	.110	.024	.030	.025	.000	.001	.098	.010	.002	.022	.000	.019	.005	.010	.026	.006	.072	.031	.035	****	YGSL
	AUST	BLGM	BLGR	CNDA	CZCH	DNMK	FNLD	FRNC	FRG	GDR	GRCE	HNGR	ICLD	IRLD	ITLY	NTHL	NRWY	PLND	PRTG	RMNA	SPAN	SWDN	SWTZ	TRKY	USSR	UK	USA	YGSL	

0 = No relationship
1 = Exclusive Bilateral Relationship

Table A3.35. Measures of Proximity Between CSCE Nations: Trade, 1975

	AUST	BLGM	BLGR	CNDA	CZCH	DNMK	FNLD	FRNC	FRG	GDR	GRCE	HNGR	ICLD	IRLD	ITLY	NTHL	NRWY	PLND	PRTG	RMNA	SPAN	SWDN	SWTZ	TRKY	USSR	UK	USA	YGSL	
AUST	****	.014	.008	.004	.026	.016	.012	.023	.191	.011	.013	.032	.003	.002	.058	.021	.011	.029	.010	.015	.008	.030	.067	.016	.023	.035	.020	.033	AUST
BLGM	.014	****	.003	.009	.005	.021	.013	.173	.182	.005	.019	.004	.010	.014	.047	.186	.019	.012	.022	.006	.026	.032	.035	.018	.013	.072	.046	.009	BLGM
BLGR	.008	.003	****	.000	.036	.002	.001	.010	.029	.056	.008	.019	.000	.000	.013	.003	.001	.037	.001	.025	.002	.003	.004	.005	.359	.004	.003	.013	BLGR
CNDA	.004	.009	.000	****	.002	.005	.003	.015	.019	.000	.006	.001	.001	.006	.017	.008	.013	.005	.006	.006	.010	.010	.008	.006	.008	.053	.636	.004	CNDA
CZCH	.026	.005	.036	.002	****	.005	.005	.010	.042	.125	.008	.077	.006	.001	.011	.007	.004	.091	.001	.050	.003	.008	.009	.004	.237	.010	.003	.048	CZCH
DNMK	.016	.021	.002	.005	.005	****	.037	.026	.110	.005	.006	.004	.041	.005	.029	.033	.073	.018	.014	.004	.012	.133	.018	.011	.009	.099	.040	.005	DNMK
FNLD	.012	.013	.001	.003	.005	.037	****	.026	.069	.007	.004	.005	.011	.006	.012	.018	.038	.016	.010	.002	.012	.131	.015	.002	.125	.079	.026	.001	FNLD
FRNC	.023	.173	.010	.015	.010	.026	.026	****	.201	.011	.051	.013	.010	.029	.159	.093	.028	.030	.052	.027	.104	.040	.095	.040	.031	.090	.071	.025	FRNC
FRG	.191	.182	.029	.019	.042	.110	.069	.201	****	.081	.146	.044	.049	.044	.183	.243	.088	.052	.076	.073	.090	.106	.144	.145	.054	.084	.099	.109	FRG
GDR	.011	.005	.056	.000	.125	.005	.007	.011	.081	****	.007	.097	.001	.001	.006	.007	.005	.095	.001	.053	.003	.013	.004	.003	.272	.005	.001	.032	GDR
GRCE	.013	.019	.008	.006	.008	.006	.004	.051	.146	.007	****	.003	.005	.001	.066	.030	.011	.009	.006	.012	.024	.017	.011	.000	.019	.038	.043	.016	GRCE
HNGR	.032	.004	.019	.001	.077	.004	.005	.013	.044	.097	.003	****	.000	.000	.022	.008	.002	.043	.000	.037	.002	.008	.010	.005	.249	.008	.005	.019	HNGR
ICLD	.003	.010	.000	.001	.006	.041	.011	.010	.049	.001	.005	.000	****	.000	.011	.021	.036	.006	.035	.000	.017	.024	.006	.000	.057	.061	.098	.003	ICLD
IRLD	.002	.014	.000	.006	.001	.005	.006	.029	.044	.001	.001	.000	.000	****	.016	.018	.003	.004	.003	.000	.008	.011	.005	.002	.006	.337	.037	.001	IRLD
ITLY	.058	.047	.013	.017	.011	.029	.012	.159	.183	.006	.066	.022	.011	.016	****	.055	.014	.024	.031	.035	.043	.026	.068	.052	.036	.054	.084	.069	ITLY
NTHL	.021	.186	.003	.008	.007	.033	.018	.093	.243	.007	.030	.008	.021	.018	.055	****	.030	.011	.022	.013	.032	.039	.030	.021	.009	.100	.062	.011	NTHL
NRWY	.011	.019	.001	.013	.004	.073	.038	.028	.088	.005	.011	.002	.036	.003	.014	.030	****	.008	.016	.002	.009	.160	.013	.005	.008	.102	.044	.004	NRWY
PLND	.029	.012	.037	.005	.091	.018	.016	.030	.052	.095	.009	.043	.006	.004	.024	.011	.008	****	.002	.039	.012	.025	.010	.005	.229	.022	.024	.030	PLND
PRTG	.010	.022	.001	.006	.001	.014	.010	.052	.076	.001	.006	.000	.035	.003	.031	.022	.016	.002	****	.004	.031	.036	.023	.007	.009	.102	.071	.000	PRTG
RMNA	.015	.006	.025	.006	.050	.004	.002	.027	.073	.053	.012	.037	.000	.000	.035	.013	.002	.039	.004	****	.014	.010	.008	.010	.142	.012	.023	.026	RMNA
SPAN	.008	.026	.002	.010	.003	.012	.012	.104	.090	.003	.024	.002	.017	.008	043	.032	.009	.012	.031	.014	****	.023	.027	.011	.009	.064	.116	.005	SPAN
SWDN	.030	.032	.003	.010	.008	.133	.131	.040	.106	.013	.017	.008	.024	.011	.026	.039	.160	.025	.036	.010	.023	****	.030	.016	.022	.098	.045	.010	SWDN
SWTZ	.067	.035	.004	.008	.009	.018	.015	.095	.144	.004	.011	.010	.006	.005	.068	.030	.013	.010	.023	.008	.027	.030	****	.035	.009	.070	.050	.016	SWTZ
TRKY	.016	.018	.005	.006	.004	.011	.002	.040	.145	.003	.000	.005	.000	.002	.052	.021	.005	.005	.007	.010	.011	.016	.035	****	.022	.044	.063	.005	TRKY
USSR	.023	.013	.359	.008	.237	.009	.125	.031	.054	.272	.019	.249	.057	.006	.036	.009	.008	.229	.009	.142	.009	.022	.009	.022	****	.024	.029	.118	USSR
UK	.035	.072	.004	.053	.010	.099	.079	.090	.084	.005	.038	.008	.061	.337	.054	.100	.102	.022	.102	.012	.064	.098	.070	.044	.024	****	.116	.016	UK
USA	.020	.046	.003	.636	.003	.040	.026	.071	.099	.001	.043	.005	.098	.037	.084	.062	.044	.024	.071	.023	.116	.045	.050	.063	.029	.116	****	.038	USA
YGSL	.033	.009	.013	.004	.048	.005	.001	.025	.109	.032	.016	.019	.003	.001	.069	.011	.004	.030	.000	.026	.005	.010	.016	.005	.118	.016	.038	****	YGSL
	AUST	BLGM	BLGR	CNDA	CZCH	DNMK	FNLD	FRNC	FRG	GDR	GRCE	HNGR	ICLD	IRLD	ITLY	NTHL	NRWY	PLND	PRTG	RMNA	SPAN	SWDN	SWTZ	TRKY	USSR	UK	USA	YGSL	

0 = No relationship
1 = Exclusive Bilateral Relationship

A3.5 HUMAN RIGHTS AND HUMAN CONTACTS: ADDITIONAL DATA

Table A3.36. Number of Political Sanctions in WTO Countries

YEAR	GDR	PLND	HNGR	CZCH	BLGR	RMNA	USSR	MEAN
1960	48	25	6	11	2	4	33	18
1961	71	32	8	10	3	1	36	23
1962	96	11	16	8	1	0	57	27
1963	28	12	5	9	5	0	37	14
1964	25	12	8	7	2	0	23	11
1965	32	7	10	4	2	1	19	11
1966	34	31	11	5	1	1	45	18
1967	13	21	8	12	0	3	42	14
1968	19	52	2	38	5	1	30	21
1969	17	3	0	75	1	0	33	18
1970	8	17	1	28	0	0	30	12
1971	4	2	0	12	0	1	37	8
1972	6	0	2	17	0	1	47	10
1973	10	0	0	2	0	0	55	10
1974	0	0	2	3	1	0	87	13
1975	2	2	0	1	0	0	35	6
1976	12	6	0	3	0	0	25	7
1977	3	7	0	30	0	9	58	15

Note: MEAN = mean of GDR, PLND, HNGR, USSR

Table A3.37. Unemployment in Europe as Percent of Total Labor Force

YEAR	AUST	BLGM	CNDA	DNMK	FNLD	FRG	IRLD	ITLY	NRWG	SPAN	SWDN	UK	USA	NATO	N+N
1960	3.7	5.4	7.0	.	1.5	1.3	6.7	5.6	.	.	.	1.6	5.5	4.4	.
1961	2.9	4.2	7.1	.	1.2	.8	5.7	5.1	.	.	.	1.5	6.7	4.2	.
1962	2.7	3.3	5.9	.	1.2	.7	5.7	4.6	.	.	1.5	1.9	5.5	3.6	2.8
1963	2.9	2.7	5.5	.	1.5	.8	6.1	3.9	.	.	1.7	2.3	5.7	3.5	3.0
1964	2.7	2.2	4.7	.	1.5	.8	5.7	4.3	.	1.8	1.6	1.7	5.2	3.1	2.9
1965	2.7	2.4	3.9	.	1.4	.7	5.6	5.4	.	1.6	1.2	1.4	4.5	3.0	2.7
1966	2.5	2.7	3.6	.	1.6	.7	6.1	5.9	.	.9	1.6	1.5	3.8	3.0	2.9
1967	2.7	3.7	4.1	.	2.8	2.1	6.7	5.4	.	1.1	2.1	2.3	3.8	3.6	3.6
1968	2.9	4.5	4.8	.	4.0	1.5	6.7	5.7	.	1.1	2.2	2.4	3.6	3.7	3.9
1969	2.8	3.7	4.7	.	2.8	.9	6.4	5.7	.	1.0	1.9	2.4	3.5	3.5	3.5
1970	2.4	3.0	5.7	1.3	1.9	.7	7.2	5.4	.	1.1	1.5	2.5	4.9	3.7	3.2
1971	2.1	2.9	6.2	1.7	2.3	.9	7.2	5.4	.	1.5	2.5	3.3	5.9	4.1	3.5
1972	1.9	3.4	6.2	1.7	2.5	1.1	8.1	6.4	.9	2.1	2.7	3.7	5.6	4.4	3.8
1973	1.6	3.6	5.7	1.1	2.3	1.3	7.2	6.4	.8	2.3	2.5	2.6	4.9	4.1	3.4
1974	1.5	4.0	5.5	2.5	1.7	2.6	7.9	5.4	.6	2.6	2.0	2.6	5.6	4.3	3.3
1975	2.1	6.7	6.9	6.0	2.2	4.7	12.2	5.9	1.1	4.0	1.6	3.9	8.5	6.1	4.5
1976	2.0	8.6	7.1	6.1	4.0	4.6	12.3	6.7	1.1	5.0	1.6	5.3	7.7	6.7	5.0
1977	1.8	9.8	8.1	7.7	6.1	4.5	11.9	7.2	.9	5.7	1.8	5.8	7.1	7.1	5.4
1978	2.1	10.5	8.4	7.4	7.5	4.3	10.7	7.2	1.1	7.5	2.2	5.8	6.0	7.0	5.6
1979	2.0	10.9	7.5	6.0	6.2	3.8	.	7.7	1.3	9.2	2.1	5.4	5.8	6.8	.
1980	.	.	.	.	.	.	.	.	.	.	.	.	.	.	.

NATO = mean of BLGM, CNDA, FRG, ITLY, UK, US
N + N = mean of AUST, FNLD, IRLD, SWDN

Table A3.38. Tourism Between East and West for Selected Pairs of Countries (number of persons on the basis of frontier checks; missing data interpolated where possible)

YEAR	FRNC TO USSR	FRG TO USSR	UK TO USSR	USA TO USSR	FRNC TO PLND	FRG TO PLND	UK TO PLND	USA TO PLND	CZCH TO FRG	PLND TO FRG	USSR TO FRG
1960	17750	30784	19261	17392	9426	.	7328	10796	7209	9392	5459
1961	23270	30700	26025	16156	9363	.	8343	8234	7466	9385	4998
1962	19720	29680	29377	17041	9271	.	8406	8910	7723	9378	4537
1963	21590	31900	24090	19535	11802	.	10016	9859	9956	7707	4435
1964	31700	29700	31402	22553	15071	.	13416	11190	15054	12487	7384
1965	36996	35696	26811	23041	34190	26635	30093	19547	21778	13206	7073
1966	40100	41680	33440	30355	39110	31806	28466	21791	28585	14363	9511
1967	49232	44113	32047	29322	37341	31588	29406	21418	36649	15770	10619
1968	34270	53110	28807	26566	33597	22880	27212	20622	62333	13130	10126
1969	38189	74171	33651	53583	34519	25662	27019	24230	88006	14747	13571
1970	39327	95277	43490	66365	38115	36284	29489	27926	42203	16464	13499
1971	42517	92700	44862	66515	38760	54527	29596	28849	32097	19395	13428
1972	45707	90124	46234	66665	46459	73825	31666	38373	30350	27049	17280
1973	57047	109054	65249	91254	55822	168286	43256	47134	29349	31192	20277
1974	57694	100416	65965	84637	56700	219700	38000	43000	29033	31274	21506
1975	73127	117239	58475	98774	73100	253500	45500	46300	28657	31356	22735
1976	71203	129260	57381	97844	80034	262672	43190	50838	28312	31439	23965
1977	81465	116247	42640	91840	87154	291286	48871	52143	31280	31386	24093
1978	.	.	.	.	.	.	.	.	.	.	.
1979	.	.	.	.	.	.	.	.	.	.	.
1980	.	.	.	.	.	.	.	.	.	.	.

Table A3.39. The Exchange of Visitors Between the GDR and the FRG

YEAR	GDR TO FRG *	GDR TO FRG **	FRG TO GDR *
1960	807	.	.
1961	675	.	.
1962	27	.	.
1963	50	.	.
1964	664	.	.
1965	1219	.	.
1966	1055	.	.
1967	1072	.	1424
1968	1047	.	1261
1969	1042	.	1107
1970	1048	.	1254
1971	1045	.	1267
1972	1080	11.421	1540
1973	1299	41.498	2279
1974	1354	38.298	1919
1975	1371	40.442	3124
1976	1371	42.751	3121
1977	1365	41.462	2988
1978	1433	48.659	3177
1979	1410	41.474	3617
1980	.	.	.

* TOTAL IN 1000 PERSONS

** ONLY WORKKING AGE PERSON IN 1000

Table A3.40. Migration from East to West in Europe and Associated Indicators (Persons and Numbers)

YEAR	PLND TO FRG	USSR TO FRG	CZCH TO FRG	RMNA TO FRG	TOTAL GDR TO FRG	GDR TO FRG WITH OFF. PERMIT	ISRAELI VISA GRANTED	SOVIET JEWISH EMIGRANTS	VISOVS GRANTED
1960	7739	3272	1394	2124	199188	.	.	.	.
1961	9303	345	1207	3303	207026	.	.	.	.
1962	9675	894	1228	1675	21356	5300	.	.	.
1963	9522	209	973	1321	42632	29665	.	.	.
1964	13611	234	2712	818	41876	30012	.	.	.
1965	14644	366	3210	2715	29552	17666	.	.	.
1966	17315	1245	5925	609	24131	15675	.	.	.
1967	10856	1092	11628	440	19573	13188	.	.	.
1968	8435	598	11854	614	16036	11134	379	229	6786
1969	9536	316	15602	2675	16975	11702	2902	2979	27301
1970	5624	342	4207	6519	17519	12472	1046	1027	4830
1971	25241	1145	2337	2848	17408	11565	14310	13022	40794
1972	13482	3420	894	4374	17164	11627	31478	31681	31652
1973	8903	4493	525	7577	15189	8667	34922	34733	58216
1974	7825	6541	378	8484	13252	7928	20181	20682	16816
1975	7040	5985	516	5077	16285	10274	13193	13221	34145
1976	29364	9704	849	3766	15168	10058	14138	14261	36104
1977	32857	9274	612	10989	12078	8041	17159	16736	43062
1978	36102	8455	904	12120	12117	8274	30594	28865	107212
1979	.	.	.	.	12515	9003	.	.	.
1980	.	.	.	.	.	.	.	.	.

A3.6 SOVEREIGNTY AND INDEPENDENCE: INTRA- AND INTERSYSTEMIC INTERACTIONS

Table A3.41. Cooperative Interactions Between "Camps" as Percentage of Total Cooperative Interactions (computed on the basis of COPDAB index values for cooperative interaction)

YEAR	NATO WITH NATO	NATO WITH WTO	NATO WITH N+N	WTO WITH NATO	WTO WITH WTO	WTO WITH N+N	N+N WITH NATO	N+N WITH WTO	N+N WITH N+N
1960	74.8	5.3	19.9	26.1	61.5	12.4	59.3	28.8	11.9
1961	85.3	9.4	5.2	9.5	79.1	11.4	57.7	35.5	6.8
1962	77.0	11.4	11.7	10.1	80.0	9.9	51.5	39.8	8.8
1963	70.3	24.0	5.7	31.0	56.5	12.5	56.8	38.3	4.9
1964	63.6	29.1	7.2	32.1	51.8	16.2	39.2	52.8	8.0
1965	67.5	25.0	7.5	17.6	76.5	5.8	35.7	59.3	5.0
1966	59.1	23.5	17.4	27.9	63.3	8.8	52.9	39.7	7.4
1967	70.1	19.7	10.2	24.3	68.8	6.9	40.8	49.7	9.6
1968	67.2	10.2	22.6	19.1	70.3	10.7	55.2	29.4	15.5
1969	77.6	8.0	14.4	11.2	83.2	5.6	58.6	31.1	10.3
1970	73.3	15.8	11.0	20.2	77.8	2.0	84.8	14.3	.9
1971	71.4	14.3	14.3	9.9	89.8	.3	58.6	36.7	4.8
1972	78.7	7.8	13.5	28.3	61.7	10.0	77.2	22.0	.8
1973	71.5	9.4	19.1	44.2	45.2	10.6	75.0	10.7	14.3
1974	72.7	15.9	11.4	15.8	76.3	7.9	55.3	41.2	3.5
1975	71.4	16.0	12.6	20.7	73.0	6.4	54.2	32.5	13.3
1976	87.5	2.1	10.4	23.5	59.8	16.7	53.7	20.3	26.0
1977	72.8	10.5	16.8	14.3	83.0	2.6	61.3	28.6	10.1
1978	90.8	3.4	5.8	32.8	64.6	2.6	75.4	14.7	10.0
MEAN	73.8	13.7	12.5	22.0	69.6	8.38	58.1	32.9	9.04

Table A3.42. Cooperative Interactions with NATO Countries, in Percent of Total Cooperative Interactions with CSCE Countries (computed on the basis of COPDAB index values for cooperative interaction)

YEAR	AUST	BLGM	BLGR	CNDA	CYPR	CZCH	DNMK	FNLD	FRNC	FRG	GDR	GRCE	HNGR	IRLD	ITLY
1960	71.5	82.1	25.4	69.8	93.1	2.5	70.7	15.2	90.9	79.1	36.0	70.5	23.2	79.6	70.7
1961	74.8	87.9	8.0	87.3	47.8	4.4	75.2	27.9	90.6	93.7	13.1	73.7	6.9	.	87.3
1962	53.2	85.1	8.3	62.3	44.6	1.1	56.7	30.9	87.5	94.6	16.9	50.3	23.7	100	92.0
1963	71.9	91.5	39.2	51.3	73.5	10.8	29.6	37.9	88.1	84.6	22.4	46.1	33.4	100	87.6
1964	15.1	89.5	36.2	72.3	39.7	32.9	23.0	0.0	68.5	84.6	15.7	44.7	32.4	0.0	76.6
1965	13.7	89.3	34.2	100	49.1	13.4	30.6	12.2	69.4	84.1	15.0	50.0	3.5	76.7	86.2
1966	24.2	90.8	50.8	51.3	64.8	27.4	10.1	36.9	61.9	80.9	12.1	33.2	10.8	100	86.1
1967	33.8	96.3	33.3	83.0	77.8	31.8	31.4	13.4	82.3	83.1	11.4	57.7	10.6	.	88.0
1968	9.3	93.8	23.0	68.8	100	3.0	15.2	73.7	86.9	88.2	8.2	52.4	13.3	0.0	95.3
1969	43.9	93.1	14.6	64.5	72.2	4.5	39.3	28.6	86.8	80.2	4.6	95.9	18.1	.	91.2
1970	100	95.8	28.7	65.1	100	5.0	35.9	58.5	84.2	80.0	33.3	29.2	0.0	.	93.9
1971	63.9	97.1	9.7	67.4	50.0	1.0	56.9	30.5	88.0	87.7	12.5	0.0	4.1	100	94.4
1972	93.7	96.5	22.2	69.6	87.7	0.0	95.8	62.0	80.0	77.5	27.0	28.3	33.0	100	86.9
1973	69.1	73.6	26.4	69.1	80.9	41.0	73.6	66.2	70.6	67.8	50.1	58.8	48.6	86.2	75.9
1974	73.2	88.0	10.0	80.8	49.5	11.5	67.7	18.5	78.2	45.1	21.6	82.3	1.8	100	75.2
1975	54.8	76.5	20.8	67.1	54.1	15.2	87.8	43.5	67.8	65.0	24.9	68.3	17.8	100	71.1
1976	81.8	90.8	22.2	72.3	35.6	8.8	90.2	55.9	85.8	77.7	48.3	93.0	0.0	100	90.3
1977	81.6	72.8	.9	77.0	66.7	13.8	75.7	0.0	70.3	68.4	24.7	80.7	5.9	56.5	65.1
1978	62.8	92.1	24.0	95.0	91.0	28.0	90.5	74.1	92.3	88.1	45.9	96.0	37.2	89.1	91.8
MEAN	57.5	88.6	23.0	72.3	67.3	13.5	55.6	36.1	80.5	79.5	23.3	58.5	17.1	79.2	84.5

YEAR	LXBG	MLTA	NTHL	NRWY	PLND	PRTG	RMNA	SPAN	SWDN	SWTZ	TRKY	USSR	UK	USA	YGSL
1960	79.6	.	83.6	66.7	31.7	66.7	38.1	79.4	76.4	76.2	66.5	0.0	67.3	69.6	23.3
1961	100	.	96.4	58.5	10.4	100	14.1	82.1	80.8	88.0	87.5	32.7	85.6	72.6	26.9
1962	96.5	100	85.3	59.3	9.0	100	1.4	78.2	77.4	81.4	71.3	40.6	82.7	70.1	21.4
1963	100	100	96.5	27.4	32.5	100	47.7	100	51.0	100	64.2	55.8	76.6	68.0	6.3
1964	89.7	.	77.1	33.8	36.7	100	38.4	100	79.6	82.0	52.9	51.7	51.0	67.1	18.8
1965	100	.	100	0.0	24.3	.	15.6	86.0	35.3	.	34.3	18.5	66.0	59.5	16.6
1966	100	.	92.9	0.0	26.8	100	39.3	89.8	73.4	93.0	35.5	74.7	66.4	55.2	24.9
1967	97.4	100	93.3	38.5	28.1	100	30.7	58.1	45.9	55.4	24.5	31.7	66.3	64.6	18.2
1968	96.2	0.0	95.6	0.0	14.4	52.0	52.6	49.6	60.1	68.2	49.5	38.3	64.2	56.5	19.8
1969	97.9	66.7	91.9	43.4	10.1	100	15.6	59.5	84.5	85.4	71.4	27.3	75.9	64.5	36.9
1970	96.1	100	92.3	80.6	29.5	100	24.7	100	77.5	96.2	52.4	44.0	73.5	56.9	76.6
1971	98.5	100	97.2	23.2	4.3	100	28.1	100	87.2	66.7	70.0	75.9	76.6	55.8	53.1
1972	88.0	100	87.6	81.8	50.9	100	36.5	0.0	89.4	95.6	69.6	57.6	83.3	54.3	34.8
1973	72.4	40.0	72.9	73.1	47.6	60.4	51.3	75.5	72.6	88.8	78.2	60.5	71.9	44.9	72.7
1974	87.5	.	87.1	59.6	24.4	41.8	25.7	72.7	48.9	100	56.0	36.7	64.2	33.8	41.6
1975	76.5	50.0	75.8	69.0	22.0	54.7	23.3	52.6	55.7	75.4	62.5	40.8	68.8	59.3	41.9
1976	89.1	0.0	90.5	91.7	30.4	0.0	31.4	86.0	41.1	66.7	91.0	58.0	87.9	50.5	41.3
1977	74.1	66.7	69.3	91.1	23.3	76.3	17.4	60.0	75.9	77.2	62.8	46.9	65.8	57.8	66.6
1978	91.0	.	91.7	90.9	16.8	97.8	44.7	77.2	81.9	78.5	80.8	60.5	88.9	75.2	64.0
MEAN	91.1	68.6	88.3	52.0	24.9	80.5	30.3	74.0	68.1	81.9	62.2	44.8	72.8	59.8	37.1

Table A3.43. Cooperative Interactions with WTO Countries, in Percent of Total Cooperative Interactions with CSCE Countries (computed on the basis of COPDAB index values for cooperative interaction)

YEAR	AUST	BLGM	BLGR	CNDA	CYPR	CZCH	DNMK	FNLD	FRNC	FRG	GDR	GRCE	HNGR	IRLD	ITLY
1960	4.6	.6	66.9	7.1	6.9	80.6	0.0	84.8	9.1	5.1	48.6	6.6	68.2	0.0	14.1
1961	13.0	6.5	72.1	10.6	52.2	90.7	12.2	67.3	7.2	4.2	84.1	17.5	87.8	.	8.5
1962	37.2	3.4	70.4	12.5	55.4	92.6	7.9	60.9	2.2	.8	82.4	45.5	64.5	0.0	4.0
1963	25.9	6.5	48.3	46.2	26.5	72.4	62.0	42.9	9.7	11.7	77.6	42.1	55.8	0.0	11.2
1964	78.5	10.5	51.1	27.7	60.3	44.3	60.9	85.9	26.0	15.0	69.0	38.8	46.1	0.0	20.7
1965	86.3	10.7	55.2	0.0	50.9	84.7	69.4	75.7	30.6	14.9	85.0	10.7	89.8	23.3	13.8
1966	62.6	6.9	41.5	44.9	35.2	61.3	42.0	45.2	35.8	16.3	77.3	38.0	79.8	0.0	11.2
1967	56.7	3.7	60.3	17.0	22.2	62.8	52.1	69.1	16.4	13.4	83.0	0.0	81.9	.	12.0
1968	69.0	2.3	64.8	13.3	0.0	88.9	0.0	3.6	11.0	6.5	91.8	0.0	72.7	0.0	0.0
1969	56.1	1.9	80.2	11.2	0.0	93.1	2.5	57.5	8.6	11.9	95.4	4.1	67.1	.	3.3
1970	0.0	.3	71.3	14.3	0.0	95.0	27.3	41.5	11.5	14.7	64.7	37.5	100	.	1.5
1971	36.1	1.3	90.3	25.4	50.0	99.0	2.8	53.7	10.7	11.1	87.5	81.8	94.4	0.0	2.5
1972	6.3	.9	47.6	30.4	12.3	94.9	.5	38.0	9.2	11.2	55.9	0.0	64.9	0.0	1.7
1973	16.4	6.0	66.3	20.2	0.0	44.9	3.5	21.4	10.3	14.1	36.6	20.0	43.0	.9	3.4
1974	19.0	0.0	82.3	12.9	50.5	77.6	12.2	77.3	16.0	41.9	70.4	0.0	85.9	0.0	16.6
1975	28.9	10.4	73.6	20.6	24.3	77.6	4.3	42.0	23.6	23.2	69.3	17.5	75.1	0.0	16.0
1976	9.1	0.0	66.7	6.9	18.3	78.9	0.0	18.4	4.6	9.5	25.2	0.0	77.0	0.0	0.0
1977	9.4	10.8	99.1	13.7	0.0	76.9	1.8	100	17.2	21.2	71.3	0.0	94.1	4.8	15.8
1978	20.8	1.6	72.7	1.7	9.0	70.1	1.9	9.6	3.6	6.2	49.1	.4	62.8	4.9	1.5
MEAN	33.5	4.43	67.4	17.7	25.0	78.2	19.1	52.3	13.9	13.3	69.7	19.0	74.3	2.25	8.31

YEAR	LXBG	MLTA	NTHL	NRWY	PLND	PRTG	RMNA	SPAN	SWDN	SWTZ	TRKY	USSR	UK	USA	YGSL
1960	0.0	.	1.9	3.0	51.5	0.0	53.2	0.0	0.0	0.0	7.2	100	8.6	20.5	76.7
1961	0.0	.	0.0	23.1	68.6	0.0	71.5	0.0	9.6	0.0	12.5	29.4	10.9	19.0	70.9
1962	3.5	0.0	4.2	13.6	80.8	0.0	89.2	0.0	6.4	0.0	28.7	59.4	10.5	19.4	78.6
1963	0.0	0.0	2.6	56.2	62.2	0.0	22.9	0.0	45.0	0.0	26.7	32.6	13.6	22.3	89.6
1964	10.3	.	22.9	46.5	50.9	0.0	49.2	0.0	10.2	3.3	28.9	34.7	41.3	22.6	78.7
1965	0.0	.	0.0	63.6	69.2	.	75.1	14.0	54.4	.	62.7	52.1	24.0	28.6	83.4
1966	0.0	.	3.0	9.4	69.4	0.0	50.7	10.2	18.9	7.0	53.0	13.7	21.4	37.2	69.4
1967	2.6	0.0	6.1	34.6	62.2	0.0	62.5	33.5	40.5	36.5	47.6	64.1	30.5	30.7	72.9
1968	1.4	50.0	.6	35.6	78.4	0.0	24.9	0.0	25.7	0.0	30.0	46.7	22.2	33.6	77.8
1969	.4	0.0	2.1	4.7	89.5	0.0	73.6	24.4	2.1	8.2	28.6	71.2	16.7	26.5	63.1
1970	0.0	0.0	2.3	12.9	66.8	0.0	68.8	0.0	16.8	3.8	47.6	50.8	19.6	33.2	23.4
1971	1.5	0.0	1.2	20.7	95.7	0.0	71.9	0.0	0.0	33.3	0.0	15.4	12.3	39.3	46.9
1972	0.0	0.0	0.0	18.2	43.5	0.0	63.5	100	5.5	4.4	18.8	30.9	2.5	41.3	65.2
1973	6.2	20.0	6.0	6.0	39.9	19.1	40.7	6.2	11.0	0.0	11.1	21.1	6.1	47.8	15.1
1974	0.0	.	0.0	40.4	69.9	52.3	71.3	27.3	42.0	0.0	36.0	63.3	15.2	54.9	58.4
1975	9.3	23.3	11.8	16.7	72.5	30.5	69.8	25.5	30.4	24.6	19.1	49.9	19.9	33.7	44.9
1976	0.0	0.0	0.0	0.0	61.9	100	48.8	14.0	23.8	7.4	1.6	17.9	2.5	30.0	44.8
1977	2.7	0.0	12.4	0.0	74.1	17.1	82.6	34.3	15.5	13.2	10.9	41.7	19.0	32.3	33.4
1978	1.7	.	1.9	1.5	79.0	0.0	54.0	0.0	3.2	9.4	14.3	24.2	4.8	18.6	36.0
MEAN	2.09	7.78	4.16	21.4	67.7	12.2	60.2	15.2	19.0	8.39	25.5	43.1	15.9	31.1	59.4

Table A3.44. Cooperative Interactions with Neutral and Nonaligned Countries, in Percent of Total Cooperative Interactions with CSCE Countries (computed on the basis of COPDAB index values for cooperative interaction)

YEAR	AUST	BLGM	BLGR	CNDA	CYPR	CZCH	DNMK	FNLD	FRNC	FRG	GDR	GRCE	HNGR	IRLD	ITLY
1960	23.8	17.3	7.7	23.1	0.0	16.9	29.3	0.0	0.0	15.8	15.4	22.9	8.6	20.4	15.2
1961	12.2	5.6	19.8	2.1	0.0	4.9	12.5	4.8	2.3	2.1	2.8	8.8	5.3	.	4.2
1962	9.6	11.6	21.3	25.2	0.0	6.3	35.4	8.3	10.4	4.6	.7	4.1	11.8	0.0	4.1
1963	2.2	2.0	12.5	2.5	0.0	16.8	8.5	19.2	2.2	3.7	0.0	11.8	10.8	0.0	1.2
1964	6.4	0.0	12.7	0.0	0.0	22.9	16.1	14.1	5.5	.5	15.4	16.5	21.4	100	2.7
1965	0.0	0.0	10.6	0.0	0.0	2.0	0.0	12.2	0.0	1.0	0.0	39.3	6.7	0.0	0.0
1966	13.2	2.3	7.7	3.8	0.0	11.2	47.9	17.9	2.3	2.8	10.6	28.8	9.4	0.0	2.7
1967	9.5	0.0	6.3	0.0	0.0	5.4	16.5	17.5	1.4	3.4	5.6	42.3	7.4	.	0.0
1968	21.8	4.0	12.2	17.9	0.0	8.1	84.8	22.7	2.1	5.3	0.0	47.6	14.1	100	4.7
1969	0.0	4.9	5.2	24.3	27.8	2.4	58.2	13.9	4.6	7.9	0.0	0.0	14.8	.	5.5
1970	0.0	3.9	0.0	20.6	0.0	0.0	36.8	0.0	4.4	5.3	1.9	33.3	0.0	.	4.6
1971	0.0	1.6	0.0	7.2	0.0	0.0	40.4	15.8	1.3	1.2	0.0	18.2	1.5	0.0	3.1
1972	0.0	2.5	30.2	0.0	0.0	5.1	3.6	0.0	10.8	11.3	17.1	71.7	2.1	0.0	11.4
1973	14.5	20.4	7.3	10.7	19.1	14.1	22.9	12.4	19.1	18.2	13.3	21.2	8.4	12.9	20.7
1974	7.8	12.0	7.6	6.3	0.0	10.9	20.1	4.2	5.8	12.9	8.1	17.7	12.3	0.0	8.2
1975	16.3	13.1	5.6	12.3	21.6	7.2	7.9	14.6	8.6	11.7	5.8	14.2	7.1	0.0	12.9
1976	9.1	9.2	11.1	20.8	46.1	12.3	9.8	25.7	9.6	12.8	26.5	7.0	23.0	0.0	9.7
1977	9.0	16.5	0.0	9.3	33.3	9.3	22.5	0.0	12.5	10.3	4.0	19.3	0.0	38.8	19.1
1978	16.5	6.2	3.3	3.3	0.0	1.9	7.6	16.3	4.1	5.7	5.0	3.6	0.0	6.0	6.6
MEAN	9.04	7.01	9.54	9.97	7.78	8.30	25.3	11.6	5.63	7.19	6.95	22.5	8.66	18.5	7.18

YEAR	LXBG	MLTA	NTHL	NRWY	PLND	PRTG	RMNA	SPAN	SWDN	SWTZ	TRKY	USSR	UK	USA	YGSL
1960	20.4	.	14.6	30.2	16.8	33.3	8.7	20.6	23.6	23.8	26.3	0.0	24.1	9.9	0.0
1961	0.0	.	3.6	18.3	21.0	0.0	14.4	17.9	9.6	12.0	0.0	37.9	3.5	8.4	2.3
1962	0.0	0.0	10.5	27.1	10.2	0.0	9.4	21.8	16.2	18.6	0.0	0.0	6.8	10.4	0.0
1963	0.0	0.0	.9	16.4	5.4	0.0	29.5	0.0	4.0	0.0	9.1	11.6	9.8	9.8	4.2
1964	0.0	.	0.0	19.7	12.4	0.0	12.4	0.0	10.2	14.8	18.1	13.6	7.8	10.3	2.6
1965	0.0	.	0.0	36.4	6.5	.	9.3	0.0	10.3	.	3.0	29.5	10.0	11.9	0.0
1966	0.0	.	4.1	90.6	3.8	0.0	10.0	0.0	7.7	0.0	11.5	11.6	12.2	7.6	5.7
1967	0.0	0.0	.5	26.9	9.6	0.0	6.8	8.4	13.5	8.1	27.9	4.1	3.2	4.7	8.9
1968	2.4	50.0	3.9	64.4	7.2	48.0	22.5	50.4	14.2	31.8	20.6	15.0	13.6	9.9	2.4
1969	1.8	33.3	6.0	51.9	.4	0.0	10.8	16.1	13.5	6.4	0.0	1.5	7.4	9.1	0.0
1970	3.9	0.0	5.4	6.5	3.7	0.0	6.5	0.0	5.6	0.0	0.0	5.2	6.9	9.9	0.0
1971	0.0	0.0	1.5	56.0	0.0	0.0	0.0	0.0	12.8	0.0	30.0	8.7	11.1	4.9	0.0
1972	12.0	0.0	12.4	0.0	5.6	0.0	0.0	0.0	5.1	0.0	11.6	11.5	14.2	4.3	0.0
1973	21.3	40.0	21.0	20.9	12.4	20.6	8.1	18.3	16.3	11.2	10.7	18.4	22.0	7.3	12.2
1974	12.5	.	12.9	0.0	5.7	5.9	2.9	0.0	9.2	0.0	8.0	0.0	20.6	11.3	0.0
1975	14.2	26.7	12.4	14.3	5.5	14.8	6.9	21.9	13.9	0.0	18.4	9.3	11.3	6.9	13.2
1976	10.9	100	9.5	8.3	7.7	0.0	19.8	0.0	35.1	26.0	7.5	24.1	9.6	19.5	13.9
1977	23.2	33.3	18.3	8.9	2.5	6.6	0.0	5.7	8.6	9.6	26.4	11.4	15.3	9.9	0.0
1978	7.3	.	6.4	7.6	4.2	2.2	1.3	22.8	15.0	12.1	4.9	15.4	6.3	6.2	0.0
MEAN	6.84	23.6	7.58	26.6	7.40	7.30	9.43	10.7	12.9	9.69	12.3	12.0	11.4	9.07	3.44

Appendix A4

Index Values Computed for the Master Dimensions of East–West Relations

Table A4.1. Standardized Index Values for the Master Dimensions of East–West Relations (scale: 0–100; increasing figures indicate improvements)

YEAR	PEACE AND CONFLICT	ECONOMIC COOPERATION	DISARMAMENT SECURITY	HUMAN RIGHTS SANCTIONS	HUMAN RIGHTS UNEMPLOYMENT	SOVEREIGNTY INDEPENDENCE	INDEX 1	INDEX 2
1960	40	23	100	45	66	48	51	55
1961	41	0	83	22	70	0	29	39
1962	0	23	63	0	84	2	18	34
1963	72	14	57	66	88	62	54	58
1964	71	14	62	77	96	65	58	62
1965	57	18	65	79	100	23	49	53
1966	48	27	44	43	100	53	43	55
1967	60	36	16	63	86	43	44	48
1968	64	36	3	33	82	28	33	43
1969	72	73	3	41	88	5	39	48
1970	54	73	14	71	83	31	48	51
1971	78	73	18	90	73	1	52	49
1972	82	68	13	79	66	54	59	57
1973	100	82	16	82	74	100	76	74
1974	90	100	13	65	69	18	57	58
1975	89	91	12	100	24	32	65	50
1976	73	91	15	96	11	40	63	46
1977	64	82	8	61	0	14	46	34
1978	45	82	4	.	2	67	.	40
1979	.	95	0	.	6	.	.	.
1980	.	.	.	.	.	.	.	.

Index 1 = mean of peace/conflict, economic cooperation, disarmament/security, sanctions (in WTO countries), sovereignty/independence

Index 2 = mean of peace + conflict, economic cooperation, disarmament/security, unemployment (in NATO countries), sovereignty/independence

Appendix A5

The Future of East-West Relations: A Computer Simulation of Five Scenarios

Pierre Allan and Urs Luterbacher

INTRODUCTION

How shall East-West relations evolve in the future? What effects could a new cold war or a prolonged "détente" period have on the arms race? On the other hand, what impact would a unilateral US decision to reduce its military forces really have on the Soviet Union? Is a "negotiating-from-strength" policy effective? These are some of the questions addressed in this appendix. They are analyzed by use of a dynamical mathematical model describing the evolution of the complex interrelationships within and among major powers with their main European allies. This model is first described briefly in verbal form, with the main hypotheses used to generate the alternative scenarios stemming from the preceding questions.

A word of caution is in order before proceeding. We do not purport to predict what will happen, even though our simulations extend to the year 2000; the objective is rather to analyze "what would happen if...." The international system is so complex that it is probably impossible to make exact predictions about specific politico-economic and strategic constellations in time. But that should not mean that nothing can be done. On the contrary, we have to try to understand the system by describing it through its main dimensions and gain insight by manipulating this construct. Our mathematical model thus purports to capture the main socioeconomic, political, and strategic trends and analyze the deviations that might result if certain plausible events happen. Mathematics being a very precise language, it forces the analyst to be quite explicit in his formulations and as a result allows him to gain greater insight in the subject matter. Thus in this chapter we analyze certain crucial links in the "détente" system, mainly those between political maneuvering on the international scene—détente, cold war—and decision-making in the military sphere. The internal political and socioeconomic impacts of different policies are also assessed.

The data basis used for calibrating the model, especially the construction of indices used for the measurement of armament levels, cannot be discussed here. Further details are to be found in the current working papers of the Center for Empirical Research at the Institute for Advanced Studies, Geneva.

SIMULATION OF POLITICAL, ECONOMIC, AND STRATEGIC INTERACTIONS (SIMPEST MODEL)

The SIMPEST model used for this analysis will be described through its political and military sectors that are linked to the rest of the model, that is, to the internal political, demographic, and economic sectors.

The model can be described verbally without going into its mathematical details. It concentrates on US and USSR decision-making. China (People's Republic) is included because of its military importance, as numerous Soviet divisions are stationed at its borders. These three states are described in a detailed way in the model because of their importance for the international strategic situation. The European allies of the two major powers are only included in their military dimensions. National decision-making thus determines military strength, which then defines the military balance when the different nations are compared. The dimensions security and disarmament then result from the state and the evolution of this balance.

Decision-making in military affairs is determined by two classes of factors: external and internal. The external ones compare the military strength of (the) adversary (ies) and the prevailing diplomatic climate. The external threat is thus given in terms of words and deeds in the political or diplomatic sphere and in terms of the threat means of the adversary, that is, its military power. The internal factors are essentially of an economic and political nature.

Traditionally, external factors were considered predominant. Military policy was envisioned as originating from dynamic action-reaction processes between states increasing (usually) their military strength in response to an adversary's moves. More recently a number of authors have put internal factors in the foreground. In such a conception, armament races, for example, do not result only from a reaction to the adversary but can be fueled by bureaucratic and organizational inertia, which lead to regular increases in the military budget. Technological progress or the "military-industrial complex"—as President Eisenhower called it—are similar internal factors also leading to rather continuous increases in the military sector. These different elements are translated into political pressures for arms investments and are present even when no external threat exists. The preceding factors are essentially demand factors tending to increase the size of the military. But internal factors also include supply factors, mainly the economic situation and the internal political climate. The state of the economy determines to a large extent the resources that can be channeled to the defense sector. Elites or public opinion also influence the allocation process between the military and civilian sectors.

These two sets of factors—external and internal—are both included in this analysis. Both can be considered as indispensable: without any resources or political support, defense investments are not possible; without an external threat, neither. Indeed, in the latter case, the army would have no military role any more but rather an internal police role.

The evolution of the armament levels proceeds according to the logic of actions stipulating respective reactions by the opponent. The diplomatic climate is formed by present and past conflictual moves—remaining in memory and forming current perceptions—of the East with respect to the West and vice versa. Given the crucial weight of the US and the USSR, it is their conflict interactions that are determining the decision-making.

The internal factors manifest themselves differently according to the political systems considered. For the United States, the proportion of resources devoted to each of the four military sectors depends mainly on the popularity of the government—which in turn is a function of several factors: economic conditions (unemployment, inflation, evolution in real consumption)—and the perceived security. Thus the military sector is closely linked to the political and economic ones setting the possibilities and constraints of defense spending. These processes are characterized by much inertia.

The internal allocation process of the Soviet Union is determined mainly by military and more civilian-oriented elites favoring somewhat different shares of total production for military expenditures, investments, and private consumption. Detailed information on the structure of the model is presented in Allan and Luterbacher 1981.

SIMULATIONS AND SCENARIOS

This section describes the results of our analyses. (1) First, a base run of the model is presented for the period 1965 to year 2000. It describes the major political, economic, and strategic trends among the major powers with their European allies. Then five basic scenarios are described and the derived simulations are analyzed. (2) The first one examines the impact of a prolonged détente period upon the international system. (3) The second looks at the possible effects of a new cold war of various intensities. (4) This is followed by the study of a hypothetical unilateral reduction in armaments by the United States, and (5) another scenario analyzes unilateral Soviet disarmament. (6) Finally, the policy of "negotiating from strength," which came to the foreground during the Reagan administration, is examined for its effects on the Soviet Union.

The Base Run 1965–2000

The base run extends over a very long period of thirty-five years up to the end of the twentieth century. The length of the simulation was chosen so as to picture clearly the effects of current trends on the long-term future.

The model's parameters were estimated on the basis of 1955–1975 data (when available, otherwise a shorter time period had to be taken). We collected data up to 1979, and the SIMPEST model tracks these fairly well, in a completely endogenous way, thus bolstering our confidence in it.

The base run assumes a diplomatic or international political climate that is that of the period 1965–1978 characterized mainly by "détente." It shows certain developments already visible in the late seventies, notably the persistence of the arms race between the major powers. The American politico-economic system is characterized by an expanding economy and a fairly high but deteriorating popularity of the government. On the other hand, the Soviet Union experiences slower growth due to demographic and economic problems and to increased internal dissatisfaction. But these factors only significantly lower Soviet defense efforts in the nineties. The military balance between the two major powers with their allies shows little changes up to the year 2000: parity in the strategic sector, superiority for the USSR on the ground, superiority for the US on sea and in the air.

The US economy witnesses a development of its foreign sector, with imports and exports more than doubling as a proportion of the gross national product. The share of total investments also increases somewhat, to the detriment of private consumption and governmental expenditures. Unemployment is fairly low in the eighties and nineties while inflationary pressures subsist and even intensify. The popularity of the government is boosted during the early eighties but constantly decreases later on.

Even though the share of total US governmental expenditures decreases slowly, military expenditures rise from 1978 on, after the decrease following the Vietnam war. The model thus pictures the rises that came about the last two years of the Carter administration as well as the increase in military expenditures of the Reagan administration. These increases remain in the 1980s and 1990s but tamper off very slowly. Historically the model pictures the large growth years of the Vietnam war 1965–1967—with, for instance, yearly increases of the army index of 13 to 16 percent—as well as the disengagement, with decreases of 2 to 8 percent per year till 1973 to 1975 depending on the military sector (see Graph A5.1).

The Soviet Union also reinforces considerably its military power in the eighties and nineties, according to our base run (see Graph A5.2). But the rates of increase in the different sectors are somewhat smaller than the American rates for the eighties and nineties. In the strategic sector, the US keeps its edge (see Graph A5.1), due principally to the qualitative improvements of American forces that are given much weight by the indicator used, taking into account both precision and yield of warheads. The strategic balance significantly improves for the USSR during the sixties up to the early eighties, but it still appears to be to the advantage of the United States. This stems mainly from the large increase in nuclear warheads with a better precision on the Western side. For instance, at the beginning of the seventies, American warheads numbered approximately 4,000, increasing to 9,000 at the beginning of the eighties, whereas the Soviet evolution was from 1,600 to 4,000. The precision of American missiles also seems higher than that of Soviet ones, but the USSR has, of course, a larger number of nuclear vectors. Since our lethality index gives much weight to effectiveness factors, the United States comes ahead. But, given the destructive potential of the Soviet nuclear forces and the large number of imponderable factors in a nuclear conflict, we feel that our indicators portray in fact a picture of a relative parity between the two superpowers—even though the American edge increases from 1984 on, due to increases of the order of 8 to 11 percent from 1983 to 1989 that are only partly matched by the Soviet Union.

In the conventional domain, Soviet superiority in ground forces remains even though the United States and its allies increase their efforts so that the Soviet four-to-one advantage decreases to a three-to-one ratio in the year 2000. This result depends, of course, on the indicator chosen that gives much weight to tanks. US and Western superiority in the air, on the other hand, remains up to the twenty-first century. The Soviet navy build-up allows it in the eighties almost to attain parity, but due to the US reaction, the American lead increases during the 1990s (see Graphs A5.1 and A5.2). In summary:

1. Base The East–West arms race accelerates during the 1980s. The pace is slower in the nineties.

Graph A5.1. Strategic, Army, and Naval Forces Index for the US

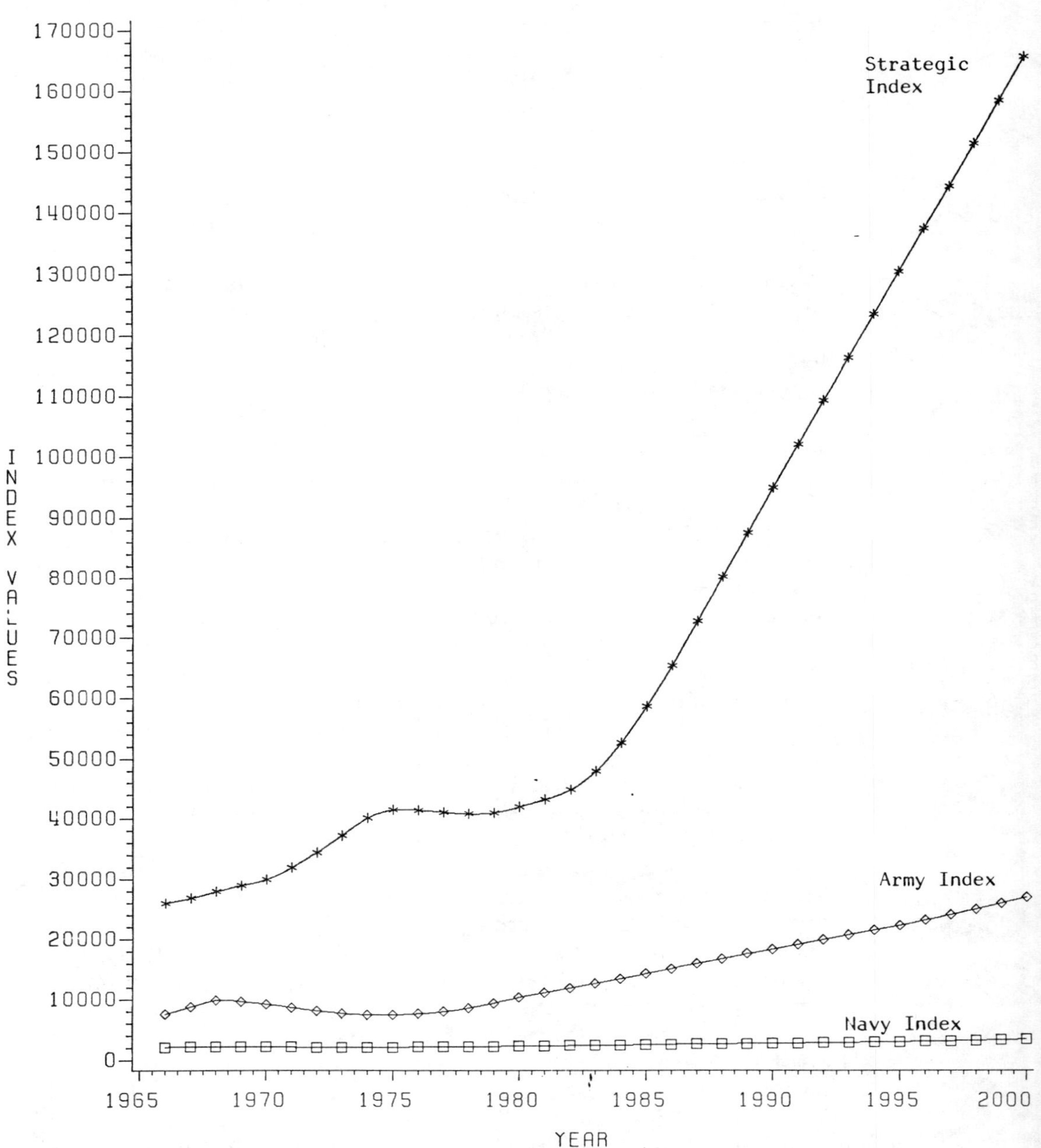

Graph A5.2. Soviet Strategic, Army, and Naval Forces Index

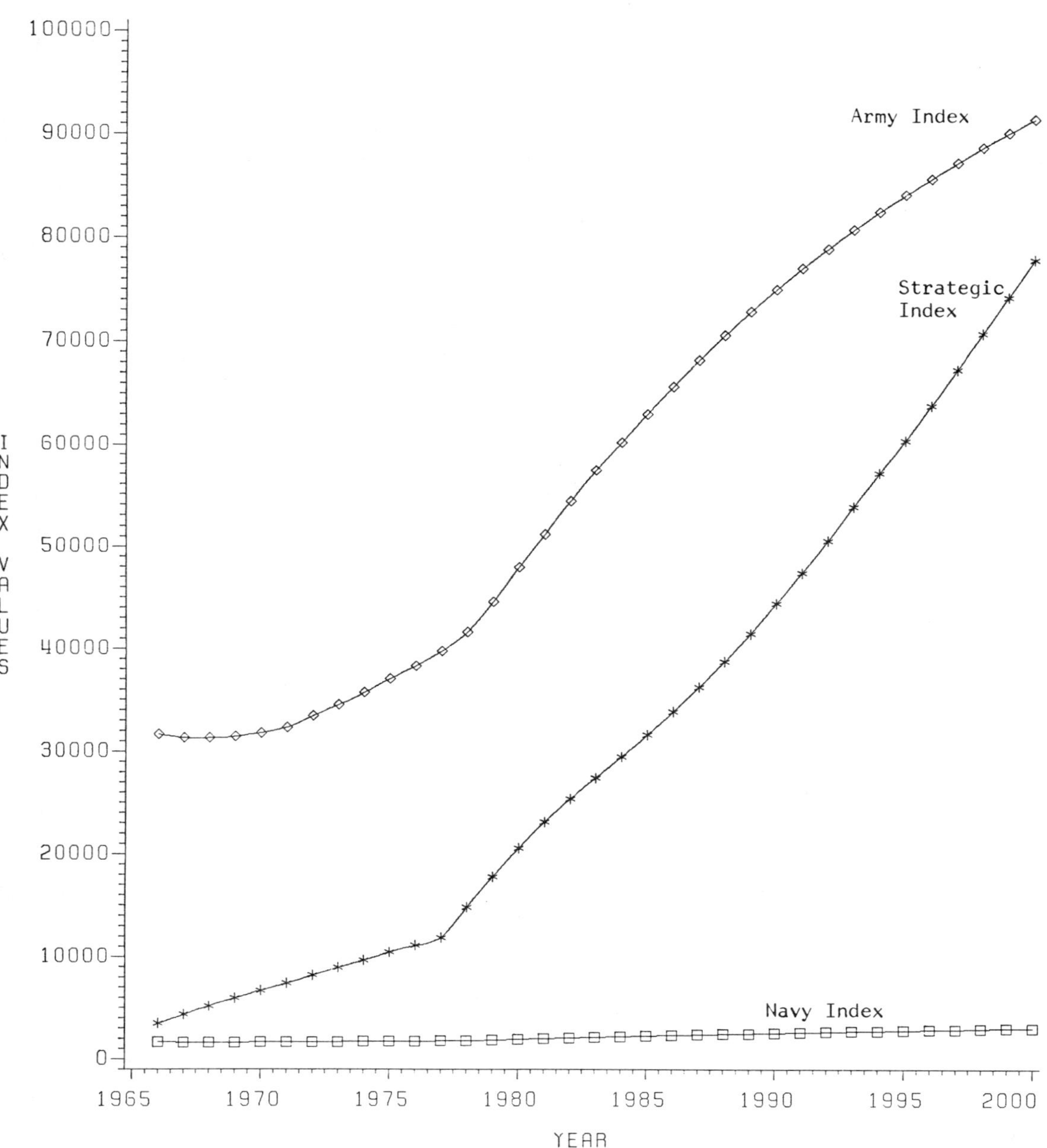

2. Base The USSR has practically caught up with the United States in the strategic sector in the sixties and seventies, but in terms of a lethality index, the US stays ahead, marginally increasing its lead from 1983 on. American and Soviet forces seem overall to be at parity for the rest of the century.
3. Base In the conventional domain, the superiority of the Soviet army will remain even though decreasing somewhat due to Western armament efforts. The Soviet navy comes close to parity with the United States in the eighties but remains No. 2. The West retains its air superiority.

The arms race thus accelerates during the eighties and declerates later on. Let us examine the reasons for these changes. In the United States, the Soviet build-up of the seventies becomes a major concern in the late seventies, early eighties. Improved economic conditions and especially a relatively high popularity provide for the means to increase military expenditures. In addition, the diplomatic climate worsens, thus also prompting a faster pace of the arms race. Whereas the American defense effort seems to stimulate the economy to some extent, the situation is opposite in the USSR, where defense spending takes a larger share of total resources. This increases, of course, the military elites' satisfaction index in the model, but these increases are fairly small and do not compensate for the large decreases of the civilian elites' satisfaction index as well as the satisfaction of the population at large.

Civilian elites were most satisfied during the period 1965 to 1975 after which the situation started deteriorating. The main reasons for all this lie in a poorer performance of the economy. Even though investments grow faster than output, production increases at rates of approximately 3 percent in the eighties and 2–3 percent during the nineties. This is in terms of overall production because the agricultural output increases even less, barely more than the population (see Graph A5.4). The economy slows down because of a slower demographic growth and also due to lower productivity stemming from increased dissatisfaction of the masses—which in the model has a direct effect on labor productivity. Thus we have a positive feedback from dissatisfaction to lesser productivity to smaller production leading to a smaller consumption, which again increases the masses' dissatisfaction. But this dissatisfaction seems to be a bearable one for the elites. Increased imports of Western machinery do not help much even though the productivity of this equipment is larger than for the Soviet one. Like the US, the USSR becomes more dependent on foreign trade whose share more than doubles between the year 1965 and the year 2000.

The economic slowdown in the Soviet Union increases the constraints put upon the military sector, but significantly only in the nineties where our different military indicators show annual

Graph A5.3. Satisfaction of the Military Elite, the Civilian Elites, and the Population in the Soviet Union

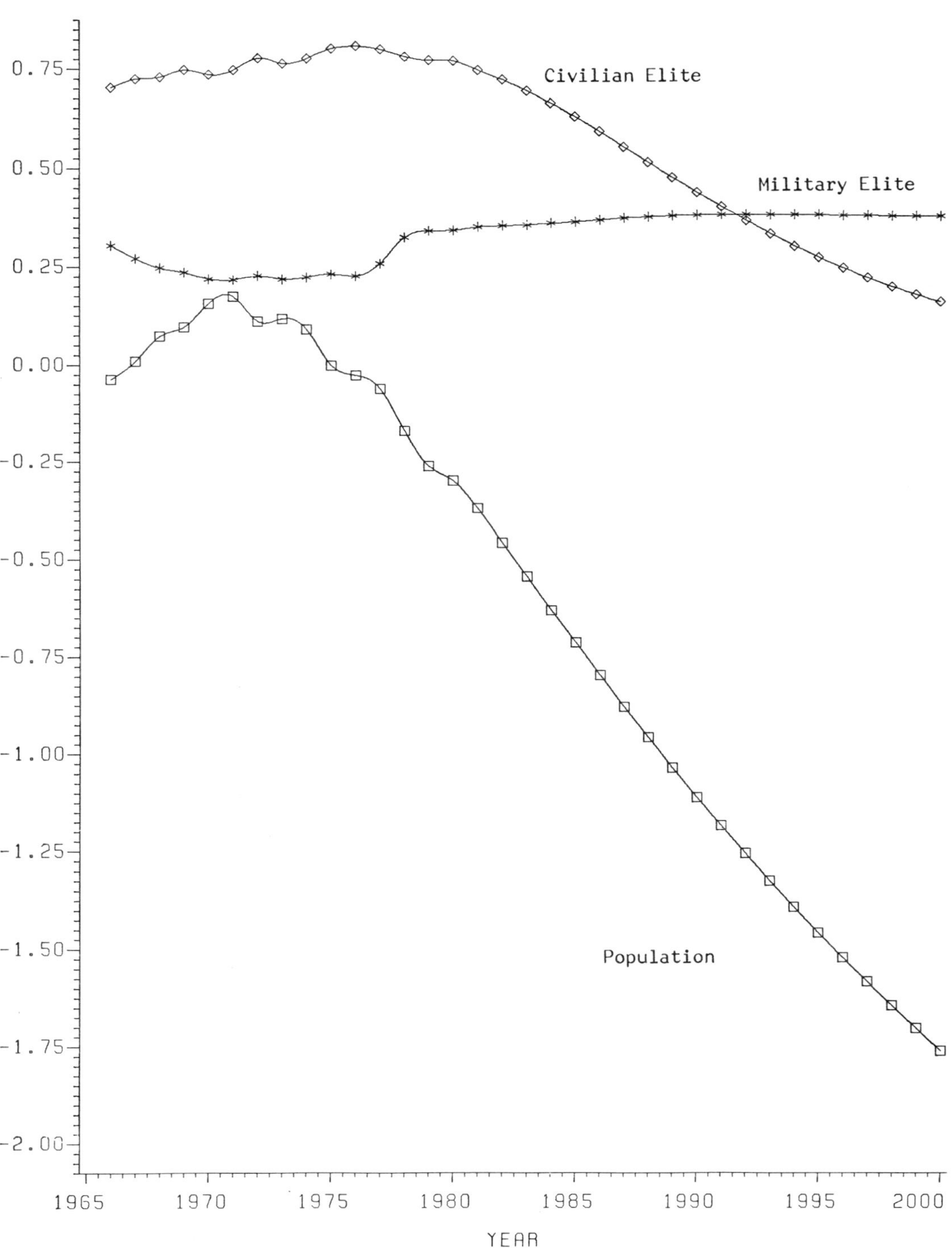

Graph A5.4. Soviet Agricultural and Nonagricultural Production (in billions of rubles at 1970 prices)

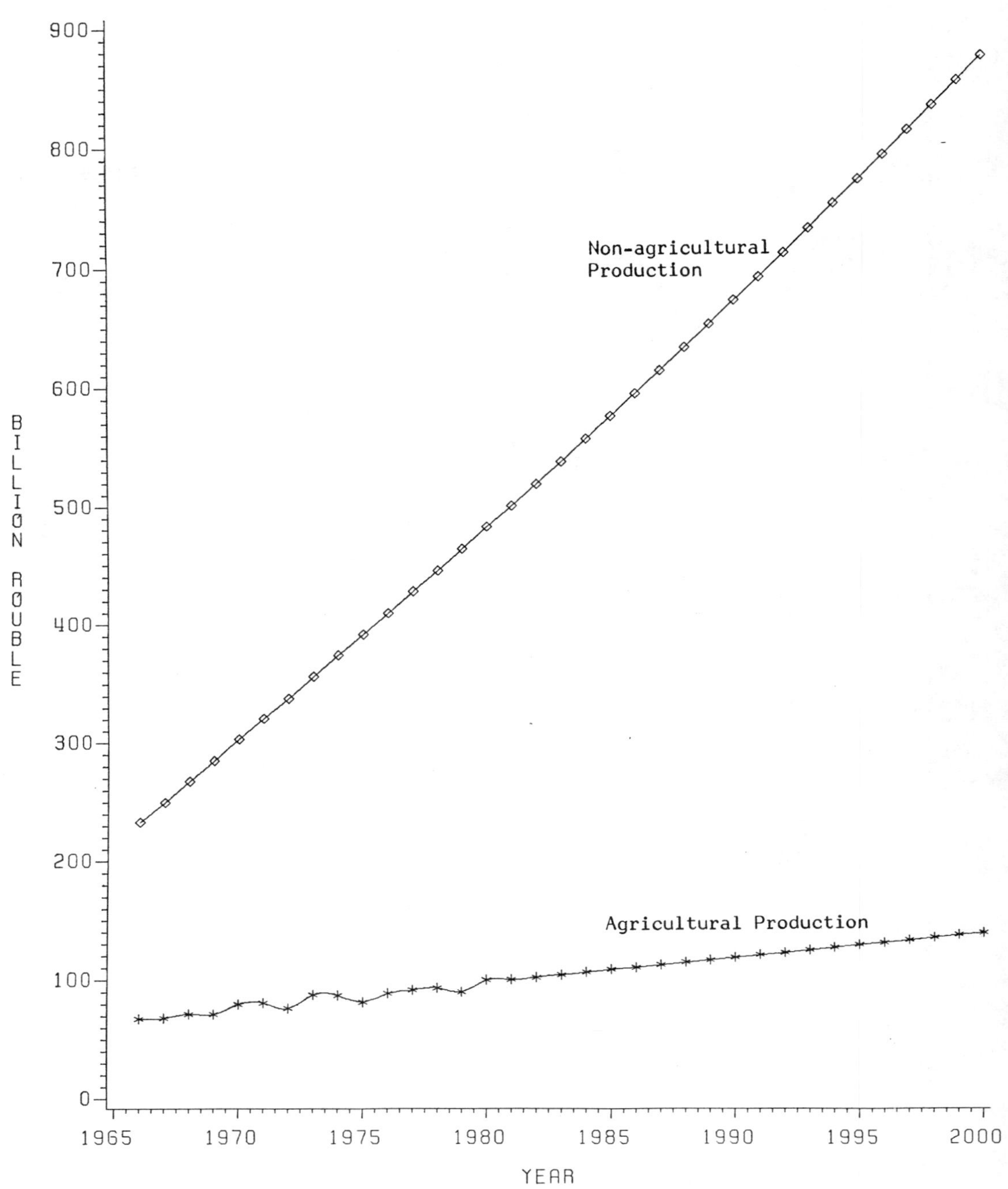

growth of 1.5–2 percent in the conventional sectors and 4.5–6 percent in the strategic one. Thus

4. Base It appears that the Soviet military effort is approaching internal politico-economic limits. The situation is far from explosive but is slowly worsening in the 1980s and becoming more critical only in the nineties. No such limits seem present for the US whose economy is helped on the contrary by higher demand originating in the military sector.

The overall military ratio between East and West was calculated on the basis of different indicators. The concept of security was constructed taking this military ratio and adding to it three times the evolution or change of this ratio, to take into account the expectations and perceptions of future developments. To obtain a unique "security" index, the ratios in the strategic, army, air forces, and navy sectors where aggregated. Different weights were tried for this aggregation procedure, generally giving the same picture of the resulting security evaluations. We made the plausible assumption that the strategic forces were given a weight of about one-third in the overall comparison, but even this hypothesis did not appear crucial for the general assessment, which shows a remarkably stable picture whose changes are quite small (see Graph A5.5):

5. Base Western "security" in terms of composed military capabilities and its evolution is rather favorable in the 1960s and diminishes in the 1970s, with the lowest point in 1978 before increasing mainly during the eighties and getting better during the 1990s. Eastern "security" is lower than Western essentially because of the military weight of China and Soviet threat perceptions amplifying its importance. It remains approximately at the same level but for a small increase at the end of the seventies and diminishes somewhat during the 1980s and 1990s.

All these projections are to some extent at variance with the view presented in 1980–1981 in the West, notably in the press. They result mainly from two factors: (1) the inclusion of qualitative elements in the appreciation of the military balance, and (2) the inclusion of China as a potential threat for the security of the Soviet Union. The consideration of China in the East-West picture was prompted by our empirical studies of the question (see Allan 1979 and Luterbacher et al. 1979). The Soviet Union appears to have a superiority in almost all fields only if purely quantitative indicators (such as the number of missiles or tanks) are considered, and that only with respect to the United States considered in isolation.

Graph A5.5. Eastern and Western Security Index Values

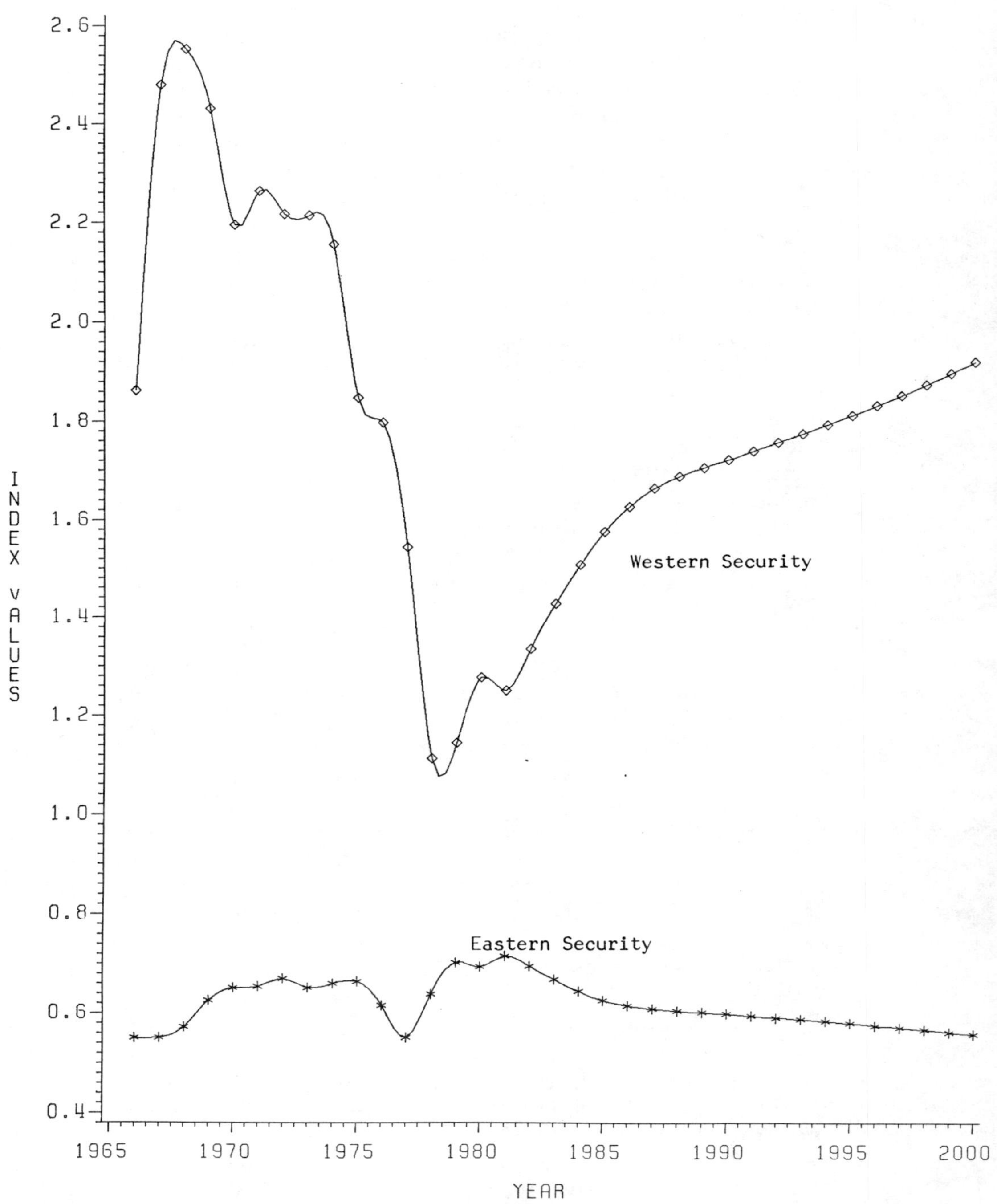

The base run was examined in detail since all the simulations that now follow take deviations from it. Let us now turn to these, starting with the effects of a prolonged détente period up to the year 2000.

A New Détente Period 1981-2000

The base run made the assumption that the diplomatic climate in the years ahead will remain at the average level it had in the 1965-1978 period. Thus it already makes the hypothesis of a fairly cooperative relationship among major powers, with few crises and a low conflict level. The following scenario is based on the hypothesis that the diplomatic climate becomes even better. Two simulations are performed. Both imply a counterfactual bettering of the diplomatic climate starting with the Reagan administration on 20 January 1981. The first one postulates a diplomatic climate analogous to the best periods of US-USSR détente in the seventies. The second one goes even beyond to see what difference that would make.

What are the results? The overall picture is one of a less intense but still strong arms race because both parties keep on threatening each other with their huge military forces. The overall balance changes little, with the Western security increasing marginally while the Eastern one decreases somewhat. As for the internal politico-economic repercussions, they are quite interesting. The US economy experiences less growth, due to lower military expenditures of up to 8 percent annum in the year 2000—with respect to the base simulation—in the first run of the model and 16 percent in the second simulation. GNP is 4 and 8 percent lower. Thus there is less private consumption (4 and 7 percent). Investments decrease even more, by 6 and 11 percent respectively. The other major variables, including the popularity of the president and government, are hardly affected.

In the Soviet Union, the lower share of military expenditures in GNP (only 0.9 percent and 1.6 percent less of GNP) is almost integrally transferred to private consumption. The rest of the economy is unaffected. The great impacts appear on the satisfaction of the military elites, as expected. Interestingly, the civilian elites' and the population-at-large's satisfaction indices are only marginally affected.

Let us now look in more detail at the changes in the arms race. Graphs A5.6-A5.8 portray the strategic, army, and navy indices of the US and the USSR, with the "highest" curve always picturing the evolution in the base run to be compared to the two simulations (S1 and S2) with a new détente period starting in 1981 and remaining up to the year 2000.

Overall, the Soviet Union moderates its arms build-up to a larger extent than the United States. The Soviet decreases—rather, lesser increases—at the end of the simulation are approximately one-

Graph A5.6. Strategic Indices for the Détente Scenario

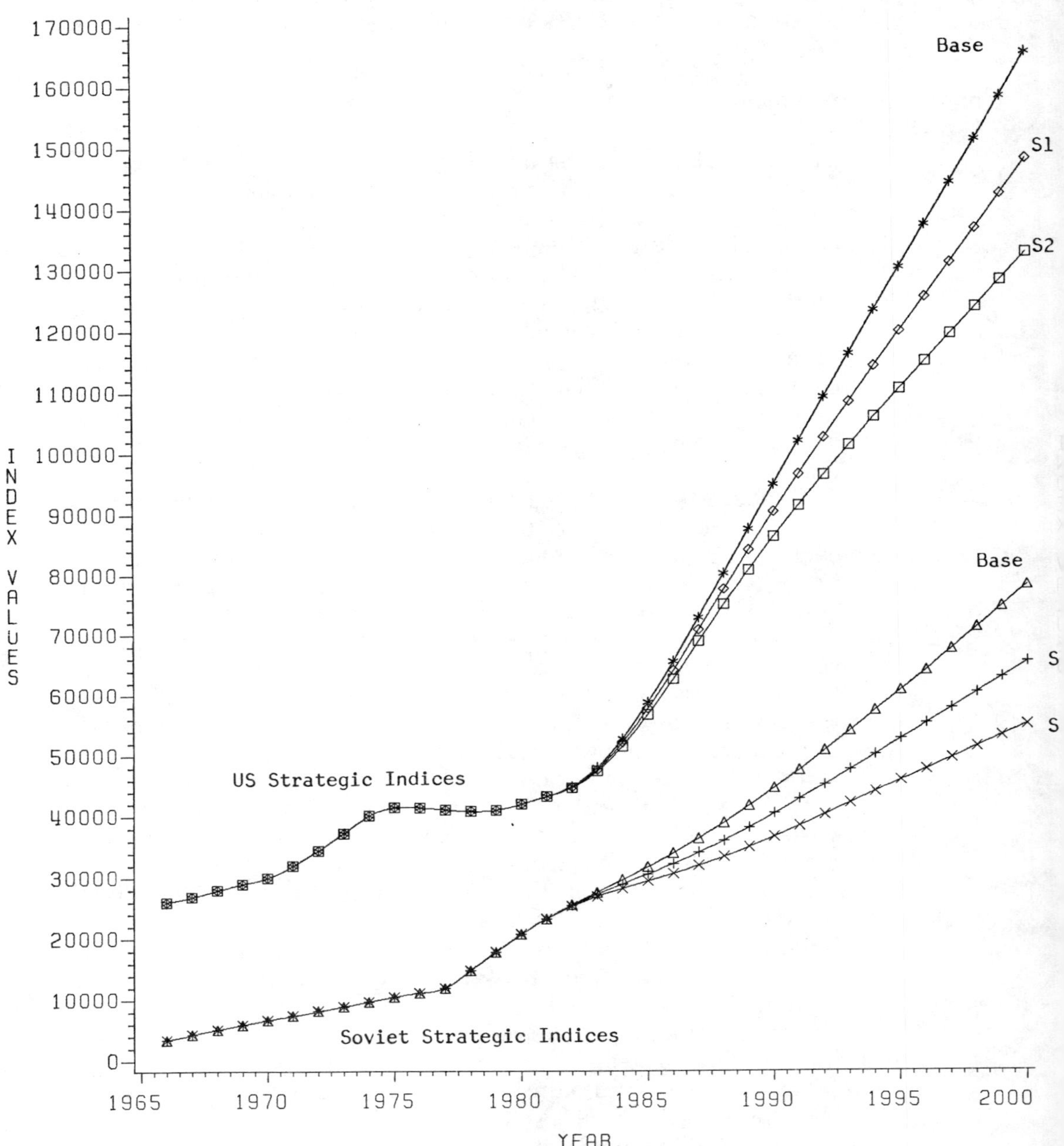

Graph A5.7. Army Indices for the Détente Scenario

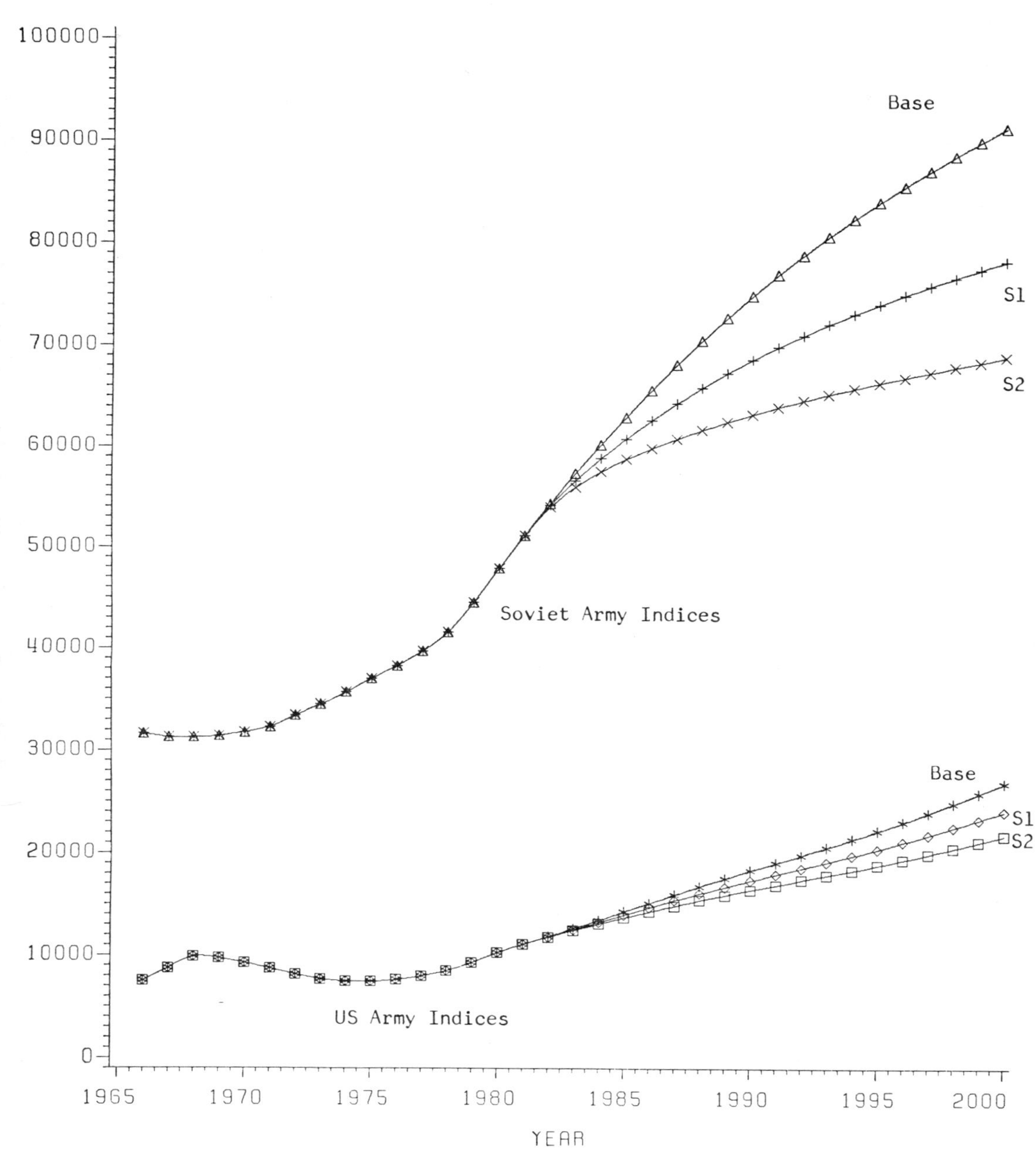

Graph A5.8. Navy Indices for the Détente Scenario

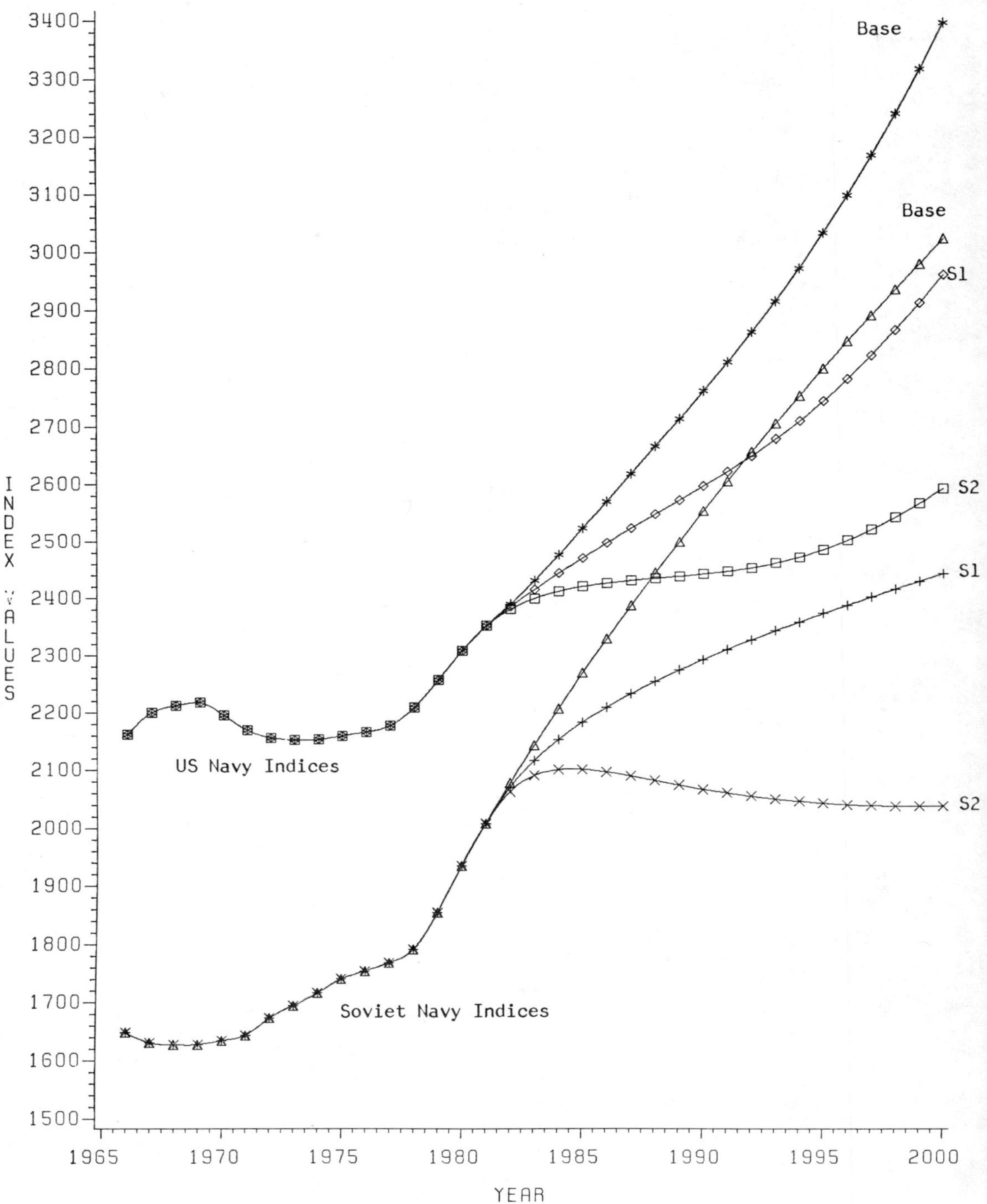

halfth larger, in percentage terms, than the American ones. In the strategic sector, the US index is 11 percent, smaller in the year 2000 for the first simulation, and 20 percent) for the second one; for the USSR, the respective percentages are 16 and 30 percent. For the army indices, US decreases are similar, whereas USSR decreases are smaller than those it showed for the strategic sector. Détente seems to have the largest impact on the two navies, which increase only moderately, at a pace of one-half percent per annum for the US in the second simulation, which sees a USSR navy in the year 2000 barely larger than the one in 1981 and smaller than the one in 1985: In summary:

6. Détente Détente (in terms of a bettering of the diplomatic or international political climate) brings about a lessening of the pace of the arms race, but it does not stop it since both parties still feel threatened by their respective military forces. Smaller military expenditures induce a slower economic growth in the US whereas the decreases in the USSR military budget are almost integrally transferred to consumers but dissatisfying military elites without satisfying anybody else to a large extent.

A New Cold War 1981–2000

Currently a more realistic scenario is that of a new cold war, similar in tension to the 1950s and early 1960s. The computer run shows opposite results to the preceding one about détente. In the first simulation, we postulated a revival of the Cold War between the major powers, starting with the Reagan administration, and with an intensity somewhat less conflictual than the historical Cold War. The second simulation is based on conditions similar to the Cold War of the 1950s and early 1960s.

The Soviet Union exhibits again its greater sensitivity to changes in the diplomatic climate. Its reactions in the military sector are fairly important. The strategic index is greater by 20 percent in the first simulation and by 44 percent in the second one (at the end of the period) with respect to the standard run of the model; the US increase is only 12 percent and approximately one-quarter. The changes in the army indices are approximately the same. It is with the navy indices that the largest changes appear. The Soviet navy is 27 percent greater in the first simulation and two-thirds larger in the second; the US increases are only 14 and 32 percent. This allows the Soviet navy to be almost at parity by the year 2000 in the base run, be the first in the world by the year 1989 in the first simulation (see Graph A5.9)

Graph A5.9. Navy Indices for the Cold War Scenario

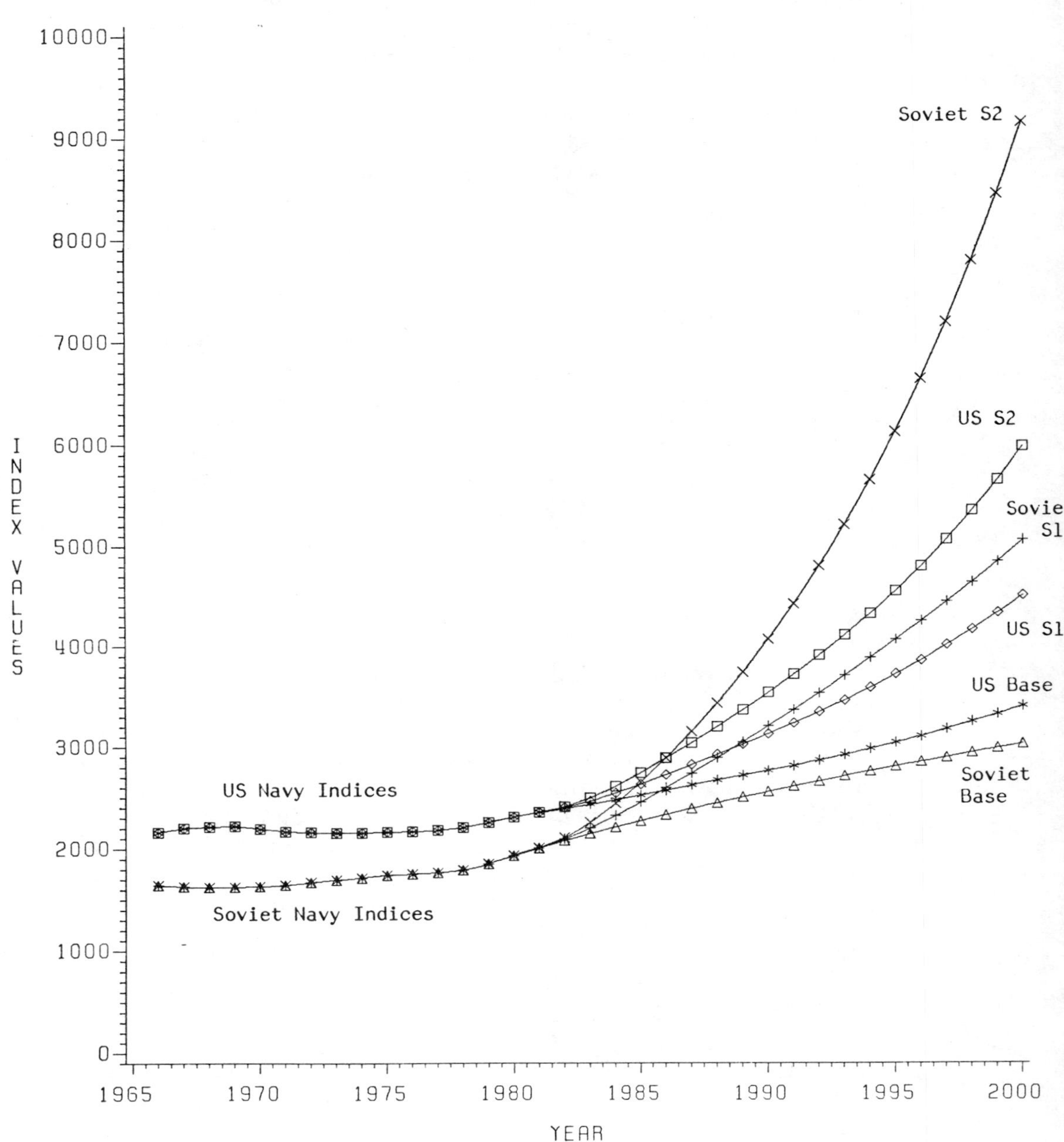

The results of this simulation run must be interpreted with caution, however, because the build-up in Soviet military capabilities is associated by a significant decrease in consumption per capita. The consequences of decreasing popularity of the regime are very likely security problems, which are not included in the model. In the United States, the increase in military expenditures stimulates the economy adding ½ percent to the yearly growth rate, with a similar inflation—as US investments increase more than private consumption. In summary:

7. Cold War A revival of the Cold War (in terms of a worsening of the diplomatic or international political climate) increases the arms race and especially the Soviet reaction. But in the long run, it seems unlikely that the USSR can react to such an extent while the US can muster to the challenge.

The Results of Unilateral American Disarmament

So far the consequences of changes in the international political situation were examined. The simulations that follow present scenarios where changes occur in the overall strategic picture. Among the cures proposed to end the ongoing arms race, unilateral disarmament is perhaps the most interesting since representatives of the Peace Research community and the new peace movements in Western Europe have argued in favor of unilateral disarmament. It is also part of the program of the British Labor party. The following computer run starts with the counterfactual assumption of a unilateral American disarmament initiative starting in 1981.

The main consequences are twofold. First, the Soviet Union does not disarm but keeps on arming, albeit at somewhat lower rates. Second, after a few years, the US politico-economic system shows signs of trouble as popularity of the president decreases and economic growth slows down appreciably.

Graph A5.10 portrays the changes in the military balance of the strategic sector. The Soviet index only increases by a yearly 2 percent with respect to a 6 ½ percent in the base run of the model (having a value of less than half in the year 2000) and is larger by 46 percent than in 1981. US disarmament is thus not followed by the USSR, which uses this opportunity to go ahead. With respect to the army, the simulation even shows a higher Soviet index *with* American disarmament than without it (see Graph A5.11). The difference is one of a third of a percent more yearly growth resulting in an index 5 percent higher at the end of the simulation period. The same phenomenon happens for the air-force index. The Soviet navy index shows very little changes even though Soviet expansion on sea is slightly slower.

The US internal consequences are pictured in Graphs A5.12 and A5.13. They are not very important during the first two or three

Graph A5.10. Strategic Indices for the US Unilateral Disarmament Scenario

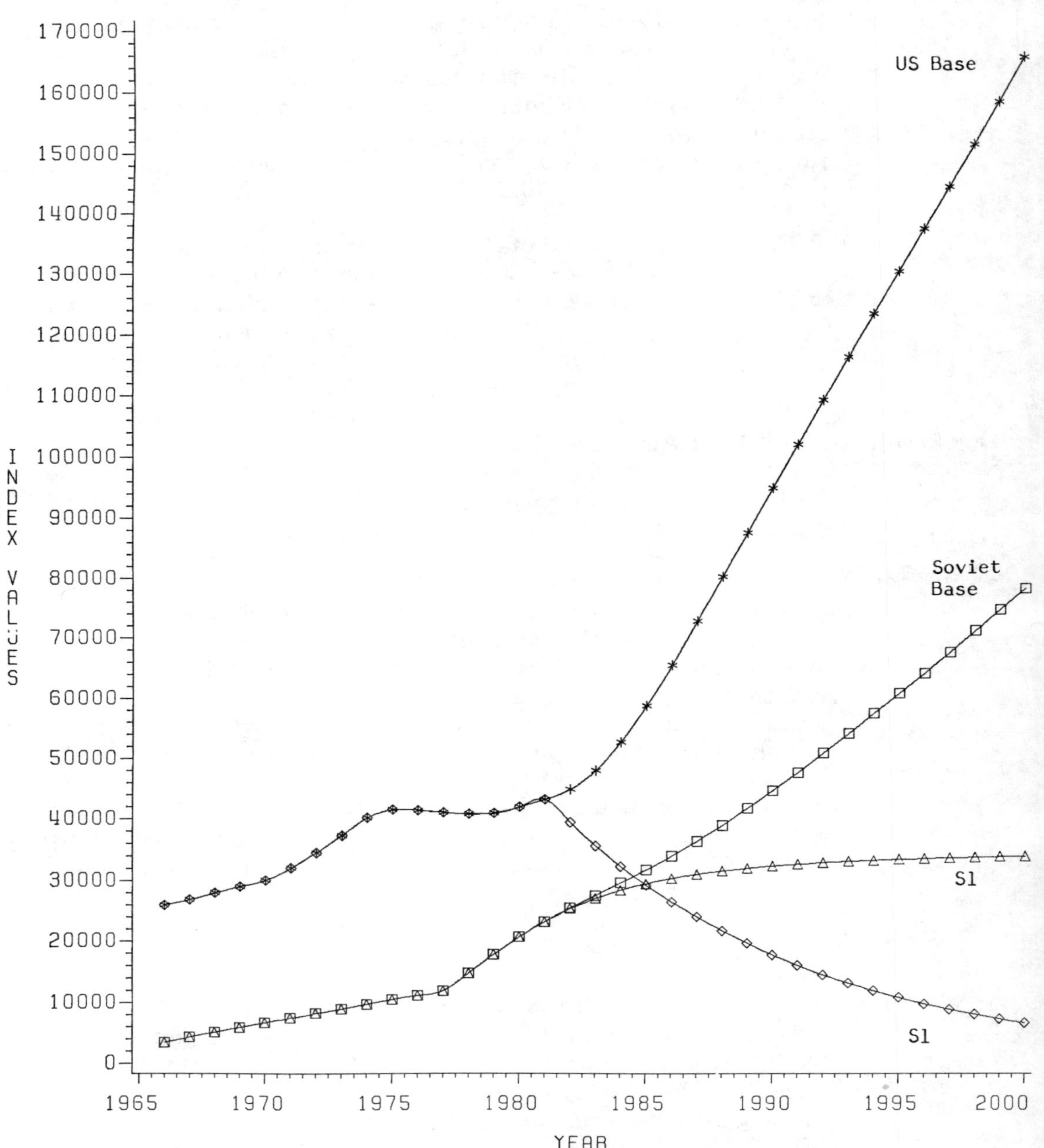

Graph A5.11. Army Indices for the US Unilateral Disarmament Scenario

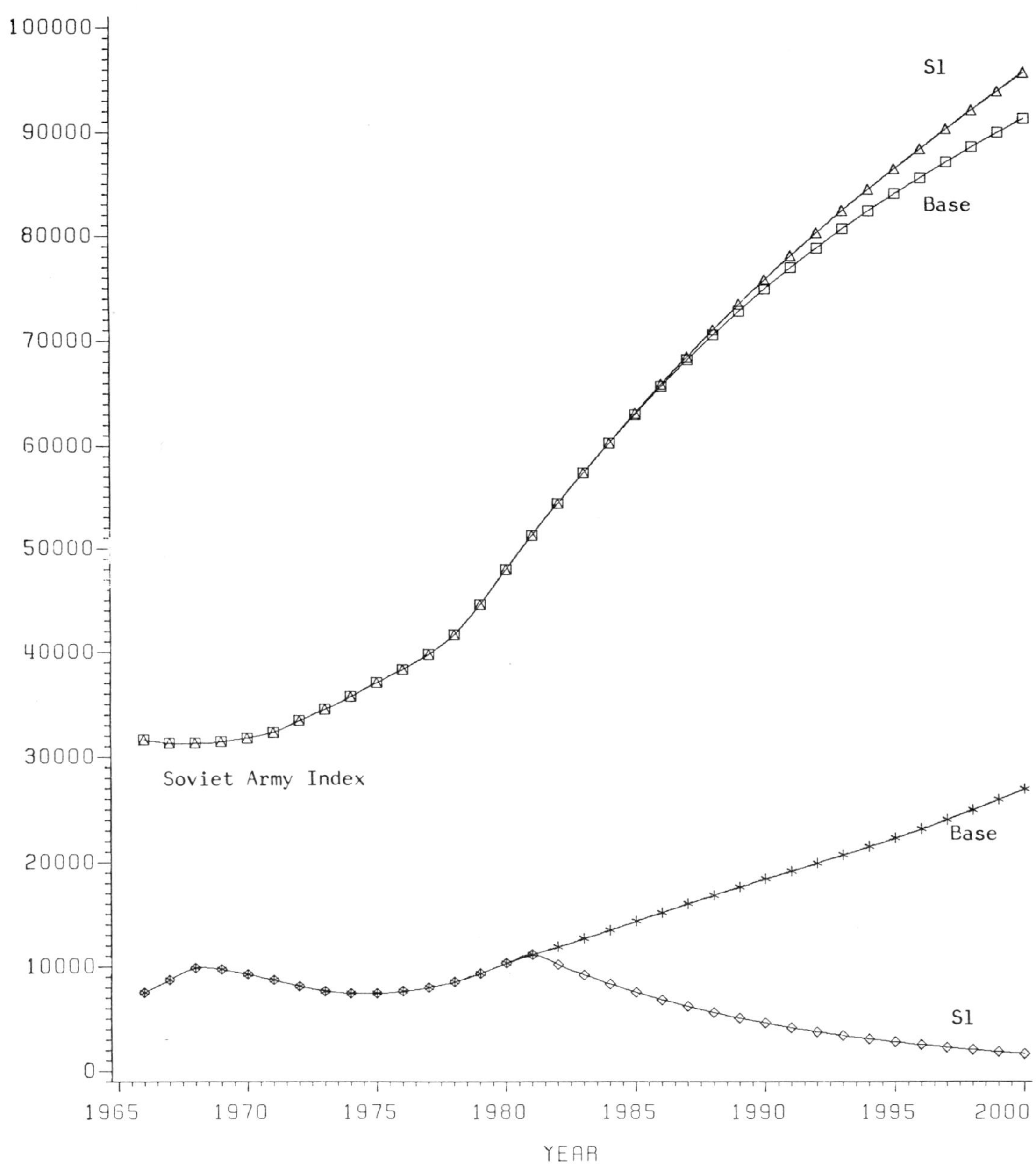

Graph A5.12. US GNP Figures for the Scenario of a Unilateral American Disarmament (in billions of US dollars, 1965 prices)

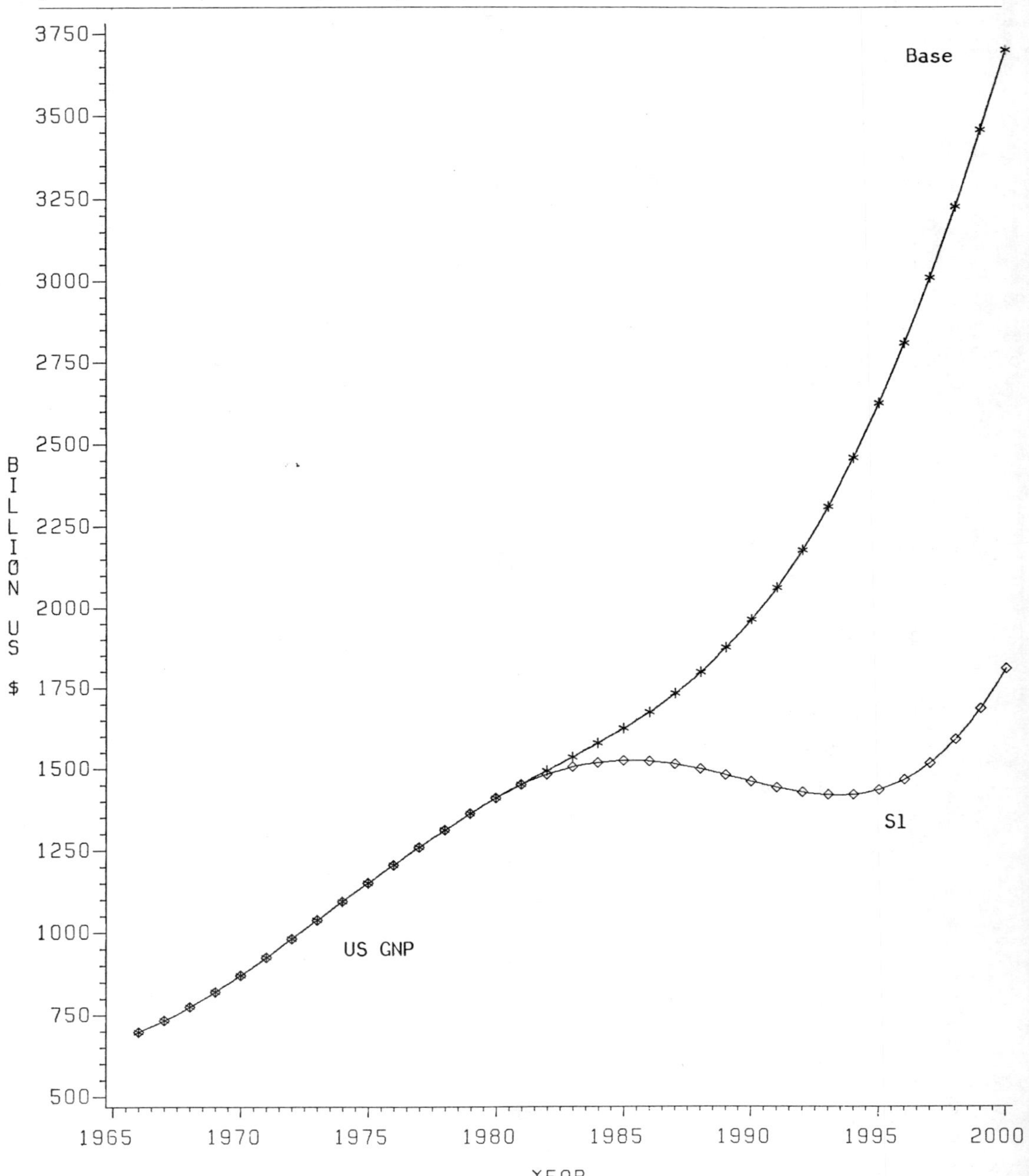

Graph A5.13. US Military Expenditure for the Scenario of a Unilateral American Disarmament (in millions of US dollars, 1965 prices)

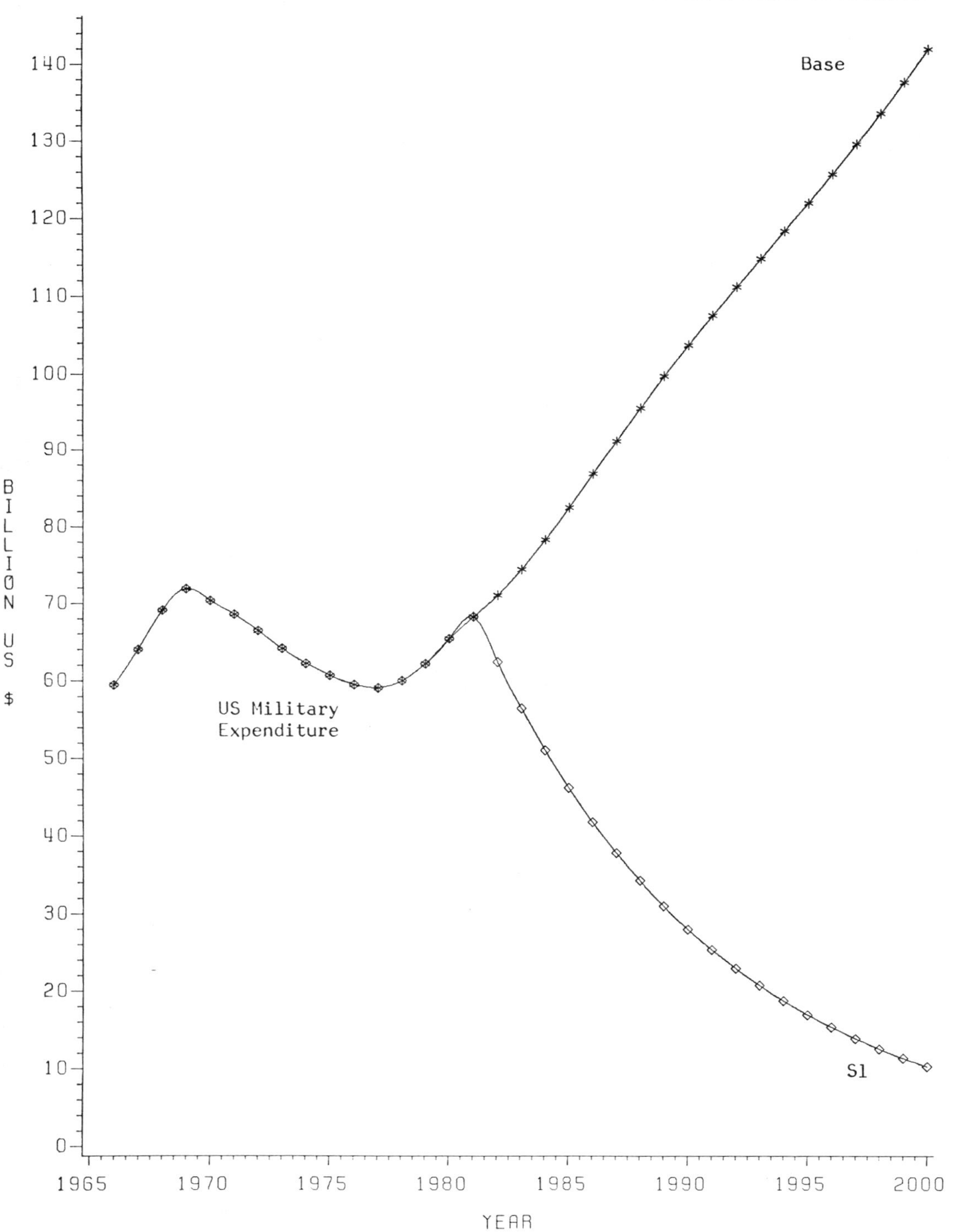

Graph A5.14. US Private Consumption for the Scenario of a Unilateral American Disarmament (in billions of US dollars, 1965 prices)

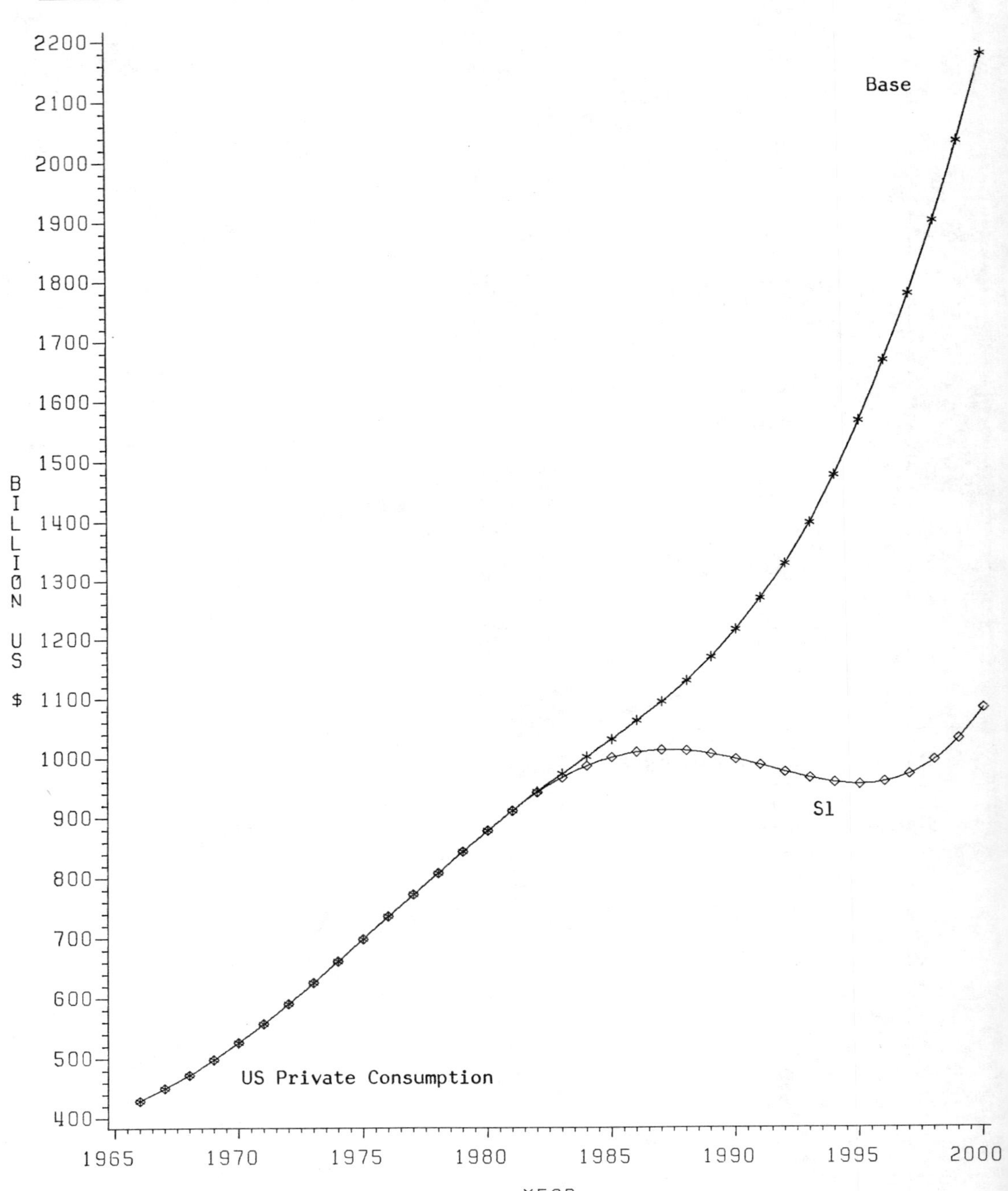

years but become acute later on. Military expenditures decrease drastically being lower by 50 percent by 1985 already. As a result, GNP grows at a much slower rate of a little above 1 percent over the whole period. Private total consumption keeps increasing up to 1987 but decreases later on as can be seen in Graph A5.14. These developments have a large impact on presidential-governmental popularity, but only from 1986 on (see Graph A5.15).

The Soviet internal consequences are relatively minor. Soviet military expenditures take up 3 percent less of GNP, which is transferred to consumption. In summary:

8. US disarmament — A US unilateral disarmament of 10 percent per annum does not decrease the USSR's armament, which, on the contrary, keeps building up its forces. The US cannot sustain this very long because of much slower economic growth, a decrease in consumption, and dismal presidential popularity.

The Result of Unilateral Soviet Disarmament

Also the assumption of a Soviet unilateral disarmament is of course counterfactual, although Western security planners would be pleased very much. Having studied the consequences of American unilateral steps toward disarmament, it appears to be only fair when testing the same measures on behalf of the Soviet Union.

The scenario for Soviet unilateral disarmament sees a 3-percent yearly decrease in Soviet forces from 1981 on. The results are quite similar to the ones in the American case (see Graphs A5.16 and A5.17). The other party, the US, keeps on arming although at a slower rate than before. US armaments grow by about 2 percent less in the strategic sector and by 1 percent less for the army. In the air force and navy, the changes are even smaller, but in all cases, the US arms less. Soviet armament is approximately one-third of what it would have been in the normal case, that is, in the base simulation.

Whereas there are only small changes in the US politico-economic system, the Soviet polity sees its military elites becoming dissatisfied. With higher disarmament rates, the whole Soviet system becomes unstable showing resistance toward disarmament. In summary:

9. Soviet disarmament — Soviet unilateral disarmament does not induce the United States to disarm but only to arm at a slower pace. High Soviet disarmament is limited by internal political constraints.

Graph A5.15. Approval of the US President's Policies (Popularity), in Percentages

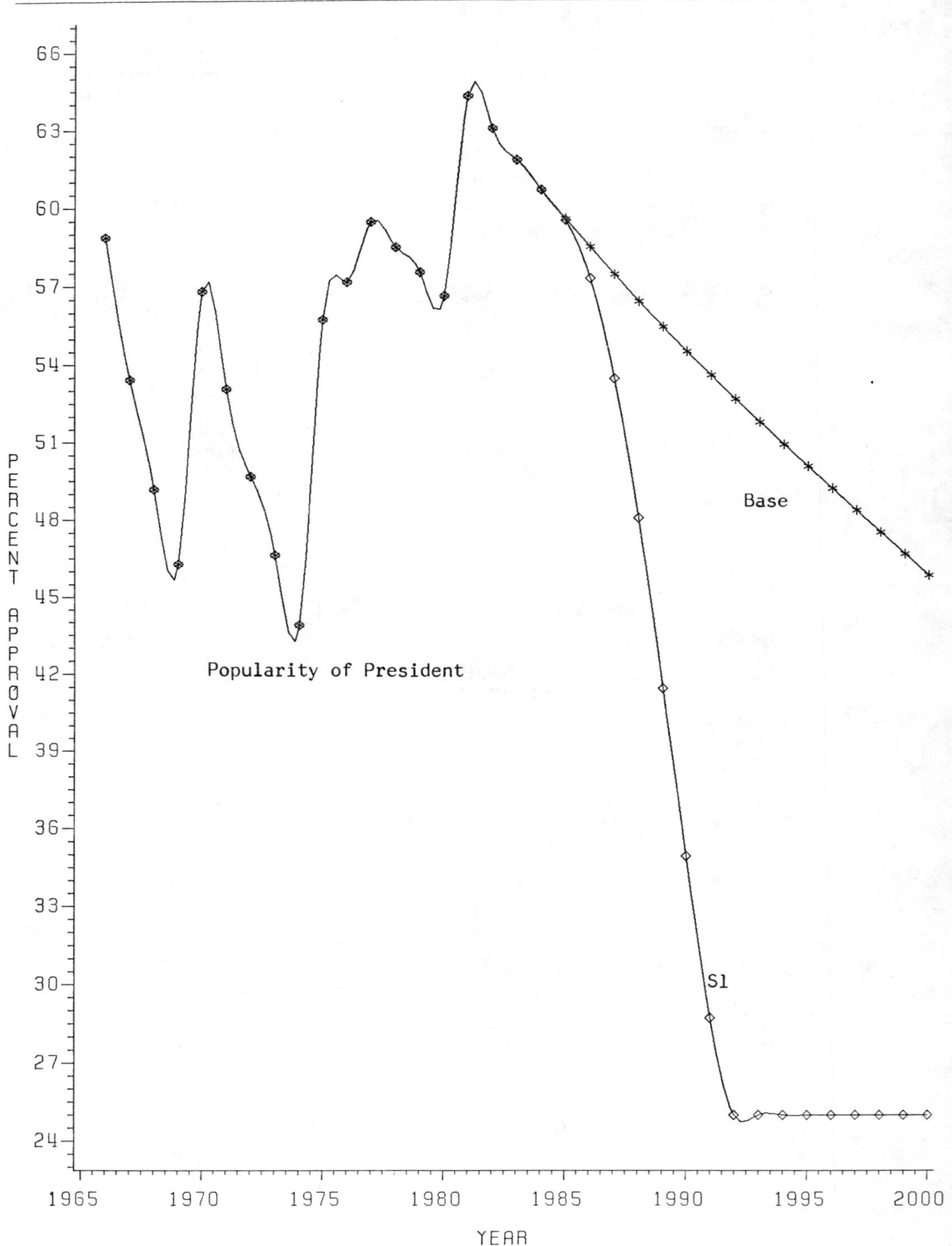

Graph A5.16. Strategic Indices for the Scenario of Unilateral Soviet Disarmament

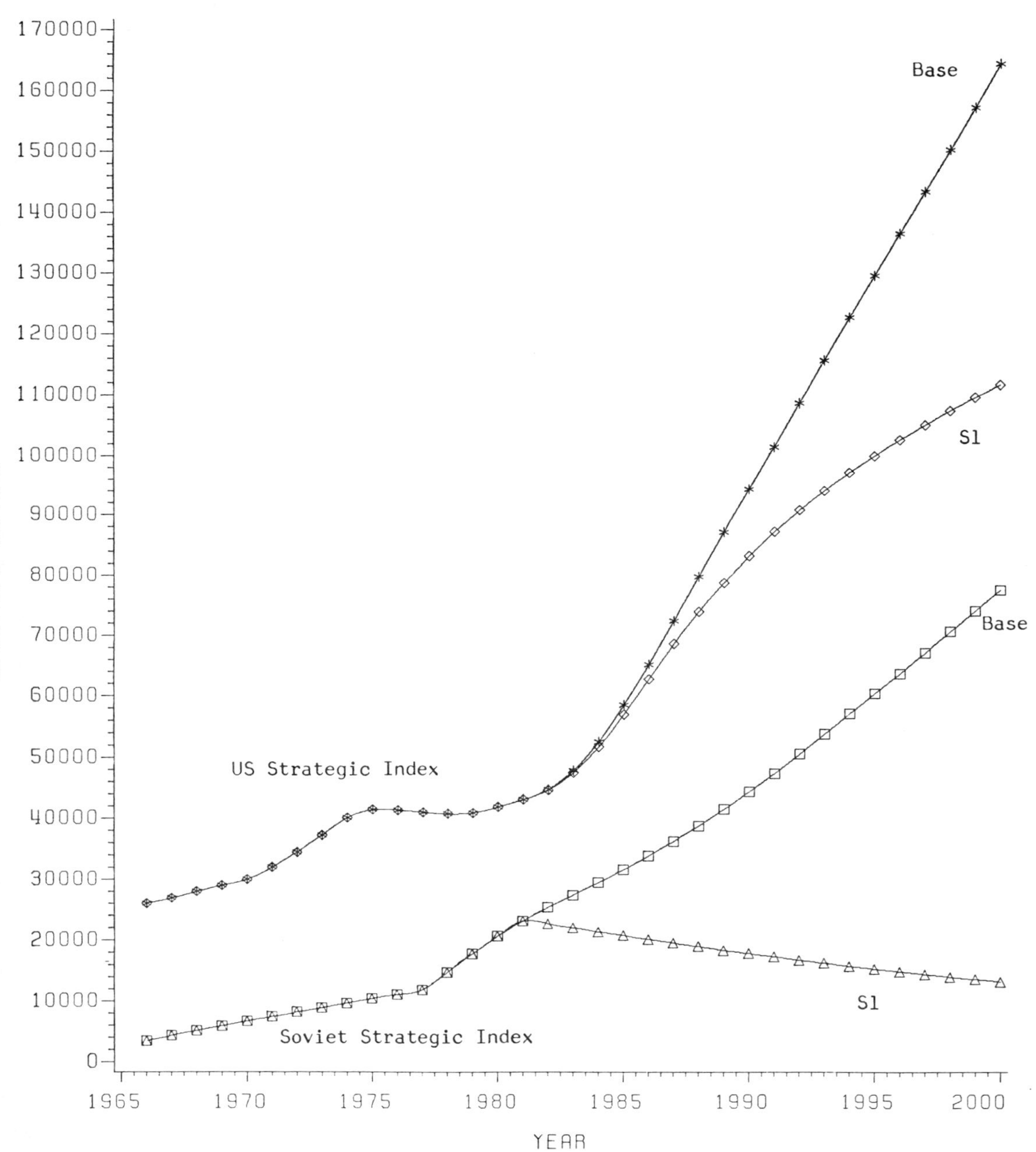

Graph A5.17. Army Indices for the Scenario of Soviet Unilateral Disarmament

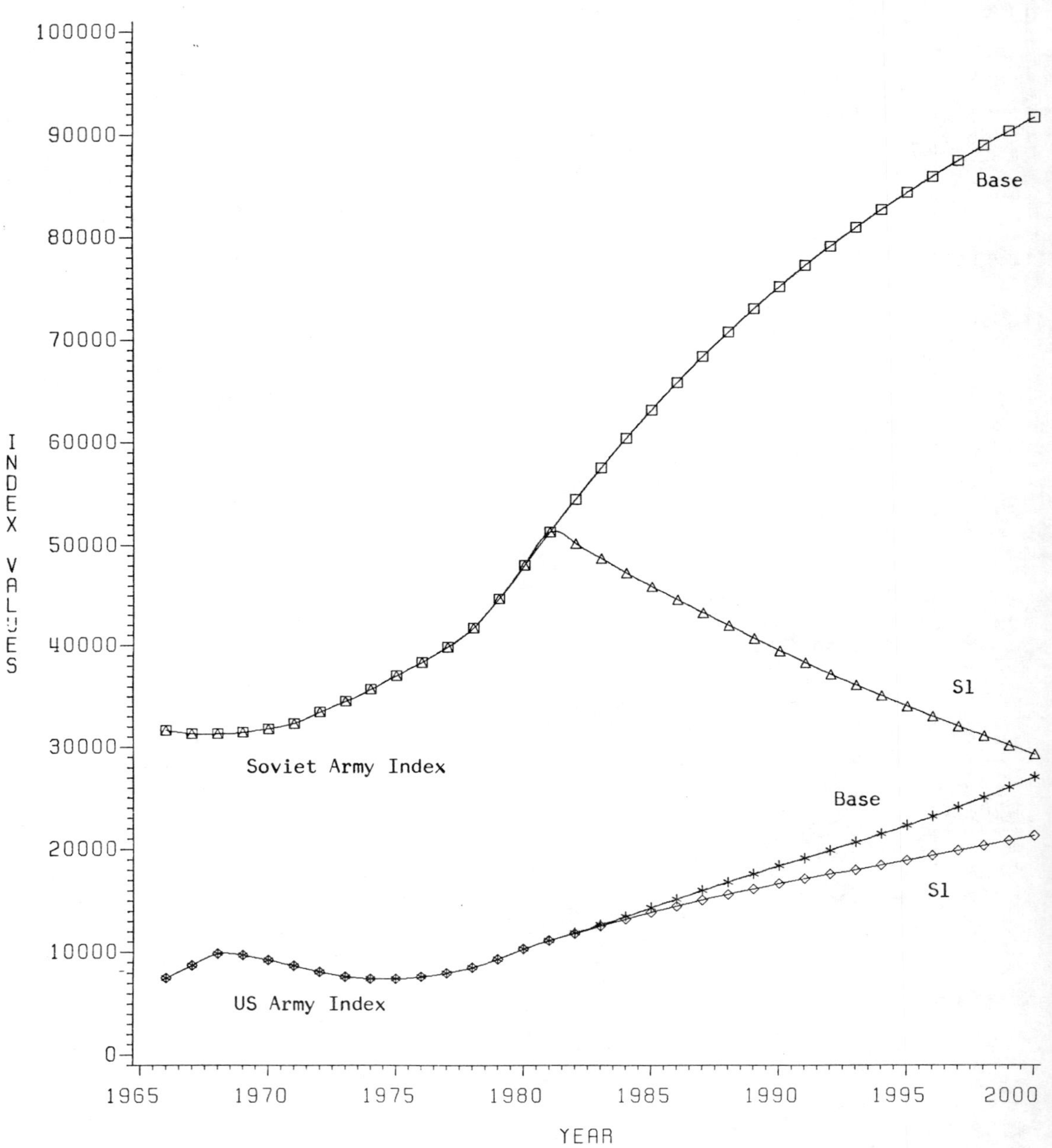

Negotiating from a Position of Strength

The slogan "negotiating from strength" has acquired notoriety during the Reagan administration. It refers to the policy advice: arm first, negotiate later. The reasoning behind it runs that the USSR will be accommodating only when the US is strong, especially in terms of its military posture. Thus we made this simulation where US armaments increase to a much larger extent than in the base run, to observe the effects this might have on the USSR as well as the effect upon the US itself.

This scenario is played according to two variants, both starting 20 January 1981. In the first run, US military expenditures increase at an annual rate of 6 percent (US 4 percent for the base run). The second run sees American defense spending increasing yearly at a 7 percent rate but with larger increases most of the years because a cyclical effect manifests itself and constrains military expenditures to "normal" increases (see Graph A5.18). The decreases in the budget that arise in the years 1992 to 1994 result not from internal political or economic constraints but from more technical ones related to the rapid expansion. In some sense these are bottleneck and production problems that may arise with a long-term investment. The curves thus generated by the model should not be taken at face value but as the expression of the above-mentioned problems occuring.

Graphs A5.19 and A5.20 display the evolution of the strategic and army indices. The strategic forces' curves in Graph A5.16 show a constant evolution of the American strategic index, with only a short slowing down of the growth during the midnineties. The growth problems are better displayed with the evolution of the army index in Graph A5.17. This index is decreasing during the period 1987–1991, being *smaller*—during the early nineties—in the second variant of the scenario postulating a larger growth in American forces than the first variant.

What is the effectiveness of this strategy of negotiating from a position of strength? How does the Soviet reaction look like? Is it characterized by what could be called submissiveness—in the conventional sector. Graph A5.17 shows slight decreases in the Soviet army from the mideighties on with the index being 6 percent lower with respect to the base run in the first variant and 10 percent in the second. Similar results occur for the other conventional indices for the air force and the navy. It is only in the strategic sphere that the USSR is reacting vigorously. But its response (+44 percent in year 2000 in the first simulation and +64 percent in the second) is only approximately one-half of the American evolution.

This huge build-up stimulates the US economy, adding 1 to 1½ percent to the growth rate. The USSR encounters difficulties following this build-up because its reaction in the strategic sector puts high demands on the economy. Even though the conventional

Graph A5.18. US Military Expenditure for the Scenario of Negotiating from a Position of Strength (in billions of US dollars, 1965 prices)

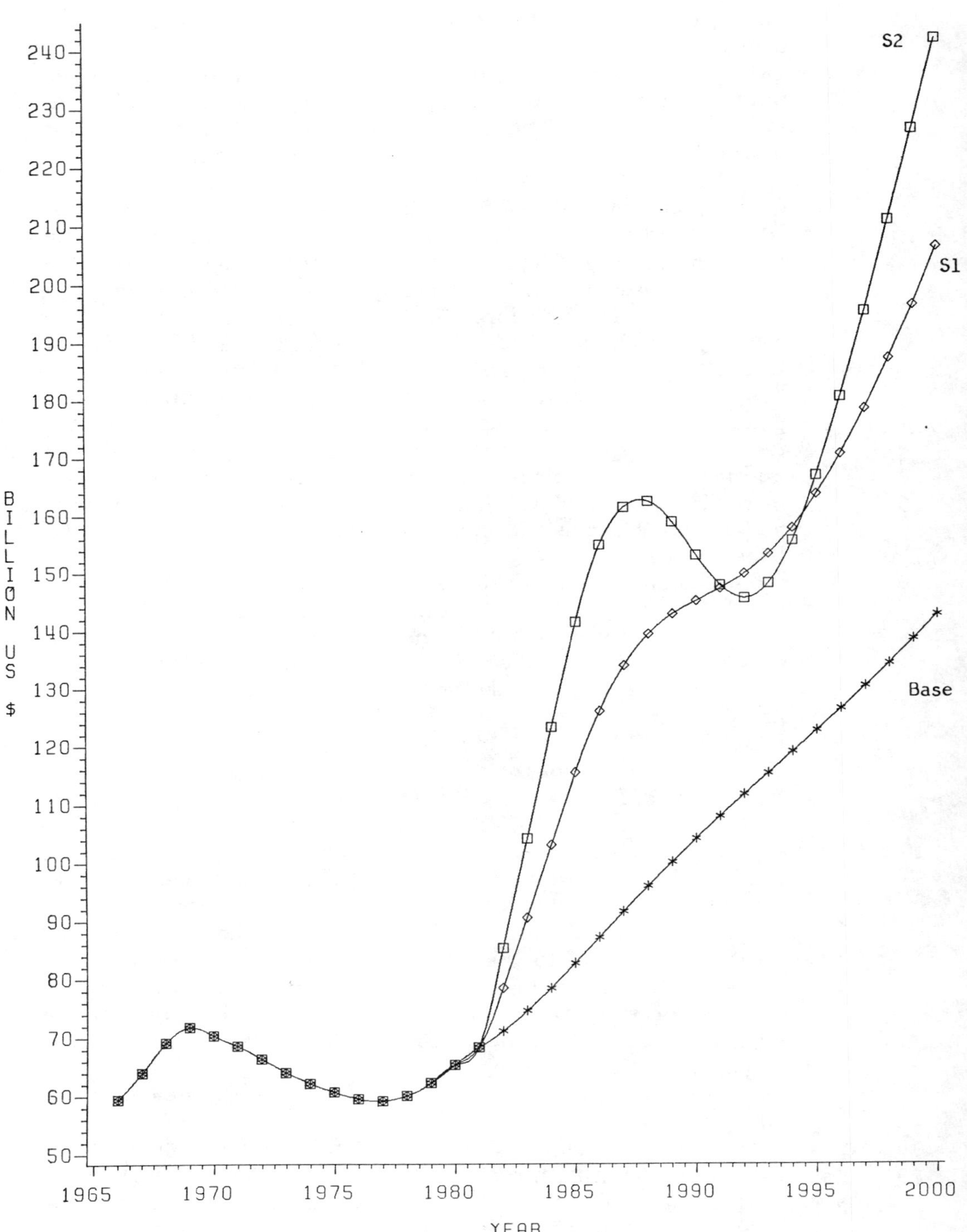

Graph A5.19. Strategic Indices for the Scenario of Negotiations from a Position of Strength

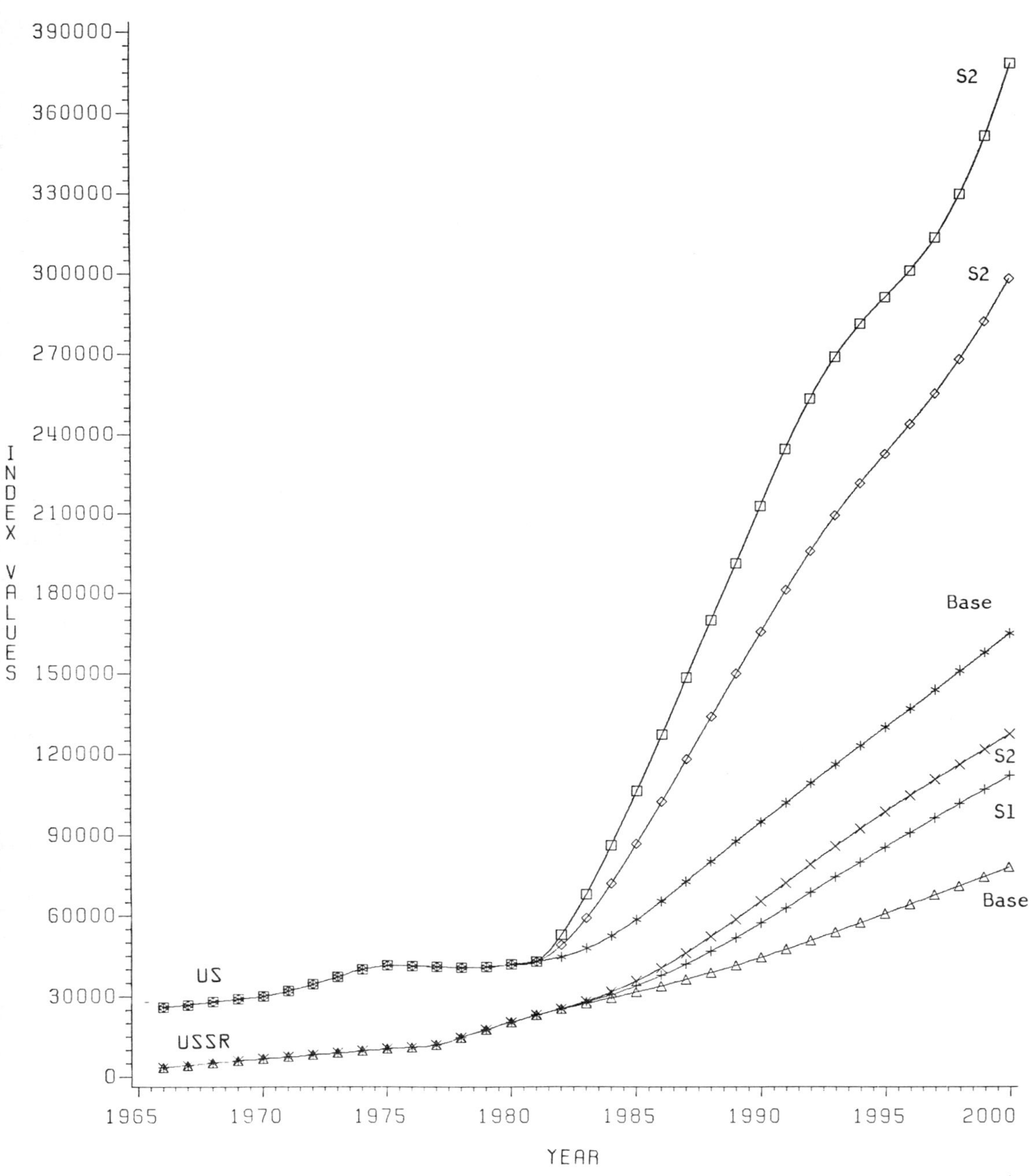

Graph A5.20. Army Indices for the Scenario of Negotiations from a Position of Strength

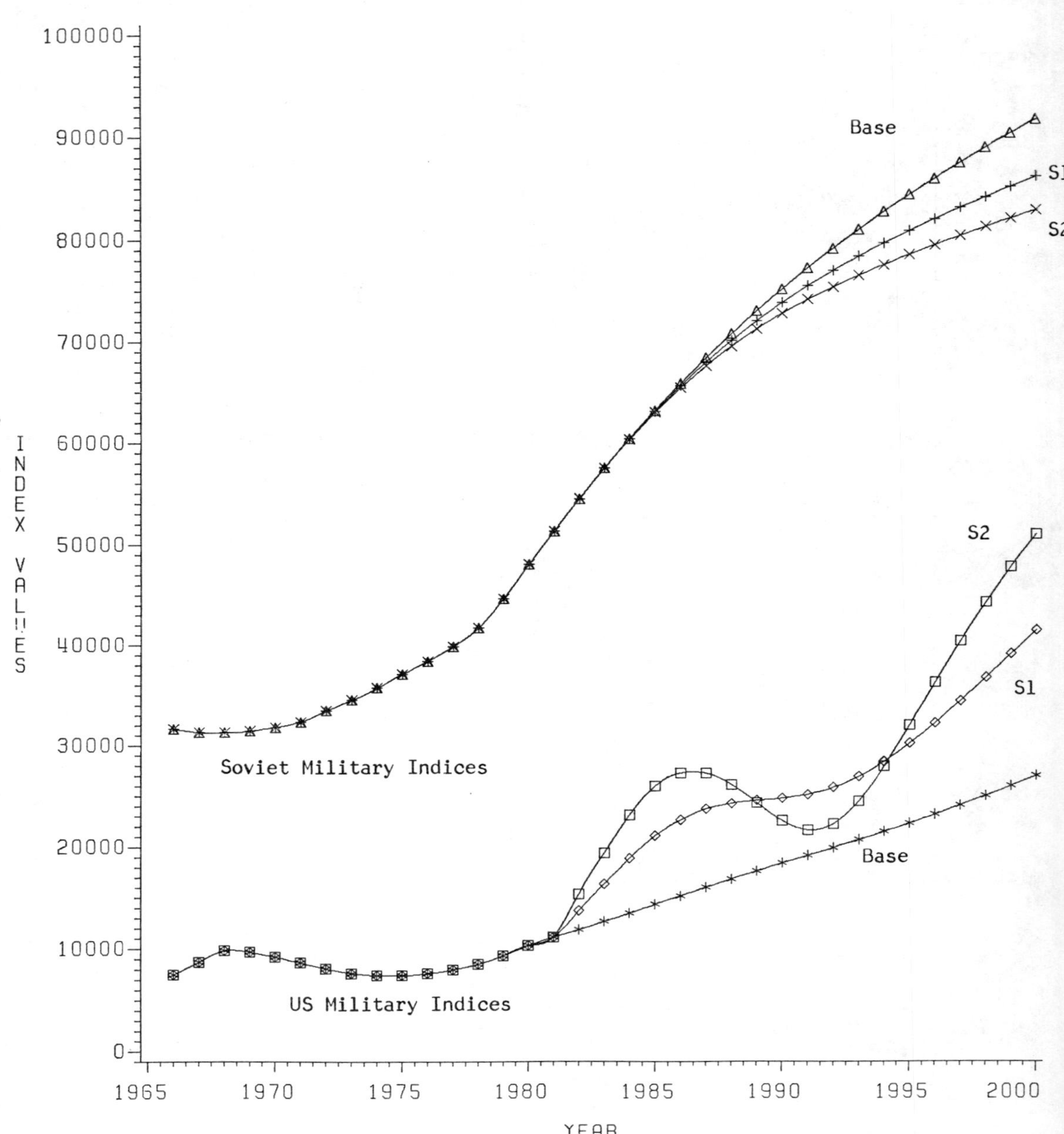

indices do not increase as much as in the base run, Soviet military expenditures take up a larger share of production (in relative terms to GNP share, they increase by 15 to more than 20 percent). Consumption is thus directly affected with decreases in per-capita consumption during the late nineties. In summary:

10. Negotiating from strength	A large US armament build-up to follow a policy of negotiating from strength seems to put some constraints on the USSR in the long run, especially in the conventional sector.

SYNTHESIS OF THE RESULTS

This appendix examined one of the most central aspects of East-West relations: the connection between political and economic interactions, between the political or diplomatic climate and arms races as described in Section A5.2. For that purpose, a mathematical model linking these détente dimensions through national policy decision-making was used. The model portrays the evolution of the main political, strategic, and economic trends of the United States and the Soviet Union with their major allies in Europe. How do these evolve?

The arms race is driven mostly by its own dynamics. Détente—in terms of a bettering of the diplomatic or international political climate—while lessening the pace of the arms build-up, does not stop it. Both East and West keep feeling threatened by their huge military forces. Accordingly, détente in the political sphere is clearly not sufficient to induce the parties to reduce their armaments. It can help lead to negotiations about arms reductions by a bettering of the climate, but these negotiations need to be desired by both parties. Our simulations of a counterfactual unilateral US or USSR disarmament seem to show that the other party does in general not follow suit but keeps on arming, albeit at a smaller rate than before. In addition, unilateral disarmament entails internal political—and sometimes economic—costs that will most probably deter politicians from embarking on such a course of action.

In our base run of the model for the period 1965 to the year 2000—empirically estimated from data from the 1950s to the mid-1970s—the East-West arms race accelerates during the 1980s and slows down in the 1980s. The military balance between East and West is only marginally affected. The model shows the important Soviet build-up of the 1960s and 1970s, especially in its strategic and navy sectors. It also portrays its superiority in ground forces. But the USSR never attains superiority in the strategic field where it has parity. This result runs counter to the prevalent theses (in the early eighties) of a Soviet superiority; it is based on the choice made for the indicators, which include not only quantitative factors—where the USSR usually has a lead over the US—but also qualitative ones. If Western security—in terms of the overall military balance and the projections of this balance—is compared to Eastern security, the West is in a better position. Western security decreased sharply in the 1970s but will increase during the 1980s and get better during the 1990s. Eastern security is lower because of the military weight of the People's Republic of China and especially Soviet threat perceptions, which amplify its importance. Eastern prospects are not as good as Western ones because their large efforts do not seem to do more than to keep security at a constant—or even slightly declining—relatively low level.

Why is that so? Mainly because Eastern economies, and above all the Soviet one, experience lesser growth in the industrial and mainly in the agricultural sector during the coming two decades. Lesser demographic growth and lower productivity increases due partly to workers' apathy and dissatisfaction—stemming from smaller private consumption growth—lead to a vicious cycle of decreasing growth and increasing dissatisfaction. Huge capital investments are not sufficient to offset this phenomenon, neither are increased imports, in particular of machinery from the developed West. In the United States, on the contrary, the arms build-up seems to stimulate the economy to some extent.

A revival of the Cold War has thus not a very large impact on the US politico-economic system but will put larger strains on the USSR. The USSR will react to the resulting American build-up in its forces but will face increasing difficulties should the Cold War extend into the nineties. A US policy of "negotiating from strength," that is, arm first, negotiate later, also puts constraints on the Soviet Union but only if it can be pursued for a number of years. But such a policy can be very dangerous if it increases Soviet external and internal problems to such an extent that Soviet decision-makers could see no solution to these but the recourse to extreme measures. Such considerations are very important: The analyses in this appendix were done precisely to give a better picture of East-West relations and show some of the crucial interconnections that need more scrutiny by politicans, commentators of the international scene, and by the scholarly community.

Bibliography

Abouchar, A. (1979). *Economic Evaluation of Soviet Socialism.* New York: Pergamon Press.

Alker, Hayward R., and Puchala, Donald (1968). "Trends in Economic Partnership in the North Atlantic Area, 1928-1963," in J. David Singer (ed.), *Quantitative International Politics.* New York: Free Press, pp. 287-316.

Allan, Pierre (1979). "L'impact du climat international sur les dépenses militaires soviétiques," *Annuaire suisse de science politique* 19, pp. 15-24.

Allan, Pierre, and Luterbacher, Urs (1981). "Détente Processes in Europe: A Tentative Model," in Daniel Frei (ed.), *Definitions and Measurement of Détente: East and West Perspectives.* Cambridge, Mass.: Oelgeschlager, Gunn & Hain, pp. 173-194.

Alting von Geusau, Frans A. M. (1981). "Economic Cooperation and Political Détente in Europe: Actors, Interactions, and Implications," in Bo Huldt and Atis Lejins (eds.), *East-West Economic Interaction: Possibilities, Problems, Politics, and Prospects.* Stockholm: The Swedish Institute of International Affairs, pp. 79-100.

Andrén, Nils (1980). "Expectations and Disillusionment," in: Nils Andrén and Karl E. Birnbaum (eds.), *Belgrade and Beyond: The CSCE Process in Perspective.* Alphen, pp. 89-98.

Andriole, Stephen J., and Young, Robert A. (1977). "Toward the Development of an Integrated Crisis Warning System," *International Studies Quarterly* 21, pp. 107-150.

Arbatow, Georgij A., and Oltmans, Willem (1981). *Der sowjetische Standpunkt. Über die Westpolitik der USSR.* Munich: Rogner & Bernard.

Arbeitsgruppe "Entspannung" (1977). *Indikatoren der Entspannung in Europa* (Kleine Studien zur Politischen Wissenschaft, No. 118-119). Zürich: Universität Zürich.

Ash, Robert W. (1980). "Power Parity and the Outbreak of War," in Daniel Frei (ed.), *Beiträge zur Kriegsursachenforschung* (Zürcher Beiträge zur Politischen Wissenschaft, No. 187). Zürich, pp. 51-58.

Axelrod, R. (ed.) (1976). *Structure of Decision*. The Cognitive Maps of Political Elites. Princeton, N.J.: Princeton University Press.

Azar, Edward E. (1975). "Ten Issues in Events Research," in Edward E. Azar and Joseph D. Ben-Dak (eds.), *Theory and Practice of Events Research*. New York: Gordon & Breach, pp. 1-17.

——. (1977). Codebook and User's Package for the Conflict and Peace Data Bank (COPDAB). Chapel Hill: University of North Carolina, mimeo.

Azar, Edward E., and Ben-Dak, Joseph D. (eds.) (1975). *Theory and Practice of Events Research. Studies on Inter-Nation Actions and Interactions*. New York: Gordon and Breach.

Azar, Edward E., and Havener, Thomas (1974). "Discontinuities in the Symbolic Environment: A Problem in Scaling Events," New Orleans: International Studies Association, mimeo.

Azar, Edward E.; McLaurin, R.D.; Havener, Thomas; Murphy, Craig; Sloan, Thomas; and Wagner, Charles A. (1977). "A System for Forecasting Strategic Crises: Findings and Speculations About Conflict in the Middle East," *International Interactions* 3, pp. 193-222.

Azar, Edward E., and Sloan, Thomas J. (1975). *Dimensions of Interactions: A Source Book for the Study of the Behavior of 31 Nations from 1948-1973*. Pittsburgh: International Studies Association.

Baumer, Max, and Jacobsen, Hanns-Dieter (1980). "Die Wirtschaftsbeziehungen des RGW mit dem Westen im Spannungsfeld zwischen weltweiten Beschränkungen und europäischen Möglichkeiten," in *DGFK-Jahrbuch 1979/80*. Baden-Baden: Nomos, pp. 557-577.

Bell, Coral (1977). *The Diplomacy of Détente*. London.

Bertsch, Gary K. et al. (1979). "Technology Transfer, Export Controls, and East-West Relations." Paper presented to the 1979 IPSA World Congress.

Bethkenhagen, Jochen; Kupper, Siegfried; and Lambrecht, Horst (1980). "Aussenwirtschaftliche Interessen der DDR und Entspannung," in *Die DDR im Entspannungsprozess*. Köln, pp. 1-17.

Bindschedler, Rudolf (1978). "Die Konferenz von Belgrad—Episode oder Wendepunkt?" *Europäische Rundschau*, no. 3, pp. 15-24.

Bonham, G. Matthew, and Shapiro, Michael J. (1973). "Simulation in the Development of a Theory of Foreign Policy Decision-Making," in P.J. McGowan (ed.), *Sage International Yearbook of Foreign Policy Studies*. Beverly Hills, Calif.: Sage, pp. 55-71.

——. (1976). "Explanation of the Unexpected: The Syrian Intervention in Jordan in 1970", in R. Axelrod (ed.), *Structure of Decision*. Princeton: Princeton University Press, pp. 113-141.

——. (1977). *Thought and Action in Foreign Policy*. Basel: Birkhäuser.

Bonham, G.M.; Shapiro, M.J.; and Nozicka, G.J. (1976). "A Cognitive Process Model of Foreign Policy Decision Making," *Simulation and Games* 7, pp. 123-152.

Borst, G., et al. (1977). *Militärwesen in der Sowjetunion*. Wehrforschung Aktuell 5. München: Bernard & Graefe.

Brainard, Lawrence J. (1981). "Eastern Europe's Uncertaint Future: The Outlook for East-West Trade and Finance," in Bo Huldt and Atis Lejins (eds.), *East-West Economic Interaction: Possibilities, Problems, Politics, and Prospects*. Stockholm: The Swedish Institute of International Affairs, pp. 39-53.

Bredow, Wilfried von (1979). *Die Zukunft der Entspannung*. Köln: Pahl-Rugenstein.

Brock, Lothar (1976). "Möglichkeiten und Grenzen einer konstruktiven Abrüstungspolitik in den intersystemaren Beziehungen," in Gerda Zellentin (ed.), *Annäherung, Abrenzung und friedlicher Wandel in Europa*. Boppard: Boldt, pp. 191-216.

Bundesminister der Verteidigung (1980). *Die nuklearen Mittelstreckenwaffen. Modernisierung und Rüstungskontrolle*. Bonn: Planning Staff of the Federal Ministry of Defense of the FRG.

Burzig, Arno (1977). "Intersystemare ökonomische Beziehungen und Entspannung in Europa," in Annemarie Grosse-Jütte and Rüdiger Jütte (eds.), *Entspannung ohne Frieden*. Frankfurt: S. Fischer, pp. 207-217.

Calvocoressi, Peter (1968). *World Politics since 1945*. London: Longman.

Cherkasov, P.P., and Proektor, D.M. (1978). "The Problem of Deepening the European Détente," in Soviet Committee for European Security and Cooperation (ed.), *European Security and Cooperation*. Moscow: Progress, pp. 306-346.

Cherry, Colin (1967). *Kommunikationsforschung-Eine neue Wissenschaft*, 2nd ed. Hamburg.

Choucri, Nazli, and North, Robert C. (1976). *Nations in Conflict (Code Book)*. Ann Arbor: ICPSR.

Corson, Walter H. (1970a). "Conflict and Co-operation in East-West Relations: Measurement and Explication" Ann Arbor: Institute for Social Research, mimeo.

———. (1970b). "Measuring Conflict and Cooperation Intensity Between Nations." Ann Arbor: Institute for Social Research, mimeo.

Czempiel, Ernst-Otto, et al. (1980). "Amerikanisch-sowjetische Beziehungen im weltpolitischen Kontext: Rahmenbedingungen der Entspannungspolitik in Europa," in: *DGFK-Jahrbuch 1979/80*. Baden-Baden: Nomos, pp. 35-64.

Daly, Judith A., and Andriole, Stephen J. (1980). "The Use of Events/Interaction Research by the Intelligence Community," *Policy Science* 12, pp. 215-236.

Deutsch, Karl W., and Eckstein, Alexander (1960/61). "National Industrialization and the Declining Share of the International Sector, 1890-1959," *World Politics*, vol. 13, pp. 267-299.

Deutsch, Karl W., and Isard, Walter (1966). "A Note on a Generalized Concept of Effective Distance," *Behavioral Science* 6, pp. 308-311.

Dobroczynski, Michal (1980). "Abhängigkeiten, Strukturen und Perspektiven einer Politik der Zusammenarbeit in Europa," in Hansjürgen von Kries (ed.), *Friede durch Zusammenarbeit in Europa*. Berlin: Berlin-Verlag, pp. 114-126.

Dobrosielski, Marian (1977). "Aspects of European Security After the Helsinki Conference," *Studies in International Relations*, No. 8, pp. 7-16.

Entspannungsbegriff und Entspannungspolitik in Ost und West (1979). Berlin: Duncker & Humblot.

Etzioni, Amitai (1962). *The Hard Way to Peace*. New York: Knopf.

Feger, Hubert (1976). "Annäherung und Abgrenzung politisch-sozialer Systeme aus sozialpsychologischer Sicht," in Gerda Zellentin (ed.), *Annäherung, Abgrenzung und friedlicher Wandel in Europa*. Boppard: Bolt, pp. 451-490.

Ferraris, Luigi Vittorio (1979). *Report on a Negotiation*. Alphen: Sijthoff & Nordhoff.

Finsterbusch, Kurt (1975). "Trends in International Integration as Indicated by Trends in International Mail Flows," in Edward E. Azar and Joseph D. Ben-Dak (eds.), *Theory and Practice of Events Research*. New York: Gordon & Breach, pp. 128–141.

Forrester, Jay W. (1970). *Urban Dynamics*. Cambridge and London: MIT Press.

Frankel, Joseph (1975). *British Foreign Policy, 1945–1973*. London: Oxford University Press.

Frei, Daniel (1980). *Evolving a Conceptual Framework of Inter-Systems Relations*. New York: UNITAR.

—— (ed.) (1981). *Definitions and Measurement of Détente: East and West Perspectives*. Cambridge, Mass.: Oelgeschlager, Gunn & Hain.

Friedliche Koexistenz in Europa (1977). Berlin: Staatsverlag der DDR.

Füllenbach, Josef, and Schulz, Eberhard (eds.) (1980). *Entspannung am Ende?* München: Oldenbourg.

Galtung, Johan (1975). "East–West Interaction Patterns," in Edward E. Azar and Joseph D. Ben-Dak (eds.), *Theory and Practice of Events Research*. New York: Gordon & Breach, pp. 95–120.

Gamson, William, and Modigliani, André (1971). *Untangling the Cold War: A Strategy for Testing Rival Theories*. Boston: Little, Brown.

Gantman, Vladimir (1977). "Zwischen Helsinki und Belgrad." Paper presented to the HSFK Conference on European Security, Frankfurt.

Garnham, David (1976). "Power Parity and Lethal International Violence, 1969–1973," *Journal of Conflict Resolution* 20, pp. 379–394.

Gastil, Raymond D. (1978). *Freedom in the World: Political Rights and Civil Liberties*. New York: Freedom House.

Gaupp, Peter (1976). *Die Rollentheorie als Analyseinstrument von Aussenpolitik und internationalen Beziehungen* (Kleine Studien zur Politischen Wissenschaft, No. 75–77). Zürich: Universität Zürich.

Goldman, Marshall I. (1980). *The Enigma of Soviet Petroleum: Half-Empty of Half-Full?* London: George Allen and Unwin.

Goldmann, Kjell (1972). "Bipolarization and Tension in International Systems: A Theoretical Discussion," *Cooperation and Conflict* 7, pp. 37–63.

——. (1973). "East–West Tensions in Europe, 1946–1970: A Conceptual Analysis and a Quantitative Description," *World Politics* 26, pp. 106–112.

——. (1974). *Tension and Détente in Bipolar Europe*. Stockholm: Esselte Studium.

——. (1979). *Is My Enemy's Enemy My Friend's Friend?* Lund: Studentlitteratur.

——. (1980). "Cooperation and Tension Among Great Powers: A Research Note," *Cooperation and Conflict* 15, pp. 31–45.

——. (1981). "Change and Stability in Foreign Policy: Détente as a Problem of Stabilization." Stockholm, mimeo.

Goldmann, Kjell, and Lagerkranz, Johan (1977). "Neither Tension nor Détente: East–West Relations in Europe, 1971–1975," *Cooperation and Conflict* 12, pp. 251–264.

Greven, Michael Th. (1976). "Internationale Politik und Gesellschaftsformation," in Gerda Zellentin (ed.), *Annäherung, Abgrenzung und friedlicher Wandel in Europa*. Boppard: Boldt, pp. 217–291.

Guetzkow, Harold, and Ward, Michael Don (eds.) (1981). *Simulated International Processes: Theories and Research in Global Modeling*. Beverly Hills, Calif.: Sage.

Haftendorn, Helga (1975). "Versuch einer Theorie der Entspannung," *Sicherheitspolitik heute* 2, pp. 223–242.

Hart, Thomas G. (1976). *The Cognitive World of Swedish Security Elites*. Stockholm: Esselte Studium.

———. (1979). *The Spread of Extra-European Conflicts to Europe: Concepts and Analysis*. Stockholm: The Swedish Institute of International Affairs (Research Report UI-79-1).

Havener, Thomas, and Peterson, Alan (1975). "Measuring Conflict/Cooperation in International Relation. A Methodological Inquiry," in Edward E. Azar and Joseph D. Ben-Dak (eds.), *Theory and Practice of Events Research*. New York: Gordon & Breach, pp. 57–61.

Hermann, Charles F. (1973). "Indikatoren internationaler politischer Krisen," in Martin Jänicke (ed.), *Herrschaft und Krise*. Opladen: Westdeutscher Verlag, pp. 44–63.

———. (1981). "Some Initial Problems and Possible Solutions in Measuring Détente Processes: Prospective of an American Social Scientist," in: Daniel Frei (ed.), *Definitions and Measurement of Détente: East and West Perspectives*. Cambridge, Mass.: Oelgeschlager, Gunn & Hain, pp. 11–23.

Hermann, Charles F., and Hermann, Margaret G. (1976). "CREON: Comparative Research on the Events of Nations," *Quarterly Report* 1. Columbus: Mershon Center.

Hermann, Margaret G. (1979). "Acceptance and Rejection." Columbus: Mershon Center (draft manuscript, unpublished).

Hinkel, Günter, and Nicolai, Wolfgang (1978). *Entspannung und wirtschaftliche Zusammenarbeit in Europa*. Berlin: Staatsverlag der DDR.

Hoffmann, Stanley (1976). "Paris Dateline. The Case of the Vanishing Foreign Policy," *Foreign Policy* 23, pp. 221–230.

———. (1981). "Voraussetzungen und Ziele der Entspannung in den 80er Jahren," in *Protokoll Nr. 67 des Bergedorfer Gesprächskreises*. Hamburg, pp. 11–19.

Hoggard, Gary D. (1975). "An Analysis of the 'Real' Data," in Edward E. Azar and Joseph D. Ben-Dak (eds.), *Theory and Practice of Events Research*. New York: Gordon & Breach, pp. 19–27.

Hopple, Gerald W. (1980). "Automatic Crisis Warning and Monitoring: Exploring a Staircase Display Option." McLean, Va., mimeo.

Holsti, Ole R. (1966). "External Conflict and International Cohesion: The Sino-Soviet Case," in P.J. Stone et al. (eds.), *The General Inquirer*. Cambridge, Mass.: MIT Press, pp. 343–358.

———. (1969a). *Content Analysis for the Social Sciences and Humanities*. Reading, Mass.: Addison-Wesley.

———. (1969b). "The Belief System and National Images: A Case Study," in J.N. Rosenau (ed.), *International Politics and Foreign Policy*. New York: Free Press, pp. 543–550.

———. (1972). *Crisis, Escalation, War*. Montreal: McGill/Queen University Press.

Holsti, Ole R.; Brody, R.A.; and North, R.C. (1965). "Measuring Affect and Action in International Reaction Models: Empirical Materials from the 1962 Cuban Crisis," *Papers of the Peace Research Society (International) II*, pp. 170–190.

———. (1968). "Perception and Action in the 1914 Crisis," in J.D. Singer (ed.), *Quantitative International Politics: Insights and Evidence*. New York: Free Press, pp. 123–158.

Hopman, Terry (1967). "International Conflict and Cohesion in the Communist System," *International Studies Quarterly* 11, pp. 212-136.

Hutchins, Gerald (1979). "Affect." Columbus: Mershon Center (draft chapter of manuscript).

Iker, H. P. (1974). "A Historical Note and the Use of Word-Frequency Contiguities in Content Analysis," *Computers and the Humanities* 8, pp. 93-98.

———. (1974/75). "SELECT: A Computer Program to Identify Associationally Rich Words for Content Analysis. I. Statistical Results; II. Substantive Results," *Computers and the Humanities* 8, pp. 313-319; 9, pp. 3-12.

Iker, H. P., and Klein, R. (1974). "WORDS: A Computer System for the Analysis of Content," *Behavior Research Methods and Instrumentation* 6, pp. 430-438.

Iker, H. P., and Harway, N. I. (1969). "A Computer System Approach to the Recognition and Analysis of Content," in G. Gerbner et al. (eds.), *Analysis of Communication Content.* New York: John Wiley & Sons.

Inozemtsev, Nikolai N. (ed.) (1980). *Europe Before a Choice: Confrontation or Relaxation of Military Tension.* Moscow.

International Institute for Strategic Studies (1959/60). *The Military Balance.* London.

Institut für Internationale Beziehungen an der Akademie für Staats- und Rechtswissenschaft der DDR (1979). *Konfrontation, Entspannung, Zusammenarbeit.* East Berlin: Staatsverlag der Deutschen Demokratischen Republik.

———. (1980). *Die DDR und die Verwirklichkung der Schlussakte von Helsinki. Dokumente und Materialien.* East Berlin: Staatsverlag der Deutschen Demokratischen Republik.

Jacobsen, Hans-Adolf (1980). "Bedingungsfaktoren realistischer Entspannungspolitik," in *DGFK-Jahrbuch 1979/80.* Baden-Baden: Nomos, pp. 65-90.

Jacobsen, Hanns-Dieter (1976). "Kooperation und Abgrenzung in den wirtschaftlichen Beziehungen zwischen Ost- und Westeuropa," in Gerda Zellentin (ed.), *Annäherung, Abgrenzung und friedlicher Wandel in Europa.* Boppard: Boldt, pp. 417-443.

Jahn, Egbert (1977). "Die Wiedergeburt funktionalistischer Theorie in der Ost-West-Kooperation: Eine Kritik," in Annemarie Grosse-Jütte and Rüdiger Jütte, *Entspannung ohne Frieden.* Frankfurt: S. Fischer, pp. 183-190.

———. (1977a). "Zur Ambivalenz der Entspannungspolitik nach der KSZE," in Dalbrücke Jost et al. (eds.), *Grünbuch zu den Folgewirkungen der KSZE.* Köln: Verlag Wissenschaft und Politik, pp. 57-78.

Jenkins, Robin (1969). "Perception in Crises," in *IPRA Studies in Peace Research,* IInd Conference, vol. 1, Assen, pp. 157-175.

Jodice, David A., and Taylor, Charles L. (1979). "Quantitative Materials for the Study of East-West Relations." Paper for Delivery at the Moscow IPSA Congress.

———. (1981). "Détente and Its Effects: A Measurement of East-West Trade," in Daniel Frei (ed.), Definitions and Measurement of Détente. Cambridge, Mass.: Oelgeschlager, Gunn & Hain, pp. 153-172.

Johnson, Stephen C. (1967). "Hierarchical Clustering Schemes," *Psychometrika* 32, pp. 241-254.

Jütte, Rüdiger (1979). "Europäische Friedensstruktur," in Annemarie Jütte-

Grosse and Rüdiger Jütte (eds.), *Entspannung ohne Frieden*. Frankfurt: S. Fischer, pp. 148–172.

Kadushin, Charles (1968). "Reason Analysis," in *International Encyclopaedia of the Social Sciences*, vol. 13. New York: Macmillan, pp. 338–343.

Kaltefleiter, W. (1976). "Entspannung und Eskalation," in *Zeitschrift für Politik* 23, pp. 30–40.

Katzenstein, Peter (1975). "International Interdependence," *International Organization* 29, pp 1021–1034.

Kipp, Jacob W. (1978). "Détente Politics and the US–USSR Military Balance," in Della W. Sheldon (ed.), *Dimension of Détente*. New York: Praeger, pp. 197–216.

Kiss, Laszlo J. (1978). "Western Conceptions of Détente," in *Külpolitika (Foreign Policy)*. A Selection from the 1978 Issues of the Periodical. Budapest: Hungarian Institute of Foreign Affairs, pp. 38–51.

Klein, Peter, et al. (1977). *Friedliche Koexistenz in Europa*. Berlin: Staatsverlag der DDR.

Knight, Albion W. (1980). "The Changing Strategic Balance: Its Effect on European Security," in Alfred Domes (ed.), *Ost-West: Erfahrungen und Perspektiven*. München: Hanns-Seidel-Stiftung, pp. 148–157.

Knirsch, Peter (1980). "Die Möglichkeit der Weiterführung der Ost-West-Wirtschaftsbeziehungen nach der sowjetischen Intervention in Afghanistan," in *DGFK-Jahrbuch 1979/80*. Baden-Baden: Nomos, pp. 667–675.

———. (1981). "Economic and Political Interdependence Between East and West Reconsidered," in Bo Huldt and Atis Lejins (eds.), *East-West Interaction: Possibilities, Problems, Politics, and Prospects*. Stockholm: The Swedish Institute of International Affairs, pp. 55–78.

Kohl, W. L. (1971). *French Nuclear Diplomacy*. Princeton, N.J.: Princeton University Press.

Köhler, Gernot (1975). "Ein Verfahren zur Messung internationaler Spannungen auf der Basis von Ereignisdaten," in *Konfliktforschung* 5, pp. 87–99.

Kolodziej, Edward A. (1974). *French International Policy under de Gaulle and Pompidou.: The Politics of Grandeur,* Ithaca, N.Y.: Cornell University Press.

———. (1979). "Measuring French Arms Transfer: A Problem of Sources and Some Sources of Problems with ACDA Data," *Journal of Conflict Resolution* 23, pp. 195–227.

Koloskov, I. A. (1978). "Prerequisites for a Security System in Europe," in Soviet Committee for European Security and Cooperation (ed.), *European Security and Cooperation*. Moscow: Progress, pp. 27–47. *Konfrontation, Entspannung, Zusammenarbeit* (1979). Berlin: Staatsverlag der DDR.

Kulish, Vasily (1977). "Détente, International Relations, and Military Might," *Co-Existence* 14, pp. 175–195.

Kulski, Wladyslaw W. (1966). *De Gaulle and the World: The Foreign Policy of the Fifth Republic*. Syracuse, N.Y.: Syracuse University Press.

Kusnezow, Wladlen (1975). *Internationale Entspannungspolitik aus sowjetischer Sicht*. Vienna: Europa Verlag.

Lasswell, Harold. D.; Lerner, Daniel; and Pool, Ithiel de Sola (1952). *The Comparative Studies of Symbols*. Stanford, Calif.: Stanford University Press.

Lawrence, E. J., and Sherwin, R. G. (1978). "The Measurement of Weapons-Systems Balances: Building Upon the Perceptions of Experts," in D. C.

Daniel (ed.), *International Perceptions of the Superpower Military Balance.* New York: Praeger.

Lebedev, Nikolai I. (1978). *Eine neue Etappe der internationalen Beziehungen.* Berlin: Staatsverlag der DDR.

Lee, William T. (1980). *The Estimation of Soviet Defense Expenditures, 1955–75: An Unconventional Approach,* New York: Praeger Publishers.

Leitenberg, M. (1979). "The Counterpart of Defense Industry Conversion in the United States: The USSR Economy, Defense Industry, and Military Expenditure," *Journal of Peace Research* 26, pp. 262–277.

Leng, Russell J. (1975). "The Future of Events Data Marriages," *International Interactions* 2, pp. 45–62.

Lerner, Daniel; Pool, Ithiel de Sola; and Lasswell, Harold D. (1951). "Comparative Analysis of Political Ideologies: A Preliminary Statement," *Public Opinion Quarterly* 15, pp. 713 ff.

Link, Werner (1980). *Der Ost-West-Konflikt.* Stuttgart: Kohlhammer.

Lomejko, Wladimir B. (1980). "Stabilität, Gleichgewicht und Zusammenarbeit in Europa," in Hansjürgen von Kries (ed.), *Friede durch Zusammenarbeit in Europa.* Berlin: Berlin-Verlag, pp. 92–106.

Luhn, H.P. (1958). "The Automatic Creation of Literature Abstracts," *IBM Journal of Research and Development* 2, pp. 159–165.

——. (1959/68). "Keywood-in-Context for Technical Literature (KWIC Index)." New York: IBM Corporation. Reprinted in C.K. Schultz (ed.), *H.P. Luhn: Pioneer of Information Science.* New York: Spartan Books.

Luterbacher, Urs (1976). "Towards a Convergence of Behavioral and Strategic Conceptions of the Arms Race: The Case of American and Soviet ICBM Build-up," *Papers, Peace Science Society (International),* 26, pp. 1–21.

Luterbacher, Urs; Allan, Pierre; and Imhoff, André (1979). "SIMPEST: A Simulation Model of Political, Economic, and Strategic Interactions Among Major Powers." Paper presented at 1979 IPSA World Congress.

Luttwak, Edward N. (1979). Statement Before the Committee on Foreign Relations, in John Sparkman (ed.), *Perceptions: Relations Between the United States and the Soviet Union.* Washington, D.C.: Committee on Foreign Relations, United States Senate, pp. 340–343.

Lutz, Dieter S. (1980a). "Das militärische Kräfteverhältnis bei den euronuklearen Waffensystem," in *DGFK-Jahrbuch 1979/80.* Baden-Baden: Nomos, pp. 357–399.

——. (1980b). "Das militärische Kräfteverhältnis im Bereich der 'Nuklearkräfte in und für Europa,'" in Gert Krell and Dieter S. Lutz (eds.), *Nuklearrüstung im Ost- und West-Konflikt: Potentiale, Doktrinen, Rüstungssteuerung.* Baden-Baden: Nomos pp. 13–89.

Mateew, W.A. (1981). "Voraussetzungen und Ziele der Entspannung in den 80er Jahren," in *Protokoll Nr. 67 des Bergedorfer Gesprächskreises.* Hamburg, pp. 5–11.

Mazrui, Ali A. (1977). "State of the Globe Report 1977," *Alternatives* 3, pp. 151–320.

McCamant, John I. (1981). "A Critique of Present Measures of Human Rights Development and an Alternative," in Ted P. Nanda et al. (eds.), *Global Human Rights.* Boulder, Colo.: Westview Press, pp. 123–146.

McClelland, Charles A. (1972). "The Beginning, Duration, and Abatement of International Crises," in Charles F. Hermann (ed.), *International Crises: Insights from Behavioral Research.* New York: Free Press, pp. 83–105.

McClelland, Charles A., and Hoggard, Gary D. (1969). "Conflict Patterns in the Interactions Among Nations," in James N. Rosenau (ed.), *International Politics and Foreign Policy: A Reader in Research and Theory*. New York: Free Press, pp. 711-724.

Merritt, R. L. (1966). *Symbols of American Community, 1735-1775*. New Haven, Conn.: Yale University Press.

Milstein, Jeffrey S., and Mitchell, William Charles (1968). "Dynamics of the Vietnam Conflict: A Quantitative Analysis and Predictive Computer Simulation," in *Papers, Peace Science Society (International)* 10, pp. 163-187.

Mitrovic, Tomislav (1977). "La continuité et l'institutionalisation de la Conférence sur la sécurité et la coopération en Europe," *Jugoslavenska Revija za Medunarodno Pravo* 24, pp. 160-177.

Morawiecki, Wojciech (1977). "Die Struktur der Ost-West Beziehungen im europäischen System," in Annemarie Grosse-Jütte and Rüdiger Jütte (eds.), *Entspannung ohne Frieden*. Frankfurt: S. Fischer, pp. 110-130.

Moses, Lincoln E.; Brody, Richard A.; Holsti, Ole R.; Kadane, Joseph B.; and Milstein, Jeffrey S. (1967). "Scaling Data on Inter-Nation Action," *Science* 156, pp. 1054-1059.

Mouritzen, Hans (1981). "Prediction on the Basis of Official Doctrines," *Cooperation and Conflict* 16, pp. 25-38.

Müller, Hans-Gerhard; Neubert, Wolfram; and Pirsch, Hans (1980). *Friedliche Koexistenz, Konfrontationspolitik, bürgerliche Entspannungstheorie* (IPW-Forschungshefte 4). East Berlin: Staatsverlag der DDR.

Nastasescu, Stefan (1980). "The Dialectic of Détente," *Revue Roumaine d'Etudes Internationales* 14, pp. 362-365.

Newcombe, A. G.; Newcombe, N. S.; and Landrons, G. D. (1974). "The Development of an Inter-Nation Tensiometer," *International Interactions* 1, pp. 3-18.

Newcombe, Alan G., and Andrighetti, Robert (1977). "Nations at Risk: A Prediction of Nations Likely to Be in War," *International Interactions* 3, pp. 135-160.

Newcombe, Hanna, and Wert, James (1979). *The Affinities of Nations: Tables of Pearson Correlation Coefficients of U.N. General Assembly Roll-Call Votes* (1946-1973). Dundas, Ontario: Peace Research Institute-Dundas.

Nogee, Joseph L., and Donaldson, Robert H. (1981). *Soviet Foreign Policy Since World War II*. New York/Oxford: Pergamon Press.

North, Robert C.; Holsti, Ole R.; Zaninovich, M. George; and Zinnes, Diana A. (1963). *Content Analysis: A Handbook with Applications for the Study of International Crisis*. Evanston, Ill.: Northwestern University Press.

Nygren, Bertil (1979). *Peaceful Interaction in Ten Great Power Relations* (Research Report UI-79-2). Stockholm: Swedish Institute of International Affairs.

Nygren, Bertil, and Lavery, Donald (1981). Cooperation Between the Soviet Union and Three Western Great Powers, 1950-1975 (Research Report 6). Stockholm: Swedish Institute of International Affairs.

Osgood, Charles E. (1959). "The Representative Model and Relevant Research Methods," in Ithiel de Sola Pool (ed.), *Trends in Content Analysis*. Urbana, Ill.: The University of Illinois Press, p. 33ff.

———. (1962). "Studies on the Generality of Affective Meaning Systems," *American Psychologist* 17, pp. 10-28.

——. (1962a). *An Alternative to War and Surrender*. Chicago: The University of Illinois Press.
——. (1966). *Perspectives in Foreign Policy*. San Francisco: Pacific Press.
——. (1969). "Calculated De-escalation as a Strategy," in Dean G. Pruitt and Richard C. Snyder (eds.), *Theory and Research on the Causes of War*. Englewood Cliffs, N.J.: Prentice-Hall, pp. 213–216.
Osgood, Charles E., and Anderson, Louis (1956). "Certain Relations Between Experienced Contingencies Association Structure, and Contingencies in Encoded Messages," *American Journal of Psychology* 70, pp. 411ff.
Osgood, C.E.; Suci, George J.; and Tannenbaum, Percy M. (1957). *The Measurement of Meaning*. Urbana, Ill.: The University of Illinois Press.
Pastusiak, Longin (1978). "Objective and Subjective Premises of Détente," *Polish Round Table* 8, pp. 53–72.
Phillips, Warren (1968). "Investigations into Alternative Techniques for Developing Empirical Taxonomies: The Results of 2 Plasmodes" (Research Report No. 14). University of Hawaii, Dimensionality of Nations Project.
Pool, Ithiel de Sola (1951). *Symbols of Internationalism*. Stanford, Calif.: Stanford University Press.
——. (1952). *The "Prestige Press": A Survey of Their Editorials*. Stanford, Calif.: Stanford University Press.
——. (1962). *Symbols of Democracy*. Stanford, Calif.: Stanford University Press.
Poser, G. (1977). *Militärmacht Sowjetunion 1977. Daten, Tendenzen, Analyse*. München: Olzog.
Richardson, Lewis F. (1960). *Arms and Insecurity*. Pittsburgh: Boxwood, and Chicago: Quadrangle.
Ropers, Norbert (1977). "Die KSZE und ihre Folgewirkungen," in Jost Delbrück et al. (eds.), *Grünbuch zu den Folgewirkungen der KSZE*. Köln: Verlag Wissenschaft und Politik, pp. 477–509.
——. (1980a). "Transnationale Reisen und Kontakte zwischen Ost und West," in *DGFK-Jahrbuch 1979/80*. Baden-Baden: Nomos, pp. 701–748.
——. (1980b). "Entspannungspolitik in Europa 1979/80," in *DGFK-Jahrbuch 1979/80*. Baden-Baden: Nomos, pp. 835–881.
Rossa, Paul J.; Hopple, Gerald W.; and Wilkenfeld, Jonathan (1980). "Crisis Analysis: Indicators and Models," *International Interactions* 7, pp. 123–163.
Rotfeld, Adam Daniel (1977). "Implementation of the CSCE Final Act and the Development of Détente in Europe" (Studies on International Relations, No. 8). Warsaw: Polish Institute of International Affairs.
Ruloff, Dieter (1975). *Konfliktlösung durch Vermittlung: Computersimulation zwischenstaatlicher Krisen*. Basel: Birkhäuser.
Rummel, Rudolph J. (1972). *The Dimensions of Nations*. Beverly Hills, Calif.: Sage.
——. (1976). *The Dimensionality of Nations Project (Codebook)*. Ann Arbor, Mich.: ICPR.
Russett, Bruce M. (1970). "Indicators for America's Linkages with the Changing World Environment," *The Annals* 388 (March), pp. 82–96.
Samoschkin, Juri, and Gantman, Wladimir (1980). "Die marxistische Konzeption der Ideologie, Ethik und Aussenpolitik in den frühen achtziger Jahren," *Wissenschaft und Frieden*, No. 4, pp. 4–13.
Scarritt, James R. (1981). "Definitions, Dimensions, Data, and Designs,"

in Ved P. Nanda et al. (eds.), *Global Human Rights*. Boulder, Colo.: Westview Press, pp. 115–122.

Scoble, Harry M., and Laurie S. Wiseberg (1981). "Problems of Comparative Research on Human Rights," in Ved P. Nanda et al. (eds.), *Global Human Rights*. Boulder, Colo.: Westview Press, pp. 147–171.

Schissler, Jakob (1980). *Symbolische Sicherheitspolitik. Die Bedeutung der KSZE-Schlussakte für die Sicherheitspolitik der Bundesrepublik Deutschland*. München: Minerva.

Schneider, William (1980). "Factors Affecting East–West Economic Relations," in Alfred Domes (ed.), *Ost-West Erfahrungen und Perspektiven*. München: Seidel-Stiftung, pp. 205–223.

Schössler, Dietmar (1977). "Détente im Meinungsbild von sicherheitspolitischen Experten der Bundesrepublik Deutschland" (mimeo). Mannheim: University of Mannheim.

Schwarz, Günter, and Lutz, Dieter S. (1980). *Sicherheit und Zusammenarbeit. Eine Bibliographie zu MBFR, SALT, KSZE*. Baden-Baden: Nomos.

Schwarz, Hans-Peter (1979). "Die Entspannungspolitik der westlichen Staaten," in *Entspannungsbegriff und Entspannungspolitik in Ost und West*. Berlin: Dunker & Humblot, pp. 45–60.

———. (1979a). "Supermacht und Juniorpartner. Ansätze amerikanischer und westdentscher Ostpolitik," in H.-P. Schwarz and Boris Meissner (eds.), *Entspannungspolitik in Ost und West*. Köln: Heymanns, pp. 147–191.

———. (1979b). "Die Alternative zum Kalten Krieg? Bilanz der bisherigen Entspannung," in H.-P. Schwarz and Boris Meissner (eds.), *Entspannungspolitik in Ost und West*. Köln: Heymanns, pp. 275–303.

Shuell, T. J. (1969). "Clustering and Organization in Free Recall," *Psychological Bulletin* 72, pp. 353–374.

Simes, Dimitri K. (1980). "The Death of Détente?" *International Security* 5, pp. 1–25.

Singer, J. David, and Small, Melvin (1974a). *The Wages of War, 1816–1965 (Codebook)*. Ann Arbor, Mich.: ICPSR.

———. (1974b). "Foreign Policy Indicators: Predictors of War in History and in the State of the World Message," *Policy Sciences* 5, pp. 271–296.

SIPRI (1968/69–1981). *SIPRI Yearbook: World Armaments and Disarmament*. Stockholm: Stockholm International Peace Research Institute (various publishers).

Sloan, Thomas J. (1975). "The Development of Cooperation and Conflict Interaction Scales," in Edward E. Azar and Joseph D. Ben-Dak (eds.), *Theory and Practice of Events Research*. New York: Gordon & Breach, pp. 29–39.

———. (1978). "The Association between Domestic and International Conflict Hypothesis Revisited," *International Interactions* 4, pp. 3–32.

Snyder, Richard D.; Hermann, Charles F.; and Lasswell, Harold D. (1976). "A Global Monitoring System: Appraising the Effects of Government on Human Dignity," *International Studies Quarterly* 20, pp. 221–260.

Sonnenfeldt, Helmut (1977/78). "Russia, America and Détente," *Foreign Affairs* 56, pp. 274–294.

Spröte, Wolfgang (1980). "Die Rolle der ökonomischen Zusammenarbeit im Entspannungsprozess," in Hansjürgen von Kries (ed.), *Friede durch Zusammenarbeit in Europa*. Berlin: Berlin-Verlag, pp. 230–237.

Stankovsky, Jan (1980). "Handels-und Kreditbeziehungen zwischen Ost und West," *DGFK-Jahrbuch 1979/80*. Baden-Baden: Nomos, pp. 527–555.

———. (1981). Industrial East–West Cooperation: "Motivations, Developments, and Prospects," in Bo Huldt and Atis Lejins (eds.), East–*West Economic Interaction: Possibilities, Problems, Politics, and Prospects*. Stockholm: The Swedish Institute of International Affairs, pp. 9–27.

Stehr, Uwe (1980). *Wirtschaft und Politik in den Sowjetischen Westbeziehungen*. Frankfurt: Campus.

Stone, P.J.; Dunphy, D.C.; Smith, M.S.; and Ogilvie, D.M. (1966). *The General Inquirer: A Computer Approach to Content Analysis in the Behavioral Sciences*. Cambridge, Mass.: MIT Press.

Stone, P.J., and Mochmann, E. (1976). "Erweiterung des Instrumentariums der Sozialforschung durch inhaltsanalytische Techniken," in M.R. Lepsius (ed.), *Zwischenbilanz der Soziologie. Verhandlungen des 17. Deutschen Soziologentages*. Stuttgart; Enke, pp. 163–174.

Stratmann, K.-Peter (1981). *Kritische Anmerkungen zu Darstellungen des "Euro-strategischen" Kräfteverhältnisses von NATO und Warschauer Pakt* (Arbeitspapier 2284). Ebenhausen: Stiftung Wissenschaft und Politik, FRG.

Sullivan, Michael P. (1976). *International Relations—Theories and Evidence*. Englewood Cliffs, N.J.: Prentice-Hall.

Sütö, Otto (1978). "Détente in Europe," *Külpolitika (Foreign Policy). A Selection from the 1978 Issues of the Periodical*. Budapest: Hungarian Institute of Foreign Affairs, pp. 3–16.

Taylor, Charles L. (1981). *The World Handbook of Political and Social Indicators*, 3rd ed. Vol. I: *Aggregate Data;* Vol. II (together with David A. Jodice): *Political Events Data*. Berlin: International Institute for Comparative Social Research (Reports 80–127 and 81–124).

Teunissen, Paul J. (1980). "Strukturen und Perspektiven der Sicherheit und Zusammenarbeit in Europa," in Hansjürgen von Kries (ed.), *Friede durch Zusammenarbeit in Europa*. Berlin: Berlin-Verlag, pp. 13–49.

Thalheim, Karl C. (1980). "Wirtschaftliche Beziehungen im Wandel," in Alfred Domes (ed.), *Ost West: Erfahrungen und Perspektiven*. München: Hanns-Seidel-Stiftung, pp. 183–204.

Thompson, William R., and Modelski, George (1977). "Global Conflict Intensity and Great Power Summitry Behavior," *Journal of Conflict Resolution* 21, pp. 339–376.

Timberlake, Charles E. (1978). *Détente. A Documentary Record*. New York: Praeger.

Urban, G.R. (1976). *Détente*. New York: Universe Books.

US Arms Control and Disarmament Agency (1975; 1976; 1977). *World Military Expenditures and Arms Trade*, 1963–1973; 1965–1975; 1966–1975. Washington, D.C.

Vahl, Winfried (1979). "Von der Vision zum Pragmatismus: Französische Entspannungspolitik von de Gaulle bis Giscard d'Estaing," in H.P. Schwarz and Boris Meissner (eds.), *Entspannungspolitik in Ost und West*. Köln: Carl Heymans, pp. 227–243.

Väyrynen, Raimo (1977). "Abrüstung und Entspannung: Divergierende oder konvergierende Phänomene?" in Annemarie Grosse-Jütte and Rüdiger Jütte (eds.), *Entspannung ohne Frieden*. Frankfurt: S. Fischer, pp. 218–241.

———. (1977a). "Zur Dynamik des Unfriedens in Europa," in Annemarie Grosse-Jütte and Rüdiger Jütte (eds.), *Entspannung ohne Frieden*. Frankfurt: S. Fischer, pp. 60–67.

Wallace, Michael D. (1979). "Early Warning Indicators from the 'Correlates of War Project'," in David J. Singer and Michael D. Wallace (eds.), *To Augur Well. Early Warning Indicators in World Politics*. Beverly Hills, Calif.: Sage, pp. 17-36.

Walter, F. (1977). "Zum Problem der Belastung der Sowjetwirtschaft durch die Militäraufwendungen," *Wehrforschung Aktuell* 7 (München: Bernard & Graefe), pp. 90-111.

Weede, Erich (1981). "Methods, Problems and Some Results in Evaluating Détente-Related Policies," in Daniel Frei (ed.), *Definitions and Measurement of Détente: East and West Perspectives*. Cambridge, Mass.: Oelgeschlager, Gunn & Hain, pp. 141-151.

Weltman, John (1979). "Détente and the Decline of Geography," *Jerusalem Journal of International Relations* 4, pp. 75-94.

Wettig, Gerhard (1981). *Die Sowjetischen Sicherheitsvoestellungen und die Möglichkeiten eines Ost-West-Einvernehmens*. Baden-Baden: Nomos.

Weymann, A. (1973). "Bedeutungsfeldanalyse," *Kölner Zeitschrift für Soziologie und Sozialpsychologie* 25, pp. 761-776.

White Book (1979). *Weissbuch 1979*-Zur Sicherheit der Bundesrepublik Deutschland und zur Entwicklung der Bundeswehr. Edited by the Federal Minister of Defense on behalf of the Federal Government of the FRG. Bonn: Federal Government of the FRG.

Wiberg, Hakan (1979). "Détente in Europe?" *Current Research on Peace and Violence* 2, pp. 104-113.

Wilkenfeld, Jonathan; Hopple, Gerald W.; and Rossa, Paul J. (1979). "Sociopolitical Indicators of Conflict and Cooperation," in David J. Singer and Michael D. Wallace (eds.), *To Augur Well. Early Warning Indicators in World Politics*. Beverly Hills, Calif.: Sage, pp. 104-151.

——. (1980). "Crisis Analysis: Indicators and Models," *International Interactions* 7, pp. 123-163.

Willms, Bernard (1976). "Zur Dialektik von Kooperation und Abgrenzung im Entspannungsprozess zwischen Ost und West," in Gerda Zellentin (ed.), *Annäherung, Abgrenzung und friedlicher Wandel in Europa*. Boppard: Boldt, pp. 45-78.

Wojnar, Marian (1981). "Patterns of East-West Trade and Cooperation," in Bo Huldt and Atis Lejins (eds.), *East-West Economic Interaction: Possibilities, Problems, Politics, and Prospects*. Stockholm: The Swedish Institute of International Affairs, pp. 29-37.

Wright, Quincy (1942). *A Study of War*. Chicago: The University of Chicago Press.

Wrightson, M.T. (1976). "The Documentary Coding Method," in R. Axelrod (ed.), *Structure of Decision*. Princeton, N.J.: Prince for University Press, pp. 291-332.

Zaleski, Eugene, and Wienert, Helgard (1980). *Technology Transfer between East and West*. Paris: OECD.

Zinnes, Dina A. (1968). "The Expression and Perception of Hostility in Prewar Crisis: 1914," in J.D. Singer (ed.), *Quantitative International Politics: Insights and Evidence*. New York: Free Press, pp. 85-119.

About the Authors

Daniel Frei is professor of Political Science at the University of Zurich and director of the Political Science Research Institute, University of Zurich. He was educated at Zurich University, the London School of Economics and Political Science, the University of Michigan, and the Geneva Graduate Institute of International Studies. He is the author of several publications (most of them in German) on theory of international relations, security problems, and neutrality. He is also the editor of *Definitions and Measurement of Détente: East and West Perspectives* (1981).

Dieter Ruloff is lecturer of Political Science at the University of Zurich and research associate at the Political Science Research Institute, University of Zurich. He received his M.A. in Political Science and History from the University of Constance (Federal Republic of Germany), and his Ph.D. in Political Science from the University of Zurich. His work includes publications on computer simulation in the field of International Relations and methodological questions of both Political Science and History.